Lecture Notes in Computer Science 9503

Commenced Publication in 1973
Founding and Former Series Editors:
Gerhard Goos, Juris Hartmanis, and Jan van Leeuwen

More information about this series at http://www.springer.com/series/7410

Ho-won Kim · Dooho Choi (Eds.)

Information Security Applications

16th International Workshop, WISA 2015
Jeju Island, Korea, August 20–22, 2015
Revised Selected Papers

 Springer

Editors
Ho-won Kim
Pusan National University
Busan
Korea (Republic of)

Dooho Choi
Electronics and Telecommunications
Research Institute
Daejeon
Korea (Republic of)

ISSN 0302-9743   ISSN 1611-3349 (electronic)
Lecture Notes in Computer Science
ISBN 978-3-319-31874-5   ISBN 978-3-319-31875-2 (eBook)
DOI 10.1007/978-3-319-31875-2

Library of Congress Control Number: 2016934676

LNCS Sublibrary: SL4 – Security and Cryptology

Printed on acid-free paper

This Springer imprint is published by Springer Nature
The registered company is Springer International Publishing AG Switzerland

Preface

The 16th International Workshop on Information Security Applications (WISA 2015) was held at Ocean Suites Jeju Hotel, Jeju Island, Korea, during August 20–22, 2015. The workshop was hosted by Korea Institute of Information Security and Cryptology (KIISC) and sponsored by the Ministry of Science, ICT and Future Planning (MSIP). It was also co-sponsored by Korea Internet and Security Agency (KISA), Electronics and Telecommunications Research Institute (ETRI), National Security Research Institute (NSR), AhnLab, Korea Information Certificate Authority (KICA), REDBC, and UNET systems. The excellent arrangements were led by the WISA 2015 general chair, Prof. ChoonSik Park, and organizing chair, Prof. Souhwan Jung.

This year WISA 2015 provided an open forum for exchanging and sharing of ongoing hot issues and results of research, development, and applications in information security areas. The Program Committee prepared for an interesting program including an invited talk from Mr. Harry Wechsler of George Mason University, USA. The workshop had roughly nine tracks such as Hardware Security (Track 1), Cryptography 1 (Track 2), Side Channel Attacks and Countermeasures (Track 3), Security and Threat Analysis (Track 4), IoT Security 1 (Track 5), Network Security (Track 6), Cryptography 2 (Track 7), Application Security (Track 8), IoT Security 2 (Track 9). We would like to thank all authors who submitted papers. Each paper was reviewed by at least three reviewers. External reviewers as well as Program Committee members contributed to the reviewing process from their particular areas of expertise. The reviewing and active discussions were provided by a Web-based system, EDAS. Through the system, we could check the amount of similarity between the submitted papers and previously published papers to prevent plagiarism and self-plagiarism.

Following the strict reviewing processes, 35 outstanding papers from 12 countries were accepted for publication in this volume of Information Security Applications. There were five papers for Track 1, four papers for Track 2, four papers for Track 3, four papers for Track 4, three papers for Track 5, three papers for Track 6, four papers for Track 7, five papers for Track 7, and three papers for Track 7.

Many people contributed to the success of WISA 2015. We would like to express our deepest appreciation to each of the WISA Organizing and Program Committee members as well as the paper contributors. Without their endless support and sincere dedication and professionalism, WISA 2015 must have been impossible.

August 2015

Ho-won Kim
Dooho Choi

Organization

Executive Committee

General Chair

ChoonSik Park   Seoul Women's University, Korea

Organizing Committee Chair

Souhwan Jung   Soongsil University, Korea

Organizing Committee

Tae-Sung Kim	Chungbuk University, Korea
Taekyoung Kwon	Yonsei University, Korea
SeungWook Jung	Soongsil University, Korea
Namhi Kang	Duksung Women's University, Korea
Huy Kang Kim	Korea University, Korea
Minho Park	Soongsil University, Korea
Jin Kwak	Ajou University, Korea
Kyungho Lee	Korea University, Korea
Hyoungshick Kim	Sungkyunkwan University, Korea
JeongHyen Yi	Soongsil University, Korea
Im-Yeong Lee	Soonchunhyang University, Korea
Gi-Wook Son	NSR, Korea
JeongNyeo Kim	ETRI, Korea
KyungHo Chung	KISA, Korea
Jaecheol Ryou	Chungnam National University, Korea
Yongtae Shin	Soongsil University, Korea
Okyoen Yi	Kookmin University, Korea
Kyung-Hyune Rhee	Pukyong National University, Korea
YooJae Won	MSIP, Korea
Sangchoon Kim	Kangwon National University, Korea

Program Committee Co-chairs

Ho-won Kim	Pusan National University, Korea
Dooho Choi	ETRI, Korea

Program Committee

Man Ho Au	The Hong Kong Polytechnic University, Hong Kong, SAR China
Aziz Mohaisen	Verisign Labs, VA, USA
Selcuk Baktir	Bahcesehir University, Turkey
Sang Kil Cha	Carnegie Mellon University, USA
Seong-je Cho	Dankook University, Korea
Daesun Choi	ETRI, Korea
Hyoung-Kee Choi	Sungkyunkwan University, Korea
Yoon-Ho Choi	Pusan National University, Korea
Jinguang Han	Nanjing University of Finance and Economics, China
Swee-Huay Heng	Multimedia University, Malaysia
Eul Gyu Im	Hanyang University, Korea
Seung-Hun Jin	ETRI, Korea
Namhi Kang	Duksung Women's University, Korea
You Sung Kang	ETRI, Korea
Huy Kang Kim	Korea University, Korea
Hyoungshick Kim	Sugkyunkwan University, Korea
DaeYoub Kim	Korea University, Korea
Jong Kim	POSTECH, Korea
Yongdae Kim	KAIST, Korea
Jun Ho Kwon	Pusan National University, Korea
Taekyoung Kwon	Yonsei University, Korea
Dong Geon Lee	NSR, Korea
Mun-Kyu Lee	Inha University, Korea
Zhen Ling	Southeast University, China
Kirill Morozov	Kyushu University, Japan
Elizabeth O'Sullivan	Queen's University Belfast, UK
Jeahoon Park	NSR, Korea
Kyung Hyune Rhee	Pukyong University, Korea
Junghwan Rhee	NEC Laboratories America, USA
Kouichi Sakurai	Kyushu University, Japan
Seungwon Shin	KAIST, Korea
Chao Yang	Texas A&M University, USA
Chung-Huang Yang	National Kaohsiung Normal, Taiwan
Yanjiang Yang	Institute for Infocomm Research, Singapore
Dae-Hyun Yum	Myongji University, Korea
Taek-Young Youn	ETRI, Korea
Xuehui Zhang	Oracle, USA
Raphael C.-W. Phan	Multimedia University, Malaysia

Keynote Speech

Cyber Security Using Adversarial Learning and Conformal Prediction

Harry Wechsler

George Mason University, Fairfax, USA

This talk reviews new directions for cyber security built around machine learning and using adversarial learning and conformal prediction to enhance network and computing services defenses against adaptive, malicious, persistent, and tactical threats. The motivation for using conformal prediction and its immediate offspring, those of semi-supervised learning and transduction, comes from them supporting discriminative and non-parametric methods using likelihood ratios; demarcation using cohorts, local estimation, and non-conformity measures; randomness for hypothesis testing and inference using sensitivity and stability analysis; reliability indices on prediction outcomes using credibility and confidence to assist meta-reasoning and information fusion; and open set recognition including novelty detection and the reject option for negative selection. The solutions proffered are built around active learning, meta-reasoning, randomness, semantics and stratification using topics and most important and above all using adaptive Oracles that are effective and valid for the purpose of model selection and prediction. Effective to be resilient to malicious attacks aimed at subverting promptness, selective in separating the wheat (e.g., informative patterns) from the chaff (e.g., obfuscation), and valid and well - calibrated to not overrate the accuracy and reliability of the predictions made.

Contents

Side Channel Attacks and Countermeasures

Security and Threat Analysis

IoT Security

Network Security

Application Security

Hardware Security

M-ORAM: A Matrix ORAM with Log N Bandwidth Cost

Steven Gordon[4], Atsuko Miyaji[1,2,3], Chunhua Su[1],
and Karin Sumongkayothin[1,4(✉)]

[1] Japan Advance Institute of Science and Technology (JAIST), Nomi, Japan
{miyaji,chsu,s1420209}@jaist.ac.jp
[2] Japan Science and Technology Agency (JST) CREST, Tokyo, Japan
[3] Graduate School of Engineering, Osaka University, Suita, Japan
[4] Sirindhorn International Institute of Technology (SIIT), Thammasat University,
Bangkok, Thailand
steve@siit.tu.ac.th

Abstract. Oblivious RAM can hide a client's access pattern from an untrusted server. However current ORAM algorithms incur large communication or storage overheads. We propose a novel ORAM construction using a matrix structure for server storage where a client downloads blocks from each row, choosing the column randomly to hide the access pattern. Both a normal and recursive construction are presented, achieving bandwidth cost of $O(1)$ and $O(\log N)$, respectively, and client storage similar to Path ORAM. We show under the same conditions, our matrix ORAM reduces bandwidth cost compared to Path ORAM by $\frac{\log N}{2}$.

1 Introduction

Oblivious RAM (ORAM) [4] is seen as beneficial for cloud computing, specifically for hiding access patterns from client to server. Encrypting the data before uploading to the server is not sufficient for privacy as it has been shown that the sequence of server storage locations read/written by the client can reveal valuable information to the server [6,8]. Therefore ORAM can be used to hide the access pattern by making the reads/write indistinguishable from random access to the server. The basic approach is when a client wants to access a block of data on the server, the client reads multiple blocks (including the block of interest) and writes back multiple blocks. The multiple blocks accessed are selected to make it impossible for the server to identify which block is of interest to the client and what operation is being performed. Despite many ORAM schemes being designed [1–3,5,7,9,12–14], achieving a satisfactory performance tradeoff remains a challenge. Key performance objectives for ORAM are:

K. Sumongkayothin–This study is partly supported by Grant-in-Aid for Scientific Research (C) (5K00183) and (15K00189) and Grant-in-Aid for Young Scientists (15K16004).

H. Kim and D. Choi (Eds.): WISA 2015, LNCS 9503, pp. 3–15, 2016.
DOI: 10.1007/978-3-319-31875-2_1

– Minimize client storage, the persistent and temporary storage needed.
– Minimize bandwidth cost, the total blocks transferred between client and server in order to write (or read) one block of real data.
– Maximize server storage usage efficiency, that is given the server can store N blocks of data, ensure as much as possible is available for storing real data.

In this paper we introduce a new ORAM that uses a Matrix data structure on the server; we call it M-ORAM. The design of the matrix data structure allows us to keep the bandwidth cost independent of the number of blocks stored on the server, thereby reducing bandwidth cost compared to other similar schemes. In addition, M-ORAM's read and write operations are performed using a simple random permutation function without any complex operations such as shuffling, sorting and merging.

1.1   Related Work

ORAM algorithms can generally be divided by the server storage structure: either a hierarchical structure [1–3,5,7,9,12–14] where each layer is independent from each other; or a tree–structure [10,11,15,16] where nodes in neighboring layers have relation of child and parent. A comparison of the asymptotic performance of key ORAM schemes is given in Table 1.

Table 1. Performance comparison of Different ORAM schemes

Scheme	Client storage (#Block)	Bandwidth cost (#Block)	Server storage usage
Hierarchical structure			
GO-ORAM [4]	$O(1)$	$O(\log^3 N)$	50 %
SSS-ORAM [14]	$O(N)$	$O(\log N)$	50 %
Recurisve SSS-ORAM [14]	$O(\sqrt{N})$	$O(\log^2 N)$	50 %
Tree structure			
Tree-ORAM [11]	$O(N)$	$O(\log^2 N)$	50 %
Recursive Tree-ORAM [11]	$O(1)$	$O(\log^3 N)$	50 %
Path-ORAM [15]	$O(N)$	$O(\log N)$	100 %
Recursive Path-ORAM [15]	$O(\log N) \cdot \omega(1)$	$O(\log^2 N)$	100 %
Matrix structure			
M-ORAM	$O(N)$	$O(1)$	100 %
Recursive M-ORAM	$O(\log N)$	$O(\log N)$	100 %

The original ORAM used a hierarchical structure [4]. Each hierarchy level is larger than its previous level which incurs $O(\log^3 N)$ bandwidth cost. Emil Stefanov *et al.* [14] introduced the idea of using ORAM for cloud storage with SSS-ORAM. By making several ORAM partitions and using concurrent access via an amortizer module, they can achieve $O(\log N)$ bandwidth cost with $O(N)$ client storage. In addition, they proposed *recursive ORAM*, which reduces client storage to $O(\sqrt{N})$ by storing client data structures in a 2nd ORAM on the server. The new method that dramatically reduces local storage requirement to $O(\sqrt{N})$. However compared to the normal ORAM construction, the recursive constructions come with the increased bandwidth cost.

Binary tree based ORAM was first proposed by Elaine Shi *et al.* [11] with $O(\log^2 N)$ bandwidth cost and $O(N)$ client storage when using the normal construction and $O(\log^3 N)$ bandwidth cost and $O(1)$ client storage with the recursive construction. Emil Stefanov *et al.* enhance it by reducing the processes that consume processing time and bandwidth, such as shuffling and sorting. This lead to $O(\log N)$ bandwidth cost and $O(N)$ client storage (normal) or $O(\log^2 N)$ bandwidth cost and $O(\log N) \cdot \omega(1)$ client storage (recursive).

Unlike any existing schemes, M-ORAM is built upon a matrix data structure for server storage. With the normal construction, it achieves $O(1)$ bandwidth cost when using constant size of stash buffer and N blocks of position-map. For the recursive construction, M-ORAM can achieve the best bandwidth cost at $O(\log N)$ and $O(\log N)$ client storage.

1.2   Contribution and Paper Organization

One aspect of ORAM's inefficiency is the bandwidth cost. To hide access patterns ORAM requires the client to download/upload multiple blocks, even though it is interested in just one of those blocks. The number of blocks to access usually depends on the total number of blocks the server may store. This paper provides an alternative ORAM structure that makes the bandwidth cost independent of the total number of blocks; instead dependent on the matrix height which is controllable by the designer. Our contributions are:

- Propose a new ORAM scheme based on matrix structure at server such that bandwidth cost is independent from the size of ORAM server storage.
- Design two constructions for M-ORAM: the normal construction and a recursive construction that recursively stores client data structures (stash) on the server, thereby reducing client storage.
- Show that with the M-ORAM recursive construction the bandwidth cost is better than other recursive models.
- Analyse performance and security for both M-ORAM constructions.

The rest of the paper is organized as follows. In Sect. 2 we provide an overview of M-ORAM construction and the process of secret key management for re-encryption method, and then its operations are presented in Sect. 3. In Sect. 4 we compare the performance of M-ORAM with other schemes and in Sect. 5 discuss the security issues. We conclude in Sect. 6.

2   M-ORAM Structure and Key Management

Two key design issues with ORAM are the data structures and the operations for accessing data. In this section we describe the server and client storage structures used by M-ORAM; the operations are described in Sect. 3. The notation used in this paper is summarized in Table 2.

The M-ORAM storage architecture is illustrated in Fig. 1. The physical addresses of server storage are mapped to the set of logical addresses in the

Table 2. Notation

Parameter	Description
N	Total number of data blocks stored in server [unit: blocks]
B	Size of each data block [Bytes]
H	Height of ORAM logical structure in server-side
W	N/H, Width of ORAM logical structure in server-side
S	Size of each stash buffer [Blocks]
$SecretKey$	Common secret key for encryption/decryption key generator
K	Encryption/Decryption Key
$dataID$	Data identification number
$stash$	Temporary buffer for downloaded information
x, y	Position of column and row in matrix structure
m	Number of address in single block of ORAM position-map
r	Number of recursions per single access request operation
P	Size of position-map information [Bytes]
$counter$	Individual counter of each information
$Pos[i]$	$[ctr_i, x_i, y_i]$, Position map of data i
$loclist$	Temporary address list of downloaded data
$oldlist$	Address list of previous access operation
$PRP()$	Pseudo-Random Permutation function

matrix format, x and y as described in Sect. 2.1. Those logical addresses are stored within the client and they will be accessed whenever the client needs to retrieve content from the server. The client also uses temporary storage called a stash; in M-ORAM logically separate stashes are used on conjunction with the matrix data structure. Section 2.2 describes the stash and position map in detail. The alternative structure for minimizing the client storage cost, recursive M-ORAM is presented in Sect. 2.3. Another role of the client is re-encrypting data and storing necessary keys. We explain how M-ORAM performs key management in Sect. 2.4.

2.1 Server Storage Structure

Path-ORAM [15] is one of the best ORAM schemes in terms of bandwidth cost. A binary–tree structure is used (for N blocks of data the tree height is $\log N$) where the client downloads all blocks from a path in the tree between root and a leaf node (the block of interest is on that path). Hence the bandwidth cost is $O(\log N)$. Our aim is to improve on this bandwidth cost. We do so by introducing a matrix structure for server storage. Rather than a binary–tree, a matrix with H rows and N/H columns is used. In M-ORAM a client downloads one block from each row. For the rows which do not contain data of interest, the column

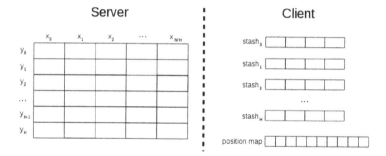

Fig. 1. M-ORAM structure

is chosen uniformly at random. The motivation for the matrix data structure is that the bandwidth cost depends on H. By selecting an appropriate H, the bandwidth cost can be less than Path-ORAM (and similar schemes). Section 4 analyses the bandwidth cost, while Sect. 5 discusses the security implications of using the matrix structure.

2.2   Client Storage Structure

Similar to other ORAM schemes, an M-ORAM client uses a stash buffer to temporarily store downloaded blocks and a position map for mapping logical block addresses to dataIDs. However unlike other schemes, M-ORAM uses a separate stash buffer for each row in the matrix. We denote each stash buffer as $stash_i$ where i is the matrix row number as illustrated in Fig. 1. The content in $stash_i$ will be uploaded to row_i but the downloaded content from row_i is not necessarily stored in $stash_i$ (Fig. 2). Furthermore, we can keep the size of the stash as constant during read/write operation (see Sect. 3).

In the normal M-ORAM construction every address of the data is in the client's position map. To reduce the client storage requirements, the position map may be stored on the server, with a second (smaller) position map storing the address of the data on the first position map. This recursive M-ORAM construction is described in the next section.

2.3   Recursive M-ORAM Construction

The position map on the client can introduce a significant storage overhead. Different ORAM schemes [11,14,15] have therefore proposed a recursive construction where the majority of the position map is stored on the server with ORAM and the remaining part of the position map is on the client. Further client storage space reduction is achieved by continuing the recursion. This recursive construction reduces client storage but increases bandwidth cost. In Path-ORAM (and other) recursive construction there is one position map ORAM for each level of recursion. A position map ORAM stores m addresses per data block, where these addresses point to either the data ORAM or another position map ORAM.

With N data blocks in the data ORAM, $\log_m N$ recursions are needed to cover every address of the N data blocks.

Instead of using multiple position map ORAMs as Path ORAM does, M-ORAM integrates all content (eg. data and position-map) into a single ORAM. The reason is to reduce the number of download elements during recursive operation. Suppose M-ORAM's height is H and it needs $\log_m N$ recursions for retrieving the requested information. The bandwidth cost per access operation is therefore $2H \log_m N$ blocks. However, we can dramatically reduce this overhead by slightly changing the traditional recursion protocol. Rather than downloading then uploading in every single recursion, M-ORAM will download and keep every block content within the stash until the requested information is retrieved and then uploads the same number of blocks back to the server. During each recursion the number of downloaded blocks is selected by uniform random from 1 to H. Hence, the expected value of downloaded elements is $\frac{H}{2}$, giving $H \log_m N$ bandwidth cost. Regarding the security of this approach, although the amount of downloaded elements is varied in each round, this distinction cannot be differentiated by server due to the consecutive downloading and consecutive uploading. A disadvantage is that we need at least $\frac{H \cdot (\log_m N)}{2}$ blocks of stash to contain information during the download operation. It means our stash size is bounded by $O(\log_m N)$ instead of $O(1)$ as the Path ORAM operation.

2.4   Encryption/Decryption Key Management

As with other ORAM schemes, data is re-encrypted by using a different key before being uploaded to the server. Therefore the server cannot identify if a subsequent upload is the same data as a previous upload. The details of the encryption algorithm and management of encryption keys differs amongst ORAM schemes. In our construction we use AES as our encryption method and use the counter, dataID, and a common secret key as the initial elements for generating the block's encryption key. Every counter is kept within the position-map along with its associated block location and is increased whenever the information has been downloaded. To generate the encryption key, the client will use those three elements as input into a pseudo-random permutation function (PRP) as described in Algorithm 1.

Algorithm 1. Secret Key Management

Input: $dataID, SecretKey$
$counter \leftarrow Pos[dataID]$
$K \leftarrow \mathrm{PRP}(dataID, ctr, SecretKey)$
$text \leftarrow \mathrm{Decrypt}_K(data)$
$counter \leftarrow counter + 1$
$Pos[dataID] \leftarrow ctr$
$K \leftarrow \mathrm{PRP}(dataID, counter, SecretKey)$
$data \leftarrow \mathrm{Encrypt}_K(text)$

---

3   M-ORAM Operation

In this section the detailed operation of our scheme will be discussed. Operation of M-ORAM can be categorized into Read, Write, Add and Delete operation. The Read and Write are major operation that are used to produce indistinguishable access pattern while the Add and Delete are a minor operation are used for locally inserting and deleting the elements in stash buffer. We give the functional descriptions that will be used in algorithm description as Table 3.

Table 3. Functional description

Function Name	Description
$ReadBl(x, y)$	Read information from server at position x and y
$RndStash(stash_i, data)$	Randomly put data to $stash_i$ without duplication
$RndData(stash_i)$	Randomly pick up data from $stash_i$ without duplication
$RndOld(oldlist, n)$	Randomly pick up n addresses from $oldist$
$UpdatePos(dataID_i, x, y)$	Update position-map of $dataID_i$
$WriteBl(x, y)$	Write information to server at position x and y

3.1   Read/Write Operation

In ORAM, whenever the client wishes to read or write data, it must actually read multiple blocks and then write multiple blocks back and forth to server. One among the many downloaded blocks must be the information that is required by client, whereas the uploaded blocks are not necessarily the same set as previously downloaded.

In M-ORAM, an extremely simple read/write operation will be utilized. The operation will begin whenever the client requests information from server. The address of requested information is derived from the position-map by using its dataID, then the read operation is invoked. To simplify, we first define the *height* and *width* of matrix structure as the number of *row:* y and *column:* x. The intersection of a distinct x and y is represented as the position of the block of information. As described in Algorithm 2, x_i will be uniformly randomly chosen if y_i does not belong to the requested information. Information within that location will be retrieved whether it is real information or not. The same process will be repeatedly applied to the next row and so on. The dummy contents are thrown away and only real information is randomly spread to $stash_i$ without duplication (See Fig. 2a). With this method the location in Y-axis of every content is changed without relevance to its original position.

The randomization in the X-axis will take place during the write operation as illustrated in Fig. 2b. The information will be uploaded by uniformly randomly selecting from the stash, starting from $stash_0$ to $stash_H$. This is to ensure the write access pattern is deterministic over indistinguishable information. Furthermore, the uploaded information can be either dummy or real information.

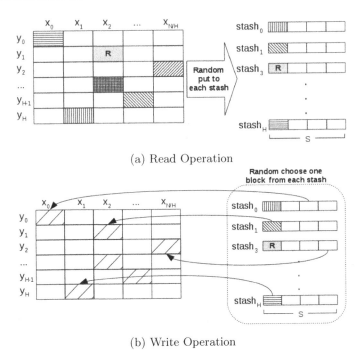

(a) Read Operation

(b) Write Operation

Fig. 2. M-ORAM Operatoin

The dummy information will be uploaded if the empty column is hit by randomization. The chosen content will be stored at the previous accessed position based on the stash buffer. Specifically, the selected block from $stash_i$ will be written back to the last accessed location of y_i, where $i \in \{0, 1, \ldots, H\}$. Note that to avoid the information being distinguishable between different read/write operations, at least one block location of the previous operation must be "randomly" selected for the next operation. To achieve this we randomly select n locations from the previous operation. In a binary tree structure the same node at level h will be chosen twice in a row of operation with the probability $\frac{1}{2^{h-1}}$. Hence, we should select n from between 1 and some upper limit that gives similar probability as binary-tree structure. In our design we select n blocks from the previous operation where $1 \leq n \leq 5$. In this case H in M-ORAM should be at least 10 blocks for distribution of the random selection. A read/write operation will push a single downloaded element and pop a single element to and from each stash respectively. Therefore the stash will not overflow under the operation although each stash has a constant size. However, the distribution of information during the operation depends on the height of storage and the stash size. With H being at least 10 blocks, the stash size should be at least 10 blocks to keep the probability of duplication when writing back under 1 %.

Algorithm 2. Read Operation	**Algorithm 3.** Write Operation
Input: $dataID, data^*$	**Input:** $loclist, stash$
$x_d, y_d \leftarrow Pos[dataID]$	**for** $i \in \{0, 1, 2, 3, \dots, H\}$ **do**
$n \xleftarrow{\$} \{1, 2, 3 \dots, 5\}$	$\quad x_i, y_i \leftarrow loclist[i]$
$j \leftarrow \text{RndOld}(oldlist, n)$	$\quad dataID, data \leftarrow \text{RndData}(stash_i)$
for $i \in \{0, 1, 2, 3, \dots, H\}$ **do**	$\quad \text{UpdatePos}(dataID, x_i, y_i)$
$\quad$ **if** $y_i = y_d$ **then**	$\quad \text{WriteBl}(x_i, y_i, data)$
$\quad\quad data \leftarrow \text{ReadBl}(x_d, y_d)$	**end for**
$\quad\quad loclist \leftarrow loclist \cup (x_d, y_d)$	
$\quad\quad$ **if** update operation **then**	
$\quad\quad\quad data \leftarrow data^*$	
$\quad\quad$ **end if**	
$\quad\quad \text{RndStash}(stash_i, data)$	
$\quad$ **else**	
$\quad\quad$ **if** $y_i \in j$ **then**	
$\quad\quad\quad loclist \leftarrow loclist \cup (x_*, y_i)$	
$\quad\quad\quad \text{RndStash}(stash_i, \text{ReadBl}(x_*, y_i))$	
$\quad\quad$ **else**	
$\quad\quad\quad x_i \xleftarrow{\$} \{0, 1, 2, 3, \dots, \frac{N}{H}\}$	
$\quad\quad\quad loclist \leftarrow loclist \cup (x_i, y_i)$	
$\quad\quad\quad \text{RndStash}(stash_i, \text{ReadBl}(x_i, y_i))$	
$\quad\quad$ **end if**	
$\quad$ **end if**	
end for	
return $data$	

3.2 Add/Delete Operation

In M-OORAM, the Add/Delete features are included as additional operations. Adding information will be locally operated by randomly choosing empty blocks within the stash buffer. The Delete operation, on the other hand, has the same procedure as read operation. However, after downloading the data that is to be deleted, it is not stored in the stash buffer.

4 Performance Analysis

The key aim of M-ORAM is to decrease the communication overhead when the client accesses data on the server. In Sect. 4.1 we analyse the bandwidth cost in the normal and recursive case of M-ORAM. In Sect. 4.2 we show that our construction consumes less bandwidth cost even if we use the same height structure as binary tree ORAM.

4.1 M-ORAM Communication Overhead

The server in (normal) M-ORAM stores data of up to N blocks in a matrix with H rows (the height). When the client accesses data it must read/write an element from each of the H rows. Therefore to access one real data block, M-ORAM has a bandwidth cost of $2H$ blocks. Reducing the matrix height reduces the bandwidth cost. In Sect. 5 we analyse the security impact of reducing the height, and claim that the height can be fixed, irrespective of N. Therefore the bandwidth cost is independent of N, i.e. is bounded by $O(1)$.

In the recursive construction of M-ORAM the bandwidth cost depends on two aspects which are the number of recursion and the height of matrix. In traditional recursion method the number of downloaded and uploaded element for each round is equal to height of position-map ORAM. For more precise we suppose our position-map in server: $posORAM$ has height equal to H and we need r recursions for retrieving the position of requested information. According to our construction, we have $2rH$ as our bandwidth cost for access operation. Suppose each block of $posORAM$ contains m blocks position of next recursion, it needs $log_m N$ rounds to keep the amount of block of the first recursion equal to 1. As was mentioned, we can keep height of our structure as constant thus our construction can achieve $O(\log_m N)$ bandwidth cost. If we consider $m = 2$, the bandwidth consumption for our recursive construction is bounded by $O(\log N)$.

4.2 Comparison of Bandwidth Cost with Binary Tree Based ORAM

We already explained that our bandwidth consumption is bounded by $O(\log N)$. Now we will show that we can achieve better bandwidth cost even when our construction has the same height as binary tree ORAM. In binary tree ORAM the amount of cyclic requests depends on $\log N$ (height of binary tree structure) and m. Furthermore, after running $\log_m N$ recursions, we can construct the general equation of amount downloaded as (using geometric series formula):

$$\sum_{i=0}^{\log_m N} \log \frac{N}{m^i} = \sum_{i=0}^{\log_m N} \log N - \sum_{i=0}^{\log_m N} \log m^i$$
$$= (\log N)(\log_m N + 1) - \frac{(\log m)(\log_m N)(\log_m N + 1)}{2}$$
$$= \frac{\log^2 N}{2 \log m} + \frac{\log N}{2}$$

According to Sect. 2, the height of our structure is independent from the number of blocks of information. It is clear that our scheme can achieve better bandwidth overhead by adjusting H. Even if we are forced to use the same height as binary tree, our scheme achieves better performance. To be more precise, lets assume that our structure uses same height as binary tree which is $\log N$. As the uniform randomization of number of downloaded block is 1 to H for each request, the average amount per request is $\frac{H}{2}$. In the case we make a request $\log_m N$ times, the total amount of downloaded blocks is, $\frac{\log^2 N}{2 \log m}$. This is $\frac{\log N}{2}$ less downloaded blocks that what is used for the Path ORAM recursion method.

5 Security Analysis

In this section we state the security requirements of ORAM schemes and then explain why M-ORAM achieves the requirements.

5.1   Security Requirements

The security requirements of M-ORAM are:

1. The server cannot observe the relationship between data and the address position that is stored on the server.
2. The server cannot distinguish between updated and non-updated information when the client writes back to the server.
3. The server (or other clients) cannot observe the requested data, i.e. each request message cannot be differentiated from a random bit string.
4. The server cannot recognise any patterns of access by the client.

To achieve requirement 1 and 2, random re-encryption is needed. Section 5.2 explains the role of random re-encryption in M-ORAM and the reason M-ORAM achieves requirement 3 and 4 is explained in Sect. 5.3.

When a client makes a series of access requests (read/write $dataID_i$, read/write $dataID_{i-1}$, ..., read/write $dataID_1$), the server sees the sequence:

$$A = (pos_i[dataID_i]), pos_{i-1}[dataID_{i-1}], \ldots, pos_1[dataID_1])$$

where for data item $dataID_j$, $pos_j[dataID_j]$ is the set of block position for retrieving $dataID_j$ where $j \in \{1, 2, \ldots, i\}$. Each block information given in the format $(counter_j, x_n, y_m)$, where $counter_j$ is a counter, and x_n and y_m are the column m and row n, respectively.

5.2   Random Re-encryption

As described in Sect. 2.4, every time the client has data to upload, the client first encrypts the data. A different key is used for each encryption. We use the set of $(dataID_j, counter_j)$ together with a shared $SecretKey$ as the inputs to a strong pseudo random permutation function (PRP) to generate a secret key for encrypting the data. The reasons for using these three inputs are first the $dataID$ is unique per data block. Second, the $counter$ is introduced so that each time the same data block is uploaded a different value input to the PRP is used (to ensure the server cannot identify multiple uploads of the same data). Third, the $SecretKey$ is a secret known by the client and is necessary as the server may be able to learn the $dataID$ and $counter$. Combining these three values as input to the PRP ensures that a unique, secret encrypt key will be used before the upload. Assuming $SecretKey$ is secure, the server cannot distinguish encrypted information uploaded by the client.

5.3   Indistinguishable Access Pattern

The indistinguishable access pattern consists of two factors which are server cannot determine what data will be written to which location, and the client's requested information cannot be distinguished by the server.

In M-ORAM the client downloads H blocks where, as described in Sect. 3, the junk blocks are selected from each row (other than the row with the requested block) with the column chosen uniformly at random, then randomly be pushed to each stash without duplication. At this point the way of downloaded data being stored at *stashes* without duplication is $H!$. Suppose each *stash* has S blocks. It is precise that the way to choose the data from each stash for writing back is S, Hence, the probability that downloaded contents will be written back to their previous location is:

$$\Pr(pos_j(dataID_j)) = \frac{1}{H! \cdot S^H}, \text{where} j \in \{1, 2, \ldots, i\}.$$

Suppose we have access request sequence A size i and $j < k \in \{1, 2, \ldots, i\}$. When the $pos_j(dataID_j)$ is revealed to the server, it will be randomly remapped to the new position as previous mentioned. Therefore the $pos_j(dataID_j)$ is statically independent from $pos_k(dataID_k)$, with $dataID_j = dataID_k$. In the case of $dataID_j \neq dataID_k$, the address of difference information does not has any relation, thus those addresses are statically independent from each other. As Bayes rule, we can describe the statistically independent of A as:

$$\prod_{j=1}^{i} \Pr(pos_j(dataID_j)) = \left(H! \cdot S^H\right)^{-i}$$

By considering that H and S are greater than 10 for each request operation. It proves that the series of access request is indistinguishable from a random sequence of bit string. Regarding the recursive construction, the single access request is started from read set of information and then write set of information. We can replace $dataID_j$ with set of information, $dataID_j[z], z \in \{0, 1, \ldots, m\}$, where $dataID_j[z]$ is a set of data d blocks during m recursions. The statistically independent of single request under recursive construction is

$$\Pr(pos_j(dataID_j[z])) = \left[\left(\prod_{k=1}^{d-1}(HS - (\varphi - k))\right) \cdot \left(\prod_{k=1}^{d-1}(HS - (\omega - k))\right)\right]^{-1}$$

where φ is the amount of remaining elements in stash and ω is the amount of block that cannot be updated position map which $HS - \omega \leq d \leq HS - \varphi$. Hence, the probability of sequence request i is:

$$\prod_{j=1}^{i} \Pr(pos_j(dataID_j[z])) = \left[\left(\prod_{k=1}^{d-1}(HS - (\varphi - k))\right) \cdot \left(\prod_{k=1}^{d-1}(HS - (\omega - k))\right)\right]^{-i}$$

In the same manner as the normal construction, we can claim that the series of access requests from recursive construction is also indistinguishable from a random sequence of bit strings.

6   Conclusion

M-ORAM uses a matrix storage structure on the server to provide the same security as other ORAM schemes (such as Path ORAM), while reducing the bandwidth cost. In the normal construction it gives $O(1)$ bandwidth cost with

$O(N)$ client storage, while with the recursive construction $O(\log N)$ bandwidth cost with $O(\log N)$ client storage. We show an bandwidth cost improvement over binary tree based ORAM of $\frac{\log N}{2}$ when the two schemes use the same height. We believe the matrix structure is favorable for using with cache memory, further improving bandwidth cost; this analysis is left for future research.

References

1. Boneh, D., Mazieres, D., Popa, R.A.: Remote oblivious storage: Making oblivious RAM practical (2011)
2. Dautrich, J., Stefanov, E., Shi, E.: Burst ORAM: Minimizing oram response times for bursty access patterns. In: 23rd USENIX Security Symposium (USENIX Security 14), pp. 749–764. USENIX Association, San Diego, August 2014
3. Gentry, C., Goldman, K.A., Halevi, S., Julta, C., Raykova, M., Wichs, D.: Optimizing ORAM and using it efficiently for secure computation. In: De Cristofaro, E., Wright, M. (eds.) PETS 2013. LNCS, vol. 7981, pp. 1–18. Springer, Heidelberg (2013)
4. Goldreich, O., Ostrovsky, R.: Software protection and simulation on oblivious RAMs. J. ACM (JACM) **43**(3), 431–473 (1996)
5. Goodrich, M.T., Mitzenmacher, M., Ohrimenko, O., Tamassia, R.: Privacy-preserving group data access via stateless oblivious RAM simulation. In: Proceedings of the Twenty-third Annual ACM-SIAM Symposium on Discrete Algorithms, pp. 157–167 (2012)
6. Islam, M.S., Kuzu, M., Kantarcioglu, M.: Access pattern disclosure on searchable encryption: ramification, attack and mitigation. In: NDSS, vol. 20, p. 12 (2012)
7. Karvelas, N.P., Peter, A., Katzenbeisser, S., Biedermann, S.: Efficient privacy-preserving big data processing through proxy-assisted ORAM. IACR Cryptology ePrint Archive **2014**, 72 (2014)
8. Liu, C., Zhu, L., Wang, M., Tan, Y.A.: Search pattern leakage in searchable encryption: Attacks and new construction. Inf. Sci. **265**, 176–188 (2014)
9. Pinkas, B., Reinman, T.: Oblivious RAM revisited. In: Rabin, T. (ed.) CRYPTO 2010. LNCS, vol. 6223, pp. 502–519. Springer, Heidelberg (2010)
10. Ren, L., Fletcher, C.W., Yu, X., Kwon, A., van Dijk, M., Devadas, S.: Unified oblivious-RAM: Improving recursive ORAM with locality and pseudorandomness. IACR Cryptology ePrint Archive **2014**, 205 (2014)
11. Shi, E., Chan, T.-H., Stefanov, E., Li, M.: Oblivious RAM with $O((\log N)^3)$ worst-case cost. In: Lee, D.H., Wang, X. (eds.) ASIACRYPT 2011. LNCS, vol. 7073, pp. 197–214. Springer, Heidelberg (2011)
12. Sion, R., Williams, P.: Fast oblivious storage. Assoc. Comput. Mach. **15**(4), 1–28 (2013)
13. Stefanov, E., Shi, E.: ObliviStore: high performance oblivious cloud storage, pp. 253–267. IEEE, May 2013
14. Stefanov, E., Shi, E., Song, D.: Towards practical oblivious RAM. arXiv preprint (2011). arxiv:1106.3652
15. Stefanov, E., Van Dijk, M., Shi, E., Fletcher, C., Ren, L., Yu, X., Devadas, S.: Path ORAM: an extremely simple oblivious ram protocol. In: Proceedings of the 2013 ACM SIGSAC Conference on Computer & Communications Security, pp. 299–310. ACM (2013)
16. Zhang, J., Ma, Q., Zhang, W., Qiao, D.: KT-ORAM: a bandwidth-efficient ORAM built on k-ary tree of pir nodes. Cryptology ePrint Archive, Report 2014/624 (2014)

Process Variation Evaluation Using RO PUF for Enhancing SCA-Resistant Dual-Rail Implementation

Wei He[1]([⊠]), Dirmanto Jap[2], and Alexander Herrmann[1]

[1] Physical Analysis and Cryptographic Engineering (PACE),
Nanyang Technological University, SPMS, MAS 05-31,
Singapore 637371, Singapore
{he.wei,aherrmann}@ntu.edu.sg
[2] School of Physical and Mathematical Sciences (SPMS),
Nanyang Technological University, SPMS, MAS 05-31,
Singapore 637371, Singapore
dirm0002@e.ntu.edu.sg

Abstract. The security of the implemented cryptographic algorithm in hardware has been certified to be vulnerable against physical-level Side-Channel analysis. As a typical countermeasure, dual-rail precharge logic theoretically thwarts Side-Channel analysis because of its compensated data-dependent fluctuations in observable power or EM traces. However the security grade of the dual-rail behavior is significantly impacted by silicon technological bias due to its non identical alterations to each rail's electrical characteristics. In this paper, a technique is proposed to evaluate the in-die process variation, which relies on the Hamming Distance of the PUF responses by intentionally heating up the silicon. Based on the observed PV distribution, a secure dual-rail placement against SCA in FPGA is devised. To validate the security variants, EM based surface scan is performed for investigating the leakage distribution. Correlation and mutual information analyses are used for jointly evaluating the security variants of a lightweight crypto coprocessor in variant placements. Experimental results demonstrated enhanced dual-rail symmetry owing to the reduced process variation in the interleaved placement.

Keywords: Side-Channel Attack (SCA) · Process Variation · Physical Unclonable Function (PUF) · Dual-Rail Precharge Logic (DPL) · CEMA · MIA

1 Introduction

In modern cryptography, data is protected by utilizing strong cryptographic algorithms, which inevitably draws into numerous vulnerabilities within its implementations. Conventional cryptanalysis centers to the exploitations of algorithmic decipherable weaknesses. Impeded by complex cipher systems, pure mathematic cryptanalysis became far to be viable when attacking the mathematically robust

© Springer International Publishing Switzerland 2016
H. Kim and D. Choi (Eds.): WISA 2015, LNCS 9503, pp. 16–27, 2016.
DOI: 10.1007/978-3-319-31875-2_2

crypto algorithms. In Contrast, Side-Channel attacks specially exploit the unintentionally leaked physical information for retrieving the hidden *things*. Side-Channel Attack in this context was originally sketched in [9] by Paul Kocher, *et al.* for analyzing the implementation basing on the tiny data-dependent fluctuations from the real-time power consumption.

A typical protection approach is to remove the data-dependent variations from the security critical logic elements. In this way, the dual-rail precharge logic (DPL) can be used which bases on a *'dual-rail'* and *'dual-phase'* protocol, where each logic value a is replaced by a pair of complementary values a_t and b_t respectively in two rails (*True* (T) and *False* (F) rails). In the *'evaluation'* phase, all the effective values are propagated through the combinatorial logic chain, and in the *'precharge'* phase, all the non-register values are reset to a fixed state (normally '0'). A proper realization of this structure ensures one and only one switch in each clock cycle in view of each compound gate, where in view of the two rails the logic behavior is constant. Hence the data dependencies can be theoretically removed. Since the continuously shrinking size of transistors, *Process Variation* (PV) is posing significant impacts to security assurances that makes some design essentials probabilistic and unpredictable [2,3,13]. Numerous researches have certified that silicon process variation affects power consumption within both routings and gates (output capacitive load [17]). This influence become even prominent in term of dual-rail logics, wherein a phenomena arose is that the mismatch between the logic behavior over complementary rails is likely to emit revealable Side-Channel leakage.

In this paper, a novel PV evaluation technique is proposed relying on the thermal influenced Ring-Oscillator Physical Unclonable Function (RO PUF), for bolstering the secure placement scheme of a SCA-hardened dual-rail logic. The remainder of paper is organised as follows: Sect. 2 describes the prior relevant work; The silicon process variation evaluation using RO PUF is detailed in Sect. 3; Sect. 4 demonstrates the dual-rail implementation of a lightweight crypto coprocessor; The selections of analysis models and platform setup are presented in Sect. 5; Sect. 6 gives the security evaluations basing on the EM surface scan, using correlation and mutual information approaches. Section 7 draws the conclusions and perspectives.

2 Technical Background

2.1 Silicon Process Variation and Dual-Rail Impacts

Process variation is the innate silicon feature of the randomly dispersed articles and etching deviations introduced from the chip manufacture. These non identical distributions unfavorably cause tiny spatial differences in electrical characteristics. The parasitic capacitances of ideally implemented net pair must consume the same amount of power. In Eq. (1), P_w denotes the power consumption from a routing assuming its parasitic capacitance is C_{pc}, working on the average flip frequency f and voltage swing V.

$$P_w = \frac{1}{2} \cdot C_{pc} \cdot f \cdot V^2 \qquad (1)$$

For DPL researches in FPGA, routings in a long-term exist as a concern since the innate C_{pc} for each complementary routing pair should be as identical as possible. As previously stressed, parasitic parameters differ across the entire chip owing to the uncontrollable silicon bias. Hence, the rigorous requirements for a nicely constructed dual-rail circuit mainly reside within how to diminish the PV influence.

2.2 Silicon Process Variation Alleviation

A number of logics have been proposed in literatures, which helps to alleviate the security defects from process variations. In [14], the interconnect pairs are randomly swapped using a bit masking, which makes the routing bias ignorable. But the unbalanced routings still performs as the main leakage sources. A technique described in [10] increases the transistor channel lengths to mitigate the PV influence, using *Spice* simulation. However, a new fabrication technology is required which greatly increases the design cost. A technique proposed in [12] purposely minimizes the skews between T/F routing delays in a swapped dual-rail format. Since the routing pairs are estimated by length, instead of the precise shapes, the T/F routing pairs still leave exploitable leakage due to the unbalanced parasitic capacitances. In order to effectively remove the influence from technological biases, some expensive efforts must be devoted.

2.3 RO PUF Architecture

Inverter Based Ring Oscillator: RO is a low-cost logic that has been widely used in security specific Random Number Generator (RNG). The basic framework of RO is a cascaded delay stages in a closed chain, for yielding regulated and stable frequency oscillation at a fixed temperature. Figure 1(a) illustrates a generic inverter based Ring Oscillator in digital logic.

The flip frequency f of this RO can be computed by:

$$f = \frac{1}{\sum_{i=1}^{n}(d_{G_i} + d_{L_i})} \tag{2}$$

RO PUF: Because of the variations of physical characteristics in silicon, d_{G_i} and d_{L_i} have slight difference from different chips, locations, and even thermal environments, hence the observed frequencies can also be different. One of the most important RO usages in security domain is the RO based Physical Unclonable Function (PUF) [15], which takes into account of the unclonable and chip unique features. In an ordinary RO based PUF, identically laid-out ROs are implemented together. Due to the manufacturing variations across the chip, each RO delivers different frequencies that cannot be cloned to another chip. By deploying a number of identical ROs and comparing the frequencies obtained from the same sequence of RO pairs, a particular output bit combination can be achieved. Importantly, due to the PV from chip to chip, these bit orders are not able to be duplicated even if the internal structure and sequence are disclosed. Hence this logic can be safely used as a unique signature for security authentication. Figure 1(b) sketches a type of RO based PUF.

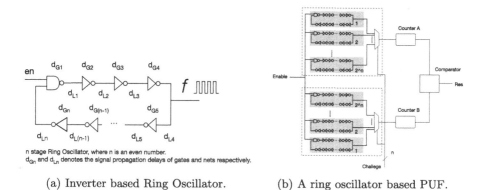

(a) Inverter based Ring Oscillator.   (b) A ring oscillator based PUF.

Fig. 1. Ring oscillator based physical unclonable function.

3   Dual-Rail PV Evaluation Using RO PUF

3.1   Thermal Effect to RO Pair

Temperature alters the physical behavior of a silicon circuit by influencing the mobility of the dopant electrons (n-type) and holes (p-type). More concretely, the higher thermal environment, the lower the signal propagation is. Since the frequency of a RO is determined by the summed up signal delays (see Eq. 2), the temperature can hence change the RO frequency in a predictable direction, *i.e.,* increasing the temperature would slow down the frequency as illustrated in Fig. 2(a). Assuming that identical ROs have different base frequencies at temperature T0. If the silicon where RO_a and RO_b are placed have smaller process variation than that between RO_a and RO_c, RO_a should have closer base frequency to RO_b, and larger base frequency to RO_c. Furthermore, owing to the similar physical characteristics, the frequency-temperature plots should be more likely to be a pair of parallel lines between RO_a and RO_b. An immediate hypothesis can be deduced that by increasing the temperature, the frequency flip between RO_a and RO_c occurs earlier (at T1) than that between RO_a and RO_b (at T2), which has been elaborated in Fig. 2(b).

3.2   FPGA Evaluation

To further certify this phenomenon, we employed two RO PUF in the Virtex-5 FPGA on SASEBO-GII board, where each RO has the same placement and route configuration to guarantee that the response variability is only rooted at the technological bias. For any challenges, frequencies from two unique ROs

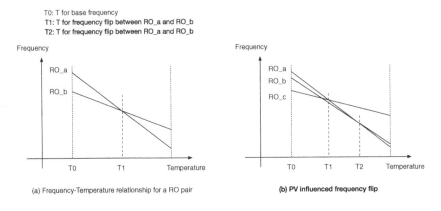

T0: T for base frequency
T1: T for frequency flip between RO_a and RO_b
T2: T for frequency flip between RO_a and RO_b

(a) Frequency-Temperature relationship for a RO pair

(b) PV influenced frequency flip

Fig. 2. Process variation influenced frequency flip for RO pair in changing temperature.

are compared, we can hence ensure the weakest dependency among each RO. Our work is based on the comparison of two settings: (i) All the ROs are randomly deployed in the logic array. We set the distance relevant process variation between any pair of ROs as $PV_{(a)}$, as shown in Fig. 3(a). (ii) The two ROs from any of the 64 RO pairs are intentionally deployed in an interleaved fashion, as given in Fig. 3(b), hence the distance relevant process variation is set as $PV_{(b)}$. Since all the RO pairs are interleaved in (b), the distances are all minimized and unified. By scanning the 6-bit challenge vector, we can extract 64 response bits respectively from the two settings. The two implemented RO PUF are shown in Fig. 4. To test the temperature influence to the PUF response, we used the hair dryer to heat up the silicon.

Table 1 shows the flipped response bits at the beginning (lowest temperature T_{low}) till the ending point (highest temperature T_{high}) to the differently placed PUFs in Fig. 4. The number of the flipped bits to the randomly placed

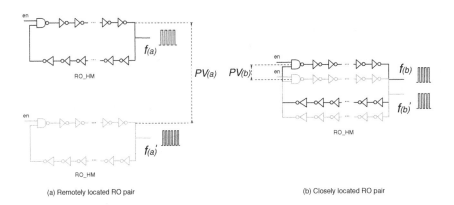

(a) Remotely located RO pair

(b) Closely located RO pair

Fig. 3. Distance relevant process variation to Ring-Oscillator pair.

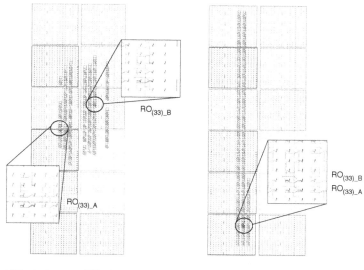

(a) Randomly scattered RO pair array in PUF. (b) Interleaved RO pair array in PUF.

Fig. 4. FPGA editor view of the implemented RO pairs in PUF.

Table 1. Thermal influenced RO PUF responses

PUF_1	T_{low}	0	7	E	0	3	D	5	7	F	6	0	3	9	8	B	7	HD:13
	T_{high}	2	F	2	0	7	D	3	7	F	5	8	3	1	B	9	7	
PUF_2	T_{low}	F	D	C	F	F	4	6	8	6	B	F	4	E	E	C	0	HD:2
	T_{high}	F	D	C	F	F	C	6	8	4	B	F	4	E	E	C	0	

*A smaller HD represents fewer flipped response bits by heating up the silicon, time window for heating is 5 min.

PUF (PUF_1 in Table 1) during the heating process is 13 (*e.g.*, Hamming Distance (HD) of responses from T_{low} to T_{high}). In contrary, the counterpart HD to the interleaved PUF (PUF_2 in Table 1) is only 2. This observation shows that the thermal influence to the interleaved RO pairs are generally more identical, so they are comparatively difficult to be flipped (see RO_a and RO_b in Fig. 2(b)) by altering the temperature, which in turn implies smaller PVs between the corresponding logic and routing segments if the two identical rails can be interleaved.

4 Dual-Rail Implementation

4.1 Dual Core Placement

The viable placements of the paired rails reside on twofold metrics: (a) the resource configuration in FPGA device and (b) the logic structure to be handled. Since the selected DPL is a separate dual-rail format, or more precisely, the two

T/F networks have no swapped signals between each logic intermediates. Three placement styles are schemed which consists of (1) unprotected single-rail circuit, Fig. 5(i); (2) separate dual-rail one, Fig. 5(ii); (3) interleaved dual-rail, Fig. 5(iii).

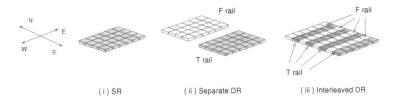

(i) SR   (ii) Separate DR   (iii) Interleaved DR

Fig. 5. Schemed dual-rail placements in FPGA resource array.

A lightweight *Present* block cipher [1] is selected in our experiments, which follows the principle of *Substitution-Permutation network* [11], to use either 80 bit or 128 bit key for en-/de-crypting 64-bit plaintext/ciphertext in 32 computation rounds. Figure 6 briefs the basic parallel architecture of the selected cipher.

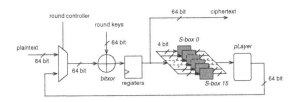

Fig. 6. Structure of *Present* lightweight crypto core.

4.2 Symmetric Dual-Rail Precharge Logic (DPL)

In our work, Precharge Absorbed-DPL (PA-DPL) [6] is selected for its high symmetry in dual-rail routing networks. Figure 7 presents the logic frameworks of the generic WDDL logic [16] and the used PA-DPL. The main difference here is that WDDL requires the swapped T/F routings to realize the *inverse factor* in logic functions, as seen in Fig. 7(a). Hence the routing pairs are impossible to be maintained physically identical in FPGAs. In contrary, the T/F rails in PA-DPL are independent, so a pair of identical T/F routing networks are possibly to be achieved, as shown in Fig. 7(b).

The implementation is approximately similar to the described 2-stage design flow in [12,18], which consists of: (1) the generic FPGA single-rail implementation stage; (2) the back-end Xilinx Design Language (XDL) dual-rail transformation stage. We used the technique presented in [7] for the entire design flow for the following automatic routing repair process for finding non-identical or conflict routings, and restoring the identical T/F paths.

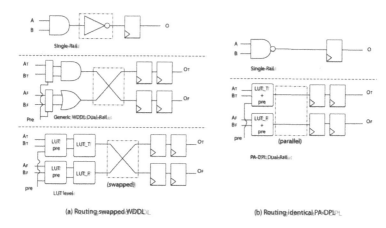

Fig. 7. WDDL and PA-DPL comparison.

5   Experimental Analysis

5.1   Selection of Distinguisher

Correlation EM Analysis (CEMA). The most widely utilized analysis metric is Correlation Power/EM Analysis (CPA/CEMA), which was originally proposed in [4]. Pearson correlation is used as distinguisher to determine the linear relationship between the hypothetical model and the measured leakage, using the following model:

$$r_{x,y} = \frac{\sum_{i=1}^{n}(x_i - \bar{x})(y_i - \bar{y})}{\sqrt{\sum_{i=1}^{n}(x_i - \bar{x})^2 \sum_{i=1}^{n}(y_i - \bar{y})^2}} \tag{3}$$

For any pair of vectors $x = \{x_1, ..., x_n\}$ and $y = \{y_1, ..., y_n\}$, $\bar{x}$ and $\bar{y}$ denote the means of x and y respectively. The x and y are substituted with the vector of measured traces and the hypothetical value. A higher $|r_{x,y}|$ shows some linear dependencies between x and y. The main restriction using correlation analysis is that it only reveals the linear relationship. Hence, if the constructed analysis model doesn't fit the circuit quite well, or the environmental noise is high, the correlation analysis might not be preferable.

Mutual Information Analysis (MIA). Mutual Information Analysis (MIA) was sketched in [5], which is constructed on the information theory for measuring the dependency between any two random variables. The entropy of random variable X in its space $\mathcal{X}$ (discrete) is defined by:

$$H(X) = - \sum_{x \in \mathcal{X}} Pr[X = x] \cdot log_2(Pr[X = x]) \tag{4}$$

$Pr[X = x]$ denotes the probability of $X = x$.

The higher the mutual information is, the stronger the relation among X and Y. Mutual information only concerns about general dependencies and thus, it could be generalized to construct both linear and non-linear relations between the logic value and the Side-Channel leakage. Hence in some cases, it outperforms the correlation analysis in condition of higher environmental noise and vague analysis model. Kernel Density Estimation (KDE) is utilized for estimate the probability distribution:

$$Pr[Y = y] = \frac{1}{qh} \sum_{i=1}^{q} K\left(\frac{y - y_i}{h}\right) \tag{5}$$

5.2   EM Surface Scan Acquisition

The cipher system is implemented in SASEBO-GII board [8], wherein *Present* is deployed into the main Virtex-5 cipher FPGA and the peripheral part is situated into the Spartan-3A controller FPGA. The main Virtex-5 FPGA is mechanically decapsulated (Thermal Interface Material(TIM) layer is EM transparent), hence the micro EM probe can be closely situated to the bottom-layer logic/routing elements. Riscure EM Station is used to perform the EM trace acquisition.

We conducted a preliminary thorough chip scan for positioning the logic region. An EM-proof shield is wrapped to the EM probe to increase the SNR. To collect the EM traces, a more precise EM acquisition is mounted to the pre-positioned clock regions. We set the surface rectangle region roughly over the clock regions where the cipher part resides. More precisely, the scanning matrix is set as 30×30. In each location, 50,000 EM traces are collected, which exclusively aim at the time window between the last and the second last encryption rounds of *Present* cryptography at a sampling rate of 1GS/s.

6   Security Evaluation

6.1   CPA Analysis

For every 50,000 traces in each of the 900 locations, we performed the correlation coefficient analyses respectively for each of the total 16 4-bit subkey nibbles. The 2D correlation values for the scanned region yielded from the three implementations can be seen in Fig. 8, where the pixels showing the dark red colour refer to the locations where strong EM leakage appear, and vice versa. It is clear that Single Rail (SR) circuit shows the strongest local leakages in the locations where the cipher core is implemented (center in the array). Note that in the left-down corner, the leakage is also strong, which is generally due to the nearby IO pins that emanate strong EM information. Comparatively, the two dual-rail circuits demonstrate much lower leakage and smoother correlation distributions. More precisely, the separate Dual-Rail (DR) circuit still shows distinguishable leakages in the cipher part, while the interleaved DR shows even weaker leakages in the cipher deployed regions.

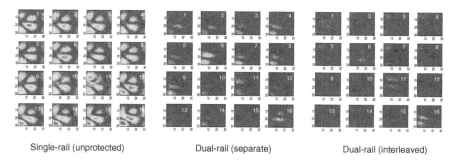

Single-rail (unprotected)   Dual-rail (separate)   Dual-rail (interleaved)

Fig. 8. 2D correlation plots of the EM scanning for different implementations.

6.2 MIA Analysis

MIA analysis is advantageous compared to correlation solution in case the data-leak relevancy is not linear, or the environmental noise is strong. As demonstrated in Fig. 9, the strong leakages widely exist in the unprotected single rail one (left in Fig. 9). The leakage distribution is similar to the CPA result where high leakages appear in crypto parts. For the DR candidates, leakages are significantly reduced because of the rail compensations. The separate DR (middle in Fig. 9) reveals some strong and distinguishable leakage in certain nibbles, and comparatively, the interleaved DR (right in Fig. 9) shows low and unidentifiable leakages in positions of all nibbles.

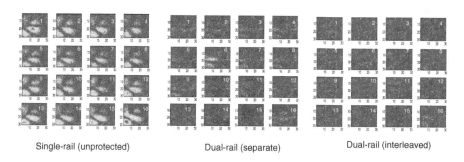

Single-rail (unprotected)   Dual-rail (separate)   Dual-rail (interleaved)

Fig. 9. 2D correlation plots of the EM scanning for different implementations.

6.3 Experimental Summary

According to the observations of the CPA and MIA leakages to the scanned region on chip, CPA shows high and distinct leakage peaks at the expected leak points where the cipher cores are deployed. MIA, in contrary, as well demonstrates the local leakages, while the distributions are not sharp *w.r.t.*, CPA, *i.e.*, the leakage locations are not precisely localized. This is mainly owing to the MIA nature, which is functional for revealing not just linear relevancy, but also non-linear dependency, which inevitably introduces of considerable environmental noise that partially matches the hypothesized relationship between the EM field and the processed data. However, the leakage maps of the interleaved DR circuit from both correlation and mutual information analyses jointly certify a higher security grade. Since all the experiments are done in the same setups and similar temperature/EM environments, we can safely conclude that the interleaved DR placement outperforms the separate DR placement in term of correlation and mutual information based SCAs.

7 Conclusions

In this paper, we have reported a technique for evaluating the dual-rail influence from in-die silicon process variations. This approach depends on the thermal influence to the RO PUF in different placements, for validating that the paired ROs in the interleaved PUF have less influence from heating. This result in turn certifies smaller process variations between each interleaved RO pairs. A lightweight block cipher - *Present* is implemented in a symmetric dual-rail logic (PA-DPL). Based on the achieved outcomes, a complete security evaluation has been performed, where an EM surface scan is mounted to collect the local emanations. By drawing the leakage map using both CPA and MIA analyses to each measured logic location in the scan array, the leakage distributions can be plotted. The experimental results certified significantly decreased information leakage by employing DR protections. More concretely, the interleaved DR placement provides an even higher security grade due to the reduced process variations between any paired T/F logic rails.

In the subsequent work, we plan to find more proper distinguisher to evaluate the leakage distribution of a wide variety of DPL styles.

References

1. Bogdanov, A.A., Knudsen, L.R., Leander, G., Paar, C., Poschmann, A., Robshaw, M.J., Seurin, Y., Vikkelsoe, C.: PRESENT: An ultra-lightweight block cipher. In: Paillier, P., Verbauwhede, I. (eds.) CHES 2007. LNCS, vol. 4727, pp. 450–466. Springer, Heidelberg (2007)
2. Boning, D., Chung, J.: Statistical metrology: Understanding spatial variation in semiconductor manufacturing. In: Microelectronic Manufacturing Yield, Reliability, and Failure Analysis II: SPIE 1996 Symp. On Microelectronic Manufacturing (1996)
3. Bowman, K.A., Duvall, S.G., Meindl, J.D.: Impact of die-to-die and within-die parameter fluctuations on the maximum clock frequency distribution for gigascale integration. IEEE J. Solid-State Circuits **37**(2), 183–190 (2002)
4. Brier, E., Clavier, C., Olivier, F.: Correlation power analysis with a leakage model. In: Joye, M., Quisquater, J.-J. (eds.) CHES 2004. LNCS, vol. 3156, pp. 16–29. Springer, Heidelberg (2004)
5. Gierlichs, B., Batina, L., Tuyls, P., Preneel, B.: Mutual information analysis. In: Oswald, E., Rohatgi, P. (eds.) CHES 2008. LNCS, vol. 5154, pp. 426–442. Springer, Heidelberg (2008)

6. He, W., de la Torre, E., Riesgo, T.: A precharge-absorbed DPL logic for reducing early propagation effects on FPGA implementations. In: International Conference on Reconfigurable Computing and FPGAs (ReConFig), pp. 217–222. IEEE (2011)
7. He, W., Otero, A., de la Torre, E., Riesgo, T.: Customized and automated routing repair toolset towards side-channel analysis resistant dual rail logic. Elsevier J. Microprocess. Microsyst. **38**(8), 899–910 (2014)
8. Katashita, T., Satoh, A., Kikuchi, K., Nakagawa, H., Aoyagi, M.: Evaluation of DPA characteristics of SASEBO for board level simulations. In: International Workshop on Constructive Side-Channel Analysis and Secure Design (COSADE), vol. 36, p. 39 (2010)
9. Kocher, P.C., Jaffe, J., Jun, B.: Differential power analysis. In: Wiener, M. (ed.) CRYPTO 1999. LNCS, vol. 1666, pp. 388–397. Springer, Heidelberg (1999)
10. Lin, L., Burleson, W.: Analysis and mitigation of process variation impacts on power-attack tolerance. In: 46th ACM/IEEE Design Automation Conference, DAC 2009, pp. 238–243. IEEE (2009)
11. Menezes, A.J., Van Oorschot, P.C., Vanstone, S.A.: Handbook of Applied Cryptography. CRC Press, Boca Raton (2010)
12. Moradi, A., Immler, V.: Early propagation and imbalanced routing, how to diminish in FPGAs. In: Batina, L., Robshaw, M. (eds.) CHES 2014. LNCS, vol. 8731, pp. 598–615. Springer, Heidelberg (2014)
13. Nassif, S.R.: Modeling and forecasting of manufacturing variations. In: Proceedings of the ASP-DAC 2001 Design Automation Conference, pp. 145–149 (2001)
14. Popp, T., Mangard, S.: Masked dual-rail pre-charge logic: DPA-resistance without routing constraints. In: Rao, J.R., Sunar, B. (eds.) CHES 2005. LNCS, vol. 3659, pp. 172–186. Springer, Heidelberg (2005)
15. Suh, G.E., Devadas, S.: Physical unclonable functions for device authentication and secret key generation. In: Proceedings of the 44th Annual Design Automation Conference, pp. 9–14. ACM (2007)
16. Tiri, K., Verbauwhede, I.: A logic level design methodology for a secure DPA resistant ASIC or FPGA implementation. In: Proceedings of the Conference on Design, Automation and Test in Europe, vol. 1, p. 10246. IEEE Computer Society (2004)
17. Tiri, K., Verbauwhede, I.: Place and route for secure standard cell design. In: Quisquater, J.-J., Paradinas, P., Deswarte, Y., El Kalam, A.A. (eds.) Smart Card Research and Advanced Applications VI. IFIP, vol. 153, pp. 143–158. Springer, Heidelberg (2004)
18. Yu, P., Schaumont, P.: Secure FPGA circuits using controlled placement and routing. In: 2007 5th IEEE/ACM/IFIP International Conference on Hardware/Software Codesign and System Synthesis (CODES+ ISSS), pp. 45–50. IEEE (2007)

Compact Implementations of LEA Block Cipher for Low-End Microprocessors

Hwajeong Seo[1], Zhe Liu[2], Jongseok Choi[1], Taehwan Park[1], and Howon Kim[1(✉)]

[1] School of Computer Science and Engineering, Pusan National University,
San-30, Jangjeon-Dong, Geumjeong-Gu, Busan 609-735, Republic of Korea
{hwajeong,jschoi85,pth5804,howonkim}@pusan.ac.kr
[2] Laboratory of Algorithmics, Cryptology and Security (LACS),
University of Luxembourg, 6, rue R. Coudenhove-Kalergi,
1359 Luxembourg-Kirchberg, Luxembourg
zhe.liu@uni.lu

Abstract. In WISA'13, a novel lightweight block cipher named LEA was released. This algorithm has certain useful features for hardware and software implementations, i.e., simple ARX operations, non-S-box architecture, and 32-bit word size. These features are realized in several platforms for practical usage with high performance and low overheads. In this paper, we further improve 128-, 192- and 256-bit LEA encryption for low-end embedded processors. Firstly we present speed optimization methods. The methods split a 32-bit word operation into four byte-wise operations and avoid several rotation operations by taking advantages of efficient byte-wise rotations. Secondly we reduce the code size to ensure minimum code size. We find the minimum inner loops and optimize them in an instruction set level. After then we construct the whole algorithm in a partly unrolled fashion with reasonable speed. Finally, we achieved the fastest LEA implementations, which improves performance by 10.9 % than previous best known results. For size optimization, our implementation only occupies the 280B to conduct LEA encryption. After scaling, our implementation achieved the smallest ARX implementations so far, compared with other state-of-art ARX block ciphers such as SPECK and SIMON.

Keywords: Low-power encryption algorithm · AVR · Speed optimization

This work was partly supported by Institute for Information & communications Technology Promotion (IITP) grant funded by the Korea government (MSIP) (No. 10043907, Development of high performance IoT device and Open Platform with Intelligent Software) and the MSIP (Ministry of Science, ICT and Future Planning), Korea, under the ITRC(Information Technology Research Center) support program (IITP-2015-H8501-15-1017) supervised by the IITP (Institute for Information & communications Technology Promotion).

H. Kim and D. Choi (Eds.): WISA 2015, LNCS 9503, pp. 28–40, 2016.
DOI: 10.1007/978-3-319-31875-2_3

1 Introduction

In 2013, Low-power Encryption Algorithm (LEA) was announced by the Attached Institute of ETRI [7]. This algorithm has software-friendly architecture and efficient implementation results on wide range of computational devices from high-end machines such as personal computers and smart phones, to low-end microprocessors such as AVR and ARM processors are also drawn in previous papers [7,8]. In this paper, we re-visit previous results on low-end devices and further improve performance in various platforms. This result can contribute to compact design of LEA in terms of high speed and low capacity and ensure the secure and robust communications between low-end devices.

The remainder of this paper is organized as follows. In Sect. 2, we recap the basic specifications of LEA and target platform. In Sect. 3, we present the compact implementations of LEA block cipher. In Sect. 4, we evaluate the performance of proposed methods in terms of clock cycles and code size. Finally, Sect. 5 concludes the paper.

2 Related Works

2.1 LEA Block Cipher

In 2013, Low-power Encryption Algorithm (LEA) was announced by the Attached Institute of ETRI [4]. This algorithm has simple Addition-Rotation-eXclusive-or (ARX) and non-S-box architecture for high performance on both software and hardware environments. LEA is a block cipher with 128-bit block and word size is 32-bit. Various security levels including 128-bit, 192-bit and 256-bit are available. The number of rounds is 24, 28 and 32 for 128-, 192- and 256-bit keys, respectively. The algorithm consists of key schedule, encryption and decryption operations.

2.2 8-Bit Embedded Platform AVR

The 8-bit AVR embedded processor is equipped with an ATmega128 8-bit processor clocked at 7.3728 MHz [2]. It has a 128 KB EEPROM chip and 4 KB RAM chip. The ATmega128 processor has RISC architecture with 32 registers. Among them, 6 registers (R26~R31) serve as the special pointers for indirect addressing. The remaining 26 registers are available for arithmetic operations. One arithmetic instruction incurs one clock cycle, and memory instructions or 8-bit multiplication incur two processing cycles. In Table 1, the detailed instructions used in this paper are drawn.

Previous 8-bit microprocessor results show that LEA is estimated to run at around 3,040 cycles for encryption on AVR AT90USB82/162 where AES best record is 1,993 cycles [6,7]. Former implementation used separated mode to optimize performance in terms of speed by considering high performance. In case of AES, they used the conventional approach [6] to reduce memory

Table 1. Instruction set summary for AVR [2]

Mnemonics	Operands	Description	Operation	#Clock
ADD	Rd, Rr	Add without Carry	Rd ← Rd+Rr	1
ADC	Rd, Rr	Add with Carry	Rd ← Rd+Rr+C	1
EOR	Rd, Rr	Exclusive OR	Rd ← Rd⊕Rr	1
LSL	Rd	Logical Shift Left	C|Rd ← Rd <<1	1
LSR	Rd	Logical Shift Right	Rd|C ← 1>>Rd	1
ROL	Rd	Rotate Left Through Carry	C|Rd ← Rd<<1||C	1
ROR	Rd	Rotate Right Through Carry	Rd|C ← C||1>>Rd	1
LD	Rd, X	Load Indirect	Rd ← (X)	2
ST	Z, Rr	Store Indirect	(Z) ← Rr	2

Table 2. 32-bit instructions over 8-bit AVR, where R12–R15, R16–R19 and R20 represent destination, source and temporal registers, respectively

Addition	Exclusive-or	Right rotation	
ADD R12, R16	EOR R12, R16	CLR R20	ROR R12
ADC R13, R17	EOR R13, R17	LSR R15	ROR R20
ADC R14, R18	EOR R14, R18	ROR R14	EOR R15, R20
ADC R15, R19	EOR R15, R19	ROR R13	

consumption and high speed. The lookup tables are the forward and inverse S-boxes, each 256 bytes, because 32-bit look-up table access is not favorable due to limited storages over low-end devices. S-box pointer is always placed in Z register and the variable is stored into SRAM for fast access speed. For efficient MixColumn computation, a left shift with conditional branch to skip the bit-wise exclusive-or operation is established. Finally, the MixColumns step is implemented without the use of lookup tables as a series of register copies, xors operations, taking a total of 26 cycles. The InvMixColumns step is implemented similarly, but is more complicated and takes a total of 42 cycles. Recently, ARX-based block ciphers (SPECK and SIMON) are introduced [3,4]. They provides efficient rotation operation by multiplying the byte and general multi-precision addition, rotation and exclusive-or operations are studied.

3   Proposed Method

Unlike modern processors, embedded processor provides limited computing power and storage capacities. We need to carefully re-design the algorithm to meet the requirements of speed and size factors over resource constrained environments. In this section, we introduce LEA implementation techniques for low-end microprocessors.

Algorithm 1. Efficient Shift Offset and Direction in AVR

Require: direction d, offset o
Ensure: direction d, offset o
1: $o = o \bmod 8$
2: **if** o>4 **then** $o = 8 - o$, $d =!d$
3: **return** d, o

3.1 On the Fly Versus Separate Computation Modes

LEA block cipher consists of key schedule and encryption/decryption. The key schedule generates each round pair to be used for encryption. If target platform has enough storages, whole round key pairs can be pre-computed in offline and stored into storages. By selecting the methods of round key generation, we can achieve the two opposite properties including size and speed. Firstly, on the fly method generates round key on the spot and then directly encrypts plaintext with these round key pairs. The main benefits are two-fold. Additional storages for round keys are not needed and source code size is reduced by rolling the encryption and key scheduling. Secondly, separated computation mode literally executes key schedule and encryption processes separately. The round keys are computed in offline and then stored into temporal storages. After then these values are simply loaded and used during encryption or decryption process. The method can avoid the key generation process.

3.2 Speed Optimization

Core operations of LEA are 32-bit wise addition, bit-wise exclusive-or and rotation. When it comes to a 8-bit processor, 32-bit wise instruction is not straightforwardly computable. For this reason, we sliced a 32-bit instruction into four 8-bit instructions. The detailed process is described in Table 2. In case of addition and bit-wise exclusive-or, four 8-bit instructions are conducted for 32-bit single instruction. From 9th to 32th bit, carry bits are concerned during addition operation. In case of rotation, we shift four 8-bit registers and then conduct carry handling to rotate the carry bits. Among operations, rotation operation is particularly crucial operation in microprocessors, because there is no 32-bit wise rotation supported and carry handling is complicated process than any other operations. In order to overcome this problem, we set several efficient computation strategy. Firstly, shift operation over 8-bit offset is omitted because 8-bit shift is simply established by ordering of inner word. Secondly, as we can find in [1], shift operation by $(5, 6, 7)$-bit is simply replaced by $(3, 2, 1)$-bit shifts in opposite direction. The detailed 8-bit shift process is available in Algorithm 1. Firstly offsets in multiple times of 8-bit are reduced and then remaining bits over 4-bit is changed into opposite direction. For left rotation by 9-bit, we simply conduct one bit left shift with register arrangements so this approach saves 8-bit left rotation instructions.

For further improvements of performance, we retained variables in registers rather than memory. For encryption, we allocate sixteen registers (R0 $\sim$ R15)

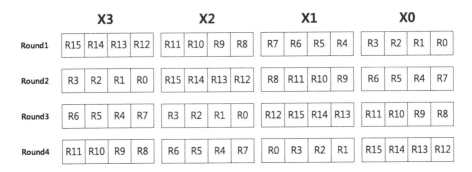

Fig. 1. Register alignments for LEA encryption in AVR

for plaintext (X0, X1, X2, X3) and eight registers (R16 ~ R23) are reserved for purpose of temporal storages. Combining proposed rotation techniques and register allocation, we can schedule registers described in Fig. 1. The figure describes from round 1 to round 4 of encryption, where each box represents 8-bit and remaining steps are iterated in same order. As we explained before, shift with over 8-bit is computed without cost by ordering the results. In case of 128-bit key scheduling, sixteen registers are assigned for master key and remaining registers are used for temporal registers. The delta variable is not retained into registers due to limited number of registers so it is obtained from memory in every round.

3.3 Size Optimization

In previous section, we show the highest speed record with loop unrolled optimizations. This ensures the best possible performance but it increases code size significantly. In order to minimize the code size, an implementation with "rolled" loops is the most feasible choice. The size-first method rolls whole source codes by number of iteration (N). If size of source code is (S), the size of looped version is calculated in $(\frac{S}{N} + A)$, where (A) represents overheads of counter, offset and branch operations. However, the performance is relatively slower than that of unrolled version. One possible solution is to partially unroll the loops. For instance, the body of the loop can be replicated multiple times, which replaces a number of loop iterations by non-iterated straight-line code.

Minimum Loop Implementation. 128-bit LEA block cipher consists of 24 rounds. As described in Fig. 2, each round again boiled down to three addition, six exclusive-or and three rotation operations. These operations are grouped into three inner loops and iterated by three times in a round. In order to minimize the source code, we only implemented single inner loop operation and then iterated the inner loop by three times[1]. This process computes one round function. After

---

[1] The 32-bit wise inner loops are optimal choice because each instruction set occupies 2 bytes and 32-bit instruction only needs four consecutive instructions(8 bytes = 4 × 2) If we use 8-bit instruction as a minimum loop for 32-bit addition, we should use 1 ADD, 1 MOV, 1 INC, 1 CPSE and 1 RJMP and total 10 bytes with far slow performance.

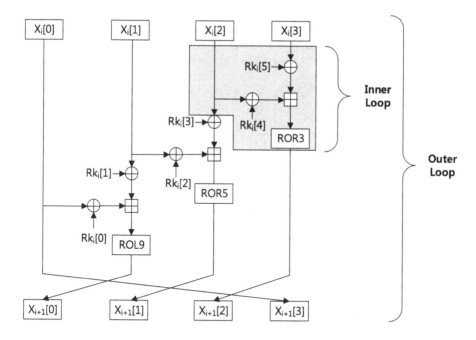

Fig. 2. Inner and outer loops of LEA encryption

then, 24 times of round operations are iterated. Of the 26 registers, the 16 registers are assigned for plaintext and four registers for rotation counter, one for round counter and five for temporal registers. Since the number of general purpose registers is highly limited, efficient scheduling of register is important. We firstly computed value in Xi[3] and then stored the results, because Xi[3] is once used but not used in following operations. After each round, the variable X is shifted by one word size (32-bit) to align the variables for looped operation. Cases of 192-, 256-bit implementations are also achieved with same program but different number of rounds (28 and 32 times), because their basic architectures are identical to that of 128-bit encryption.

Since LEA decryption has a similar structure of encryption. The techniques for encryption can be applied to the decryption with simple modification. Each round in Fig. 3 consists of three subtraction, six exclusive-or and three rotation operations. This inner loop is iterated by three times in a round and then each round operation is repeated by 24 times for 128-bit decryption. The decryption computes opposite way in that of encryption, so we firstly use Xi[0] and then store the results into Xi[0] registers, because following operations do not need Xi[0] variables any more. After each round operation, variable alignments follow by word size (32-bit). The 16 registers are assigned for ciphertext and four registers for rotation offsets, one for round counter and five for temporal registers.

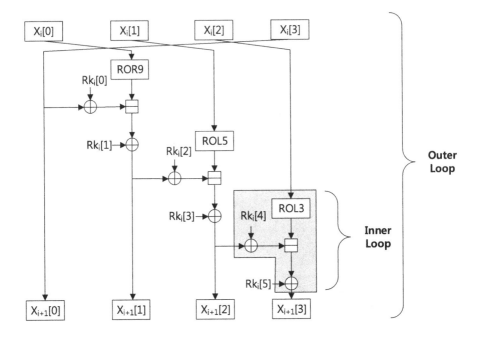

Fig. 3. Inner and outer loops of LEA decryption

Key scheduling consists of eight rotation and four addition operations. The loop is grouped into four identical inner loops. The loop contains two rotation and four addition operations. Firstly whole keys are loaded into registers and then key scheduling is conducted by size of inner loop. Each round has different rotation count and delta variables. Due to limited number of registers, we re-load delta variables every time when it is in needs. The counter values are also re-loaded from memory. Since rotation and delta variables are changed in every round, we should schedule these offsets with counter variables. For efficient 128-bit loop encryption implementations, we stored duplicated six 32-bit round key pairs. The 16 registers are assigned for secret/round key and four registers for rotation counter, two for round counter and six for temporal registers. In order to reduce the source code size, program is written in looped fashion. For looped version, we re-aligned plaintext, ciphertext and round keys in every inner round. Looped version always accesses to same index of registers but we should ensure that the registers contain different variables by the round. We rotated destination registers by word size in an every inner round to align the variables properly.

Separated Method. Block cipher can be computed in separated key scheduling and encryption/decryption operations. This method firstly computes whole key chains once and stores them into storages. And then encryption/decryption operations follow. Since key scheduling method is executed once before encryption process, separated mode can avoid overheads of key generation.

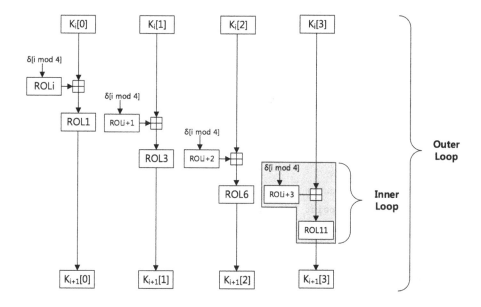

Fig. 4. Inner and outer loops of LEA key scheduling

For key scheduling operation, we firstly load secret key pairs and delta variables by the number of rounds. After key generation, we stored whole round key pairs into RAM. For encryption operation, we load plaintext and round keys by 128-bit and 192-bit to conduct encryption process. In case of decryption, we load ciphertext and access round keys in reverse order to conduct decryption process (Fig. 4).

On-the-fly Method. On-the-fly method is the challenging task over resource constrained embedded processors because this operation mode is required to retain more number of parameters including delta, round key, plaintext and counter variables for rotation and round. Since the storages for these parameters are beyond capacity of registers in embedded processors, additional memory is in needs. Memory access is one of the most expensive operations but we should retain intermediate variables to memory due to limited number of registers. For on-the-fly computations, we firstly load secret key, delta and counter variables and then generate round keys in every session. The round key pairs are not placed within registers because sub-sequent operations also need many registers for plaintext and counter variables. In each inner round, we re-load round keys to generate the next round key pairs and intermediate ciphertext pairs are also re-loaded and placed back to memory after computations. This process is iterated by the number of rounds.

Decryption is conducted in reverse way of encryption process. In the case of encryption, round key pairs are generated from initial secret keys and each key

Table 3. Scaled overheads of block ciphers in 128-bit encryption cases

Features	LEA	SPECK	SIMON
Scaled in 32-bit addition	3	2	-
Scaled in 32-bit bit-wise and	-	-	2
Scaled in 32-bit exclusive-or	6	4	10
Scaled in 32-bit rotation (offset)	7	6	6
Size of master key (bit)	128	128	128
Total size of round key (bit)	4608	2048	2176
Number of Rounds	24	32	34
Scaled panelty point in speed (clock)	-	+40	-19
Scaled panelty point in size (proportion)	-	1.57	1.1

is used directly for the encryption computations. On the other hand, decryption conducts the operation from last round key pairs to first. For starter, we conduct key scheduling in ordinary way to get final round key pairs after then we traced back from last to first round keys. While conducting key scheduling in reverse order, decryption process is conducted by each round. The key scheduling in reverse order follows reverse order of ordinary key scheduling. Firstly delta variables are rotated by number of i. And then round keys are rotated. For better performance, we conduct right rotation. Right rotation can compute the inverse operation of left rotation. After then both values are subtracted. The loops are iterated by the number of rounds.

Scalable Implementation. In order to support various protocols and environments, we need to ensure diverse security levels. If we implement one by one over the embedded processors, it would consume more capacities to store. For this reason, we implemented scalable encryption and decryption operations. Thanks to simple architecture of LEA block cipher, we can easily implement scalable encryption/decryption operations. LEA block cipher provides three different key sizes including 128-, 192-, and 256-bit. The basic instruction is same for all key sizes but only the number of round is varied. By assigning the number of rounds differently, we can readily scale the three different encryption models. In case of decryption, opposite order of encryption operations are conducted. As like encryption case, we can only alter the round numbers to conduct the operations.

Loop Friendly Instruction Set. For register realignments, MOVW instruction relocates two adjacent register to destination within single clock cycle. In case of memory load/store, we can use post increment or pre-decrement accesses. This does not impose additional clock costs to calculate the indirect address. In order to set the counter, we use LDI instruction to assign the value directly. The ADIW and SBIW conduct addition and subtraction by word with immediate value.

These are used to modify memory address. Finally, INC and DEC operations are used to increase and decrease the counter variables.

3.4   Implementations for 16-Bit MSP Embedded Processors

The proposed techniques are not limited to 8-bit AVR processors. We also applied to other resource constrained devices such as 16-bit MSP processors. As like 8-bit AVR, 32-bit wise ARX instructions are split into two consecutive 16-bit operations. In case of rotation operation, we also adopted efficient rotation method in Algorithm 1. For left rotation by 9-bit, we can replace the operations into right shift by 7-bit (16-9) together with register ordering. Of twelve 16-bit registers, two or three registers are assigned for pointer and remaining ten or nine registers are available for general purposes. However, plaintext and round keys are larger than register capacities. For this reason, register utilizations should be taken into accounts.

For LEA encryption process, we allocate eight registers (R4 ~ R11) for plaintext (X0, X1, X2, X3) and remaining registers are used for temporal storages. The order of plaintext is also aligned by using techniques introduced in Fig. 1. In case of 128-bit key scheduling, eight registers are assigned for master key and remaining registers are used for temporal registers. The delta variable is not kept in the registers due to lack of register. The variables are re-loaded from memory in every session. Finally we compute the LEA key scheduling and encryption in 206.4 and 157.6 cycles/byte. This is the first LEA implementation on MSP processors. We compared results with AES implementations. The results show that 180 cycles/byte for AES encryption [5].

4   Results

4.1   Speed Optimization

In Table 4, comparison results of speed factor on AVR are described[2]. The results introduced in WISA'13 [7] computes LEA encryption within 190 cycles/byte. Our optimized implementation achieved 169.2 cycles/byte, which improves performance by 10.9 %. We also compared with other block ciphers. Of many methods, we selected the most well known block cipher AES. AES follows SPN architecture but LEA is ARX architecture. For fair comparison, we brought the most well-known ARX based block ciphers such as SPECK and SIMON.

Firstly, optimized LEA shows lower performance than optimized AES by 26.4 %. This is obvious that LEA is targeting the 32-bit processor but AES is for 8-bit processors. Secondly, we compared with SPECK and SIMON. Direct comparison with both algorithm is also unfair because number of arithmetic is different to each other. In case of 128-bit SPECK encryption, each round consists of 64-bit rotation by 3-bit and one 64-bit addition and two 64-bit exclusive-or

---

[2] The performance is measured in clock cycles and bytes for timing and code size. Precise results are measured in AVR studio and program is complied with optimization level 2.

Table 4. Speed optimized results on AVR, encryption is measured in cycles/byte and code size in bytes, *: estimated results, P/C: Pre-computed

Method	ARCH	KEY	ENC	ENC(scaled)	ROM(byte)	RAM(byte)
Speed(Separated)						
LEA 128-bit	ARX	P/C	169.2	**169.2**	924	592
LEA 192-bit	ARX	P/C	224.6	N/A	1004	688
LEA 256-bit	ARX	P/C	256.1	N/A	1004	784
LEA 128-bit [7]	ARX	P/C	190	**190**	N/A	N/A
SPECK 128-bit [3]	ARX	P/C	143	**183**	452	256
SPECK 192-bit [3]	ARX	P/C	147	N/A	632	272
SPECK 256-bit [3]	ARX	P/C	151	N/A	522	288
SIMON 128-bit [3]	ARX	P/C	337	**318**	510	544
SIMON 192-bit [3]	ARX	P/C	339	N/A	646	552
SIMON 256-bit [3]	ARX	P/C	357	N/A	522	576
AES 128-bit [6]	SPN	P/C	124.5	N/A	956*	N/A

operations. When they are scaled into 32-bit operations each 64-bit operation is split into 2 32-bit operation. Another factor is round key size. If round key is getting large, memory access frequently happens and latency should be lower. The SPECK has relatively small round key sizes (2048 bits). In case of 128-bit SIMON encryption, each round consists of 64-bit rotation by 3-bit and one 64-bit logical AND and five 64-bit exclusive-or operations. When they are scaled into 32-bit operation, the operations are changed into 10-bit rotation, two AND and six exclusive-or. The SIMON has also small round key sizes by 2176 bits. We scaled the operation by calculating the overheads of each operation. One 32-bit operation needs four 8-bit operations (4 clock cycles) and 1 byte memory accesses needs 2 clock cycles. With this conversion, we can draw objective complexity (cycles/byte) of LEA ($168 = \frac{16 \times \#round(24) \times 4 + 2 \times \frac{roundkey(4608)}{8}}{16}$), SPECK ($128 = \frac{12 \times 32 \times 4 + 2 \times \frac{2048}{8}}{16}$) and SIMON ($187 = \frac{18 \times 34 \times 4 + 2 \times \frac{2176}{8}}{16}$). The detailed comparison in Table 3. After scaling, our work is faster than SPECK and SIMON by 7.5 % and 46.8 %, respectively.

4.2 Size Optimization

One 32-bit operation consists of four 8-bit operations. Each 8-bit operation needs 2 bytes for program instructions. In case of memory accesses, one byte access operation needs 2 bytes. We calculated the relative costs in each round of block cipher as follows. In case of LEA, its complexity is ($176 = \#operation(16) \times 4 \times 2 + roundkey(192)/8 \times 2$) and for SPECK it is ($112 = \#operation(12) \times 4 \times 2 + roundkey(64)/8 \times 2$) and for SIMON it is ($160 = \#operation(18) \times 4 \times 2 + roundkey(64)/8 \times 2$). We compute relative complexity and after scaling LEA implementation is 35 % smaller than SPECK and SIMON. Furthermore, we presented on-the-fly and parameterized version with only 1286 and 592 bytes, respectively. The parameterized version is readily available in LEA because it shares same structures throughout the all security levels (Table 5).

Table 5. Size optimized results on AVR, Key and Enc are measured in cycles/byte and code size in bytes. P/C: Pre-computed

Method	KEY	ENC	DEC	ROM(byte)	ROM(scaled)	RAM(byte)
Size(On-the-fly)						
LEA 128-bit	N/A	2576	5029	1286	**1286**	88
Size(Parameterized)						
LEA 128-bit	N/A	729.8	748.8	592	**592**	596
LEA 192-bit	N/A	849.8	871.8	592	N/A	692
LEA 256-bit	N/A	969.8	994.8	592	N/A	788
Size(Separated)						
LEA 128-bit	P/C	729.6	N/A	280	**280**	592
LEA 192-bit	P/C	849.6	N/A	280	N/A	688
LEA 256-bit	P/C	969.6	N/A	280	N/A	784
SPECK 128-bit [3]	P/C	169	N/A	278	**436**	264
SPECK 192-bit [3]	P/C	174	N/A	330	N/A	272
SPECK 256-bit [3]	P/C	179	N/A	348	N/A	280
SIMON 128-bit [3]	P/C	346	N/A	392	**431**	544
SIMON 192-bit [3]	P/C	351	N/A	392	N/A	552
SIMON 256-bit [3]	P/C	366	N/A	404	N/A	576

5 Conclusion

One of the biggest challenges for Internet of Things is secure communications between small and resource constrained embedded processors. In order to ensure secure and robust transactions, we should conduct the encryption operation on sensitive and important information. In this paper, we explore the optimal implementations pursuing high speed and small memory footprint for new light-weight block cipher, LEA. This paper presents several optimization techniques including efficient 32-bit wise ARX operations and minimum inner loop scheduling. Furthermore, to the best of our knowledge, this is first scalable LEA block cipher implementations over AVR processor. The program can compute various key sizes with single code and no further modifications.

References

1. Aranha, D.F., Dahab, R., López, J., Oliveira, L.B.: Efficient implementation of elliptic curve cryptography in wireless sensors. Adv. Math. Commun. 4(2), 169–187 (2010)
2. Atmel Corporation. ATmega128(L) Datasheet (Rev. 2467O-AVR-10/06), October 2006. http://www.atmel.com/dyn/resources/prod_documents/doc2467.pdf
3. Beaulieu, R., Shors, D., Smith, J., Treatman-Clark, S., Weeks, B., Wingers, L.: The SIMON and SPECK block ciphers on AVR 8-bit microcontrollers
4. Beaulieu, R., Shors, D., Smith, J., Treatman-Clark, S., Weeks, B., Wingers, L.: The SIMON and SPECK families of lightweight block ciphers. IACR Cryptology ePrint Archive, 2013:404 (2013)
5. Gouvêa, C.P.L., López, J.: High speed implementation of authenticated encryption for the MSP430X microcontroller. In: Hevia, A., Neven, G. (eds.) LatinCrypt 2012. LNCS, vol. 7533, pp. 288–304. Springer, Heidelberg (2012)
6. Osvik, D.A., Bos, J.W., Stefan, D., Canright, D.: Fast software AES encryption. In: Hong, S., Iwata, T. (eds.) FSE 2010. LNCS, vol. 6147, pp. 75–93. Springer, Heidelberg (2010)
7. Hong, D., Lee, J.-K., Kim, D.-C., Kwon, D., Ryu, K.H., Lee, D.-G.: LEA: a 128-Bit block cipher for fast encryption on common processors. In: Kim, Y., Lee, H., Perrig, A. (eds.) WISA 2013. LNCS, vol. 8267, pp. 1–24. Springer, Heidelberg (2014)
8. Seo, H., Liu, Z., Park, T., Kim, H., Lee, Y., Choi, J., Kim, H.: Parallel implementations of LEA. In: Lee, H.-S., Han, D.-G. (eds.) ICISC 2013. LNCS, vol. 8565, pp. 256–274. Springer, Heidelberg (2014)

Compact Implementations of LSH

Taehwan Park[1], Hwajeong Seo[1], Zhe Liu[2], Jongseok Choi[1],
and Howon Kim[1(✉)]

[1] School of Computer Science and Engineering, Pusan National University,
San-30, Jangjeon-Dong, Geumjeong-Gu, Busan 609-735, Republic of Korea
{pth5804,hwajeong,jschoi85,howonkim}@pusan.ac.kr
[2] Laboratory of Algorithmics, Cryptology and Security (LACS),
University of Luxembourg, 6, rue R. Coudenhove-Kalergi,
1359 Luxembourg-Kirchberg, Luxembourg
zhe.liu@uni.lu

Abstract. In ICISC'14, a new hash function family named LSH was released. The algorithm is secure against all critical hash function attacks and has simple ARX architecture with multiple data sets, which are computed in same operation. This nice features are well suited on modern parallel computer architectures such as SIMD (Single Instruction Multiple Data). The software efficiency of LSH is four times faster than SHA-3 and 1.5–2.3 times faster than other SHA-3 finalists over modern SIMD architectures. In this paper, we introduce the implementations of LSH hash functions for low-end embedded processors. The results show that LSH function are efficient enough to perform the operation over resource challenging processors so far.

Keywords: Hash function · ARX operations · Software implementation · AVR · MSP · ARM

1 Introduction

In ICISC'14, a new hash function family named LSH was released [7]. The algorithm is secure against all critical hash function attacks and has simple ARX architecture with multiple data sets, which are computed in same operation. This nice features are well suited on modern parallel computer architectures such as SIMD (Single Instruction Multiple Data).The software efficiency of LSH is four times faster than SHA-3 and 1.5–2.3 times faster than other SHA-3 finalists

This work was partly supported by Institute for Information & communications Technology Promotion (IITP) grant funded by the Korea government (MSIP) (No. 10043907, Development of high performance IoT device and Open Platform with Intelligent Software) and the MSIP (Ministry of Science, ICT and Future Planning), Korea, under the ITRC(Information Technology Research Center) support program (IITP-2015-H8501-15-1017) supervised by the IITP(Institute for Information & communications Technology Promotion).

H. Kim and D. Choi (Eds.): WISA 2015, LNCS 9503, pp. 41–53, 2016.
DOI: 10.1007/978-3-319-31875-2_4

over modern SIMD architectures. In this paper, we introduce the implementations of LSH hash functions over low-end embedded processors. The results show that LSH function are efficient enough to perform the operation over resource challenging processors so far.

The remainder of this paper is organized as follows. In Sect. 2, we recap the basic specifications of LSH and target platforms. In Sect. 3, we present the novel implementation designs. In Sect. 4, we evaluate the performance of proposed methods in terms of clock cycles. Finally, Sect. 5 concludes the paper.

2 Related Works

2.1 Hash Structure

The n-bit hash function based on w-bit word, LSH-$8w$-n, has the wide-pipe Merkle-Damgard structure with one-zeros padding. The message hashing process of LSH-$8w$-n consists of the following three stages.

Initialization

- One-zeros padding of a given bit string message.
- Conversion to 32-word array message blocks from the padded bit string message.
- Initialization of a chaining variable with the initialization vector.

Let m be a given bit string message. The m is padded by one-zeros, i.e., the bit '1' is appended to the end of m, and the series of bit '0' are appended until a bit length of a padded message is $32wt$-bit, where $t = \lceil \frac{|m|+1}{32w} \rceil$ and $\lceil x \rceil$ is the smallest integer not less than x. Let $m' = m_0 || m_1 || ... || m_{32wt-1}$ be the one-zeros-padded $32wt$-bit string of m. Then m' is considered as a $4wt$-byte array $m = (m[0], ..., m[4wt-1])$, where $m[l] = m_{8l} || m_{8l+1} || ... || m_{8l+7}$ for all l. The $4wt$-byte array m conversion a $32t$-word array $M = (M[0], .., M[32t-1])$. From the word array M, we define the t 32-word array message blocks $\{M^i\}_{i=0}^{t-1}$. $M^i \leftarrow (M[32i], M[32i+1], ..., M[32i+31])$. The 16-word array chaining variable CV^0 is initialized to the initialization vector IV of LSH-$8w$-n, i.e., $CV^0 \leftarrow IV$.

Compression

- Updating of chaining variables by iteration of a compression function with message blocks.

In this stage, the t 32-word array message blocks $\{M^i\}_{i=0}^{t-1}$, which are generated from a message m, are compressed by iteration of compression functions. The compression function $CF : W^{16} \times W^{32} \to W^{16}$ has two inputs; the i-th 16-word chaining variable CV^i and the i-th 32-word message block M^i and returns the $(i+1)$-th 16-word chaining variable $CV^{(i+1)}$.

Table 1. Instruction set summary for AVR [2]

Mnemonics	Operands	Description	Operation
ADD	Rd, Rr	Add without Carry	Rd ← Rd+Rr
ADC	Rd, Rr	Add with Carry	Rd ← Rd+Rr+C
EOR	Rd, Rr	Exclusive OR	Rd ← Rd⊕Rr
LSL	Rd	Logical Shift Left	C|Rd ← Rd<<1
LSR	Rd	Logical Shift Right	Rd|C ← 1>>Rd
ROL	Rd	Rotate Left Through Carry	C|Rd ← Rd<<1||C
ROR	Rd	Rotate Right Through Carry	Rd|C ← C||1>>Rd

Finalization

– Generation of an n-bit hash value from the final chaining variable.

The finalization function FIN_n return n-bit hash value h from the final chaining variable $CV^t = (CV^t[0], ..., CV^t[15])$. Let $h = (h[0], ..., h[w-1])$ be an w-byte array. $h \leftarrow (CV^t[0] \oplus CV^t[8], CV^t[1] \oplus CV^t[9], ..., CV^t[7] \oplus CV^t[15])$, $h \leftarrow (h[0]||...||h[w-1])_{[0:n-1]}$.

2.2   8-Bit Embedded Platform: AVR

The representative 8-bit AVR embedded processor is an ATmega128 processor which clocked at 7.3728 MHz and supports a 128 KB EEPROM chip and 4 KB RAM chip [2]. The ATmega128 processor has RISC architecture with 32 registers. Of 32 registers, 6 registers (R26–R31) serve as the special pointers for indirect addressing. The remaining 26 registers are available for arithmetic operations. One arithmetic instruction incurs one clock cycle, and memory instructions or 8-bit multiplication incur two processing cycles. In Table 1, the detailed instructions used in this paper are drawn.

2.3   16-Bit Embedded Platform: MSP

The MSP430 is a representative 16-bit processor board with a clock frequency of 8 MHz, 32–48 KB of flash memory, 10 KB of RAM, and 12 general purpose registers from R4 to R15 available [5]. Since this register shares pointer and user defined registers, the number of registers is much constrained than AVR platforms. The device also provides various operations supporting full functions of ARX. The detailed instructions are described in Table 2.

2.4   32-Bit Embedded Platforms: ARM

Advanced RISC Machine (ARM) is an instruction set architecture (ISA) designed by ARM for high-performance 32-bit embedded applications. Although ARM cores are usually larger and more complex than AVR and MSP, most ARM

Table 2. Instruction set summary for MSP [10]

Mnemonics	Operands	Description	Operation
ADD	Rr, Rd	Add without Carry	Rd ← Rd+Rr
ADDC	Rr, Rd	Add with Carry	Rd ← Rd+Rr+C
AND	Rr, Rd	Logical AND	Rd ← Rd&Rr
XOR	Rr, Rd	Exclusive OR	Rd ← Rd⊕Rr
RLA	Rd	Logical Shift Left	C|Rd ← Rd<<1
RRA	Rd	Logical Shift Right	Rd|C ← 1>>Rd
RLC	Rd	Rotate Left Through Carry	C|Rd ← Rd<<1||C
RRC	Rd	Rotate Right Through Carry	Rd|C ← C||1>>Rd

Table 3. Instruction set summary for ARM [11]

Mnemonics	Operands	Description	Operation
ADD	Rd, Rr	Add without Carry	Rd ← Rd+Rr
EOR	Rd, Rr	Exclusive OR	Rd ← Rd⊕Rr
ROL	Rd	Rotate Left Through Carry	C|Rd ← Rd<<1||C
ROR	Rd	Rotate Right Through Carry	Rd|C ← C||1>>Rd

designs are also well regarded for their low power consumption and high code density and the ARM is one of the most widely used 32-bit processors in mobile applications [6]. The ARM family has developed from the traditional ARM1 to advanced Cortex (ARMv8) in these days [9]. They provide large number of pipeline stages and various caches, SIMD extensions and simple load/store architecture. The processor has 37 32-bit registers. Among them only sixteen 32-bit registers are visible by users [8]. Most instructions of the ARM compute in a single cycle. The inline barrel shifter provides free shift or rotation operations on second operands before the target operation is performed. The load and store-multiple instructions copy any number of general-purpose registers from/to a block of sequential memory addresses. Their 32-bit wise instructions are described in Table 3.

3 Proposed Method

In this section, we introduce our implementation techniques for low-end microprocessors.

3.1 8-Bit AVR Platform

Core operations of LSH are 32-bit and 64-bit wise addition, bit-wise exclusive-or and rotation operations for 256-bit and 512-bit hash functions. Since, on the 8-bit processor, 32-bit and 64-bit wise instructions are not straight-forwardly

Table 4. 32-bit instructions over 8-bit AVR, where R12–R15, R16–R19 and R20 represent destination, source and temporal registers, respectively

Addition	Exclusive-or	Right rotation
ADD R12, R16	EOR R12, R16	CLR R20 ROR R16
ADC R13, R17	EOR R13, R17	LSR R19 ROR R20
ADC R14, R18	EOR R14, R18	ROR R18 EOR R19, R20
ADC R15, R19	EOR R15, R19	ROR R17

Table 5. 64-bit instructions over 8-bit AVR, where R8–R15, R16–R23 and R24 represent destination, source and temporal registers, respectively

Addition	Exclusive-or	Right rotation
ADD R8, R16	EOR R8, R16	CLR R24 ROR R16
ADC R9, R17	EOR R9, R17	LSR R23 ROR R20
ADC R10, R18	EOR R10, R18	ROR R22 EOR R23, R20
ADC R11, R19	EOR R11, R19	ROR R21
ADC R12, R20	EOR R12, R20	ROR R20
ADC R13, R21	EOR R13, R21	ROR R19
ADC R14, R22	EOR R14, R22	ROR R18
ADC R15, R23	EOR R15, R23	ROR R17

computable, we sliced 32-bit and 64-bit wise instructions into several 8-bit instructions. The detailed 32-bit and 64-bit operations are described in Tables 4 and 5, respectively. In case of addition and bit-wise exclusive-or, four and eight 8-bit instructions are required for 32-bit and 64-bit wise operations. In case of rotation, we shift four and eight 8-bit registers and then conduct carry handling with the overflow bit. Among operations, rotation operation is particularly crucial operation in microprocessors, because there is no 32-bit and 64-bit wise rotation supported and carry handling is much more complicated than any other operations. In order to overcome this problem, we set several efficient computation strategy. Firstly, shift operation over 8-bit offset is omitted because 8-bit shift is simply established by ordering the word. Secondly, as we can find in [1], shift operation by $(5, 6, 7)$-bit is simply replaced by $(3, 2, 1)$-bit shifts in opposite direction. The

---

Algorithm 1. Efficient Shift Offset and Direction in AVR

Require: direction d, offset o
Ensure: direction d, offset o
1: $o = o \bmod 8$
2: **if** o>4 **then** $o = 8 - o$, $d = !d$
3: **return** d, o

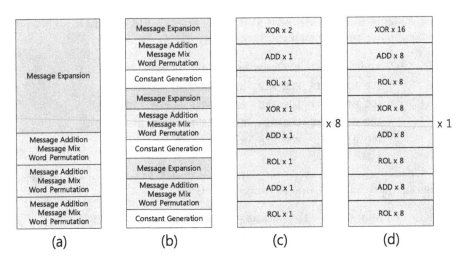

Fig. 1. (AVR, MSP): abstraction of compression function, (a) offline, (b) online approaches/comparison of message add and mix operation in different order of loops, (c) outer-loop-first, (d) inner-loop-first

detailed 8-bit shift process is available in Algorithm 1. Firstly whole offsets over 8-bit are eliminated and then remaining bit over 4-bit is changed to opposite direction. For left rotation by 9-bit, we simply conduct one bit left shift with register arrangements and this eliminates 8-bit left rotation instructions.

Furthermore, AVR processor is a storage challenging embedded device which normally provides 4KB RAM or lower, so we should consider about small memory consumptions as well. For high speed implementations, constant value can be computed in off-line by sacrificing the RAM storages. However, this is not proper way over storage challenging device like AVR processor because pre-computed constant table occupies 832 and 1792 bytes for 256-bit and 512-bit LSH which are almost a quarter or half of RAM resources. Moreover the message expansion also consumes 1728 and 3712 bytes so we choose to use online computation for both cases.

In Fig. 1, comparison of online and offline(naive) compression function methods is described. The offline(naive) approach doesn't need to compute constant variables by storing whole constant variables into storages. Furthermore, the offline(naive) approach firstly computes whole message expansion and stored into memory. After then, remaining operations including message addition, message mix and word permutation are conducted. On the other hands, online approach computes part of message expansion and constant in every round. As we can see in case (b), the computation is conducted in following order: message expansion, message addition, message mix, word permutation and constant generation. With this approach, we can reduce the storage consumption with small sacrifice of speed factors.

In Fig. 1, comparison of loop orders for message addition and mix operation is described. The case (c) conducts different 64-bit ARX operations in mixed form and iterated the loops by eight times. However in case (d), we fully conduct

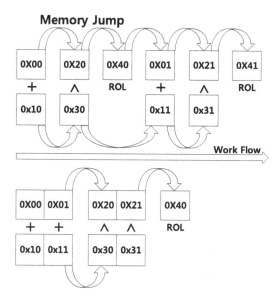

Fig. 2. (AVR, MSP): comparisons of memory access patterns for outer-loop-first (upper) and inner-loop-first (lower)

Algorithm 2. Efficient Shift Offset and Direction in MSP

Require: direction d, offset o
Ensure: direction d, offset o
1: $o = o \bmod 16$
2: **if** $o > 8$ **then** $o = 16 - o$, $d = !d$
3: **return** d, o

---

one ARX operation and then move to different ARX operations. This approach provides efficient memory accesses. In Fig. 2, the comparison of memory access pattern is described. The upper case shows outer-loop-first memory accesses. The addition of two operands located in addresses (0x00) and (0x10) is conducted after then the bit-wise exclusive-or is conducted with operands of addresses (0x20) and (0x30). This means memory access pattern is not a regular form so this causes additional memory calculation costs. On the other hands, our inner-loop-first approach (lower figure) conducts addition on incrementally aligned operand sets. This only needs memory calculation when operations are changed into others. Furthermore, we can exploit incremental and decremental address accesses which eliminates the memory calculations.

3.2   16-Bit MSP Platform

As like 8-bit AVR, 16-bit MSP platform should slice 32-bit and 64-bit wise instructions into two and four 16-bit operations, respectively. The 32-bit and

Table 6. 32-bit instructions over 16-bit MSP, R8-R9, R10-R11 and R12 represent destination, source and temporal registers, respectively

Addition	Exclusive-or	Right rotation
ADD R8, R10	XOR R8, R10	CLR R12 RRC R12
ADDC R9, R11	XOR R9, R11	RRA R11 AND #0X1FFF, R11
		RRC R10 ADD R12, R11

Table 7. 64-bit instructions over 16-bit MSP, R4-R7, R8-R11 and R12 represent destination, source and temporal registers, respectively

Addition	Exclusive-or	Right rotation
ADD R4, R8	XOR R4, R8	CLR R12 RRC R8
ADDC R5, R9	XOR R5, R9	RRA R11 RRC R12
ADDC R6, R10	XOR R6, R10	RRC R10 AND #0X1FFF, R11
ADDC R7, R11	XOR R7, R11	RRC R9 ADD R12, R11

64-bit addition and bit-wise exclusive-or operations are realized with two and four 16-bit instructions. In case of rotation, we adopted the efficient rotation method, which is discussed in previous section. The detailed rotation method for MSP processor is depicted in Algorithm 2. For left rotation by 9-bit, we can replace the operations into right shift by 7-bit (16-9) with register ordering. The detailed 32-bit and 64-bit ARX operations are available in Tables 6 and 7. For further enhancements of 8-bit wise rotations, we exploit 8-bit wise swap and mask operations and detailed descriptions are available in Fig. 3, Given two 16-bit registers, we firstly swap the two registers by 8-bit wise with single instruction. After then we masked each operand with higher mask(0xffff0000) and lower mask(0x0000ffff), respectively. This ensures 8-bit wise shifted results in four parts. After then we can combine the two higher and lower 8-bit elements to get 8-bit shifted results. This method realizes the 8-bit shift operations with only two swap, four mask and two addition operations rather than 8 times of shift operations.

3.3   32-Bit ARM Platform

Modern ARM instruction is proper 32-bit wise operations due to its word size. In following subsections, we give a detailed techniques to reach the highest performance in ARM architectures. 256-bit LSH hash function is perfectly fit into 32-bit ARM processor, because the platform provides 32-bit wise addition, bit-wise exclusive-or and rotation, described in Table 8 with one clock cycle. There is no further concern to optimize the basic instruction. Instead, we optimize the rotation operation with barrel shifter. This operation provides cost-free rotation by inserting inline rotation into second operand. The bit-wise exclusive-or instruction needs two operands. The second operand should be rotated before to be inputted to next operation. We added inline barrel shifter to conduct rotation

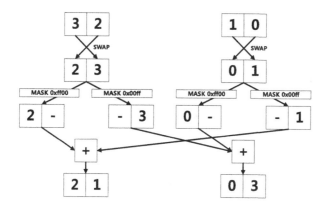

Fig. 3. MSP: 8-bit wise rotation with swap and mask operations

operation on second operand. Without inline barrel shifter, whole intermediate results are rotated before next round. Unlike former implementation, we didn't conduct rotation independently in former round. Instead of this, we wrote rotation operation known as inline barrel shifter into second operand of bit-wise exclusive-or operation. This approach reduces the independent rotation computations and improve the performance by number of rotation operations. We further exploit barrel shifter for combined way of rotation operations. As we explored before, barrel shifter does not impose overheads so we can delay the rotation operation. In Table 9, comparisons of sequential and combined ways of rotation operations are described. The computation of rotation, addition and rotation is conducted in three independent operations in the conventional sequential way. However, our combined way uses barrel shifter to delay the complete rotation and reduces one clock cycle. Barrel shifter does not change the value of input but generates proper intermediate results. For this reason, we can delay the rotation operation and combine two rotation operations. This techniques is available in byte permutation. Normal approach needs to conduct two 17 and 8-bit left shift operations but we conduct one in barrel shifter and in second step we directly conduct 25-bit left shift operation. This nice approach can avoid one rotation operation in similar conditions. Unlike 256-bit LSH, 512-bit LSH is not straight-forwardly implemented over 32-bit ARM processor because the size of operands is 64-bit and it is twice of word size. As like 8-bit AVR and 16-bit MSP, 32-bit ARM platform should slice 64-bit wise instructions into two 32-bit operations. The 64-bit addition and bit-wise exclusive-or are realized with two 32-bit instructions. The detailed operations are available in Table 10. For efficient 64-bit wise rotation, we introduce the barrel shifter based rotation. In Fig. 4, we describe two 32-bit operands and show 24-bit left rotation operation. Firstly, we conduct the 24-bit left shift on two operands. This outputs 24-bit shifted results with zero paddings. Secondly, we conduct right shift by 8-bit and then add the results with first 24-bit left shifted results. Since the operations are executed in barrel shifter form, we can save one clock cycle for each 24-bit left rotation.

Table 8. 32-bit instructions over 32-bit ARM, where R8 and R3 represent destination and source registers

Addition	Exclusive-or	Right rotation by 31
ADD R8, R8, R5	EOR R8, R8, R5	ROR R8, #31

Table 9. Comparisons of sequential and combined ways of rotation operations

Sequential way	Combined way
A = ROL32(A, 17)	–
B = B + A	B = B + ROL32(A, 17)//Barrel Shifter
A = ROL32(A,8)	A = ROL32(A, 25)

4 Results

4.1 8-Bit AVR Platform

AVR results are implemented in AVR studio 6.2 and complied with optimization level 3. The performance is scaled in clock cycle/byte. In Table 11, comparison results on AVR are described. Three different sizes of messages are evaluated including 500, 100 and 50 bytes. Since reference code is written in C language and there is no optimization techniques applied, proposed 256 and 512-bit implementations improved performance by 40 and 64 % than naive C implementations. Compared with other SHA-3 candidates, LSH implementation ranked at fourth place because LSH has long operand operation sets (32, 64-bit) with long messages (512-bit). This degrades the performance over embedded processor with limited number of registers and word lengths.

4.2 16-Bit MSP Platform

MSP programs are implemented in IAR studio for TI MSP430 and compiled with optimization level 3. The performance is scaled in clock cycle/byte. In Table 12, comparison results on MSP430 are described. To the best of our knowledge, there are no hash implementation results, so we mainly compared

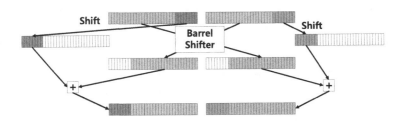

Fig. 4. ARM: 24-bit left rotation operation with barrel shifter for 64-bit word

Table 10. 64-bit instructions over 32-bit ARM, where R8 and R3 represent destination and source registers

Addition	Exclusive-or	Left rotation by 23
ADDS R8, R8, R5	EOR R8, R8, R5	MOV R8, R5, LSL#23
ADCS R9, R9, R6	EOR R9, R9, R6	MOV R9, R6, LSL#23
		ORR R8, R8, R6, LSR#9
		ORR R9, R9, R5, LSR#9

Table 11. Comparison results of LSH implementations on AVR.

Method	500 Byte	100 Byte	50 Byte
Proposed LSH-256	788	1031	2061
Reference LSH-256	1319	1695	3388
SHA2-256 [3]	532	668	672
SHA3-256 [3]	1432	1794	3560
SKEIN-256 [3]	4787	7982	10647
BLAKE-256 [3]	562	708	714
GROESTL-256 [3]	685	1012	1220
JH-256 [3]	5062	7855	10490
Proposed LSH-512	830	2132	4263
Reference LSH-512	2351	5930	11855

with naive C implementations. Compared with the C implementations, proposed 256 and 512-bit implementations improved performance by 12 and 33 %. The performance gap between naive and proposed methods is smaller than that of 8-bit processor because 16-bit processor can handle 32/64-bit operations more efficiently.

Table 12. Comparison results of LSH implementations on MSP.

Method	500 Byte	100 Byte	50 Byte
Proposed LSH-256	597	781	1561
Reference LSH-256	675	878	1755
Proposed LSH-512	652	1672	3343
Reference LSH-512	976	2480	4960

4.3   32-Bit ARM Platform

ARM programs are implemented in Android 4.3 and compiled with optimization level 3. The performance is measured in millisecond and scaled into clock cycle with CPU frequency. In Table 13, comparison results on ARM are described.

Our LSH256 and LSH512 implementations show higher performance improvements than C language results by 36 and 60 %, respectively. Compared with other SHA2 and SHA3 candidates, our implementation ranked at fifth place out of seven cases. Since LSH algorithm is SIMD friendly architecture, SISD implementation is degraded.

Table 13. Comparison results of LSH implementations on ARM

Method	Long Message	4096 Byte	64 Byte
Proposed LSH-256	63.5	65.4	148.0
Reference LSH-256	99.8	103.9	214.3
SHA2-256 [4]	22.9	23.8	80.7
SHA3-256 [4]	48.9	51.1	188.1
SKEIN-256 [4]	31.4	32.5	98.7
BLAKE-256 [4]	30.6	31.6	96.3
GROESTL-256 [4]	74.9	77.5	237.2
JH-256 [4]	165.7	168.7	363.2
Proposed LSH-512	75.7	82.0	323.7
Reference LSH-512	194.1	204.3	772.1
SHA2-512 [4]	47.7	49.8	133.6
SHA3-512 [4]	58.7	61.4	180.0
SKEIN-512 [4]	31.4	32.5	99.4
BLAKE-512 [4]	71.2	74.1	179.5
GROESTL-512 [4]	107.4	112.9	353.6
JH-512 [4]	165.7	168.8	362.7

5   Conclusion

In this paper, we presented various implementation techniques of LSH hash function. The results achieve high performance enhancements with novel approaches. The detailed implementation results would be good materials for following researchers.

References

1. Aranha, D.F., Dahab, R., López, J., Oliveira, L.B.: Efficient implementation of elliptic curve cryptography in wireless sensors. Adv. Math. Commun. 4(2), 169–187 (2010)
2. Atmel Corporation. ATmega128(L) Datasheet (Rev. 2467O-AVR-10/06) October 2006. http://www.atmel.com/dyn/resources/prod_documents/doc2467.pdf
3. Balasch, J., et al.: Compact implementation and performance evaluation of hash functions in ATtiny devices. In: Mangard, S. (ed.) CARDIS 2012. LNCS, vol. 7771, pp. 158–172. Springer, Heidelberg (2013)

4. eBACS. ECRYPT Benchmarking of Cryptographic Systems. http://bench.cr.yp.
   to/supercop.html
5. Gouvêa, C.P., Oliveira, L.B., López, J.: Efficient software implementation of public-
   key cryptography on sensor networks using the MSP430X microcontroller. J.
   Crypt. Eng. **2**(1), 19–29 (2012)
6. Klami, K., Hammond, B.: ARM Announces 10 Billionth Mobile Processor (2009).
   http://www.arm.com/news/24403.html
7. Kim, D.-C., Hong, D., Lee, J.-K., Kim, W.-H., Kwon, D.: Lsh: a new fast secure
   hash function family. In: Lee, J., Kim, J. (eds.) ICISC. LNCS, vol. 8949, pp. 286–
   313. Springer, Heidelberg (2014)
8. Seal, D.: ARM Architecture Reference Manual. Pearson Education, Harlow (2001)
9. Sloss, A., Symes, D., Wright, C.: ARM System Developer's Guide: Designing and
   Optimizing System Software. Morgan Kaufmann, San Francisco (2004)
10. Texas Instruments. MSP430 instruction set. http://cnx.org/content/m23503/
    latest/
11. Texas Instruments. Cortex-M3 Instruction Set (2010). http://cnx.org/content/
    m23503/latest/

Detection of Rogue Devices in WLAN by Analyzing RF Features and Indoor Location of the Device

Hyeokchan Kwon$^{(\boxtimes)}$, Kwang-Il Lee, Gaeil An, Byung-Ho Chung, and Jeong-Nyeo Kim

Electronics and Telecommunications Research Institue, 218 Gajeong-ro, Yuseong-gu, Daejeon, Korea
{hckwon, leeki, fogone, cbh, jnkim}@etri.re.kr

Abstract. In this paper, we present rogue device detection mechanism in WLAN (Wireless Local Area Network) by analyzing radio frequency (RF) features and estimating indoor location of the device. The presented mechanism analyzes error vector magnitude (EVM) as a RF feature and it also utilizes indoor location to improve detection rates. To estimate location, we use the triangulation method with Gauss–Seidel iterative technique to find approximate coordinate. We developed the proposed mechanism in the wireless sensor hardware and wireless intrusion prevention server platform, and we provide experimental results.

1 Introduction

Currently, to prevent attack against WLAN (Wireless Local Area Network), the various kinds of Wireless Intrusion Prevention System (WIPS) has been developed. The WIPS system detects and prevents WLAN intrusion such as man-in-the middle attack, wireless DoS, session hijacking, rogue device, unauthorized network access and so forth in the enterprise network [1]. Figure 1 shows a brief architecture of WIPS system. Among above attacks, we focus on the security attack related to rogue devices. Actually a lot of wireless attacks can be made by rogue devices. Currently, commercial WIPS check MAC address of the device in order to determine whether the device is authorized or not. To do this, WIPS utilize white-list that contains MAC addresses of the pre-registered (i.e., authorized) device. When a new device is detected, it analyzes an RF signal such as beacon, probe response message of the detected device to extract the MAC address and then checks whether the extracted MAC address is included in the white-list. However, the white-list based approaches can't detect the device that forges its MAC address (i.e. MAC spoofing).

In this paper, we present security mechanism to detect a rogue device which has a spoofed (i.e., cloned) MAC in WLAN by analyzing RF features and indoor-location of the device. The RF features contains Error Vector Magnitude (EVM), frequency offset, I/Q offset, sync correlation and so on. The mechanism analyzes analog characteristics of RF signal of a device for detecting MAC cloned device and it also utilizes location information for improving detection rates.

© Springer International Publishing Switzerland 2016
H. Kim and D. Choi (Eds.): WISA 2015, LNCS 9503, pp. 54–61, 2016.
DOI: 10.1007/978-3-319-31875-2_5

We developed WIPS sensor hardware platform that support RF feature extraction. The previous works [4, 5] extracts RF features using technical measuring equipment such as agilent spectrum analyzer and so on. Up to now, there has not been implementing the RF feature extraction functions to the wireless sensor hardware platform. And, we implemented the proposed mechanism with considering EVM as a RF feature and triangulation with Jacobi and Gauss–Seidel method [2] as a indoor location estimation. In our experiments, the detection rate of rogue device is improved about 4.7 % compared to the mechanism without consider device location.

The rest of the paper is organized as follows. Section 2 introduces related studies. The rogue device detection mechanism and experiment result is described in Sect. 3. Finally, conclusion is given in Sect. 4.

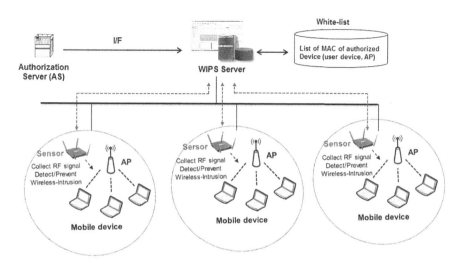

Fig. 1. The brief architecture of wireless intrusion prevention system

2 Related Study

To detect rogue devices which has a spoofed (i.e., cloned) MAC, various kinds of mechanisms has been presented.

In case of the AP is installed at a fixed location, to detect cloned AP, [3] uses pre-registered MAC address and RSSI of the AP. When a device having MAC address of the authorized AP is found, it compares RSSI values to determine whether the MAC is forged or not. This mechanism cannot detect when the rogue device having forged MAC is located at the same location as the authorized AP. Furthermore, it cannot detect when the attacker device is located at the different location but same distance with the authorized AP. It is possible because even when directions are different, the same RSSI values can be measured.

[3] also propose the mechanism using pre-registered MAC and configuration of the AP. When a device having the MAC of the authorized AP is detected, it compares the configuration such as security configuration, channel number and so on., to determine

whether the MAC is forged or not. However this mechanism cannot detect when the attacker having same configuration values as the authorized AP. The forging the configuration of the authorized AP is relatively easy, because configurations values are exposed by broadcasted RF signals such as beacon, probe response and so on.

Another approach [4, 5], to detect cloned device, uses RF features of the device such as EVM, Frequency offset, sync correlation and so on. For this work, the system generates unique RF fingerprint of the device using machine learning of the collected RF signals of the device.

Since the RF characteristics forgery is not possible, the last mechanism can obtain high detection rates of the cloned device. But in order to obtain high detection rates, it is required to extract accurate meaningful RF features and to apply appropriate learning algorithm. And RF features are somewhat different depends on the location, so it is need to compensate the defect.

3   Rogue (MAC Spoofing) Device Detection Mechanism

In order to detect rogue devices, this mechanism utilizes the location information in addition to RF features. In the training phase, the wireless sensor collects and analysis RF signals of the device by moving the physical zone (i.e., location) of the device. In the detection phase, it estimates indoor location of the suspected device, and it analyzes RF fingerprint data with the best nearby RF features in current location of the device. Figure 2 shows the overall architecture of this mechanism.

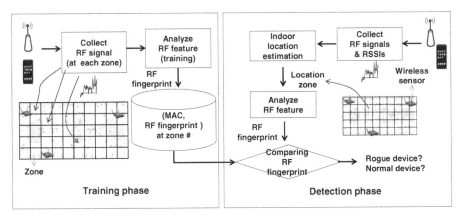

Fig. 2. Detection process of MAC spoofing rogue device by analyzing RF features and indoor-location of the device

3.1   Training Phase

In the training phase, the network manager registers MAC address of the authorized device. And determines a wireless signal measurement zone (location xyz), and moves wireless device to the measurement location and generates wireless packets. The sensor collects RF signals from the authorized device, and the analysis server operates machine learning algorithm such as K-NN, SVM and so on, and creates RF fingerprint of the authorized device. In this paper, we employ K-NNDD (K-Nearest Neighbor Data Description) [6] for training RF feature of authorized devices.

The location information and RF fingerprint data is stored in fingerprint database.

In this paper, we consider EVM as a RF feature. EVM is a vector magnitude difference between an ideal reference signal and measured signal. Figure 3 shows the concept of error vector magnitude (EVM). The formula 1 shows a mathematical formula for deriving EVM value.

$$EVM = \sqrt{Err_I{}^2 + Err_Q{}^2}, \quad \text{where} \begin{cases} Err_I = I_{reference} \cdot I_{measured} \\ Err_Q = Q_{reference} \cdot Q_{measured} \end{cases} \tag{1}$$

EVM is calculated by comparing the actual measured signal with a reference (ideal) signal to determine the error vector. The EVM value is the root mean square value of the error vector over time at the instants of the symbol clock transitions. There are various reasons of mismatching measured signal with reference ideal signal such as hardware impairment, channel characteristics, noise at the receiver and modulation error. By using modulation error, we can identify particular wireless devices with different manufacturer or different wifi-chipset or even the same manufacturer/ wifi-chipset.

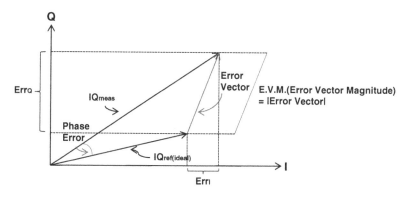

Fig. 3. Error vector magnitude (EVM)

3.2 Detection Phase

In the detection phase, the wireless sensor collects and analyzes the RF signal of the device and extracts MAC address, RSSI and RF features. And it sends this information to the device identification server. The device identification server estimates location of the device using collected RSSIs and information of the collected sensor location. In this paper, we used following three steps for location estimation; (1) Filtering RSSI value (2) distance estimation (3) location estimation using triangulation.

To calculate distance from RSSI values we used the formula (2). The correction factors (−12.5,−36.5) are derived through iterative experiments by minimizing the difference from the value by distance estimation algorithm with real distance. The notation d in formula (2) is a distance. To estimate location, we use the triangulation method. And we use the Gauss–Seidel iterative technique to find approximate coordinate.

$$RSSI = -12.5Ln(d) - 36.25 \tag{2}$$

The device identification server then selects the RF features having the highest P (RF features| RSSI) of the MAC of the device. P(RF features | RSSI) means a probability of RF features in a given RSSI value. Then it creates RF signature from the RF features by using machine learning algorithm. Then it determines whether the device having forged MAC by comparing the RF signature of the device with the device having same MAC in the database. In this paper, we employ K-NN(K-Nearest Neighbor) algorithm for comparing measured RF signature with reference RF signature (Fig. 4).

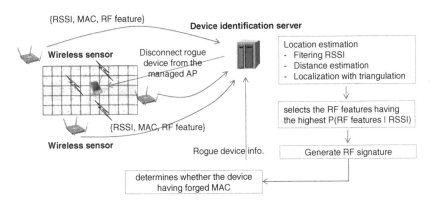

Fig. 4. Detection process of rogue device

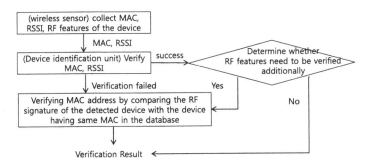

Fig. 5. The simple Rogue AP detection mechanism when the verifying AP is in a fixed location

If case of access point which is installed in a fixed location, the mechanism can be simplified like Fig. 5. In this case, since the RSSI of the AP is relatively consistent, device identification unit detects MAC forgery by verifying MAC and RSSI at first. And then if necessary, it verifies RF signature additionally.

3.3   Experiments

We developed wireless sensor hardware platform that support RF feature extraction. Figure 6 shows the developed sensor HW platform which supporting RF feature extraction. The sensor consists of Atheros 9380 WLAN chipset, intel atom CPU, 4 GB memory, PoE and so on.

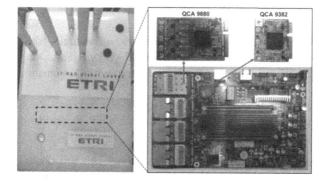

Fig. 6. Wireless intrusion prevention sensor H/W platform which supporting RF feature(EVM) extraction

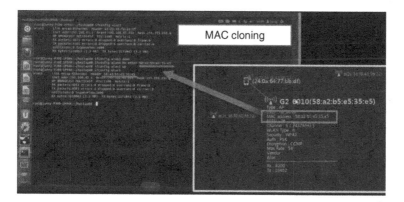

Fig. 7. MAC spoofing process (screenshot of attack tool)

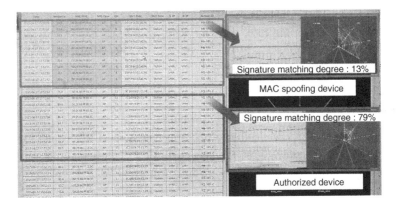

Fig. 8. RF signature verification process (screenshot of the wireless threat management server)

And we also developed wireless server system with related user interface and dashboard. And we developed wireless attack tool for evaluating developed system. Figure 7 shows the screenshots to create spoofed MAC by out attacking tool. Figure 8 shows the server UI for Rogue AP detection through RF signature analysis and verification.

Table 1 shows the experiment result. In Table 1, the detection rate of rogue device is improved about 4.7 % compared to the mechanism without consider device location. The testing device is as follows.

- Mobile device with different chipset: smart phone with Broadcom chipset, laptop computer with intel chipset, laptop computer with atheros chipset
- Mobile device with same chipset: iphone4 s smart phone with broadcom's BCM 4330, iphone4 smart phone with broadcom's BCM 4329

Table 1. Experiment Result

Condition	Approach	Threshold	FAR (False Accept Rate)	FRR (False Reject Rate)	EER (Equal Error Rate)
Mobile device with different chipset	EVM	0.90	4.35%	0%	1.09%
	EVM +location		3.97%	0%	0.93%
Mobile device with same wi-fi chipset	EVM	0.76	63.04%	0%	31.52%
	EVM +location		61.58%	0%	30.3%

4 Conclusions

In this paper, we present security mechanism to detect a rogue device which has a spoofed (i.e., cloned) MAC in WLAN by analyzing RF features and location of the device. The proposed mechanism analyzes analog characteristics of radio frequency signal of a device for detecting MAC spoofing device and it also utilizes physical indoor location for improving detection rates. We developed wireless intrusion prevention sensor hardware platform that support RF feature extraction. We implemented the proposed mechanism with considering EVM as a RF feature and triangulation with Jacobi and Gauss–Seidel methods as location estimation. We also developed wireless attacking tool to evaluate our results.

In our experiments, the proposed mechanism works well in detecting MAC spoofed rogue device. The detection rate of rogue device can be improved about 4.7 % compared with EVM only detection mechanism by additionally applying physical location information. However detection rate should be improved in sophisticated case such as rogue devices have same manufacturers and wi-fi chipset with authorized one. Currently, we are refining the implementation consider additional RF features such as IQ offset, sync correlation, frequency offset and so on.

Acknowledgement. This work was supported by ICT R&D program of MSIP/IITP. [R0166-15-1012, Safety and Test International Standard Development for Integrated Shipborne Network]

References

1. Sobh, T.S.: Wired and wireless intrusion detection system: Classifications, good characteristics and state-of-the-art. Comput. Stand. Interfaces **28**(6), 670–694 (2006). Elsevier
2. Gauss–Seidel method. https://en.wikipedia.org/wiki/Gauss%E2%80%93Seidel_method
3. AirTight Patent, Method and system for monitoring a selected region of an airspace associated with local area networks of computing devices, Patent# US 7,002,943, February 2006
4. Shi, Y., Jensen, M.A.: Improved radiometric identification of wireless devices using MIMO transmission. IEEE Trans. Inf. Forensics Secur. **6**, 1346–1354 (2011)
5. Brik, V., Banerjee, S., Gruteser, M., Oh, S.: Wireless device identification with radiometric signatures. In: ACM MobiCom, pp. 116–127 (2008)
6. Son, J., Kim, S.: kNNDD-based one-class classification by nonparametric density estimation. J. Korean Inst. Ind. Eng. **38**(3), 191–197 (2012)
7. An, G., Kim, S.H.: MAC Spoofing Attack Detection based on EVM in 802.11 WLAN. UBICOMM 2013 (2013)
8. Kwon, H., An, G., Kim, S.H., Chung, B.H.: Detecting cloned devices in wireless network using RSSI and RF Features. ICONI, December 2014

Cryptography

Security Analysis on RFID Mutual Authentication Protocol

You Sung Kang[1]([✉]), Elizabeth O'Sullivan[2], Dooho Choi[1], and Maire O'Neill[2]

[1] Cyber Security Research Division, Electronics and Telecommunications
Research Institute, Daejeon 305-350, Korea
{youskang,dhchoi}@etri.re.kr
[2] Centre for Secure Information Technologies,
Queen's University Belfast, Belfast BT3 9DT, UK
e.osullivan@qub.ac.uk, m.oneill@ecit.qub.ac.uk

Abstract. Radio frequency identification (RFID) has received much attention both in industry and academia in recent years. To this extent, the international standards group, ISO/IEC JTC 1/SC 31, is in the midst of standardization activity to define the security extension to the EPC-global Generation 2 (Gen2) ultra high frequency (UHF) air interface protocols for secure RFID communications. In this paper, we investigate a vulnerability of an RFID mutual authentication protocol that was highlighted in a recent letter [5]. Our analysis presents that the attack on the mutual authentication protocol is just a relay operation between a legitimate reader and a legitimate tag. We also propose the threshold values of data rate between a reader and a tag based on link timing parameters of passive UHF RFID systems.

Keywords: RFID security · Mutual authentication · RFID Gen2 · ISO/IEC 29167-6 · Man-in-the-middle attack

1 Introduction

Radio frequency identification (RFID) technology is rapidly emerging as a leading ubiquitous computing technology. RFID systems provide the ability to automatically identify and track objects and/or personnel in a non-contact, non-line-of-sight manner. This enables the development of very efficient automated item management frameworks and as such provides a compelling business case for the rapid adoption of RFID systems. However, due to the very nature of being able to read an RFID tag without line-of-sight, presents significant security challenges that must be addressed in order for this technology to transfer seamlessly and securely into industry.

A typical RFID system consists of a reader, R, composed of a set of transceivers together with a backend database, and a set of tags, T_i ($1 \leq i \leq N$, N is the total number of tags), where each tag is a passive transponder identified by a unique ID. The communication between a reader and the tags is defined by

© Springer International Publishing Switzerland 2016
H. Kim and D. Choi (Eds.): WISA 2015, LNCS 9503, pp. 65–74, 2016.
DOI: 10.1007/978-3-319-31875-2_6

the EPCglobal Generation 2 (Gen2) specification. This specification includes the physical layer and medium access control parameters for ultra high frequency (UHF) RFID passive tags operating in the frequency band between 860 MHz and 960 MHz [1]. The international standard group, ISO/IEC JTC 1/SC 31, is in the process of standardizing the security extension to the ISO/IEC 18000-63 standard that is based on the EPCglobal Gen2 protocol [2]. Amongst several candidates, ISO/IEC 29167-14 that is based on advanced encryption standard-output feedback (AES-OFB) mode of operation has been proposed to define a variety of authentication protocols and session key generation applicable to the ISO/IEC 18000-63 standard [3].

The initial proposal that defines an RFID mutual authentication protocol and session key generation was ISO/IEC working draft (WD) 29167-6 [4]. ISO/IEC 29167-6 WD proposal describes three security protocols, namely **Protocol 1, 2, and 3**. ISO/IEC 29167-14 succeeds this and includes the authentication protocols and main contents of ISO/IEC 29167-6 WD proposal. **Protocol 1** considers the RFID mutual authentication and secure communication in security mode. In a recent letter [5], it was highlighted that **Protocol 1** is vulnerable to an attack that results in the manipulation of a communication parameter, called the *Handle*, such that the tag and the reader fail to share the same *Handle* for subsequent communications during a run of the protocol. This attack is named as a man-in-the-middle attack in the letter. In the same letter, a cryptographic countermeasure was presented that introduced dependency between security parameters in a message using a more complex variable length shift technique, and constructed the *Handle* as the concatenation of the challenge from the reader and the challenge from the tag.

In this paper, we review the vulnerability to the man-in-the-middle attack proposed in [5] and introduce different points of view about the man-in-the-middle attack presented in [6,7]. In addition, we point out that the effect of the man-in-the-middle attack on the RFID mutual authentication protocol is just a relay between a legitimate reader and a legitimate tag. We also analyze a correlation between link timing parameters and the man-in-the-middle attack. The remainder of this paper is organized as follows. We review the man-in-the-middle attack together with an improved mutual authentication protocol proposed in [5] in Sect. 2. In Sect. 3, we analyze the attack effects in terms of security weakness and link timing parameters. Finally, we conclude the paper in Sect. 4.

2   Review of *Handle* Manipulation Attack

For the sake of completeness, we review **Protocol 1** of ISO/IEC 29167-6 WD (shown in Fig. 1) and the *Handle* manipulation attack together with the associated countermeasure presented in [5]. **Protocol 1** assumes that the tag shares the same 128-bit master key with the reader and that the key stream is produced using AES algorithm as the encryption engine. Step 0 to step 9 (see Fig. 1) are concerned with the setting up of the secure channel. During this exchange of messages, the security parameters $RnInt$ (step 7) and $RnTag$ (step 8), which are

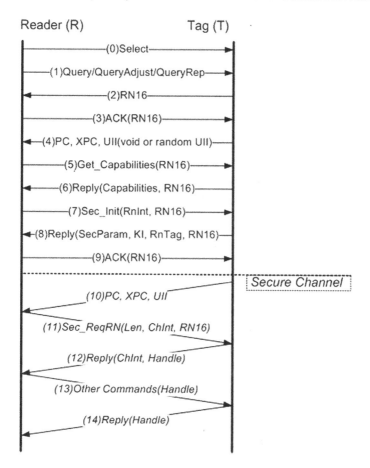

Fig. 1. Protocol 1 - RFID mutual authentication protocol.

64-bit random numbers, are generated and exchanged by the reader and tag, respectively. $RnInt$ and $RnTag$ are then concatenated to create the initial vector (IV) as input to the AES algorithm and the master key is used as the AES key for the first iteration of key stream generation. Subsequent iterations of AES uses the output generated from the previous iteration as the input to AES algorithm. We note that even though $RnInt$ and $RnTag$ are sent in the clear, without knowledge of the master key the key stream cannot be determined.

The secure channel commences upon a successful acknowledgement of the 16-bit random number $RN16$ at step 9. Taking k_i to be consecutive blocks of the key stream whose block length is determined by the length of the parameter it is XOR'd with, the first message of the secure channel (step 10) is sent from the tag to the reader and is given as,

$$T \rightarrow R : (PC, XPC, UII) = (PC \oplus k_1, XPC \oplus k_2, UII \oplus k_3) \tag{1}$$

where PC is the protocol control, XPC is the extended protocol control and UII is the actual unique item identifier (note a random or void UII was sent earlier in step 4 of the protocol procedure). It is at the next step that the attack described in [5] begins.

The message sent from the reader to the tag in step 11 is

$$R \rightarrow T : \textbf{Sec\_ReqRN}(Len, ChInt, RN16)$$
$$= (Len \oplus k_4, ChInt \oplus k_5, RN16 \oplus k_6) \tag{2}$$

where $RN16$ is the encrypted version of $RN16$ that was sent earlier in the clear, $ChInt$ is a random challenge from the reader and Len is a 3 bit indicator of the wordlength of $ChInt$ (one word is 16 bits). Hence the value of Len can range from 0 to 7, where all zeros are interpreted as a value of 8. This implies that the length of $ChInt$ can range from 16 bits to 128 bits. In the attack, the adversary intercepts and changes the random parameter 2 of this message denoted by Eq. (2), with a different random number, so that the message becomes

$$R \rightarrow T : (Len \oplus k_4, R_1, RN16 \oplus k_6) \tag{3}$$

Upon receiving this message the tag will decrypt using the key stream and check that the $RN16$ parameter matches the $RN16$ that was sent earlier in the clear, if true the tag authenticates the reader. At this point, however, the tag does not contain the actual challenge that was sent by the reader, but instead it registers $R_1 \oplus k_5$ as the challenge.

Step 12 contains the reply from the tag to the reader and according to **Protocol 1** the message is intended to be

$$T \rightarrow R : \textbf{Reply}(ChInt, Handle) = (ChInt \oplus k_7, Handle \oplus k_8) \tag{4}$$

however, because of the manipulation of the previous message (shown in Eq. (3)), which results in the tag registering $R_1 \oplus k_5$ as the challenge from the reader, the actual message sent from the tag is

$$T \rightarrow R : ((R_1 \oplus k_5) \oplus k_7, Handle \oplus k_8) \tag{5}$$

where $Handle$ is defined as a 16 bits temporary tag identification number, that the tag generates and backscatters to the reader, and is thus used in subsequent communications by the tag and the reader.

The adversary continues with the attack by manipulating parameter 1 of Eq. (5) with $ChInt \oplus k_5$, observed in step 11 of the protocol (see Eq. (2)), together with the random number R_1 that was injected in step 11 (see Eq. (3)), and further manipulates parameter 2 of Eq. (5) to produce

$$T \rightarrow R : ((R_1 \oplus k_5) \oplus k_7 \oplus (ChInt \oplus k_5) \oplus R_1, R_2) = (ChInt \oplus k_7, R_2) \tag{6}$$

The reader decrypts using the key stream and checks that the $ChInt$ sent from the tag matches the reader's $ChInt$, if true the reader authenticates the tag. However, at this point the reader and the tag fail to share the same $Handle$

as the reader's *Handle* is now $R_2 \oplus k_8$. Note here that the manipulation of *ChInt* in steps 11 and 12 does not contribute to the manipulation of the *Handle*, the *Handle* manipulation attack would have just as easily occurred had the adversary only intercepted and manipulated parameter 2 of the message in step 12. Also note that at no point in the attack is the security of the key stream compromised.

We now turn our attention to the proposed countermeasure presented in [5]. The idea here is to create a dependency between the parameters of the message by using a variable length shift to build integrity into the message. In the countermeasure the message in step 11 becomes,

$$
\begin{aligned}
R \to T : (Len, ChInt &\ll k_5, RN16 \oplus L_{16}(ChInt)) \\
= (Len \oplus k_4, (ChInt &\ll k_5) \oplus k_6, RN16 \oplus L_{16}(ChInt) \oplus k_7)
\end{aligned}
\tag{7}
$$

where now parameter 2 contains a bitwise rotation by k_5 whose bit length is determined by the value of *Len* and is given as $\lceil \log_2(Len \times 16) \rceil$, hence the bit length of k_5 can range from 4 bits to 7 bits. The left-most 16 bits of the challenge parameter *ChInt* (i.e., $L_{16}(ChInt)$) is included in parameter 3 XOR'd with $RN16$. Thus *ChInt* is now contained within two parameters of the message in different formats (one rotated by a secret amount and one not), so that any manipulation en-route may be detected by the tag.

Step 12 of the countermeasure then becomes

$$
\begin{aligned}
T \to R : (ChTag &\ll k_8, ChInt \oplus ChTag) \\
= ((ChTag \ll k_8) &\oplus k_9, (ChInt \oplus ChTag) \oplus k_{10})
\end{aligned}
\tag{8}
$$

where $\text{BitLen}(k_8) = \lceil \log_2(Len \times 16) \rceil$, and $\text{BitLen}(k_9) = \text{BitLen}(k_{10}) = \text{BitLen}(ChInt)$. Here the tag now also produces a challenge, *ChTag*, which is of the same bit length as *ChInt* (i.e. from 16 bits to 128 bits). *ChTag* is bitwise rotated by a secret amount and is delivered to the reader in both the parameters of the **Reply** message, again in different formats so that any manipulation may be detected by the reader. Upon decryption the reader checks for a match on the *ChInt* and *ChTag* and the *Handle* now becomes a shared parameter that comprises both the tag and the reader challenges as,

$$
Handle = L_8(ChInt) \| R_8(ChTag) \tag{9}
$$

where $\|$ denotes concatenation.

Recently, Bagheri *et al.* [6] showed that the improved protocol presented in [5] suffers from the same man-in-the-middle attack as **Protocol 1**. In [5,6], the attack is considered as an man-in-the-middle attack. However, Kang *et al.* [7] pointed out that the attack of [5] comes from a misunderstanding regarding a communication parameter called *Handle* and claimed that the attack is not a security threat. In the next Section, we analyze the practical effects of the man-in-the-middle attack in terms of a role of *Handle* and link timing parameters.

3   Analysis of Attack Effects

3.1   Attack Effects

We analyze tag access operations and tag authentication under the man-in-the-middle attack. The first analysis is related to tag access operations. In the passive UHF RFID system, tags located within communication range of a reader can receive all access commands from the reader. Tags check whether the received *Handle* is the same as the *Handle* backscattered by them, and only a tag with the same *Handle* executes the access command. A Reader utilizes a *Handle* in the same manner for a tag access operation. In general, the reader and the tag use the same *Handle* value in the same session. It is, however, possible to use dual *Handles* in a session. That is, all a tag needs to do is to check the *Handle* backscattered by itself and a reader has only to use the *Handle* received at step 12.

Figure 2 illustrates the procedures of the man-in-the-middle attack. Assuming that E can intercept and replace the air interface data, it can replace the tag's *Handle* $\oplus k_8$ with R_2 at step 12. And, E can relay an access command to T and forward the tag's **Reply** to R like Steps 13 and 14 in Fig. 2, respectively. It is, however, a real-time data injection over the radio rather than a man-in-the-middle attack. In the general man-in-the-middle attack, the role of E in a tag access operation is to fake and forward data. In the case that someone can manipulate air interface data, he/she can perform the same operations as the man-in-the-middle attack without *Handle* manipulation. Steps 13 and 14 are the same situation as an attacker intervenes in tag-reader communication to change the payload into fake data over the radio.

Figure 3 is equivalent to Fig. 2. The practical effect of the man-in-the-middle attack is that **Protocol 1** utilizes the dual *Handles* such as *Handle$_T$* and *Handle$_R$*. The *Handle$_T$* is the backscattered *Handle* which is the same as the *Handle* of step 12 in Fig. 2, and the *Handle$_R$* is $R_2 \oplus k_8$ which is accepted by R. In other words, even though the man-in-the-middle attack manipulates the *Handle* between T and R, it is practically only the dual *Handles*. In addition, E can neither decrypt the original ciphertext nor encrypt any of its own data because it has no session key. Furthermore, it is impossible to reuse the current fabricated information at other sessions or other tags because E's intervention works only when a legitimate reader communicates with a legitimate tag in the current session. As a result, there is no meaning to E's intervention using *Handle* manipulation. That is, the man-in-the-middle attack of [5] does not interfere with tag access operations, but is just a relay using the dual *Handles* between a legitimate reader and a legitimate tag.

The second analysis is related to tag authentication. In the general man-in-the-middle attack, R authenticates E as T when it receives the returned challenge number which is intercepted and replaced by E. However, in the man-in-the-middle attack of [5], despite a successful authentication, E cannot send any data independently of a legitimate reader because it knows neither session key nor original *Handle*. The man-in-the-middle attack manipulates only the encrypted version of *Handle*. That is, there is no effect from fake authentication.

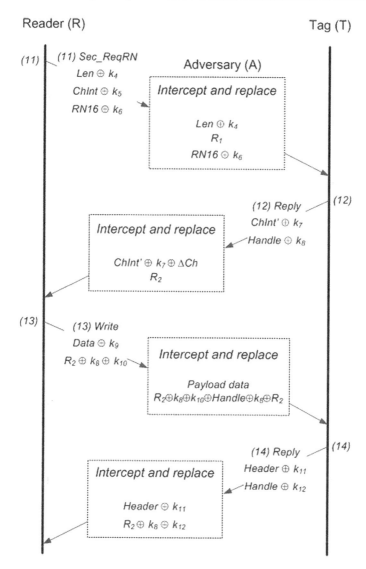

Fig. 2. Procedures of the man-in-the-middle attack on **Protocol 1**.

Furthermore, it does not matter whether E intervenes in tag authentication procedure or not, because the fake authentication is successful only if the legitimate tag exists in the authentication procedure at the current session. It is no more than the authentication for the legitimate tag. As a result, the man-in-the-middle attack of [5] does not interfere with tag authentication.

3.2   Link Timing Analysis

ISO/IEC 18000-63 defines two link timing parameters related to single tag reply [2,8]. The first parameter, T_1, is the time from reader transmission to

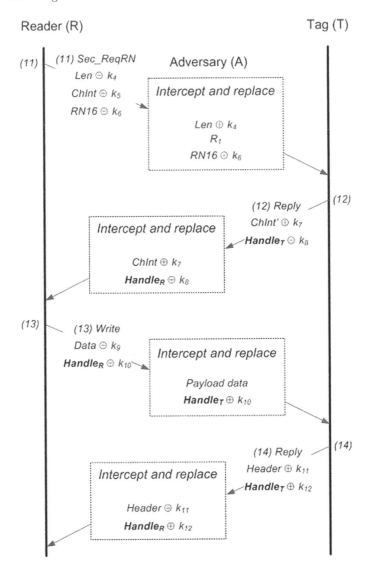

Fig. 3. Practical effect of the man-in-the-middle attack on **Protocol 1**.

tag response (specifically, the time from the last rising edge of the last bit of the reader transmission to the first rising edge of the tag response), measured at the tag's antenna terminals. That is, a reader starts a new session if it receives no reply from a tag in defined time. The nominal value of T_1 is MAX($RTcal$, $10 \cdot T_{pri}$), where, $RTcal$ is reader-to-tag calibration symbol and T_{pri} is backscatter-link pulse-repetition interval. According to [2], the values for $RTcal$ and T_{pri} are in the range of $[15.625\mu s, 75\mu s]$ and $[1.5625\mu s, 25\mu s]$, respectively. The second parameter, T_2, is the reader response time required if a tag is to demodulate the reader signal, measured from the end of the last bit of the tag response to the first falling edge of the reader transmission. That is, a tag transitions to the **arbitrate** state if T_2 expires. The value of T_2 is $3 \cdot T_{pri}$ to $20 \cdot T_{pri}$. (refer to [2] for notations and values.) Therefore, the T_1 time is $15.625\mu s$ ($=$ minimum $RTcal$) to $250\mu s$ ($=$ maximum $10 \cdot T_{pri}$), and the T_2 time is $4.6875\mu s$ ($=$ minimum $3 \cdot T_{pri}$) to $500\mu s$ ($=$ maximum $20 \cdot T_{pri}$). In other words, E shall intercept, replace, and forward **Sec_ReqRN** of step 11 in T_2 time (at most, $500\mu s$) and **Reply** of step 12 in T_1 time (at most, $250\mu s$).

In Fig. 2, the minimum length of **Seq_ReqRN** is 35 bits ($= Len$ of 3 bits, $ChInt$ of 16 bits, and $RN16$ of 16 bits). The first action of E is to intercept **Seq_ReqRN** over the radio. Assuming the maximum T_2 time (that is, $500\mu s$), E needs a reader-to-tag data rate ($RTrate$) of 70 kbps ($= 35$ bits/$500\mu s$) in order to intercept **Seq_ReqRN** of step 11. In other words, if $RTrate$ is less than 70 kbps, the man-in-the-middle attack cannot work because the T_2 time expires during intercepting 35 bits data. Therefore, a simple countermeasure against the man-in-the-middle attack is to adjust the $RTrate$ to less than 70 kbps. Link timing-constrained condition is applied to **Reply** of step 12 in the same way. The minimum length of **Reply** is 32 bits ($= ChInt'$ of 16 bits and $Handle$ of 16 bits). Assuming the maximum T_1 time (that is, $250\mu s$), the required tag-to-reader data rate ($TRrate$) for intercepting **Reply** is at least 128 kbps ($= 32$ bits/$250\mu s$). Therefore, the man-in-the-middle attack cannot work if $TRrate$ is less than 128 kbps. According to [2], the $RTrate$ ranges between 26.7 kbps and 128 kbps and the $TRrate$ ranges between 5 kbps and 320 kbps in case of Miller encoding. The proposed threshold values of 70 kbps for $RTrate$ and 128 kbps for $TRrate$ exist in the allowable ranges. So, the proposed link timing countermeasure has no influence on the existing passive UHF RFID system.

4   Conclusion

In this paper, we have reviewed the man-in-the-middle attack on the RFID mutual authentication protocol of ISO/IEC 29167-6 WD and the subsequent countermeasure recently presented in [5]. After reviewing the attack scenario, we have analyzed practical security effects of the man-in-the-middle attack in terms of tag authentication service and link timing conformance. Our analysis shows that the attack does not interfere with tag access operations and tag authentication service, but is just a relay using the dual $Handles$ between a legitimate reader and a legitimate tag. We have also drawn the threshold values of 70 kbps for $RTrate$ and 128 kbps for $TRrate$ which can fundamentally protect the passive UHF RFID system from the data manipulation by any man-in-the-middle attack. We hope that our analysis helps the reader understand security features of the passive UHF RFID system.

Acknowledgments. This work was supported by the K-SCARF project, the ICT R&D program of ETRI [Research on Key Leakage Analysis and Response Technologies].

References

1. EPCglobal Specification for RFID Air Interface, "Radio-frequency identity protocols class-1 generation-2 UHF RFID protocol for communications at 860 MHz - 960 MHz," version 1.0.9, January 2005
2. "ISO, IEC 18000–63, Information Technology - Automatic Identification, Data Capture Techniques - Radio Frequency Identification(RFID) for Item Management - Part 63: Parameters for air interface communications at 860 MHz to 960 MHz Type C," International Organization for Standardization, February 2013
3. "ISO, IEC FDIS 29167–14, Information technology - Automatic identification, data capture techniques - Part 14: Crypto suite AES OFB security services for air interface communications," International Organization for Standardization, May 2015
4. "ISO, IEC WD 29167–6, Information technology - Automatic identification, data capture techniques - Part 6: Air interface for security services and file management for RFID at 860–960 MHz," International Organization for Standardization, August 2010
5. Song, B., Hwang, J., Shim, K.: Security improvement of an RFID security protocol of ISO/IEC WD 29167–6. IEEE Commun. Lett. **15**(12), 1375–1377 (2011)
6. Bagheri, N., Safkhani, M., Peris-Lopez, P., Tapiador, J.: Comments on "security improvement of an RFID security protocol of ISO/IEC WD 29167–6". IEEE Commun. Lett. **17**(4), 805–807 (2013)
7. Kang, Y., Choi, D., Park, D.-J.: Comments on an improved RFID security protocol for ISO/IEC WD 29167–6. J. ETRI **35**(1), 170–172 (2013)
8. Engels, D., Kang, Y., Wang, J.: On security with the new Gen2 RFID security framework. In: 7th IEEE International Conference on RFID, pp. 144–151. IEEE Press, New York (2013)

How Much Randomness Can Be Extracted from Memoryless Shannon Entropy Sources?

Maciej Skorski$^{(\boxtimes)}$

Cryptology and Data Security Group, University of Warsaw, Warsaw, Poland
`maciej.skorski@mimuw.edu.pl`

Abstract. We revisit the classical problem: given a memoryless source having a certain amount of Shannon Entropy, how many random bits can be extracted? This question appears in works studying random number generators built from physical entropy sources.

Some authors proposed to use a heuristic estimate obtained from the Asymptotic Equipartition Property, which yields roughly n extractable bits, where n is the total Shannon entropy amount. However best precise results of this form give only $n - O(\sqrt{\log(1/\epsilon)n})$ bits, where ϵ is the distance of the extracted bits from uniform. In this paper we show a matching $n - \Omega(\sqrt{\log(1/\epsilon)n})$ upper bound. Therefore, the loss of $\Theta(\sqrt{\log(1/\epsilon)n})$ bits is necessary. As we show, this theoretical bound is of practical relevance. Namely, applying the imprecise AEP heuristic to a mobile phone accelerometer one might overestimate extractable entropy even by 100 %, no matter what the extractor is. Thus, the "AEP extracting heuristic" should not be used without taking the precise error into account.

Keywords: Shannon entropy · Randomness extractors · Asymptotic equipartition property

1 Introduction

1.1 Entropy

RANDOMNESS SOURCES. Important computer applications, like generating cryptographic keys, building countermeasures against side-channel attacks or gambling, demand randomness of excellent quality, that is uniformly or almost uniformly distributed sequences of bits. Unfortunately, in practice we cannot generate pure randomness. Even best physical sources of randomness produce bits that are slightly biased or correlated. Sources which provide some (not maximal) amount of randomness are called *weak sources*. In practice, randomness can be gathered based on a physical phenomena (like radiation [hot], photons transmission, thermal noise [BP99], atmospheric noise [ran], jitters) or even from

---

M. Skorski–This work was partly supported by the WELCOME/2010-4/2 grant founded within the framework of the EU Innovative Economy Operational Programme.

H. Kim and D. Choi (Eds.): WISA 2015, LNCS 9503, pp. 75–86, 2016.
DOI: 10.1007/978-3-319-31875-2_7

a human-device interaction (like timing I/O disk and network events [dev], keystrokes or mouse movements [pgp], shaking accelerators in mobile phones [VSH11] and other ideas). Such raw randomness must be further post-processed before use, in order to eliminate bias and correlations between individual bits. While this task can be easily achieved by general-purpose tools called *randomness extractors* [BST03], the main problem is in evaluating the quality of a random source. One needs to ensure that enough randomness has been collected, depending on the chosen post-processing technique. This is the major concern in designing so called *true random number generators*, which combine randomness sources with postprocessing algorithms to generate random output of high quality from underlying weak sources. The design of a typical TRNG is illustrated in Fig. 1 below [BST03].

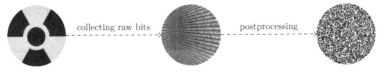

Weak Randomness Source   Extractor   Strongly Random Output

Fig. 1. True Random Number Generators. The scheme illustrates the typical design, where the building blocks are: (a) an entropy source (b) a harvesting mechanism and (c) a postprocessor (extractor). The main issue is how to ensure that enough raw bits have been collected?

QUANTIFYING RANDOMNESS IN THEORY. From a theoretical point of view, to evaluate randomness within a *known* probability distribution one uses the notion of entropy. One uses different entropy definitions depending on the context. In information theory most widely used is Shannon entropy, which quantifies the encoding length of a given distribution. For any discrete random variable X its Shannon Entropy equals

$$H(X) = -\sum_x \Pr[X = x] \log \Pr[X = x]. \tag{1}$$

In turn, cryptographers use the more conservative notion called min-entropy, which quantifies unpredictability (in particular, min-entropy provides a bound on how much randomness can be extracted). The min-entropy of a probability distribution X is defined as

$$H_\infty(X) = \min_x (1/\log \Pr[X = x]). \tag{2}$$

In general, there is a large gap between these two measures: the min-entropy of an n-bit string may be only $O(1)$ whereas its Shannon entropy as big as $\Omega(n)$[1].

---

[1] Consider simply a n-bit distribution X which puts the weight 0.5 on the string 0^n and is uniform elsewhere.

QUANTIFYING RANDOMNESS IN PRACTICE. From a practical point of view, often it happens that not only the distribution of X is unknown, but it may be even hard to assign a fitting theoretical model with some degrees of freedom (for example if we knew that X comes from a particular paremetrized family of distributions, not knowing the concrete parameters). This is in particular the case when randomness is being gathered from different sources (for example the linux random number generator). In such cases, we have no understanding of the underlying physical process and cannot conclude anything about its characteristics (like the entropy), which would be the recommended solution [KMT15]. Instead, we can only observe output samples of the source, considering it a black-box device. In this setting, we need an *entropy estimator*, which guess the entropy of an *unknown* distribution X based on its samples.

1.2   Entropy Estimating

MOTIVATIONS FOR ENTROPY ESTIMATING. We have already seen that we need entropy estimators to evaluate the quality of a source and thus the quality of the extractor output. Also, entropy estimating is motivated in practice by the fact that actually many parties may be interested in evaluating the source entropy in the context of TRNGs [BL05,KMT15]: (a) designers, when they fail to fit a good model to the source (b) testing labs, when verifying quality claimed by manufacturers and (c) developers, especially when working with multiple sources.

SHANNON ENTROPY OR MIN-ENTROPY? Technically speaking, extractable randomness is quantified in terms of min-entropy, not Shannon entropy. However, there are two reasons for why we actually makes sense to work with Shannon entropy

(a) *Shannon entropy is easier to be reliably estimated.*
(b) *For memoryless sources, Shannon and min-entropy are comparable*

Regarding (a), we note that to estimate Shannon entropy one can use fairly general source models based on Markov chains like Maurer-Coron tests [Cor99] or measures based on mutual information [YSK13]. Also, Shannon Entropy is much easier (and efficient) to estimate in an *online* manner, where the source distribution may change over time. Such estimators are an active research area and find important applications not only in cryptography [BL05,LPR11] but also in learning, data mining or network anomaly detection [HJW15].

   To discuss (b), recall that *memoryless source* (called also *stateless*) is a source which produces consecutive samples independently. While this is a restriction, it is often assumed as a part of the model by practitioners working on random number generators (cf. [LRSV12,BKMS09,BL05,DG07]) or enforced be under some circumstances (so called *certification mode* which enforces fresh samples, see [BL05,DG07]). An important result is obtained from a more general fact called Asymptotic Equipartition Property (AEP). Namely, for a stateless source the min-entropy rate (min-entropy per sample) is close to its Shannon entropy per bit (conditionally with probability almost 1), for a large number of samples.

AEP AND EXTRACTING FROM MEMORYLESS SHANNON SOURCES. We start
with the following general fact, which easily follows by the Weak Law of Large
Numbers.

Theorem 1 (Asymptotic Equipartition Property). *The min entropy per
bit in a sequence $X_1, \ldots, X_n$ of i.id. samples from X, for large n and with high
probability, is* close *to the Shannon entropy of X. More precisely*

$$-\frac{1}{n} \log P_{X_1, \ldots, X_n}(x_1, \ldots, x_n) \longrightarrow H(X) \tag{3}$$

where the convergence holds in probability (over $(x_1, \ldots, x_n) \leftarrow X_1, \ldots, X_n)$.

Intuitively, the AEP simply means that, conditionally with large probability,
the product of many independent copies is flat and its min-entropy approaches
Shannon entropy.

Thus, the AEP is a bridge connecting the heuristic use of Shannon entropy
as a measure of extractable randomness (practice) and the provable security
(randomness extractors theory). The best known quantitative form of Eq. (3)
appears in [Hol06].

Theorem 2 (Quantitative Asymptotic Equipartition Property *[Hol06]*).
*Let $X^n = X_1, \ldots, X_n$ be a sequence of i.i.d. samples from a distribution X of
Shannon entropy k. Then the sequence $(X_1, \ldots, X_n)$ is ϵ-close in the variational
distance to a distribution of min entropy $kn - O\left(\sqrt{kn \log(1/\epsilon)}\right)$.*

Now we restate the same result in language of randomness extractors

**Corollary 1 (Extracting from Memoryless Shannon Sources, Lower
Bound).** *In particular, in the above setting, one can extract at least*

$$m = kn - O\left(\sqrt{kn \log(1/\epsilon)}\right) - 2\log(1/\epsilon) \tag{4}$$

*bits which are ϵ-close to uniform (e.g. using independent hash functions [HILL99]
as an extractor). Since in most settings we have[2] $\epsilon \gg 2^{-kn}$, we extract*

$$m = H(X^n) - O\left(\sqrt{H(X^n) \log(1/\epsilon)}\right) \tag{5}$$

bits, that is we extract all the Shannon entropy but $O\left(\sqrt{kn \log(1/\epsilon)}\right)$ bits.

1.3   Problem Statement

We have already seen that in case of many independent copies the amount of
extractable bits approaches asymptotically the Shannon entropy. We note that
some works, including works on entropy estimating [BL05,LPR11] suggest to
use a simplified (asymptotic) version of Eq. (5), namely

---

[2] Because $\epsilon \approx 2^{-kn}$ provides exponential security which is already overkill in most
cases.

$$m \approx H(X^n) \tag{6}$$

bits ϵ-close to uniform, ignoring a smaller order term $O\left((H(X^n)\log(1/\epsilon))^{\frac{1}{2}}\right)$. The question which naturally arises is how much do we lose by this approximation. Is it safe to assume (heuristically) that the equality (6) holds in practical parameter regimes?

Question: What is the exact error of the AEP heuristic Eq. (6)?

We rewrite this problem as the task of finding upper bounds on the extraction rate of Shannon entropy memoryless sources.

Question (Reformulated): Suppose that we have a source which produces i.i.d samples $X_1, X_2, \ldots$ each of Shannon entropy k. How much almost uniform bits can be extracted from n such samples?

This question is well-motivated as no upper bounds to Theorem 2 have been known so far (though some other works [Hol11] also address lower bounds), and because of the popularity of the AEP herustic (6).

1.4 Our Results and Applications

THE TIGHT NO-GO RESULT. We answer the posted question, showing that the convergence rate in Eq. (3) given in Theorem 2 is optimal.

Theorem 3 (An Upper Bound on the Extraction Rate from Shannon Sources). *From any sequence of i.i.d. binary random variables $X^n = X_1, \ldots, X_n$ we no extract can get more than*

$$m = H(X^n) - \Theta(\sqrt{H(X^n)\log(1/\epsilon)}) \tag{7}$$

bits which are ϵ-close (in the variation distance) to uniform. This matches the lower bound in [Hol06] (the constant under $\Theta(\cdot)$ depends on the source X).

Corollary 2 (A Significant Entropy Loss in the AEP Heuristic Estimate). *In the above setting, the gap between the Shannon entropy and the number of extractable bits ϵ-close to uniform equals at least $\Theta(\sqrt{\log(1/\epsilon)kn})$. In particular, for the recommended security level ($\epsilon = 2^{-80}$) we obtain the loss of $kn - m \approx \sqrt{80kn}$ bits, no matter what an extractor we use.*

AN APPLICATION TO TRNGS: NOT TO OVERESTIMATE SECURITY. Imagine a mobile phone where the accelerometer is being used as an entropy source. Such a source was studied in [LPR11] and the Shannon entropy rate was estimated to be roughly 0.125 per bit. Since the recommended security level for almost random bits is $\epsilon = 2^{-80}$. According to the heuristic (3) we need roughly $m = 128/0.125 = 1024$ samples to extract a 128-bit key. However taking into account the true error in our Theorem 3 we see that we need at least $m \approx 2214$ bits!

AN APPLICATION TO THE AEP: CONVERGENCE SPEED. Let $X^n =$ $X_1, X_2, \ldots, X_n$ be a sequence of i.i.d. bit random variables. By the standard AEP we know that with probability $1 - \epsilon$ over $x \leftarrow X^n$ we have $P_{X^n}(x) \leqslant$ $2^{-nH(X_1)+O\left(\sqrt{nH(X_1)\log(/\epsilon)}\right)}$. Our result implies that for *any* event E of probability $1-\epsilon$ for some $x \in E$ we have $P_{X^n}(x) \geqslant 2^{-nH(X_1)+\Omega\left(\sqrt{nH(X_1)\log(1/\epsilon)}\right)}$. This proves that the error term for the convergence is really $\Theta\left(\sqrt{nH(X_1)\log(1/\epsilon)}\right)$.

1.5   Organization

The remainder of the paper is structured as follows. In Sect. 2 we give some basic facts and auxiliary technical results that will be used later. The proof of the main result, that is Theorem 3, is given in Sect. 3. Finally, Sect. 4 concludes the work.

2   Preliminaries

2.1   Basic Definitions

The most popular way of measuring how two distributions are close is the statistical distance.

Definition 1 (Statistical Distance). *The statistical (or total variation) distance of two distributions X, Y is defined as*

$$\mathrm{SD}\left(X; Y\right) = \sum_x |\Pr[X = x] - \Pr[Y = x]| \tag{8}$$

We also simply say that X and Y are ϵ-close.

Below we recall the definition of Shannon entropy and min entropy. The logarithms are taken at base 2.

Definition 2 (Shannon Entropy). *The Shannon Entropy of a distribution X equals $H(X) = -\sum_x \Pr[X = x] \log \Pr[X = x]$.*

Definition 3 (Min Entropy). *The min entropy of a distribution X equals $H_\infty(X) = \min_x(1/\log \Pr[X = x])$.*

2.2   Extractors

Extractors are functions which transform inputs of some required min-entropy amount into an almost uniform string of known length. To extract from every high-entropy source (that is, to have an extractor of general purpose), one needs to allow extractors to use small amount of auxiliary randomness, which can be "reinvested" as in the case of catalysts in chemistry. Also, one has to accept some small deviation of the output from being uniform (small enough to be acceptable for almost every application) and some entropy loss [RTS00]. Good extractors, simple, provable-secure and widely used in practice, are obtained from universal hash families [CW79]. We refer the reader to [Sha11] for a survey.

Definition 4 (Randomness Extractors). *A function* $\mathsf{Ext} : \{0,1\}^n \times \{0,1\}^d \to \{0,1\}^m$ *is a* (k, ϵ)-*extractor*

$$\mathrm{SD}\left(\mathsf{Ext}(X, U_d), U_d; U_{m+d}\right) \leqslant \epsilon$$

for any distribution X *of min-entropy at least* k *and independent* d-*bit string* U_d.

Definition 5 (Extractable Entropy, [RW04]). *We say that* X *has* k *extractable bits within distance* ϵ, *denoted* $H^\epsilon_{\mathrm{ext}}(X) \geqslant k$, *if for some randomized function* Ext *we have* $\mathrm{SD}\left(\mathrm{Ext}(X, S); U_k, S\right) \leqslant \epsilon$, *where* U_k *is a uniform* k-*bit string and* S *is an independent uniform string (called the seed).*

The so called Leftover Hash Lemma [HILL88] ensures that $H^\epsilon_{\mathrm{ext}}(X) \geqslant H_\infty(X) - 2\log(1/\epsilon)$.

2.3   Technical Facts

Our proof uses the following characterization of "extractable" distributions.

Theorem 4 (An Upper Bound on Extractable Entropy, [RW04]). *If* $H^\epsilon_{\mathrm{ext}}(X) \geqslant k$ *then* X *is* ϵ-*close to* Y *such that* $H_\infty(Y) \geqslant k$.

The second important fact we use is the sharp bound on binomial tails.

Theorem 5 (Tight Binomial Tails [McK]). *Let* $B(n, p)$ *be a sum of independent Bernoulli trials with success probability* p. *Then for* $\gamma \leqslant \frac{3}{4}q$ *we have*

$$\Pr\left[B(n, p) \geqslant pn + \gamma n\right] = Q\left(\sqrt{\frac{n\gamma^2}{pq}}\right) \cdot \psi(p, q, n, \gamma) \tag{9}$$

with the error term satisfies

$$\psi(p, q, n, \gamma) = \exp\left(\frac{n\gamma^2}{2pq} - n\mathrm{KL}\left(p + \gamma \parallel p\right) + \frac{1}{2}\log\left(\frac{p+\gamma}{p} \cdot \frac{q}{q-\gamma}\right) + O_{p,q}\left(n^{-\frac{1}{2}}\right)\right) \tag{10}$$

where $\mathrm{KL}\left(a \parallel b\right) = a\log(a/b) + (1-a)\log((1-a)/(1-b))$ *is the Kullback-Leibler divergence, and* Q *is the complement of the cumulative distribution function of the standard normal distribution.*

3   Proof of Theorem 3

3.1   Characterizing Extractable Entropy

We state the following fact with an explanation in Fig. 2.

Lemma 1 (An Uppper Bound on the Extractable Entropy). *Let* X *be a distribution. Then for every distribution* Y *which is* ϵ-*close to* X, *twe have* $H_\infty(Y) \leqslant -\log t$ *where* t *satisfies*

$$\sum_x \max(\mathbf{P}_X(x) - t, 0) = \epsilon. \tag{11}$$

Proof (of Lemma 1). The proof follows easily by observation that the optimal mass rearrangement (which maximizes $H_\infty(Y)$) is to decrease probability mass at biggest points. Indeed, we have to find the optimal value of the following optimization program.

$$\begin{aligned} \text{maximize } & H_\infty(Y) \\ \text{s.t.} \quad & \text{SD}(X;Y) \leqslant \epsilon \end{aligned} \qquad (12)$$

Note that we can write $P_Y = \epsilon(x) + P_X$ where $\sum_x \epsilon(x) = 0$ and $\sum_x |\epsilon(x)| = 2\epsilon$, transforming program (12) into

$$\begin{aligned} \text{maximize } & \min_x \left(\log \frac{1}{P_X(x) + \epsilon(x)} \right) \\ \text{s.t.} \quad & \begin{cases} \sum_x \epsilon(x) = 0 \\ \sum_x |\epsilon(x)| = 2\epsilon \end{cases} \end{aligned} \qquad (13)$$

where the optimization runs over the numbers $\epsilon(x)$. Since $u \to \log u^{-1}$ is an decreasing function when $u \in (0,1)$, the program has the same maximizer as the solution of

$$\begin{aligned} \text{maximize } & \min_x (P_X(x) + \epsilon(x)) \\ \text{s.t.} \quad & \begin{cases} \sum_{x'} \epsilon(x') = 0 \\ \sum_{x'} |\epsilon(x')| \leqslant 2\epsilon \end{cases} \end{aligned} \qquad (14)$$

For the set $S = \{x : \epsilon(x) < 0\}$, we claim that the optimal solution satisfies $P_X(x) + \epsilon(x) = \text{const}$ on $x \in S$. Indeed, otherwise we have

$$P_X(x_1) + \epsilon(x_1) < P_X(x) + \epsilon(x) \leqslant P_X(x_2) + \epsilon(x_2)$$

for some $x_1, x_2 \in S$ and every $x \in S \setminus \{x_1\}$. Then replacing $\epsilon(x_1), \epsilon(x_2)$ by $\frac{\epsilon(x_1) + \epsilon(x_2)}{2}$ increases the objective keeping the constraint, a contradiction. Thus $P_X(x) + \epsilon(x) = t_0$ whenever $\epsilon(x) < 0$. Similarly, we prove that $P_X(x) + \epsilon(x) \leqslant t_0$ for any x. Going back to Eq. (13), it suffices to observe that we have

$$\min_x \left(\log \frac{1}{P_X(x) + \epsilon(x)} \right) \leqslant -\log t_0.$$

Finally, since $-\epsilon(x) = P_X(x) - t_0$ when $x \in S$, we get $\epsilon \geqslant -\sum_x \epsilon(x) = \sum_x \max(P_X(x) - t_0, 0)$. In particular, $t_0 \geqslant t$ which gives $-\log t_0 \leqslant -\log t$ and the result follows. $\qquad \square$

Without losing generality, we assume from now that $X \in \{0,1\}$ where $\Pr[X = 1] = p, q = 1 - p$. Define $X^n = (X_1, \ldots, X_n)$. For any $x \in \{0,1\}^n$ we have

$$\Pr[X^n = x] = p^{\|x\|} q^{n - \|x\|}. \qquad (15)$$

According to the last lemma and Theorem 4, we have

$$H_{\text{ext}}^\epsilon(X^n) \leqslant -\log t \qquad (16)$$

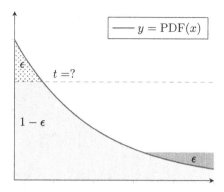

Fig. 2. The Entropy Smoothing Problem. For a given probability density function, we want to cut a total mass of up to ϵ above a possibly highest threshold (in dotted red) and rearrange it (in green), to keep the upper bound smallest possible.

where $t \in (0,1)$ is such that

$$\sum_x \max\left(\mathbf{P}_{X^n}(x) - t, 0\right) = \epsilon. \tag{17}$$

From now we assume that

$$t = p^{pn+\gamma n} q^{qn-\gamma n}. \tag{18}$$

3.2 Determining the Threshold t

The next key observation is that t is actually small and can be omitted. That is, we can simply cut the $(1 - \epsilon)$-quantile. This is stated in the lemma below.

Lemma 2 (Replacing the Threshold by the Quantile). *Let $x_0 \in \{0,1\}^n$ be a point such that $\|x_0\| = pn + \gamma n$. Then we have*

$$\sum_{x:\ \|x\| \geqslant \|x_0\|} \max\left(\mathbf{P}_{X^n}(x) - \mathbf{P}_{X^n}(x_0)\right) \geqslant \frac{1}{2} \sum_{x:\ \|x\| \geqslant \|x_0\|} \mathbf{P}_{X^n}(x) \tag{19}$$

To prove the lemma, note that from Theorem 5 it follows that setting

$$\gamma' = \gamma + n^{-1} \log\left(\frac{p}{q}\right) \tag{20}$$

we obtain

$$\sum_{j \geqslant pn+\gamma'n} \binom{n}{j} \geqslant \frac{3}{4} \cdot \sum_{j \geqslant pn+\gamma n} \binom{n}{j} \tag{21}$$

when γ is sufficiently small comparing to p and q (formally this is justified by calculating the derivative with respect to γ and noticing that it is bigger by at most a factor of $1 + \frac{\gamma}{\sqrt{npq}}$). But we also have

$$p^j q^{n-j} \geqslant 2 \cdot p^{(p+\gamma)n} q^{(q-\gamma)n} \quad \text{for } j \geqslant \gamma' n \tag{22}$$

Therefore,

$$\sum_{j \geqslant pn+\gamma n} \binom{n}{j} p^j q^{n-j} \geqslant \sum_{j \geqslant pn+\gamma' n} \binom{n}{j} p^j q^{n-j}$$

$$\geqslant 2 \cdot p^{(p+\gamma)n} q^{(q-\gamma)n} \cdot \sum_{j \geqslant pn+\gamma' n} \binom{n}{j}$$

$$\geqslant 2 \cdot \frac{3}{4} \cdot p^{(p+\gamma)n} q^{(q-\gamma)n} \cdot \sum_{j \geqslant pn+\gamma n} \binom{n}{j} \tag{23}$$

which finishes the proof.

3.3   Putting This All Together

Now, by combining Lemmas 1 and 2 and the estimate $Q(x) \approx x^{-1} \exp(-x^2/2)$ for $x \gg 0$ we obtain

$$\epsilon \geqslant \exp\left(-n\mathrm{KL}\left(p+\gamma \parallel p\right) - \log\left(\frac{n\gamma^2}{2pq}\right) + O_{p,q}(1)\right) \tag{24}$$

which, because of the Taylor expansion $\mathrm{KL}\left(p+\gamma \parallel p\right) = \frac{\gamma^2}{2pq} + O_{p,q}(\gamma^3)$, gives us

$$\gamma \geqslant \Omega\left(\sqrt{\frac{\log(1/\epsilon)}{pqn}}\right) \tag{25}$$

Setting $\gamma = c \cdot \sqrt{\frac{\log(1/\epsilon)}{pqn}}$, with sufficiently big c, we obtain the claimed result.

4   Conclusion

We show an upper bound on the amount of random bits that can be extracted from a Shannon entropy source. Even in the most favourable case, that is for independent bits, the gap between the Shannon entropy and the amount of randomness that can be extracted is significant. In practical settings, the Shannon entropy may be even 2 times bigger than the extractable entropy. We conclude that the hard error term in the AEP needs to be taken into account when extracting from memoryless Shannon sources.

Acknowledgments. The author is grateful to the organizers of the 8th Annual North American School of Information Theory in San Diego, and the organizers of the conference LATINCRYPT 2015 in Guadalajara, for the opportunity to present preliminary versions of this work.

References

[BKMS09] Bouda, J., Krhovjak, J., Matyas, V., Svenda, P.: Towards true random number generation in mobile environments. In: Jøsang, A., Maseng, T., Knapskog, S.J. (eds.) NordSec 2009. LNCS, vol. 5838, pp. 179–189. Springer, Heidelberg (2009)

[BL05] Bucci, M., Luzzi, R.: Design of testable random bit generators. In: Rao, J.R., Sunar, B. (eds.) CHES 2005. LNCS, vol. 3659, pp. 147–156. Springer, Heidelberg (2005)

[BP99] Benjamin, J., Paul, K.: The intel random number generator (1999)

[BST03] Barak, B., Shaltiel, R., Tromer, E.: True random number generators secure in a changing environment. In: Walter, C.D., Koç, Ç.K., Paar, C. (eds.) CHES 2003. LNCS, vol. 2779, pp. 166–180. Springer, Heidelberg (2003)

[Cor99] Coron, J.-S.: On the security of random sources (1999)

[CW79] Carter, J.L., Wegman, M.N.: Universal classes of hash functions. J. Comput. Syst. Sci. 18(2), 143–154 (1979)

[dev] http://www.cs.berkeley.edu/~daw/rnd/linux-rand

[DG07] Dichtl, M., Golić, J.D.: High-speed true random number generation with logic gates only. In: Paillier, P., Verbauwhede, I. (eds.) CHES 2007. LNCS, vol. 4727, pp. 45–62. Springer, Heidelberg (2007)

[HILL88] Hstad, J., Impagliazzo, R., Levin, L.A., Luby, M.: Pseudo-random generation from one-way functions. In: Proceedings of the 20th STOC, pp. 12–24 (1988)

[HILL99] Hastad, J., Impagliazzo, R., Levin, L.A., Luby, M.: A pseudorandom generator from any one-way function. SIAM J. Comput. 28(4), 1364–1396 (1999)

[HJW15] Han, Y., Jiao, J., Weissman, T.: Adaptive estimation of shannon entropy. CoRR abs/1502.00326 (2015)

[Hol06] Holenstein, T.: Pseudorandom generators from one-way functions: A simple construction for any hardness. In: Halevi, S., Rabin, T. (eds.) TCC 2006. LNCS, vol. 3876, pp. 443–461. Springer, Heidelberg (2006)

[Hol11] ——: On the randomness of repeated experiment

[hot] Hotbits project homepage. www.fourmilab.ch/hotbits/

[KMT15] Kelsey, J., McKay, K.A., Turan, M.S.: Predictive models for min-entropy estimation. IACR Cryptology ePrint Arch. 2015, 600 (2015)

[LPR11] Lauradoux, C., Ponge, J., Röck, A.: Online Entropy Estimation for Non-Binary Sources and Applications on iPhone. Rapport de recherche, Inria, June 2011

[LRSV12] Lacharme, P., Röck, A., Strubel, V., Videau, M.: The linux pseudorandom number generator revisited, Cryptology ePrint Archive, Report 2012/251 (2012). http://eprint.iacr.org/

[McK] McKay, B.D.: On littlewood's estimate for the binomial distribution. In: Advances in Applied Probability

[pgp] Pgp project homepage. http://www.pgpi.org

[ran] Random.org project homepage. www.random.org

[RTS00] Radhakrishnan, J., Ta-Shma, A.: Bounds for dispersers, extractors, and depth-two superconcentrators. SIAM J. Discrete Math. 13, 2000 (2000)

[RW04] Renner, R., Wolf, S.: Smooth Renyi entropy and applications. ISIT 2004, 232 (2004)

[Sha11] Shaltiel, R.: An introduction to randomness extractors. In: Aceto, L., Henzinger, M., Sgall, J. (eds.) ICALP 2011, Part II. LNCS, vol. 6756, pp. 21–41. Springer, Heidelberg (2011)

[VSH11] Voris, J., Saxena, N., Halevi, T.: Accelerometers and randomness: Perfect together. In: WiSec 2011, pp. 115–126. ACM (2011)

[YSK13] Bong, H., Young, C., Kim, S., Yeom, Y.: Online test based on mutual information for true random number generators. J. Korean Math. Soc. **504**, 879–897 (2013)

Two Types of Special Bases for Integral Lattices

Renzhang Liu[1,2(✉)] and Yanbin Pan[1,2]

[1] Key Laboratory of Mathematics Mechanization,
Academy of Mathematics and Systems Science, NCMIS,
Chinese Academy of Sciences, Beijing 100190, China
{liurenzhang,panyanbin}@amss.ac.cn
[2] Science and Technology on Communication Security Laboratory,
Chengdu 610041, China

Abstract. Lattice basis reduction algorithms, such as LLL, play a very important role in cryptography, which usually aim to find a lattice basis with good "orthogonality". However, not every lattice has an orthogonal basis, which means that we can only find some nearly orthogonal bases for these lattices. In this paper, we show that every integral lattice must have two types of special bases related to the orthogonality. First, any integral lattice with rank more than 1 has a class of bases such that the angle between any two basis vectors lies in $[\frac{\pi}{3}, \frac{2\pi}{3}]$. Second, any integral lattice with rank more than 2 has a class of bases such that any basis can be divided into two sets and the vectors in every set are pairwise orthogonal. To obtain such results, we introduce the technique called unimodular congruence transformation for the Gram matrix.

Keywords: Lattice · Gram matrix · Unimodular congruence transformation · Orthogonality

1 Introduction

Lattices are discrete additive subgroup in $\mathbb{R}^n$, which have very wide applications in cryptology, both in cryptographic constructions and cryptanalysis, such as in the constructions of quantum-resistant encryption schemes [7,8], signature schemes [2], fully homomorphic encryption schemes [6], multilinear maps [4] and attacking the knapsack-based public-key cryptosystems [11], analyzing the weak keys of RSA [1].

Lattice basis reduction algorithms, such as the famous LLL algorithm [10], are one of the basic tools for employing lattice in cryptography and hence have drawn considerable attention. Usually, the lattice basis reduction algorithms aim to find a lattice basis with good "orthogonality", since with an orthogonal basis, the well-known hard problems as the shortest vector problem (SVP) and

This research is supported by the NNSF of China (No. 11201458, No. 11471314, No. 61121062, and No. 61572490), in part by 973 Project (No. 2011CB302401) and in part by the National Center for Mathematics and Interdisciplinary Sciences, CAS.

H. Kim and D. Choi (Eds.): WISA 2015, LNCS 9503, pp. 87–95, 2016.
DOI: 10.1007/978-3-319-31875-2_8

the closest vector problem (CVP) can be easily solved. However, not all lattices have orthogonal basis, which means that for most lattices only nearly orthogonal basis can be found. Therefore, a natural problem is that what kinds of nearly orthogonal bases can be found. Moreover, once a new kind of nearly orthogonal basis is proposed, we can design the corresponding algorithm to find such a basis, which may provide a new idea to solve the SVP or CVP. Therefore, it is important to study the nearly orthogonal basis of lattice.

In this paper, we show that every integral lattice must have two types of special bases related to the orthogonality.

First, any integral lattice with rank more than 1 has a class of bases such that for any basis the angle between any two basis vectors lies in $[\frac{\pi}{3}, \frac{2\pi}{3}]$. An algorithm is also proposed to find such basis, which can be seen as the generalization of the Gauss's algorithm for 2-dim lattice [5,9]. However, we only prove that the algorithm must terminate but can not show that it will terminate in polynomial time although it always terminates in rational time in practice. Nevertheless, by the proof we can show that the algorithm can be used to improve the quality of the basis outputted by the other algorithms, such as LLL algorithm. More precisely, the algorithm will produce shorter vectors when taking the LLL-reduced basis as input.

Second, it is well-known that every lattice can be decomposed into indecomposable sublattices which are pairwise orthogonal uniquely up to the order [3], where a lattice is called decomposable if it can be written as an orthogonal direct sum of two non trivial sublattices. More precisely, every lattice $\mathcal{L}$ can be decomposed into $\mathcal{L}_1 \oplus \cdots \oplus \mathcal{L}_k$ with $\mathcal{L}_i \perp \mathcal{L}_j$. However, it is very hard to find such a decomposition. In this paper we show that any integral lattice with rank more than 2 has a class of bases such that any basis can be divided into two sets and the vectors in every set are pairwise orthogonal. That is, any integral lattice $\mathcal{L}$ can be decomposed into $\mathcal{L}_1 \oplus \mathcal{L}_2$, where $\mathcal{L}_i$ has an orthogonal basis. However, we have not found any direct applications for solving SVP or CVP with such a basis by now.

To obtain the results above, we introduce the technique called unimodular congruence transformation for the Gram matrix.

ROADMAP. The remainder of the paper is organized as follows. In Sect. 2, we give some preliminaries needed. We give our main results in Sect. 3. Finally, a short conclusion is given in Sect. 4.

2   Preliminaries

We denote by $\mathbb{R}$ the field of real numbers and by $\mathbb{Z}$ the integer ring. We use bold letters to denote vectors, in column notation. Let $\mathbf{v}_i$ be the i-th component of vector $\mathbf{v}$, $\langle \mathbf{v}, \mathbf{u} \rangle$ be the dot product of vectors $\mathbf{v}$ and $\mathbf{u}$ and $\|\mathbf{v}\| = \langle \mathbf{v}, \mathbf{v} \rangle^{\frac{1}{2}}$ be the Euclidean norm of $\mathbf{v}$. If A is a matrix, then we denote by A_i the i-th column of A and by A^T its transpose.

For any $x \in \mathbb{R}$, we denote $\lfloor x \rfloor$ the maximal integer less than or equal to x and $\lceil x \rfloor$ the integer nearest to x.

2.1 Lattice

A lattice $\mathcal{L}$ is a discrete additive subgroup of $\mathbb{R}^n$ and can be also defined as below:

Let $\mathbf{b}_1, \mathbf{b}_2 \cdots, \mathbf{b}_d \in \mathbb{R}^n$ be linearly independent vectors, the lattice $\mathcal{L}$ spanned by them is

$$\mathcal{L}(\mathbf{b}_1, \mathbf{b}_2, \cdots, \mathbf{b}_d) = \{\sum_{i=1}^{d} a_i \mathbf{b}_i | a_i \in \mathbb{Z}\}.$$

$B = [\mathbf{b}_1, \mathbf{b}_2, \cdots, \mathbf{b}_d]$ is called the basis of $\mathcal{L}$. Usually, if $B \in \mathbb{R}^{n \times d}$ has d linearly independent columns, we denote by $\mathcal{L}(B)$ the lattice spanned by $\mathbf{b}_1, \mathbf{b}_2, \cdots, \mathbf{b}_d$. d is called the rank of the lattice and n is the dimension of the lattice.

For any lattice $\mathcal{L}$ with $d \geq 2$, there are infinity bases generating $\mathcal{L}$. However, for any two of its bases A and B, there must be a unimoduar matrix U, which is defined as a square integer matrix with determinant 1 or -1, such that $A = BU$. In another word, for any basis $\{\mathbf{b}_1, \mathbf{b}_2, \cdots, \mathbf{b}_d\}$ of $\mathcal{L}$, arbitrary combination of the following operations will yield another basis of $\mathcal{L}$.

- Multiplying $\mathbf{b}_i$ by ± 1 for $1 \leq i \leq d$;
- Exchanging $\mathbf{b}_i$ and $\mathbf{b}_j$ for $1 \leq i \neq j \leq d$;
- Adding $\alpha \mathbf{b}_i$ to $\mathbf{b}_j$ for any $\alpha \in \mathbb{Z}$ and $1 \leq i \neq j \leq d$. In terms of matrix, this operation can be seen as multiplying a matrix $U(i, j, \alpha)$ $(i \neq j)$, where $U(i, j, \alpha)$ is defined as follows:

$$U(i, j, \alpha)_{st} \begin{cases} 1, & \text{if } s = t; \\ \alpha, & \text{if } s = i, t = j; \\ 0, & \text{otherwise.} \end{cases}$$

Since the orthogonality of any two vectors can be described by their inner product, it is natural to consider the Gram matrix for the lattice basis. For any basis B of lattice $\mathcal{L}$, the corresponding Gram matrix G is defined as $B^T \cdot B$, which is always a square matrix. A simple analysis concludes that $G_{i,j} = \langle B_i, B_j \rangle$.

Definition 1 (Integral Lattice). *A lattice is called integral if the Gram matrix for any basis is a integral matrix.*

2.2 Hermite Normal Form

The Hermite Normal Form is a useful tool to study integer matrix. We just give the definition for square nonsingular integer matrix.

Definition 2. *A square nonsingular matrix $H \in \mathbb{Z}^{n \times n}$ is in Hermite Normal Form (HNF) if*

- *H is upper triangular, i.e., $h_{ij} = 0$ for all $i > j$;*
- *All diagonal elements are positive, i.e., $h_{ii} > 0$ for all i;*
- *All non diagonal elements are bounded by the corresponding diagonal element at the same row, i.e., $0 \leq h_{ij} < h_{ii}$ for all $i < j$.*

A famous result for HNF is:

Theorem 1. *For every square nonsingular matrix $A \in \mathbb{Z}^{n \times n}$, there exists a unique $n \times n$ matrix B in Hermite Normal Form with $B = AU$ where U is a unimodular matrix. Moreover, B can be found in polynomial time.*

In fact, we just need the following lemma about the HNF of integer matrix with rank 1.

Lemma 1. *For any nonzero $[a_1, a_2, \cdots, a_n] \in \mathbb{Z}^{1 \times n}$, there exists a unimodular matrix $U \in \mathbb{Z}^{n \times n}$ such that*

$$[a_1, a_2, \cdots, a_n]U = [g, 0, \cdots, 0],$$

where $g = GCD(a_1, a_2, \cdots, a_n)$.

3   Two Types of Bases for Any Integral Lattice

We mainly investigate the lattice basis which has better orthogonality. The main tool is the unimodular congruence transformation for a Gram matrix. More precisely, for any Gram matrix G of a lattice basis B, we try to find some unimodular matrix U such that $G' = U^T G U$ has a special form, for example, the non-diagonal elements are all small enough. Then we could say the orthogonality of the new basis BU is better.

3.1   First Type

In this subsection, we will show that any integral lattice with rank $d > 1$ has a basis such that any angle between any two basis vectors lies in $[\frac{\pi}{3}, \frac{2\pi}{3}]$. First we give a lemma.

Lemma 2. *Any integral lattice $\mathcal{L}$ with rank $d > 1$ has a basis B such that the corresponding Gram matrix G satisfying*

$$|G_{ij}| \leq \frac{1}{2} G_{ii},$$

for any $i \neq j$.

Proof. For the Gram matrix G, the i-th row is called Angle-Reduced if for every $j \neq i$,

$$|G_{ij}| \leq \frac{1}{2} G_{ii}.$$

We show that we can construct such a basis B from any basis A of $\mathcal{L}$ by the following algorithm.

Input: a integral lattice basis $A \in \mathbb{R}^{n \times d}$.
Output: a lattice basis $B \in \mathbb{R}^{n \times d}$.

---

1. Compute $G = A^T A$.
2. While there is a row of G not Angle-reduced, WLOG, the i-th row, do 3-6
3.   for j from 1 to d and $j \neq i$,
4.   if $|G_{ij}| > \frac{1}{2} G_{ii}$
5. $A = A * U(i, j, \lceil -\frac{G_{ij}}{G_{ii}} \rfloor)$.
6. $G = U(i, j, \lceil -\frac{G_{ij}}{G_{ii}} \rfloor)^T * G * U(i, j, \lceil -\frac{G_{ij}}{G_{ii}} \rfloor)$,
7. Output $B = A$.

For simplicity, Steps 5 and 6 are called the reduction step. WLOG, we assume $A = [\mathbf{b}_1, \mathbf{b}_2, \cdots, \mathbf{b}_d]$ that will be reduced and hence $|\langle \mathbf{b}_i, \mathbf{b}_j \rangle| > \frac{1}{2} \langle \mathbf{b}_i, \mathbf{b}_i \rangle > 0$ by Step 4. Notice that after the reduction step, we have

$$A' = A * U(i, j, \lceil -\frac{G_{ij}}{G_{ii}} \rfloor)$$
$$= [\mathbf{b}_1, \mathbf{b}_2 \cdots, \mathbf{b}_{i-1}, \mathbf{b}_i, \mathbf{b}_{i+1}, \cdots, \mathbf{b}_{j-1}, \mathbf{b}_j + \lceil -\frac{G_{ij}}{G_{ii}} \rfloor \mathbf{b}_i, \mathbf{b}_{j+1}, \cdots, \mathbf{b}_d]$$

and

$$G' = U(i, j, \lceil -\frac{G_{ij}}{G_{ii}} \rfloor)^T * G * U(i, j, \lceil -\frac{G_{ij}}{G_{ii}} \rfloor) = A'^T A'.$$

Hence it is obvious that if the algorithm terminates, then the lemma follows. We next show the algorithm will indeed terminate.

Notice that after each reduction step,

$$\| \mathbf{b}_j + \lceil -\frac{G_{ij}}{G_{ii}} \rfloor \mathbf{b}_i \|^2 < \| \mathbf{b}_j \|^2. \tag{1}$$

Notice that the reduction step happens if $|G_{ij}| > \frac{1}{2} G_{ii}$, that is, $(\frac{G_{ij}}{G_{ii}})^2 > \frac{1}{4}$. The Eq. (1) holds since

$$\| \mathbf{b}_j + \lceil -\frac{G_{ij}}{G_{ii}} \rfloor \mathbf{b}_i \|^2 - \| \mathbf{b}_j \|^2 = \lceil -\frac{G_{ij}}{G_{ii}} \rfloor^2 \langle \mathbf{b}_i, \mathbf{b}_i \rangle + 2 \lceil -\frac{G_{ij}}{G_{ii}} \rfloor \langle \mathbf{b}_i, \mathbf{b}_j \rangle$$
$$= \lceil \frac{G_{ij}}{G_{ii}} \rfloor^2 \langle \mathbf{b}_i, \mathbf{b}_i \rangle - 2 \lceil \frac{G_{ij}}{G_{ii}} \rfloor \langle \mathbf{b}_i, \mathbf{b}_j \rangle$$
$$= \langle \mathbf{b}_i, \mathbf{b}_i \rangle (\lceil \frac{G_{ij}}{G_{ii}} \rfloor^2 - 2 \lceil \frac{G_{ij}}{G_{ii}} \rfloor \frac{G_{ij}}{G_{ii}})$$
$$= \langle \mathbf{b}_i, \mathbf{b}_i \rangle ((\lceil \frac{G_{ij}}{G_{ii}} \rfloor - \frac{G_{ij}}{G_{ii}})^2 - (\frac{G_{ij}}{G_{ii}})^2)$$
$$< \langle \mathbf{b}_i, \mathbf{b}_i \rangle (\frac{1}{4} - \frac{1}{4})$$
$$< 0.$$

For each basis $A = [\mathbf{b}_1, \mathbf{b}_2, \cdots, \mathbf{b}_d]$, define $\mathcal{D}_A = \sum_{i=1}^{d} \| \mathbf{b}_i \|^2$. By the discussion above, $\mathcal{D}_A$ decreases by at least 1 after each reduction step since $\mathcal{D}_A$ is an integer. Together with the fact that $\mathcal{D}_A > 0$, the algorithm terminates.

Easily we have the following theorem.

Theorem 2. *Any integral lattice with rank $d > 1$ has a basis such that any angle between any two basis vectors lies in $[\frac{\pi}{3}, \frac{2\pi}{3}]$.*

Proof. Notice that by the symmetry of G, we have

$$|\langle \mathbf{b}_i, \mathbf{b}_j \rangle| = |G_{ij}| = |G_{ji}| \leq \min\{G_{ii}, G_{jj}\} = \min\{\|\mathbf{b}_i\|, \|\mathbf{b}_j\|\},$$

and

$$|\cos(\mathbf{b}_i, \mathbf{b}_j)| = \frac{|\langle \mathbf{b}_i, \mathbf{b}_j \rangle|}{\|\mathbf{b}_i\|\|\mathbf{b}_j\|} \leq \frac{|\langle \mathbf{b}_i, \mathbf{b}_j \rangle|}{\max\{\|\mathbf{b}_i\|, \|\mathbf{b}_j\|\}^2} \leq \frac{1}{2}.$$

Then the theorem follows.

Remark 1. For this type of bases, we have some remarks.

- In fact, there are some other bases for any lattices such that any angle between any two basis vectors lies in $[\frac{\pi}{3}, \frac{2\pi}{3}]$, taking the Minkowski reduced basis as an example.
- We can not prove that the algorithm will terminate in polynomial time. However, the algorithm will terminate in rational time in practice. We suggest that the algorithm can be used to improve the quantity of the basis outputted by the LLL algorithm. More precisely, the algorithm will produce shorter vectors when taking the LLL-reduced basis as input since the reduction step will decrease the length of one basis vector. We implemented the algorithm on an Intel(R) Core(TM) i7 2.93 GHz PC using Shoup's NTL library version 5.4.1 [12]. For any dimension n, we generated lattice with entries uniformly randomly chosen from $[0, 10000]$. For every lattice, we run the LLL algorithm first and computed the length Len_{LLL} of the shortest vector in the outputted basis and then we run the reduction algorithm on the LLL-reduced basis and computed the length Len_R of the shortest vector in the outputted basis. We compared Len_{LLL} and Len_R and found that for nearly 70 % of the lattices, the length of the shortest vector could be improved. The results are listed as below:

Dimension	150	200	250	300
Number of tested lattices	100	100	100	50
Number of lattices with $Len_R < Len_{LLL}$	62	74	69	35

3.2 Second Type

In this subsection, we will show that any integral lattice with rank $d \geq 3$ has a basis that can be divided into two sets such that the vectors in every set are pairwise orthogonal. First, we give a lemma.

Lemma 3. *Any integral lattice $\mathcal{L}$ with rank $d \geq 3$ has a basis B such that the corresponding Gram matrix G is a tridiagonal matrix.*

Proof. We will prove the lemma by induction.

(i). For $d = 3$, we can write the Gram matrix G_1 of any lattice basis B_1 as

$$G_1 = \begin{pmatrix} G_{11} & G_{12} & G_{13} \\ G_{21} & & G_1' \\ G_{31} & & \end{pmatrix}.$$

If G_{12}, G_{13} are both zero, then the Gram matrix G_1 of B_1 is already a tridiagonal matrix. Otherwise, by Lemma (1), we know that there is a unimodular matrix $U \in \mathbb{Z}^{2\times2}$ such that

$$[G_{12}, G_{13}]U = [g_1, 0].$$

Let

$$\overline{U} = \begin{pmatrix} 1 & 0 & 0 \\ 0 & & U \\ 0 & & \end{pmatrix},$$

Notice that $\overline{U}$ is also a unimodular matrix in $\mathbb{Z}^{3\times3}$ and we have

$$\overline{U}^T G_1 \overline{U} = \begin{pmatrix} 1 & 0 & 0 \\ 0 & & U^T \\ 0 & & \end{pmatrix} \begin{pmatrix} G_{11} & G_{12} & G_{13} \\ G_{21} & & G_1' \\ G_{31} & & \end{pmatrix} \begin{pmatrix} 1 & 0 & 0 \\ 0 & & U \\ 0 & & \end{pmatrix} = \begin{pmatrix} 1 & g_1 & 0 \\ g_1 & & U^T G_1' U \\ 0 & & \end{pmatrix},$$

which is a tridiagonal matrix. Moreover, $G = \overline{U}^T G_1 \overline{U}$ is a Gram matrix of basis $B_1 \overline{U}$. Hence the holds for $d = 3$.

(ii). Assume the lemma holds for $d - 1$. In the following we prove the lemma for d.

Given a basis B_1, we can write its Gram matrix $G_1 \in \mathbb{Z}^{d\times d}$ as

$$G_1 = \begin{pmatrix} G_{11} & G_{12} \cdots G_{1d} \\ G_{21} & \\ \vdots & G_1' \\ G_{d1} & \end{pmatrix}.$$

If $G_{12}, \cdots, G_{1d}$ are not all zero, by Lemma (1), we know that there is a unimodular matrix $U_1 \in \mathbb{Z}^{(d-1)\times(d-1)}$ such that

$$[G_{12}, \cdots, G_{1d}]U_1 = [g_1, 0, \cdots, 0].$$

(Notice that if we allow g_1 to be zero, the equation still holds even if $G_{12}, \cdots, G_{1d}$ are all zero.) Let

$$\overline{U}_1 = \begin{pmatrix} 1 & 0 \cdots 0 \\ 0 & \\ \vdots & U_1 \\ 0 & \end{pmatrix},$$

then it is obvious that $\overline{U}_1$ is also a unimodular matrix in $\mathbb{Z}^{d\times d}$. Considering the transformation

$$G_2 = \overline{U}_1^T G_1 \overline{U}_1 = \begin{pmatrix} G_{11} & g_1 & 0 & \cdots & 0 \\ g_1 & & & & \\ 0 & & & & \\ \vdots & & U_1^T G_1' U_1 & & \\ 0 & & & & \end{pmatrix},$$

we know that $G_2' = U_1^T G_1' U_1$ is a Gram matrix with dimension $d-1$, hence there exists a unimodular matrix U_2 such that $G_3' = U_2^T G_2' U_2$ is a tridiagonal matrix by the induction hypothesis. Let

$$\overline{U}_2 = \begin{pmatrix} 1 & 0 & \cdots & 0 \\ 0 & & & \\ \vdots & & U_2 & \\ 0 & & & \end{pmatrix},$$

then $\overline{U}_2$ is also a unimodular matrix in $\mathbb{Z}^{d\times d}$. Finally we have that

$$G = \overline{U}_2^T G_2 \overline{U}_2 = \overline{U}_2^T \overline{U}_1^T G_1 \overline{U}_1 \overline{U}_2 = \begin{pmatrix} G_{11} & g_1 & 0 & \cdots & 0 \\ g_1 & & & & \\ 0 & & & & \\ \vdots & & & G_3' & \\ 0 & & & & \end{pmatrix}$$

is a tridiagonal matrix and a Gram matrix of basis $B = B_1 \overline{U}_1 \overline{U}_2$. Hence the lemma follows.

Theorem 3. *Any integral lattice with rank $d \geq 3$ has a basis $\{b_1, b_2, \cdots, b_d\}$ which can be divided into two sets A and B such that*

- $\#A = \lfloor \frac{n+1}{2} \rfloor$ *and the vectors in A are pairwise orthogonal;*
- $\#B = \lfloor \frac{n}{2} \rfloor$ *and the vectors in B are also pairwise orthogonal.*

Proof. Considering the basis $[b_1, b_2, \cdots, b_d]$ such that the corresponding Gram matrix G is a tridiagonal matrix. Let A be the set of those b_i's with odd index i and B be the set of the b_i's with even index. It is easy to check A and B satisfy the conditions. Hence the theorem holds.

4   Conclusion and Open Problems

Since the orthogonality between any two vectors is related to their inner product, it is natural to consider the Gram matrix to investigate the orthogonality of the lattice basis. In this paper, we introduce the technique called unimodular congruence transformation to study the nearly orthogonality of the lattice basis and show that any integral lattice with rank more than 1 has a class of bases such that for any basis the angle between any two basis vectors lies in $[\frac{\pi}{3}, \frac{2\pi}{3}]$ and any integral lattice with rank more than 2 has a class of bases such that any basis can be divided into two sets and the vectors in every set are pairwise orthogonal. However, we have not known that whether we can find the first type of lattice basis in polynomial time yet. Another problem is how we can use the second type of lattice basis to find the solution of SVP or CVP more efficiently. To find more applications of the unimodular congruence transformation technique is also an interesting problem.

Acknowledgement. We very thank the anonymous referees for their valuable suggestions on how to improve the presentation of this paper.

References

1. Boneh, D., Durfee, G.: Cryptanalysis of RSA with private key d less than $N^{0.292}$. In: Stern, J. (ed.) EUROCRYPT 1999. LNCS, vol. 1592, pp. 1–11. Springer, Heidelberg (1999)
2. Ducas, L., Durmus, A., Lepoint, T., Lyubashevsky, V.: Lattice signatures and bimodal gaussians. In: Canetti, R., Garay, J.A. (eds.) CRYPTO 2013, Part I. LNCS, vol. 8042, pp. 40–56. Springer, Heidelberg (2013)
3. Eichler, M.: Note zur Theorie der Kristallgitter. Math. Ann. **125**, 51–55 (1952)
4. Garg, S., Gentry, C., Halevi, S.: Candidate multilinear maps from ideal lattices. In: Johansson, T., Nguyen, P.Q. (eds.) EUROCRYPT 2013. LNCS, vol. 7881, pp. 1–17. Springer, Heidelberg (2013)
5. Gauss, C.F.: Disquisitiones Arithmeticae. Springer, New York (1801)
6. Gentry, C.: Fully homomorphic encryption using ideal lattices. In: 41st ACM Symposium on Theory of Computing, pp. 169–178. ACM, Maryland (2009)
7. Gentry, C., Peikert, C., Vaikuntanathan, V.: Trapdoors for hard lattices and new cryptographic constructions. In: 40st ACM Symposium on Theory of Computing, pp. 197–206. ACM, Canada (2008)
8. Hoffstein, J., Pipher, J., Silverman, J.H.: NTRU: a ring-based public key cryptosystem. In: Buhler, J.P. (ed.) ANTS 1998. LNCS, vol. 1423, pp. 267–288. Springer, Heidelberg (1998)
9. Lagrange, J.L.: Recherches d'arithmétique. Nouveaux Mémoires de l'Académie de Berlin (1773)
10. Lenstra, A.K., Lenstra, H.W., Lovász, L.: Factoring polynomials with rational coeffcients. Math. Ann. **261**, 515–534 (1982)
11. Odlyzko, A.M.: The rise and fall of knapsack cryptosystems. In: Symposia in Applied Mathematics, vol. 42, pp. 75–88. A.M.S. (1990)
12. Shoup, V.: NTL: A library for ng number theory. http://www.shoup.net/ntl/

Keyword Updatable PEKS

Hyun Sook Rhee[1] and Dong Hoon Lee[2]([✉])

[1] Printing Solutions, Samsung Electronics Co. Ltd.,
Suwon-si, Gyeonggi-do, Korea
hyunsook.rhee@gmail.com
[2] Graduate School of Information Security, CIST,
Korea University, Seoul, Korea
donghlee@korea.ac.kr

Abstract. Secure keyword search in the asymmetric setting, also known as public-key encryption with keyword search (PEKS), enables a receiver to search the encrypted messages with a keyword without revealing any information on the messages to the server in the store-and-forward system such as an e-mail system. To make this possible, a sender encrypts a keyword with a receiver's public-key and tags the encrypted keyword to the messages. In the paper, we propose PEKS with keyword updatablility (KU-PEKS), where a tagged keyword can be updated upon the receiver's request. The proposed KU-PEKS is generically constructed and provides *ciphertext confidentiality* and *keyword-update privacy*. This keyword updatability enables synonym search and/or similarity search in PEKS. We also propose a generic transformation from KU-PEKS to secure keyword search in the symmetric setting, that is the first attempt to generically construct secure keyword search in the symmetric setting providing *trapdoor privacy*.

Keywords: Keyword updatable PEKS · Searchable encryption · Trapdoor privacy

1 Introduction

Secure keyword search enables a user to search the encrypted data with a keyword without revealing any information on the data. As increasing the concern of efficient searching techniques on massive encrypted data for providing data privacy against inside adversaries, secure keyword search has been extended to accommodate various queries such as equality, subset, range and inner product queries [1,6,8,9,11,17,19].

Secure keyword search can be classified into two types. (1) Secure keyword search in the asymmetric setting, also known as public-key encryption with keyword search (PEKS), was introduced by Boneh et al. [4], considering an application to the store-and-forward systems such as an e-mail system. In a PEKS, a sender generates a *ciphertext* CT_w of a keyword w under the public key of a receiver and sends the ciphertext CT_w along with an encrypted message to a server.

© Springer International Publishing Switzerland 2016
H. Kim and D. Choi (Eds.): WISA 2015, LNCS 9503, pp. 96–109, 2016.
DOI: 10.1007/978-3-319-31875-2_9

To retrieve the encrypted email messages containing a keyword w' from the server, a receiver asks to the server a query, that is a *trapdoor* $T_{w'}$ generated under the receiver's secret key. The server then runs a test function with inputs CT_w and $T_{w'}$ to decide whether or not $w = w'$, and forwards the corresponding email messages to the receiver. (2) In secure keyword search in the symmetric setting [5,17], the ciphertext CT_w of a keyword w is generated under a symmetric key and only the owner of the key can generate queries by using the symmetric key. Here a symmetric key is not shared, but owned by one client. The symmetric setting is suitable for a blog and web-hard service, where the same client uploads and downloads his/her data.

This paper firstly proposes a PEKS scheme with keyword updatability, called *keyword-updatable PEKS* scheme (*KU-PEKS* for short). Keyword updatability means that the server can update a ciphertext CT_w of keyword w into $\mathsf{CT}_{w'}$ of keyword w' by using a value, called keyword update value $k_{w\to w'}$ provided by a receiver in advance. This update process is different from re-encryption in the literature [2,10]. Keyword update process changes a corresponding plaintext of a ciphertext while re-encryption changes a person who can decrypt the ciphertext.

We can intuitively and straightforwardly construct a direct construction from identity-based proxy reencryption (IBPRE) [10]. An IBPRE scheme is an identity-based one where a proxy can transform convert a ciphertext computed under Alice's ID into one that can be decrypted by Bob's secret key. In the direct construction, the server is provided with trapdoor T_w for finding CT_w and a keyword update key to transform CT_w into $\mathsf{CT}_{w'}$, where the key is derived from T_w. This implies that the server with T_w can derive any key to transform CT_w, say into $\mathsf{CT}_{w''}$, for any keyword w''. This is not intended by the receiver. To remedy this drawback, we construct an improved KU-PEKS scheme, where keyword update key can be generated only by the receiver. The improved scheme satisfies ciphertext confidentiality and consistency. In addition, KU-PEKS should satisfy the property, called keyword-update privacy which can update ciphertext without revealing any information on a keyword.

Application. One of the main applications of PEKS is an e-mail system, where a receiver retrieves e-mails with a keyword [4]. For example, the receiver may want to retrieve urgent e-mails with keyword "urgent". However it is highly possible that urgent e-mails in fact do not contain keyword "urgent". A sender might have selected a proper synonym as a keyword to express suitable situation. That is, urgent e-mail may contain "urgency", "emergency", or "burning" other than "urgent". It is certain that PEKS with enabling synonym search capability would be practically useful. This type of synonym search can be exploited for similarity search if we select a similar word with a few character difference instead of synonym. For example, "urgent" could be mistyped into urgant", "urgenk", and so on. Similarity search is not known to be possible in secure keyword search on encrypted data yet, while it is possible in web search engines. Similarity search in PEKS has been considered not attainable since one bit difference in a plaintext results in unexpected difference in the corresponding ciphertext.

One naive approach to enable similarity search in PEKS would be that a receiver tries each of all possible similar keywords, one by one. This inevitably delays retrieval time. Furthermore, more trapdoors available makes keyword guessing easier. Hence this is not a wise approach for similarity search. The generic construction to reduce retrieval time would be to provide the server with trapdoors for similar keywords in advance. For example, for keyword urgent a receiver provides ciphertext CT_{urgent} and similar trapdoors $T_{urgency}$, $T_{emergency}$, $T_{burning}$ and so on. When a ciphertext CT of a keyword similar to urgent is sent, the server runs the test function with inputs CT and each of the similar trapdoors. If the result of test function is true, the server replaces CT with CT_{urgent}. This approach results in an identical ciphertext for similar keywords. That is, both $CT_{urgency}$ and $CT_{emergency}$ are transformed into CT_{urgent}. However, this approach reveals the information that two original ciphertexts $CT_{urgency}$ and $CT_{emergency}$ encrypted two similar keywords even without keyword guessing. KU-PEKS construction makes the server transform CT into CT_{urgent} even without providing a trapdoor, where only the receiver can generate a keyword-update key. Furthermore, the transformed ciphertexts for similar keywords are random. That is, both $CT_{urgency}$ and $CT_{emergency}$ are transformed into independent random objects.

2   Preliminaries

We review the notation and the definitions of an identity-based proxy re-encryption (IBPRE) scheme. We assume that IBPRE satisfies (1) *unidirectionality* that IBPRE scheme permits a user U_1 to delegate to another user U_2 without permitting U_1 to decrypt U_2's ciphertexts and (2) *multiple-use capability* that IBPRE scheme permits the proxy to perform multiple consecutive re-encryptions on a ciphertext [2,10].

Notation: For any string x, $|x|$ denotes its length. For any set S, $|S|$ denotes its size. The symbol λ denotes a security parameter. We let $a \leftarrow b$ denote the assignment to a the result of evaluating b. We say a function μ is *negligible* if for any constant λ, there exists N such that $\mu(n) < 1/n^\lambda$ for $n > N$.

2.1   Identity-Based Proxy Re-encryption

An identity-based proxy re-encryption (IBPRE) scheme is an extension of identity based encryption (IBE) scheme in which the decryption capability of a user to another user via a third party called a *proxy*. Via $(PP, msk) \leftarrow \mathbf{Setup}(1^\lambda)$ the setup algorithm produces a pair of public parameters and master secret key for security parameter λ; via $sk_{id} \leftarrow \mathbf{KeyGen}(PP, msk, id)$ the key generation algorithm takes the public parameters PP and the master secret key msk and an identity $id \in \{0,1\}^*$ as input and produces a secret key sk_{id} corresponding to that identity id; via $c_{id} \leftarrow \mathbf{Enc}(PP, id, m)$ the encryption algorithm encrypts a message m to create a ciphertext c_{id} under the specified identity; via $rk_{id_1 \rightarrow id_2} \leftarrow \mathbf{RKGen}(PP, sk_{id_1}, id_1, id_2)$ the re-encryption key generation algorithm generates a re-encryption key $rk_{id_1 \to id_2}$ for converting a ciphertext for one identity id_1 into for the other identity id_2, which are given to the proxy; via $c_{id_2} \leftarrow$ **Reencrypt**(PP, $rk_{id_1 \to id_2}$, c_{id_1}) the re-encryption algorithm reencrypts a ciphertext c_{id_1} to produce a "re-encrypted"ciphertext c_{id_2}; via $m \leftarrow$ **Decrypt**(PP, sk_{id}, c_{id}) the decryption algorithm decrypts a ciphertext c_{id} to recover a message m.

Correctness of IBPRE: In [10], Green and Ateniese identified the concept of the correctness of IBPRE schemes. Suppose that $(PP, msk) \leftarrow$ **Setup**(1^λ), $d_{id} \leftarrow$ **KeyGen**(PP, msk, id). Let id and id_1 be any identities. Suppose that $rk_{id_1 \to id} \leftarrow$ **RKGen**(PP, sk_{id_1}, id_1, id) and $C_{id_1} \leftarrow$ **Enc**(PP, id_1, m). If $C_{id} \leftarrow$ **Enc**(PP, id, m) or $C_{id} \leftarrow$ **Reencrypt**(PP, $rk_{id_1 \to id}$, C_{id_1}), then the following propositions hold:

- **Decrypt**(PP, sk_{id_1}, C_{id_1}) $= m$
- **Decrypt**(PP, sk_{id}, **Reencrypt**(PP, $rk_{id_1 \to id}$, C_{id_1})) $= m$

Game$_1$: The game for *ciphertext confidentiality* [10] between the adversary $\mathcal{A}$ and the challenger $\mathcal{B}$ proceeds as follows.

- **Setup:** $\mathcal{B}$ runs the **Setup**(1^λ) algorithm to obtain (PP, msk) and sends the public parameter PP to $\mathcal{A}$.
- **Phase 1:** $\mathcal{A}$ makes the following queries and $\mathcal{B}$ adaptively responses as follows.
  - For any extraction query id, $\mathcal{B}$ returns d_{id} =**KeyGen**(PP, msk, id) to $\mathcal{A}$.
  - For any reencryption key query (id_1, id_2), $\mathcal{B}$ extracts the key d_{id_1}=**KeyGen** (PP, msk, id_1) and returns $rk_{id_1 \to id_2}$ =**RKGen**(PP, sk_{id_1}, id_1, id_2).
- **Challenge:** $\mathcal{A}$ sends identity id^* and messages m_0 and m_1 to the challenger. $\mathcal{B}$ picks a random $\beta \in \{0, 1\}$ and returns $c_\beta \leftarrow$ **Enc**(PP, id^*, m_β) to $\mathcal{A}$. The restriction is as follows.
  - The extraction query id^* and the re-encryption key query (id^*, id') and the extraction query id' should not be queried previously, for any identity id'.
- **Phase 2:** $\mathcal{A}$ makes the following queries as in the **Phase 1**, except for the following queries.
  - The extraction query id^* and the re-encryption key query (id^*, id') and the extraction query id' should not be queried previously, for any identity id'.
- **Guess:** The adversary returns a guess $\beta' \in \{0, 1\}$ of β.

The advantage of $\mathcal{A}$ in breaking IND-CPA security in an **IBPRE** scheme is defined as

$$\mathbf{Adv}^{\mathsf{ibpre\text{-}ind\text{-}cpa}}_{\mathbf{IBPRE}, \mathcal{A}}(\lambda) = |\Pr[\beta = \beta'] - 1/2| \ .$$

Definition 1. *We say that **IBPRE** satisfies a ciphertext confidentiality (IND-CPA-secure) if the advantage $\mathbf{Adv}^{ibpre\text{-}ind\text{-}cpa}_{\mathbf{IBPRE}, \mathcal{A}}(\lambda)$ of any probabilistic polynomial-time (PPT) adversary $\mathcal{A}$ is negligible in the security parameter λ.*

Game$_2$: The game for *anonymity of IBPRE* between the adversary $\mathcal{A}$ and the challenger $\mathcal{B}$ proceeds as follows.

- **Setup**: $\mathcal{B}$ runs the **Setup**(1^λ) algorithm to obtain $(\mathsf{PP}, \mathsf{msk})$ and sends the public parameter PP to $\mathcal{A}$.
- **Phase 1**: $\mathcal{A}$ makes the following queries and $\mathcal{B}$ adaptively responses as follows.
  - For any extraction query id, $\mathcal{B}$ returns $d_{id} = \mathbf{KeyGen}(\mathsf{PP}, \mathsf{msk}, id)$ to $\mathcal{A}$.
  - For any re-encryption key query (id_1, id_2), $\mathcal{B}$ extracts the key $d_{id_1} = \mathbf{KeyGen}(\mathsf{PP}, \mathsf{msk}, id_1)$ and returns $rk_{id_1 \to id_2} = \mathbf{RKGen}(\mathsf{PP}, sk_{id_1}, id_1, id_2)$.
- **Challenge**: $\mathcal{A}$ sends identities id_0^* and id_1^* and a message m^* to the challenger, and $id_0^* \neq id_1^*$. $\mathcal{B}$ picks a random $\beta \in \{0,1\}$ and returns $C_\beta \leftarrow \mathbf{Enc}(\mathsf{PP}, id_\beta^*, m^*)$ to $\mathcal{A}$. The restriction is that $\mathcal{A}$ does not hold a secret keys $d_{id_0^*}$ and $d_{id_1^*}$, and reencryption keys $rk_{id_0^* \to id}$, $rk_{id_1^* \to id}$ and a secret key d_{id}, for any identity id.
- **Phase 2**: $\mathcal{A}$ makes the following queries as in the **Phase 1**, except for the following queries.
  - The extraction query id_1^* and re-encryption key extraction queries (id_1^*, id') and the extraction query id' should be restricted, for any id'.
- **Guess**: The adversary returns a guess $\beta' \in \{0,1\}$ of β.

The advantage of $\mathcal{A}$ in breaking ANO-CPA security in an **IBPRE** scheme is defined as
$$\mathbf{Adv}_{\mathbf{IBPRE}, \mathcal{A}}^{\mathrm{ibpre\text{-}ano\text{-}cpa}}(\lambda) = |\Pr[\beta = \beta'] - 1/2| .$$

Definition 2. *We say that **IBPRE** satisfies the anonymity (ANO-CPA-secure) if the advantage $\mathbf{Adv}_{\mathbf{IBPRE}, \mathcal{A}}^{ibpre\text{-}ano\text{-}cpa}(\lambda)$ of any probabilistic polynomial-time (PPT) adversary $\mathcal{A}$ is negligible in the security parameter λ.*

Remark 1. The notion of *key-privacy* or *anonymity* [3] in public-key encryption schemes has been considered as the security requirements of encryption schemes as well as *semantic security*. Ateniese et al. introduced a notion of key privacy of proxy re-encryption scheme [2]. For anonymity in **IBPRE**, an adversary cannot distinguish the intended recipient from the ciphertexts and re-encryption keys even when given re-encryption keys and re-encryption oracles. As mentioned in [2], the anonymity of ciphertext (Definition 3) as well as the re-encryption key privacy (Definition 4) should be considered in **IBPRE**.

We can infer that the IBPRE scheme proposed by Green and Ateniese [10] satisfies the anonymity (IBPRE-ANO-CPA security) against chosen-plaintext attacks.

Re-encryption key privacy of IBPRE: We first define the anonymity (IBPRE-REKey-CPA security) of the IBPRE scheme against adaptive chosen-plaintext attacks using **Game**$_3$.

Game$_3$: The game for *re-encryption predicate privacy* between the adversary $\mathcal{A}$ and the challenger $\mathcal{B}$ proceeds as follows.

- **Setup**: $\mathcal{B}$ runs the **Setup**(1^λ) algorithm to obtain $(\mathsf{PP}, \mathsf{msk})$ and sends the public parameter PP to $\mathcal{A}$.
- **Phase 1**: $\mathcal{A}$ makes the following queries and $\mathcal{B}$ adaptively responses as follows.

- For any extraction query id, $\mathcal{B}$ returns $d_{id} =$ **KeyGen**(PP, msk, id) to $\mathcal{A}$.
- For any reencryption key query (id_1, id_2), $\mathcal{B}$ extracts the key $d_{id_1} =$ **KeyGen** (PP, msk, id_1) and returns $rk_{id_1 \to id_2} =$ **RKGen**(PP, sk_{id_1}, id_1, id_2).

– **Challenge**: $\mathcal{A}$ sends identities id_0^* and id_1^* and a message m^* to the challenger, and $id_0^* \neq id_1^*$. $\mathcal{B}$ computes $s \leftarrow$ **RKGen**(PP, $sk_{id_0^*}$, id_0^*, id_1^*) and picks a random $\beta \in \{0, 1\}$. $\mathcal{B}$ returns $c_\beta = s$ to $\mathcal{A}$ if $\beta = 1$ and a random key in the key space otherwise. The restriction is that $\mathcal{A}$ does not hold secret keys $d_{id_0^*}$ and $d_{id_1^*}$, and a reencryption key $rk_{id_0^* \to id_1^*}$.

– **Phase 2**: $\mathcal{A}$ makes the following queries as in the **Phase 1**, except for the following queries.
- The extraction query id_1^* should be restricted.
- The re-encryption key extraction queries (id_1^*, id') and the extraction query id' should be restricted, for any id'.

– **Guess**: The adversary returns a guess $\beta' \in \{0, 1\}$ of β.

The advantage of $\mathcal{A}$ in breaking REKey-CPA security in an **IBPRE** scheme is defined as
$$\mathbf{Adv}_{\mathbf{IBPRE}, \mathcal{A}}^{\text{ibpre-rekey-cpa}}(\lambda) = |\Pr[\beta = \beta'] - 1/2| \ .$$

Definition 3. *We say that **IBPRE** satisfies a privacy of re-encryption key (REKey-CPA-secure) if the advantage $\mathbf{Adv}_{IBPRE, \mathcal{A}}^{ibpre-rekey-cpa}(\lambda)$ of any probabilistic polynomial-time (PPT) adversary $\mathcal{A}$ is negligible in the security parameter λ.*

3   Keyword-Updatable PEKS

Definition 4. *(Keyword Updatable PEKS Scheme) A keyword-updatable PEKS scheme (**KU-PEKS**) consists of six PPT algorithms as follows.*

- **Gen**(λ) takes a security parameter λ as input, and generates a pair of public and secret keys (PK, SK) of the receiver R.
- **Td**(SK, w) takes as inputs a receiver's secret key SK and a keyword, w. It then generates a trapdoor T_w.
- **PEKS**(PK, w) takes as inputs a receiver's public key PK and a keyword, w. It returns a ciphertext CT on the keyword w.
- **Test**(CT, T_w) takes as inputs a ciphertext CT and a trapdoor T_w. It outputs '1' if $w = w'$ and '0' otherwise, where $CT =$ **PEKS**(PK, w').
- **kuTd**(PK, T_{w_1}, w_1, w_2) takes as inputs a receiver's public key PK, a trapdoor T_{w_1}, and keywords w_1 and w_2. It then outputs a keyword-update value $\mathsf{kuTd}_{w_1 \to w_2}$.
- **kuPEKS**($PK, CT, \mathsf{kuTd}_{w_1 \to w_2}$) takes as inputs a receiver's public key PK, a ciphertext $CT =$ **PEKS**(PK, w), and a keyword-update value $\mathsf{kuTd}_{w_1 \to w_2} =$ **kuTd**(PK, T_{w_1}, w_1, w_2). It outputs CT $' =$ **PEKS**(PK, w_2) if $w = w_1$ and aborts otherwise.

Table 1. Consistency of KU-PEKS.

$\mathbf{Exp}_{\mathbf{kuPEKS},\mathcal{A}}^{\text{kupeks-cons}}(\lambda)$

    $(PK, SK) \leftarrow \mathbf{Gen}(\lambda)$; $(w, w') \leftarrow \mathcal{A}(PK)$; $\mathsf{CT} \leftarrow \mathbf{PEKS}(PK, w)$

    $\mathsf{kuTd}_{w_1 \to w_2} \leftarrow \mathbf{kuTd}(SK, PK, T_{w_1}, w_1, w_2)$; $T_{w'} \leftarrow \mathbf{Td}(SK, w')$

    $\mathsf{CT}' \leftarrow \mathbf{kuPEKS}(PK, \mathsf{CT}, \mathsf{kuTd}_{w_1 \to w_2})$

    If $w \neq w_1$ or $w_2 \neq w'$ and $\mathbf{Test}(T_{w'}, \mathsf{CT}') = 1$ then return 1 else return 0

Suppose there exists an adversary $\mathcal{A}$ that wants to make consistency fail. A computational consistency for KU-PEKS scheme is defined as follows (Table 1). The advantage of $\mathcal{A}$ is defined as follows.

$$\mathbf{Adv}_{\mathbf{kuPEKS},\mathcal{A}}^{\text{kupeks-cons}}(\lambda) = \Pr[\mathbf{Exp}_{\mathbf{kuPEKS},\mathcal{A}}^{\text{kupeks-cons}}(\lambda) = 1],$$

where the probability is taken over all possible coin flips of all the algorithms involved.

Definition 5. *We say that **KU-PEKS** satisfies "computationally consistency" if for any PPT adversary $\mathcal{A}$ attacking **KU-PEKS** scheme the advantage $\mathbf{Adv}_{kuPEKS,\mathcal{A}}^{kupeks-cons}(\lambda)$ is negligible.*

Game$_4$: The game for *ciphertext confidentiality* between the adversary $\mathcal{A}$ and the challenger $\mathcal{B}$ proceeds as follows.

- **Setup**: $\mathcal{B}$ runs the $\mathbf{Gen}(1^\lambda)$ algorithm to obtain (PK, SK) and sends the public key PK to $\mathcal{A}$.
- **Phase 1**: $\mathcal{A}$ makes the following queries and $\mathcal{B}$ adaptively responses as follows.
  - **Trapdoor queries**: For any trapdoor query of the form $w \in \{0,1\}^*$, $\mathcal{B}$ returns $T_w = \mathbf{Td}(SK, w)$ to $\mathcal{A}$.
  - **Keyword-Update Key queries**: For any keyword-update key query (w_1, w_2), $\mathcal{B}$ returns $\mathsf{kuTd}_{w_1 \to w_2} = \mathbf{kuTd}(PK, T_{w_1}, w_1, w_2)$.
- **Challenge**: $\mathcal{A}$ sends keywords w_0^* and w_1^* to the challenger. The restriction is that $\mathcal{A}$ did not previously make both (1) the trapdoor query of w_b^* and (2) the keyword-update value $\mathsf{kuTd}_{w_b^* \to w}$ as well as the trapdoor query T_w, for any keyword w and $b = 0, 1$. $\mathcal{B}$ picks a random $\beta \in \{0,1\}$ and returns the challenge ciphertext $\mathsf{CT}_\beta^* \leftarrow \mathbf{PEKS}(PK, w_\beta^*)$.
- **Phase 2**: $\mathcal{A}$ makes the following queries as in the **Phase 1**, except for the following queries.
  - The trapdoor query of the form w_0^* and w_1^* should be restricted.
  - The keyword-update key queries of the form (w_b^*, w') and the trapdoor query of the form w' should be not queried, for any keyword $w' \in \{0,1\}^*$ and $b = 0, 1$.
- **Guess**: The adversary returns a guess $\beta' \in \{0,1\}$ of β.

The advantage of $\mathcal{A}$ in breaking the ciphertext confidentiality (kuPEKS-IND-CPA security) in **KU-PEKS** scheme is defined as

$$\mathbf{Adv}_{\mathbf{KU\text{-}PEKS},\mathcal{A}}^{\text{kupeks-ind-cpa}}(\lambda) = |\Pr[\beta = \beta'] - 1/2| .$$

Definition 6. *We say that a KU-PEKS scheme provides the ciphertext confidentiality against an adaptive chosen-plaintext attack (kuPEKS-IND-CPA security) if for any PPT adversary $\mathcal{A}$, $Adv_{kuPEKS,\ \mathcal{A}}^{kupeks\text{-}ind\text{-}cpa}(\lambda)$ is negligible.*

Game$_5$: The game for *keyword-update key privacy* between the adversary $\mathcal{A}$ and the challenger $\mathcal{B}$ proceeds as follows.

- **Setup:** $\mathcal{B}$ runs the **Gen**(1^λ) algorithm to obtain (PK, SK) and sends the public key PK to $\mathcal{A}$.
- **Phase 1:** $\mathcal{A}$ makes the following queries and $\mathcal{B}$ adaptively responses as follows.
  - **Trapdoor queries:** For any trapdoor query of the form $w \in \{0,1\}^*$, $\mathcal{B}$ returns $T_w = \mathbf{Td}(SK, w)$ to $\mathcal{A}$.
  - **Keyword-Update Key queries:** For any keyword-update key query (w_1, w_2), $\mathcal{B}$ returns $\mathsf{kuTd}_{w_1 \to w_2} = \mathbf{kuTd}(PK, T_{w_1}, w_1, w_2)$.
- **Challenge:** $\mathcal{A}$ queries w to obtain $T_w \leftarrow \mathbf{Td}(SK, w)$, for any keyword $w \neq w_b^*$ ($b = 0,1$) and sends T_w as well as keywords w_0^* and w_1^* to the challenger $\mathcal{B}$. The restriction is that $\mathcal{A}$ did not previously make both (1) the trapdoor query of w_b^* and (2) the keyword-update key $\mathsf{kuTd}_{w_b^* \to w}$ as well as the trapdoor query T_w, for any keyword w and $b = 0,1$. $\mathcal{B}$ picks a random $\beta \in \{0,1\}$ and returns the challenge keyword-update key $\mathsf{kuTd}_{w \to w_\beta^*} \leftarrow \mathbf{kuTd}\ (PK, T_w, w, w_\beta^*)$ to $\mathcal{A}$.
- **Phase 2:** $\mathcal{A}$ makes the following queries as in the **Phase 1**, except for the following queries.
  - The trapdoor query of the form w_0^* and w_1^* should be restricted.
  - The keyword-update key queries of the form (w_b^*, w') and the trapdoor query of the form w' should be not queried, for any keyword $w' \in \{0,1\}^*$ and $b = 0,1$.
- **Guess:** The adversary returns a guess $\beta' \in \{0,1\}$ of β.

The advantage of $\mathcal{A}$ in breaking the keyword-update key privacy (kuTd-IND-CPA security) in **KU-PEKS** scheme is defined as

$$Adv_{KU\text{-}PEKS,\ \mathcal{A}}^{kuTd\text{-}ind\text{-}cpa}(\lambda) = |\Pr[\beta = \beta'] - 1/2|\ .$$

Definition 7. *We say that KU-PEKS scheme provides the keyword-update key privacy against an adaptive chosen-plaintext attack (kuTd-IND-CPA security) if for any PPT adversary $\mathcal{A}$, $Adv_{kuPEKS,\ \mathcal{A}}^{kuTd\text{-}ind\text{-}cpa}(\lambda)$ is negligible.*

4   Construction of KU-PEKS

In an IBE scheme $\mathcal{IBE} = (\mathbf{Setup}_{\mathcal{IBE}}, \mathbf{KeyDer}_{\mathcal{IBE}}, \mathbf{Enc}_{\mathcal{IBE}}, \mathbf{Dec}_{\mathcal{IBE}})$, the key generator with master public/private key pair (PK, SK) generates the secret key sk_{ID} corresponding to an identity ID by computing $\mathbf{KeyDer}_{\mathcal{IBE}}\ (SK, \mathsf{ID})$.

We now propose a generic construction *keyword updatability* PEKS from IBPRE. We can intuitively and straightforwardly construct a direct construction from IBPRE along the line of the approach in [1]. The idea of providing keyword-updatability is that re-encryption key $rk_{w \to w'}$ that converts C_w into

$C_{w'}$ without changing the message in IBPRE is used in generating keyword-update key $k_{w \to w'}$ for converting ciphertext CT_w with ciphertext $CT_{w'}$ in KU-PEKS. Unfortunately, the direct construction inherits the property from IBPRE that anyone with secret key sk_w can generate re-encryption key $rk_{w \to w''}$, for any identity w'', by the re-encryption key generation algorithm. Moreover, it is required that anyone with re-encryption key $rk_{w \to w'}$ and secret key $sk_{w'}$ can generate re-encryption key $rk_{w \to w''}$, for any identity w'' that is called collusion attacks of a proxy and a delegator [16]. This property in KU-PEKS means that anyone who obtains trapdoor $T_w (= sk_w)$ or keyword-update key $k_{w \to w'} = [T_w, rk_{w \to w'}]$ can generate new keyword-update key $k_{w \to w''} = [sk_w, rk_{w \to w''}]$ for any keyword w''. To overcome this weakness, the underlying IBPRE needs to be secure against collusion attacks. Koo et al.'s collusion-resistant IBPRE scheme [16] can be a proper candidate for the underlying IBPRE.

A generic approach transforms an IBPRE scheme secure against collusion attacks [16] into a secure KU-PEKS scheme. To perform the keyword update, the server first needs to find the PEKS ciphertexts that a receiver wants to retrieve. For this purpose, the server in the first approach is given a trapdoor information together with a keyword-update key. The novel idea of the second approach is that the server is enabled to find the corresponding PEKS ciphertexts without any trapdoor information. Let $rk_{w_1 \to w_2}$ be a re-encryption key in IBPRE. The keyword-update key $k_{w_1 \to w_2}$ of the transformed KU-PEKS consists of two re-encryption keys $rk_{w_1 \to rand}$ and $rk_{w_1 \to w_2}$ and secret key sk_{rand} for random $rand$. Here, $rk_{w_1 \to rand}$ and sk_{rand} are used in searching a ciphertext CT_{w_1}, and $rk_{w_1 \to w_2}$ is used in converting CT_{w_1} into CT_{w_2}. As stated above, if the underlying IBPRE scheme is secure against collusion attacks, anyone with $rk_{w_1 \to rand}$, sk_{rand} and $rk_{w_1 \to w_2}$ cannot obtain sk_{w_1} or $rk_{w_1 \to w_2'}$ for some keyword $w_2'(\neq w_2)$ from the given information.

The generic construction of KU-PEKS scheme **KU-PEKS** =(**Gen, Td, PEKS, kuTd, kuPEKS, Test**), using **IBPRE**=(**Setup, KeyGen, Enc, RKGen, Reencrypt, Decrypt**), proceeds as follows.

– **Gen**(1^λ): This algorithm runs **Setup**(1^λ) to obtain (PP, msk). The public key is $PK = PP$ and the secret key is $SK = msk$. It outputs $(PK, SK) = (PP, msk)$.
– **Td**(SK, w): Let $w \in \{0,1\}^n$ be a keyword. To generate a trapdoor T_w of w, the trapdoor algorithm runs $d_w \leftarrow$ **KeyGen**(PP, msk, w). The trapdoor is $T_w = d_w$.
– **PEKS**(PK, w): To encrypt a keyword $w \in \{0,1\}^*$ under the public key PK, this algorithm picks a random message $R \in \mathcal{M}$ and computes $C \leftarrow$ **Enc**(PK, w, R) and outputs $CT = [C_1, C_2] = [R, C]$.
– **Test**($PK, CT, T_{w'}$) : To obtain the test result, this algorithm parses the ciphertext CT as $[C_1, C_2]$. It computes $R' \leftarrow$ **Decrypt**($PK, T_{w'}, C_2$). It outputs '0' if $C_1 \neq R'$ and '1' otherwise.
– **kuTd**(PK, T_{w_1}, w_1, w_2) : To generate a keyword-update key from w_1 to w_2, this algorithm chooses a random identity $id \in \{0,1\}^*$ and computes $d_{id} \leftarrow$ **KeyGen**(PP, msk, id). It computes $rk_{w_1 \to w_2} \leftarrow$ **RKGen**($PK, T_{w_1}, w_1,$

w_2) and $rk_{w_1 \to id} \leftarrow \textbf{RKGen}(PK, T_{w_1}, w_1, id)$ and outputs $\mathsf{kuTd}_{w_1 \to w_2} = [rk_{w_1 \to w_2}, rk_{w_1 \to id}, T_{id}]$.

– $\textbf{kuPEKS}(PK, \mathsf{CT}, \mathsf{kuTd}_{w_1 \to w_2})$: Let $\mathsf{kuTd}_{w_1 \to w_2} = [K_1, K_2, K_3]$ be a keyword-update key and $\mathsf{CT} = [C_1, C_2]$ be a ciphertext. This algorithm proceeds as follows.

   • It computes $C_2' \leftarrow \textbf{Reencrypt}(PK, K_1, C_2)$ and $C_2'' \leftarrow \textbf{Reencrypt}(PK, K_2, C_2)$.
   • It aborts if $\textbf{Decrypt}(PK, K_3, C_2'') \neq C_1$ and outputs $\mathsf{CT}_{w_2} = [C_1, C_2']$ otherwise.

We now prove that our generic construction provides the ciphertext confidentiality, the keyword-update key privacy and the computational consistency as follows. We note that this proof approach follows from [1].

Theorem 1. *If the underlying IBE scheme of* **IBPRE** *scheme provides IBE-ANO-CPA security, then our generic construction provides the kuPEKS-IND-CPA security.*

Proof. Suppose that there exists a PPT adversary $\mathcal{A}$ attacking the kuPEKS-IND-CPA security of KU-PEKS scheme. We can construct a PPT adversary $\mathcal{B}$ attacking the IBE-ANO-CPA security of the underlying IBE scheme of IBPRE scheme. Let $\mathcal{C}$ denote a challenger against $\mathcal{B}$. $\mathcal{C}$ begins by supplying $\mathcal{B}$ with the public parameters PP of **IBPRE** and $\mathcal{B}$ forwards PP (as the public key PK of KU-PEKS) to $\mathcal{A}$.

In its find stage, given public key PP, $\mathcal{A}$ runs $\mathcal{B}(\mathtt{find}, \mathsf{PP})$ to obtain challenge keywords w_0^* and w_1^*. $\mathcal{B}$ chooses a random message $R^* \in \mathcal{M}$ and gives a challenge query (w_0^*, w_1^*, R^*) to $\mathcal{C}$. $\mathcal{B}$ mounts an IBPRE-ANO-CPA attack on **IBPRE** by interacting with $\mathcal{A}$ as follows.

- On trapdoor query w, $\mathcal{B}$ makes an extraction query with an identity w to $\mathcal{C}$. Upon receiving w, $\mathcal{C}$ runs the KeyGen algorithm in **IBPRE** to obtain the private key d_w. $\mathcal{C}$ returns the trapdoor $d_w(= T_w)$.
- On keyword-update key query (w, w'), $\mathcal{B}$ makes a re-encryption key query with an identity (w, w') to $\mathcal{C}$. Upon receiving (w, w'), $\mathcal{C}$ runs the RKGen algorithm in **IBPRE** to obtain the re-encryption key $rk_{w \to w'}$. $\mathcal{C}$ returns the keyword-update key $rk_{w \to w'}(= \mathsf{kuTd}_{w_1 \to w_2})$.

On receiving $C_b^* = \textbf{Enc}(\mathsf{PP}, w_b^*, R^*)$ from $\mathcal{C}$, $\mathcal{B}$ gives back his challenge ciphertext $[R^*, C_b^*]$ to $\mathcal{A}$ in its guess stage. It is easy to see from the definition of the KU-PEKS scheme that CT^* is equal to the output of the encryption algorithm in **KU-PEKS** for the input (PP, w_b^*). For any keyword $w \in \{0,1\}^*$, we insist that if $\mathcal{B}$ makes a trapdoor query on w_b^* ($b = 0, 1$) or a keyword-update key $rk_{w_b \to w}$ on (w_b, w) in some phases, then $\mathcal{B}$ aborts. Eventually, $\mathcal{A}$ must guess b' for b. Then $\mathcal{B}$ outputs b' as its guess for b. It is easy to see that for any $b (\in \{0,1\})$,

$$\Pr[\textbf{Exp}_{\textbf{IBPRE},\mathcal{B}}^{\text{ibe-ano-cpa-b}}(k) = 1] = \Pr[\textbf{Exp}_{\textbf{KU-PEKS},\mathcal{A}}^{\text{kupeks-ind-cpa-b}}(k) = 1].$$

Therefore, $\mathbf{Adv}_{\mathbf{KU\text{-}PEKS},\mathcal{A}}^{\text{kupeks-ind-cpa}}(k) \leq \mathbf{Adv}_{\mathbf{IBPRE},\mathcal{B}}^{\text{ibe-ano-cpa}}(k)$.

Theorem 2. *If **IBPRE** scheme provides the IBPRE-ANO-CPA security, then our generic construction provides the kuTd-IND-CPA security.*

Proof. Suppose that there exists a PPT adversary $\mathcal{A}$ attacking the kuTd-IND-CPA security of KU-PEKS scheme. We can construct a PPT adversary $\mathcal{B}$ attacking the IBPRE-ANO-CPA security of IBPRE scheme. Let $\mathcal{C}$ denote a challenger against $\mathcal{B}$. $\mathcal{C}$ begins by supplying $\mathcal{B}$ with the public parameters PP of **IBPRE** and $\mathcal{B}$ forwards PP (as the public key PK of KU-PEKS) to $\mathcal{A}$.

In its find stage, given public key PP, $\mathcal{A}$ runs $\mathcal{B}(\text{find}, \text{PP})$ to obtain challenge keywords w_0^* and w_1^*. $\mathcal{B}$ chooses a random message $R^* \in \mathcal{M}$ and keyword w_1 and computes $\text{CT}_{w_1} \leftarrow \mathbf{Enc}(\text{PP}, w_1, R^*)$ and queries w_1 to the private-key generation oracle to obtain $d_{w_1} \leftarrow \mathbf{KeyGen}(\text{PP}, \text{msk}, w_1)$. $\mathcal{B}$ gives a challenge query $(T_{w_1}, w_1, w_0^*, w_1^*)$ to $\mathcal{C}$. $\mathcal{B}$ mounts an IBPRE-ANO-CPA attack on **IBPRE** by interacting with $\mathcal{A}$ as follows.

- On trapdoor query w, $\mathcal{B}$ makes an extraction query with an identity w to $\mathcal{C}$. Upon receiving w, $\mathcal{C}$ runs the KeyGen algorithm in **IBPRE** to obtain the private key d_w. $\mathcal{C}$ returns the trapdoor $d_w(= T_w)$.
- On keyword-update key query (w, w'), $\mathcal{B}$ makes a re-encryption key query with an identity (w, w') to $\mathcal{C}$. Upon receiving (w, w'), $\mathcal{C}$ runs the RKGen algorithm in **IBPRE** to obtain the re-encryption key $rk_{w \to w'}$. $\mathcal{C}$ returns the keyword-update key $rk_{w \to w'}(= \text{kuTd}_{w_1 \to w_2})$.

On receiving $rk_{w_1 \to w_b^*} = \mathbf{RKGen}(\text{PP}, d_{w_1}, w_b^*)$ from $\mathcal{C}$, $\mathcal{B}$ randomly chooses $id \in \{0,1\}^*$ and runs the private-key generation oracle to obtain T_{id} and computes $rk_{w_1 \to id}$ with d_{w_1}. $\mathcal{B}$ gives back his challenge keyword update key $kuTd_{w_1 \to w_b^*} = [rk_{w_1 \to w_b^*}, rk_{w_1 \to id}, T_{id}]$ to $\mathcal{A}$ in its guess stage. It is easy to see from the definition of the KU-PEKS scheme that $kuTd_{w_1 \to w_b^*}$ is equal to the output of the keyword update key generation algorithm in **KU-PEKS** for the input $(PK, T_{w_1}, w_1, w_b^*)$.

For any keyword $w \in \{0,1\}^*$, we insist that if $\mathcal{B}$ makes a trapdoor query on w_b^* $(b = 0,1)$ or a keyword-update key $rk_{w_b \to w}$ on (w_b, w) in some phases, then $\mathcal{B}$ aborts. Eventually, $\mathcal{A}$ must guess b' for b. Then $\mathcal{B}$ outputs b' as its guess for b. It is easy to see that for any $b (\in \{0,1\})$,

$$\Pr[\mathbf{Exp}_{\mathbf{IBPRE},\mathcal{B}}^{\text{ibpre-ano-cpa-b}}(k) = 1] = \Pr[\mathbf{Exp}_{\mathbf{KU\text{-}PEKS},\mathcal{A}}^{\text{kuTd-ind-cpa-b}}(k) = 1].$$

Therefore, $\mathbf{Adv}_{\mathbf{KU\text{-}PEKS},\mathcal{A}}^{\text{kuTd-ind-cpa}}(k) \leq \mathbf{Adv}_{\mathbf{IBPRE},\mathcal{B}}^{\text{ibpre-ano-cpa}}(k)$.

Theorem 3. *If **IBPRE** scheme satisfies the correctness, then our construction is computationally consistent.*

Proof. Suppose that there is a PPT adversary $\mathcal{A}$ attacking the computational consistency of KU-PEKS scheme **KU-PEKS**. We can construct a PPT adversary $\mathcal{B}$ attacking the IBPRE-IND-CPA security of IBPRE scheme **IBPRE**.

To show the computational consistency of **IBPRE**, we will show that if $\mathcal{A}$ successes to attack the computational consistency of **KU-PEKS** then $\mathcal{B}$ successes to attack the IBPRE-IND-CPA security of **IBPRE** or it contradicts the correctness constraint of **IBPRE**. We can construct algorithms $\mathcal{B}$ as follows.

Let $\mathcal{C}$ denote a challenger against $\mathcal{B}$. $\mathcal{C}$ begins by supplying $\mathcal{B}$ with the public parameters PP of **IBPRE**. Given public parameters $\mathsf{PP} = PK$, $\mathcal{B}$ runs $\mathcal{A}(\mathsf{PP})$ to obtain keywords w and w' such that $\mathbf{Test}(\mathsf{CT}_w, T_{w'}) = 1$, where $\mathsf{CT}_w = \mathbf{PEKS}(\mathsf{PP}, w)$, (or $\mathsf{CT}_w = \mathsf{kuPEKS}(\mathsf{PP}, T_{w_0}, w_0, w)$, for some $w_0 \in \{0,1\}^*$) and $T_{w'} = \mathbf{Td}(\mathsf{msk}, w')$.

In simulation, $\mathcal{B}$ will eventually obtain in one of two different ways:

Case I $\mathcal{A}$ will obtain keywords w and w' such that $\mathbf{Test}(\mathsf{CT}_w, T_{w'}) = 1$, where $\mathsf{CT}_w = \mathbf{PEKS}(\mathsf{PP}, w)$ and $T_{w'} = \mathbf{Td}(\mathsf{msk}, w')$. In this case, $\mathcal{B}$ needs to generate all secret keys, except the key d_w.

Case II $\mathcal{A}$ will obtain keywords w and w' such that $\mathbf{Test}(\mathsf{CT}_w, T_{w'}) = 1$, where $\mathsf{kuTd}_{w_0 \to w} = \mathbf{kuTd}(PK, T_{w_0}, w_0, w)$, $\mathsf{CT}_w = \mathsf{kuPEKS}(\mathsf{PP}, \mathsf{CT}_{w_0}, \mathsf{kuTd}_{w_0 \to w})$ and $T_{w_0} = \mathbf{Td}(\mathsf{msk}, w_0)$ (for some $w_0 \in \{0,1\}^*$) and $T_{w'} = \mathbf{Td}(\mathsf{msk}, w')$. In this case, $\mathcal{B}$ needs to generate all secret keys, except the key d_w and d_{w_0}.

$\mathcal{B}$ chooses random messages $R_0^*, R_1^* \in \mathcal{M}$ and gives a challenge query (w, R_0^*, R_1^*) to $\mathcal{C}$. $\mathcal{B}$ gets back a ciphertext $C^* = \mathbf{Enc}(\mathsf{PP}, w, R_b^*)$ from $\mathcal{C}$. $\mathcal{B}$ uses its key-derivation oracle to obtain a trapdoor $T_{w'}$ (a private key $d_{w'}$ corresponding to an identity w') for a keyword w'.

Case I: If $\mathbf{Dec}(C^*, T_{w'}) = R_{b'}^*$ (for some $b' = 0, 1$) then $\mathcal{B}$ wins attacking IBPRE-IND-CPA security of **IBPRE**. Hence, if $\mathbf{Dec}(C^*, T_{w'}) = R_1^*$ then it returns 1 else it returns 0. Otherwise, we can assume that there exists $R^* \in \mathcal{M}$ ($R^* \neq R_0^*, R_1^*$) such that $\mathbf{Dec}(C_2^*, T_{w'}) = R^*$. It is contradict to $\mathbf{Test}(\mathsf{CT}_w, T_{w'}) = 1$ in the definition of the consistency of KU-PEKS scheme.

Case II: Suppose that $\mathbf{Dec}(C^*, T_{w'}) = R_{b'}^*$ (for some $b' = 0, 1$). There exist a keyword $w_0 \in \{0,1\}^*$ and $R^* \in \mathcal{M}$ such that $\mathsf{CT}_{w_0} = \mathbf{PEKS}(\mathsf{PP}, w_0) = [R^*, \mathbf{Enc}(\mathsf{PP}, w_0, R^*)]$, $T_{w_0} = \mathbf{Td}(\mathsf{msk}, w_0)$, $\mathsf{kuTd}_{w_0 \to w} = \mathbf{kuTd}(\mathsf{PP}, T_{w_0}, w_0, w)$, $\mathsf{CT}^* = [R_{b'}^*, C^*] = \mathsf{kuPEKS}(\mathsf{PP}, \mathsf{CT}_{w_0}, \mathsf{kuTd}_{w_0 \to w})$, and $T_{w'} = \mathbf{Td}(\mathsf{msk}, w')$.

Suppose that $R^* \neq R_0^*, R_1^*$ and $\mathbf{Reencryt}(\mathsf{PP}, \mathbf{Enc}(\mathsf{PP}, w_0, R^*), \mathsf{kuTd}_{w_0 \to w}) = C^*$. If $\mathbf{Dec}(C^*, T_{w'}) = R_{b'}^*$ (for some $b' = 0, 1$) then it is contradict to the definition of the correctness of IBPRE scheme. Meanwhile, if $\mathbf{Dec}(C^*, T_{w'}) = R_{b'}^*$ (for some $b' = 0, 1$) then $\mathcal{B}$ wins attacking IBPRE-IND-CPA security of **IBPRE**. Hence, if $\mathbf{Dec}(C^*, T_{w'}) = R_1^*$ then it returns 1 else it returns 0. It is easy to see that

$$\Pr[\mathbf{Exp}_{\mathbf{IBPRE}, \mathcal{B}}^{\text{ibpre-ind-cpa-1}}(k) = 1] \geq \Pr[\mathbf{Exp}_{\mathbf{KU\text{-}PEKS}, \mathcal{A}}^{\text{kupeks-cons}}(k) = 1],$$
$$\Pr[\mathbf{Exp}_{\mathbf{IBPRE}, \mathcal{B}}^{\text{ibpre-ind-cpa-0}}(k) = 1] \leq 2^{-k}.$$

Therefore, $\mathbf{Adv}_{\mathbf{KU\text{-}PEKS}, \mathcal{A}}^{\text{kupeks-cons}}(k) \leq \mathbf{Adv}_{\mathbf{IBPRE}, \mathcal{B}}^{\text{ibpre-ind-cpa}}(k) + 2^{-k}$.

5 Applications

As efforts to improve an efficiency of database management, the research of relational database management system (RDBMS) is very mentally active. To convert from one keyword into another keyword in an encrypted email system, we proposed a keyword-updatable PEKS scheme. This had improved the problem of keyword inconsistency residing in PEKS system processed by guessable keywords without previous commitments. After converting the ciphertexts, if only the converted ciphertexts remain open over the public database then these ciphertexts confidentiality and the corresponding queries privacy against an outside adversary also are provided.

References

1. Abdalla, M., Bellare, M., Catalano, D., Kiltz, E., Kohno, T., Lange, T., Malone-Lee, J., Neven, G., Paillier, P., Shi, H.: Searchable encryption revisited: consistency properties. Relat. Anonymous IBE, Extensions, J. Crypt. **21**(3), 350–391 (2008)
2. Ateniese, G., Benson, K., Hohenberger, S.: Key-Private proxy re-encryption. In: Fischlin, M. (ed.) CT-RSA 2009. LNCS, vol. 5473, pp. 279–294. Springer, Heidelberg (2009)
3. Bellare, M., Boldyreva, A., Desai, A., Pointcheval, D.: Key-Privacy in public-key encryption. In: Boyd, C. (ed.) ASIACRYPT 2001. LNCS, vol. 2248, pp. 566–582. Springer, Heidelberg (2001)
4. Boneh, D., Di Crescenzo, G., Ostrovsky, R., Persiano, G.: Public key encryption with keyword search. In: Cachin, C., Camenisch, J.L. (eds.) EUROCRYPT 2004. LNCS, vol. 3027, pp. 506–522. Springer, Heidelberg (2004)
5. Blundo, C., Iovino, V., Persiano, G.: Private-Key hidden vector encryption with key confidentiality. In: Garay, J.A., Miyaji, A., Otsuka, A. (eds.) CANS 2009. LNCS, vol. 5888, pp. 259–277. Springer, Heidelberg (2009)
6. Baek, J., Safavi-Naini, R., Susilo, W.: Public key encryption with keyword search revisited. In: Proceedings of ACIS2006 (2006)
7. Boyen, X., Waters, B.: Anonymous hierarchical identity-based encryption (without random oracles). In: Dwork, C. (ed.) CRYPTO 2006. LNCS, vol. 4117, pp. 290–307. Springer, Heidelberg (2006)
8. Boneh, D., Waters, B.: Conjunctive, subset, and range queries on encrypted data. In: Vadhan, S.P. (ed.) TCC 2007. LNCS, vol. 4392, pp. 535–554. Springer, Heidelberg (2007)
9. Chor, B., Kushilevitz, E., Goldreich, O., Sudan, M.: Private information retrieval. J. ACM **45**(6), 965–981 (1998)
10. Green, M., Ateniese, G.: Identity-based proxy re-encryption. In: Katz, J., Yung, M. (eds.) ACNS 2007. LNCS, vol. 4521, pp. 288–306. Springer, Heidelberg (2007)
11. Gentry, C., Silverberg, A.: Hierarchical ID-Based cryptography. In: Zheng, Y. (ed.) ASIACRYPT 2002. LNCS, vol. 2501, pp. 548–566. Springer, Heidelberg (2002)
12. Garg, S., Sahai, A., Waters, B.: Efficient fully collusion-resilient traitor tracing scheme, Cryptology ePrint Archive, in report /532 (2009). http://eprint.iacr.org/2009/532/
13. Horwitz, J., Lynn, B.: Toward hierarchical identity-based encryption. In: Knudsen, L.R. (ed.) EUROCRYPT 2002. LNCS, vol. 2332, pp. 466–481. Springer, Heidelberg (2002)

14. Jeong, I.R., Kwon, J.O., Hong, D., Lee, D.H.: Constructing PEKS schemes secure against keyword guessing attacks is possible? Elsevier's Comput. Commun. **32**(2), 394–396 (2009)

15. Kiltz, E., Galindo, D.: Direct chosen-ciphertext secure identity-based key encapsulation without random oracle. J. Theor. Comput. Sci. **410**(47–49), 5093–5111 (2009)

16. Koo, W., Hwang, J., Lee, D.: Collusion-resistatn identity-based proxy re-encryption scheme. In: Proceedings of International Conference, Information Science and Technology, pp. 265–269 (2012)

17. Katz, J., Sahai, A., Waters, B.: Predicate encryption supporting disjunctions, polynomial equations, and inner products. In: Smart, N.P. (ed.) EUROCRYPT 2008. LNCS, vol. 4965, pp. 146–162. Springer, Heidelberg (2008)

18. Rhee, H.S., Park, J.H., Susilo, W., Lee, D.H.: Improved searchable public key encryption with designated tester. In: Proceedings of ASIACCS, pp. 376–379 (2009)

19. Rhee, H.S., Park, J.H., Susilo, W., Lee, D.H.: Trapdoor security in a searchable public-key encryption scheme with a designated tester. J. Syst. Softw. **83**(5), 763–771 (2010)

20. Seo, J.H., Kobayashi, T., Ohkubo, M., Suzuki, K.: Anonymous hierarchical identity-based encryption with constant size ciphertexts. In: Jarecki, S., Tsudik, G. (eds.) PKC 2009. LNCS, vol. 5443, pp. 215–234. Springer, Heidelberg (2009)

21. Shen, E., Shi, E., Waters, B.: Predicate privacy in encryption systems. In: Reingold, O. (ed.) TCC 2009. LNCS, vol. 5444, pp. 457–473. Springer, Heidelberg (2009)

On Partitioning Secret Data Based on Concept of Functional Safety

Seira Hidano[(✉)] and Shinsaku Kiyomoto

KDDI R&D Laboratories, Inc., 2-1-15 Ohara,
Fujimino-shi, Saitama 356-8502, Japan
se-hidano@kddilabs.jp

Abstract. It is frequently reported that large volumes of secret data stored online, such as passwords and PINs, leak out. Since most of these incidents resulted from potential vulnerabilities, such as human error, bugs and intentional misconduct, it was not easy to eliminate the underlying causes. In this paper, we focus on the concept of functional safety where the goal is to ensure that systems work correctly in a worst case scenario, such as in the situations referred to above. Our goal is to minimize the impact of information leakage. In this paper, we first present some metrics for evaluating the security of a cloud system where the secret data of several users have been compromised. We also propose a partitioning method to store secret data on the cloud system more securely, thereby making it possible to diminish the impact on the secret data of other users.

Keywords: Functional safety · Database partitioning · Renyi entropy · Guessing difficulty

1 Introduction

In recent years, there have been frequent incidents where secret data stored online, such as passwords and PINs, have leaked out, and then there have been a number of reports of damage from misuse of compromised information. However, most of these incidents were due to potential vulnerabilities, such as human error, bugs and intentional misconduct. It is therefore not easy to eliminate the underlying causes. Accordingly, it is considered extremely difficult to preclude all the risks related to information leakage. This paper therefore focuses on the concept of functional safety where the goal is to ensure that systems work correctly even in a worst case scenario. In other words, assuming that information leakage actually occurs, we plan to resolve these problems by establishing a method that minimizes the impact on systems. In particular, the following case is dealt with in this paper since many services are developed on cloud systems.

Several physical servers are virtually unified under a cloud system so there is a high possibility that incidents may occur involving more than one server. For instance, if bugs are found on one server, an adversary would aim at this server,

© Springer International Publishing Switzerland 2016
H. Kim and D. Choi (Eds.): WISA 2015, LNCS 9503, pp. 110–121, 2016.
DOI: 10.1007/978-3-319-31875-2_10

and also if the administrators are different for each server, one administrator may act dishonestly. If the potential vulnerabilities are obvious, secret data from a number of users will be compromised. It makes no sense to encrypt secret data in cases when administrator authorities are abused and when the administrator becomes involved in dishonest activity. Soon after information leakage is discovered, affected users may change the secret information, but other users may not be willing to do so because they use the same secret information for several services. There are also several types of information that cannot be changed, such as biometric information. To make matters worse, some secret data such as passwords, biometric information and physical sources are not uniformly distributed (such data are referred to as non-uniform data below) [4]. Although it is not easy to model non-uniformity, if secret data from some users are known, it would be possible to estimate the bias of secret data from other users because the statistical properties are similar. By using the bias, adversaries can execute their attacks more effectively than by brute-force attacks. In this paper, we discuss a method that minimizes the effects on the secret data of the remaining users, assuming that numerous secret data from several users are compromised.

For related work based on the concept of functional safety in the field of security, there has been some research on leakage-resilient cryptography, in which it is assumed that any information about other secret information is obtained illicitly by attacks such as side-channel attacks [1,5]. In these studies, the leakage model is constructed with leakage information $f(X)$ where X is secret information and f is a leakage function, in order to prove that cryptographic primitives are sufficiently secure even though secret information has been compromised. However, those models consider only the case when partial bits of secret information are compromised and do not assure security in the situation assumed in this paper, where large volumes of secret data are leaked from the system.

Differential privacy [6] also falls into a category of studies that examine the concept of functional safety. In this model, it is assumed that the adversary guesses values of a targeted database D_1 by using another database D_2 that differs by one element at most. The concept is formally defined as the difference between the probability that values will occur from D_1 and the probability that the adversary can guess the same values with D_2. Our model is considered to be a variation of this model if D_1 and D_2 are regarded as the remaining secret data and the leaked data, respectively. However, in most of studies related to differential privacy, D_2 is not regarded as secret data per se but the processed data, and so envisaged attack models and the countermeasures are not suitable for our model.

In this paper, we first present metrics for evaluating the security of the system from which large volumes of secret data have been leaked (see Sect. 3). There have been several metrics concerning the difficulty of guessing the secret information using non-uniformity [2,3]. These metrics are defined by only the probability distribution of secret data stored in a target system, which means the adversary is fully acquainted with this distribution. However, even if some secret data are compromised, it is not easy to guess the complete distribution of the remaining secret data. We redefine the above metrics while distinguishing the target distribution of secret data and the distribution the adversary can know. We also explain how to enhance security in terms of the redefined metrics. Moreover, we propose a partitioning method to store secret data on a cloud system more securely under the concept of functional safety (see Sect. 4). This method is developed on the basis of redefined quadratic Renyi entropy and makes it possible to diminish the impact on the secret data of other users when the secret data from some users are leaked. The usability of our partitioning method is demonstrated through simulations in Sect. 5.

2   Preliminaries

The definitions of Renyi entropy and Euclidean distance between random variables are explained.

Renyi Entropy. Let X be a random variable on a discrete set $\mathcal{X}$. The quadratic Reny entropy [8] of X is defined as:

$$H_\alpha(X) = \frac{1}{1-\alpha} \log \sum_{x \in \mathcal{X}} p(x)^\alpha, \tag{1}$$

where $p(x)$ is a probability mass function (PMF) of X. Note that the base of the logarithm is 2 throughout this paper.

Euclidean Distance. Let X and Y be random variables on a discrete set $\mathcal{X}$. The Euclidean distance between random variables is defined as:

$$D(X,Y) = \left[\sum_{x \in \mathcal{X}} d_x(X,Y)^2 \right]^{\frac{1}{2}}, \tag{2}$$

where $p(x)$ and $q(x)$ are PMFs of X and Y, respectively, and $d_x(X,Y) = p(x) - q(x)$. Here, assume that $|\mathcal{X}| = 2^n$ and $H_2(X) = r$. If $q(x)$ is a uniform distribution, the Euclidean distance between X and Y can be written as:

$$E(X) = \left(2^{-r} - 2^{-n} \right)^{\frac{1}{2}}. \tag{3}$$

3   Security Analysis

This section analyses the security in the case when large volume of secret data are compromised from the system. If the secret data from some users are leaked from the system, this leakage will wreak havoc on the other users from which secret data does not leak out, as mentioned in Sect. 1.

   In this section, we first present the concept of attacks using the compromised secret data and provide three concrete metrics to evaluate the attacks and new security notions. We also discuss how to enhance the security of the system in terms of these metrics.

3.1 Attack Model

Let us consider an adversary who obtains secret data from some users and who guesses secret data of other users in the same system. The adversary seeks to estimate the distribution of secret data from other users by taking advantage of statistical properties of obtained data because his/her attack can be executed more effectively by using the estimated distribution as compared to brute-force attacks. In this paper, let $p(x)$ and $q(x)$ be the probability distribution of the target secret data and the one that adversary estimates, respectively. Additionally, we assume that the target system has two inputs and one output. One input is for an identifier to specify a user, and the other is for secret data. The system conducts some processes using the secret data and outputs some result. The user who inputs the secret data can confirm from the output whether the secret data was correct or not. In our model, the adversary chooses a user from which secret data are not leaked, guesses the secret data while using $q(x)$ and inputs the guessed data to the system as secret data from the user. The attack is successful if the guessed data operate as the correct secret data.

3.2 Metrics and Security Notions

There have been several metrics for attacks based on the probability distribution, and these metrics are classified into two classes, which are known as Renyi entropy and α-guesswork [2]. In this paper, we focus on quadratic Renyi entropy and min-entropy, which are variants of Renyi entropy, and guessing entropy, which is the guesswork with $\alpha = 1$. This is because only quadratic Renyi entropy and min-entropy can be related to practical attacks in all variants of Renyi entropy. Also, since the variants of α-guesswork except guessing entropy take account of scenarios where attacks end in failure, these metrics are not suitable for our attack model. However, the above three metrics are defined under the assumption that the adversary knows the complete distribution of the target secret data. It is not easy to fully estimate the distribution even though the adversary has data with similar properties. We redefine the above three metrics taking into account the difference between the distribution of the target secret data and the distribution the adversary can know.

Quadratic Renyi Entropy. Quadratic Renyi entropy $H_2(X)$ is often used as a metric of coincidence. In the attack model on $H_2(X)$, however, it is assumed that both the target user and the adversary choose secret data at random according to the same distribution $p(x)$. Here, if the adversary randomly chooses secret data according to $q(x)$, this metric can be written as follows:

$$H_2'(X) = -\log \sum_{x \in \mathcal{X}} p(x)q(x). \tag{4}$$

If an adversary having no knowledge guesses secret data that the target user chooses, that is, if $q(x)$ is a uniform distribution over $\mathcal{X}$, Eq. (4) can be represented by the Renyi entropy for $\alpha = 0$: $H_2'(X) = -\log \sum_{x \in \mathcal{X}} p(x) \cdot \frac{1}{|\mathcal{X}|} = -\log \frac{1}{|\mathcal{X}|} = H_0(X)$. Even though $q(x)$ is not a uniform distribution, if the system achieves the same level of security as in the case when the adversary executes brute-force attacks, the system is considered sufficiently secure in terms of the attack model on $H_2'(X)$.

Definition 1 (H_2'-secure). *A system is H_2'-secure if $H_2'(X) \geq H_0(X)$.*

Min-entropy. Let us consider the attack model on min-entropy. It is assumed that adversary only uses the value x such that $p(x)$ is the greatest over $\mathcal{X}$ and attempts to crack secret data of an arbitrary user. So if the adversary uses value x such that $q(x)$ is the greatest, this metric can be written as follows:

$$H_\infty'(X) = -\log p(\arg \max_{x \in \mathcal{X}} q(x)). \tag{5}$$

If $q(x)$ is a uniform distribution, the adversary has no alternative but to choose value x at random. In this case, $H_\infty'(X)$ is also represented by $H_0(X)$. We thus have the following definition as with the discussion on $H_2'(X)$.

Definition 2 (H_∞'-secure). *A system is H_∞'-secure if $H_\infty'(X) \geq H_0(X)$.*

Guessing Entropy. In the attack model on guessing entropy, the adversary attempts to crack the secret data of a particular user continuously by choosing value x in decreasing order of $p(x)$. The guessing entropy is defined as the expected value of the number i of trials. Assuming that the adversary conducts this attack according to the order of $q(x)$, the metric can be written as follows:

$$G'(X) = \sum_{x_i \in \mathcal{X}} i \cdot p(x_i), \tag{6}$$

where $q(x_1) \geq \ldots \geq q(x_i) \geq \ldots \geq q(x_{2^n})$. If $q(x)$ is a uniform distribution, the guessing entropy is given by $G'(X) = \sum_{x_i \in \mathcal{X}} i \cdot \frac{1}{|\mathcal{X}|} = \frac{1+|\mathcal{X}|}{2}$.

Definition 3 (G'-secure). *A system is G'-secure if $G'(X) \geq \frac{1+|\mathcal{X}|}{2}$.*

3.3 How to Enhance Security

We first consider how to enhance security in terms of quadratic Renyi entropy. From Eq. (4), we intuitively know that the security varies depending on the statistical difference between $p(x)$ and $q(x)$. We use the following Lemma to discuss that more formally:

Lemma 1. *Let X and Y be random variables with PMFs $p(x)$ and $q(x)$ on $\mathcal{X}$. Let $H_2(X) = r$ and $H_2(Y) = s$. Assuming that $r \leq s$, the following inequality holds:*

$$H_2'(X) \geq -\log \left[2^{-r} - \frac{D(X,Y)^2}{2} \right]. \tag{7}$$

Proof. From $r \leq s$,

$$-\log \sum_{x \in \mathcal{X}} p(x)^2 \leq -\log \sum_{x \in \mathcal{X}} q(x)^2 \tag{8}$$

$$-\log \sum_{x \in \mathcal{X}} p(x)^2 \leq -\log \sum_{x \in \mathcal{X}} (p(x) - d_x(X, Y))^2 \tag{9}$$

$$-\log \sum_{x \in \mathcal{X}} p(x) d_x(X, Y) \leq -\log \frac{\sum_{x \in \mathcal{X}} d_x(X, Y)^2}{2}. \tag{10}$$

Hence,

$$H_2'(X) = -\log \sum_{x \in \mathcal{X}} p(x)(p(x) - d_x(X, Y)) \tag{11}$$

$$\geq -\log \left[\sum_{x \in \mathcal{X}} p(x)^2 - \frac{\sum_{x \in \mathcal{X}} d_x(X, Y)^2}{2} \right]. \tag{12}$$

The Lemma 1 indicates that if the Euclideanean distance between $p(x)$ and $q(x)$ can be made larger, the security is enhanced in terms of quadratic Renyi entropy. Furthermore, we see from the Lemma 1 that $D(X, Y)^2 \geq 2E(X)^2$ is a sufficient condition to satisfy $H_2'(X) \geq H_0(X)$, and the following theorem holds:

Theorem 1. *A system is H_2'-secure when $r \leq s$ and $D(X, Y)^2 \geq 2E(X)^2$.*

On the other hand, security in terms of min-entropy and guessing entropy is improved provided the one quadratic Renyi entropy concerned can be sufficiently enhanced. Min-entropy increases if the value of $|p(x) - q(x)|$ regarding value x such that $q(x)$, as the highest among all possible values of $\mathcal{X}$, can be made larger. In the case of guessing entropy, it is clear from rearranging the inequality that the more different the ranks of probabilities of the same x are, the higher the number of trials [7]. When the Euclidean distance between $p(x)$ and $q(x)$ is sufficiently large, the value of $|p(x)-q(x)|$ is large for any value x, and consequently the ranks would differ significantly. Thus, the above requirements to enhance security in terms of min-entropy and guessing entropy are dependently satisfied by giving sufficient consideration to an increase in quadratic Renyi entropy. For this reason, we particularly focus on quadratic Renyi entropy in Sect. 4.

4   Proposed Method

We focus on a cloud system composed of two sets of storage areas (we plan to extend this method to the case of multiple sets after presenting the validity of the concept in the this paper). Secret data are partitioned into databases DB1 and DB2, and these DBs are each kept in a different storage area. As mentioned in Sect. 1, since there is a possibility that secret data from only one DB will be compromised, when secret data are partitioned into these DBs, the statistical properties of data in one DB should be made as different as possible from that in the other DB.

In this section, the preconditions of a system and an adversary are described, and an optimization problem to enhance security in terms of quadratic Renyi entropy is set on the basis of those conditions. We also produce an algorithm for partitioning secret data into DB1 and DB2.

4.1   Problem Settings

Let us consider policies to partition secret data into DB1 and DB2. First, assume the following three conditions:

1. When one DB is compromised, an adversary uses a histogram of compromised secret data as $q(x)$ of Eq. (4). In this paper, it is not assumed that the adversary would guess $p(x)$ using more complicated algorithms.
2. Our method does not degrade the security when $p(x)$ is estimated completely, as compared to the case when the secret data are randomly partitioned. Although it is assumed that the adversary does not use the complicated estimation algorithms in condition 1, this condition is also set for the worst case.
3. Secret data in either DB take values of the same set. This condition is required to prevent attacks such that the adversary chooses the secret data of which value is not included in the compromised DB.

Let $p_1(x)$ and $p_2(x)$ be histograms of secret data in DB1 and DB2, respectively, and let X_1 and X_2 be random variables according to $p_1(x)$ and $p_2(x)$, respectively. By condition 1, if DB2 is compromised, $q(x)$ is given by $p_1(x)$, otherwise, it is given by $p_2(x)$.

To uniform security levels of both DBs, let $H_2(X_1) = H_2(X_2) = r$. By Lemma 1, $H_2'(X)$ can be written as:

$$H_2'(X) = -\log\left[2^{-r} - \frac{D(X_1, X_2)^2}{2}\right].\qquad(13)$$

We see from Eq. (13) that in order to enhance security in terms of quadratic Renyi entropy taking condition 2 into account, the values of both r and $D(X_1, X_2)$ should be increased. However, the value of r cannot be more than the value in the case where the secret data are randomly partitioned since it is assumed that $H_2(X_1) = H_2(X_2)$. Thus r should be set to satisfy the following condition:

$$r = H_2(X_1) = H_2(X_2) = H_2(X),\qquad(14)$$

where X is a random variable that depends on the distribution of all the data in DB1 and DB2.

Then let $\mathcal{X}_1$ and $\mathcal{X}_2$ be sets of possible values of secret data in DB1 and DB2, respectively, and let $\mathcal{X} = \mathcal{X}_1 \bigcup \mathcal{X}_2$. In order to satisfy condition 3, we set the following condition:

$$\mathcal{X}_1 = \mathcal{X}_2 = \mathcal{X}.\qquad(15)$$

Therefore the value of $D(X_1, X_2)$ of Eq. (13) should be as large as possible under the conditions of Eqs. (14) and (15) to enhance security in terms of quadratic Renyi entropy. However, since a large increase in the secret data increases exponentially the number of combinations by which these data can be partitioned, brute-force solutions for this problem are difficult to achieve.

4.2 Partitioning Algorithm

Let $c_1(x)$ and $c_2(x)$ be the frequency of value x in DB1 and DB2, respectively. The total number of secrets taking value x is then given by $c(x) = c_1(x) + c_2(x)$. The problem set in Sect. 4.1 can be reduced to the following one:

$$\underset{p(x),q(x)}{\text{maximize}} \quad \sum_{x \in \mathcal{X}} [c_1(x) - c_2(x)]^2 \tag{16}$$

$$\text{subject to} \quad \sum_{x \in \mathcal{X}} c_1(x)^2 = \sum_{x \in \mathcal{X}} c_2(x)^2 = \sum_{x \in \mathcal{X}} \frac{c(x)^2}{4} \tag{17}$$

$$\sum_{x \in \mathcal{X}} c_1(x) = \sum_{x \in \mathcal{X}} c_2(x) = \sum_{x \in \mathcal{X}} \frac{c(x)}{2} \tag{18}$$

$$1 \leq c_1(x), 1 \leq c_2(x) \tag{19}$$

An algorithm for solving this problem is explained below.

Step 1: This step is an initialization process. N sets of secret data are partitioned into DB1 and DB2 whose sizes are equal. This process is carried out under the condition of $c_1(x) = c_2(x)$ for all $x \in \mathcal{X}$. Then $\Delta = \{\delta(x) = c(x) - 2\}_{x \in \mathcal{X}}$ is generated.

Step 2: Value x, such that the value of $\delta(x)$ is the greatest in Δ, is focused on, and $[\delta(x) - |c_1(x) - c_2(x)|]/2$ sets of the secret data taking the value are moved from DB2 to DB1.

Step 3: $[\delta(x) - |c_1(x) - c_2(x)|]/2$ sets of secret data are moved from DB1 to DB2 to satisfy Eq. (17). This move is performed using a greedy algorithm.

Step 4: Let $\delta(x) = \perp$ and update Δ. However, if the move to satisfy Eq. (17) at Step 3 could not be conducted, DB1 and DB2 revert to the states before the moves of Step 2 and Step 3 are conducted and let $\delta(x) = \delta(x) - 2$.

Step 5: The processes from Step 2 to Step 4 are repeatedly run until $\delta(x) \leq 0$ or $\delta(x) = \perp$ for all x. This process is performed according to the following conditions:

  – In Step 2, if $c_2(x) \geq c_1(x)$, secret data are moved from DB1 to DB2. In this case, at Step 3, secret data are moved from DB2 to DB1.
  – At Step 2, the secret data of x such that $|c_1(x) - c_2(x)| \geq \delta(x)$ are not moved. In this case, let $\delta(x) = \perp$ and go to the processes for next x.
  – At Step 3, only the secret data of x such that $\delta(x) \neq \perp$ are moved.

Greedy Algorithm. The greedy algorithm used in Step 2 is explained below. When e sets of secret data taking the value x are moved from DB2 to DB1, the variation in $c_2(x)^2 - c_1(x)^2$ is given by:

$$[(c_2(x) + e)^2 - (c_1(x) - e)^2] - [c_2(x)^2 - c_1(x)^2]$$
$$= 2 \cdot [c_2(x) + c_1(x)] \cdot e = 2 \cdot c(x) \cdot e. \tag{20}$$

We see from the result that when secret data taking the value x such that the value of $c(x)$ is the highest are moved, there are major variations in the value of $|\sum_{x \in \mathcal{X}} c_1(x)^2 - \sum_{x \in \mathcal{X}} c_2(x)^2|$. Thus in our greedy algorithm, secret data taking value x are moved in decreasing order of the value of $c(x)$.

Computational Complexity. We consider the computational complexity of our partitioning algorithm in a worst case scenario. The computational complexity of the greedy algorithm of Step 2 is $N/2$. Since that of Step 3 increases in proportion to the number of updates of Δ, it is $N/2$. Thus the total cost is $\mathcal{O}(N^2)$.

Application to Real System. The value of $H_2'(X)$ would vary every time a new user registers secret information or when an existing user changes it. However, this algorithm does not need to be executed every time because the variation in $H_2'(X)$ for one event would be minor. The system just has to decide whether to execute our algorithm or not with a threshold of $H_2'(X)$. The system needs to calculate the value of $H_2'(X)$ after the event such that $p_1(x)$ or $p_2(x)$ is changed. If the calculated value is less than the threshold, the system should execute our partitioning algorithm, otherwise it does not have do anything. Thereby, the load on the system will be substantially reduced as compared to each execution.

5   Experimental Evaluation

We conducted experiments on the partitioning algorithm proposed in Sect. 4.2. Three data sets were generated according to a standard normal distribution, each of which consisted of 1,000 sets of secret data. We assumed that the secret data had 32 possible values and assigned each value to 32 intervals into which range $[-3\sigma, 3\sigma]$ of the standard normal distribution was divided.

5.1   Results for Quadratic Renyi Entropy

Table 1 shows the effects on quadratic Renyi entropy from this experiment. All values in Table 1 were calculated under the assumption that DB2 was compromised. $H_2(X_1)$ means $H_2'(X_1)$ in the case where our partitioning algorithm was not applied, that is, when secret data were partitioned randomly. $H_2'(X_1)$ were calculated with Eq. (4). $D(X_1, X_2)^2$ is the square Euclidean distance between

Table 1. Quadratic Renyi entropy.

Index	1	2	3
$H_2(X_1)$	3.334	3.688	4.026
$H_2'(X_1)$	6.276	5.069	4.433
$D(X_1, X_2)^2$	0.169	0.0956	0.0278
$2E(X_1)^2$	0.136	0.0927	0.0603

Table 2. Other entropies.

Index	1	2	3
$H_\infty(X_1)$	2.75	2.76	2.99
$H_\infty'(X_1)$	7.94	8.95	4.48
$G(X_1)$	5.78	7.11	8.41
$G'(X_1)$	19.1	14.7	10.7

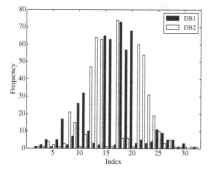

Fig. 1. Histogram of data set 1.

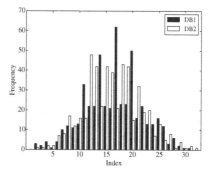

Fig. 2. Histogram of data set 3.

the histograms of DB1 and DB2, and $E(X_1)^2$ is the square Euclidean distance between the histogram of DB1 and the histogram such that each value occurs with a probability of $1/32$.

We see from Table 1 that our partitioning method was useful for enhancing security in terms of quadratic Renyi entropy since the value of $H_2'(X_1)$ was greater than the value of $H_2(X_1)$ for every data set. In particular, the greater the value of $D(X_1, X_2)^2$, the greater the difference between the values of $H_2'(X_1)$ and $H_2(X_1)$, and the more the security was enhanced. For data sets 1 and 2, the values of $H_2'(X_1)$ exceeded $H_0(X_1) = -\log \frac{1}{32} = 5$, and consequently the systems achieved H_2'-secure. However, for data set 3, H_2'-secure was not achieved. Here, see Figs. 1 and 2, which show the histograms of data sets 1 and 3, respectively. The horizontal axis shows the index of a possible value for secret data while the vertical axis shows the frequency. In Fig. 1, for almost all indexes, the frequencies were completely different between DB1 and DB2. On the other hand, in Fig. 2, frequencies were nearly equal for most indexes. Taking the values of $H_2(X_1)$ in Table 1, this value for data set 3 was greater than that for data set 1. If the value of quadratic Renyi entropy is large, variations in frequencies are minor. In this case, from Eq. (20), the number of types of variations in quadratic Renyi entropy associated with the move of one set of data between DBs are also minor. The low number of types of variations made it much more likely that Steps 2 and 3 of our partitioning algorithm could not be conducted several times because there were not enough sets of data for fine-tuning in order to satisfy the Eq. (17). Thus, as

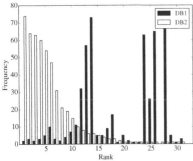 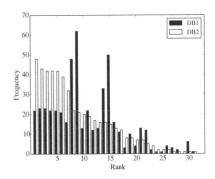

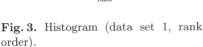

Fig. 3. Histogram (data set 1, rank order).

Fig. 4. Histogram (data set 3, rank order).

shown in Table 1, it would appear that the values of $D(X_1, X_2)$ decreased in descending order of the values of $H_2(X_1)$. From the above discussion, it can be seen that our partitioning method is particularly appropriate for non-uniform secret data.

5.2 Discussions on Min-entropy and Guessing Entropy

The security of our partitioning method is discussed here from the perspective of min-entropy and guessing entropy as redefined in Sect. 3. Table 2 shows the values for min-entropy and guessing entropy, which were calculated from the results presented in Sect. 5.1. As with Table 1, it was assumed that DB2 was compromised. $H'_\infty(X_1)$ and $G'(X_1)$ respectively mean $H_\infty(X_1)$ and $G(X_1)$ in the case where secret data were partitioned randomly. The values of $H'_\infty(X_1)$ and $G'(X_1)$ were calculated with Eqs. (5) and (6), respectively.

Taking up the values of $H'_\infty(X_1)$, we see that security was enhanced in terms of min-entropy since the value of $H'_\infty(X_1)$ was greater than that of $H_\infty(X_1)$ for every data set. In our partitioning algorithm, the data of value x, which allowed the greatest difference in frequencies, is preferentially moved by using Δ. Thereby, even though the probability of value x is the highest in one DB, it is unlikely that the probability of value x is the highest in the other DB. H_∞-secure was achieved for data sets 1 and 2 as $H_0(X_1) = 5$.

Security was also enhanced in terms of guessing entropy since the value of $G'(X_1)$ was greater than that of $G(X_1)$ for every data set. Figures 3 and 4 show the histograms such that bins of Figs. 1 and 2 are rearranged in descending order of frequency for DB2. As explained in Sect. 3, the more different the ranks of value x concerning the probability between $p(x)$ and $q(x)$, the more the value of guessing entropy. In Fig. 3, the ranks are very different between DBs, and in Fig. 4, the ranks are nearly equal except for some values with high frequency. This is why $G'(X_1)$ for data set 1 was improved more as compared to that for data set 3. G'-secure was achieved only for data set 1 as $\frac{1+|\mathcal{X}|}{2} = 16.5$.

In both cases, the security was improved more greatly for data sets 1 and 2 as compared to data set 3. This is due to the same reason as Table 1, that is, because there were few sets of data to fine-tune in data set 3. We can say again that our partitioning method is particularly appropriate for the non-uniform secret data.

6 Conclusion

In this paper, we focus on the concept of functional safety and discuss a method that minimizes the effects on the other secret data in the case when numerous secret data are compromised from the same system. Quadratic Renyi entropy, min-entropy, and guessing entropy, which were metrics for the difficulty in guessing secret information, were redefined with consideration for the difference between the distribution of secret data stored in the target system and the distribution the adversary could know. How to enhance security in terms of quadratic Renyi entropy were then discussed, and we proposed a new partitioning method for secret data stored in a cloud system with two storage areas. We observed through simulations that our partitioning method made the target system more secure in terms of not only quadratic Renyi entropy but also min-entropy and guessing entropy and was more effective for non-uniform secret data.

In feature research, we will extend the proposed method and establish a partitioning method that can be implemented in cloud systems with any number of storage areas. Furthermore, although how this can be applied to real systems was mentioned in Sect. 4.2, it still does not appear to be an elegant solution. We will thus consider new models where some secret data are rearranged dynamically according to the change in secret data and the registration of new users.

References

1. Akavia, A., Goldwasser, S., Vaikuntanathan, V.: Simultaneous hardcore bits and cryptography against memory attacks. In: Reingold, O. (ed.) TCC 2009. LNCS, vol. 5444, pp. 474–495. Springer, Heidelberg (2009)
2. Bonneau, J.: The science of guessing: analyzing an anonymized corpus of 70 million passwords. In: Proceedings of the 2012 IEEE Symposium on Security and Privacy (SP 2012), pp. 538–552 (2012)
3. Burr, W.E., Dodson, D.F., Polk, W.T.: Electronic authentication guideline. NIST Special Publication 800–63 Version 1.0.2 (2006)
4. Dodis, Y., Yu, Y.: Overcoming weak expectations. In: Sahai, A. (ed.) TCC 2013. LNCS, vol. 7785, pp. 1–22. Springer, Heidelberg (2013)
5. Duc, A., Dziembowski, S., Faust, S.: Unifying leakage models: from probing attacks to noisy leakage. In: Nguyen, P.Q., Oswald, E. (eds.) EUROCRYPT 2014. LNCS, vol. 8441, pp. 423–440. Springer, Heidelberg (2014)
6. Dwork, C.: Differential privacy. In: Bugliesi, M., Preneel, B., Sassone, V., Wegener, I. (eds.) ICALP 2006. LNCS, vol. 4052, pp. 1–12. Springer, Heidelberg (2006)
7. Hardy, G.H., Littlewood, J.E., Polya, G.: Inequalities (Cambridge Mathematical Library). Cambridge University Press, Cambridge (1988)
8. Renyi, A.: On measures of entropy and information. In: Proceedings of the 4th Berkeley Symposium on Mathematical Statistics and Probability, pp. 547–561 (1960)

Unbounded Hierarchical Identity-Based Encryption with Efficient Revocation

Geumsook Ryu, Kwangsu Lee, Seunghwan Park, and Dong Hoon Lee[✉]

CIST, Korea University, Seoul, Republic of Korea
{madeby_r,kwangsu.lee,sgusa,donghlee}@korea.ac.kr

Abstract. Hierarchical identity-based encryption (HIBE) is an extension of identity-based encryption (IBE) where an identity of a user is organized as a hierarchical structure and a user can delegate the private key generation to another user. Providing a revocation mechanism for HIBE is highly necessary to keep a system securely. Revocable HIBE (RHIBE) is an HIBE scheme that can revoke a user's private key if his credential is expired or revealed. In this paper, we first propose an unbounded HIBE scheme where the maximum hierarchy depth is not limited and prove its selective security under a q-type assumption. Next, we propose an efficient unbounded RHIBE scheme by combining our unbounded HIBE scheme and a binary tree structure, and then we prove its selective security. By presenting the unbounded RHIBE scheme, we solve the open problem of Seo and Emura in CT-RSA 2015.

Keywords: Identity-based encryption · Hierarchical identity-based encryption · Revocation · Unbounded hierarchy depth · Bilinear maps

1 Introduction

Identity-based encryption (IBE) is a kind of public key encryption (PKE) that uses any bit-string (e.g., e-mail address, phone number, or identity) as a public key of a user. Although the concept of IBE was introduced by Shamir [24], the first realization of IBE was achieved by Boneh and Franklin [4] by using bilinear maps. In IBE, a single key generation center (KGC) should issue private keys and establish secure channels to transmit private keys of users. To reduce the cost of private key generation of the KGC in IBE, the concept of hierarchical IBE (HIBE) was introduced such that the KGC delegates the key generation functionality to a lower level KGC [7,8]. After that, many IBE and HIBE schemes were suggested with additional functionalities [2,3,5,14,25,26].

To maintain a whole system securely, a revocation mechanism is absolutely necessary when a user's contract is expired or the user's private key is revealed. Boldyreva, Goyal and Kumar [1] introduced the concept of revocable IBE (RIBE) and proposed a scalable RIBE scheme by combining a fuzzy IBE scheme of Sahai Waters [20] and a tree based revocation system of Naor et al. [16]. In RIBE, each user initially obtains a private key from a KGC, and then the KGC periodically

© Springer International Publishing Switzerland 2016
H. Kim and D. Choi (Eds.): WISA 2015, LNCS 9503, pp. 122–133, 2016.
DOI: 10.1007/978-3-319-31875-2_11

publishes an update key for non-revoked users. If a user is not revoked in the update key, then he can derive a decryption key from his private key and the update key. After the work of Boldyreva et al., many different RIBE scheme were proposed [11,15,17,22].

It is a natural research direction to devise an efficient revocation mechanism for HIBE. By following the design strategy of Boldyreva et al. [1], Seo and Emura proposed efficient revocable HIBE (RHIBE) schemes [21,23]. In RHIBE, a KGC can delegate the key generation functionality and the revocation functionality to a lower level KGC or a user. Seo and Emura [21] first proposed a concrete RHIBE scheme by combining the HIBE scheme of Boneh and Boyen and a binary tree structure. After that, they also proposed new efficient RHIBE schemes by using the history-free update approach to reduce the size of private keys [23]. Although they proposed efficient RHIBE schemes, their RHIBE schemes have the inherent limitation that the size of public parameters linearly grows to the maximum hierarchy depth. Thus, they left it as an interesting problem to devise an unbounded RHIBE scheme [23].

1.1 Our Contributions

In this paper, we give an answer to the above problem of Seo and Emura by presenting an unbounded RHIBE scheme. Before presenting an unbounded RHIBE scheme, we first propose an HIBE scheme with no limitation in maximum hierarchy, denoted by unbounded HIBE. Our unbounded HIBE scheme is derived from the key-policy attribute-based encryption (KP-ABE) scheme of Rouselakis and Waters [18]. We use the observation that an HIBE scheme can be derived from a KP-ABE scheme if the KP-ABE scheme can be modified to support the delegation of private key generation. We prove the selective security of our unbounded HIBE scheme under the q-type assumption introduced by Rouselakis and Waters. Next, we propose an unbounded RHIBE scheme by combining our unbounded HIBE scheme and a tree-based revocation system. Mainly we follow the design strategy of the previous RHIBE scheme of Seo and Emura [23]. To prove the selective security of our RHIBE scheme, we show that our RHIBE scheme is selectively secure if our HIBE scheme is selectively secure.

1.2 Related Work

IBE and Its Extensions. As mentioned before, the concept of IBE was introduced by Shamir [24] where a public key can be the identity string of a user such as an e-mail address. The first IBE scheme that uses bilinear maps was constructed by Boneh and Franklin [4]. Since the pioneering work of Boneh and Franklin, many IBE schemes were proposed in bilinear maps [2,6,25]. The notion of IBE has been extended to several other encryption systems like HIBE [8], attribute-based encryption (ABE), predicate encryption (PE), and functional encryption (FE). The concept of HIBE was introduced by Horwitz and Lynn [8] and it additionally provides a key delegation mechanism by which the private key of a low level user is generated by a upper level user. After the introduction of HIBE, many HIBE schemes with different properties have been suggested in bilinear maps [2,3,5,7,12,13,26]. One inherent limitation of previous HIBE schemes is that the maximum hierarchy depth should be fixed in the setup phase. To remove this restriction, an unbounded HIBE scheme was proposed by Lewko and Waters [14].

Revocation in IBE. Boneh and Franklin [4] proposed the first IBE scheme that supports key revocation, but their scheme is not scalable since each user periodically connects to a KGC to receive a new private key. Boldyreva et al. [1] proposed a scalable RIBE scheme by combining the fuzzy IBE scheme of Sahai and Waters [20] and the tree based revocation system of Naor et al. [16]. Libert and Vergnaud [15] proposed first fully secure RIBE scheme by using a fully secure IBE scheme that is a variant of the Waters IBE [25]. Seo and Emura [22] refined the security model of RIBE by considering decryption key exposure attacks and proposed a fully secure RIBE scheme in their security model. To improve the efficiency of RIBE, Lee et al. [11] proposed a new RIBE scheme based on the subset difference method and Park et al. [17] proposed an RIBE scheme from multilinear maps. An efficient RHIBE scheme was first presented by Seo and Emura [21] and its improvement was also proposed by using the history-free update approach [23]. In RIBE, revoked user on the time T is still accessible to ciphertext that were encrypted before the time T in the cloud storage environment. To solve this problem, Sahai et al. [19] introduced revocable storage ABE (RS-ABE) for cloud storage by using the idea of RIBE. The improved RS-ABE schemes were presented in [9,10].

2   Preliminaries

In this section, we introduce the complexity assumption for our schemes and define the syntax of RHIBE and its security model.

2.1   Bilinear Groups

Let $\mathbb{G}$ and $\mathbb{G}_T$ be multiplicative cyclic groups of prime order p and g be a generator of $\mathbb{G}$. The bilinear map $e : \mathbb{G} \times \mathbb{G} \to \mathbb{G}_T$ has the following properties: (1) Bilinearity: for all $u, v \in \mathbb{G}$ and for all $a, b \in \mathbb{Z}_p$, $e(u^a, v^b) = e(u, v)^{ab}$. (2) Non-degeneracy: for generator $g \in \mathbb{G}$, $e(g, g) \neq 1_{\mathbb{G}_T}$, where $1_{\mathbb{G}_T}$ is an identity element in $\mathbb{G}_T$. Furthermore, we assume the existence of a group generator algorithm $\mathcal{G}$ which takes as input a security parameter λ and outputs a bilinear group $(p, \mathbb{G}, \mathbb{G}_T, e)$ where p is a prime of $\Theta(\lambda)$ bits.

2.2   Complexity Assumption

For the proof of our schemes, we introduce the q-RW2 assumption of Rouselakis and Waters [18] that was used to prove the security of their attribute-based encryption schemes.

Assumption 1 (q-RW2, [18]). *Let $(p, \mathbb{G}, \mathbb{G}_T, e)$ be a description of the bilinear groups of prime order p. Let g be a random generator of $\mathbb{G}$. The q-RW2 assumption is that if the challenge tuple*

$$D = \Big((p, \mathbb{G}, \mathbb{G}_T, e), g, g^x, g^y, g^z, g^{(xz)^2}, \{g^{b_i}, g^{xzb_i}, g^{xz/b_i}, g^{x^2 zb_i}, g^{y/b_i^2}, g^{y^2/b_i^2}\}_{\forall i \in [q]},$$

$$\{g^{xzb_i/b_j}, g^{yb_i/b_j^2}, g^{xyzb_i/b_j^2}, g^{(xz)^2 b_i/b_j}\}_{\forall i,j \in [q], i \neq j} \Big) \text{ and } Z$$

are given, no probabilistic polynomial time (PPT) algorithm $\mathcal{A}$ can distinguish $Z = Z_0 = e(g, g)^{xyz}$ from $Z = Z_1 = e(g, g)^f$ with more than a negligible advantage. The advantage of $\mathcal{A}$ is defined as $\mathbf{Adv}_{\mathcal{A}}^{q\text{-}RW2}(\lambda) = \big| \Pr[\mathcal{A}(D, Z_0) = 0] - \Pr[\mathcal{A}(D, Z_1) = 0] \big|$ where the probability is taken over random choices of $x, y, z, \{b_i\}_{i \in [q]}, f \in \mathbb{Z}_p$.

Lemma 1 ([18]). *The q-RW2 assumption holds in the generic group model.*

2.3 Hierarchical IBE

HIBE is an extension of IBE where an identity of a user is represented as a hierarchical structure such as $ID|_k = (I_1, \ldots, I_k)$ [7]. The syntax of HIBE is given as follows:

Definition 1 (HIBE). *An HIBE scheme consists of five algorithms **Setup**, **GenKey**, **Delegate**, **Encrypt**, and **Decrypt**, which are defined as follows:*

Setup(1^λ). *The setup algorithm takes as input a security parameter 1^λ. It outputs a master key MK and public parameters PP.*

GenKey($ID|_k, MK, PP$). *The key generation algorithm takes as input an identity $ID|_k = (I_1, \ldots, I_k) \in \mathcal{I}^k$, the master key MK, and the public parameters PP. It outputs a private key $SK_{ID|_k}$ for $ID|_k$.*

Delegate($ID|_k, SK_{ID|_{k-1}}, PP$). *The delegation algorithm takes as input an identity $ID|_k$, a private key $SK_{ID|_{k-1}}$ for an identity $ID|_{k-1}$, and the public parameters PP. It outputs a delegated private key $SK_{ID|_k}$ for $ID|_k$.*

Encrypt($ID|_k, M, PP$). *The encryption algorithm takes as input an identity $ID|_k$, a message $M \in \mathcal{M}$, and the public parameters PP. It outputs a ciphertext $CT_{ID|_k}$ for $ID|_k$ and M.*

Decrypt($CT_{ID|_k}, SK_{ID'|_\ell}, PP$). *The decryption algorithm takes as input a ciphertext $CT_{ID|_k}$ for an identity $ID|_k$, a private key $SK_{ID'_\ell}$ for an identity ID'_ℓ, and the public parameters PP. It outputs an encrypted message M.*

*The correctness of HIBE is defined as follows: For all MK, PP generated by **Setup**, all $ID|_k, ID'|_\ell$, any $SK_{ID|_k}$ generated by **GenKey**, and any M, it is required that*

- *If $ID|_k$ is a prefix of $ID'|_\ell$, then **Decrypt**(**Encrypt**($ID'|_\ell, M, PP$), $SK_{ID|_k}$, PP) $= M$.*
- *If $ID|_k$ is not a prefix of $ID'|_\ell$, then **Decrypt**(**Encrypt**($ID'|_\ell, M, PP$), SK_{ID}, PP) $= \bot$.*

We follow the security model of HIBE given in [14]. The exact security of HIBE is given in the full version of this paper.

2.4 Revocable HIBE

RHIBE is an extension of HIBE that provides revocation functionality [21]. The syntax of RHIBE is given as follows:

Definition 2 (Revocable HIBE). *An RHIBE scheme for the identity space* $\mathcal{I}$, *the time space* $\mathcal{T}$, *and the message space* $\mathcal{M}$, *consists of seven algorithms* **Setup**, **GenKey**, **UpdateKey**, **DeriveKey**, **Encrypt**, **Decrypt**, *and* **Revoke**, *which are defined as follows:*

Setup(1^λ): *This algorithm takes as input a security parameter* 1^λ. *It outputs a master key* MK, *an (empty) revocation list* RL, *a state information* ST, *and public parameters* PP.

GenKey$(ID|_k, ST_{ID|_{k-1}}, PP)$: *This algorithm takes as input an identity* $ID|_k = (I_1, \ldots, I_k) \in \mathcal{I}^k$, *the state* $ST_{ID|_{k-1}}$, *and public parameters* PP. *It outputs a private key* $SK_{ID|_k}$.

UpdateKey$(T, RL_{ID|_{k-1}}, DK_{ID|_{k-1},T}, ST_{ID|_{k-1}}, PP)$: *This algorithm takes as input time* $T \in \mathcal{T}$, *the revocation list* $RL_{ID|_{k-1}}$, *the decryption key* $DK_{ID|_{k-1},T}$, *and public parameters* PP. *It outputs an update key* $UK_{ID|_{k-1},T}$.

DeriveKey$(SK_{ID|_k}, UK_{ID|_{k-1},T}, PP)$: *This algorithm takes as input a private key* $SK_{ID|_k}$ *for an identity* $ID|_k$, *an update key* $UK_{ID|_{k-1},T}$ *for time* T, *and the public parameters* PP. *It outputs a decryption key* $DK_{ID|_k,T}$.

Encrypt$(ID|_\ell, T, M, PP)$: *This algorithm takes as input an identity* $ID|_\ell = (I_1, \ldots, I_\ell) \in \mathcal{I}^\ell$, *time* T, *a message* M, *and the public parameters* PP. *It outputs a ciphertext* $CT_{ID|_\ell,T}$.

Decrypt$(CT_{ID|_\ell,T}, DK_{ID'|_k,T'}, PP)$: *This algorithm takes as input a ciphertext* $CT_{ID|_\ell,T}$, *a decryption key* $DK_{ID'|_k,T'}$ *and the public parameters* PP. *It outputs an encrypted message* M.

Revoke$(ID|_k, T, RL_{ID|_{k-1}}, ST_{ID|_{k-1}})$: *This algorithm takes as input an identity* $ID|_k$, *revocation time* T, *the revocation list* $RL_{ID|_{k-1}}$, *and the state* $ST_{ID|_{k-1}}$. *It outputs the updated revocation list* $RL_{ID|_{k-1}}$.

The correctness of RHIBE is defined as follows: For all MK, RL, ST, *and* PP *generated by* **Setup**(1^λ), SK_{ID} *generated by* **GenKey**(ID, MK, ST, PP) *for any* ID, $UK_{T,R}$ *generated by* **UpdateKey**(T, RL, MK, ST, PP) *for any* T *and* RL, $CT_{ID',T'}$ *generated by* **Encrypt**(ID', T', M, PP) *for any* ID', T', *and* M, *it is required that*

- *If* $ID|_k$ *is not revoked on time* T, *then* **DeriveKey**$(SK_{ID|_k}, UK_{ID|_{k-1},T}, PP) = DK_{ID|_k,T}$.
- *If* $ID|_k$ *is revoked on time* T, *then* **DeriveKey**$(SK_{ID|_k}, UK_{ID|_{k-1},T}, PP) = \perp$.
- *If* $(ID' = ID) \wedge (T' = T)$, *then* **Decrypt**$(CT_{ID',T'}, DK_{ID,T}, PP) = M$.
- *If* $(ID' \neq ID) \vee (T' \neq T)$, *then* **Decrypt**$(CT_{ID',T'}, DK_{ID,T}, PP) = \perp$.

The security model of RHIBE was introduced by Seo and Emura [21]. We follow the stronger security model of Seo and Emura [23] that considers decryption key exposure attackers and inside attackers. The detailed definition of the security model is given as follows:

Definition 3 (Selective IND-CPA Security). *The selective IND-CPA security of RHIBE is defined in terms of the following experiment between a challenger $\mathcal{C}$ and a PPT adversary $\mathcal{A}$:*

1. ***Init:*** $\mathcal{A}$ *initially submits a challenge identity $ID^*|_k = (I_1^*, \ldots, I_k^*)$ and challenge time T^*.*
2. ***Setup:*** $\mathcal{C}$ *runs **Setup**(1^λ) and obtains a master key MK, a revocation list RL, a state information ST, and public parameters PP. It keeps MK, RL, ST to itself and gives PP to $\mathcal{A}$.*
3. ***Phase 1:*** $\mathcal{A}$ *adaptively requests a polynomial number of queries. These queries are processed as follows:*
   - *If it is a private key query for an identity $ID|_k$, then $\mathcal{C}$ gives a private key $SK_{ID|_k}$ and a state information $ST_{ID|_k}$ by running **GenKey**$(ID|_k, ST_{ID|_{k-1}}, PP)$. There is a restriction: If $\mathcal{A}$ requested a private key query for $ID^*|_{k'}$ that is a prefix of $ID^*|_k$ where $k' \leq k$, then the identity $ID^*|_{k'}$ or one of its ancestors should be revoked at some time T where $T \leq T^*$.*
   - *If it is an update key query for an identity $ID|_{k-1}$ and time T, then $\mathcal{C}$ gives an update key $UK_{ID|_{k-1},T}$ by running **UpdateKey**$(T, RL_{ID|_{k-1}}, DK_{ID|_{k-1}}, ST_{ID|_{k-1}}, PP)$.*
   - *If it is a decryption key query for an identity $ID|_k$ and time T, then $\mathcal{C}$ gives a decryption key $DK_{ID|_k,T}$ by running **DeriveKey**$(SK_{ID|_k}, UK_{ID|_{k-1}}, PP)$. There is a restriction: $\mathcal{A}$ cannot request a private key query for the challenge identity $ID^*|_k$ or its ancestors on the challenge time T^*.*
   - *If it is a revocation query for an identity $ID|_k$ and time T, then $\mathcal{C}$ updates a revocation list $RL_{ID|_{k-1}}$ by running **Revoke**$(ID|_k, T, RL_{ID|_{k-1}}, ST_{ID|_{k-1}})$. There is a restriction: $\mathcal{A}$ cannot request a revocation query for $ID|_k$ on time T if he already requested an update key query for $ID|_k$ on time T.*

   Note that we assume that update key, decryption key, and revocation queries are requested in non-decreasing order of time.
4. ***Challenge:*** $\mathcal{A}$ *submits two challenge messages M_0^*, M_1^* with the same length. $\mathcal{C}$ flips a random coin $\mu \in \{0,1\}$ and gives the challenge ciphertext $CT_{ID^*|_k,T^*}$ to $\mathcal{A}$ by running **Encrypt**$(ID^*|_\ell, T^*, M_\mu^*, PP)$.*
5. ***Phase 2:*** $\mathcal{A}$ *may continue to request a polynomial number of queries subject to the same restrictions as before.*
6. ***Guess:*** *Finally, $\mathcal{A}$ outputs a guess $\mu' \in \{0,1\}$, and wins the game if $\mu = \mu'$.*

The advantage of $\mathcal{A}$ is defined as $\mathbf{Adv}_{\mathcal{A}}^{RHIBE}(\lambda) = \left| \Pr[\mu = \mu'] - \frac{1}{2} \right|$ where the probability is taken over all the randomness of the experiment. An RHIBE scheme is selectively secure under a chosen plaintext attack if for all PPT adversary $\mathcal{A}$, the advantage of $\mathcal{A}$ in the above experiment is negligible in the security parameter λ.

3   Hierarchical Identity-Based Encryption

In this section, we propose an unbounded HIBE scheme from the key-policy ABE scheme of Rouselakis and Waters [18] and prove its security.

3.1   Construction

Let $\mathcal{I} = \{0,1\}^\lambda$ be the identity space where λ is a security parameter. Our unbounded HIBE scheme is described as follows:

HIBE.Setup(1^λ): This algorithm takes as input a security parameter λ. It first runs the group generator $\mathcal{G}$ and obtains a bilinear group $(p, \mathbb{G}, \mathbb{G}_T, e)$. Let g be a generator of $\mathbb{G}$. Next, it selects random elements $g, u, h \in \mathbb{G}$ and random exponents $x, y \in \mathbb{Z}_p$. It sets $w = g^x, v = g^y, \alpha = xy$. It outputs a master key $MK = \alpha$ and public parameters $PP = \big((p, \mathbb{G}, \mathbb{G}_T, e), g, u, h, w, v, \Omega = e(g,g)^\alpha\big)$.

HIBE.GenKey$(ID|_k, MK, PP)$: This algorithm takes as input an identity $ID|_k = (I_1, \ldots, I_k) \in \mathcal{I}^k$, the master key MK, and the public parameters PP. It chooses random exponents $r_1, \ldots, r_k \in \mathbb{Z}_p$ and outputs a private key
$$SK_{ID|_k} = \big(K_0 = g^\alpha \textstyle\prod_{i=1}^k w^{r_i}, \; \{K_{i,1} = (u^{I_i}h)^{-r_i}, \; K_{i,2} = g^{r_i}\}_{i=1}^k\big).$$

HIBE.RandKey$(ID|_k, \gamma, SK_{ID|_k}, PP)$: This algorithm takes as input an identity $ID|_k = (I_1, \ldots, I_k) \in \mathcal{I}^k$, an exponent $\gamma \in \mathbb{Z}_p$, a private key $SK_{ID|_k} = (K_0', \{K_{i,1}', K_{i,2}'\}_{i=1}^k)$, and the public parameters PP. It chooses random exponents $r_1, \ldots, r_k \in \mathbb{Z}_p$ and outputs a re-randomized private key $SK_{ID|_k} = \big(K_0 = K_0' \cdot g^\gamma \prod_{i=1}^k w^{r_i}, \; \{K_{i,1} = K_{i,1}' \cdot (u^{I_i}h)^{-r_i}, \; K_{i,2} = K_{i,2}' \cdot g^{r_i}\}_{i=1}^k\big)$.

HIBE.Delegate$(ID|_k, SK_{ID|_{k-1}}, PP)$: This algorithm takes as input an identity $ID|_k = (I_1, \ldots, I_k) \in \mathcal{I}^k$, a private key $SK_{ID|_{k-1}} = (K_0', \{K_{i,1}', K_{i,2}'\}_{i=1}^{k-1})$ for $ID|_{k-1}$, and the public parameters PP. It chooses a random exponent $r_k \in \mathbb{Z}_p$ and creates a temporal delegated private key $TSK_{ID|_k} = \big(K_0 = K_0' \cdot w^{r_k}, \; \{K_{i,1} = K_{i,1}', \; K_{i,2} = K_{i,2}'\}_{i=1}^{k-1}, \; \{K_{k,1} = (u^{I_k}h)^{-r_k}, K_{k,2} = g^{r_k}\}\big)$. Next, it outputs a delegated private key $SK_{ID|_k}$ by running **HIBE.RandKey**$(ID|_k, 0, TSK_{ID|_k}, PP)$.

HIBE.Encrypt$(ID|_\ell, M, PP)$: This algorithm takes as input an identity $ID|_\ell = (I_1, \ldots, I_\ell) \in \mathcal{I}^\ell$, a message $M \in \mathcal{M}$, and the public parameters PP. It chooses random exponents $t, s_1, \ldots, s_k \in \mathbb{Z}_p$ and outputs a ciphertext
$$CT_{ID|_\ell} = \big(C = \Omega^t \cdot M, \; C_0 = g^t, \; \{C_{i,1} = g^{s_i}, \; C_{i,2} = (u^{I_i}h)^{s_i}w^{-t}\}_{i=1}^\ell\big).$$

HIBE.Decrypt$(CT_{ID|_\ell}, SK_{ID'|_k}, PP)$: This algorithm takes as input a ciphertext $CT_{ID|_\ell} = (C, C_0, \{C_1, C_2\}_{i=1}^\ell)$ for $ID|_\ell$, a private key $SK_{ID'|_k} = (K_0, \{K_{i,1}, K_{i,2}\}_{i=1}^k)$ for $ID'|_k$, and the public parameters PP. If $ID'|_k$ is a prefix of $ID|_\ell$, it outputs an encrypted message by computing $M = C \cdot e(C_0, K_0)^{-1} \cdot \prod_{i=1}^k \big(e(C_{i,1}, K_{i,1}) \cdot e(C_{i,2}, K_{i,2})\big)^{-1}$. Otherwise, it outputs $\perp$.

3.2   Security Analysis

Theorem 2. *The above HIBE scheme is selectively IND-CPA secure if the q-RW2 assumption holds.*

Due to the lack of space, we briefly sketch the proof of our HIBE scheme. At first, HIBE can be considered as a kind of KP-ABE since an attribute is corresponding to an identity and an access policy in a private key just consists of the AND gate only. Our HIBE scheme is based on the KP-ABE scheme of Rouselakis and Waters [18] and the first component K_0 of a private key in our HIBE scheme is the multiplication of every components $\{K_{\tau,0}\}$ of their KP-ABE scheme. Thus, the security proof of our HIBE scheme can be easily simulated like that of their KP-ABE scheme.

4   Revocable Hierarchical Identity-Based Encryption

In this section, we propose an unbounded RHIBE scheme by using our unbounded HIBE scheme in the previous section. To provide the revocation functionality, we basically follow the design strategy of previous RIBE (or RHIBE) schemes that use a binary tree structure [1,21,23].

4.1   KUNode Algorithm

We use the KUNode algorithm of Boldyreva et al. [1] for our RHIBE scheme.

Definition 4 (KUNode Algorithm). *This algorithm takes as input a binary tree BT, a revocation list RL, and time T. It outputs a set of nodes. If η is a non-leaf node, then the left and right child node of η is denoted by η_{left} and η_{right}, respectively. Users are assigned to leaf nodes, and **Path**(η) means the set of nodes on the path from η to the root node. If a user assigned to η is revoked on time T, then $(\eta, T) \in RL$. The algorithm is given below.*

$KUNode(BT,RL,T)$:
    $X, Y \leftarrow \emptyset$
    $\forall (\eta_i, T_i) \in RL$
        If $T_i \leq T$ then add $Path(\eta_i)$ *to* X
    $\forall x \in X$
        If $x_{left} \notin X$ then add x_{left} to Y
        If $x_{right} \notin X$ then add x_{right} to Y
    If $Y \neq \emptyset$ then add root to Y
    Return Y

When a user requests a private key to a KGC, the KGC assigns a user to the leaf node η of a binary tree BT, and generates a private key. A private key is associated with the set of nodes **Path**(η). The KGC publishes the update key for a set **KUNode**(BT, RL, T) at time T, then only unrevoked users have at least one node in **Path**(η) $\cap$ **KUNode**(BT, RL, ST). Unrevoked users can derive the decryption key combining the secret key and the update key in that node.

4.2   Construction

Let $\mathcal{I} = \{0,1\}^\lambda$ be the identity space and $\mathcal{T} = \{0,1\}^\lambda$ be the time space where λ is a security parameter. Our RHIBE scheme from our HIBE scheme is described as follows:

RHIBE.Setup(1^λ): This algorithm takes as input a security parameter 1^λ. It first runs the group generator $\mathcal{G}$ and obtains a bilinear group $(p, \mathbb{G}, \mathbb{G}_T, e)$. Let g be a generator of $\mathbb{G}$. Next, it selects random elements $u, h, u_0, h_0 \in \mathbb{G}$ and random exponents $x, y \in \mathbb{Z}_p$. It sets $w = g^x, v = g^y, \alpha = xy$. It outputs a master key $MK = \alpha$ and public parameters $PP = \big((p, \mathbb{G}, \mathbb{G}_T, e), g, u, h, w, v, \Omega = e(g, g)^\alpha, u_0, h_0\big)$.

RHIBE.GenKey$(ID|_k, ST_{ID|_{k-1}}, PP)$: This algorithm takes as input an identity $ID|_k = (I_1, \ldots, I_k) \in \mathcal{I}^k$, the state $ST_{ID|_{k-1}}$, and public parameters PP. Note that the state $ST_{ID|_{k-1}}$ contains $BT_{ID|_{k-1}}$.

1. It first assigns $ID|_k$ to a random leaf node in $BT_{ID|_{k-1}}$. Let *Path* be a path node set defined by **Path**$(ID|_k) \in BT_{ID|_{k-1}}$.
2. For each node $\theta \in Path$, it performs the following steps: It first retrieves $\gamma_\theta \in \mathbb{Z}_p$ from $BT_{ID|_{k-1}}$ where γ_θ is associated to the node θ. Note that if γ_θ is not defined, then it chooses a random exponent $\gamma_\theta \in \mathbb{Z}_p$ and stores it to the node θ. Next, it creates a partial private key $PSK_\theta = \big(K_0, \{K_{i,1}, K_{i,2}\}_{i=1}^k\big)$ by running **HIBE.GenKey**$(ID|_k, \gamma_\theta, PP)$.
3. Finally, it outputs a private key $SK_{ID|_k} = \big(\{\theta, PSK_\theta\}_{\theta \in Path}\big)$.

RHIBE.UpdateKey$(T, RL_{ID|_{k-1}}, DK_{ID|_{k-1},T}, ST_{ID|_{k-1}}, PP)$:
This algorithm takes as input time $T \in \mathcal{T}$, the revocation list $RL_{ID|_{k-1}}$, the decryption key $DK_{ID|_{k-1},T}$, the state $ST_{ID|_{k-1}}$ where it contains $BT_{ID|_{k-1}}$, and public parameters PP. Recall that $RL_{ID|_0} = RL_0$ and $ST_{ID|_0} = ST_0$. Note that $DK_{ID|_0,T} = \big(D_0 = g^\alpha (u_0^T h_0)^{-r_0}, D_1 = g^{r_0}\big)$ can be easily generated by using MK.

1. Let *KUNode* be a covering set that is obtained by running **KUNode**$(BT_{ID|_{k-1}}, RL_{ID|_{k-1}}, T)$.
2. For each node $\theta \in KUNode$, it performs the following steps: It first retrieves $\gamma_\theta \in \mathbb{Z}_p$ from $BT_{ID|_{k-1}}$ where γ_θ is associated to the node θ. It obtains $DK'_{ID|_{k-1},T} = \big(D'_0, D'_1, \{D'_{i,1}, D'_{i,2}\}_{i=1}^{k-1}\big)$ by running **RHIBE.RandDK**$(DK_{ID|_{k-1},T}, PP)$. Next, it creates a time-constrained update key $TUK_\theta = \big(U_0 = g^{-\gamma_\theta} \cdot D'_0, U_1 = D'_1, \{U_{i,1} = D'_{i,1}, U_{i,2} = D'_{i,2}\}_{i=1}^{k-1}\big)$.
3. Finally, it outputs an update key $UK_{ID|_{k-1},T} = \big(\{\theta, TUK_\theta\}_{\theta \in KUNode}\big)$.

RHIBE.DeriveKey$(SK_{ID|_k}, UK_{ID|_{k-1},T}, PP)$: This algorithm takes as input a private key $SK_{ID|_k}$ for an identity $ID|_k$, an update key $UK_{ID|_{k-1},T}$ for time T and the public parameters PP.

1. If $ID|_k \notin RL_{ID|_{k-1}}$, then it finds a unique node $\theta^* \in$ **Path**$(ID|_k) \cap$ **KUNode**$(BT_{ID|_{k-1}}, RL_{ID|_{k-1}}, T)$. Otherwise, it outputs $\perp$.
2. It derives $PSK_{\theta^*} = \big(K_0, \{K_{i,1}, K_{i,2}\}_{i=1}^k\big)$ from $SK_{ID|_k}$ and $TUK_{\theta^*} = \big(U_0, U_1, \{U_{i,1}, U_{i,2}\}_{i=1}^{k-1}\big)$ from $UK_{ID|_{k-1},T}$ for the node θ^*. Next, it creates a decryption key $DK_{ID|_k,T} = \big(D_0 = K_0 \cdot U_0, D_1 = U_1, \{D_{i,1} = K_{i,1} \cdot U_{i,1}, D_{i,2} = K_{i,2} \cdot U_{i,2}\}_{i=1}^{k-1}, \{D_{k,1} = K_{k,1}, D_{k,2} = K_{k,2}\}\big)$ and re-randomizes it by running **RHIBE.RandDK**.

3. Finally, it outputs a (re-randomized) decryption key $DK_{ID|_k,T} = (D_0, D_1, \{D_{i,1}, D_{i,2}\}_{i=1}^k)$.

RHIBE.RandDK$(DK_{ID|_k,T}, PP)$: This algorithm takes as input a decryption key $DK_{ID|_k} = (D'_0, D'_1, \{D'_{i,1}, D'_{i,2}\}_{i=1}^k)$ for an identity $ID|_k = (I_1, I_2, \ldots, I_k) \in \mathcal{I}^k$ and time T, and the public parameters PP. It selects random exponents $r_0, r_1, \ldots, r_k \in \mathbb{Z}_p$ and outputs a re-randomized decryption key $DK_{ID|_k,T} = (D_0 = D'_0 \cdot (u_0^T h_0)^{-r_0} \prod_{i=1}^k w^{r_i}, \; D_1 = D'_1 \cdot g^{r_0}, \; \{D_{i,1} = D'_{i,1} \cdot (u^{I_i} h)^{-r_i}, \; D_{i,2} = D'_{i,2} \cdot g^{r_i}\}_{i=1}^k)$.

RHIBE.Encrypt$(ID|_\ell, T, M, PP)$: This algorithm takes as input an identity $ID|_\ell = (I_1, \ldots, I_\ell) \in \mathcal{I}^k$, time T, a message M, and the public parameters PP. It first chooses random exponents $t, s_1, \ldots, s_\ell \in \mathbb{Z}_p$ and outputs a ciphertext $CT_{ID|_k,T} = (C = \Omega^t \cdot M, \; C_0 = g^t, \; C_1 = (u_0^T h_0)^t, \; \{C_{i,1} = g^{s_i}, \; C_{i,2} = w^{-t}(u^{I_i} h)^{s_i}\}_{i=1}^\ell)$.

RHIBE.Decrypt$(CT_{ID|_\ell,T}, DK_{ID'|_k,T'}, PP)$: This algorithm takes as input a ciphertext $CT_{ID|_\ell,T} = (C, C_0, C_1, \{C_{i,1}, C_{i,2}\}_{i=1}^\ell)$, a decryption key $DK_{ID'|_k,T'} = (D_0, D_1, \{D_{i,1}, D_{i,2}\}_{i=1}^k)$ and the public parameters PP. If $ID'|_k$ is a prefix of $ID|_\ell$ and $T = T'$, then it outputs an encrypted message $M = C \cdot (e(C_0, D_0) \cdot e(C_1, D_1) \cdot \prod_{i=1}^k (e(C_{i,1}, D_{i,1}) \cdot e(C_{i,2}, D_{i,2})))^{-1}$. Otherwise, it outputs $\perp$.

RHIBE.Revoke$(ID|_k, T, RL_{ID|_{k-1}}, ST_{ID|_{k-1}})$: This algorithm takes as input an identity $ID|_k$, revocation time T, the revocation list $RL_{ID|_{k-1}}$, and the state $ST_{ID|_{k-1}}$. If $(ID|_k, -) \notin ST_{ID|_{k-1}}$, then it outputs $\perp$ since the private key of $ID|_k$ was not generated. Otherwise, it adds $(ID|_k, T)$ to $RL_{ID|_{k-1}}$ and outputs the updated revocation list $RL_{ID|_{k-1}}$.

4.3 Security Analysis

Theorem 3. *The above RHIBE scheme is selectively IND-CPA secure if the underlying HIBE scheme is selectively IND-CPA secure.*

The proof of this theorem is given in the full version of this paper.

5 Conclusion

In this paper, we proposed the first unbounded RHIBE scheme using proposed HIBE and the history-free approach of Seo and Emura [23]. To achieve our scheme, we first proposed an unbounded HIBE scheme from the KP-ABE scheme of Rouselakis and Waters [18]. Our proposed RHIBE scheme makes it efficient to generate private keys in IBE for a large number of users since it allows the delegation of the key generation using a hierarchical structure among users and provides the revocation functionality. Furthermore it solves the open problem of removing the limitation on maximum hierarchy.

The security of our RHIBE scheme was proved in the selective model. It will be interesting to construct a fully secure RHIBE scheme with no limitations on maximum hierarchy. Our RHIBE scheme essentially uses the complete subtree (CS) method for revocation. We expect that the subset difference (SD) method also can be applied to our RHIBE scheme since Seo and Emura [23] also proposed an RHIBE scheme that uses the SD method by following the methodology of Lee et al. [11].

Acknowledgments. This work was supported by the National Research Foundation of Korea (NRF) grant funded by the Korea government (MEST) (No. 2010-0029121). The first two authors (Geumsook Ryu and Kwangsu Lee) equally contributed to this work.

References

1. Boldyreva, A., Goyal, V., Kumar, V.: Identity-based encryption with efficient revocation. In: Ning, P., Syverson, P.F., Jha, S., (eds.) ACM Conference on Computer and Communications Security, pp. 417–426. ACM (2008)
2. Boneh, D., Boyen, X.: Efficient selective-ID secure identity-based encryption without random oracles. In: Cachin, C., Camenisch, J.L. (eds.) EUROCRYPT 2004. LNCS, vol. 3027, pp. 223–238. Springer, Heidelberg (2004)
3. Boneh, D., Boyen, X., Goh, E.-J.: Hierarchical identity based encryption with constant size ciphertext. In: Cramer, R. (ed.) EUROCRYPT 2005. LNCS, vol. 3494, pp. 440–456. Springer, Heidelberg (2005)
4. Boneh, D., Franklin, M.: Identity-based encryption from the weil pairing. In: Kilian, J. (ed.) CRYPTO 2001. LNCS, vol. 2139, p. 213. Springer, Heidelberg (2001)
5. Boyen, X., Waters, B.: Anonymous hierarchical identity-based encryption (without random oracles). In: Dwork, C. (ed.) CRYPTO 2006. LNCS, vol. 4117, pp. 290–307. Springer, Heidelberg (2006)
6. Gentry, C.: Practical identity-based encryption without random oracles. In: Vaudenay, S. (ed.) EUROCRYPT 2006. LNCS, vol. 4004, pp. 445–464. Springer, Heidelberg (2006)
7. Gentry, C., Silverberg, A.: Hierarchical ID-based cryptography. In: Zheng, Y. (ed.) ASIACRYPT 2002. LNCS, vol. 2501, pp. 548–566. Springer, Heidelberg (2002)
8. Horwitz, J., Lynn, B.: Toward hierarchical identity-based encryption. In: Knudsen, L.R. (ed.) EUROCRYPT 2002. LNCS, vol. 2332, pp. 466–481. Springer, Heidelberg (2002)
9. Lee, K.: Self-updatable encryption with short public parameters and its extensions. Des. Codes Crypt. 1–41 (2015). http://dx.doi.org/10.1007/s10623-015-0039-9
10. Lee, K., Choi, S.G., Lee, D.H., Park, J.H., Yung, M.: Self-updatable encryption: time constrained access control with hidden attributes and better efficiency. In: Sako, K., Sarkar, P. (eds.) ASIACRYPT 2013, Part I. LNCS, vol. 8269, pp. 235–254. Springer, Heidelberg (2013)
11. Lee, K., Lee, D.H., Park, J.H.: Efficient revocable identity-based encryption via subset difference methods. Cryptology ePrint Archive, Report 2014/132.(2014). http://eprint.iacr.org/2014/132
12. Lee, K., Park, J.H., Lee, D.H.: Anonymous HIBE with short ciphertexts: full security in prime order groups. Des. Codes Crypt. **74**(2), 395–425 (2015)

13. Lewko, A., Waters, B.: New techniques for dual system encryption and fully secure HIBE with short ciphertexts. In: Micciancio, D. (ed.) TCC 2010. LNCS, vol. 5978, pp. 455–479. Springer, Heidelberg (2010)
14. Lewko, A., Waters, B.: Unbounded HIBE and attribute-based encryption. In: Paterson, K.G. (ed.) EUROCRYPT 2011. LNCS, vol. 6632, pp. 547–567. Springer, Heidelberg (2011)
15. Libert, B., Vergnaud, D.: Adaptive-ID secure revocable identity-based encryption. In: Fischlin, M. (ed.) CT-RSA 2009. LNCS, vol. 5473, pp. 1–15. Springer, Heidelberg (2009)
16. Naor, D., Naor, M., Lotspiech, J.: Revocation and tracing schemes for stateless receivers. In: Kilian, J. (ed.) CRYPTO 2001. LNCS, vol. 2139, pp. 41–62. Springer, Heidelberg (2001)
17. Park, S., Lee, K., Lee, D.H.: New constructions of revocable identity-based encryption from multilinear maps. IEEE Trans. Inf. Forensic Secur. **10**(8), 1564–1577 (2015)
18. Rouselakis, Y., Waters, B.: Practical constructions and new proof methods for large universe attribute-based encryption. In: Sadeghi, A.R., Gligor, V.D., Yung, M., (eds.) ACM Conference on Computer and Communications Security, pp. 463–474. ACM (2013)
19. Sahai, A., Seyalioglu, H., Waters, B.: Dynamic credentials and ciphertext delegation for attribute-based encryption. In: Safavi-Naini, R., Canetti, R. (eds.) CRYPTO 2012. LNCS, vol. 7417, pp. 199–217. Springer, Heidelberg (2012)
20. Sahai, A., Waters, B.: Fuzzy identity-based encryption. In: Cramer, R. (ed.) EUROCRYPT 2005. LNCS, vol. 3494, pp. 457–473. Springer, Heidelberg (2005)
21. Seo, J.H., Emura, K.: Efficient delegation of key generation and revocation functionalities in identity-based encryption. In: Dawson, E. (ed.) CT-RSA 2013. LNCS, vol. 7779, pp. 343–358. Springer, Heidelberg (2013)
22. Seo, J.H., Emura, K.: Revocable identity-based encryption revisited: security model and construction. In: Kurosawa, K., Hanaoka, G. (eds.) PKC 2013. LNCS, vol. 7778, pp. 216–234. Springer, Heidelberg (2013)
23. Seo, J.H., Emura, K.: Revocable hierarchical identity-based encryption: history-free update, security against insiders, and short ciphertexts. In: Nyberg, K. (ed.) CT-RSA 2015. LNCS, vol. 9048, pp. 106–123. Springer, Heidelberg (2015)
24. Shamir, A.: Identity-based cryptosystems and signature schemes. In: Blakely, G.R., Chaum, D. (eds.) CRYPTO 1984. LNCS, vol. 196, pp. 47–53. Springer, Heidelberg (1985)
25. Waters, B.: Efficient identity-based encryption without random oracles. In: Cramer, R. (ed.) EUROCRYPT 2005. LNCS, vol. 3494, pp. 114–127. Springer, Heidelberg (2005)
26. Waters, B.: Dual system encryption: realizing fully secure IBE and HIBE under simple assumptions. In: Halevi, S. (ed.) CRYPTO 2009. LNCS, vol. 5677, pp. 619–636. Springer, Heidelberg (2009)

Publishing Graph Data with Subgraph Differential Privacy

Binh P. Nguyen[1(✉)], Hoa Ngo[2], Jihun Kim[2], and Jong Kim[2]

[1] Division of IT Convergence Engineering, POSTECH,
Pohang, Republic of Korea
phuongbinh@postech.ac.kr
[2] Department of Computer Science and Engineering,
POSTECH, Pohang, Republic of Korea
{hoanx,jihun735,jkim}@postech.ac.kr

Abstract. The eruption of social networks, communication networks etc. makes them become valuable resources for the research community. However, the graph data owners hesitate to share their data due to the barrier of privacy leakage. In this work, we propose a new privacy definition, called subgraph-differential privacy (subgraph-DP), for graph data publishing based on the conventional differential privacy definition. Subgraph-DP is against the subgraph-based attacks by restricting the adversaries predict the true subgraph with a high confidence. We provide the mechanism that gives subgraph-DP in which noise will be added to a small set of edges to make sure that all k-vertices connected subgraphs are perturbed. The experimental results show that our perturbation mechanism preserves most of the important statistic features of graph while still guarantees privacy.

Keywords: Differential privacy · Graph pertubation

1 Introduction

In recent years, more and more data has been collected and stored on the Internet. These information are not independent but have relationships such as social networks, communication networks etc. Many applications are improved with information from the social networks such as network-based recommendation systems [9], sybil defenses [10]. However, the graph owners hesitate to publish their data because that may result in leaking the confidential information. Graph perturbation emerges as an inevitable solution and receives more attention from the research community. The re-identification on Netflix [6] is a typical example showing that simply anonymizing graph is not enough because adversaries can easily get desired information about a particular person if the personal privacy is not considered carefully in graph publishing.

Differential privacy [1] is an in-focus paradigm for publishing useful statistical information over sensitive data with the rigorous privacy's guarantees. Differential privacy has been successfully applied to a wide range of data analysis tasks

© Springer International Publishing Switzerland 2016
H. Kim and D. Choi (Eds.): WISA 2015, LNCS 9503, pp. 134–145, 2016.
DOI: 10.1007/978-3-319-31875-2_12

and found to have tight relations to other fields such as cryptography, statistics, complexity, combinatorics, mechanism design and optimization. However, it is not easy to apply differential privacy to non-tabular databases like graphs where relationships exist among separated entities.

In this paper, we propose a new privacy definition, subgraph-differential privacy, which applies the conventional differential privacy to graphs. We also introduce a mechanism satisfying subgraph-differential privacy. Finally, we evaluate the mechanism on real graphs and show that our mechanism provides strong privacy while retaining utility.

The paper is organized as follows. In Sect. 2, we summarize the related work. Section 3 reviews the basic concepts of differential privacy. In Sect. 4, we focus on our proposal, called subgraph-differential privacy, the definition and mechanism. In Sect. 5, we show our experiments and evaluate our scheme on real graphs. The conclusion and future work is addressed in Sect. 6.

2   Related Work

Several existing works try to apply the robust privacy definition, differential privacy, to graph data. There are two approaches in literature of graph data publishing: the interactive and non-interactive mechanism. In the so-called interactive setting, information is protected inside a graph handled by the data owner, and access is allowed only through an interface. In the non-interactive setting these problems are addressed by releasing once and for all the graph or its model which we think is interest to most analysts, while still preserving privacy.

In the perspective of the interactive publishing, [12] designs the node differentially private algorithms, that are, algorithms whose the output distribution does not change significantly when a node and all its adjacent edges are added/deleted to a graph. The main idea behind their techniques is to project the input graph onto a set of graphs with their maximum degree below a certain threshold. By this way, node privacy is easier to achieve in bounded-degree graphs since the insertion of one node affects only a relatively small part of the graph.

In the perspective of the non-interactive publishing, F. Ahmed et al. [4] propose a random projection approach which publishes the adjacency matrix of a given graph. This approach utilizes random matrix theory to reduce the dimensions of the adjacency matrix and achieves differential privacy by adding small amount of noise. A. Sala et al. [5] describes graph into dK-graph model. They introduce the dK-perturbation algorithm that computes the noise injected into dK-2 to obtain differential privacy. This approach becomes more efficient if dK-series is clustered.

3   Background

Differential privacy ensures that the outcome of any analysis on database is not influenced substantially by the existence of any individual. An adversary therefore hardly inference attacks on any data rows.

Definition 1. *(Differential Privacy [1]): A randomize function $\mathcal{K}$ gives ϵ-differential privacy if for all datasets D_1 and D_2 differing on at most one element, and all $S \subseteq Range(\mathcal{K})$*

$$Pr[\mathcal{K}(D_1) \in S] \leq \exp(\epsilon)Pr[\mathcal{K}(D_2) \in S] \tag{1}$$

where $Range(\mathcal{K})$ *denotes the output range of the algorithm* $\mathcal{K}$.

The most popular mechanism achieving ϵ -DP is calibrating Laplace noise to query answer. The standard deviation of noise depends on the *sensitivity* of function $\mathcal{K}$.

Theorem 1. *(Laplace mechanism [2]): For all randomize function $\mathcal{K} : D \rightarrow \mathbb{R}^d$, the following mechanism is ϵ-DP:*

$$San_{\mathcal{K}}(\boldsymbol{x}) = \mathcal{K}(\boldsymbol{x}) + (Y_1, .., Y_d) \tag{2}$$

where the Y_d are drawn i.i.d. from $Lap(\Delta\mathcal{K}/\epsilon)$

4   Subgraph-Differential Privacy

4.1   Problem

Given a graph G representing graph data, the graph owner wants to release the anonymized and possibly sanitized network graphs to commercial partners and academic researchers. Therefore, we take it for granted that attackers will access to such data.

The structural attack model on graph data is a class of attacks that adversaries somehow can collect a set of vertices and their trust relationships which are represented as edges between those vertices. [3] proposes the k-neighborhood graph attack in which adversaries possess a subgraph formed from a specific vertex and its neighborhoods in d-hops distance. Another attack assume that an adversary can collect a relatively large graph whose memberships partially overlap with the original graph [7].

In our work, we consider subgraph attack model which is similar to Neighborhood Attack Graph (NAG) in [8]. Assume that adversary can somehow collect an arbitrary connected graph made from any set of vertices. General speaking, adversary only has partial neighborhoods of a target user/vertex but he may know neighborhoods of the target's neighborhoods. Our model does not limit vertices having relationship with the target vertex.

4.2   Definition

The conventional DP limits the adversaries' ability to conclude which neighbor database the output database comes from. In context of tabular datasets, two datasets are considered as neighbor datasets if they exactly differ from one tuple. This definition is no longer appropriate in the context of graph data. We define a new neighbor graph definition in which a separated entity is a subgraph.

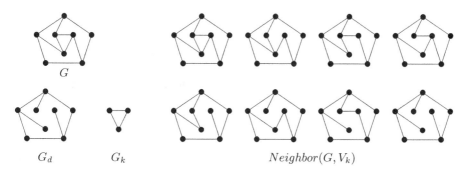

G G_d G_k $Neighbor(G, V_k)$

Fig. 1. Example of subgraph-based neighbor graphs

Definition 2. *(Subgraph-based neighbor graphs): Given graph $G = (V, E)$, the set of k vertices $V_k \subseteq V$ and $E_k \subseteq E$ is set of edges between vertices in V_k. $Neighbor(G, V_k)$ is defined as follows:*

$$Neighbor(G, V_k) = \{G_i | \forall G_k \in \mathbb{G}^k, G_i = G_d \parallel G_k\}$$

in which $G_d = G \setminus \{e | e \in E_k\}$

Intuitively, two graphs are neighbors if they are different from exactly one subgraph, given the set of k vertices V_k (Fig. 1).

Definition 3. *(Subgraph-Differential privacy): A randomized function $\mathcal{K}$: $\mathbb{G}^n \rightarrow \mathbb{G}^n$ is (k, ϵ)-subgraph-differential-privacy if given graph $G = (V, E)$; for all connected subgraph $G_k = (V_k, E_k)$, in which $V_k \subseteq V$ is a set of k vertices, $E_k \subseteq E$ is set of edges between vertices in V_k; for all pair of graphs $G_1, G_2 \in Neighbor(G, V_k)$; for all $S \in Range(\mathcal{K})$*

$$Pr[\mathcal{K}(G_1) \in S] \leq \exp(\epsilon) Pr[\mathcal{K}(G_2) \in S] \qquad (3)$$

Subgraph-DP is against subgraph-based attacks. By observing the perturbed subgraph, adversaries cannot figure out which subgraph that observed subgraph comes from with a high confidence.

Privacy parameter ϵ and k control how much privacy leaks. Parameter k is introduced as a new parameter for graph data. Obviously, k measures how large subgraph is. In fact, the graph owners do not need configure a large value of k. We suggest $k = 3$ is enough.

4.3   Mechanism

Consider a given graph $G = (V, E)$ as a complete graph. E_r is the set of real edges in G, $E_r = E$ and E_v is the set of virtual edges which do not exist in G. The underlining idea of our mechanism is very simple. The graph is perturbed by rewiring edges. Rewiring an edge means that the edge changes its state, from real to virtual and vice versa. A set of edges, including real and virtual edges, is selected such that every k-vertices connected subgraph in G is perturbed. Each edge is assigned a weight w. The range of w is $[0, 1]$. The weight measures how "*important*" that edge is. Its weight closes to 0 means that it is not *important* and we can rewire it without too much changes in the graph features. Note that the terminology *important* here is an abstract definition that we define.

Overall, the mechanism comprises three stages. In stage 1, we select a set of edges which are injected noise in the perturbation process. The execution of our mechanism needs some parameters, therefore, these parameters are configured in the stage 2. In the final step, Laplace noise is generated and injected to weight of selected edges. Noise makes a change in the *importance* of an edge to graph features toward two tendencies, namely the edge becomes more or less *important*. A pre-defined threshold θ is used to decide whether an edge is rewired or not. We will explain in detail in the rest of this section.

Algorithm 1. Subgraph-DP Mechanism

1: **procedure** PERTURBGRAPH(G,k,ϵ)
2:     $E_s = $ SELECTEDGES(G,k)
3:     $\sigma = -\frac{1}{\ln\left(\frac{2}{\exp(\epsilon_i)+1}\right)}$ $\triangleright$ ($\epsilon_i = \frac{\epsilon}{N_k}$ and $N_k = \frac{k(k-1)}{2}$)
4:     $M = $ COMPUTEMETRIC(G)
5:     $C = $ COMPUTECOST(G)
6:     $\alpha = $ SETPARAMETER(E_s,σ)
7:     $M = $ SCALE(M,α) $\triangleright$ Re-compute metric M
8:     $G' = $ ADDNOISE($G,E_s,\sigma,\theta = 0$)
9:     Return G'
10: **end procedure**

Selection Strategy. For every vertex $v \in G$, we construct Breadth First Search (BFS) on G, starting from v. Because we consider subgraphs with exactly k vertices, we only need traversal the vertices within $(k-1)$-hops distance from v. The purpose of constructing BFS with root v is that we want to select edges which have one vertex is v, and put them in E_s. Certainly, E_s should be minimum while it still guarantees the condition. However, it is not trivial task. In our work, we propose a flexible selection strategy which does not give the optimal set but it is simple and still satisfies the condition.

For each BFS, if all real edges are selected, the condition satisfies certainly. But the graph features may change significantly due to a large amount of edges are deleted without any compensation of new edges introduced in the perturbed graph. Therefore, virtual edges should be selected even though only real edges are enough. Random selecting is the most simple way that we can consider. Selecting the edges having maximum or minimum weight among candidates is another strategy. This strategy, actually, depends on which feature we want to preserve.

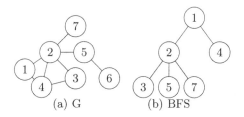

Fig. 2. An example of the edges selection. (a) The original graph G; (b) The BFS starts from 1

We introduce β, the ratio between the number of real edges and that of virtual edges when the selection performs in a particular BFS. It is noted that neither the ratio always is β in each BFS nor after the whole selection.

Figure 2 is an example of a graph G and its BFS starting from vertex 1. Every vertices, excluding 1, in BFS are candidates for selection. If the random selection strategy is used and $\beta = 1$, two edges in $\{(1,3),(1,5),(1,7)\}$ are selected randomly; for instance, $(1,3)$ and $(1,5)$ are selected. In summary, from this BFS, $\{(1,2),(1,4),(1,3),(1,5)\}$ are supplemented to E_s.

Graph Perturbation. In the final step, an appropriately pre-defined random noise will be injected into weight of each $e \in E_s$. For each edge, if the new weight is smaller than threshold θ that edge is rewired and remains unchanged if the new weight is larger than θ. The random noise follows Laplace distribution with $\mu = 0$ and σ depends on the privacy budget ϵ.

The injected noise should be large enough to guarantee subgraph-DP Eq. (3). Theoretically, we can select θ in the range of $[0,1]$, which is the range of weight. However, we fix $\theta = 0$ for following reason. Intuitively, according to the definition of subgraph-DP, when ϵ is large, injected noise becomes small, whereby the graph feature changes a little bit. Given large enough ϵ, G' should be the same as G, which means no edge or just very little edges are injected noise. If $\theta \in [0,1]$, even though given large enough ϵ, a fixed part of edges is still injected noise. This seems quite odd.

Theorem 2. *Algorithm 1 satisfies Subgraph-DP given privacy parameter ϵ*

Proof. SELECTEDGES(G,k) in line 2 guarantees that every k-vertices connected subgraph in G is perturbed as the above explanation.

Consider a set of k vertices V_k and $G_1, G_2 \in Neighbor(G, V_k)$ and $S \in Range(\mathcal{K})$.

$$Pr[\mathcal{K}(G_1) \in S] = \Pi_{i=1}^{N_k} Pr_{G_1,i}$$

in which $N_k = \frac{k(k-1)}{2}$ and $Pr_{G_1,i}$ is probability of the ith edge changing its state in G_1 to that in G'

Given p_i is probability of rewiring the ith edge.

$$p_i = Pr[w_i + noise \leq \theta] = Pr[Lap(\sigma) \leq \theta - w_i]$$

$\theta = 0$ and noise is Laplace noise $Lap(\sigma)$ with $\mu = 0$

Basically, p_i is the cumulative distribution at $(\theta - w_i)$

$$p_i = \frac{1}{2}\exp(-\frac{w_i}{\sigma})$$

For the ith edge, $p_i \leq \frac{1}{2}$ because $w_i \in [0,1]$, therefore

$$\frac{Pr_{G_1,i}}{Pr_{G_2,i}} \leq \frac{1 - p_i}{p_i} = \frac{1}{\frac{1}{2}\exp(-\frac{w_i}{\sigma})} - 1 \leq \frac{1}{\frac{1}{2}\exp(-\frac{1}{\sigma})} - 1 = \exp(\epsilon_i)$$

$$\frac{Pr[\mathcal{K}(G_1) \in S]}{Pr[\mathcal{K}(G_2) \in S]} = \frac{\Pi_{i=1}^{N_k} Pr_{G_1,i}}{\Pi_{i=1}^{N_k} Pr_{G_2,i}} \leq \Pi_{i=1}^{N_k} \exp(\epsilon_i) = \exp(\Sigma_{i=1}^{N_k}\epsilon_i) = \exp(\epsilon)$$

Parameter Setting. Given w is weight of the edge (i,j), regardless real or virtual edge, between two vertices i and j, w is computed from metric m of this edge.

$$w(i,j) = -\sigma \log(m(i,j)) \tag{4}$$

The metric $m(i,j)$ measures how strong the connection between i and j is. We introduce the normalized mutual friends as the metric.

$$m(i,j) = \frac{[\#mutual friends]}{2}(\frac{1}{deg(i)} + \frac{1}{deg(j)}) \tag{5}$$

in which $deg(i)$ is node degree of vertex i.

Note that different metrics have different specific ranges, however, the range of the weight is fixed in $[0,1]$. Therefore, we have to translate the original range of metric to a new range $[\exp(-\frac{1}{\sigma}), 1]$.

We define a *target equation* which decides which feature we want to preserve in the perturbed graph.

$$\sum_{e \in E_s \cap E_r} p_e c_e = \sum_{e \in E_s \cap E_v} p_e c_e \tag{6}$$

in which, p_e is the probability of rewiring an edge and c_e is the cost for rewiring that edge.

The cost c_e measures how much an edge impacts a specific graph feature. The target equation means that the cost for deleting the edges should be the same as the cost for adding new edges. In fact, appraising judiciously the cost c_e is not trivial in some cases. We introduce two case studies.

Case 1: Preserving Average Node Degree. It is easily seen that the cost for deleting an edge and adding an edge is the same. Therefore, the target function is re-written as follow:

$$\sum_{e \in E_s \cap E_r} p_e = \sum_{e \in E_s \cap E_v} p_e \tag{7}$$

Case 2: Preserving the Number of Triangles. Triangles play an important role in graph analysis. If an edge (i, j) is deleted or added, the decrease/increase in the number of triangles exactly equals the number of mutual friends of i and j. Therefore, we can use the number of mutual friends as the cost of deleting/adding an edge. This cost, in fact, does not assess thoroughly triangle counting. However, our experimental results prove that the number of mutual friends is accurate enough to achieve triangle counting preservation if the number of the selected real and virtual edges approximatively are the same.

$$\sum_{e \in E_s \cap E_r} p_e m u_e = \sum_{e \in E_s \cap E_v} p_e m u_e \tag{8}$$

in which mu_e is the number of mutual friends of two vertices connected by edge e.

Unfortunately, it is difficult to achieve both Eqs. (7) and (8) in practice. To guarantee the target equation has a solution, the naive method we can consider is to scale again the range of metric to new range $[\exp(-\frac{1}{\sigma}), \alpha]$ such that the target equation satisfies. The new range is also a subset of $[\exp(-\frac{1}{\sigma}), 1]$. Solving that condition, we can get ϵ_{min} such that for $\epsilon \geqslant \epsilon_{min}$, the target equation has a solution. We do not describe in detail how to compute α and ϵ_{min} here because of the space limitation.

5 Evaluation

We collect real graphs to demonstrate that our proposed privacy definition and mechanism work well in practice, guarantee privacy while is useful in analysis. We run the mechanism in both cases: preserving average node degree and preserving triangle counting and then measure the features of both the original graphs and the perturbed graphs to evaluate the differences between them. Note that we do not consider the case of preserving number of triangles in directed graphs. We implement our mechanism using NetworkX which is a Python language software package for processing complex networks.

We use the data sets that are available on https://snap.stanford.edu/data/. The data sets and their characteristics are described in the Table 1.

Table 1. Data sets and their characteristics

Data set	Type	#nodes	#edges	Average node degree	#triangles	Clustering coefficient	Power law
Facebook	Undirected	4039	88234	43.69	1612010	0.61	1.2588
Twitter	Directed	81306	1768149	43.49	-	-	1.3189
DBLP	Undirected	425957	1049867	6.62	2224385	0.63	1.4803
Enron	Undirected	36692	183831	10.02	727044	0.50	1.5127
Stanford	Directed	281903	2312497	16.41	-	-	1.4367

"-" indicates that this value cannot be specified. We do not consider the number of triangles and thus clustering coefficient in directed graphs.

5.1 Preserving Average Node Degree

Table 2 shows the average node degree of the perturbed graphs with $k = 3$ and $\beta = 0.5$. The average node degree in all cases is preserved in general. The main trend is that the average node degree of perturbed graphs is slightly higher than that of the original graph.

Table 2. Average node degree of perturbed graphs

ϵ	Facebook	Twitter	DBLP	Enron	Stanford
1	43.54	44.45	6.99	10.93	16.57
2	43.56	44.27	6.90	10.74	16.55
3	43.81	44.09	6.85	10.59	16.53
4	43.81	43.95	6.80	10.49	16.49
5	43.67	43.87	6.75	10.35	16.46

Simultaneously, we also compute other statistical graph features to verify that how our mechanism influences other features while preserving average node degree. We compute the power law exponent and the clustering coefficient.

Even though power law exponent is also preserved in this case, the clustering coefficient changes much (Fig. 3). Note that in case of preserving average node degree, we expect the number of added and deleted edges are relatively similar. Due to the cost of real and virtual edges are generally different, namely deleting a real edge tends to lose more triangles than an new edge brings in. Therefore the number of triangles decreases dramatically, especially with a small ϵ.

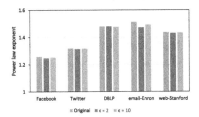 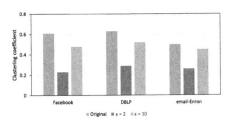

Fig. 3. Power law exponent and clustering coefficient of perturbed graphs in case of preserving average node degree

5.2 Preserving Triangle Counting

Table 3 shows the changes of the perturbed graphs in clustering coefficient. Three graphs are preserved with respect of clustering coefficient. However, all three graphs incur a relatively high ϵ_{min}.

Table 3. Clustering coefficient of perturbed graphs

ϵ	Facebook	DBLP	Enron
6	0.50	-	-
7	0.51	-	-
8	0.51	-	-
9	0.51	0.60	-
10	0.52	0.61	0.53
11		0.61	0.53
12		0.61	0.53
13		0.62	0.53
14			0.53

"-" indicates that this value
is not specified because of
ϵ_{min} or we do not measure

Similar to the case of preserving average node degree, power law exponent is also preserved in this case (Fig. 4). All graphs have slightly higher average node degree because the cost of a selected real edge in general is higher than that of a selected virtual edge because two vertices with relationship tend to have more mutual friends than two vertices without relationship. If we want to preserve the number of triangle, we have to add more new edges to make sure that the cost for adding and deleting are the same. However, we believe that the difference in the average node degree is acceptable.

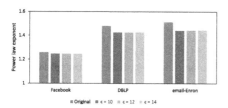 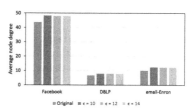

Fig. 4. Power law exponent and average node degree of perturbed graphs in case of preserving the number of triangles

6 Conclusions and Future Work

In this study, we propose a novel privacy framework, subgraph-DP, which is based on definition of differential privacy. Subgraph-DP is a robust framework for graph data where entities have relationships with others. Subgraph-DP is against subgraph-based attacks. We also propose a mechanism which gives subgraph-DP. We introduce the mechanism in two cases: preserving average node degree and preserving the number of triangles. The perturbed graph preserves most of the statistical features of graph. The database owners can appropriately adapt subgraph-DP for their purposes.

However, our work incurs some limitations. Firstly, ϵ_{min} in case of preserving the number of triangles is high, which means we cannot protect much privacy in these cases. Secondly, measuring how much an edge effects on specific graph feature is a challenge, especially with complex features such as spectral analysis and node degree distribution. Thirdly, our mechanism works well with small and medium graphs, however, with large graphs running time reaches several hours. As the future work, we plan to overcome these limitations.

Acknowledgments. We are grateful to anonymous reviewers who give us helpful advices, support us improve our work. This work was supported by Institute for Information and communications Technology Promotion (IITP) grant funded by the Korea government (MSIP) (No. H0510-14-1004, Subgraph differential privacy for graph data publishing)

References

1. Dwork, C.: Differential privacy. In: Bugliesi, M., Preneel, B., Sassone, V., Wegener, I. (eds.) ICALP 2006. LNCS, vol. 4052, pp. 1–12. Springer, Heidelberg (2006)
2. Dwork, C., McSherry, F., Nissim, K., Smith, A.: Calibrating noise to sensitivity in private data analysis. In: Halevi, S., Rabin, T. (eds.) TCC 2006. LNCS, vol. 3876, pp. 265–284. Springer, Heidelberg (2006)
3. Zhou, B., Pei, J.: Preserving privacy in social networks against neighborhood attacks. In: ICDE (2008)
4. Ahmed, F., Jin, R., Liu, A.X.: A random matrix approach to differential privacy and structure preserved social network graph publishing. ArXiv preprint (2013). arXiv:1307.0475
5. Sala, A., Zhao, X., Wilson, C., Zheng, H., Zhao, B.Y.: Sharing graphs using differentially private graph models. In: IMC, pp. 81–98 (2011)
6. Narayanan, A., Shmatikov, V.: Robust de-anonymization of large sparse datasets. In: S&P, pp. 111–125 (2008)
7. Nilizadeh, S., Kapadia, A., Ahn, Y.Y.: Community-enhanced De-anonymization of online social networks. In: CCS (2014)
8. Cheng, J., Fu, A.W.C., Fu, J.: K-Isomorphism: privacy preserving network publication against structural attacks. In: SIGMOD (2010)
9. Jamali, M., Ester, M.: TrustWalker: a random walk model for combining trust-based and item-based recommendation. In: KDD, pp. 397–406, Paris, France (2009)
10. Alvisi, L., Clement, A., Epasto, A., Lattanzi, S., Panconesi, A.: The evolution of sybil defense via social networks. In: S&P (2013)
11. Harel, D., Koren, Y.: On clustering using random walks. In: Hariharan, R., Mukund, M., Vinay, V. (eds.) FSTTCS 2001. LNCS, vol. 2245, pp. 18–41. Springer, Heidelberg (2001)
12. Kasiviswanathan, S.P., Nissim, K., Raskhodnikova, S., Smith, A.: Analyzing graphs with node differential privacy. In: Sahai, A. (ed.) TCC 2013. LNCS, vol. 7785, pp. 457–476. Springer, Heidelberg (2013)

13. McSherry, F.D.: Privacy integrated queries: an extensible platform for privacy-preserving data analysis. In: SIGMOD, pp. 19–30 (2009)
14. Le Ny, J., Pappas, G.J.: Differentially private filtering. In: CDC, pp. 3398–3403 (2012)
15. Cover, T.M., Thomas, J.A.: Elements of Information Theory. Wiley-interscience, Hoboken (2006)
16. Hay, M., Rastogi, V., Miklau, G., Suciu, D.: Boosting the accuracy of differential-lyprivate histograms through consistency. Proc. VLDB Endow. **3**(1–2), 1021–1032 (2010)
17. Chen, S., Zhou, S., Bhowmick, S.S.: Integrating historical noisy answers for improving data utility under differential privacy. In: EDBT, pp. 62–73 (2012)

An Improved Analysis of Broadcast Attacks on the GGH Cryptosystem

Maoning Wang[✉]

Key Laboratory of Cryptologic Technology and Information Security,
Ministry of Education, School of Mathematics, Shandong University,
Jinan 250100, China
wangmaoning@mail.sdu.edu.cn

Abstract. In recent years, lattice-based cryptosystems have attracted widespread attention due to the increased prevalence of cloud computing and the big data background. Among such cryptosystems, the GGH cryptosystem is an important, practice-oriented system. In addition, the concept behind this cryptosystem continues to be used in fully homomorphic encryptions and other cutting-edge designs for cryptographic applications. This paper considers the security of the GGH cryptosystem and provides a further analysis of its broadcast attacks presented by Plantard et al. in 2009. Concretely, we first correct a doubtable step in their attack, which Plantard et al. did not describe in a rigorous way; subsequently, the number of instances required in a successful attack is given and is used to explain the success of their attacks. Moreover, this paper presents a new attack algorithm via a CVP solver, which rectifies the original attack that has not been proven. Our conclusions are of theoretical and practical significance to the analysis and the design of new cryptosystems in the big data context.

Keywords: Cryptography · Information security · Lattice-based cryptosystems · GGH · Broadcast attack

1 Introduction

Lattice-based cryptosystems are a class of novel cryptographic schemes whose security is related to the hardness of solving lattice problems. These cryptosystems have numerous advantages over conventional cryptosystems. From a theoretical perspective, they have a higher theoretical security strength due to their resistance to quantum attacks, the average-case hardness of lattice problems, and so on [7,15]. From a practical perspective, they can be used in a greater number of applications, such as the fully homomorphic encryptions and the randomized multilinear maps used to construct attribute-based encryptions and witness encryptions [5,6].

This work was supported by National Natural Science Foundation of China (GrantNo. 61133013,61272091), China's 973 Program(GrantNo. 2013CB834205) and Nature Science Foundation of Shandong Province (GrantNo. ZR2012FM005).

H. Kim and D. Choi (Eds.): WISA 2015, LNCS 9503, pp. 146–158, 2016.
DOI: 10.1007/978-3-319-31875-2_13

The GGH cryptosystem, which was proposed by Goldreich, Goldwasser and Halevi in 1996 [8], is an important lattice-based cryptosystem. Its design concept originates from McEliece [16], a classic code-based cryptosystem, and its security is based on the hard lattice problem–the closest vector problem. The GGH cryptosystem also uses linear algebra operations to ensure implementation efficiency, which makes GGH a practice-oriented cryptosystem and thus attracts substantial attention from researchers in the field of cryptanalysis. The authors of GGH provided five groups of challenge parameters, corresponding to lattice instances with dimensions of 200, 250, 300, 350, and 400. In 1999, certain parameters (200–350 dimensions) were successfully attacked in the way of message recovery by Nguyen [19]. Subsequently, [11] demonstrated an attack for the 400-dimensional parameter challenge; [13] provided a more efficient 350-dimensional message recovery attack and key recovery attacks of 200–300 dimensions. Currently, GGH is generally considered to be secure at higher dimensions, but a similar structure remains popular in recent cryptographic designs. For example, in fully homomorphic encryption schemes, the component of somewhat homomorphic encryption can be observed as GGH on ideal lattices [6].

More importantly, because lattice-based cryptosystems can be used in a wide range of applications, we have to consider their potential weaknesses under different circumstances, i.e., in more application backgrounds. One such attack type is called the broadcast attack, proposed by Hastad in 1988 [9], which corresponds to the cryptosystems' weakness that appears when they are used in broadcasting, i.e., the case in which the same plaintext message needs to be sent to a plurality of users after being encrypted by different public keys for different users. In addition, the attacker's objective is to restore the plaintext message while observing the ciphertexts without knowledge about the private keys. Such a background tends to be increasingly more useful because an attacker or unauthentic server can more easily create such conditions today in cloud computing environments. Hence, it is of theoretical and practical significance to consider the security of lattice-based cryptosystems, particularly the GGH cryptosystem, under broadcast circumstances [3,12,21,24,25]. Among such type attacks, [22] developed very efficient broadcast attacks on GGH by employing a technique called lattice intersection. Concretely, they presented two attacks: one using a shortest-vector-problem-solving algorithm and one using a closest-vector-problem-solving algorithm. This is the first time that the lattice-intersection technique has been employed in cryptanalysis. The authors also performed various experiments that demonstrated that the attacks are very efficient. However, their theoretical analysis was somewhat rough and hence not sufficient to explain the good performance.

In this letter, we provide a further analysis of the broadcast attacks presented by Plantard et al. Concretely, we present a formal proof that a statement in their basic attack is actually not true, and we provide a correction to the corresponding doubtable step in their attack. In addition, after a more elaborate study of the properties of random integer lattices, the number of instances required in a successful attack is given and is shown to explain the success of their attacks.

Moreover, we also present a new attack algorithm via a CVP solver, which rectifies the original, yet-to-be-proven algorithm. Therefore, our results are of theoretical significance for the analysis and design of new lattice-based cryptosystems in the big data context.

2 Preliminaries

2.1 The Basic Concepts of Lattices and Lattice Hard Problems

We first introduce some basic knowledge about a relevant mathematical concept: lattices. More detailed descriptions can be found in the literature [17,18].

Definition 1. *Let $B = [\boldsymbol{b}_1, \ldots, \boldsymbol{b}_n] \in \mathbb{R}^{d \times n}$ be n vectors in the real space $\mathbb{R}^d$. The set*

$$L(B) = \{B\boldsymbol{x} : \boldsymbol{x} = (x_1, \ldots, x_n)^T \in \mathbb{Z}^n\} = \{\sum_{i=1}^{n} x_i \cdot \boldsymbol{b}_i : \forall i, x_i \in \mathbb{Z}\}$$

of all the integer linear combinations of the columns of the matrix B is called the lattice generated by B. If the columns of matrix B are linearly independent, B is called a basis for the lattice $L(B)$. The integer n is called the rank or dimension of the lattice. If $n = d$, then $L(B)$ is called a full-rank or full-dimensional lattice in $\mathbb{R}^d$.

Definition 2. *For any given lattice basis $B \in \mathbb{R}^{d \times n}$, the lattice's determinant $\det(L(B))$ is defined by*

$$\det(L(B)) = \sqrt{\det(B^T B)}.$$

In particular, if $B \in \mathbb{R}^{n \times n}$ is a full-rank matrix, i.e., $L(B)$ is a full-rank lattice, then $\det(L(B)) = |\det(B)|$.

The following theorem provides an upper bound of the determinant of a lattice:

Theorem 1 *(Hadamard inequality). For the lattice $L = L(B)$, $\det(L) \leq \prod_i \|\boldsymbol{b}_i\|$.*

Definition 3. *Given two lattices L_1 and L_2, their intersection is defined by*

$$L_1 \cap L_2 = \{\boldsymbol{x} : \boldsymbol{x} \in L_1, \boldsymbol{x} \in L_2\}.$$

It can be verified that the intersection of two lattices remains a lattice.

Definition 4. *For any lattice L, if a subset $L' \subseteq L$ of L remains a lattice, i.e., it can be written as a combination of linearly independent vectors with integer coefficients, then L' is called a sublattice of L. If the sublattice L' is of the same rank (or dimension) as L, L' is called a full-rank sublattice.*

Theorem 2. *If L is an n-dimensional full-rank lattice and $L' \subseteq L$ is a full-rank sublattice of L, then $\det(L')$ is an integer multiple of $\det(L)$.*

There are two main types of hard problems on lattices, SVP and CVP, which are defined as follows:

Definition 5 *(Shortest Vector Problem, SVP). For a given lattice L, find a non-zero vector v satisfying the condition that for any non-zero vector $u \in L, ||v|| \leq ||u||$.*

The earliest and best-known algorithm for solving the shortest vector problem is the LLL lattice basis reduction algorithm [20]. This algorithm runs in polynomial time and finds an approximate solution to the shortest vector problem. Such algorithms have been proven to be capable of finding a lattice vector with a length that is no greater than $2^{n \log \log n / \log n} \cdot \lambda_1(L)$, in which $\lambda_1(L)$ represents the length of the shortest lattice vector. Furthermore, if the lengths of all the lattice vectors different from the shortest one are $\geq 2^{n \log \log n / \log n} \cdot \lambda_1(L)$, the vector that the algorithm finds is the shortest one.

Definition 6 *(Closest Vector Problem, CVP). Given a lattice L and a target vector $t \in \mathbb{R}^n$, find a lattice vector v such that for any vector $u \in L, ||v - t|| \leq ||u - t||$. This problem has a variant, namely, the bounded distance decoding problem (BDD, for short): Given a lattice L and a target vector t satisfying $dist(t, L) < f(n) \det(L)^{1/n}$, where the distance $dist(t, L)$ between the target vector t and the lattice L is defined as $\min_{v \in L} ||v - t||$ and where $f(n)$ is a function of the dimension n, find the closest vector in L to t, i.e., a lattice vector v such that for any vector $u \in L, ||v - t|| \leq ||u - t||$.*

The nearest plane algorithm is an approximation algorithm used to solve the closest vector problem in polynomial time [1]. For its BDD variant, for the lattice L of dimension n, which enables preprocessing, [1] further stated that when the distance of the target to the lattice is less than $O(\frac{1}{n}) \cdot \det(L)^{\frac{1}{n}}$, the nearest plane algorithm can solve the problem; [14] combines the method to decide the range of the distance between the target vector and the lattice and the gradient descent criteria and provides an algorithm that improves the result to $O(\sqrt{\frac{\log n}{n}}) \cdot \det(L)^{\frac{1}{n}}$.

2.2   GGH Cryptosystem

Definition 7 *(GGH). Parameter Generation: Compute a "good basis" A and a "bad basis" B of a lattice L; now, $L(A) = L(B)$. Take B as public, and take A as secret.*

Encryption: To encrypt a message vector m, use the bad basis to create a random vector Br of L. Publish the encrypted message, which is the sum of the vector message with the random vector, i.e., $c = m + Br$.

Decryption: Use the good basis to find the closest vector in the lattice of the encrypted message c. The closest vector of the encrypted message c is the random *vector Br. Subtract the random vector of the encrypted message to obtain the vector message m.*

Remark 1. Here, the private key A, as the "good basis", should ensure that the ciphertext vector can be correctly decrypted, i.e., the lattice vector Br can be found. If the nearest plane algorithm is used in the decryption step to seek the lattice vector, then according to the condition for the algorithm to succeed, which is for each dimension, the lattice vector we are looking for should lie in the plane nearest to the target vector, A needs to satisfy the condition that $\frac{1}{2} \min_i \|a_i^*\| > \rho$, where ρ is the distance between the ciphertext vector c and the lattice $L(A) = L(B)$, decided by the norm of m; and a_i^* is the vertical component to the plane spanned by $a_1, \ldots, a_{i-1}$ of a_i, the i's column of A. By contrast, the "bad group" public key B should satisfy the condition that $\frac{1}{2} \min_i \|b_i^*\|$ is considerably less than ρ. In addition, the "good" and "bad" basis can also be defined by the orthogonality defect of the basis matrix.

In [8], the authors show several methods for selecting the private key A, for example, randomly selecting an $n \times n$-dimensional matrix whose elements are integers selected from $[-4, 4]$ according to a uniform distribution or setting $A = \sqrt{n}I + Q$, in which I is the unit matrix and Q is a random matrix with elements uniformly selected from $[-4, 4]$. The public key B can be constructed by performing random elementary column operations on A. Then, we can consider the public key B in GGH to be a random integer matrix.

2.3   Plantard et al.'s Broadcast Attack on the GGH Cryptosystem

The authors in [22] abstracted the objective of broadcast attacks as the following mathematical problems:

Definition 8 *(GGH challenge (Type A)). Let B be an $n \times n$-dimensional integer matrix, and $c \in \mathbb{Z}^n$ is a vector such that there exist two vectors $r, m \in \mathbb{Z}^n$ with $c = Br + m$. Then, (B, c) is called a group of GGH challenge (Type A) instance.*

Definition 9 *(GGH challenge (Type B)). Let B' be an $n \times n$-dimensional integer matrix, and $c' \in \mathbb{Z}^n$ is a vector such that there exist two vectors $r, m \in \mathbb{Z}^n$ with $c' = B'm + r$. Then, (B', c') is called a group of GGH challenge (Type B) instance.*

Definition 10 *(Broadcast attack on GGH). Given k groups of GGH challenge (Type A) instances (B_i, c_i) or GGH challenge (Type B) instances (B_i', c_i') encrypting the same message vector m, find m.*

[22] presented two types of broadcast attacks, i.e., one that uses an SVP-solving algorithm (Algorithm 1) and one uses a CVP-solving algorithm (Algorithm 2). The high efficiency of both of the attacks can be experimentally verified; however, only some of the steps in the first attack have been theoretically proven to be correct (by Theorem 3), and no concrete parameters for the efficiency, i.e., the number of instances required, have been given for the two attacks in their paper.

Input: k groups of GGH challenge (Type A) instances (B_i, c_i) encrypting the same message vector m

Output: $m \in \mathbb{Z}^n$

begin

Compute $B_i' = \begin{bmatrix} B_i & c_i \\ 0 & 1 \end{bmatrix}$;

Compute $L = \bigcap_{i=1}^{k} L(B_i')$;

Find the shortest vector of L: $\begin{bmatrix} m \\ 1 \end{bmatrix}$.

end

Algorithm 1. Broadcast Attack on GGH (Type A) Challenges

Input: k groups of GGH challenge (Type B) instances (B_i', c_i') encrypting the same message vector m

Output: $m \in \mathbb{Z}^n$

begin

Compute $B' = \sum_{i=1}^{k} B_i'$;

Compute $c' = \sum_{i=1}^{k} c_i'$;

Find the closest vector v of c' in $L(B')$;

Compute $m = B'^{-1}v$.

end

Algorithm 2. Broadcast Attack on GGH (Type B) Challenges

Theorem 3 *(Theorem 7 in [22]). Let L_1, L_2 be two lattices, and let v be a vector such that v is the shortest vector of both L_1 and L_2. Then, v is the shortest vector of the lattice $L_1 \cap L_2$,*

$$\gamma(L_1 \cap L_2) \leq \gamma(L_1), \gamma(L_2). \tag{1}$$

Here, $\gamma(L)$ is defined by $\gamma(L) = \frac{\lambda_1(L)}{\det(L)^{1/\dim(L)}}$.

3   A Correction to Plantard et al.'s SVP Broadcast Attack

In the description of Algorithm 1, Plantard et al. stated that $\begin{bmatrix} m \\ 1 \end{bmatrix}$, the vector m with one more coordinate 1 appended, is the shortest vector of intersection lattice $L = \bigcap_{i=1}^{k} L(B_i')$. However, this cannot be deduced trivially, and they did not provide a rigorous proof. In this section, we provide a formal proof that this statement is not always true. Fortunately, however, our conclusion shows that with high probability in random conditions, this statement is true.

Theorem 4. *If each element of the matrix B is a random integer independently selected from the range $[-\beta, \beta]$ and the shortest nonzero vector in the*

$(n+1)$-*dimensional lattice* $L = L(\begin{bmatrix} B & c \\ 0 & 1 \end{bmatrix})$ *is* s, *then* $s \neq \pm[m,1]^T$ *occurs with a probability not exceeding*

$$P = \frac{(2(1+||m||^2)^{1/2}+1)N(n,||m||^2+1)}{(2\beta+1)^n},$$

where $N(n,\alpha)$ *represents the number of integer points within an* n-*dimensional sphere of radius* $\sqrt{\alpha}$.

Proof. Because m satisfies $c = Br + m$ and lattice L is of the form $L = L(\begin{bmatrix} B & c \\ 0 & 1 \end{bmatrix})$, the $(n+1)$-dimensional vector $[m,1]^T$ is a vector in lattice L. Additionally, if s is a vector in lattice L, then there are an n-dimensional integer x and an integer t such that $s = \begin{bmatrix} Bx + tc \\ t \end{bmatrix}$, i.e., $s = \begin{bmatrix} Bx + t(Br + m) \\ t \end{bmatrix} = \begin{bmatrix} Bz + tm \\ t \end{bmatrix}$, where $z = x + tr$. Because s is the shortest vector in L,

$$||s||^2 \leq ||[m,1]^T||^2 = ||m||^2 + 1,$$

and as a coordinate of s, t satisfies

$$t^2 \leq ||m||^2 + 1. \tag{2}$$

Let us denote $Bz + tm$ by u; then, $||u|| \leq ||s||$. Consider the case in which $s \neq \pm[m,1]^T$; then, for t, we have the following two cases.

Case 1: $t = 0$. Because s is nonzero, we have $u \neq 0$. Then, $Bz = u$, i.e.,

$$Bx = u. \tag{3}$$

Therefore, for every possible u, if (3) has integer solutions, it has a unique nonzero solution x, where W.L.O.G., we can assume that $x_1 \neq 0$. Hence, for a group of fixed u, x, consider each row $b_{i1}x_1 + \cdots + b_{in}x_n = u_i$ of $Bx = u$, i.e.,

$$b_{i1}x_1 = u_i - (b_{i2}x_1 + \cdots + b_{in}x_n). \tag{4}$$

For randomly selected $b_{i2}, \cdots, b_{in}$, there is at most 1 value that can be taken as b_{i1} independent with these $b_{i2}, \cdots, b_{in}$ such that (4) holds in the range $[-\beta, \beta]$. Then, for the random elements in B, each row in (3) holds with a probability not exceeding $\frac{1}{2\beta+1}$, and all the rows in (3) hold with a probability not exceeding $\frac{1}{(2\beta+1)^n}$. According to $||u||^2 \leq ||s||^2 \leq ||m||^2 + 1$, the number of ways to choose u is $N(n,||m||^2+1)$. In other words, Case 1 occurs with a probability of less than

$$\frac{N(n,||m||^2+1)}{(2\beta+1)^n}.$$

Case 2: $t \neq 0$. First, we can conclude that $u - tm \neq 0$. Otherwise, we have $u = tm$. Then, if $t = \pm 1$, we obtain $s = \pm[m,1]^T$, which is not the condition we consider; if $|t| > 1$, then $||\boldsymbol{u}|| > ||\boldsymbol{m}||$, and $||\boldsymbol{s}|| > ||[\boldsymbol{m}, 1]^T||$, which contradicts the condition that $\boldsymbol{s}$ is the nonzero shortest vector. Now, for a given group of $\boldsymbol{u}$, t, if $B\boldsymbol{z} = \boldsymbol{u} - t\boldsymbol{m}$ has solutions, it has a nonzero solution. Therefore, similar to Case 1, we can see that $B\boldsymbol{z} = \boldsymbol{u} - t\boldsymbol{m}$ holds with $\leq \frac{1}{(2\beta+1)^n}$. According to (2), there are $2(1 + ||\boldsymbol{m}||^2)^{1/2}$ ways to choose t. Because $||\boldsymbol{u}||^2 \leq ||\boldsymbol{m}||^2 + 1$, there are $N(n, ||\boldsymbol{m}||^2 + 1)$ ways to choose $\boldsymbol{u}$; in other words, Case 2 occurs with a probability of less than

$$\frac{2(1 + ||\boldsymbol{m}||^2)^{1/2}N(n, ||\boldsymbol{m}||^2 + 1)}{(2\beta + 1)^n}.$$

Thus, we obtain the conclusion in the theorem.   □

Remark 2. Theorem 4 shows that, for each lattice $L(\begin{bmatrix} B_i & c_i \\ 0 & 1 \end{bmatrix})$, $\begin{bmatrix} \boldsymbol{m} \\ 1 \end{bmatrix}$ is its shortest nonzero vector with a probability of at least $1 - P$. We can conclude from the estimation of $N(n, \alpha)$ in [2,23] and GGH's parameter setting that P is exponentially small. It is also easy to see that $\begin{bmatrix} \boldsymbol{m} \\ 1 \end{bmatrix}$ is the shortest nonzero vector in the intersection lattice $L = \bigcap_{i=1}^k L(B_i')$ when it is the shortest nonzero vector simultaneously in each lattice $L(B_i')$. This holds with probability $\geq (1 - P)^k \geq 1 - kP$, which tends to 1 exponentially. Therefore, we can conclude that the broadcast attack succeeds with high probability, which tends to 1 rather than exactly succeeding.

Thus, the correct way to describe the attack algorithm (Algorithm 1) is to change Step 3 "Find the shortest vector of L: $\begin{bmatrix} \boldsymbol{m} \\ 1 \end{bmatrix}$" to "Find the shortest vector of L. With high probability, it is $\begin{bmatrix} \boldsymbol{m} \\ 1 \end{bmatrix}$".

4   Efficiency Analysis of the Attack Using the SVP Algorithm

Intuitively, the idea of the attack in Algorithm 1 is to employ the intersection of lattices to increase the volume (determinant) of the lattices, while maintaining the length of the shortest vector, and make the lattice reach the range such that the LLL algorithm is able to find its shortest vector.

Hence, to consider the efficiency of the attack is to consider the value of k that ensures that the shortest vector can be effectively found in the intersection lattice $L = \bigcap_{i=1}^k L(B_i')$. Theorem 3 given by [22] shows that the use of more instances would be more beneficial to constructing the lattice whose shortest vector is able to be found, but the conclusion of this theorem is too simple to obtain the number of necessary instances.

To this end, we now provide an estimate of the lower bound of the volume of the lattice $L = \bigcap_{i=1}^k L(B_i')$. If $L = \bigcap_{i=1}^k L(B_i')$, then L is a sublattice of each $L(B_i'), i = 1, 2, \cdots, k$. Thus, each $\det(L(B_i'))$ divides $\det(L)$, and hence, $\det(L)$ is an integer multiple of $\mathrm{lcm}(\det(L(B_1')), \cdots, \det(L(B_k')))$, where lcm denotes the least common multiple. Therefore, the expectation value of $\mathrm{lcm}(\det(L(B_1')), \cdots, \det(L(B_k')))$ under the random condition can be regarded as a lower bound of $\det(L)$. [4] provides results regarding the distribution of the lcm of a series of random integers. In particular, we have the following theorem:

Theorem 5 *(Theorem 2 in [4]). Denote by $X_1^{(N)}, \ldots, X_r^{(N)}$ a series of independent random variables uniformly selected from $\{1, 2, \ldots, N\}$; then, the expectation $\mathbb{E}(\mathrm{lcm}(X_1^{(N)}, \ldots, X_r^{(N)})) \asymp N^r$.*

[10] noted that the determinant of a matrix whose elements are integers selected at random from $[-\beta, \beta]$ can be seen as a random value in its Hadamard bound $\beta^n \cdot 2^{n \log n}$. Combined with Theorem 5, we have that $\mathbb{E}(\mathrm{lcm}(\det(L(B_1')), \cdots, \det(L(B_k')))) \asymp (\beta^n \cdot 2^{n \log n})^k$. Thus, a lower bound of $\det(L)$ is $C \cdot (\beta^n \cdot 2^{n \log n})^k$, where C is a constant. Thus, taking

$$k \geq \frac{n \log \log n / \log n + \log \|\boldsymbol{m}\|}{\log \beta + \log n} \approx \frac{n \log \log n}{(\log n)^2}, \tag{5}$$

we have $\frac{\det(L)^{\frac{1}{n}}}{\|\boldsymbol{m}\|+1} \geq 2^{n \log \log n / \log n}$, where "$\approx$" is derived from the fact that in actual GGH, $\|\boldsymbol{m}\|$ is generally taken as $O(\sqrt{n})$. It is also easily proven that with high probability, $\dim(L) = n + 1$. As a random integer lattice, other vectors in L that are different from the shortest vector are not shorter than $\det(L)^{1/n}$; moreover, $\geq 2^{n \log \log n / \log n} \cdot (\|\boldsymbol{m}\| + 1)$. Thus, as the shortest vector of L (with high probability), $\begin{bmatrix} \boldsymbol{m} \\ 1 \end{bmatrix}$ can be found by the LLL algorithm. Therefore, when the value of k satisfies (5), the attack of Algorithm 1 can be considered as a successful attack.

As shown from the above result, compared with the dimension n, the number of instances required in the broadcast attack is relatively small.

5   The New Attack Using the CVP Algorithm

For the attack presented in Algorithm 2, the original authors did not conduct a detailed analysis and only stated that their Theorem 3 cannot explain why the attack is successful.

To this end, we provide a clearer broadcast attack on GGH that uses the technique of lattice intersection and that calls the CVP algorithm. Note that B', c' in Type B challenges are B^{-1} and $B^{-1}c$ in Type A challenges; therefore, the two types of challenges are equivalent. We might still consider only Type A challenges. The idea behind our attack is as follows.

Given k groups of GGH challenge instances (B_i, c_i) encrypting the same message vector $\boldsymbol{m}$, we need to construct a vector $\boldsymbol{y}$ that satisfies

$$\boldsymbol{y} = B_1 \boldsymbol{r}_1' + \boldsymbol{c}_1 = B_2 \boldsymbol{r}_2' + \boldsymbol{c}_2 = \cdots = B_k \boldsymbol{r}_k' + \boldsymbol{c}_k. \tag{6}$$

Here, y is required to simultaneously meet all of the equal signs in 6. Thus, according to $m = -B_i r_i + c_i$, we have $y - m = B_i(r_i' + r), i = 1, 2, \ldots, k$, i.e., $y - m$ is in each lattice $L(B_i)$; hence,

$$y - m \in L = \bigcap_{i=1}^{k} L(B_i).$$

Now, the distance between y and the vector $y - m$ in the lattice is $||m||$; hence, when the length of m, $||m||$, is sufficiently small, $y - m$ can be viewed as the closest vector to the target vector y, which holds with high probability and will be later proven in Theorems 4 and 7 and Remark 3. If the conditions on the lattice L and the target vector y are such that the CVP can be solved, we can then call the CVP solver to obtain $y - m$ and hence m.

The method we use to obtain y satisfying (6) is to solve the equations

$$\begin{cases} B_1 r_1' - y = -c_1 \\ B_2 r_2' - y = -c_2 \\ \vdots \\ B_k r_k' - y = -c_k \end{cases}. \tag{7}$$

in which each $B_i r_i' - y = -c_i$ is

$$\begin{cases} b_{11} r_1^{(i)} + \cdots + b_{1n} r_n^{(i)} - y_1 = -c_1^{(i)} \\ \vdots \\ b_{n1} r_1^{(i)} + \cdots + b_{nn} r_n^{(i)} - y_n = -c_n^{(i)} \end{cases}, \tag{8}$$

Thus, in equations (7), we have in total $(k + 1)n$ unknowns $y_1, \ldots, y_n$, $r_1^{(i)}, \ldots r_n^{(i)}, i = 1, 2, \ldots k$ and kn equations. Therefore, according to the law concerning the solving of Diophantine Equations, we can determine a set $y_1, \ldots, y_n$, i.e., y. According to the GGH encryption process, we can see that the equations do have at least one set of solutions $(m, r_1, \cdots, r_k)$. In addition, the vector y we obtain can be observed as a translation of m along a vector in the lattice $L = \bigcap_{i=1}^{k} L(B_i')$ in the space $\mathbb{R}^n$.

Theorem 6. *If each element of the matrix B is a random integer independently selected from the range $[-\beta, \beta]$, the n-dimensional vector m satisfies $c = Br + m$, the n-dimensional vector y satisfies $y = Br' + c$, and the closest vector to y in the n-dimensional lattice $L = L(B)$ is a, then $a \neq y - m$ occurs with a probability not exceeding*

$$P = \frac{N(n, ||m||^2)}{(2\beta + 1)^n},$$

where $N(n, \alpha)$ represents the number of integer points within an n-dimensional sphere of radius $\sqrt{\alpha}$.

Proof. First, it is clear that the vector $\boldsymbol{y}-\boldsymbol{m} = B\boldsymbol{r}'+(B\boldsymbol{r}+\boldsymbol{m})-\boldsymbol{m} = B(\boldsymbol{r}'-\boldsymbol{r})$ is in the lattice $L = L(B)$. Because $\boldsymbol{a} \in L$, there exists $\boldsymbol{r}''$ such that $\boldsymbol{a} = B\boldsymbol{r}''$; hence, we let $\boldsymbol{m}' = B(\boldsymbol{r}'-\boldsymbol{r}'') + \boldsymbol{c}$, and $\boldsymbol{a}$ can be written as $\boldsymbol{y}-\boldsymbol{m}'$. Because $\boldsymbol{a}$ is the closest vector to $\boldsymbol{y}$, we have

$$||\boldsymbol{m}'|| \leq ||\boldsymbol{m}||. \tag{9}$$

Consider $\boldsymbol{a} \neq \boldsymbol{y}-\boldsymbol{m}$; now, we have $\boldsymbol{m}' \neq \boldsymbol{m}$, i.e., $\boldsymbol{m}'-\boldsymbol{m} \neq \boldsymbol{0}$. According to the expressions of $\boldsymbol{m}'$ and $\boldsymbol{m}$,

$$\boldsymbol{m}'-\boldsymbol{m} = B\boldsymbol{r}^*. \tag{10}$$

For a given $\boldsymbol{m}'$, if Eq. (10) has solutions, it has a unique non-zero solution (we may suppose W.L.O.G for the solution $\boldsymbol{r}^* = [r_1^*, \ldots, r_n^*]^T \in \mathbb{Z}^n$, r_1^* is not 0). Then, for a given $\boldsymbol{m}'$, which is also a given group of $\boldsymbol{m}', \boldsymbol{r}^*$, we have that for each equation in (10) $b_{i1}r_1^* + \cdots + b_{in}r_n^* = m_i' - m_i$, i.e.,

$$b_{i1}r_1^* = m_i' - m_i - (b_{i2}r_2^* + \cdots + b_{in}r_n^*), \tag{11}$$

for any selection of $b_{i2}, \cdots, b_{in}$, there is at most 1 value in the range $[-\beta, \beta]$ that can be chosen as b_{i1}, which is independent of $b_{i2}, \cdots, b_{in}$, such that (11) holds. Therefore, for randomly chosen elements in B, each equation in (10) holds with probability of no higher than $\frac{1}{2\beta+1}$; hence, all equations of (10) simultaneously hold with a probability of no higher than $\frac{1}{(2\beta+1)^n}$. In addition, according to (9), there are $N(n, ||\boldsymbol{m}||^2)$ ways to choose $\boldsymbol{m}'$; thus, $\boldsymbol{a} \neq \boldsymbol{y}-\boldsymbol{m}$ occurs with a probability that does not exceed $\frac{N(n, ||\boldsymbol{m}||^2)}{(2\beta+1)^n}$. $\square$

Theorem 7. *For a target vector $\boldsymbol{y}$, and if $\boldsymbol{a}$ is the closest vector to $\boldsymbol{y}$ in both of the lattices L_1 and L_2, then $\boldsymbol{a}$ is the closest vector to $\boldsymbol{y}$ in lattice $L = L_1 \cap L_2$.*

Proof. Clearly, $\boldsymbol{a} \in L = L_1 \cap L_2$. If $\boldsymbol{a}' \in L, \boldsymbol{a}' \neq \boldsymbol{a}$, $||\boldsymbol{y}-\boldsymbol{a}'|| < ||\boldsymbol{y}-\boldsymbol{a}||$, the conclusion that $\boldsymbol{a}'$ is also in L_1, L_2 will lead to a contradiction with the condition that $\boldsymbol{a}$ is the closest vector in L_1, L_2. Hence, there cannot be a vector in L different from $\boldsymbol{a}$ and closer to $\boldsymbol{y}$ than $\boldsymbol{a}$. $\square$ Namely, we establish our conclusion.

Remark 3. Theorem 6 shows that, for each lattice $L(B_i)$, $\boldsymbol{y}-\boldsymbol{m}$ is the closest vector to $\boldsymbol{y}$ with a probability of at least $1-P$. We can conclude from the estimation of $N(n, \alpha)$ in [2,23] and GGH's parameter setting that P is exponentially small. From Theorem 7, for $\boldsymbol{y}$ satisfying (6), $\boldsymbol{y}-\boldsymbol{m}$ is the closest vector to $\boldsymbol{y}$ in each lattice with probability $\geq (1-P)^k \geq 1 - kP$, namely, the closest vector to $\boldsymbol{y}$ in the lattice $L = \bigcap_{i=1}^k L(B_i')$. Therefore, we presented above a feasible broadcast attack.

Next, we consider the efficiency of the attack, which is the value of the number of instances k such that $L, \boldsymbol{y}$ meets the conditions such that the CVP can be effectively solved. Specifically, we consider the case that the CVP solver is the BDD variant, with preprocessing of the lattices allowed. This is reasonable because the lattice bases are public keys. If there is an algorithm that is able to determine the closest vector under the condition that the distance between the n-dimensional lattice L and the target vector does not exceed $f(n) \cdot \det(L)^{1/n}$, then we need to use k instances to construct L such that it satisfies

$$\|\boldsymbol{m}\| \leq f(n) \cdot \det(L)^{1/n}, \tag{12}$$

and then call the CVP solver to determine $\boldsymbol{y}$'s closest vector. Based on the similar analysis in the last section, we can see that when k is taken as $k \geq \frac{\log(\|\boldsymbol{m}\|/f(n))}{\log \beta + \log n}$, the condition (12) holds. For example, if the solver here is taken as the algorithm in [12], which is a polynomial time algorithm and $f(n) = \sqrt{\log n/n}$, then we can take $k \geq \frac{\log(\frac{n}{\sqrt{\log n}})}{\log n}$ to perform a successful attack. As a summary, we can see that the number of required instances is quite low.

6 Conclusion

In this paper, by considering properties of random integer lattices, we describe and analyze an application of lattice intersection in cryptanalysis. The results show that the current parameters of GGH cannot be considered to be secure in broadcast backgrounds. Because its structure remains in use today in cryptography in the cloud computing and big data era, the results are of theoretical and practical significance.

References

1. Babai, L.: On Lovászlattice reduction and the nearest lattice point problem. Combinatorica **6**(1), 1–13 (1986)
2. Bi, J., Cheng, Q.: Lower bounds of shortest vector lengths in random knapsack lattices and random NTRU lattices. Cryptology ePrint Archive, Report 2011/153 (2011). http://eprint.iacr.org/
3. Ding, J., Pan, Y., Deng, Y.: An algebraic broadcast attack against NTRU. In: Susilo, W., Mu, Y., Seberry, J. (eds.) ACISP 2012. LNCS, vol. 7372, pp. 124–137. Springer, Heidelberg (2012)
4. Fernández, J.L., Fernández, P.: On the probability distribution of the gcd, lcm of r-tuples of integers (2013). arXiv preprint arXiv:1305.0536
5. Garg, S., Gentry, C., Halevi, S.: Candidate multilinear maps from ideal lattices. In: Johansson, T., Nguyen, P.Q. (eds.) EUROCRYPT 2013. LNCS, vol. 7881, pp. 1–17. Springer, Heidelberg (2013)
6. Gentry, C.: A fully homomorphic encryption scheme. Ph.D. thesis, Stanford University (2009)
7. Gentry, C., Peikert, C., Vaikuntanathan, V.: Trapdoors for hard lattices and new cryptographic constructions. In: Proceedings of the Fortieth Annual ACM Symposium on Theory of Computing, pp. 197–206. ACM (2008)
8. Goldreich, O., Goldwasser, S., Halevi, S.: Public-key cryptosystems from lattice reduction problems. In: Kaliski Jr., B.S. (ed.) CRYPTO 1997. LNCS, vol. 1294, pp. 112–131. Springer, Heidelberg (1997)

9. Hastad, J.: Solving simultaneous modular equations of low degree. SIAM J. Comput. **17**(2), 336–341 (1988)
10. Girko, V.L.: Theory of Random Determinants. Springer, Dordrecht (1990)
11. Lee, M.S., Hahn, S.G.: Cryptanalysis of the GGH cryptosystem. Math. Comput. Sci. **3**(2), 201–208 (2010)
12. Li, J., Pan, Y., Liu, M., Zhu, G.: An efficient broadcast attack against NTRU. In: 7th ACM Symposium on Information, Compuer and Communications Security, ASIACCS 2012, Seoul, Korea, May 2–4, pp. 22–23 (2012)
13. Liu, M., Nguyen, P.Q.: Solving BDD by enumeration: an update. In: Dawson, E. (ed.) CT-RSA 2013. LNCS, vol. 7779, pp. 293–309. Springer, Heidelberg (2013)
14. Liu, Y.-K., Lyubashevsky, V., Micciancio, D.: On bounded distance decoding for general lattices. In: Díaz, J., Jansen, K., Rolim, J.D.P., Zwick, U. (eds.) APPROX 2006 and RANDOM 2006. LNCS, vol. 4110, pp. 450–461. Springer, Heidelberg (2006)
15. Lyubashevsky, V.: SIS and worst-case to average-case reductions. Bar-Ilan University, Israel (2012). http://www.di.ens.fr/lyubash/talks/SISWtoAv.pdf
16. McEliece, R.J.: A public-key cryptosystem based on algebraic coding theory. DSN Prog. Rep. **42**(44), 114–116 (1978)
17. Micciancio, D., CSE206A: Lattices algorithms and applications, (Spring 2014). http://cseweb.ucsd.edu/classes/sp14/cse206A-a/index.html
18. Micciancio, D., Goldwasser, S.: Complexity of Lattice Problems: A Cryptographic Perspective. The Kluwer International Series in Engineering and Computer Science, vol. 671. Kluwer Academic Publishers, Boston, Massachusetts (2002)
19. Nguyên, P.Q.: Cryptanalysis of the goldreich-goldwasser-halevi cryptosystem from Crypto'97. In: Wiener, M. (ed.) CRYPTO 1999. LNCS, vol. 1666, pp. 288–304. Springer, Heidelberg (1999)
20. Nguyen, P.Q., Valle, B.: The LLL Algorithm: Survey and Applications, 1st edn. Springer Publishing Company, Incorporated, Heidelberg (2009)
21. Pan, Y., Deng, Y.: A broadcast attack against NTRU using ding's algorithm. IACR Cryptology ePrint Archive **2010**, 598 (2010)
22. Plantard, T., Susilo, W.: Broadcast attacks against lattice-based cryptosystems. In: Abdalla, M., Pointcheval, D., Fouque, P.-A., Vergnaud, D. (eds.) ACNS 2009. LNCS, vol. 5536, pp. 456–472. Springer, Heidelberg (2009)
23. Nguyen, P.Q., Stern, J.: Adapting density attacks to low-weight knapsacks. In: Roy, B. (ed.) ASIACRYPT 2005. LNCS, vol. 3788. Springer, Heidelberg (2005). doi:10.1007/11593447_3
24. Jun, X., Lei, H., Sun, S.: Cryptanalysis of two cryptosystems based on multiple intractability assumptions. IET Commun. **8**(14), 2433–2437 (2014)
25. Jun, X., Lei, H., Sun, S., Xie, Y.: Cryptanalysis of countermeasures against multiple transmission attacks on NTRU. IET Commun. **8**(12), 2142–2146 (2014)

Side Channel Attacks
and Countermeasures

Secure Binary Field Multiplication

Hwajeong Seo[1], Chien-Ning Chen[2], Zhe Liu[3], Yasuyuki Nogami[4],
Taehwan Park[1], Jongseok Choi[1], and Howon Kim[1(✉)]

[1] School of Computer Science and Engineering, Pusan National University,
San-30, Jangjeon-Dong, Geumjeong-Gu, Busan 609–735, Republic of Korea
{hwajeong,pth5804,jschoi85,howonkim}@pusan.ac.kr
[2] Physical Analysis and Cryptographic Engineering (PACE),
Nanyang Technological University, Singapore, Singapore
chienning@ntu.edu.sg
[3] Laboratory of Algorithmics, Cryptology and Security (LACS),
University of Luxembourg, 6, rue R. Coudenhove-Kalergi,
1359 Luxembourg-kirchberg, Luxembourg
zhe.liu@uni.lu
[4] Graduate School of Natural Science and Technology, Okayama University,
3-1-1, Tsushima-naka, Kita, Okayama 700–8530, Japan
yasuyuki.nogami@okayama-u.ac.jp

Abstract. Binary field multiplication is the most fundamental building block of binary field Elliptic Curve Cryptography (ECC) and Galois/Counter Mode (GCM). Both bit-wise scanning and Look-Up Table (LUT) based methods are commonly used for binary field multiplication. In terms of Side Channel Attack (SCA), bit-wise scanning exploits insecure branch operations which leaks information in a form of timing and power consumption. On the other hands, LUT based method is regarded as a relatively secure approach because LUT access can be conducted in a regular and atomic form. This ensures a constant time solution as well. In this paper, we conduct the SCA on the LUT based binary field multiplication. The attack exploits the horizontal Correlation Power Analysis (CPA) on weights of LUT. We identify the operand with only a power trace of binary field multiplication. In order to prevent SCA, we also suggest a mask based binary field multiplication which ensures a regular and constant time solution without LUT and branch statements.

Keywords: Binary field multiplication · Embedded processors · Side channel attack · Horizontal correlation power analysis

This work was partly supported by Institute for Information & communications Technology Promotion(IITP) grant funded by the Korea government (MSIP) (No.10043907, Development of high performance IoT device and Open Platform with Intelligent Software) and the MSIP (Ministry of Science, ICT and Future Planning), Korea, under the ITRC(Information Technology Research Center) support program (IITP-2015-H8501-15-1017) supervised by the IITP(Institute for Information & communications Technology Promotion).

H. Kim and D. Choi (Eds.): WISA 2015, LNCS 9503, pp. 161–173, 2016.
DOI: 10.1007/978-3-319-31875-2_14

1   Introduction

Elliptic Curve Cryptography (ECC) scalar multiplication (point addition and doubling) consists of field arithmetic including addition/subtraction, multiplication/squaring and inversion [9]. Of these operations, multiplication/squaring is the most performance-critical operations of point addition and doubling. Any efforts spent in optimizing these operations are deserved. The binary field multiplication is normally established with a combination of exclusive-or and bit-shift operations. The advanced binary field implementations achieved remarkably good performance by reducing the number of partial products and replacing bit operations into consecutive look-up table accesses known as Lopez et al.'s method [12,14,17]. The alternative approach, Block-Comb based multiplication, is introduced in [18]. Several operands are grouped in block-wise and multiple operands are computed at once. Later, an unbalanced fashion of Block-Comb method is presented by Seo et al. in [15]. This method increases the size of block by exploiting the additional registers with instruction set level optimization techniques and then computes the multiplication in block-wise way as like former Block-Comb approaches. There is nice way to reduce the multiplication overheads into sub-quadratic complexity known as Karatsuba algorithm. This method efficiently replaces multiplication into several addition and subtraction operations. There exist several papers which have considered the Karatsuba's technique for speeding-up the performance of binary field multiplication over embedded processors. Lopez et al. in [12] conducts Karatsuba multiplication with look-up table accesses. This trial reduces the number of multiplication but it increases overheads for constructing the look-up table which is beyond benefits of Karatsuba approach. Oliveira et al. in [14] also mentioned that Lopez et al.'s normal method is faster than Karatsuba's multiplication by a factor of 44 %. Recently, an alternative combination of Karatsuba algorithm and Block-Comb method is introduced [16]. The method exploits 3-term Karatsuba and reduces 3 63-bit partial products out of 9. The results show high performance gains in 163-bit Koblitz curve. There is relatively few number of papers considering Side Channel Attack (SCA) on these binary field multiplication. While the fastest implementations over embedded processors were a quite important factor in the past, because implementations of binary field ECC over embedded processor were too slow due to limited computing power and storages. However without secure implementations against side channel attack, practical applications are limited [2,3,11]. In this paper, we explore all binary field multiplication on embedded processors in terms of side channel attack and show the vulnerability of LUT based binary field multiplication as well. Lastly, we introduce a secure mask based binary field multiplication.

Summary of Research Contributions

The main contributions of our work are summarized as follows.

1. *Side channel attacks on LUT based binary field multiplication.*We present side channel attacks on consecutive memory access patterns. We used horizontal

Correlation Power Analysis (CPA) on weights of LUT. The method success-fully extracts the correlation co-efficient from power traces of binary field multiplication and identifies the operands used in the operations.

2. *Develop the secure binary field multiplication techniques.* Unlike previous binary field multiplication methods, we designed a new mask based binary field multiplication. Since this regular and atomic method is branch-free and LUT-free, proposed method is much secure against simple power analysis than previous approaches. In order to boost the performance, we exploit several levels of Karatsuba multiplication.

The remainder of this paper is organized as follows. In Sect. 2, we overview the previous binary field multiplication methods. In Sect. 3, we point out the vulnerability of previous approaches in terms of side channel attack and show our side channel attack results on LUT based binary field multiplication. In Sect. 4, we present a mask based binary field multiplication. Finally, Sect. 5 concludes the paper.

2   Binary Field Multiplications

The look-up table based binary field multiplication, introduced in [12,14], replaces the bit operations into look-up table access operations. In order to utilize the method, we should compute the look-up table by one operand and place them into memory as pre-computed results. Typically, the range is chosen to 4, indicating a 4-bit value (0x0~0xf) for 16 (2^4) cases. The look-up table occupies memory size at least $16 \times m$, where m is size of operands. After gener-ating the look-up table with target operand, we access the look-up table by 4-bit wise and then update intermediate results with the pre-computed results from LUT, thereby reducing complex shift or bit-wise exclusive-or operations. The alternative approach is Block-Comb method. The method executes consecutive bit-wise exclusive-or on intermediate results under condition of bit setting by block-wise [18]. In every session, one bit of block is tested from the least signif-icant to the most significant bits. If the bit is set to 1, the intermediate results are updated by block-wise operand. After then intermediate result is left-shifted by 1-bit to align the location of result. This process is iterated by size of word. Since, whole processes are conducted in block-wise fashion, the intermediate result and operand bit test are handled efficiently. The unbalanced Block-Comb method optimizes the utilization of general purpose registers [15] to retain more operands into registers. A key feature of the method is the computation of par-tial products using extra bits in operands. After bit test of the operand, the least significant bit of the operand is not used anymore. We can store the carry bit of intermediate result into the least significant bit of operand. The advan-tage of exploiting additional registers is that we can compute partial products in large block size, which reduces the number of block-wise partial products. Karatsuba method is a general technique to reduce the complexity of multi-plication with small number of addition operations. In [19], Karatsuba method is applied to Lopez et al.'s method but it increases overheads for constructing the look-up table in on-line which is beyond benefits of Karatsuba approach. Oliveira et al. in [14] also mentioned that original Lopez et al.'s method is faster than Karatsuba's multiplication by a factor of 44 %. Since Karatsuba method divides long integers into half and conducts multiplication operations on them, as many as we divide multiplication blocks, the pre-computation costs significantly increase. Block-Comb method is grouping several bytes of the operand into a block and then computes the multiplication in block-wise fashion. A Karatsuba Block-Comb (KBC) firstly groups the operand and then Karatsuba multiplication is conducted in block-wise fashion. However, the Block-Comb approach is vulnerable toward timing attacks. The computation time is highly relied on bit setting. In order to remove the timing information, constant time solution was introduced. In the method, each bit is evaluated and conduct operations in a regular timing. If the bit is set, it conduct bit-wise exclusive-or with operand. Otherwise it conducts bit-wise exclusive-or with zero register. Even though this method eliminates the timing information, it still leaks power consumption from branch operations.

3   Side Channel Attacks on Binary Field Multiplications

Real world multiplication can be conducted with dedicated 8-, 16-, or 32-bit multipliers of Arithmetic Logic Unit (ALU). In terms of binary field multiplication, high-end processors such as ARM and Intel chip-sets support polynomial multiplier. However, low-end 8-bit and 16-bit embedded processors do not support polynomial multiplications yet. In order to get acceptable speed performance over low-end devices, previous binary field multiplication operations exploit the basic logical operations or LUT computations. However, the works mainly focus on speed optimizations rather than secure implementations which expose information leakages. In this paper, we conduct the side channel attacks on binary field multiplication over the popular embedded board named ARDUINO UNO with the 8-bit 16 MHz AVR microcontroller Atmega328p. An AVR processor, such as the Atmel ATmega series, features 32 general-purpose registers, of which six are used for pointers. In particular, the register pair (R26,R27) is aliased as X pointer, the register pair (R28,R29) is aliased as Y pointer, and the register pair (R30,R31) is aliased as Z pointer. The AVR microcontrollers have separate memories and buses for program and data. It has a total of 133 instructions and each instruction has a fixed latency. Ordinary arithmetic/logical instructions (e.g. add) are executed in a single clock cycle, while a mul instruction takes two clock cycles, and also load/store instructions take two cycles. Most of the software implementation on AVR processors is written in both mixed C and Assembly code. The function-call specifies that the first three 16-bit arguments (e.g., pointers) are passed in register pairs (R24, R25), (R22,R23), and (R21,R20). It furthermore specifies that registers R2–R17, R28, and R29 are "called- saved" registers, and the register R1 is assumed by the compiler to always contain zero thus has to be set to zero before returning from a function. In order to measure the power consumption of AVR processor, we manipulate the circuit to get the chip's

Table 1. AVR program codes for constant time binary field multiplication

Constant time with NOP		Constant time with ZERO Register	
SBRS B0,0	NOPIN:	SBRS B0,0	ZEROIN:
RJMP NOPIN	NOP	RJMP ZEROIN	EOR C0, ZERO
EOR C0, A0	NOP	EOR C0, A0	EOR C1, ZERO
EOR C1, A1	NOP	EOR C1, A1	EOR C2, ZERO
EOR C2, A2	NOP	EOR C2, A2	EOR C3, ZERO
EOR C3, A3	NOP	EOR C3, A3	EOR C4, ZERO
EOR C4, A4	NOP	EOR C4, A4	EOR C5, ZERO
EOR C5, A5	NOP	EOR C5, A5	EOR C6, ZERO
EOR C6, A6	NOP	EOR C6, A6	NOP
RJMP NOPOUT	NOPOUT:	RJMP ZEROOUT	ZEROOUT:

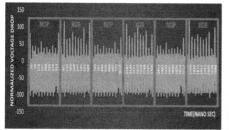 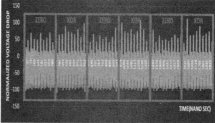

Fig. 1. Power traces for (left) NOP operations and (right) ZERO register based constant time binary field multiplication

power consumption with less noise. The power consumption of the AVR microcontroller is measured by LeCroy WaveRunner 610Zi oscilloscope with AP033 active differential probe at the sampling rate 10 G/s (Table 1).

Firstly, Block-Comb variants including original Block-Comb, unbalanced Block-Comb and Karatsuba Block-Comb need to check the bit setting of the operands. If the bit is set, the operands are added to intermediate results. If the bit is not set, the whole operations are skipped. This irregular form of program leaks timing information because it has different timing pattern between branched or non-branched cases. In order to hide timing information, we can ensure constant time solutions by inserting the NOP or adding ZERO operations for branched cases. In Table 3, the AVR program codes for constant time binary field multiplication are described. It consumes same clock cycles with padding operations. However both approaches leak another important information namely power consumption. In Fig. 1, the power traces of both methods are drawn. For NOP based operations, it vividly shows low power consumption than exclusive-or operations. For alternative approach based on ZERO register, it relatively consumes more power than NOP based approaches but it still shows different power consumption patterns compared with normal exclusive-or operation.

Algorithm 1. Lopez et al. multiplication in $\mathbb{F}_{2^m}$ [12]

Require: $A = A[0, ..., n-1], B = B[0, ..., n-1]$ where word size is 8-bit.
Ensure: $C = C[0, ..., 2n-1]$.
 1: Compute $T = U \cdot B$ for all polynomials U of degree lower than $t = 4$-bit.
 2: $C[0, ..., 2n-1] \leftarrow 0$
 3: **for** k from 0 by 1 to $n-1$ **do**
 4:    $u \leftarrow A[k] \gg t$
 5:    **for** j from 0 by 1 to $n-1$ **do**
 6:       $C[j+k] \leftarrow C[j+k] \oplus T(u)[j]$
 7:    **end for**
 8: **end for**
 9: $C \leftarrow C \cdot 2^t$
10: **for** k from 0 by 1 to $n-1$ **do**
11:    $u \leftarrow A[k] \bmod 2^t$
12:    **for** j from 0 by 1 to $n-1$ **do**
13:       $C[j+k] \leftarrow C[j+k] \oplus T(u)[j]$
14:    **end for**
15: **end for**
16: **return** C

On the other hands, Lopez et al.'s look-up table approach is relatively secure against simple power analysis than that of Block-Comb variants, because the method does not have branch statements and only consists of regular memory access operations. This nice property does not leak the irregular form of timing and power consumption. However, Messerges et al. showed that the power consumption of a smart card depends on the activity on both data and address bus [13]. Chen showed the method to identify the memory address from power consumption of consecutive memory accesses and distinguish the multiplication and squaring operations from the multiplication always based exponentiation algorithm [4]. The horizontal correlation analysis computes the correlation factor on segments corresponding to the atomic operations and extracts secret information [5]. This attack successfully finds the secret keys of RSA crypto systems from power traces.

In this paper, we attack the LUT based binary field multiplication, which has high relations between memory access pattern and weights of operands because LUT is written in online by referring the operand values and it is read by referring the another operand values. In Algorithm 1, Lopez's binary field multiplication consists of online LUT construction based on the operand (B) and consecutive LUT accesses by using another operand (A) as an offset. In Step 1, LUT is generated by multiplying the operands (B) and degree (t). The degree determines the size of LUT $(2^t)^1$. From Step 4, higher 4-bit of operands (A) are extracted by degree (t) and then the higher value (u) is used as index of LUT (T). In Step

---

[1] Normally the degree (t) is set to 4 to get 16 cases because degree 8 needs too large LUT ($2^8 = 256$). Since the other degrees including (5, 6, 7) are not the power of two, they are inefficient over 8, 16 or 32-bit machine.

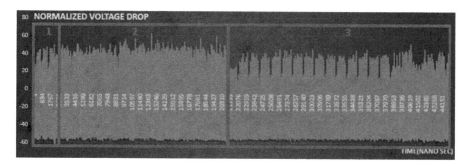

Fig. 2. Power traces of Lopez et al. method (①, ②) LUT construction, (③) 4-bit wise binary field multiplication with LUT

6, the LUT variables are added to intermediate results (C). Same procedures are conducted again for lower 4-bit of (A). In Fig. 4, the power traces of Lopez et al. with degree 4 are described. The Section ① is constructing the LUT with variable (0, 1, 2, 4, 8) and Section ② is constructing the LUT with remaining variables (3, 5, 6, 7, 9, 10, 11, 12, 13, 14, 15). The Section ③ is conducting the 4-bit wise binary field multiplication with LUT. Since, the LUT is based on operands (A), the power consumption is highly relied on weights of operands. In Table 2, the source codes for look-up table construction is described. The LUT construction conducts consecutive memory store. The ST instruction, transferring the data from register to memory storages, takes 2 clock cycles. This instruction consumes certain pattern of power consumption depending on weights of data, because bit one or zero generates different power consumption. If we extract current data patterns from power consumption, we can identify the operands used for building LUT. With the leakage information, we can identify the scalar addition and doubling from scalar multiplication where the information is the secret key of ECDH operations (Fig. 2).

In order to show the practical attack results, we target the smallest field namely sect113r1. If we succeed in attacks on the smallest field, we can readily extend to larger binary fields such as 128, 163, 193, 233, 239, 283, 409 and 571-bit. The 113-bit binary field multiplication over 8-bit processor needs 14 ($\lceil \frac{113}{8} \rceil$) bytes to store one element of LUT. For side channel attack, we collected power traces of look-up table construction cases including 0x1, 0x3, 0x5, 0x7, 0x09, 0xb, 0xd, 0xf from ① and ② in Fig. 4. Each case consists of 14 memory store operations. In one round of multiplication, we can collect 112 (8×14) operations and we conduct the horizontal correlation power analysis with their weights. We compute the correlation factor on segments corresponding to the atomic LUT access operations and identify the specific operands. AVR processor uses data bus when it stores byte-wise data from registers to memory. This causes certain power consumption patterns depending on the weights of passing data. The idea is to calculate the Pearson Correlation Coefficient ρ between power consumption and the Hamming Weight of the LUT namely $HW_{LUT}(A_i)$. If it accesses the

Table 2. AVR program codes for LUT computations of Lopez et al.

Look up table construction for 0x01 and 0x02 cases				
ST Z+, A0	ST Z+, A9	ROL A3	ROL A12	ST Z+, A6
ST Z+, A1	ST Z+, A10	ROL A4	ROL A13	ST Z+, A7
ST Z+, A2	ST Z+, A11	ROL A5	ROL A14	ST Z+, A8
ST Z+, A3	ST Z+, A12	ROL A6	ST Z+, A0	ST Z+, A9
ST Z+, A4	ST Z+, A13	ROL A7	ST Z+, A1	ST Z+, A10
ST Z+, A5	ST Z+, A14	ROL A8	ST Z+, A2	ST Z+, A11
ST Z+, A6	LSL A0	ROL A9	ST Z+, A3	ST Z+, A12
ST Z+, A7	ROL A1	ROL A10	ST Z+, A4	ST Z+, A13
ST Z+, A8	ROL A2	ROL A11	ST Z+, A5	ST Z+, A14

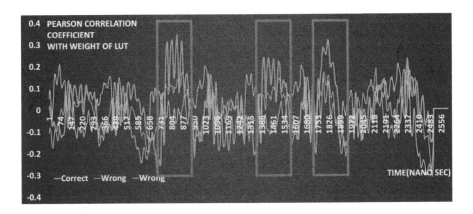

Fig. 3. Correlation value of weights and power consumptions

LUT by using i-th operand (A) at the time t, there will be a higher coefficient ρ. In the correlation graph of Fig. 3, we found distinguished three peaks colored in blue. The other lines show wrong estimations with wrong LUT and weights.

4   Secure Binary Field Multiplication

In Sect. 3, we explored the vulnerability of existing binary field multiplication methods. The main vulnerabilities of existing approaches are branch statements and predicable memory access patterns based on the weights of memory. In order to reduce the information leakages, we introduce a Masked Block-Comb method. The method avoids the branch operation and even LUT accesses but it uses an operand masking to conduct the regular and atomic form of binary field multiplication.

In Algorithm 2, 32-bit wise MBC multiplication is introduced. In Step 3, i-th bit of operand $A[j]$ is stored in BIT variable. In Step 4, zero value is subtracted from BIT and borrow bit is stored into $T1$ variable. In Step 5, zero value is

Algorithm 2. Masked Block Comb on 32-bit

Require: Two 32-bit operands A and B
Ensure: $C(64\text{-bit}) = A \cdot B$

```
 1: for i from 7 by 1 to 0 do
 2:    for j from 3 by 1 to 0 do
 3:       BIT = A[j]&(1 ≪ i)
 4:       {T1, T0} = 0 − BIT
 5:       MASK = 0 − T1
 6:       for k from 3 by 1 to 0 do
 7:          C[k + j] = C[k + j] ⊕ (B[k]&MASK)
 8:       end for
 9:    end for
10:    C = C ≪ 1
11: end for
12: return C
```

Table 3. AVR program codes for masked block comb multiplication

Constant time with masked operand			
LDI BIT, 0X80	SUB ZERO, BIT	AND M0, BIT	EOR C0, M0
AND BIT, A0	SBC BIT, BIT	AND M1, BIT	EOR C1, M1
CLR ZERO	MOVW M0, B0	AND M2, BIT	EOR C2, M2
	MOVW M2, B2	AND M3, BIT	EOR C3, M3

subtracted from $T1$. This outputs 0 if $T1$ is zero and if not it outputs 0xff. After then Step 7, operand $B[k]$ is masked with variable $MASK$ and then conduct Block-Comb style multiplication. This operation is conducted by the number of block size (4, 32-bit). After then intermediate results C is left shifted by 1-bit and this process is iterated by 7 times more. The detailed source code is available in Table 3. We set the bit with LDI operation and then conduct AND with operand A0. If the bit is set, the (SBC BIT, BIT) operation outputs 0xff. After then this masking bit are used for AND operation with operand B. If the BIT is 0xff, masked operand M is operand B. If not masked operand M is set to zero variable. The computed masked operand M is finally bit-wise exclusive-ored with intermediate results C. Since MBC method exploits many masking process, it shows low performance results than previous approaches. In order to boost the performance, we adopted the asymptotically faster multiplication namely Karatsuba multiplication.

In Algorithm 3, 64-bit wise Karatsuba Masked Block-Comb method is introduced. We selected 64-bit for practical usages because size of binary field ECC is multiple of 64-bit and modern processors including INTEL and ARM provide 64-bit polynomial multiplication. This means our method can readily adopt the other 64-bit optimization techniques to the embedded processors as well [6–8]. In Step 1, 32-bit wise MSK multiplication is conducted on $A[3 \sim 0]$ and $B[3 \sim 0]$ and outputs lower part of intermediate results ($L[7 \sim 0]$). In Step 2,

Algorithm 3. 64-bit Karatsuba Block Comb

Require: An eight 8-bit operand A(64-bit) and B(64-bit)
Ensure: C(128-bit)$= A \cdot B$
1: $L[7 \sim 0] = (A[3 \sim 0] \times_{32-bit} B[3 \sim 0])$
2: $H[7 \sim 0] = (A[7 \sim 4] \times_{32-bit} B[7 \sim 4])$
3: $M[7 \sim 0] = ((A[7 \sim 4] \oplus A[3 \sim 0]) \times_{32-bit} (B[7 \sim 4] \oplus B[3 \sim 0]))$
4: $M[7 \sim 0] = M[7 \sim 0] \oplus L[7 \sim 0] \oplus H[7 \sim 0]$
5: $C = H[7 \sim 0] \cdot 2^{64} \oplus M[7 \sim 0] \cdot 2^{32} \oplus L[7 \sim 0]$
6: **return** C

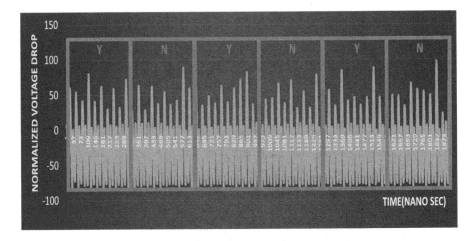

Fig. 4. Power traces of proposed method

higher part ($H[7 \sim 0]$) are computed by multiplying $A[7 \sim 4]$ and $B[7 \sim 4]$. In Step 3, high and low part of operands A and B are bit-wise exclusive-ored and then the operands are multiplied to output middle part ($M[7 \sim 0]$). In Step 4, higher and lower parts are bit-wise exclusive-ored with middle part. It Step 5, all intermediate results are bit-wise exclusive-ored. Total 64-bit Karatsuba Masked Block-Comb needs 1926 clock cycles. In order to construct binary field multiplication for sect163k1 and sect233k1 with 64-bit API, we need 192 and 256-bit multiplications. For 163-bit multiplication we adopt three terms Karatsuba multiplication. The method reduces the three multiplication out of nine multiplication operations. For 233-bit multiplication we conduct four terms Karatsuba multiplication. Firstly we construct 128-bit binary field multiplication with 1 level Karatsuba with 64-bit 1 level Karatsuba and then this 128-bit multiplication is used for 1 level of 256-bit multiplication. Totally three levels of Karatsuba multiplication is used.

As like previous Block-Comb variants, we also collected the power traces of proposed methods. The detailed descriptions are available in Fig. 4. The red blocks represent one round of Table 3. The operation consists of register based operations and there is no consecutive memory accesses. For this reason, the power traces do not leak information through timing and power consumption

Table 4. Clock cycles for 163- and 233-bit multiplication on binary fields.

Method	Technique	Vulnerability	Clock Cycle
163-bit binary field multiplication			
Kargl et al. [10]	4-bit wise Lookup Table	LUT access	5,057
Aranha et al. [1]	4-bit wise Lookup Table	LUT access	4,508
Seo et al. [15]	Unbalanced Block Comb	Branch op	4,346
Seo et al. [16]	Karatsuba Block Comb	Branch op	3,274
Seo et al. [16]	Constant Karatsuba Block Comb	Branch op	5,005
Proposed Method	**Masked Karatsuba Block Comb**	-	**14,445**
233-bit binary field multiplication			
Aranha et al. [1]	4-bit wise Lookup Table	LUT access	8,314
Proposed Method	**Masked Karatsuba Block Comb**	-	**20,537**

that is common vulnerabilities of Block-Comb methods. Since MBC method does not access memory in consecutive way, our SCA on LUT does not work properly. In Fig. 4, the symbols including Y and N represent 0xff mask and 0x00 mask, respectively. In Table 4, performance of binary field multiplication is described. LUT based approach exploits 4-bit wise lookup table accesses but it leaks memory access pattern as we pointed out in this paper. In terms of Block-Comb method, it shows the highest performance. However it is not constant time solution and branch operation leaks power consumption information. The constant Karatusba Block-Comb method is even an atomic solution but it is still based on branch operation which leaks power consumption information. Our proposed method namely masked Karatsuba Block-Comb method shows the lowest speed performance but it does not include vulnerabilities found in existing approaches. Furthermore, our method is easily scalable with Karatsuba approaches. The overheads from 163 to 233 is only 1.4 but previous works are 1.8. For this reason, our method would be better choice for large operands.

5   Conclusion

In this paper, we conduct side channel attacks on LUT based binary field multiplication by collecting the power traces from LUT accesses. We also presented the novel binary field multiplication namely masked Karatsuba Block-Comb. This method exploits masking method to get regular form of results which is also easily scalable for large operands. Our future works are attacking the other algorithms based on LUT such as window methods for exponentiation and scalar multiplication. It is also worth to note that binary field squaring is also using constant look-up table and our attack would be available in this case as well. Furthermore, for higher performance we will try to optimize the current implementation techniques for practical applications. Lastly but not least we will evaluate performance of GCM and other ECC primitives with proposed secure binary field multiplication.

References

1. Aranha, D.F., Dahab, R., López, J., Oliveira, L.B.: Efficient implementation of elliptic curve cryptography in wireless sensors. Adv. Math. Comm. 4(2), 169–187 (2010)
2. Brier, E., Clavier, C., Olivier, F.: Correlation power analysis with a leakage model. In: Joye, M., Quisquater, J.-J. (eds.) CHES 2004. LNCS, vol. 3156, pp. 16–29. Springer, Heidelberg (2004)
3. Chari, S., Jutla, C.S., Rao, J.R., Rohatgi, P.: Towards sound approaches to counteract power-analysis attacks. In: Wiener, M. (ed.) CRYPTO 1999. LNCS, vol. 1666, pp. 398–412. Springer, Heidelberg (1999)
4. Chen, C.-N.: Memory address side-channel analysis on exponentiation. In: Lee, J., Kim, J. (eds.) ICISC 2014. LNCS, vol. 8949, pp. 421–432. Springer, Heidelberg (2014)
5. Clavier, C., Feix, B., Gagnerot, G., Roussellet, M., Verneuil, V.: Horizontal correlation analysis on exponentiation. In: Soriano, M., Qing, S., López, J. (eds.) ICICS 2010. LNCS, vol. 6476, pp. 46–61. Springer, Heidelberg (2010)
6. Gouvêa, C.P.L., López, J.: Implementing GCM on ARMv8. In: Nyberg, K. (ed.) CT-RSA 2015. LNCS, vol. 9048, pp. 167–180. Springer, Heidelberg (2015)
7. Gueron, S.: AES-GCM software performance on the current high end CPUs as a performance baseline for CAESAR competition
8. Gueron, S., Kounavis, M.E.: Intel® carry-less multiplication instruction and its usage for computing the GCM mode. Intel white paper (2010), September 2012
9. Hankerson, D., Vanstone, S., Menezes, A.J.: Guide to Elliptic Curve Cryptography. Springer, New York (2004)
10. Kargl, A., Pyka, S., Seuschek, H.: Fast arithmetic on ATmega128 for elliptic curve cryptography. IACR Cryptology ePrint Archive 2008, 442 (2008)
11. Kocher, P.C., Jaffe, J., Jun, B.: Differential power analysis. In: Wiener, M. (ed.) CRYPTO 1999. LNCS, vol. 1666, pp. 388–397. Springer, Heidelberg (1999)
12. López, J., Dahab, R.: High-speed software multiplication in F2m. In: Roy, B., Okamoto, E. (eds.) INDOCRYPT 2000. LNCS, vol. 1977, pp. 203–212. Springer, Heidelberg (2000)
13. Messerges, T.S., Dabbish, E.A., Sloan, R.H.: Investigations of power analysis attacks on smartcards. In: USENIX workshop on smartcard technology, vol. 17, p. 17 (1999)
14. Oliveira, L.B., Aranha, D.F., Gouvêa, C.P., Scott, M., Câmara, D.F., López, J., Dahab, R.: TinyPBC: pairings for authenticated identity-based non-interactive key distribution in sensor networks. Comput. Commun. 34(3), 485–493 (2011)
15. Seo, H., Lee, Y., Kim, H., Park, T., Kim, H.: Binary and prime field multiplication for public key cryptography on embedded microprocessors. Secur. Commun. Netw. 7(4), 774–787 (2014)
16. Seo, H., Liu, Z., Choi, J., Kim, H.: Karatsuba-block-comb technique for elliptic curve cryptography over binary fields. Secur. Commun. Netw. 8(17), 3121–3130 (2015)
17. Seo, S.C., Han, D.-G., Kim, H.C., Hong, S.: TinyECCK: Efficient elliptic curve cryptography implementation over GF(2m) on 8-bit micaz mote. IEICE Trans. Inf. Syst. 91(5), 1338–1347 (2008)

18. Shirase, M., Miyazaki, Y., Takagi, T., Han, D.-G.: Efficient implementation of pairing-based cryptography on a sensor node. IEICE Trans. Inf. Syst. **92**(5), 909–917 (2009)

19. Szczechowiak, P., Oliveira, L.B., Scott, M., Collier, M., Dahab, R.: NanoECC: testing the limits of elliptic curve cryptography in sensor networks. In: Verdone, R. (ed.) EWSN 2008. LNCS, vol. 4913, pp. 305–320. Springer, Heidelberg (2008)

An Improved Second-Order Power Analysis Attack Based on a New Refined Expecter
- *Case Study on Protected AES* -

Hyunjin Ahn[1,2], Neil Hanley[2], Maire O'Neill[2], and Dong-Guk Han[1,3]($\boxtimes$)

[1] Department of Financial Information Security, Kookmin University, Seoul, Korea
ahz012@kookmin.ac.kr
[2] Centre for Secure Information Technologies, Queen's University, Belfast, UK
{n.hanley,maire.oneill}@qub.ac.uk
[3] Department of Mathematics, Kookmin University, Seoul, Korea
christa@kookmin.ac.kr

Abstract. This work proposes an improved second-order correlation power analysis attack based on a new *refined expecter* ($\mathcal{RE}$). The predicted $\mathcal{RE}$ with the correct secret key is related to the Hamming weight of the Sbox output mask with a correlation coefficient of 0.35. It gives an improved attack performance in comparison with a traditional second-order attack which exhibits a correlation value of 0.24. In order to verify the practicability and performance of the proposed attack, we perform experiments on both simulated data and an AES implementation on an ARM SecureCore device, protected with first-order masking and shuffling countermeasures. The results demonstrate that our proposed attack outperforms the conventional second-order attack.

Keywords: Side-channel attack · Second-order power analysis · Software countermeasure · Masking-shuffling countermeasure

1 Introduction

Kocher *et al.* proposed side-channel analysis to recover secret data from side-channel information [10]. Various techniques have subsequently been developed, for instance Correlation Power Analysis (CPA) which exploits Pearson's correlation coefficient to reveal the secret data [1].

In order to thwart side-channel attacks, a variety of countermeasures have been proposed. In particular, masking and the randomization of operations are both effective schemes for use in software implementations [3,12,15,16]. Masking acts to change the expected intermediate value of a cryptographic operation using randomly chosen masks. The randomization of operations, commonly referred to as shuffling, changes the order of operations and therefore distributes them over a period of execution time. Thus with shuffling, the intermediate value now occurs with a certain probability at any given instant, diminishing the relationship between the intermediate value and measured information.

H. Kim and D. Choi (Eds.): WISA 2015, LNCS 9503, pp. 174–186, 2016.
DOI: 10.1007/978-3-319-31875-2_15

The combination of masking and shuffling countermeasures was examined in [15] as a means of providing a good security/performance tradeoff. In particular, Herbst *et al.* proposed a combination of first-order masking and shuffling in [8]. The authors argued that since their countermeasures would require a very large number of traces to be attacked, that they could therefore be considered to be secure against second-order CPA (SOCPA) attacks [12,14]. For this reason, these types of countermeasures have been implemented in smart cards as well as compact embedded devices. However, we contend that this combination of countermeasures is fundamentally vulnerable to SOCPA.

There have been many publications relating to the retrieval of the Hamming weight value from targeted variables, which is the so called Hamming weight estimator function. Profiling attacks have been shown to be most effective in this area [4,17]. However, they have a significant limitation in that they require a programmable device similar to the targeted one. In contrast to the profiling attacks, Linge *et al.* and Cho *et al.* proposed reasonable Hamming weight estimator functions in [2,11], respectively. Additionally, an attack method was proposed in [2], Biasing Power Analysis (BPA), that defeats the combined countermeasure by applying their estimator function to the power consumption of Sbox output mask. Although reasonable methods do not yield as precise a Hamming weight value as more elaborate methods (e.g. templates), they are good at obtaining an approximation of it by using only measured traces. More precisely, they are able to extract Hamming weight values from measured signals without additional requirements such as an identical target device with a known secret key, high computational cost, etc. They therefore promoted these reasonable assumption attacks, rather than template based techniques [4,17]. The reasonable methods work for collected signals consisting of uniformly distributed data.

Contributions. In this paper, we propose an improved SOCPA attack based on a new *refined expecter* $(\mathcal{RE})$. In order to apply our attack, the measured traces incorporate the processing of a masked sensitive variable and its mask value at some point. Note that the attacker does not need to know the exact point in time where the mask occurs. Whilst the SOCPA, which considers a masked Sbox and its output mask, has the same key search space size as our attack (2^8 key candidates), our refined expecter $\mathcal{RE}$, predicts the correct key with a maximum correlation of 0.35, while the straightforward SOCPA has a correlation of 0.24. Thanks to this increased correlation value, our attack can employ Hamming weight estimator functions which are less accurate than profiling methods. However, our attack outperforms traditional SOCPA with a reasonable assumptive requirement. In this article, we present a feasible attack flow, including how to determine the *points of interest (PoI)*, and characterize the performance of our attack in simulations and real-life traces for a protected implementation of AES [5]. From a variety of experiments considering diverse noise levels, we demonstrate that our proposed attack outperforms existing attack methods, SOCPA and BPA. In particular, our attack yields considerably better result than others in noisy environments. The proposed attack yields a guessing entropy of under 10 on at most 30,300 simulation traces with a noise level of $SNR^1 = 2^{-1}$, while neither the SOCPA nor BPA methods result in a guessing entropy of under 10 on the traces (cf. Table 2). Our attack is applicable to other block ciphers protected with first-order masking and shuffling countermeasures.

Organization. The remainder of this paper is organized as follows. Section 2 summarizes an overview of our target countermeasure, conventional SOCPA attacks and both reasonable Hamming weight estimator functions. In Sect. 3, we introduce our attack with practical work flow. Section 4 describes the attack environment and presents the results for both simulated and realistic scenarios. Finally, our conclusions are stated in Sect. 5.

2 Preliminaries

2.1 Notation

In this paper, we denote a set of N measured traces as a matrix $\mathbf{T} = (\mathbf{t}_n)_{n \in [1,N]}$. In the traces, function f relates to a certain period of time, expressed as $\mathbf{T}^f = (\mathbf{t}_n^f)_{n \in [1,N]}$. If the number of points relating to this period is l, we denote $\mathbf{t}_n^f = (t_{n,i}^f)_{i \in [1,l]}$. For an effective description, we introduce the concept of a *point of interest (PoI)*, which is an instant of l. We denote a power value at PoI as t_n^f, and can therefore rewrite $\mathbf{T}^f$ as $(t_n^f)_{n \in [1,N]}$. Sometimes we use t^f to express any t_n^f. Hereafter, we focus on the PoI based expression.

For n-bit data $x = \sum_{i=0}^{n-1} x_i 2^i$ ($x_i \in \{0,1\}$), its Hamming weight is calculated as $h(x) = \sum_{i=0}^{n-1} x_i$. The notation $\oplus$ relates to the exclusive-or operation.

2.2 Masked and Randomized Countermeasure for AES

In software implementations, the combination of masking and shuffling is a reasonable choice in order to render effective protection for cryptographic algorithms. In [8], Herbst *et al.* applied first-order masking together with shuffling to AES to make it suitable for smart card implementations. For the sake of performance, the SubBytes operation is implemented as a table look-up which has 8-bit inputs and outputs. A Boolean masking scheme is not only applied to all rounds, but also to the key-schedule. All intermediate values within the masked rounds and the key schedule are exclusive-or'd with one of six different masking bytes. These masking bytes consist of the input and output masks, M and M', for use within the masked SubBytes operation, and four input masks, $M1$, $M2$, $M3$ and $M4$, for use within the MixColumns operation.

At the beginning of each AES algorithm, three pre-computations are performed. The first generates six random masks. The second computes a masked Sbox table S' such that $S'(x \oplus M) = S(x) \oplus M'$ (S denotes the Sbox table).

---

[1] An *signal-to-noise ratio (SNR)* is the ratio between variance of signal and of noise, and denoted by $\frac{\sigma^2(signal)}{\sigma^2(noise)}$ [12]. The higher *SNR*, the higher quality of the trace.

The third, outputs masks, $M1'$, $M2'$, $M3'$ and $M4'$, by performing the Mix-Columns operation using $M1$, $M2$, $M3$ and $M4$ as input values.

The first and last rounds are only interleaved with the shuffling scheme. For AddRoundKey, SubBytes and ShiftRows, the sequence of processing the 16 bytes can be dealt with independently. In MixedColumns, the order of the processing of both four-columns and four-rows within each column can be randomized simultaneously. Consequently, an intermediate value is operated with a probability $\frac{1}{16}$ at any particular instant.

2.3   Description of the SOCPA

Although a first-order masking countermeasure can thwart a first-order CPA attack, nevertheless, it is still vulnerable to a more sophisticated attack, such as the SOCPA. In the SOCPA attack, one considers two points, t^{f_1} and t^{f_2} in a measured trace which manipulates two distinct functions, f_1 and f_2 respectively. If both functions are related to a single mask, then it holds that $pre(t^{f_1}, t^{f_2})$ is related to $h(f_1 \oplus f_2)$. Specifically this equation has correlation coefficient $\rho = 0.24$, when the preprocess function $pre()$ is absolute difference and the outputs of both functions are 8-bit data [12].

There are two main approaches to perform the SOCPA attack. Firstly by targeting two distinct masked Sboxes, S_i' and S_j'. In this case, candidate keys are treated in $\{0,1\}^{16}$ for successful attack. Secondly by taking into account the masked Sbox and its mask value, S_i' and M', the key guesses are handled within $\{0,1\}^8$. From the perspective of the number of elements in the key space, the latter is a more convenient method.

2.4   The Reasonable Hamming Weight Estimator Functions

We now briefly describe the Hamming weight estimator functions of [2,11]. In the following treatments we consider N measurements manipulating a function $f()$ with input x. The function is bijective over $\{0,1\}^8$ and the input is different from one execution to another. Hereafter the Hamming weight estimator functions are denoted as φ: $\varphi(t^{f(x)}) = h(f(x))$.

Linge's Scheme. In [11], Linge et al. proposed a reasonable Hamming weight estimator function, that takes into account the distribution of processed data. This scheme is established from two properties of Hamming weight model:

- The Hamming weight value is proportional to the measured value.
- Among the measured values, $\frac{N \times C_8^p}{2^8}$ elements have a certain Hamming weight $p \in [0,8]$.

Using the above properties the Hamming weight can be estimated as follows: For a set $\{t_n^{f(x)}\}_{n \in [1,N]}$, we sort it in an ascending order. The maximum Hamming weight value 8 is assigned to the $\frac{N \times C_8^8}{2^8}$ highest elements of the sorted set.

7 is assigned to the $\frac{N \times C_8^7}{2^8}$ next highest elements. The rest of Hamming weight values p are assigned to the $\frac{N \times C_8^p}{2^8}$ elements, in the same manner.

Cho's Scheme. Another scheme is proposed by Cho *et al.* in [2]. This scheme is based on a feature that can be derived from the first property above. The property implies that distances between any two measured values which are manipulating two adjacent Hamming weight values are constant. For instance, $t^{f(z)} - t^{f(y)} = t^{f(y)} - t^{f(x)}$, where $h(f(x)) = 3$, $h(f(y)) = 4$ and $h(f(z)) = 5$.

This feature can be exploited to estimate the Hamming weight as follows: The range of values is divided into 9 equal segments between the maximum and minimum values of the sorted set $\{t_n^{f(x)}\}_{n \in [1,N]}$. The maximum Hamming weight value is assigned to all elements in the highest part. The rest of the Hamming weights are assigned to each element in consecutive order.

In addition, the authors proposed an attack method, Biasing Power Analysis (BPA), that defeats the combined countermeasure by applying their estimator function to the power consumption of Sbox output mask. We expect $h(S')$ as $h(S)$ when $\varphi(t^{M'})$ takes value corresponding to 0 and 1, or bit inversion of $h(S)$, denoted by $h(\sim S)$, when $\varphi(t^{M'})$ is 7 and 8. Finally, it reveals the secret key by comparing the expected values with signals relating to the masked Sbox.

$$h(S') = \begin{cases} h(S) & \text{if } \varphi(t^{M'}) \leq 1 \\ h(\sim S) & \text{if } \varphi(t^{M'}) \geq 7 \end{cases}$$

3   The Proposed Attack

In order to reveal the secret key, the general SOCPA methods [12] compare mask-free intermediate values with preprocessed traces which are related to the expected value. By contrast, our proposed attack requires the Sbox output mask as an intermediate value. To reveal the secret key, an attacker directly compares the intermediate value with the trace points relating to the Sbox output mask. Therefore, our attack has the same assumptions to the SOCPA which considers a masked Sbox and output mask value. The rest of this section describes the proposed attack in detail.

3.1   The Refined Expecter

Our goal is to determine the proper Hamming weight of the Sbox output mask from collected side channel information, e.g. power consumption, and guessable value.

Intuitively, taking into account the second-order preprocessing function (cf. Sect. 2.3), an attacker who is aware of $h(S')$ is readily able to infer $h(M')$ by guessing $h(S)$ with a correct key candidate. By introducing the reasonable Hamming weight estimator functions, we can exploit $\varphi(t^{S'})$ instead of the $h(S')$ within our attack assumptions. We denote the *expecter*($\mathcal{E}$) as $|\varphi(t^{S'}) - h(S)|$.

Since the expecter is based on a second-order preprocessing function, it is related to $h(M')$ as 0.24, if $\varphi(t^{S'})$ has success rate of 1.

Moreover, if we consider relations among $h(M')$, $h(S)$ and $h(S')$, we can get a refined expecter which is further related to $h(M')$. The *refined expecter* ($\mathcal{RE}$) is defined as follows:

Definition 1. $\forall \alpha, \beta \in [0, 8]$, *let* $X^{\alpha} = \{x | h(x) = \alpha, x \in \{0, 1\}^8\}$ *and* $Y^{\beta} = \{y | h(y) = \beta, y \in \{0, 1\}^8\}$. *Let a set* $U^{\alpha, \beta} = \{u_{i,j} = h(x_i \oplus y_j) | x_i \in X^{\alpha}, y_j \in Y^{\beta}$, *where* $1 \leq i \leq |X^{\alpha}|$ *and* $1 \leq j \leq |Y^{\beta}|\}$. *Define a refined expecter* $\mathcal{RE}$ *for* α *and* β, $\mathcal{RE}(\alpha, \beta)$, *as mean value of the set* $U^{\alpha, \beta}$:

$$\mathcal{RE}(\alpha, \beta) = \frac{1}{|U^{\alpha, \beta}|} \times \sum_{u_{i,j} \in U^{\alpha, \beta}} u_{i,j}.$$

For instance, if $\alpha = 1$ and $\beta = 1$, then $U^{1,1}$ consists of two types of elements, 0 and 2, and the number of both elements are 8 and 56, respectively. Therefore, $\mathcal{RE}(1, 1)$ is identical to $\frac{0 \times 8 + 2 \times 56}{64} = 1.75$. Table 1 shows overall $\mathcal{RE}(\alpha, \beta)$ according to 9×9 input pairs.

We can utilize the $\mathcal{RE}$ in our attack by applying $h(S)$ and $\varphi(t^{S'})$ instead of α and β, respectively.

Theorem 1. *Let us define two vectors* $\mathbf{V} = (v_{i,j})_{i,j \in \{0,1\}^8}$ *with* $v_{i,j} = h(i \oplus j)$ *and* $\mathbf{W} = (w_{i,j})_{i,j \in \{0,1\}^8}$ *with* $w_{i,j} = \mathcal{RE}(h(i), h(j))$. *Then*

$$\rho(\mathbf{V}, \mathbf{W}) = 0.35.$$

Proof. By performing an exhaustive search, the extracted correlation was determined to be 0.35. $\square$

From Theorem 1, we can demonstrate that the correlation coefficient between $\mathcal{RE}$ and $h(M')$ is 0.35 by taking S and $S'(= S \oplus M')$ into account as i and j, respectively. Compared with $\mathcal{E}$, this provides significant improvement in the magnitude of the relation.

3.2   Workflow

In the previous section, it is demonstrated that $\mathcal{RE}$ is more closely related than that between $\mathcal{E}$ and $h(M')$. Therefore, we describe the attack flow based on $\mathcal{RE}$. The proposed attack consists of two phases: (1) Pre-computation phase and (2) Analysis phase.

In pre-computation phase, the Hamming weight estimator function is applied at the instant of a targeted masked SubBytes in measured trace. Indeed, the performance of φ is susceptible to the considered instant. A variety of research examines the significance of *PoI* and how to determine the *PoI* when attacking masked countermeasures [6, 7, 13, 18]. They have suggested some solutions to this

Table 1. Refined expecter according to input pair

β \ α	0	1	2	3	4	5	6	7	8
0	0	1	2	3	4	5	6	7	8
1	1	1.75	2.5	3.25	4	4.75	5.5	6.25	7
2	2	2.5	3	3.5	4	4.5	5	5.5	6
3	3	3.25	3.5	3.75	4	4.25	4.5	4.75	5
4	4	4	4	4	4	4	4	4	4
5	5	4.75	4.5	4.25	4	3.75	3.5	3.25	3
6	6	5.5	5	4.5	4	3.5	3	2.5	2
7	7	6.25	5.5	4.75	4	3.25	2.5	1.75	1
8	8	7	6	5	4	3	2	1	0

problem, which often require high computational overhead. For the sake of simplicity and performance, we recommend to exploit trace compression techniques. If multiple points of the targeted operation are compressed to just one value, it can give reasonable results with low cost. In fact, this method can be employed when the portion of masked SubBytes operation is visually distinguished in a waveform, if not using an average trace may allow to eliminate some of noise effect.

Finally, the analysis phase recovers the secret key by comparing measured traces with the $\mathcal{RE}$ which is determined according to the key guess value. When the $\mathcal{RE}$ is inferred with a correct key, its correlation stands out. Note that, as previously stated, since this attack determines Hamming weight of the mask followed by comparing it with the collected signal value, the measured power traces should include instant for handling the mask. An attacker does not need to determine the specific part for mask in a measured trace. The overall attack flow is given in Algorithm 1.

Algorithm 1. Proposed Attack flow

▷ **Pre-computation Phase**
Select *PoI*
for all N measured traces **do**
    Calculate $\varphi(t^{S'})$
end for

▷ **Analysis Phase**
$CPA(\mathbf{T}^{M'}, \mathcal{RE}(h(S), \varphi(t^{S'})))$ /* $h(S)$ is depend on key candidate */
---

4   Experimentation

In this section, we empirically demonstrate the practicability and performance of the proposed attack in both simulated and real-world scenarios. In order to verify the attack performance, we compare attack results between the SOCPA targeting the masked Sbox and its output mask, the BPA, and our proposed attack. Our attack is combined with the two reasonable Hamming weight estimator functions. Hereafter, the attack using Linge's method is denoted by $\mathcal{RE} + Linge$ and utilizing Cho's scheme is denoted by $\mathcal{RE} + Cho$.

4.1   Attack Environment

The intended algorithm is a protected AES implementation with first-order masking and shuffling (cf. Sect. 2.2). To simplify our experiments, the algorithm is implemented as in Algorithm 2, however the results presented are applicable to the general case. For every execution of the algorithm, fresh masks, M and M', are randomly generated. The protected AES is considered both in simulation and practical scenarios. In particular, we focus on step 2 and 9 which treat the Sbox output mask generation and the masked SubBytes function respectively.

Algorithm 2. Structure of Target Algorithm

Input: *Plaintext* $\{pt_i\}_{i \in [0,15]}$, *Round key* $\{rk_i\}_{i \in [0,15]}$
Output: *Output* $\{out_i\}_{i \in [0,15]}$
 1: $M \leftarrow rand()$,
 2: $M' \leftarrow rand()$
 3: Generate random sequence $\{seq_i\}_{i \in [0,15]}$
 4: Generate masked Sbox S'
 5: **for all** i **do**
 6:     $temp[i] \leftarrow (pt_i \oplus M) \oplus rk_i$ /* Key Addition with masking*/
 7: **end for**
 8: **for all** i **do**
 9:     $out_i \leftarrow S'(temp[seq_i])$ /* SubBytes with masking and shuffling*/
10: **end for**

The determination of *PoI* may vary according to attack method. Concrete methodologies employed in our experiments are outlined as follows:

– SOCPA: set the most informative two distinct points for the masked Sbox and its output mask as $t^{S'}$ and $t^{M'}$, respectively.
– BPA: exploits the $t^{M'}$ which is identical to above. Additionally the *Windowing* method is employed as utilized in [2].
– $\mathcal{RE} + Linge$ and $+Cho$: utilize $t^{S'}$ which is equal to the sum of overall points for the masked SubBytes operation in a measured trace.

   In the simulation scenario, we generate $100,000 \times 50 = 5,000,000$ virtual traces for the various *SNR* in MATLAB. The power consumption values follow the Hamming weight model and have additive white gaussian noise[2].

---
[2] This follows normal distribution with $\mu = 0$ and σ^2, where μ and σ^2 indicate mean and variance, respectively.

Formally, for sub-function f of the algorithm, its input x and $noise \sim N(0, \sigma^2)$, the corresponding simulation power is generated as follows:

$$vt^{f(x)} = h(f(x)) + noise$$

For the practical attack, our *device under test (DUT)* consists of an IC-chip card based on ARM SecureCore and the target algorithm. We measure the power consumption for processing the algorithm on the IC-chip card. In total $50,000 \times 50 = 2,500,000$ traces are collected with an oscilloscope *Lecroy Wave Runner HDO 6104* at sampling rate 250MS/s. For the sake of performance and computational cost, we downsample to 5MS/s by the *Raw Integration* [12] compression method. Particularly, as previously mentioned, in order to extract relevant *PoI*, the power consumption for masked SubBytes are compressed to a single point value. From this point, we get our model $\varphi(t^{S'})$.

4.2   Experimental Results

We present here attack results on both simulation and real-life traces. For the simulated traces, for each *SNR*, we perform the experiment 50 times.

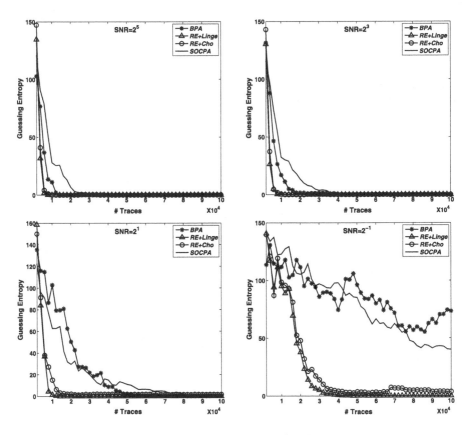

Fig. 1. Attack results on simulated traces

Figure 1 shows the guessing entropy[3] of the four considered attack methods. For all *SNR* values, both our attacks, $\mathcal{RE} + Linge$ and $+Cho$, have a lower guessing entropy than the other methods. The BPA also generally outperforms the SOCPA, however, the SOCPA has a better result when the $SNR=2^{-1}$. This reversal is caused by the low success rate of Cho's Hamming weight estimator function. From Table 3 in Appendix A, we can verify that the success rate of $SNR=2^{-1}$ is significantly lower when Hamming weight is 0, 1, 7 and 8. Table 2 shows the minimum number of traces which yields a guessing entropy of under 10 as shown in Fig. 1.

Similar to our attacks on simulated data, we conduct the experiment 50 times on actual power traces. Figure 2 also shows that $\mathcal{RE}$s outperform other methods, and $\mathcal{RE} + Linge$ yields the best result. However, there is an interesting point to note. The *DUT* has an *SNR* of about 1.07, and thus we can intuitively expect that its result can be extrapolated from the $SNR=2^1$ and $SNR=2^{-1}$ results in Fig. 1, *i.e.* the attack performance of the BPA should be either similar to or worse

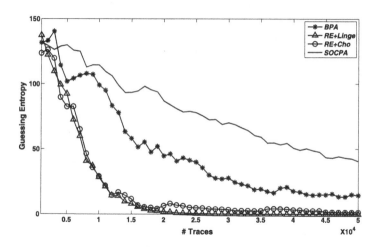

Fig. 2. Attack results on realistic traces

Table 2. The minimum number of traces producing a guessing entropy of under 10 (unit=10^4)

attack \ SNR	2^5	2^3	2^1	2^{-1}
SOCPA [14]	1.67	2.15	5.18	fail
BPA [2]	0.90	1.08	3.61	fail
$\mathcal{RE} + Cho$	0.29	0.31	0.95	3.03
$\mathcal{RE} + Linge$	0.29	0.31	0.56	2.30

---

[3] The guessing entropy indicates the average of how many key bytes remain to be guessed [9].

than the result of the SOCPA. However, the BPA outperforms the SOCPA as the real-life traces have misalignment problem and the *windowing* method used in BPA helps mitigate the problem. This is why the BPA yields more efficient results than the SOCPA on actual traces. Finally, it is demonstrated that our proposed $\mathcal{RE}$ has superior performance in noisy environments when reasonable Hamming weight estimator functions are employed.

5   Conclusion

In this paper we proposed an improved SOCPA based on a new *refined expecter*, which can overcome first-order masking combined with shuffling countermeasure. The *refined expecter* reveals the secret key with a maximum correlation value of 0.35. The proposed attack was conducted in a key space of $\{0, 1\}^8$ with identical assumptions to the SOCPA attack targeting a masked Sbox and its output mask. Through simulation and actual power traces, the performance and practicability of our proposed attack were demonstrated. We exploited 4 types of simulation traces which were applied different noise level and actual traces measured from IC card. Overall in the experiments (simulation and real-life traces), our proposed $\mathcal{RE}$ outperformed the existing attack methods, SOCPA and BPA, when using the reasonable Hamming weight estimator functions. In particular, when more noisy environments are considered, our attack yielded better performance than others. Additionally, we conducted performance evaluation of both Hamming weight estimator functions on 6 types of simulation traces according to various noise levels. From the result, we verified properties of both reasonable Hamming weight functions, according to Hamming weight values.

Though this paper took into account the AES as a case study, our attack is equally applicable to other block ciphers protected by first-order masking and shuffling schemes.

Acknowledgements. This research was supported by Basic Science Research Program through the National Research Foundation of Korea(NRF) funded by the Ministry of Education(NRF-2013R1A1A2A10062137). The authors would like to thank Dooho Choi at ETRI for supporting us with SCARF boards (http://www.k-scarf.or.kr/). The SCARF boards were supported by the KLA-SCARF project, the ICT R&D program of ETRI.

A   Performance Evaluation of Reasonable Hamming Weight Estimator Functions

Both reasonable Hamming weight estimator functions, Cho's method [2] and Linge's method [11], effectively calibrate the Hamming weight value in noise-free signals. On the contrary, in noisy environments, they are likely to have different performances. This section shows the performance evaluation of both in various *SNR* scenarios.

In this experiment, we consider simulation traces manipulating 8-bit random mask generation. For the sake of comparison, 6 different simulation traces of varying SNR were generated for exploitation in this experiment. Each type includes different white gaussian noise which is generated in MATLAB (simulator is described in Sect. 5.1 in detail). In this experiment, for each SNR, we run 50 experiments of 40,000 simulation traces $i.e.$ in total $40,000 \times 50 = 2,000,000$ traces are used for a certain SNR.

Table 3 shows that the SNR is proportional to success rate. White indicates that success rate of Linge's method is higher than Cho's, while dark gray in contrast to white. For both methods, the closer to 0 or 8 the Hamming weight, the lower the success rate. However, Linge's method outperforms Cho's for most Hamming weights except for 3–5, while the total resolution of Cho's scheme is higher than the other on noisier traces.

Table 3. Success rates of both Hamming weight estimator functions (Linge's method / Cho's method)

SNR \ $h(f(x))$	0	1	2	3	4	5	6	7	8	total
2^5	0.932	0.949	0.956	0.958	0.959	0.957	0.956	0.950	0.933	0.957
	/0.926	/0.935	/0.946	/0.954	/0.956	/0.954	/0.945	/0.932	/0.928	/0.951
2^3	0.623	0.675	0.701	0.714	0.717	0.712	0.698	0.675	0.622	0.708
	/0.402	/0.522	/0.633	/0.715	/0.742	/0.713	/0.630	/0.515	/0.389	/0.689
2^1	0.304	0.383	0.428	0.453	0.460	0.452	0.430	0.383	0.298	0.444
	/0.108	/0.211	/0.347	/0.476	/0.531	/0.483	/0.364	/0.221	/0.117	/0.447
2^{-1}	0.111	0.197	0.269	0.317	0.332	0.317	0.271	0.195	0.107	0.302
	/0.037	/0.098	/0.221	/0.356	/0.414	/0.347	/0.212	/0.091	/0.031	/0.320
2^{-3}	0.033	0.101	0.188	0.262	0.290	0.261	0.189	0.103	0.031	0.242
	/0.009	/0.050	/0.156	/0.308	/0.371	/0.277	/0.126	/0.036	/0.006	/0.263
2^{-5}	0.013	0.061	0.147	0.239	0.277	0.238	0.149	0.063	0.015	0.216
	/0.003	/0.025	/0.110	/0.268	/0.357	/0.258	/0.102	/0.023	/0.003	/0.237

References

1. Brier, E., Clavier, C., Olivier, F.: Correlation power analysis with a leakage model. In: Joye, M., Quisquater, J.-J. (eds.) CHES 2004. LNCS, vol. 3156, pp. 16–29. Springer, Heidelberg (2004)
2. Cho, J.-W., Han, D.-G.: Security analysis of the masking-shuffling based side channel attack countermeasures. J. Secur. Appl. 6(4), 207–214 (2012)
3. Chari, S., Jutla, C.S., Rao, J.R., Rohatgi, P.: Towards sound approaches to counteract power-analysis attacks. In: Wiener, M. (ed.) CRYPTO 1999. LNCS, vol. 1666, pp. 398–412. Springer, Heidelberg (1999)
4. Chari, S., Rao, J.R., Rohatgi, P.: Template attacks. In: Kaliski Jr., B.S., Koç, Ç.K., Paar, C. (eds.) CHES 2002. LNCS, vol. 2523, pp. 13–28. Springer, Heidelberg (2003)

5. FIPS PUB 197. Advanced Encryption Standard. National Institute of Standards and Technology (2001)
6. Grosso, V., Standaert, F.-X., Faust, S.: Masking vs. multiparty computation: how large is the gap for AES? J. Crypt. Eng. 4(1), 47–57 (2014)
7. Grosso, V., Standaert, F.-X., Prouff, E.: Low entropy masking schemes, revisited. In: Francillon, A., Rohatgi, P. (eds.) CARDIS 2013. LNCS, vol. 8419, pp. 33–43. Springer, Heidelberg (2014)
8. Herbst, C., Oswald, E., Mangard, S.: An AES smart card implementation resistant to power analysis attacks. In: Zhou, J., Yung, M., Bao, F. (eds.) ACNS 2006. LNCS, vol. 3989, pp. 239–252. Springer, Heidelberg (2006)
9. Köpf, B., Basin, D.A.: An information-theoretic model for adaptive side-channel attacks. In: Ning, P., Vimercati, S., Syverson, P.F. (eds.) CCS 2007, pp. 286–296 (2007)
10. Kocher, P.C., Jaffe, J., Jun, B.: Differential power analysis. In: Wiener, M. (ed.) CRYPTO 1999. LNCS, vol. 1666, pp. 388–397. Springer, Heidelberg (1999)
11. Linge, Y., Dumas, C., Lambert-Lacroix, S.: Using the joint distributions of a cryptographic function in side channel analysis. In: Prouff, E. (ed.) COSADE 2014. LNCS, vol. 8622, pp. 199–213. Springer, Heidelberg (2014)
12. Mangard, S., Oswald, E., Popp, T.: Power Analysis Attacks - Revealing the Secrets of Smart Cards. Springer, Heidelberg (2007)
13. Oswald, E., Mangard, S., Herbst, C., Tillich, S.: Practical second-order dpa attacks for masked smart card implementations of block ciphers. In: Pointcheval, D. (ed.) CT-RSA 2006. LNCS, vol. 3860, pp. 192–207. Springer, Heidelberg (2006)
14. Prouff, E., Rivain, M., Bevan, R.: Statistical analysis of second order differential power analysis. IEEE Trans. Comput. 58(6), 799–811 (2009)
15. Rivain, M., Prouff, E., Doget, J.: Higher-order masking and shuffling for software implementations of block ciphers. In: Clavier, C., Gaj, K. (eds.) CHES 2009. LNCS, vol. 5747, pp. 171–188. Springer, Heidelberg (2009)
16. Schramm, K., Paar, C.: Higher order masking of the AES. In: Pointcheval, D. (ed.) CT-RSA 2006. LNCS, vol. 3860, pp. 208–225. Springer, Heidelberg (2006)
17. Schindler, W., Lemke, K., Paar, C.: A stochastic model for differential side channel cryptanalysis. In: Rao, J.R., Sunar, B. (eds.) CHES 2005. LNCS, vol. 3659, pp. 30–46. Springer, Heidelberg (2005)
18. Waddle, J., Wagner, D.: Towards efficient second-order power analysis. In: Joye, M., Quisquater, J.-J. (eds.) CHES 2004. LNCS, vol. 3156, pp. 1–15. Springer, Heidelberg (2004)

Various Threat Models to Circumvent Air-Gapped Systems for Preventing Network Attack

Eunchong Lee, Hyunsoo Kim, and Ji Won Yoon[✉]

Center for Information Security Technologies (CIST),
Korea University, Seoul, Republic of Korea
{gr4ce,aitch25,jiwon_yoon}@korea.ac.kr

Abstract. In order to prevent incidents related with information leakage, many enterprises and organizations have installed an air-gapped system. The system is used for separating their own network from a public network such as the Internet. However, researchers have demonstrated possibilities that the air-gapped system can be inactivated by attackers, especially about their advanced attacks with various covert channels. In this paper, we analyzed how much the information could be leaked via the covert channel. We conducted experiments about data communication between a speaker and a microphone which are regarded as a conventional acoustic covert channel. At the same time, we also had expanded the attack scenario into an environment without any microphone. That is, we tested whether the critical information could be leaked and transferred via two loud-speakers as a limited environment where the air-gapped system. Finally, it is shown that the speaker based covert network can be effectively expanded to centrally controlled embedded loudspeakers which have not been considered in a conventional acoustic covert channel.

Keywords: Air-gap malware · Malware communication · Acoustic covert channel communication

1 Introduction

There have been several cyber-terror incidents throughout the world. For instance, the centrifuge of nuclear facilities in Iran was damaged by Stuxnet in 2010 [1], and computer network at Nonghyup, Korean bank, was paralyzed in 2011 due to hacking attack [2]. The computer network of a major media corporate was also stopped in the Republic of Korea [3] in March 20, 2013. Furthermore, the critical information was leaked from Korea hydro & nuclear power company in 2014 [3]. From this history, governments and enterprises have applied network separation to prevent information leakage and to protect their systems from such threats.

© Springer International Publishing Switzerland 2016
H. Kim and D. Choi (Eds.): WISA 2015, LNCS 9503, pp. 187–199, 2016.
DOI: 10.1007/978-3-319-31875-2_16

Especially, Korean government and national intelligence service (NIS) have built the air-gapped system with network separation to avoid leakage of important information [4]. In February, 2012, business operators were required to set network separation in their company if they have over one million personal information data or if their yearly sale is over 10 billion in Korean won [5].

By the effort of the government and the enterprises for resisting damages and reducing risks from leaking important information and maximizing their benefit, a network separation has been utilized in many organization such as Ministry of National Defense [6], financial computer system [6], nuclear power [7] and aviation [8]. In addition, the system has been applied to banks, public corporations, courts, and factories in order to build security system from 2009 to 2014. Several solutions exist to build an effective air-gap environment including Server Based Computing (SBC) and physical separation [9].

Although the government struggles to protect their important information by separating a network, there have been various threats to incapacitate the air-gapped system. Researchers have studied about this, they could derive meaningful results by introducing some methods which circumvent the air-gap security system. In this paper, a covert channel using voice grade sound is focused on, and various threat models via the covert channel are dealing with. Especially, we have demonstrated the possibility of communication between not only a speaker and a microphone but also a speaker to a speaker through this work. Manipulating Windows registry provides us to change the role of the speaker from an output device to an input device, we were also able to experiment in a data communication environment with a speaker to speaker.

However, Prior works mostly focused on the necessity of air-gap separation to prevent the leakage of important information. To make the system effectively, people must be aware of the fact that air-gap separation can be neutralized and the possibility of such detour around according to the solution. Throughout this research, various experiments were practiced by reproducing the air-gap separation circumvention attack via covert channels between a speaker and a microphone. In addition, we show the possibility to neutralize air-gap system and to gain information by only using speakers.

2   Related Work

In 2013, Hanspach et al. used a 5-bit address system for data communication instead of TCP/IP stack in order to reduce an unnecessary overhead [10]. Through this, they demonstrated the possibility of communicating via a speaker and a microphone within 19.7 m at a speed of 20 bit/s. This network stack adapts an emulation system into the underwater acoustic network, which is composed of four parts, called APP, NET, EC, and PHY. The applied layer uses generic underwater application language (GUWAL), from FWG/FKIE to build appropriate communication for low bandwidth [14], and has 16-byte data frame, 2-byte header, 2-byte CRC checksum. The link layer uses 16-bit error verification code and ACS modem based on frequency hopping spread spectrum (FHSS), to build communication with strong resistance of error. In 2014, Guri et al. used audio frequency-shift keying and dual-tone multiple frequency modulation systems to build the physical layer and increased performance by applying DSP such as adaptive noise filtering, equalization, and so on [11]. They could show that the communication between a computer and a cell-phone is possible by using FM signal emitted from video display unit within 1–7 m, at a speed of 13–60 bit/s. The research proved that we can make various secret channels for a covert channel. In addition, Guri et al. built the covert channel between two computers with a temperature sensor and transferred information within 0–40 cm, at a speed of 1–8 bit/s. Despite the limitation of performance [12], the possibility of information leakage remains noticeable. Additionally, Carrara et al. reveals that utilizing OFDM communication mechanism between a speaker and a microphone is possible [13]. Their approach performed at a speed of 6.7 k byte/s for overnight attack and 230 byte/s for the ultrasonic attack.

Generally, speakers are used as an output device. Nevertheless, Lee et al. (2013) show that the loud-speaker can be used as a microphone by simply modifying the operating system (OS) setting [15] and proved that the speaker can provide a certain level of signal to the attacker within 30 cm. There are a lot of similarities between the speaker and the microphone. Especially, they both have a diaphragm which is the key element for utilizing the speaker as an input device. The diaphragm is an important component for input and output of sound. It interacts with the robin and the magnetic field generated from the permanent magnet and creates a vibration from sound pressure. Whenever the speaker used as an input device, it may have different current direction and different trembling vibration due to the difference of material, yet can still play the role of a microphone [15].

Frequency hopping spread spectrum (FHSS) is one of the communication methods used in initial stage of a wireless network through 802.11 physical layer [16]. FHSS is widely used in war industry due to its resistance against jamming. This method sends the same signal through multiple frequencies to increase the reliability of signal transmission. FHSS has 23 channels and transfers data by random hopping sequence throughout the whole channels. Before the signal randomly hops to other channel, it scans a channel whether it has noise or interference of electric wave in order to find stable channel that helps to secure the data while it is transmitting or receiving [17]. In FHSS, whenever signal hops to other channel, it follows the rule of hopping code. It stays very short period of time in a frequency band and hops to another frequency band by the rule of hopping code and keep repeating this process [17].

Orthogonal frequency division multiplexing (OFDM) which is announced after FHSS and DSSS[1], is still actively developed and studied due to its adequacy for high speed data transmission, both through wired and wireless

---

[1] direct-sequence spread spectrum (DSSS) is a spread spectrum modulation technique. Spread spectrum systems are such that they transmit the message bearing signals using a bandwidth that is in excess of the bandwidth that is actually needed by the message signal.

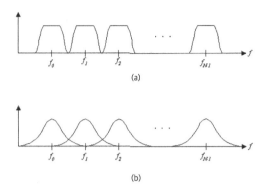

Fig. 1. Frequency Spectrum in OFDM

channels [18,19]. The OFDM has high efficiency of frequency utilization because of multiple orthogonal carrier waves. The process of modulation and demodulation of those carrier waves in the transmitting and receiving stage can be realized at a great rate. Since, the method suits for high-speed data transmission, it is chosen as a standard in IEEE 802.11a, high speed wireless LAN of HIPERLAN/2, Broadband Wireless Access of IEEE 802.16, Digital Audio Broadcasting, Digital Terrestrial Television Broadcasting, ADSL, and VDSL.

In the OFDM, the transmitting cycle increases in accordance with the a number of carrier waves increases. In 1966, the theory to send multiple carrier waves concurrently without interference between channels was introduced, which is shown above in Fig. 1(a) [20]. Later, Orthogonal multiplexing QAM[2] was proposed to prevent interference between channels, which is shown above in Fig. 1(b).

3   Threat Model

In this paper, we have classified three different threat models for air-gapped system.

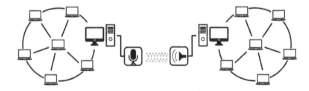

Fig. 2. Covert network between speaker and Microphone (Case 1)

---

[2] Quadrature amplitude modulation (QAM) is both an analog and a digital modulation scheme. It conveys two analog message signals, or two digital bit streams, by changing (modulating) the amplitudes of two carrier waves, using the amplitude-shift keying (ASK) digital modulation scheme or amplitude modulation (AM) analog modulation scheme.

– **Covert Network between Speaker and Microphone (Case 1)**: For the first threat model, let us assume that there are two different devices A and B which are disconnected by the separated network. B in separated networks has been infected with malware. First, a device A (the sender) and a device B (receiver) in the air-gapped system have speakers and microphones respectively. Now, A can transfer the data to B using A's speaker and B' microphone. This is a basic and traditional model to disable the air-gapped system as shown in Fig. 2. This model is well-studied as described in Sect. 2 but we also tested this for the comparison (Fig 3).

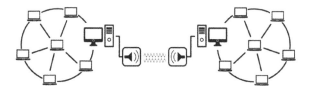

Fig. 3. Covert network between speaker and speaker (Case 2)

– **Covert Network between Speaker and Speaker (Case 2)**: The case 1 is effective and well-studied, but its usage is rather limited. In many situations, targeted system (B) does not equip any microphones physically or the targeted system removes the microphones to avoid the case 1's attack. In this case, case 1 cannot be used since B cannot receive the data from B via the covert channel. For this case, we have made an extension of Case 1 with replacement of the microphone by a speaker for the receiving device. That is, the speaker can be used both for sending and receiving devices. The attacker can use this model since it provides more flexible attack by handling only speakers.
– **Covert Network between the Speaker and Centrally Controlled, Embedded Speaker (Case 3)**: Note that the microphones and speakers in case 1 and case 2 are connected to nearby terminals or devices. However, if we use speakers as a receiver, threat model can be simply expanded as well. For example, speakers can be separately installed and connected to other speakers over a shared line in the building and they are controlled by the central control center. In this case, there is no physically connected nearby terminals or devices. However, hackers can transfer the data to the system using shared loud-speakers which are equipped on the wall. In this case, the target terminal does not have to be nearby to the sender. For example, the attacker can transmit the data using the loudspeaker in toilet of the building if the speaker on toilet wall is controlled by central server and the central server is connected to the separated local network as shown in Fig. 4.

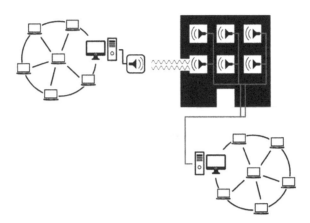

Fig. 4. Covert network between speaker and centrally control embed speaker (Case 3)

4   Technical Background

This research proposes *Speaker Based Covert Network* (SBCN), a communication network based on speakers through the acoustic band. Furthermore, we compare SBCN with existing speaker and microphone based covert network to demonstrate the possibility to communicate with only speakers. For the communication method, OFDM [13] is used to communicate at the speed of 6.7 kbit/s through acoustic frequency band and FHSS [10] is used to communicate at the speed of 20 bit/s when the environment has not any noises. In addition, hamming code is applied to our method for minimizing the error and cyclic redundancy check (CRC) and verifying received data.

4.1   Collecting Sound Signal with Redefining Terminal Pin Number

According to the paper of Lee et al. (2013) [15], loud-speakers can be used as an input device, such as a microphone. To use a speaker as a microphone, modifying terminal setting about each definition is necessary. Especially in Windows, by changing Windows registry, terminal setting for the loud-speaker can be modified simply as a terminal for the microphone. In this scenario, a malicious user can utilize the speaker for the covert network communication after modifying terminal setting of Windows registry.

Table 1 shows the description of pin number and its function. This setting is used to conduct an experiment on Windows 7. Pin numbers "10" to "1b" denote the two front side and six rear sides I/O terminals.

Figure 5 shows the Windows registry modification process in order to use the speaker as a microphone. Each pin registry key has a designated hexadecimal value according to its function, and the sound device will act differently following the value changes. Table 2 matches each hexadecimal value and its function. In this experiment, hexadecimal code "04 00 00 00" is modified to "01 00 00 00" for loud-speaker communication. A malicious code with a permission of administrator can expose normal users at the threat by simply modifying this value. Thus, attackers may be able to control sound devices and force the computer to communicate regardless of air-gap separation.

Table 1. ALC882 codec based sound card pin assignment

Pin #	Function	Pin #	Function
Pin10	Line-in(rear blue)	Pin11	Mic-in(rear pink)
Pin14	Front speakers(rear green)	Pin15	Rear Speakers(rear black)
Pin16	Center / Sub-woofer(rear orange)	Pin17	Side Speakers(rear gray)
Pin19	Front Mic-In(rear pink)	Pin1b	Front Headphone(rear green)

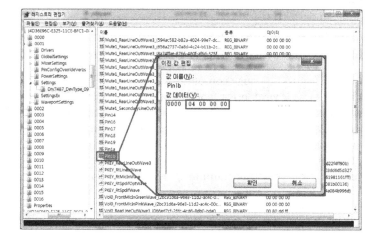

Fig. 5. Process for modifying Windows registry to use speaker

Table 2. ALC882 Codec based sound card binary value assignment

Banary	Function	Banary	Function
00 00 00 00	Line-in	01 00 00 00	Mic-in
02 00 00 00	Headphones	03 00 00 00	Front speakers 2nd Output
04 00 00 00	Front speakers	05 00 00 00	Center / Sub-woofer
06 00 00 00	Side speakers		

4.2 OFDM Communication at Acoustic Band

OFDM communication is conventionally used at a frequency over 1 GHz for high-speed communication. However, it this paper, we used the frequency band range of 3000–20000 Hz, which are that of a speaker. The frequency band is divided into multiple bands of 1 kHz. In addition, 2QAM, 4QAM and 16QAM modulation methods are applied. OFDM becomes more sensitive to noise as carrier waves in the frequency band increase, resulting in higher error rate. Thus, this paper focuses on finding the adequate balance between error and speed rate.

4.3 FHSS Communication at Acoustic Band

FHSS was developed in the United States to satisfy the need for a new modulation method which is less influenced by jamming. FHSS is also used in 802.11 and CDMA communication in accordance with this advantage. Therefore, FHSS is applied to SBCN for preventing noise affection which is a major problem in speaker based communication. The frequency band is divided into a series of 3 kHz, and acoustic bands are sorted into six channels of 3 kHz, 6 kHz, 9 kHz, 12 kHz, 15 kHz, and 18 kHz.

4.4 Verification of Transmitting Error and Recovery Code

When an error occurs during communication, retransmission is generally requested. However, forward error correction (FEC) is applied in situations where retransmissions are impossible, such as simplex transmission. In FEC, the sender encodes the message in a redundant way by using an error-correcting code. This redundancy allows the receiver to detect a limited number of errors and often attempt to correct them. In this work, we minimize errors that occur during communication by using hamming error correction code [21], which is generally used for FEC to verify and recover an error. Finally, transmitted data is verified by CRC [22].

5   Experiment Design

5.1 Environment and System Configuration

The major objective of this study is to establish a connection between an unapproved network and an external network through sound communication between speakers in an air-gapped system, measure the distance and the bit per second for communication through the relevant convert channel, and check whether there exists a possibility of private data leakage in an internal network, separated from the outside.

In order to verify the possibility of leakage in various environments, the maximum communication distance, the transmission success rate in different communication environments, the data transmission rate per second and the leakage time of each data capacity were experimented.

Lee et al. (2013) paper [15] employed an earphone and a headphone, which are passive speakers to be easily found around, to prove eavesdropping in a speaker-based environment. In this study, a passive speaker, mentioned above, was used for the SBCN communication experiment, and a room-type experiment environment that was similar to an office, was constructed at a distance of 0.1 to 7 m.

Prior to this experiment, performance of OFDM and FHSS communication was compared and analyzed. First, the OFDM algorithm was applied to SBCN communication, however it was not appropriate to use due to strong noise and interference of the speaker. The OFDM communication experiment was conducted using speaker and microphone, and FHSS, which is resistant to noise, was applied to only speaker communication.

6   Experiment and Results

6.1   The Maximum Communication Distance of Each Frequency in only Speaker Environment and with Microphone Environment

As shown in Fig. 6, the maximum communication distance experiment was performed at six frequencies ranging from 3 kHz to 21 kHz (3 kHz–6 kHz, 6 kHz–9 kHz, 9 kHz–12 kHz, 12 kHz–15 kHz, and 18 kHz–21 kHz) in the environment with only speaker and with microphone.

In the environment with microphone, communication at all the frequencies was available at a distance of 7 m, which is the maximum distance of the experiment. However in the environment with only speaker, communication was available at a long distance, as the frequency became lower, and the communication distance was rapidly shortened at higher frequencies. A frequency of 3 kHz to 6 kHz had communication with no error at a distance of 7 m, which is the maximum distance of the experiment. In the experiment with an inaudible frequency

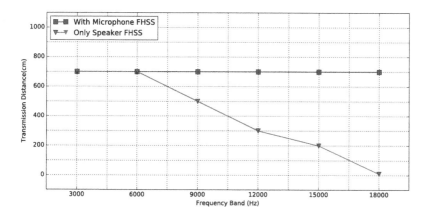

Fig. 6. Maximum Transmission Distance depend on Frequency Band

of 18 kHz to 21 kHz, communication was available only at a short distance of 10 cm. Though there might be slight differences depending on the performance of the speaker, in the inaudible domain of the only speaker environment, communication was available only under limited conditions of the short distance.

6.2 Comparison of the Transmission Success Rate of Each Frequency in the Environment with only Speaker and with Microphone

As displayed in Fig. 7, the only speaker environment and the environment with microphone both showed a perfect transmission success rate in FHSS communication. In the only speaker environment of OFDM communication, transmission was impossible due to strong noise, and in the with microphone environment, generally, the success rate of data transmission fell, as carrier waves increased. The success rate declined overall at a frequency of 3 kHz, used in human voice, and 2QAM and 4QAM showed smooth communication at all the frequencies except 3 kHz, but 16QAM showed a markedly low performance at a frequency of 6 kHz, 12 kHz, and 18 kHz.

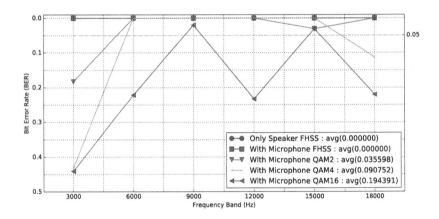

Fig. 7. Bit Error Rate on Frequency Band

6.3 Comparison of Data Transmission of Each Frequency in only Speaker Environment and with Microphone Environment

As indicated in Fig. 8, FHSS communication had a speed of 8 bit/s, which was slower than OFDM communication. 2QAM of OFDM showed stable communication with a high data success rate like FHSS, but its transmission speed was slower than that of 4QAM and 16QAM. Performance of 16QAM can fall to zero at specific frequencies (3 kHz and 18 kHz in the experiment) depending on the signal conditions, since this is sensitive to noise, compared to 2QAM and 4QAM, but in a nice signal environment, communication was available at a speed of 3.2 kbit/s, which more than doubled the speed of 2QAM and 4QAM.

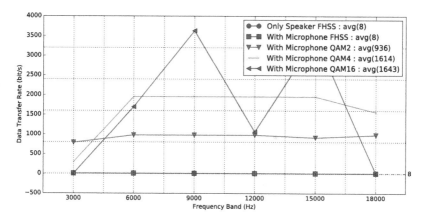

Fig. 8. Transfer Rate on Frequency Band

7 Discussion and Conclusion

7.1 Discussion

The best way to defend the attack suggested in this paper is to physically remove the speaker. Alternatively, the speaker should be deactivated from the operating system. However, in this case, a malicious code may infect the system and reactivate the speaker. If the speaker cannot be removed, the most effective way to determine such attacks is to detect the presence of abnormal signals. Methods for detecting abnormal signals have already developed. If these methods are applied to the air-gap system, the system is able to protect attacks mentioned by this paper. Particularly, the covert channel which we built could be perceived by the technique using abnormal signal detection with fast Fourier transform(FFT). The covert channel uses a high-frequency sound

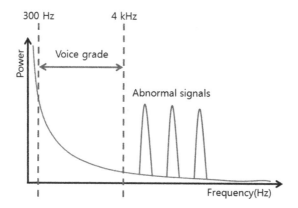

Fig. 9. Perceiving abnormal signals

for communication that is higher than voice grade. Let me show the example with Fig. 9. Basically, a range of voice grade is from 300 Hz–4 kHz. Therefore, we can assume that the sound from 300 Hz–4 kHz would be diffused in the office during business hours. Consequently, if we surveil frequency bands which are higher than voice grade and check whether there are abnormal patterns of the signal, we can perceive abnormal signals and prevent the attack.

7.2 Conclusion

To conclude, we have demonstrated various acoustic covert communications given three threat models in this paper: from a speaker to a microphone (case 1), from a speaker to another speaker (case 2) and from a speaker to a centrally controlled embedding loudspeaker on the wall(case 3). The maximum communication speed are 3.2 kbit/s when both the speaker and the microphone are attached while it is 8 bit/s when only the speakers are used. We focused on the various possibilities to circumvent air-gap system in different environments rather than their communication speed. With regard to mentioned threat models, we insist that air-gap system is not a completely secure method and at the same time, it also implies that an attacker is able to exfiltrate significant information from the separated network. Consequently, in order to protect the important information in a private network, system managers have to consider of this kind of threat models as well as network separation.

Acknowledgment. This research was supported by the Basic Science Research Program through the National Research Foundation of Korea (NRF) funded by the Ministry of Science, ICT and Future Planning (NRF-2013R1A1A1012797)

References

1. Falliere, N., Murchu, L.O., Chien, E.: W32. stuxnet dossier. White Paper Symantec Corp. Security. Response **5**, (2011)
2. Eom, J.H.: Cyber defense strategy for information superiority in cyberspace. J. Secur. Eng. **9**(5) (2012)
3. Eom, J.H.: Management plan of cyber reserve forces for cyber warfare. J. Secur. Eng. **12**(2) (2015)
4. Jeong, Y., Nam, K.-D.: An investigation of network separation solution for government network. Korea Institute of Communication Sciences, pp. 1125–1126 (2011)
5. Shim, W.J.: A Study on Considerations for Effective Network Partition. Soonsil University, Information Security 2 (2015)
6. Lindqvist, U., Jonsson, E.: A map of security risks associated with using COTS. Computer **31**(6), 60–66 (1998)
7. Sanger, D.E.: Obama Order Sped Up Wave of Cyberattacks Against Tran. The New York Times, New York (2012)
8. Zetter, K., Faa: Boeing's new 787 may be vulnerable to hacker attack. Wired (January 8) (2008). Accessed May 2009 http://www.wired.com/politics/security/news/2008/01/dreamlinersecurity

9. Lee, E., Kim, K.: A study on data protection based air-gap separate. Rev. KIISC **20**, 39–46 (2010)
10. Hanspach, M., Goetz, M. On covert acoustical mesh networks in air. arXiv preprint arXiv:1406.1213 (2014)
11. Guri, M., Kedma, G., Kachlon, A., Elovici, Y.: AirHopper: Bridging the air-gap between isolated networks and mobile phones using radio frequencies. In: 9th International Conference on Malicious and Unwanted Software: The Americas (MALWARE), pp. 58–67. IEEE (2014)
12. Guri, M., Monitz, M., Mirski, Y., Elovici, Y.: Bitwhisper: covert signaling channel between air-gapped computers using thermal manipulations, arXiv preprint arXiv:1503.07919 (2015)
13. Carrara, B., Adams, C.: On acoustic covert channels between air-gapped systems. In: Cuppens, F., Garcia-Alfaro, J., Zincir Heywood, N., Fong, P.W.L. (eds.) FPS 2014. LNCS, vol. 8930, pp. 3–16. Springer, Heidelberg (2015)
14. Nissen, I., Goetz, M.: Generic under water application language (GUWAL)-Specification of tactical instant messaging in underwater networks. In: Research Department for Underwater Acoustics and Marine Geophysics (2012)
15. Lee, S.J., Ha, Y.M., Jo, H.J., Yoon, J.W.: The danger and vulnerability of eavesdropping by using loud-speakers. J. Korea Inst. Inf. Secur. Cryptology **23**, 1157–1167 (2013)
16. Crow, B.P., Widjaja, I., Kim, J.G., Sakai, P.T.: IEEE 802.11 wireless local area networks. IEEE Commun. Mag. **35**(9), 116–126 (1997)
17. Dixon, R.C.: Spread Spectrum Systems: With Commercial Applications, 3rd edn. John Wiley & Sons Inc., New York (1994)
18. Bingham, J.A.C.: Multicarrier modulation for data transmission: an idea whose time has come. IEEE Commun. Mag. **28**(5), 5–14 (1990)
19. Sari, H., Karam, G., Jeanclaude, I.: Transmission techniques for digital terrestrial TV broadcasting. IEEE Commun. Mag. **33**(2), 100–109 (1995)
20. Chang, R.W.: Synthesis of band-limited orthogonal signals for multichannel data transmission. Bell Syst. Tech. J. **45**(10), 1775–1796 (1966)
21. Hamming, R.W.: Error detecting and error correcting codes. Bell Syst. Tech. J. **29**(2), 147–160 (1950)
22. Castagnoli, G., Brauer, S., Herrmann, M.: Optimization of cyclic redundancy-check codes with 24 and 32 parity bits. IEEE Trans. Commun. **41**(6), 883–892 (1993)

An Improved Masking Scheme for S-Box Software Implementations

Sungjun Ahn[1] and Dooho Choi[2,3(✉)]

[1] Korea Minting, Security Printing and ID Card Operating Corporation,
80-67 Gwahak-ro, Yuseong-gu, Daejeon, Korea
asj503@komsco.com
[2] Electronics and Telecommunication Research Institute,
218 Gajeong-ro, Yuseong-gu, Daejeon, Korea
dhchoi@etri.re.kr
[3] Korea University of Science and Technology,
217 Gajeong-ro, Yuseong-gu, Daejeon, Korea

Abstract. A typical approach, to protect a given symmetric key cryptographic algorithm against differential power analysis(DPA), is a masking method which is to randomize all intermediate values of the cryptographic algorithm and the main time-consuming part of the masking method is to generate masked S-Boxes. The masked S-Boxes are implemented by generating the look-up tables for most of DPA countermeasures in the software manner.

In this paper, we present an improved masking scheme that makes the efficient masked S-Boxes by revisiting the ways to use the low composite fields arithmetic. Our improved masking scheme is basically slower than the standard AES implementation, but much faster than existing method which makes a whole S-Box random with 16 masks. In addition, our scheme is 20% faster using less memory, compared to Oswald's work using the similar method with the proposed approach. In other case of our scheme, we reduce almost half of memory with 9% slow rate. We concentrate on the trade-off between memory sizes and operation speed.

Keywords: Side channel analysis · Differential power analysis · DPA countermeasure · AES

1 Introduction

AES [1] has been used in many security areas, sharing information through network as well as cryptographic implementation in devices, since AES offers good security and performance to implement in many different kinds of platforms.

It is possible to transform AES algorithm into more secure and high powered architectures. In hardware architecture, it optimizes logic gates reusing hardware resources. Satoh *et al.* [2] proposes the way to share the hardware resources between encryption and decryption and optimizes S-Box operations by presenting a composite field [4]. Another composite field by normal bases also makes

© Springer International Publishing Switzerland 2016
H. Kim and D. Choi (Eds.): WISA 2015, LNCS 9503, pp. 200–212, 2016.
DOI: 10.1007/978-3-319-31875-2_17

it cuspy [5,6]. Contrary to hardware implementation, software implementation makes normally use of look-up tables to gain output values as fast as possible using a part of memory.

Many cryptographic algorithms have been attacked by Simple Power Analysis(SPA), Differential Power Analysis(DPA) [7], Timing Attacks [8], Electromagnetic radiation [9] and so on. It is called Side Channel Analysis(SCA) since these attacks use additional information such as traces corresponding to power consumptions or electromagnetic. Adversaries are able to analyze statistical distributions of the side channel information corresponding to data flow. As a result of these attacks, guessing correct keys has been easily confirmed without countermeasures and with weak countermeasures sometimes.

It is necessary for cryptographic algorithms to counter these attacks. There are many methods to disturb information exposure such as masking [21], shuffling [19], whitening [7]. These countermeasures can make the intermediate values random to protect an important key. Especially, it is very common to use masking method. There are different types of masking to conceal the intermediate values such as addition [10,15,16] and multiplicative masking scheme [10–12]. However, algorithms masking with one random value are susceptible to second-order differential power analysis [13,14]. It means adversaries are able to analyze cryptographic algorithms with n-order masking scheme using (n+1)-order differential power analysis. Thus, it offers less performance as the size and number of masking increase.

In this paper, We show the efficient method to operate S-Box of the AES with mask in software using composite field arithmetic. We also try to find out the trade-off between speed and memory size when operating SubBytes of the AES. We technically focus on protecting important values from the first order DPA in this paper and expect that our approach can be adopted at the high-order masking scheme. With our knowledge, the masking method of S-Box, designed by Oswald and Schramm [18], is the only way to make it efficient. This paper is going to suggest a significant masking scheme of AES S-Box to make it fast in some platforms

In the next section, efficient and secure performance of AES S-Box will be shown. Some masking methods using additional and multiplicative masks in composite fields will be proposed in Sect. 2. Section 3 presents our S-Box design and performance, comparing to other methods. In Sect. 4, we prove the security of our masking scheme and implement our masking schemes on a variety of processors, followed by the summary of the results and conclusion in Sect. 5.

2   Previous Software Masking Schemes

The goal of countermeasure is to hide the intermediate values related to the side channel information of a device. Masking method, one of countermeasures, accomplishes this goal by randomizing the intermediate values and has two types such as boolean and arithmetic. Generally, the intermediate value i is concealed by operating $\circ$(boolean or arithmetic) with random values m : $i_m = i \circ m$.

Since the random value m is generated whenever it is executed, it's not easy for attackers to guess the value i from i_m.

In case of AES algorithm, the intermediate values can be covered with random values by exclusive-or since characteristic is 2 which implies that addition is equal to exclusive-or : $i_m = i \oplus m$.

Furthermore, AES algorithm uses non-linear function in SubBytes which has the property: $S(x \oplus m) \neq S(x) \oplus S(m)$. It has difficulties on changing the mask, comparing to the property of linear function: $S(x \oplus m) = S(x) \oplus S(m)$. For example, when the S-Box is masked with a random m_2, an input value should be x with a mask m_1 such that $x \oplus m_1$. Then, it gives the masked S-Box depending on random values : $MSbox(x \oplus m_1) = Sbox(x) \oplus m_2$. m_1 might be the same as m_2 and 16 different masked S-Boxes are generated with all different masks, see Algorithm 1. There is another problem about high-order masking scheme by adding more masking values than one to counter high-order differential power analysis. But we leave the question untouched since it is very expensive to implement in reality.

Algorithm 1. Masked SubBytes

Require: m_1, m_2
Ensure: Masked Sbox
 1: **for** $x \longleftarrow 0$ to 255 **do**
 2:     MSbox(x)$\longleftarrow$ Sbox(x$\oplus m_1$)$\oplus m_2$
 3: **end for**
 4: Return(MSbox)

AES could be properly implemented on an 8 bit processors because it operates each byte in 16 bytes plaintext at a time. And according to a random value, the masked tables are dissimilarly made from an original S-Box in memory.

Some papers presented some masked algorithms using the composite field operations in hardware [16,17]. And there are computations with countermeasures for AES in software. The countermeasure in [15] uses pre-computed log and $alog$ tables by discrete logarithm. But it is possible to operate when only using the conditional branches, which makes it vulnerable to power analysis attacks. And a method has been suitable for smartcard implementations introducing additional rounds at the beginning and the end and randomly chosen the sequence of operations in algorithm [19]. Oswald et $al.$ [18] offers a software implementation using a composite field faster than masked S-Box on $GF(2^8)$. The most important thing is that all input and output values should be masked while computing inversion on Galois field. Using isomorphic relation between $GF(2^4) \times GF(2^4)$ and $GF(2^8)$, masked values can be transformed into different forms to calculate inversion. Oswald's work has been done with two steps: making Pre-computed Tables and operating Masked Inversion. On the first step, four types of tables are operated on $GF(2^4)$ and stored in memory.

$$T_{d_1} : ((x + m), m) \mapsto x^2 \times \{e\} + m$$
$$T_{d_2} : ((x + m), (y + m')) \mapsto ((x + m), (y + m')) \times (y + m')$$
$$T_{mult} : ((x + m), (y + m')) \mapsto (x + m) \times (y + m')$$
$$T_{inv} : ((x + m), m) \mapsto x^{-1} + m$$

These four tables compute inverse values on $GF(2^4)$. Authors have proposed to make look-up tables to replace with many operations while masked inverse could be computed without using look-up tables in hardware [17]. This shows that it is faster than the case of making masked S-Box on $GF(2^8)$, even though they use much more memory in Read Only Memory(ROM).

In addition to boolean masking, there are another masking schemes such as multiplicative masking. Akkar et al. [10] introduces to transform boolean masking into multiplicative masking. The next year, it is more simplified algebraically, but it has turned out to be susceptible to even the standard differential power analysis [7]. Multiplicative masking method becomes the target of zero value attack [11]. Golic et al. [11] takes advantage of an extension of Galois field to avoid this attack but it is very costly to implement in software. Hence, it is still an open question to counter zero value attack for multiplicative masking.

3   An Improved Addition Masking in Software

There are many attempts to implement SubBytes part efficiently and securely. The S-Box is composed of the inversion and affine function. According to [20], it is more flexible to compute inverse elements in composite fields in hardware since it completely depends on combinational logic. If a countermeasure applies to the SubBytes transformation, and the method makes it much efficient. It is also inevitable to focus on implementing efficient algorithm without leakage of the intermediate information using composite field arithmetic in software. Thus, a masked input value on $GF(2^8)$ maps to $GF(2^4) \times GF(2^4)$ and is transformed back into $GF(2^8)$ getting an inverse by using look-up tables. It is shown in Fig. 1.

There is an approach to implement an algorithm using look up tables in software. But, if look-up tables are replaced with some operations properly, it will offer effective implementations in software. It is faster than an masking scheme in Algorithm 1 even though it needs a little more space in memory. Oswald et al. [18] has suggested a method to get SubBytes values with 4 pre-computed tables and exclusive-or operations in software. Comparing to the method, a proposed method uses less memory using an Algorithm 2 on $GF(2^4)$ and shows increment of the speed in this section.

3.1   Pre-computation

For the first time, some tables are prepared to operate multiplication on $GF(2^4)$ and store them in memory. There are two types of look-up tables for multiplication on $GF(2^4)$: Multiplication between two elements on $GF(2^4)$

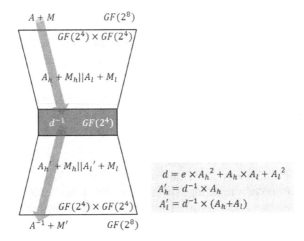

Fig. 1. The inversion process over $GF(2^4)$

and the product of a constant(we set it, $\{e\}$) and a square on $GF(2^4)$. And lastly it is very useful to array every possible inverse elements on $GF(2^4)$. The total size of multiplication tables is 288 bytes and it is stored in ROM.

$$T_{m_1} : (x, y) \mapsto z$$
$$z = x \times y \; mod \; x^4 + x + 1 \tag{1}$$

$$T_{m_2} : x \mapsto y$$
$$y = \{e\} \times x^2 \; mod \; x^4 + x + 1 \tag{2}$$

$$T_{m_3} : x \mapsto y$$
$$y = x^{-1} \; mod \; x^4 + x + 1 \tag{3}$$

Tables T_{m_1} and T_{m_2} can be in charge of every multiplication when operating in dark box in Fig. 1. And table T_{m_3} is used to compute the masked inverse value of d. The usage of the algorithm will be presented in next section.

Secondly, there are two look-up tables to map between $GF(2^8)$ and $GF(2^4) \times GF(2^4)$ by isomorphisms. Thus, masked input values map from $GF(2^8)$ to $GF(2^4) \times GF(2^4)$ and after calculating inverse values, the values go to inverse map from $GF(2^4) \times GF(2^4)$ to $GF(2^8)$. The size of each mapping is 256 bytes. Thus, 2 look-up tables are pre-computed for mapping and store them in ROM.

Thirdly, a masked inversion table is the same method as Algorithm 1. During running, masked d values could be operated with 16 elements by table T_{m_3} using Algorithm 2. it is revealed what the masked d value is in next section.

After pre-computing, Masked Inverse Dbox to use in the middle of running is saved in RAM. The size of this table is 16 bytes, but it computes 16 times in one round because of 16 bytes of a statement. Therefore the total size of a masked IDbox look-up table is 256 bytes for RAM. In summary, it is necessary to have a 16-byte space for ROM and a 256-byte space for RAM.

Algorithm 2. Masked Inverse D value

Require: m_1, m_2
Ensure: Masked Dbox
1: **for** $x \longleftarrow 0$ *to* 15 **do**
2:     MIDbox(x)$\longleftarrow$ IDbox($x \oplus m_1$) $\oplus m_2$
3: **end for**
4: Return(MIDbox)

3.2 An Improved Addition Masking

In hardware implementation, it is usually used to do arithmetic operations instead of using look-up tables since it takes short time to implement computations in comparison with operations in software. Hence, it is common to transform arithmetics into look-up tables in software. However, we try to think combination of the ways in hardware and in software respectively. There is more efficient way to implement masked algorithm by increasing operations and decreasing the number of look-up tables. And it is also an important part to mask the every single intermediate value.

At first, a value of d with an addition masking is computed. This masked d value is going to be converted into an inverse d value with a random value by Algorithm 2.

$$D_1 := \{e\} \times (a_h + m_h)^2 \ mod \ x^4 + x + 1 \tag{4}$$

$$D_2 := \mu \oplus (a_l + m_l) \times ((a_h + m_h) \oplus (a_l + m_l) \oplus m_h) \ mod \ x^4 + x + 1 \tag{5}$$

$$D_c := \{e\} \times m_h^2 \oplus m_l \times (a_h + m_h \oplus m_l \oplus m_h) \ mod \ x^4 + x + 1 \tag{6}$$

The formulas (4)–(6) could be calculated with Tables 1 and 2 easily and there is a random value μ added in formula (2) to conceal the value of d.

$$D_1 \oplus D_2 \oplus D_c = d + \mu \tag{7}$$

It is easy to confirm that exclusive-or operations with formula (4)–(6) result in the masked value of d: $d + \mu := a_h^2 \times \{e\} + a_h \times a_l + a_l^2 + \mu$. Addition operation on $GF(2^4)$ is the same as exclusive-or which is used in above formulas. And we indicate that arithmetics $\times$ and $+$ without circles represent to use look-up tables and to reuse resources. Hence, it needs 4 look-up operations and 8 exclusive-or operations for computations of the masked d value. With this result, the masked inverse of d is obtained by using Algorithm 2, *i.e.* $d^{-1} + \mu'$.

Next, we try to arrive at the inverse value on $GF(2^8)$, which is the result which we expected to get finally. It is required to get 4-bit high and 4-bit low values on $GF(2^4) \times GF(2^4)$, whose concatenation is isomorphic to an element on $GF(2^8)$. In these computations, μ is defined by m_l to make more efficient.

$$a_h' \oplus m_h := \left(d^{-1} + m_l\right) \times \underline{(a_h + m_h + m_l + m_h)}$$
$$\oplus \ m_l \times \left(d^{-1} + m_l \oplus a_h + m_h \oplus m_h\right) \oplus m_h \tag{8}$$

$$a_l' \oplus m_l := \left(d^{-1} + m_l\right) \times \underline{(a_h + m_h + a_l + m_l + m_h)}$$
$$\oplus \ m_l \times \left(d^{-1} + m_l + a_h + m_h + \underline{m_h} \oplus a_l + m_l \oplus m_l\right) \oplus m_l \tag{9}$$

It is not hard to check that results are $a_h' + m_h = d^{-1} \times (a_h) + m_h$ and $a_l' + m_l = d^{-1} \times (a_h + a_l) + m_l$. Here, it is possible to reuse resources of formulas (4)–(6) not to waste of computations. The underlined terms of formulas (8) and (9) are used from a part of computations which are stored before. It saves 6 exclusive-or operations. Therefore, it needs to use 4 look-up operations and 8 exclusive-or operations for computations of a value on $GF(2^4) \times GF(2^4)$. The value goes to a value on $GF(2^8)$ by using an inverse isomorphism.

Actually, there are another look-up operations before and after these computations. Input values with mask change their base field from $GF(2^8)$ to $GF(2^4) \times GF(2^4)$. Hence, it will change their forms such as $a+m \mapsto (a_h+m_h, a_l+m_l)$. And mapping back from $GF(2^4) \times GF(2^4)$ to $GF(2^8)$ also transforms $(a_h'+m_h, a_l'+m_l)$ into $a^{-1} + m$. SubBytes values are obtained through affine function with this inversion of input values, $i.e. SubBytes(a) + m'$. But it is possible to combine the inverse isomorphism and affine function into one look-up table.

We summarize the process of AES SubBytes operation and indicate total cost of it. It needs to take 4 look-up operations and 8 additions in (7), 2 look-up operations and 4 additions in (8) and 2 look-up operations and 4 additions in (9). Moreover, it needs to count 3 look-up operations from mapping through the isomorphism and inverse one. Two look-up operations are for masked values and masks from $GF(2^8)$ to $GF(2^4) \times GF(2^4)$ and another one is for mapping back to $GF(2^8)$. Thus, it totally needs 11 look-up operations and 16 exclusive-or operations. Furthermore, the masked inversion of d by Algorithm 2 should be remarked since it is expensive. If it is made into a look-up table, then it just needs to add a look-up table operations.

3.3 Comparison Analysis of the Improved Masking Scheme

We make a comparison between different methods and consider the implementation of AES SubBytes operation on a 8-bit smartcard. The improved masking scheme needs a space to store five look up tables in ROM. Isomorphism tables take 8-bit input and yield 8-bit output. Table T_{m_1} gives 4-bit output by 2×4-bit tables. T_{m_2} and T_{m_3} also take a 4-bit value on $GF(2^4)$ as an input and give 4-bit output value. In software, when tables are stored in memory based on 8-bit processor, it needs 4-bit space for each value because three tables give only 4-bit output. But it is more efficient to store a single 4-bit in each register since it is based on 8-bit processor.

Thus, it requires 256 bytes for table T_{m_1} and 16 bytes for tables T_{m_2} and T_{m_3} in ROM. And two isomorphic mappings between $GF(2^8)$ and $GF(2^4) \times GF(2^4)$ should be stored in ROM which is 256 bytes for each table. Therefore, it needs $1 \times 256 + 2 \times 16 + 2 \times 256 = 800$ bytes to store them in ROM. Furthermore, it is considered about the masked d value of formula (7) related to Table (3). Actually, it is possible to store all look-up tables in ROM and the masked values of d are derived from a table in ROM. The inverse value of d is stored with mask in RAM before encryption. Thus, this pre-computation needs $16 \times 16 = 256$ bytes to store them with 16 masks in RAM.

Table 1. Various AES S-Box implementations following memory size and speed for encryption

	ROM	RAM	PRE-LT	PRE-XOR	LT	XOR	cycles
unmasked	256	0	0	0	160	0	800
16 masks	256	4096	8192	8192	160	0	45696
Oswald's	1536	0	0	0	2240	2400	13600
our MS-box1	1280	0	0	0	1760	2400	11040
our MS-box2	800	256	512	512	1760	2880	14816

We implement the algorithm on the environment of smartcards based on 8-bit RISC architectures. A look-up operation which is stored in ROM takes five clock cycles and a look-up operation for reading and writing a value in RAM takes four clock cycles, which is followed by Oswald's counting method [18]. The exclusive-or operation requires a clock cycle. As we described before, we proposed the improved masking scheme for a SubBytes step and in total, it requires 11 look-up table operations and 16 exclusive-or additions. This results in $5 \times 11 \times 16 \times 10 + 1 \times 16 \times 16 \times 10 = 11360$ clock cycles for a whole AES encryption with 10 rounds. And We should take the pre-computation of the masked value of d into account. This pre-computation needs several steps: 16 exclusive-or operations to mask the index, 16 look-up operations to have unmasked values in ROM, 16 exclusive-or operations to mask the elements of the table and 16 look-up operations to store them in RAM. Following this step, a masked table is generated for the masked inversion d^{-1} on $GF(2^4)$. This method repeats 16 times to make this table with different masks and this costs $16 \times (16 + 16 \times 5 + 16 + 16 \times 4) = 2816$ clock cycles. Besides, it needs to add $4 \times 16 \times 10 = 640$ clock cycles, since it is necessary to derive the masked inversion of d from RAM. In total, it requires 14816 clock cycles for SubBytes operations of an entire AES encryption. It needs a little more time to implement our algorithm in comparison with Oswald's scheme [18]. However, the improved method uses only 800 bytes in ROM 256 bytes in RAM. It is significantly reduced by approximately 50 % in ROM even though it is 9 % slower by clock cycles. Moreover, it is possible to choose faster algorithm with more pre-computed look-up tables because it reduces operations by transforming the table T_{m_3} into a table with two 4-bit input and 4-bit output values. It means that a masked inverse table of d is made before encryption. Then it dramatically reduces the speed of algorithm by around 20 % while taking smaller spaces in ROM compared to Oswald's scheme [18], which uses 1280 bytes in ROM and results in 11040 clock cycles.

4 Implementations and Security Analysis

We performed implementation of our S-Box designs on various kinds of processors to confirm how efficient it is. In order to evaluate the practical security of masked S-Box, we carried out power analysis attacks by using Correlation

Power Analysis(CPA) attack which is a DPA attack employing correlation [22]. The specification, which is installed with our inversion scheme for attacks, is a 8-bit ATmega163 smartcard.

At first, it is shown that our scheme is much faster than 16 masking S-Box. As theoretically described before, our second masking scheme is normally 4 times faster than 16 masking scheme which makes 16 different masking values for 1 round of AES by using a S-Box table. However, when our scheme was tested on many processors, it was approximately 10 times faster than 16 masking scheme. And when our scheme is compared with Oswald's scheme, it spends a little more time than we expected. This is because reading from the memory is more expensive than we counted theoretically. We used SCARF-ARMv2 based on 32-bit ARM920T processor, SCARF-AVRv2 based on 8-bit ATmega128 processor, ATmega163 smart card based on 8-bit processor, SCARF-M430v2 based on 16-bit MSP430F2618 processor [23]. It was necessary to check out the security of our scheme by CPA attack. we used a SCARF DPA evaluation software [23] to analyze our masked S-Box. At first, AES SBox without countermeasures was implemented. And then, random values were used for masks. Encryption traces were collected with 5000 unmasked plaintexts and 100000 traces for our masked scheme. 104MXi-A Lecroy Oscilloscope was used with sampling rate of $250MS/s$. The results are shown in Figs. 2 and 3. There is a peak which assumes the correct key in Fig. 2. However, Fig. 3 doesn't show the peak even though the number of traces are collected much more. It verifies the safety of our masked scheme from DPA attacks.

Table 2. S-Box speed depending on diverse processors

	ARM	AVR	Smartcard	MSP
16 masks	$92.13\mu s$	$699.16\mu s$	$1.41ms$	$483.85\mu s$
Oswald's	$3.45\mu s$	$42.73\mu s$	$60\mu s$	$42.75\mu s$
our MS-Box1	$2.75\mu s$	$37.15\mu s$	$57\mu s$	$31.7\mu s$
our MS-Box2	$9.28\mu s$	$75.54\mu s$	$156.13\mu s$	$71.80\mu s$

Furthermore, our S-Box has been theoretically verified whether it is secure or not through some Lemmas of [16–18] which are developed from [21]. It is required to analyze output values of several tables: $T_{m_1}, T_{m_2}, T_{m_3}$, MIDbox(x), map and map^{-1} and output values from arithmetic operations in formulas (4) to (9). Lemma 3 of [18] proves the security of T_{m_1}. T_{m_2} is secure by Lemma 4 of [17]. Lemma 1 of [16] shows the security of T_{m_3}, MIDbox(x), map and map^{-1} which are bijective. Thus, it is easy to check out the security proofs by some Lemmas of previous works.(See more details in Appendix A.)

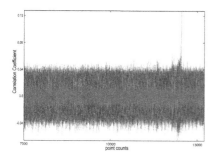

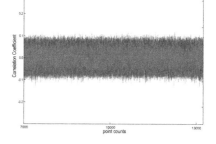

Fig. 2. CPA of the S-Box with no countermeasure

Fig. 3. CPA of the S-Box with countermeasure

5 Conclusion

We have described more efficient ideas to implement algorithm resisting DPA attacks. It is costly to compute non-linear part with mask, which makes us to think of the composite field with masked values. Intermediate values have to be always independent of the key data. Thus, we came up with a combination between software and hardware which develops efficient trade-off between speed and memory. our scheme was implemented on the various processors and platform such as ARM, AVR, MSP430, and smartcard. And it was shown that our scheme was much faster than the method to operate 16 SubBytes with different masks. It is four times faster theoretically but it is ten times faster in real implementations. We have provided the security proof of our SubBytes design. Even though our scheme is 9% slower than Oswald's method [18], it only needs a half of memory to store look up tables. Moreover, when it uses one more table, then, our scheme uses less memory with 20% speed-up compared to Oswald's method. Therefore, our scheme is properly able to implement in software with 8-bit processors.

Acknowledgments. This work was supported by the K-SCARF project, the ICT R&D program of ETRI [Research on Key Leakage Analysis and Response Technologies].

A   Appendix: Security Analysis

We show that an improved masking scheme is provably secure. For investigating all masked values, we should analyze outputs of several tables: $T_{m_1}, T_{m_2}, T_{m_3}$, MIDbox(x), map and map^{-1} and output values from arithmetic operations in formulas (4) to (9). We can follow the security analysis methods in [16–18], which are developed from [21]. In [18], Lemmas 1 to 3 show the security of four types of tables. In [17], Lemmas 1 to 4 indicate that output values of all operations are secure. Lemma 5 shows the summation of intermediate results can be also secure. We use the same Lemmas as the papers.

Lemma 1. *Let $a \in GF(2^n)$ be arbitrary. Let $m \in GF(2^n)$ be uniformly distributed in $GF(2^n)$ independent of a. Then, $a+m$ is uniformly distributed. It means that the distribution of $a+m$ is independent of a.*

This follows the Lemma 1 in [16]. This lemma implies that any values can be random values when it combines with a random value with arithmetics. Thus, the value $a + m$ doesn't depend on a. Furthermore, even though it sums more $a_i + m_i$ values, it keeps the security which is described in the next Lemma 2.

Lemma 2. *Let $a_i \in GF(2^n)$ be arbitrary. Let $m_i \in GF(2^n)$ be uniformly distributed in $GF(2^n)$ independent of a_i. Then, the distribution of $\sum_i a_i + \sum_i m_i$ is independent of a_i.*

Lemma 2 shows that a sum of values is important for secure implementation such as the order of XOR operations and independent masks [17]. Thus, Some operations of formulas (5) to (9) can be independent of important information. And we have to prove the security of our three tables. but it also follows the same Lemmas. we reuse the Lemma 3 of [18] for the security of T_{m_1} which is multiplication table in $GF(2^4)$.

Lemma 3. *Let $a_1, a_2 \in GF(2^n)$ be arbitrary. Let $m_1, m_2 \in GF(2^n)$ be independently and uniformly distributed in $GF(2^n)$. Then, the probability distribution of $T_{m_1}(a_1 + m_1, a_2 + m_2) = (a_1 + m_1) \times (a_2 + m_2)$ is*

$$Pr((a_1+m_1)\times(a_2+m_2) = i) = \begin{cases} \frac{2^{n+1}-1}{2^{2n}} & ,if\ i = 0\ i.e.,\ if m_1 = a_1\ or\ m_2 = a_2 \\ \frac{2^n-1}{2^{2n}} & ,if\ i \neq 0 \end{cases}$$

Therefore, the distribution of $(a_1 + m_1) \times (a_2 + m_2)$ is independent of a_1 and a_2.

We also reuse the Lemma 4 of [17] the security of T_{m_2} which is multiplication and square table in $GF(2^4)$. We fix a constant value as $\{e\}$ in $GF(2^4)$.

Lemma 4. *Let $a \in GF(2^n)$ be arbitrary and $0xE \in GF(2^n)$ a constant. Let $m \in GF(2^n)$ be independently and uniformly distributed in $GF(2^n)$ Then, the distribution of $(a + m)^2$ and $e \times (a + m)^2$ is independent of a.*

And T_{m_3} is a table for inverse operations which is bijective and input value of this table is $a + m$ which is independent of a. Thus, it is clearly independent from the input values. The mapping from $GF(2^8)$ to $GF(2^4) \times GF(2^4)$ and the combination of inverse mapping and affine function are bijective. Therefore, the masked output values are statistically independent of the unmasked input values.

References

1. Daemen, J., Rijmen, V.: AES proposal: Rijndael (1998)
2. Satoh, A., Morioka, S., Takano, K., Munetoh, S.: A compact Rijndael hardware architecture with S-Box optimization. In: Boyd, C. (ed.) ASIACRYPT 2001. LNCS, vol. 2248, pp. 239–254. Springer, Heidelberg (2001)
3. Rudra, A., Dubey, P.K., Jutla, C.S., Kumar, V., Rao, J.R., Rohatgi, P.: Efficient Rijndael encryption implementation with composite field arithmetic. In: Koç, Ç.K., Naccache, D., Paar, C. (eds.) CHES 2001. LNCS, vol. 2162, pp. 171–184. Springer, Heidelberg (2001)
4. Paar, C.: Effecient VLSI architecture for bit-parallel computations in Galois field, Ph.D. dissertation, Institute for Experimental Mathematics, University of Essen, Germany (1994)
5. Canright, D.: A very compact S-Box for AES. In: Rao, J.R., Sunar, B. (eds.) CHES 2005. LNCS, vol. 3659, pp. 441–455. Springer, Heidelberg (2005)
6. Canright, D., Batina, L.: A very compact "Perfectly Masked" S-Box for AES. In: Bellovin, S.M., Gennaro, R., Keromytis, A.D., Yung, M. (eds.) ACNS 2008. LNCS, vol. 5037, pp. 446–459. Springer, Heidelberg (2008)
7. Kocher, P.C., Jaffe, J., Jun, B.: Differential power analysis. In: Wiener, M. (ed.) CRYPTO 1999. LNCS, vol. 1666, pp. 388–397. Springer, Heidelberg (1999)
8. Kocher, P.C.: Timing attacks on implementations of Diffie-Hellman, RSA, DSS, and other systems. In: Koblitz, N. (ed.) CRYPTO 1996. LNCS, vol. 1109, pp. 104–113. Springer, Heidelberg (1996)
9. Gandolfi, K., Mourtel, C., Olivier, F.: Electromagnetic analysis: concrete results. In: Koç, Ç.K., Naccache, D., Paar, C. (eds.) CHES 2001. LNCS, vol. 2162, pp. 251–261. Springer, Heidelberg (2001)
10. Akkar, M.-L., Giraud, C.: An implementation of DES and AES, secure against some attacks. In: Koç, Ç.K., Naccache, D., Paar, C. (eds.) CHES 2001. LNCS, vol. 2162, pp. 309–318. Springer, Heidelberg (2001)
11. Golic, J.D., Christophe, T.: Multiplicative masking and power analysis of AES. In: Kaliski Jr., B.S., Koç, Ç.K., Paar, C. (eds.) CHES 2002. LNCS, vol. 2523. Springer, Heidelberg (2003)
12. Trichina, E., de Seta, D., Germani, L.: Simplified adaptive multiplicative masking for AES. In: Kaliski Jr., B.S., Koç, Ç.K., Paar, C. (eds.) CHES 2002. LNCS, vol. 2523. Springer, Heidelberg (2003)
13. Oswald, E., Mangard, S., Herbst, C., Tillich, S.: Practical second-order DPA attacks for masked smart card implementations of block ciphers. In: Pointcheval, D. (ed.) CT-RSA 2006. LNCS, vol. 3860, pp. 192–207. Springer, Heidelberg (2006)
14. Messerges, T.S.: Using second-order power analysis to attack DPA resistant software. In: Paar, C., Koç, Ç.K. (eds.) CHES 2000. LNCS, vol. 1965, pp. 238–251. Springer, Heidelberg (2000)
15. Trichina, E., Korkishko, L.: Secure and efficient AES software implementation for smart cards. In: Lim, C.H., Yung, M. (eds.) WISA 2004. LNCS, vol. 3325, pp. 425–439. Springer, Heidelberg (2005)
16. Blömer, J., Guajardo, J., Krummel, V.: Provably secure masking of AES. In: Handschuh, H., Hasan, M.A. (eds.) SAC 2004. LNCS, vol. 3357, pp. 69–83. Springer, Heidelberg (2004)
17. Oswald, E., Mangard, S., Pramstaller, N., Rijmen, V.: A side-channel analysis resistant description of the AES S-Box. In: Gilbert, H., Handschuh, H. (eds.) FSE 2005. LNCS, vol. 3557, pp. 413–423. Springer, Heidelberg (2005)

18. Oswald, E., Schramm, K.: An efficient masking scheme for AES software implementations. In: Song, J.-S., Kwon, T., Yung, M. (eds.) WISA 2005. LNCS, vol. 3786, pp. 292–305. Springer, Heidelberg (2006)
19. Herbst, C., Oswald, E., Mangard, S.: An AES smart card implementation resistant to power analysis attacks. In: Zhou, J., Yung, M., Bao, F. (eds.) ACNS 2006. LNCS, vol. 3989, pp. 239–252. Springer, Heidelberg (2006)
20. Wolkerstorfer, J., Oswald, E., Lamberger, M.: An ASIC implementation of the AES SBoxes. In: Preneel, B. (ed.) CT-RSA 2002. LNCS, vol. 2271, pp. 67–78. Springer, Heidelberg (2002)
21. Chari, S., Jutla, C.S., Rao, J.R., Rohatgi, P.: Towards sound approaches to counteract power-analysis attacks. In: Wiener, M. (ed.) CRYPTO 1999. LNCS, vol. 1666, pp. 398–412. Springer, Heidelberg (1999)
22. Brier, E., Clavier, C., Olivier, F.: Correlation power analysis with a leakage model. In: Joye, M., Quisquater, J.-J. (eds.) CHES 2004. LNCS, vol. 3156, pp. 16–29. Springer, Heidelberg (2004)
23. ETRI and ICTK, SCARF evaluation board SCARF-ARM. http://www.k-scarf.or.kr

Security and Threat Analysis

Open Sesame! Hacking the Password

Hwajeong Seo[1], Zhe Liu[2], Gyuwon Seo[1], Taehwan Park[1], Jongseok Choi[1], and Howon Kim[1(✉)]

[1] School of Computer Science and Engineering, Pusan National University, San-30, Jangjeon-Dong, Geumjeong-Gu, Busan 609–735, Republic of Korea
{hwajeong,wkdfekf1,pth5804,jschoi85,howonkim}@pusan.ac.kr
[2] Laboratory of Algorithmics, Cryptology and Security (LACS), University of Luxembourg, 6, rue R. Coudenhove-Kalergi, 1359 Luxembourg-kirchberg, Luxembourg
zhe.liu@uni.lu

Abstract. Wearable technology provides user friendly and customized services with multiple sensor data. However, user's sensor data is very personal and sensitive information. If malicious user abuses this information, it would cause huge social problems. In this paper, we present a novel hacking method to identify the user's password from wearable devices. We gathered three axis acceleration information from user's wearable devices and estimated the user's activity. After then we conducted post-processing to eliminate the impossible cases. This approach reduces the password complexity by 99.99 %.

Keywords: Wearable devices · Acceleration data · Password · Hacking

1 Introduction

From smart glass to smart watch, battery powered small devices can access to Internet and exchange the data in anytime and anywhere. Unlike previous platforms, wearable devices or carried mobile gadgets build much close relations with users, because they can collect the diverse and accurate sensor data such as accelerometer, gyroscope, magnetic field, proximity. These are useful resources to establish the applications such as health care and location based services. However, exposure of these sensitive information causes huge threats to the users. Recently the smart device based side channel attacks are reported. The method monitors the sensor information of smart-phone or smart gadget and then extracts the sensitive information such as user's password. In real world,

This work was partly supported by Institute for Information & communications Technology Promotion(IITP) grant funded by the Korea government (MSIP) (No.10043907, Development of high performance IoT device and Open Platform with Intelligent Software) and the MSIP (Ministry of Science, ICT and Future Planning), Korea, under the ITRC(Information Technology Research Center) support program (IITP-2015-H8501-15-1017) supervised by the IITP(Institute for Information & communications Technology Promotion).

© Springer International Publishing Switzerland 2016
H. Kim and D. Choi (Eds.): WISA 2015, LNCS 9503, pp. 215–226, 2016.
DOI: 10.1007/978-3-319-31875-2_18

there are a number of small and wearable devices introduced. These devices can monitor the user's behavior or activity more in detail. In this paper, we exploit the acceleration sensor data extracted from wearable devices and then show how to identify user's password.

Summary of Research Contributions

The main contributions of our work are summarized as the following four points.

1. *Identify user's activity with acceleration data.* With three-axis acceleration data, we identify the direction of movements and pressing activities which are basic activities of password entry.
2. *Recover passwords with single monitoring equipment.* We recover the user's password with single wearable device (acceleration sensor) over user's wrist. The device collects 3 axis acceleration data and successfully identify the password with single accelerometer trace.
3. *Provide password complexity reduction techniques.* Due to physical limitations of password keyboard, the number of possible password is limited with specific cases. By using this technique, we reduce the password complexity by 99.99 %.
4. *Investigate secure countermeasure.* We investigate the several countermeasures to mitigate the proposed side channel attack.

The remainder of this paper is organized as follows. In Sect. 2, we recap the previous works and target devices. In Sect. 3, we present the hacking process. In Sect. 4, we evaluate the performance of proposed methods in terms of password complexity. Finally, Sect. 5 concludes the paper.

2   Related Works

2.1   Previous Works

In CCS'11, Marquardt et al. presented hacking methods with user's smart-phone. They firstly placed their smart-phone next to victim's keyboard. After then the smart-phone detects and decodes the keystrokes by measuring the relative physical position and distance between each vibration [9]. In HotMobile'12, Owusu et al. shows that accelerometer readings are a powerful side channel that can be used to extract entire sequences of entered text on a smart-phone touch-screen keyboard [13]. In WiSec'12, Xu et al. studies the feasibility of inferring a user's tap inputs to a smart-phone with its integrated motion sensors [17]. In ACSAC'13, Aviv et al. shows that the accelerometer sensor can also be employed as a high-bandwidth side channel. Particularly, they demonstrate how to use the accelerometer sensor to learn user tap and gesture-based input as required to unlock smart-phones using a PIN/password or Androids graphical password pattern [2]. In SPSM'13, Simon et al. describes a new side-channel attack that makes use of the video camera and microphone to infer PINs entered on a number-only soft keyboard on a smart-phone. The microphone is used to detect touch events,

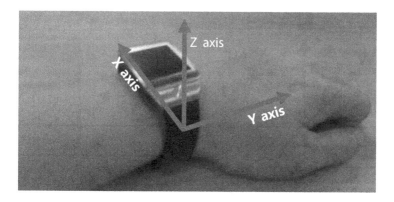

Fig. 1. Acceleration data from wearable devices

while the camera is used to estimate the smart-phone's orientation, and correlate it to the position of the digit tapped by the user [15]. In FUSION'13, Chowdhury et al. explores an efficient sensor fusion algorithm for detecting and classifying user taps on any neighboring surface even in the presence of various background acoustics [4]. In USENIX'14, Michalevsky et al. shows that the MEMS gyroscopes found on modern smart phones are sufficiently sensitive to measure acoustic signals in the vicinity of the phone [11]. In WiSec'14, Narain et al. investigates the feasibility of keystroke inference when user taps on a soft keyboard are captured by the stereoscopic microphones on an Android smart-phone. They developed algorithms for sensor-signals processing and domain specific machine learning to infer key taps using a combination of stereo-microphones and gyroscopes [12]. In SPSM'14, Spreitzer et al. propose a new type of side channel which is based on the ambient-light sensor employed in today's mobile devices [16].

Previous works generally used multiple sensor data from smart phone. Unlike previous works, we exploit the wearable devices which provide much sensitive information of user and present new side channel attacks on password inputs. This attack introduces that wearable device can be a big threats in near future.

2.2   Target Devices

Our attack target is user's password strokes through number keypad by measuring the accelerometer data from user's wearable devices. In this section, we explore the related technologies.

Personal Identification Number. A personal identification number is a numeric password shared between a user and a system, that can be used to authenticate the user to the system. Typically, the user is required to provide a non-confidential user identifier or token and a confidential PIN to gain access to the system. Upon receiving the user ID and PIN, the system looks up the

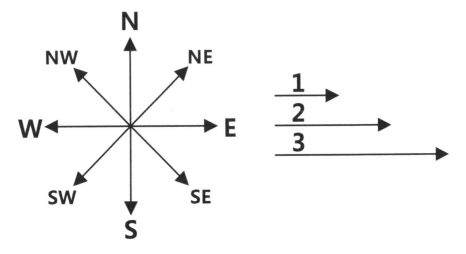

Fig. 2. User's activities, left: direction, right: distance

PIN based upon the user ID and compares the looked-up PIN with the received PIN. The user is granted access only when the number entered matches with the number stored in the system [1]. PIN based access control is widely deployed in ATM, smart phone, smart door and etc. [3,5].

Wearable Devices. Wearable devices are accessories incorporating small embedded computers. Since the device supports the several wireless network protocols such as Bluetooth and ZigBee, the device can communicate with the other devices in distance. Furthermore, they equip the multiple acceleration sensor to identify the user's movements. However, if this information can be abused by malicious users, it causes serious threats to the users. Hence, accelerator data can provide the some hints on user's movements. In our experiment, we placed STMicrolelectronics's LSM330DLC 3-axis accelerometer over our wrist and monitor the acceleration data with 40 Hz. The each button size of password keypad is set to 3 cm by 3 cm.

3   Proposed Method

We presents a novel approach to identify the password of PIN based access control systems by using wearable devices equipping the accelerometer sensors. The input numbers generally consist of 0 to 9. Each row has three different numbers and total four rows and three columns are drawn. The layout is available in Fig. 8(a).

3.1   Modeling Movements and Keystroke Events

The Fig. 1 shows that modern wearable devices provide the three axis acceleration data. This information is sensitive enough to analyze the user's activity precisely. As described in Fig. 2, user's activities are largely categorized in two different factors. One is moving direction. In order to select target number, user's hands should be placed over the number. If we identify the moving direction between each key stroke, we can identify the user's current position. Second factor is moving distance. Each number has certain gap between them. When the numbers have long distance between them, our hands should move in a long distance than shorter one. However, distance factor is difficult to get because accelerometer data contains noise factors. For this reason, we mainly focus on direction because direction information is readily available under high noise condition as well in our experiments. With this movement recognition technique, we identify the user's password with lesser complexity.

Activity Recognition. User's movements are largely divided into two activities. One is pressing the button and the other is moving the finger to the target button. In our approach, we identify the pressing and moving activities in separated way. In Fig. 3, the acceleration data of pressing activity is drawn. When we press the button, our hand approaches to the button in Y-axis after then we release the button. This basic activity is observed in V-shaped acceleration of Y-axis. When we press the button, our hand is accelerated in negative direction. After we pressed the button, our hands move in opposite direction which is positive acceleration. While pressing the button, X and Z-axis are also fluctuated but the variation from noise is quiet small to be ignored so we can identify the pressing button activity.

The other activity is moving the hands to the button. As we can see in Fig. 2, direction is largely divided into 8 factors including north, northeast, east, southeast, south, southwest, west and northwest. Firstly we identify the basic four

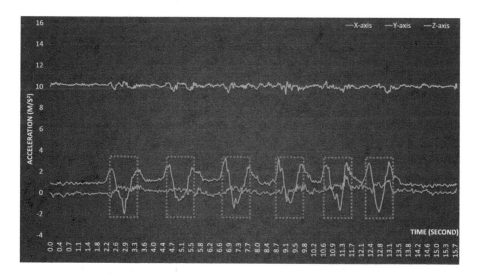

Fig. 3. Acceleration data of pressing button action

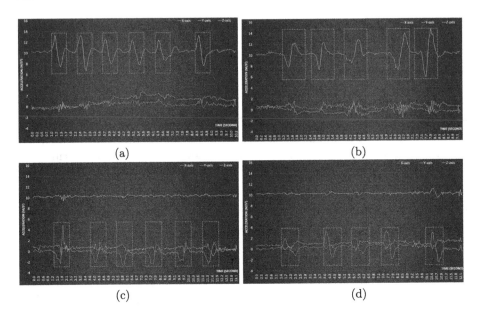

Fig. 4. Acceleration data of horizontal and vertical movements (a) up(north), (b) down(south), (c) left(west), (d) right(east).

directions including north, south, west and east. The acceleration data of four directions are available in Fig. 4. The directions are divided again in horizontal and vertical ways. The vertical movements mean our hand moves in upward or downward directions. When we move hand to the north direction as described in Fig. 4(a), Z-axis acceleration information is fluctuated. Firstly our hand moves to upward and Z-axis acceleration increases in positive direction. When our finger approaches to the destination, our finger is getting slow and negative acceleration increases. For south direction, opposite acceleration data is observed in Fig. 4(b), because our hand is moving in opposite direction of north. The horizontal movements mean our hand moves in left or right directions. When we move hand to the west as described in Fig. 4(c), X-axis acceleration information is fluctuated. Firstly our hand moves to left direction and X-axis acceleration grows in negative direction. When our finger approaches to the destination, our finger is getting slow and positive acceleration increases. For east direction, opposite acceleration data is observed in Fig. 4(d), because our hand is moving in opposite direction of west. The detailed Algorithm is available in Algorithm 1.

The diagonal movements present that our hand moves in northeast, southeast, southwest and northwest. These movements include both horizontal and vertical factors. In order to identify the diagonal movements, we should consider both X and Z-axis acceleration data. In Fig. 5(a), moving toward northeast direction is described. This diagonal movements includes north and east factors. As we can see in the figure, the features of north and east appear simultaneously which are described in Fig. 4(a) and (d), respectively. The other cases including

---

Algorithm 1. Identification of activities

Require: Variation of 3-axis accelerometers (X, Y, Z), threshold of 3-axis (X_T, Y_T, Z_T).
Ensure: Pressing the button P, moving the hand in horizontal way H, moving the hand in vertical way V.
1: $P, H, V \leftarrow NULL$
2: **if** $|Y| > Y_T$ **then**
3:     **if** $Y < 0$ **then**
4:        $P \leftarrow TRUE$
5: **if** $P = NULL$ **then**
6:     **if** $|X| > X_T$ **then**
7:        **if** $X > 0$ **then**
8:           $H \leftarrow RIGHT$
9:        **else**
10:          $H \leftarrow LEFT$
11:    **if** $|Z| > Z_T$ **then**
12:       **if** $Z > 0$ **then**
13:          $V \leftarrow UP$
14:       **else**
15:          $V \leftarrow DOWN$
16: **return** P, H, V

Algorithm 2. Inference of user's password path

Require: Movement list M
Ensure: Password path P
1: $C \leftarrow FALSE$
2: **while** $M \neq NULL$ **do**
3:     **if** $M = PRESSED$ **then**
4:        $C \leftarrow TRUE$
5:        $LIST \leftarrow CANDIDATES$
6:     $M.next$
7:     **if** $C = TRUE$ **then**
8:        **while** $LIST \neq NULL$ **do**
9:           $P \leftarrow$ possible path by referring $LIST$ and M
10:          $LIST.next$
11:       $M.next$
12:       $C \leftarrow FALSE$
13: **return** P

---

southeast, southwest and northwest also need to know both acceleration data to identify the diagonal movements. The detailed descriptions are available in Fig. 5(b), (c), and (d) respectively.

Inference of User's Password. In the previous section, we show how to identify the user's activity from acceleration data. Inserting the password consists of many movements and pressing the button activities. In this section, we show

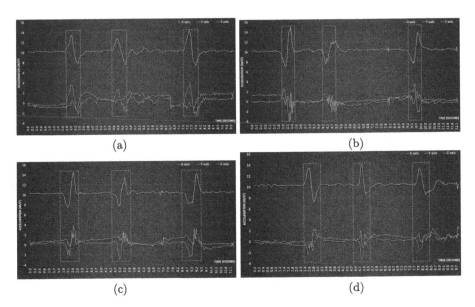

(a)   (b)

(c)   (d)

Fig. 5. Acceleration data of diagonal movements (a) northeast, (b) southeast, (c) southwest, (d) northwest.

clever idea to extract the few password candidates from thousand cases. In Fig. 6, the activity identification steps are drawn. The figure describes the case when user pressed the buttons (5 → 1 → 2 → 9) and we describe the activity in each event. The information, attacker only knows, is (pressed the button → moved to northeast → pressed the button → moved to west → pressed the button → moved to southwest → pressed the button). This information is not directly mapped into the password but we can reduce the complexity with physical limitation of input entry (refer Fig. 8a). Given input '1', it does not move to (north, northeast, southwest, west, northwest) in next steps. For this reason, this reduces the complexity of movements from 8 to 3. We applied this technique to whole user's movements and eliminate the majority of cases. The detailed algorithm is available in Algorithm 2. In Step 3 to 6, we check the movement list and if the movement is pressed activity, we set flag C to true and add possible button candidates to the $LIST$. After then we move to the next movement list. In Step 7 to 12, we generates possible password path. Firstly in Step 8 to 10, we add possible path to the P by referring the $LIST$ and M. After then movements move to the next and flag C is reset. Finally, password path P is returned.

The example of Algorithm 2 is described in Fig. 7. In Fig. 7a and b, we set the possible candidates to the (5, 6, 8, 9, 0), because other buttons cannot move to the northeast. After then possible paths are (5 → 1), (6 → 1, 2), (8 → 1, 4), (9 → 1, 2, 4, 5), (0 → 1, 4, 7). In Fig. 7c and d, we set the possible candidates to the (1, 2, 4, 5, 7), because this is destination of previous movements and can move to the west. After then possible paths are (1 → 2, 3), (2 → 3), (4 → 5, 6),

Table 1. Ideal and attacked password complexity

Password length	4	5	6	7	8	9	10	11
Ideal cases	10^4	10^5	10^6	10^7	10^8	10^9	10^{10}	10^{11}
After attack	14.3	19.2	26.5	36.2	49.9	66.5	100.0	119.5
Reduction(%)	99.85	99.98	99.99	99.99	99.99	99.99	99.99	99.99

$(5 \rightarrow 6)$, $(7 \rightarrow 8, 9)$. In Fig. 7e and f, we set the possible candidates to the $(2, 5)$, because this is destination of previous movements and other buttons cannot move to the southwest. After then possible paths are $(2 \rightarrow 6, 9)$, $(5 \rightarrow 9)$. By organizing the password path, only 13 passwords are extracted and we can find that real password $(5 \rightarrow 1 \rightarrow 2 \rightarrow 9)$ on the list.

3.2   Countermeasures

Proposed attack model exploits the pre-knowledge of input layout. In order to remove the layout information, we can randomly assign the input. In Fig. 8(b) and (c), random number order and random position order approaches are described [6–8,10,14]. This approach eliminates the relation of input and position successfully. However, this unusual layout introduces additional overheads to study this and occurs low typing speed. Another approach is access control. When user pressed the password, we can block the acceleration data access from wearable devices. These countermeasures can protect proposed attack model.

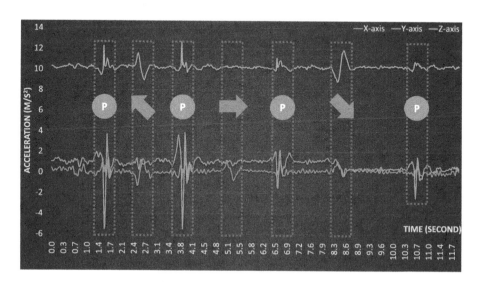

Fig. 6. Case study for identification of password path $(5 \rightarrow 1 \rightarrow 2 \rightarrow 9)$

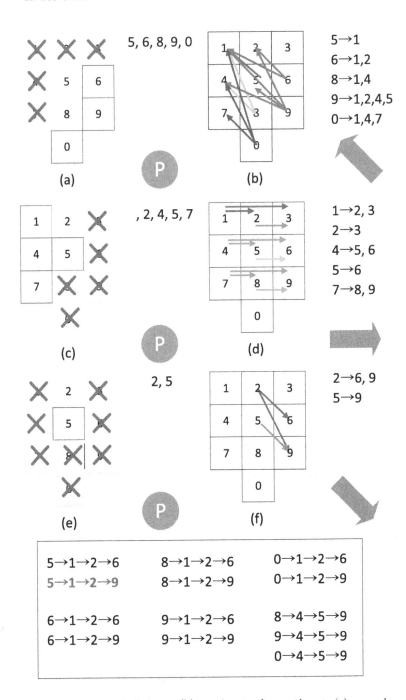

Fig. 7. (a) first pressing the button, (b) moving to the northeast, (c) second pressing the button, (d) moving to the west, (e) third pressing the button, (f) moving to the southwest

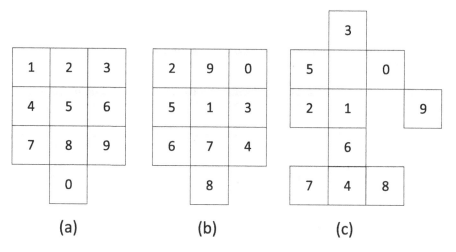

Fig. 8. Key layout: (a) normal order, (b) random number order, (c) random position order

4 Evaluation

In this section, we evaluate the performance of proposed method. In order to present fair results, we randomly generate 10,000 user's activity cases with rand() operation and then conducted the proposed Algorithm 2 with random activities. The complexity reduction is drawn in Table 1. From 4-digit to 11-digit, ideal password cases are ranging from 10^4 to 10^{11}. After taking attacks, the possible password is sharply reduced to 14.3 ~ 119.5 and this is about 99 % password reduction.

5 Conclusion

In this paper, we presented a method to reduce the password complexity with user's acceleration data of wearable devices. Firstly, we identify the user's movement directions from acceleration data. After then we distinguish the user's activity between pressing the button and moving to the button. With user's activity information, we conduct post processing to reduce the user's password complexity. In experiment, we found that the attack is successfully conducted with non-filtered single acceleration data. The most obvious future work is to analyze the distance information. Unlike direction recognition, distance information is prone to small noise so it is hard to get the accurate information. Furthermore, we should consider simultaneous pressing and moving activity and user's conditions such as taking a bus, subway or walking.

References

1. Your ID number is not a password, November 2010. http://webb-site.com/articles/identity.asp
2. Aviv, A.J., Sapp, B., Blaze, M., Smith, J.M.: Practicality of accelerometer side channels on smartphones. In: Proceedings of the 28th Annual Computer Security Applications Conference, pp. 41–50. ACM (2012)
3. Chang, A.: Your door is about to get clever 5 smart locks compared, March 2013. http://www.wired.com/2013/06/smart-locks/
4. Chowdhury, T., Aarabi, P., Zhou, W., Zhonglin, Y., Zou, K.: Extended touch mobile user interfaces through sensor fusion. In: 16th International Conference on Information Fusion (FUSION), pp. 623–629. IEEE (2013)
5. Heater, B.: Goji's Smart Lock snaps pictures welcomes you by name, July 2013. http://www.engadget.com/2013/06/04/goji-smart-lock/
6. Hoanca, B., Mock, K.J.: Screen oriented technique for reducing the incidence of shoulder surfing. In: Security and Management, pp. 334–340 (2005)
7. Kim, I.: Keypad against brute force attacks on smartphones. IET Inf. Secur. 6(2), 71–76 (2012)
8. Lee, C.: System and method for secure data entry. US Patent App. 13/093,141, 25 April 2011
9. Marquardt, P., Verma, A., Carter, H., Traynor, P.: (sp)iPhone: decoding vibrations from nearby keyboards using mobile phone accelerometers. In: Proceedings of the 18th ACM Conference on Computer and Communications Security, pp. 551–562. ACM (2011)
10. McIntyre, K.E., Sheets, J.F., Gougeon, D.A.J., Watson, C.W., Morlang, K.P., Faoro, D.: Method for secure pin entry on touch screen display. US Patent 6,549,194, 15 April 2003
11. Michalevsky, Y., Boneh, D., Nakibly, G.: Gyrophone: Recognizing speech from gyroscope signals. In: Proceeding 23rd USENIX Security Symposium (SEC 2014). USENIX Association (2014)
12. Narain, S., Sanatinia, A., Noubir, G.: Single-stroke language-agnostic keylogging using stereo-microphones and domain specific machine learning. In: Proceedings of the ACM Conference on Security and Privacy in Wireless & Mobile Networks, pp. 201–212. ACM (2014)
13. Owusu, E., Han, J., Das, S., Perrig, A., Zhang, J.: Accessory: password inference using accelerometers on smartphones. In: Proceedings of the Twelfth Workshop on Mobile Computing Systems & Applications, p. 9. ACM (2012)
14. Shin, H.-S.: Device and method for inputting password using random keypad. US Patent 7,698,563, 13 April 2010
15. Simon, L., Anderson, R.: Pin skimmer: Inferring pins through the camera and microphone. In: Proceedings of the Third ACM Workshop on Security and Privacy in Smartphones & Mobile Devices, pp. 67–78. ACM (2013)
16. Spreitzer, R.: Pin skimming: exploiting the ambient-light sensor in mobile devices. In: Proceedings of the 4th ACM Workshop on Security and Privacy in Smartphones & Mobile Devices, pp. 51–62. ACM (2014)
17. Xu, Z., Bai, K., Zhu, S.: Taplogger: Inferring user inputs on smartphone touchscreens using on-board motion sensors. In: Proceedings of the fifth ACM Conference on Security and Privacy in Wireless and Mobile Networks, pp. 113–124. ACM (2012)

BurnFit: Analyzing and Exploiting Wearable Devices

Dongkwan Kim, Suwan Park, Kibum Choi, and Yongdae Kim(✉)

Korea Advanced Institute of Science and Technology (KAIST),
291 Daehak-ro, Daejeon, Republic of Korea
{dkay,skyhwen,kibumchoi,yongdaek}@kaist.ac.kr

Abstract. Wearable devices have recently become popular, and more and more people now buy and wear these devices to obtain health-related services. However, as wearable device technology quickly advances, its security cannot keep up with the speed of its development. As a result, it is highly likely for the devices to have severe vulnerabilities. Moreover, because these wearable devices are usually light-weight, they delegate a large portion of their operations as well as permissions to a software gateways on computers or smartphones, which put users at high risk if there are vulnerabilities in these gateways. In order to validate this claim, we analyzed three devices as a case study and found a total 17 vulnerabilities in them. We verified that an adversary can utilize these vulnerabilities to compromise the software gateway and take over a victim's computers and smartphones. We also suggest possible mitigation to improve the security of wearable devices.

Keywords: Wearable device security · Communication channel analysis

1 Introduction

Wearable device, a representitive example of the *Internet of Things (IoT)*, have been increasing their market share recently. Researchers expect that this market share will reach 13 billion dollars by 2018 [23]. As increasing numbers of people are wearing these devices, adversaries may turn their attention to steal customers' private information. Despite their popularity, research on the security of wearable devices has been lacking. One can consider wearable devices as an embedded device, whose security has been actively studied recently [5,8,11,21,28]. These studies mainly focus on (semi) automatic analysis of their firmware.

In order to prepare for the IoT era, we have to understand the current state of art in designing wearable devices, as they represent the first batch of IoT devices. To this end, we decided to comprehensively evaluate the security of wearable devices through multiple steps. First, we classify the attack vectors on these devices. To save energy, wearable devices push their computational overhead and many permissions to their corresponding application on computers or smartphones, so called *software gateways*. These software gateways take the

© Springer International Publishing Switzerland 2016
H. Kim and D. Choi (Eds.): WISA 2015, LNCS 9503, pp. 227–239, 2016.
DOI: 10.1007/978-3-319-31875-2_19

role of medium between wearable devices and servers for updating the device or storing user data for customer services. Wearable devices utilize Bluetooth Low Energy (BLE) to communicate with the software gateways, and software gateways connect to the servers as usual.

We chose three popular wearable devices from a top 10 list [22], and analyzed and classified attack vectors for their update, data, and BLE channels as well as those for the device itself. From this analysis, we discovered a total of 17 vulnerabilities in the devices and showed that a user's private information can be exposed in plaintext. We successfully exploited them to take control of the software gateways as well. Finally, we present mitigations in the design stage to prevent wearable devices from being compromised.

To summarize, we make the following contributions in this study:

- We classified possible attack vectors related to the wearable devices that can be applied to most low-power IoT devices.
- We performed an analysis on our target devices and found 17 vulnerabilities. An adversary can take the control of the software gateways as well.
- We discuss mitigations for wearable devices in their operational channels to securely protect a user's private.

The rest of this paper is organized as follows: Section 2 outlines existing security research related to wearable devices and embedded systems. Section 3 overviews wearable device system as a whole and introduces our threat model. In Sect. 4, we analyze the vulnerability of wearable devices and their exploitation is described in Sect. 5. We discuss the analysis result and mitigation of these vulnerabilities in Sect. 6, and we conclude the paper in Sect. 7.

2   Related Works

Attacks on Wearable Devices. When no wearable device was available on the market in the early 2000s, there were a few studies forecasting security and privacy issues of wearable devices [3,7,13], but they were not really materialized until now. Recently, Ryan exposed vulnerabilities in the BLE interface, a dominant communication channel for wearable devices, and showed that sniffing is possible [19]. After that, Barcena at el. applied this research to actual wearable devices [6]. In particular, the authors proved that they can extract user information from the BLE interface between the target device and smartphone. In contrast to these previous studies, we perform a comprehensive study to classify possible attack vectors of the operational channels on wearable devices and analyze all.

Attacks on Embedded Devices. Security research on embedded devices is also relevant. Zaddach at el. introduced various ways to analyze the vulnerability of embedded devices [28]. In addition, Costin et al. performed a large-scale security analysis on embedded devices [10]. The authors improved their research and proposed an analysis platform for embedded devices called Avatar [27]. With this platform, firmware of embedded devices can be emulated and debugged along with the peripherals.

In addition, there have been several other approaches to embedded devices. AEG [5], Mayhem [8], FIE [11], and Firmalice [21] are frameworks for detecting vulnerabilities in firmware utilizing symbolic execution and taint analysis. These analysis methods on embedded devices can also be applied to determine vulnerabilities in the wearable devices. However, in this study, we focus on operational channels rather than their firmware. Furthermore, these studies are limited to Intel or ARM platform.

3   Background

3.1   Wearable Device Overview

A wearable device is a device that users can wear in their daily lives. Because wearable devices are light-weight and use low energy, they offload their computational overhead to software gateways. Therefore, almost all wearable devices are connected to a computer or smartphone, and this connection is usually based on Bluetooth. In this case, computers and smartphones take the role of software gateways to bridge the wearable devices to update and database servers through the Internet. Figure 1 illustrates an overview of the operational procedure of wearable devices.

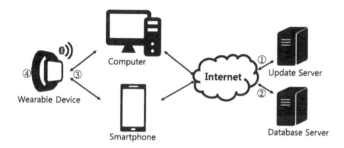

Fig. 1. General operational procedure of wearable devices

3.2   Bluetooth Low Energy (BLE)

Bluetooth Smart, also called BLE, is a relatively new protocol proposed after Bluetooth 4.0. Over the years, the security of classic Bluetooth has been improved. But BLE is a different protocol from classic Bluetooth, and, therefore, its security has to be analyzed almost from scratch.

Because BLE is designed to reduce power consumption, the randomness of the frequency hopping sequence, which protects the classic Bluetooth signal from sniffing, is replaced with an insecure modular addition. Furthermore, in classic Bluetooth, the secure simple pairing (SSP) technique effectively protects it from Man-in-the-Middle (MitM) attacks. However, this feature was only introduced in Bluetooth 4.1, meaning that devices implementing the earlier versions of Bluetooth would be vulnerable. Instead of using SSP, BLE utilizes six-digit pin numbers as a Temporary Key (TK), but this can be brute-forced within a second.

Ryan identified the vulnerabilities of the BLE interface pairing procedure in [19]. However, because many devices use customized BLE stack, their communcation should be analyzed to determine the exact meaning of the payload data in each BLE packet.

3.3   Threat Model

Wearable devices offload their operation to software gateways (i.e., applications on computers and smartphones). This includes access to various information such as health information, SMS message, calendar, email, and call history. Therefore, if an adversary can compromise the software gateway, she can take over the whole information that the wearable device can access. Furthermore, as wearable devices use more communication channels than a computer, they are likely to have more vulnerabilities.

① **Gateway to Update Server.** If there is a vulnerability in the update channel, this would be critical. An adversary can replace a benign update file to her own malicious one to compromise the software gateway as well as the wearable device. Usually this update channel is in a content management system managed by third party environment; hence, it could have vulnerabilities with respect to a link or URL access.

② **Gateway to Database Server.** As many wearable devices operate with health applications, they collect health information and send it to the database server. Based on this collected data, companies provide health-related services to their customers. However, if this channel is vulnerable, private user information can be exposed to an adversary.

③ **BLE Connection.** Wearable devices are usually connected to their software gateway through BLE. Because the BLE interface aims for low energy consumption, it is highly likely to have vulnerabilities in the pairing or communication procedure. Furthermore, the data encapsulated in the BLE signals may not be encrypted. In addition, if the channel is not authenticated, an adversary can directly send a request to the device and extract private user information.

④ **Device Analysis.** If there are vulnerabilities on the device itself, an adversary can exploit them to compromise the device itself. In this case, the adversary can control the device arbitrarily: sending multiple alarms or vibration to wake up the victim at night. Additionally, the adversary could extract a user's health information through the BLE interface.

We assume an adversary may have her own device for the analysis, but she does not have a physical access to the victim's device. In addition, we assume an adversary has access to the same or upper layer of the network so that she can perform DNS spoofing to redirect packets to her server. In addition, the adversary could be located close to the target so that she can send and receive BLE packets from the device.

4 Vulnerability Analysis of Wearable Devices

4.1 Methodology

We targeted three devices: A-fit, B-fit, and C-fit, all of which are fitness trackers that are on the list of the most popular wearable devices [22]. As we mentioned in Sect. 3, the software gateways bridging the wearable devices to the servers through the Internet may have many vulnerabilities.

We analyzed the devices as well as the operational channels: update, data, BLE. To analyze the update channel, we disassembled the software gateways using IDA Pro [14], and checked whether an adversary could substitute updates and device firmware with malicious ones. For the application analysis on Android smartphones, we utilized decompiling tools such as ApkTool [24], Smali/Baksmali [15], and dex2jar [18]. For the data channel, we analyzed the security of the health information by determining whether it is exposed as plaintext. For the analysis of BLE channel, it was determined whether sniffing or spoofing over-the-air data was possible. We sniffed BLE packets with Ubertooth [17], and analyzed them with Wireshark [9]. For device analysis, we searched for hardware debug points that could be utilized to extract firmware or other device information directly. From this analysis, we discovered total 17 vulnerabilities among three devices, as listed in Table 1.

Table 1. Vulnerabilities found on A-fit, B-fit, and C-fit. (âŬş means there was only partial obfuscation.)

Channel	Attacks	A-fit	B-fit	C-fit
Update channel	No obfuscation on app	✓	âŬş	✓
	DNS spoofing	✓	✓	✓
	App substitution	✓	✗	✓
	Firmware substitution	✗	✗	✓
Data channel	Plaintext data transfer	✓	✗	✗
BLE channel	Sniffing	✓	✓	–
	Plaintext data transfer	✓	✓	–
Device analysis	No obfuscation on firmware	✗	✗	✓
	Hidden function	✗	✗	✓
	Hidden protocol	✗	✗	✓
	Hardware debug point	✗	✗	✗

4.2   Update Channel Analysis

We performed both traffic and application analysis by respectively monitoring the network and disassembling the application to find vulnerabilities in the update channel. The A-fit has a couple of software gateways: applications on a smartphone and computer. The other devices only have a smartphone application.

A-fit. The A-fit can be connected to either a smartphone or computer using the provided Bluetooth connector. The smartphone loads its data using HTTPS, and this application was heavily obfuscated. Therefore, we chose to analyze the application on the computer, which was not obfuscated. As a result, we could easily figure out the firmware update procedure.

When a user first connects the A-fit to a computer, the device determines whether there is an update for the application on the computer. In addition, the user can directly send an update request message to the server by clicking an update button on the side of the application screen. From this analysis, we discovered that there was a hardcoded URL for the update server. Additionally, the A-fit application utilizes HTTP, which has no protection mechanism, so users are exposed to sniffing or even spoofing.

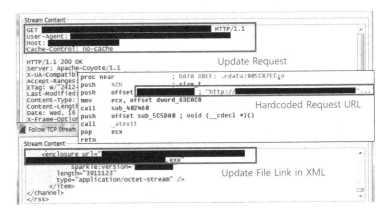

Fig. 2. XML file contents in A-fit update procedure. (Critical information was redacted to protect device.)

To update itself, the application first accesses to an XML file located at the update server of A-fit, as shown in Fig. 2. It then downloads an update file from the secondary server following the link written in the body of the XML file after checking its version. Because the A-fit application runs on Windows, this downloaded update file is an executable (.exe). After downloading it, the A-fit automatically executes the file to continue its update. From the analysis of the application we found that there is neither authentication of the downloaded file nor integrity check/verification of it. Therefore, if an adversary can perform DNS spoofing and make the A-fit application access her spoofed XML, it is possible to substitute a benign update file with a malicious one so that the application will execute it and compromise the victim's computer.

B-fit. In case of B-fit, there was only partial obfuscation on the application, and this obfuscation was not applied to the update routine. Therefore, we were able to analyze the application in a similar way to A-fit.

B-fit has similar vulnerability as A-fit; it first accesses to an XML file that contains the link of the update file. Even though it utilizes HTTPS to protect the connection from spoofing and verifies the certificate of the update server, there was no protection for the link of the update file in the XML file. The link was HTTP, which enables an adversary to perform a DNS spoofing attack to change the original update to a malicious one.

However, B-fit utilizes the update channel only for the firmware update. Because the application on the smartphone is updated from the app store, it was not able to modify the application. Furthermore, the update file was encrypted and decrypted on the B-fit device. Therefore, even though an adversary could perform DNS spoofing, she cannot create properly functioning firmware without the key.

C-fit. C-fit was the most vulnerable device in our test. Similar to B-fit, it only supports a connection with an Android smartphone that has the BLE feature. When C-fit is first connected to a smartphone, the application on the smartphone checks the firmware version as well as the application version in a similar way to A-fit. It accesses an XML file from the update server, follows the URL within it, and downloads an update file. We found that the application contains the new version of firmware in its *assets* folder. The application was not obfuscated, and there was neither integrity check nor authentication of the application and firmware, just as for A-fit. Therefore, an adversary could perform DNS spoofing and manipulate the application as well as the C-fit firmware.

4.3   Data Channel Analysis

We analyzed the security of the data channels by investigating the capability of sniffing. When A-fit transfers a user's data to the database server, it utilizes HTTP which is vulnerable to sniffing. As shown in Fig. 3, the application transfer the victim's private information in plaintext, which is only encoded in Base64. This private information includes the version of the victim's operating system, victim's private information in plaintext, health information, and device model, which is only encoded in Base64. This private information includes the version of the victim's operating system, health information, and device model.

By monitoring the network, an adversary can easily collect the private information of the users. Based on this collected data, the adversary could perform targeted attack in the real world. For example, an adversary could determine whether the target is sleeping or not before breaking into a house, or could recognize whether the target is sick. We also found that not only health information, but also the user's account information (i.e., ID and password) was exposed in plaintext. Therefore, from this analysis, we determined that the A-fit

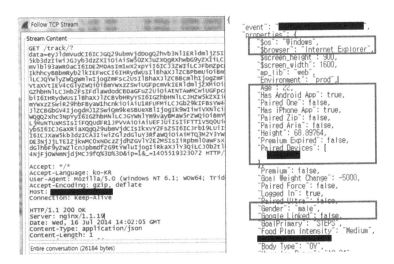

Fig. 3. Plaintext health information of a user. (The box shows user's private information and critical information of device was redacted.)

was vulnerable to sniffing because it utilized HTTP. However, in case of B-fit and C-fit, they encrypted their data using HTTPS with certificate verification, which made it difficult to extract information.

4.4 BLE Channel Analysis

As all these devices are known to use BLE, we analyzed the BLE channel to check if an adversary could access a user's health information. First, we needed to determine which version of Bluetooth was utilized. This information can be found in the BLE advertisement packets; there is a *Flags* field that indicates the configuration of BLE discoverable mode as well as the rates for data transferring.

As A-fit and B-fit only utilize BLE for communication, we were able to sniff the communication process via a pairing step. Moreover, these two devices did not have any option for BLE encryption. Because most BLE devices communicate using their own protocol implementation to increase energy efficiency, we could not understand the captured wireless packets. However, we analyzed the Android applications and figured out the data structure of the BLE packets. If an adversary is within BLE range, she can read the health information of the devices and even send fake data to the software gateways.

The C-fit supports classic Bluetooth. During our repeated experiments, we could not find any connection request in BLE protocol. This is because C-fit utilizes classic Bluetooth to send its actual data, and BLE is only used for the device ID advertisement to reduce power consumption.

4.5   Device Analysis

We also analyzed the devices to explore possible hidden functions. In the case of C-fit, the firmware consists of a file system, main executable binary, and binary for group of library functions. The firmware was not encrypted, so we could analyze it to find hidden functions and protocols.

The C-fit has an engineering mode to provide debugging at the service center. By analyzing the firmware, we could find all of the hidden functions, as listed in Table 2. Some hidden functions were published in [2], but this study did not report the full list.

Table 2. Codes for hidden functions in the C-fit engineering mode (bold codes were published in [2])

Codes for hidden menu					
#0	*#737425	*#1111	*#250	*#2222	*#251
***#1234**	*#350	*#12580*369	*#0228	***#232337**	***#2663**
*#2664	*#7353	***#7284**	***#9900**	*#22228378	*#232331
*#533881	*#533883	*#737425			

In addition, we found that C-fit has a modem feature that accepts AT commands similarly to a smartphone if it is connected to a computer with a micro USB interface. The C-fit supports multiple AT commands to configure or check device information. We discovered that there was a buffer overflow vulnerability in the AT commands. For example, if we entered an extremely long string as a parameter of the AT command, the C-fit displays the text 'Hardware Fault' on its screen and reboots itself. If an adversary can physically access the device, she can exploit this vulnerability to compromise the device. After it is compromised, she can then send fake health information to the smartphone through the Bluetooth interface and make multiple false alarms.

Furthermore, we searched for hardware debugging points that we could utilize to extract device information or firmware. Because we could not obtain the firmware of the A-fit and B-fit, we need to utilize these debugging points. We focused on exploiting the Universal Asynchronous Receiver/Transmitter (UART), Joint Test Action Group (JTAG), and Serial Wire Debug (SWD) interfaces [25,26], as many embedded devices generally contain these debugging features.

We utilized JTAGulator [16] and J-link [20] to determine if one of debugging interfaces exists. JTAGulator automatically generates signals to find debugging pins for UART and JTAG, but we could not find any such pins. In the case of SWD, we needed to input every single pin to find the debugging interface. However, as there were too many combinations of pins, we could not explore all pins. We also used a logic analyzer from Quant Asylum to directly analyze the signals from each pin, but the signal was too complicated to analyze. Therefore, we were not able to find one on the devices.

5   Exploiting Wearable Devices

We verified the exploitability of the update channel from the discovered vulnerabilities because this is the most critical part that can harm users. We prepared one phone as a victim, our own update server, and a laptop for DNS spoofing with [1]. As a result, the software gateways of the A-fit and C-fit were successfully compromised, but we were not able to take over the B-fit.

A-fit. We first performed DNS spoofing to substitute the A-fit application with our own. As we mentioned in Sect. 4.2, the application checks for updates when a user clicks on a button. We placed a malicious XML file and executable file on our server, and redirected the update traffic to it. As a result, the application on the victim's computer downloaded our file and executed it, as shown in Fig. 4. As a proof-of-concept, we utilized the Windows calculator, but any application could be executed here.

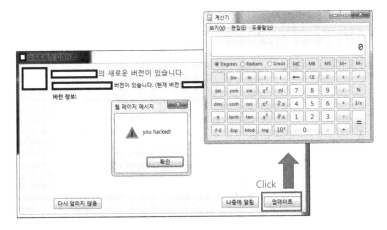

Fig. 4. Successful compromise of the victim's computer after DNS spoofing on the A-fit application. (Critical information of device was redacted. Note that words in the figure are Korean due to the OS language pack.)

C-fit. We also tried DNS spoofing the C-fit. In the case of C-fit, we were able to compromise both the Android application and the C-fit device firmware. We could install our malicious application successfully on the victim's phone. Furthermore, the installed application inherited the permissions from the original C-fit application, which includes many permissions such as accessing the phone book, extracting SMS messages, connecting to the Internet, and so on. Therefore, we could perform almost all behaviors on the victim's smartphone.

6   Discussion

6.1   Failure to Debug Hardware

Most hardware developers make debugging points to help them to remove bugs. However, these debugging points are eliminated before shipping or are located in a hidden space that only developers can recognize. Therefore, it takes a large amount of time and effort to find such points. In this experiment, we could not find any hardware debugging points among the three devices because the devices were too small and there were no public datasheets. However, even though we could not find hardware debugging interface in our target devices, we found 17 vulnerabilities from the operational channels that could enable an adversary to compromise the victim's computer and smartphone.

6.2 Improving the Security of Wearable Devices

To protect wearable devices securely, the update, data, and BLE channels should be securely protected as well as the device. Currently, the update and data channels from the software gateway to the servers are easily spoofed because they do not use encryption. Even the BLE interface has no encryption, and hence an adversary could exploit these channels. Because these channels are necessary, as light-weight wearable devices cannot directly communicate with servers, the channels should operate using SSL or TLS with certificate verification. This can prevent an adversary from manipulating packets to inject malicious update files or to extract private information from the users. Furthermore, the software gateways as well as the devices should be protected; integrity checks should be performed to prevent and detect modification of the firmware or application as in Sect. 5. In addition, TrustZone and secure boot should be applied to prohibit an adversary from bypassing the integrity check [4,12].

7 Conclusion

As wearable devices are currently becoming popular, development should be accompanied by security research. Therefore, we classified possible attack vectors related to some wearable devices. We analyzed three devices and found a total 17 vulnerabilities among them. Utilizing these vulnerabilities, we verified the exploitability of the software gateways. We also discussed ways to protect these wearable devices.

However, these issues are not only a matter for wearable devices, as other IoT devices might have similar problems. As more and more IoT devices are developed and appear on the market, researchers should take their security into account and take steps to resolve their vulnerabilities at the design stage.

Acknowledgement. This research was supported by (1) Next-Generation Information Computing Development Program through the NRF (National Research Foundation of Korea) funded by the MSIP (Ministry of Science, ICT and Future Planning) (No. NRF-2014M3C4A7030648), Korea, and by (2) the MSIP, Korea, under the ITRC (Information Technology Research Center) support program (IITP-2015-R0992-15-1006) supervised by the IITP (Institute for Information and Communications Technology Promotion).

References

1. Cain & Abel. http://www.oxid.it/cain.html. Accessed 8 June 2015
2. Redacted to protect the device
3. Al-Muhtadi, J., Mickunas, D., Campbell, R.: Wearable security services. In: 2001 International Conference on Distributed Computing Systems Workshopp, pp. 266–271. IEEE (2001)
4. Alves, T., Felton, D.: TrustZone: Integrated hardware and software security. ARM White Pap. **3**(4), 18–24 (2004)
5. Avgerinos, T., Cha, S.K., Hao, B.L.T., Brumley, D.: AEG: automatic exploit generation. In: NDSS, vol. 11, pp. 59–66 (2011)
6. Barcena, M.B., Wueest, C., Lau, H.: How safe is your quantified self. Symantech, Mountain View (2014)
7. Campbell, R.H., Al-Muhtadi, J., Naldurg, P., Sampemane, G., Mickunas, M.D.: Towards security and privacy for pervasive computing. In: Okada, M., Babu, C.S., Scedrov, A., Tokuda, H. (eds.) ISSS 2002. LNCS, vol. 2609, pp. 1–15. Springer, Heidelberg (2003)
8. Cha, S.K., Avgerinos, T., Rebert, A., Brumley, D.: Unleashing mayhem on binary code. In: 2012 IEEE Symposium on Security and Privacy (SP), pp. 380–394. IEEE (2012)
9. Combs, G., et al.: Wireshark, pp. 12–02 (2007). http://www.wireshark.org/lastmodified
10. Costin, A., Zaddach, J., Francillon, A., Balzarotti, D., Antipolis, S.: A large-scale analysis of the security of embedded firmwares. In: USENIX Security Symposium (2014)
11. Davidson, D., Moench, B., Ristenpart, T., Jha, S.: FIE on firmware: finding vulnerabilities in embedded systems using symbolic execution. In: USENIX Security, pp. 463–478 (2013)
12. Davis, D.L.: Secure boot , US Patent 5,937,063 (1999)
13. Di Pietro, R., Mancini, L.V.: Security and privacy issues of handheld and wearable wireless devices. Commun. ACM **46**(9), 74–79 (2003)
14. Eagle, C.: The IDA Pro Book: The Unofficial Guide to the World's Most Popular Disassembler. No Starch Press, San Francisco (2011)
15. Freke, J.: Smali. https://code.google.com/p/smali. Accessed 7 June 2015
16. Grand, J.: JTAGulator: assisted discovery of on-chip debug interfaces. In: 21st DefCon Conference, Las Vegas (2013)
17. Ossmann, M.: Project ubertooth, p. 23 (2012). Accessed 18 Nov 2012
18. Pan, B.: dex2jar. https://github.com/pxb1988/dex2jar. Accessed 7 June 2015
19. Ryan, M.: Bluetooth: with low energy comes low security. In: WOOT (2013)
20. SEGGE: Debug Probes - J-Link and J-Trace. https://www.segger.com/jlink-debug-probes.html. Accessed 6 June 2015
21. Shoshitaishvili, Y., Wang, R., Hauser, C., Kruegel, C., Vigna, G.: Firmalice-automatic detection of authentication bypass vulnerabilities in binary firmware. In: NDSS (2015)
22. Stables, J.: Best fitness trackers 2015: Jawbone. Misfit, Fitbit, Garmin and more, April 2015. http://www.wareable.com/fitness-trackers/the-best-fitness-tracker
23. Statista: Wearable device market value from 2010 to 2018 (2015). http://www.statista.com/statistics/259372/wearable-device-market-value. Accessed 9 June 2015

24. Tumbleson, C., Wisniewski, R.: Apktool. http://ibotpeaches.github.io/Apktool. Accessed 7 June 2015
25. Wikipedia: Joint test action group – wikipedia, the free encyclopedia (2015). http://en.wikipedia.org/w/index.php?title=Joint_Test_Action_Group& oldid=663324599. Accessed 5 June 2015
26. Wikipedia: Universal asynchronous receiver/transmitter – wikipedia, the free encyclopedia (2015). http://en.wikipedia.org/w/index.php?title=Universal_ asynchronous_receiver/transmitter&oldid=663120875. Accessed 5 June 2015
27. Zaddach, J., Bruno, L., Francillon, A., Balzarotti, D.: Avatar: a framework to support dynamic security analysis of embedded systems firmwares. In: Symposium on Network and Distributed System Security (NDSS) (2014)
28. Zaddach, J., Costin, A.: Embedded devices security and firmware reverse engineering. Black-Hat USA (2013)

Security Analysis of FHSS-type Drone Controller

Hocheol Shin[1][(✉)], Kibum Choi[1], Youngseok Park[2], Jaeyeong Choi[1],
and Yongdae Kim[1,2]

[1] School of Electrical Engineering, KAIST, Daejeon, Republic of Korea
{h.c.shin,kibumchoi,go1736,yongdaek}@kaist.ac.kr
[2] Graduate School of Information Security, KAIST, Daejeon, Republic of Korea
raccoon7@kaist.ac.kr

Abstract. Unmanned Aerial Vehicles (UAVs), or drones, have attracted
a considerable amount of attentions due to their utility to civilian as well
as military applications. However, the security issues involved in UAV
technology have not been extensively discussed in the literature. As a
first step toward analyzing these security issuxes, we investigate security
in drone controllers, especially controllers that adopt Frequency Hopping
Spread Spectrum (FHSS). In order to affect an FHSS-type controller, an
attacker first has to access its physical layer. This is difficult because of
the pseudorandomness of the hopping sequence and the rapidly changing
channels. However, these difficulties can be relaxed when the attacker
acquires the hopping sequence and when the hopping speed of the target
system is not significant. In this paper, we propose a general scheme to
extract the hopping sequence of FHSS-type controllers using a software-
defined radio (SDR). We also propose a method to address the issue of
the limited bandwidth of the SDR. We implemented our scheme on a
Universal Software Radio Peripheral (USRP), successfully extracted the
hopping sequence of the target system, and exposed the baseband signal.

Keywords: Attack · Drone · Physical layer security · Blackbox system

1 Introduction

Because of their extensive range of application, from military airstrikes [20] to
automated package delivery platforms [2,4], unmanned aerial vehicles (UAVs) or
drones have lately been the subject of increasing interest. As they become more

---

This research was supported by (1) Next-Generation Information Computing Development Program through the NRF (National Research Foundation of Korea)
funded by the MSIP (Ministry of Science, ICT & Future Planning) (No. NRF-
2014M3C4A7030648), Korea, and (2) the MSIP, Korea, under the ITRC (Information Technology Research Center) support program (IITP-2015-R0992-15-1006)
supervised by the IITP (Institute for Information & communications Technology
Promotion).

© Springer International Publishing Switzerland 2016
H. Kim and D. Choi (Eds.): WISA 2015, LNCS 9503, pp. 240–253, 2016.
DOI: 10.1007/978-3-319-31875-2_20

popular, drones are frequently flown in noisy environments, and are thus exposed to intentional/unintentional interferences. It is therefore necessary for drones to secure their control systems against such interference. As exemplified by the case of the capture by Iranian forces of a United States Air Force (USAF) drone in 2011 [21], even military drone control systems are not adequately secure.

Wireless remote controllers for radio-controlled (RC) model aircraft in the past employed fixed frequencies of tens of megahertz [1]. However, due to a shortage of spectral resources, and in order to protect against interference, current remote controllers adopt spread spectrum technology on industrial, scientific, and medical (ISM) radio bands of 2.4 GHz [1,11].

FHSS is a spread spectrum technology that continuously changes carrier frequency for anti-jamming/sniffing/spoofing capabilities. A theoretically unique hopping sequence is pre-shared by every transmitter-receiver pair through binding, which can prevent issues of mutual interference. However, even FHSS cannot completely protect links against all jamming/sniffing/spoofing threats. High-energy wideband jammers can block the entire hopping space used by an FHSS system [17]. A random jammer with a much greater hopping speed can deteriorate the signal-to-noise ratio (SNR) [17]. Furthermore, FHSS is vulnerable to reactive jammers with a sufficiently high reaction speed.

Although the above-mentioned attack vectors against FHSS are quite expensive for attackers, an exposed hopping sequence can drastically reduce the required complexity of attacks. Using the hopping sequence, attackers can proactively react to the changing center frequency, which enables the implementation of low-cost reactive jammers or baseband extractors.

In this paper, we propose a general scheme to extract the hopping sequences of FHSS-type drone controllers by using a software-defined radio (SDR). The versatility of SDRs makes it possible to deal with most FHSS-type drone controllers, which are mostly incompatible with one another [5]. We also propose a method to overcome the problem of limited SDR bandwidth when treating controllers with larger bandwidths. We applied our proposed scheme for a real-world FHSS-type controller, where the bandwidth of the target controller was approximately three times larger than that of the SDR, successfully extracted the total hopping sequence of the target system, and exposed the baseband signal.

The remainder of this paper is structured as follows: Sect. 2 provides the requisite background for our research here, whereas Sect. 3 is dedicated to a description of our proposed scheme to extract hopping sequences. In Sect. 4, we describe the implementation of the attack platform as well as the results. Sect. 5 summarizes related work in the area, and Sect. 7 contains our conclusions.

2   Background and Attack Model

2.1   Frequency Hopping Spread Spectrum

FHSS is a major spread spectrum technology along with Direct Sequence Spread Spectrum (DSSS). In wireless communications, it rapidly switches channels using

a pseudorandom sequence, which makes it difficult to eavesdrop. Rapidly changing carrier frequency also renders the system highly resistant to narrowband
interference, and enables it to share the frequency band with other systems
using different communication technologies.

FHSS has drawbacks as well. First, FHSS systems occupy much wider bandwidth than it actually requires. For example, a typical 10 channel FHSS system
occupies bandwidth ten times wider than it actually uses. Second, a transmitter-
receiver pair has to be finely synchronized, which is achieved by several ways.
A transmitter may transmit duplications of a packet for all channels, while the
receiver listens to a randomly selected channel. For another way, a transmitter-
receiver pair can share a frequency table, repeating the predefined sequence.

Most of drone controllers utilize 2.4 GHz band, which is shared by many
other wireless devices. Therefore, drone controllers can occupy only a fraction
of assigned bandwidth. Furthermore, a transmitter-receiver pair does not have
additional communication channel. Once bound at the initial stage, the pair
communicates each other without any prior pairing steps after they are turned
on. This means a consistent frequency table is shared by the pair.

2.2   Radio Control System for RC Aircraft

Drone controllers interface humans and drones. Although drones differ in their
level of autonomy, controllers always take up the most critical functions, which
makes controllers one of the most important component. Controllers vary as the
drones are. In this paper we focus on controllers for civilian RC aircraft.

A typical RC controller consists of three components: a transmitter body,
an RF module, and a receiver. The transmitter body provides the user interface, and converts user control into electrical signals. The RF module modulates
and upconverts the control signal. It characterizes the wireless link between
a transmitter and a receiver, whose robustness against interferences according
to its wireless characteristics. The receiver reconverts the wireless signal into

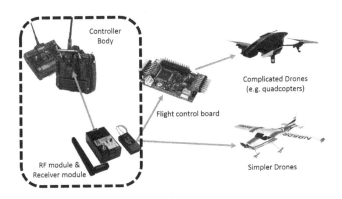

Fig. 1. RC aircraft system composition

Pulse-width modulation (PWM) pulses. Figure 1 shows the composition of the overall drone system, where components in the dashed rectangle indicate the drone controller.

Frequently, multiple RC aircraft are flown together, where multiple control signals interferes one another. In this case, control signal interference is critical for drones. They can fall into uncontrollable state, which is critical for fast moving aircraft. Therefore, RC controllers are required to resist high level of interference. To both share the band and resist mutual interference, spread spectrum technologies (FHSS and DSSS) are widely adopted.

Currently, no industrial standard for RC controllers exists. Therefore, controllers from diverse manufacturers are usually not compatible. Furthermore, the absence of the standard makes manufacturers hide details of their products. This makes the RC controller a blackbox system for third party analyst.

2.3   Attack Model

Our attack model is as follows. First, the target system is considered to be a blackbox. Though the attacker can analyze the system on her own capabilities, she cannot access any confidential information on the system a priori. Second, we assume the controller signal has at least one exclusively distinguishing characteristic. Furthermore, the attacker can exploit this characteristic to differentiate the target signal on air from other signals. The attacker can easily purchase such popular controllers and analyze their signal to reveal exclusive characteristics.

3   Methodology

3.1   Extracting the Hopping Sequence

Measuring Channel Information. Typical FHSS systems have identical channel widths. Thus, we can derive channel center frequencies and the number of channels from measurements at the lowest and the highest channels. The center frequency of the remaining channels can be identified by repeatedly adding channel bandwidth to the first channel until the last channel is reached.

Detecting Channel Activeness. In order to extract the hopping sequence through measurement, we first need to detect channel activeness. A considerable amount of past research in the area has dealt with this topic, since it is intimately related to cognitive radio [9, 18, 19, 23, 24]. Yücek et al. [24] listed various methods to determine spectral activeness according to the amount of available information regarding the target signal. The more accurate the method is, the more detailed the prior information that it requires.

Since the target system is considered to be a blackbox, applicable channel sensing methods are quite limited. Energy detection [19] and cyclostationarity-based detection [9] methods are representative techniques used to detect blackbox signals. We use energy detection to detect channel activeness for the sake of simplicity. However, this can be altered without affecting the remainder of our work here. Once we can detect channel activeness, we can record the history of the activated channels. Finally, assuming constant hopping speed, measurements of the continuous signal can be converted into a discretized sequence.

Searching the Period. The easiest way to predict the future sequence is to extract the period in hopping sequence. This can be achieved by choosing a part of the sequence and search for repetitions. While this scheme works well in most cases, there are instances of error. If the length of the chosen part is greater than twice the actual period, the period appears longer than it is. Moreover, if the chosen part is shorter than the half the actual period, the period can appear shorter than it is in some bad cases. These erroneous cases can be settled by searching repetitions by choosing multiple parts.

If the history has numerous measurement errors, the aforementioned exact matching-based search will fail. In such cases, we can find the period with similarity-based matching. This is identical to exact matching-based search except that repetitions are detected by similarity scores. Whenever the similarity score exceeds a certain threshold during the search, the relevant points are marked as repeating points. If a sufficient number of points are acquired, the intervals between any two points are aligned and compared to identify the most frequently appearing interval, which can be considered the hopping period.

Various pattern matching algorithms can be used to derive similarity scores. Matched filters are largely adopted for pattern detection [7,8]. Algorithms used to solve sequence alignment problems [22] can also be considered, since that problem is quite similar to the one here.

3.2 Overcoming Limited SDR Bandwidth

In some cases, the bandwidth of the target system can exceed the maximum bandwidth of the SDR used. In such cases, the SDR can only monitor a part of each channel. This makes it impossible to detect the activeness of channels beyond the tuned SDR bandwidth. To solve this issue, the attacker can simultaneously utilize multiple, tightly synchronized SDRs, or a more powerful SDR that can cover the entire range of the target bandwidth. However, these approaches are expensive. We suggest an alternative that enables a single narrowband SDR to acquire the full hopping sequence of the target system.

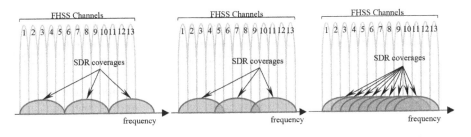

Fig. 2. Examples of SDR coverage arrangements

Measuring the number of channels and their center frequencies is not challenging, even with a narrowband SDR, since we simply need to measure the first and the last channels. However, we can only acquire a number of partial sequences with a narrowband SDR, and such partial sequences should be uniquely merged to obtain the actual total hopping sequence. In order to uniquely combine partial sequences, SDR coverage should be carefully arranged. We explore various arrangements to show that a careful arrangement can yield the total sequence without ambiguity. Note that in all examples of partial sequences presented in this subsection, all channels in a period are activated equally frequently. Although this condition is not essential to our method, typical FHSS systems meet this condition in order to uniformly utilize bandwidth.

Figure 2 shows three examples of coverage arrangement. In the left arrangement, the SDR coverages span the entire hopping space but do not overlap with one another. In this arrangement, partial hopping sequences are combined only with the duration of slots of no activity, which can lead to multiple combinations. For example, if channels under each coverage are activated in a series: "1 5 2 3 4 / 10 6 9 8 7 / 13 11 12," the partial sequences for each coverage are "1 5 2 3 4," "10 6 9 8 7," and "13 11 12," respectively. Since the channels in each coverage are contiguously activated, these partial sequences can also be combined as, for example, "1 5 2 3 4 / 13 11 12 / 10 6 9 8 7." This leads to multiple combinations.

The middle arrangement can also lead to multiple solutions when each channel is activated more than once in a period. The two example hopping sequences below show one of such cases. Overlapped channels are marked with hats and differences are bolded. It is easily verified that the two hopping periods, Eqs. (1) and (2), are different, although the corresponding partial sequences are identical.

$$\cdots 1 \hat{5} 2 3 4 \mathbf{10} 6 \hat{9} 8 7 \mathbf{13\ 11\ 12} \parallel 2 \hat{5} 3 4 1 \mathbf{11} 6 \hat{9} 8 7 \mathbf{10\ 12\ 13} \cdots \quad (1)$$

$$\cdots 1 \hat{5} 2 3 4 \mathbf{11} 6 \hat{9} 8 7 \mathbf{10\ 12\ 13} \parallel 2 \hat{5} 3 4 1 \mathbf{10} 6 \hat{9} 8 7 \mathbf{13\ 11\ 12} \cdots \quad (2)$$

By contrast, the last arrangement, which is maximally overlapped, does not lead to multiple solutions. In this arrangement, every channel, except the one at each end, overlaps with another, i.e., they are all entangled. Therefore, any rearrangement of channels different from the original will always interfere with other partial sequences. However, maximal overlap is not always optimal. In most cases, a loosely overlapped arrangement will suffice. Indeed, we can uniquely combine partial hopping sequences with a non-maximally overlapped arrangement. Therefore, repeated trials with increasing overlaps are required to find the optimally overlapped arrangement.

3.3 Possible Attack Vectors

Once the total hopping sequence has been acquired, the basic requirements of catching up the ongoing FHSS signal are met. With the hopping sequence of the target system in hand, the attack cost can be greatly reduced, and the hopping sequence can be applied to the following attack platforms.

Baseband extractors receive and record the baseband signal while continuously following FHSS signal stream. The extracted baseband signal can later be analyzed to yield information regarding the modulation, encoding, or the packet structure of the baseband. **Reactive sniffers** operate similar to baseband extractors, except that they can demodulate and decode the baseband signal to expose the bitstream or meaningful information from target systems. **Reactive jammers** transmit narrowband interfering signals whenever a channel is activated. Using the extracted hopping sequence, the level of difficulty of implementing reactive jammers can be drastically reduced, since attackers can proactively wait for the channel to be activated.

4   Implementation and Results

4.1   Equipment

Software-defined Radio - We used a USRP N210 to receive signals from the target system. USRP N210 has a gigabit Ethernet interface, and can provide up to 25 million 16-bit pair (I & Q) samples per second ($= 2 \times 2B \times M/s = 100\,MB/s$) [6]. USRP N-series devices require a separate RF frontend, called a daughterboard. We used a CBX daughterboard [3] with full duplex capability with 40 MHz of instantaneous bandwidth. It can cover 1.2~6 GHz.

Host PC - We used a general desktop with Intel Core i5-3570 and 16 GB of DDR3 memory. To interface with the USRP, we used Intel PRO/1000 PT Dual Port Server Adapter. As an OS, we used Ubuntu 12.04 LTS 64-bit.

4.2   Test Target Selection and Basic Analysis

Selected Test Target. We chose a real-world radio controller to verify our attack scheme. The target controller is composed of three components: a transmitter body, an RF module, and a receiver. The detailed brands and names are

Fig. 3. FrSKY DJT Radio Telemetry (RF module, left of left figure), FlySky FH-TH9X Transmitter (transmitter body, right of left figure), and FrSKY D4R-II 4Ch Receiver (receiver, right figure)

shown in Fig. 3. It adopts Advanced Continuous Channel Shifting Technology (ACCST), which is FrSKY's commercial name for FHSS. ACCST devices shift channels more than a hundred times per second for security and stability.

We first conducted basic examinations of the target system in order to apprehend its mechanism. We analyzed only the body and the RF module, since the analysis of the receiver is not required to verify the attack model.

Analysis of Transmitter Body. For the selected target, the transmitter body only output a series of PWM pulses and passed them to the RF module. The PWM pulses were further modulated and up converted in the RF module. Having examined the transmitter body, we concluded that the transmitter body was not related to generating FHSS signals.

Analysis of the RF Module. The RF module was powered by a pin connecting it to the transmitter body, and modulated the input PWM pulses to generate the FHSS signal output. In order to analyze only the output signal of the RF module, we connected the module's output port and the CBX input port directly using a SubMiniature version A (SMA) cable. We then ran uhd_fft to view the spectrogram of the RF module's output signal. uhd_fft is a GUI application that makes USRP work as a simple spectrometer. Since we already knew that the RF module used 2.4 GHz bands, we first tuned uhd_fft to 2.4 GHz, and gradually changed the frequency. As a result, the center frequency of the first and the last FHSS channel were found to be 2.40517 GHz and 2.41415 GHz, respectively. From these observations, we identified the total number of FHSS channels and their center frequencies.

To summarize, there were 47 channels in total, and each channel was 1.5 MHz wide. The total bandwidth was calculated as below.

$$\left[(2.40517 \times 10^9 - 1.5 \times 10^6/2) - (2.47415 \times 10^9 + 1.5 \times 10^6/2)\right] \text{Hz} \approx 70 \text{ MHz}$$

It was approximately three times larger than the maximum bandwidth of USRP N210 (25 MHz), which was the case described in Sect. 3.2

4.3 FHSS Sequence Extraction

Hopping Speed. The hopping speed of the target system is important because USRP has limited agility. If the hopping speed is too high, it is impossible to follow the changing frequency of the target system.

The simplest method of measuring hopping speed is to measure the duration of a hop, since typical FHSS systems have a constant hopping speed. To measure the duration, we first tuned the USRP to one of the channels and recorded the signal into a file. We subsequently browsed the recorded file to measure the duration of a hop, which was 0.0058 s. Converting this duration directly into hopping frequency, we derived $1/0.0058\,\text{s} \approx 172\,\text{Hops/s}$. Note that this was the upper bound of the hopping speed, since no FHSS channel is typically changed without a delay.

Based on work by Nychis et al. [13], the hopping speed was in a range that USRP can readily follow without any modifications to the field-programmable gate array (FPGA) or the firmware. In their study, the overall round trip time between the host and the USRP was measured to be 612 μs on average with a standard deviation of 789 μs. With the measured hopping speed, only more than +7σ cases would lead to missing activated hops.

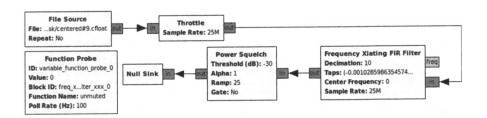

Fig. 4. GNU radio flow graph for partial sequence extraction

Partial Sequence Extraction. Following the basic analysis of the target system, we extracted the partial hopping sequences. As described in the previous subsection, the total bandwidth of the target system was approximately 70 MHz, much higher than the maximum bandwidth of the USRP (25 MHz). Therefore, we first acquired the partial hopping sequences of the target system.

In order to record the sequence, we built a GNU Radio flow graph as in Fig. 4. The flow graph was mainly composed of a Frequency Xlating FIR filter, Power Squelch, and Function Probe.

Frequency Xlating FIR filter first operates as a channel selection filter. It tunes to the target channel and filters out other signals. Power Squelch and Function Probe are core parts of this flow graph. Power Squelch allows input signals to pass though only when the power level exceeds a preset threshold, and Function Probe monitors the state of Power Squelch to determine if it is open.

We parallelized the flow graph in Fig. 4 to simultaneously record multiple channels under USRP coverage. We set seven USRP coverages, and ran Algorithm 1 for each coverage to record the corresponding partial sequence. As a result, we finally acquired all partial hopping sequences, as listed in Table 1. From the table, we see that all channels were identically activated three times for each partial period. This confirmed that the target system uniformly unitizes its bandwidth.

Combining Partial Sequences. In the final step, we combined acquired partial sequences. This step was not automated, since partial sequences can be woven manually due to their short lengths. We arranged partial sequences in a spreadsheet, and fit the activations of the overlapped channels together to find the complete hopping sequence. Though the coverages did not overlap maximally, a unique combination could be found. Table 2 shows the combined sequence.

```
build flow graph structure;
while running flow graph do
    for each interval do
        for each channel do
            if squelch active then
            |   record(channel_number);
            end
            if no activation then
            |   record(0);
            end
        end
    end
end
```

Algorithm 1. Partial sequence extraction algorithm

Table 1. Extracted partial sequences for each coverage

Coverage #	Partial hopping sequence	Length
1 (Ch1~Ch9)	7, 1, 6, 5, 4, 9, 3, 8, 2, 7, 1, 6, 5, 4, 3, 2, 1, 9, 8, 7, 6, 5, 4, 9, 3, 8, 2	27
2 (Ch1~Ch17)	7, 1, 12, 6, 11, 5, 10, 4, 9, 3, 8, 2, 7, 1, 6, 17, 5, 16, 4, 15, 3, 14, 2, 13, 1, 12, 17, 11, 16, 10, 15, 9, 14, 8, 13, 7, 12, 6, 17, 11, 5, 16, 10, 4, 15, 9, 3, 14, 8, 2, 13	51
3 (Ch9~Ch25)	12, 23, 11, 22, 10, 21, 9, 20, 25, 19, 24, 18, 23, 17, 22, 16, 21, 15, 20, 14, 25, 19, 13, 24, 18, 12, 23, 17, 11, 22, 16, 10, 21, 15, 9, 20, 14, 19, 13, 18, 12, 17, 11, 16, 10, 15, 9, 14, 25, 13, 24	51
4 (Ch17~Ch33)	26, 31, 25, 30, 24, 29, 23, 28, 22, 33, 27, 21, 32, 26, 20, 31, 25, 19, 30, 24, 18, 29, 23, 17, 28, 22, 27, 21, 26, 20, 25, 19, 24, 18, 23, 17, 22, 33, 21, 32, 20, 31, 19, 30, 18, 29, 17, 28, 33, 27, 32	51
5 (Ch25~Ch41)	41, 29, 40, 28, 39, 27, 38, 26, 37, 25, 36, 41, 35, 40, 34, 39, 33, 38, 32, 37, 31, 36, 30, 41, 35, 29, 40, 34, 28, 39, 33, 27, 38, 32, 26, 37, 31, 25, 36, 30, 35, 29, 34, 28, 33, 27, 32, 26, 31, 25, 30	51
6 (Ch33~Ch47)	44, 43, 42, 47, 41, 46, 40, 45, 39, 44, 38, 43, 37, 42, 36, 47, 41, 35, 46, 40, 34, 45, 39, 33, 44, 38, 43, 37, 42, 36, 41, 35, 40, 34, 39, 33, 38, 37, 36, 47, 35, 46, 34, 45, 33	45
7 (Ch39~Ch47)	44, 43, 42, 47, 41, 46, 40, 45, 39, 44, 43, 42, 47, 41, 46, 40, 45, 39, 44, 43, 42, 41, 40, 39, 47, 46, 45	27

Table 2. Acquired total hopping sequence

Combined partial periods	7, 1, 36, 30, 24, 12, 6, 47, 35, 29, 23, 11, 5, 46, 34, 28, 22, 10, 4, 45, 33, 27, 21, 9, 3, 44, 32, 26, 20, 8, 2, 43, 31, 25, 19, 7, 1, 42, 30, 24, 18, 6, 47, 41, 29, 23, 17, 5, 46, 40, 28, 22, 16, 4, 45, 39, 27, 21, 15, 3, 44, 38, 26, 20, 14, 2, 43, 37, 25, 19, 13, 1, 42, 36, 24, 18, 12, 47, 41, 35, 23, 17, 11, 46, 40, 34, 22, 16, 10, 45, 39, 33, 21, 15, 9, 44, 38, 32, 20, 14, 8, 43, 37, 31, 19, 13, 7, 42, 36, 30, 18, 12, 6, 41, 35, 29, 17, 11, 5, 40, 34, 28, 16, 10, 4, 39, 33, 27, 15, 9, 3, 38, 32, 26, 14, 8, 2, 37, 31, 25, 13
	(Length = 47×3 =141)

4.4   Baseband Extractor

Having successfully extracted the hopping sequence, we programmed the USRP to follow and record the target FHSS signal. In order to do that, we built a GNU radio flow graph as in Fig. 5. In the flow graph the incoming signal is first filtered by Low Pass Filter block. Power Squelch then senses the activeness of the current channel. Selector is initially headed to the null sink in order not to record meaningless signals, and is switched to the remaining flow graph when the USRP catches the FHSS signal. Once Selector is switched, PLL Carrier Tracking block finely tunes on the signal stream. Finally, the signal stream is recorded to an output file and visualized in real time. The flow graph is dynamically controlled using a Python script. It first commands the USRP to monitor one of the channels. When the channel being awaited is activated, the script compares the state of its internal counter at the moment with the incoming signal. If they match, the script switches Selector and starts recording the signal stream. Otherwise, it is reset. As a result, we successfully extracted the raw baseband signal of the target system. Figure 6 shows a part of the extracted signal.

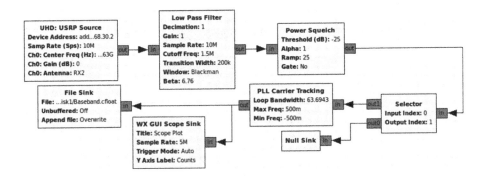

Fig. 5. GNU radio flow graph for the baseband extractor

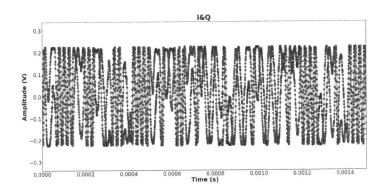

Fig. 6. Part of the extracted baseband

5 Related Work

5.1 Drone Security

Several attack trials have shown that drones are quite vulnerable. With regard, for instance, to the RQ-170 USAF drone mentioned in the introduction, the Iranian government claimed that it had captured the drone through its cyber-warfare unit [21]. Although some debates on the attack means exist, the captured drone seems quite intact, which means it was not shot down by projectiles.

With regard to civilian drones, Todd Humphreys et. al. insisted that civilian drones are threatened by GPS spoofing [10]. It was even demonstrated that drones are hijacked by spoofing GPS signals with a custom GPS spoofer [10]. Kamkar recently announced SkyJack, a specialized drone hijack platform that targets only Parrot AR drones [12]. It exploits a WiFi hotspot vulnerability in AR drones to acquire control over them.

5.2 FHSS Security

FHSS is widely adopted to various communication devices for the motive of securing transmission, as its rapid pseudorandom frequency shift apparently makes FHSS systems resilient against eavesdroppers or jammers to a certain extent. However, not a few researches indicate FHSS alone cannot completely secure the contents being transferred. Song et. al. presented several algorithms for breaking the pseudorandom FHSS sequence with external observation [16]. Presented algorithms were theoretically analyzed, and some were simulated with C++ software, which is different from our work where the attack scheme is implemented and verified in reality. Furthermore, Song et. al. assume omniscience in receiving the target signal, and thus limited receiver bandwidth was not considered in their work. Q et. al. utilized a low-cost hardware equipped with commercial RF Integrated Circuits (RFIC) to implement a hopping sequence analyzer [14]. With the tool implemented, they successfully extracted hopping pattern in the 902–928 MHz spectrum. However, their work is different from ours in some aspects. First, the presented approach can only be applied to spectrum to which the RFIC used can be tuned, whereas our SDR approach is much more flexible. Second, overcoming the limited receiver bandwidth was not covered in their work.

5.3 Bluetooth Security

Bluetooth is among the best-known communication standards that use FHSS. The wide adoption of Bluetooth in input devices suggests the likelihood of critical attacks. Especially, Bluetooth Low Energy (BLE) adopts a much simpler hopping and key sharing mechanism than classic Bluetooth. Mike Ryan has claimed [15] that the hopping sequence of BLE can be identified by collecting empty data packets, and attackers can sniff ongoing links. He used Ubertooth, a programmable BLE sniffer, to extract parameters required to acquire the hopping sequence, and brute-forced the encryption key, which enabled BLE sniffing.

6   Discussion and Future Works

Attack research on drones has not only the meaning of attacking a system. It is also highly related to privacy protection, infrastructure security, and defense, since drones are becoming severe threats against them. Drone control system is apparently one of the major attack vectors against drones. This work deals with the very first step of attacking FHSS-type control system by acquiring the hopping sequence, which is essential to realize attacks.

For future works, first, we will analyze the baseband signal to reveal its structure. If it is not encrypted, our attack platform can operate as a sniffer, which can monitor control signals. This will enable the attacker to predict the movement of the target drone. Additionally, carefully crafted spoofing waveform can take control of the target drone, which will give the defender safely capture the target drone. Second, we will automate the process of combining partial hopping sequences to make the presented attack scheme applicable to general wideband FHSS devices.

7   Conclusion

In this paper we proposed a general scheme to extract the hopping sequences of FHSS-type RC drone controllers and showed its effectiveness using an SDR. We also proposed a scheme to overcome the issue of the limited bandwidth of the SDR and showed that it was effective by successfully extracting the baseband signal of a target system in an experiment. Our work can be extended to be implemented on jammers, sniffers, and spoofers against RC controllers.

References

1. 4 GHz Radio Control Explained. http://www.rcmodelreviews.com/spread spectrum01.shtml
2. Amazon Prime Air. http://www.amazon.com/b?node=8037720011
3. CBX 1200–6000 MHz Rx/Tx (40 MHz). http://www.ettus.com/product/details/CBX
4. DHL launches first commercial drone 'parcelcopter' delivery service. http://www.theguardian.com/technology/2014/sep/25/german-dhl-launches-first-commercial-drone-delivery-service
5. How compatible are 2.4 GHz RC systems?. http://www.rcmodelreviews.com/rxcompatibility.shtml
6. USRP N210 Datasheet. http://www.ettus.com/content/files/~07495_Ettus_N200-210_DS_Flyer_HR_1.pdf
7. Chaudhuri, S., Chatterjee, S., Katz, N., Nelson, M., Goldbaum, M.: Detection of blood vessels in retinal images using two-dimensional matched filters. IEEE T-MI **8**(3), 263–269 (1989)
8. Chen, Q., Defrise, M., Deconinck, F.: Symmetric phase-only matched filtering of fourier-mellin transforms for image registration and recognition. TPAMI **16**(12), 1156–1168 (1994)

9. Gardner, W., et al.: Exploitation of spectral redundancy in cyclostationary signals. IEEE Sig. Process. Mag. **8**(2), 14–36 (1991)
10. Humphreys, T.E., Ledvina, B.M., Psiaki, M.L., OHanlon, B.W., Kintner, Jr., P.M.: Assessing the spoofing threat: Development of aportable gps civilian spoofer. In: ION GNSS+., vol. 55, p. 56 (2008)
11. James, M.: What are DSM RC Controllers and Receivers and What DoThey Do? http://rcvehicles.about.com/od/frequency/f/dsmtechnology.htm
12. Kamkar, S.: SkyJack. http://www.samy.pl/skyjack/
13. Nychis, G., Hottelier, T., Yang, Z., Seshan, S., Steenkiste, P.: Enabling mac protocol implementations on software-defined radios. NSDI **9**, 91–105 (2009)
14. Q, Atlas, Cutaway Smash, Slugs on Toast: Hop hacking hedy (2011). https://www.youtube.com/watch?v=aMBaO94Q49U
15. Ryan, M.: Bluetooth: With low energy comes low security. In: WOOT (2013)
16. Song, M., Allison, T.: Frequency hopping pattern recognition algorithms for wireless sensor networks. In: ISCA, pp. 264–269 (2005)
17. Stahlberg, M.: Radio jamming attacks against two popular mobile networks. In: Tik-110.501, vol. 3 (2000)
18. Tang, H.: Some physical layer issues of wide-band cognitive radio systems. In: DySPAN, pp. 151–159. IEEE (2005)
19. Urkowitz, H.: Energy detection of unknown deterministic signals. Proc. IEEE **55**(4), 523–531 (1967)
20. Wikipedia: General Atomics MQ-1 Predator (2015). http://en.wikipedia.org/wiki/General_Atomics_MQ-1_Predator
21. Wikipedia: Iran-U.S. RQ-170 incident (2015). http://en.wikipedia.org/wiki/Iran%E2%80%93U.S._RQ-170_incident
22. Wikipedia: Sequence alignment (2015). http://en.wikipedia.org/wiki/Sequence_alignment
23. Yücek, T., Arslan, H.: Spectrum characterization for opportunistic cognitive radio systems. In: MILCOM, pp. 1–6. IEEE (2006)
24. Yücek, T., Arslan, H.: A survey of spectrum sensing algorithms for cognitive radio applications. IEEE Commun. Surv. Tutorials **11**(1), 116–130 (2009)

Encryption is Not Enough: Inferring User Activities on KakaoTalk with Traffic Analysis

Kyungwon Park and Hyoungshick Kim$^{(\boxtimes)}$

Department of Computer Science and Engineering,
Sungkyunkwan University, Suwon, Republic of Korea
{kyungwon,hyoung}@skku.edu

Abstract. Many people started being concerned about their privacy in delivering private chats, photographs, contacts and other personal information through mobile instant messaging services. Fortunately, in the majority of mobile instant messaging services, encrypted communication channels (e.g., using the SSL/TLS protocols) are used by default to protect delivered messages against eavesdropping attacks. In this paper, however, we show that encryption is not enough. For example, in a real world service named KakaoTalk, many users' online activities can effectively be identified with 99.7 % accuracy even though traffic is encrypted. We present a practical traffic analysis attack using a supervised machine learning technique.

Keywords: Traffic analysis · Traffic classification · Mobile instant messenger · KakaoTalk

1 Introduction

The popularity of mobile instant messaging services has grown immensely over the past few years. The majority of smartphone users today are using a mobile instant messenger as their main communication tool rather than phone calls. However, as mobile instant messaging services have become the most dominant communication medium, many users also begins to become concerned about their privacy in using those services because their personal information such as private chats, photographs, contacts and user profiles can be exposed. Therefore, the communications via mobile instant messengers would have become one of the most attractive targets for eavesdroppers. For example, according to the Snowden's leaks [10], some government agencies have tracked users' online activities by intercepting their communications and eavesdropping them. Therefore, for user privacy, it is necessary to secure the communication channels between an instant messenger server and its clients. Fortunately, the majority of mobile instant messaging services have already provided a secure and authenticated communication channel (e.g., using the SSL/TLS protocols) by default to protect their users from eavesdroppers.

© Springer International Publishing Switzerland 2016
H. Kim and D. Choi (Eds.): WISA 2015, LNCS 9503, pp. 254–265, 2016.
DOI: 10.1007/978-3-319-31875-2_21

In practice, however, payload encryption is not enough; we can see that encrypted traffic can be vulnerable to traffic analysis attacks in many applications. Conti et al. [3] presented a framework to classify user activities on online social networks and email applications for smartphone, such as Facebook, Twitter, and Gmail by analyzing their encrypted traffic. We extend their framework to the traffic analysis of a mobile instant messing service named KakaoTalk (http://www.kakao.com/talk/en) which is the most widely used instant messaging service in Korea. According to a recent report [1], the number of KakaoTalk users had surpassed about 48 million global users. Although Coull and Dyer [4] already showed that several mobile instant messaging services are vulnerable to traffic analysis attacks, they only considered coarse-grained classification for detecting message types (e.g., control, image, and text) at high level. Unlike the previous study, we presented a classification method to infer users' detailed online activities in KakaoTalk even with encrypted traffic. Our key contributions can be summarized as follows:

– We proposed a framework to infer users' online activities on a mobile instant messaging service. The proposed framework was implemented with a supervised machine learning technique based on a hierarchical clustering to classify users' online activities.
– We evaluated the accuracy of the proposed inference attacks with a mobile instant messing service named KakaoTalk. The experimental results showed that the proposed classification method (with 986 clusters) is capable of achieving about 99.7 % accuracy.

The rest of this paper is organized as follows. In Sect. 2, we define the threat model in this work and introduce the important user activities on KakaoTalk. Then, we present the proposed framework for inference attacks with traffic analysis in Sect. 3. In Sect. 4, we analyze the experimental results about the accuracy of the proposed inference attacks. In Sect. 5, we suggest some reasonable defense methods to mitigate such inference attacks with traffic analysis. Some related work is discussed in Sect. 7. Finally, we conclude in Sect. 8.

2 Inferring User Activities on KakaoTalk

Previously, instant messengers were only used for exchanging text messages with other people. However, the latest instant messaging services have also served as a platform for voice calling, exchanging photographs or other files, social networking and even distributing games.

For using those features, users should send control commands and/or data via Internet. In this section, we first define the attackers' goals under the given assumptions about their capabilities and then briefly introduce the important user activities on KakaoTalk.

2.1   Threat Model

Attacker's Capabilities. We consider a passive attacker (e.g., a government agency) who can monitor traffic between users' mobile devices and the messaging service provider. We assume end-hosts are trusted and not under the control of the attacker. However, the attacker can capture the network traffic and store it for future use (e.g., analyzing its characteristics in an offline manner).

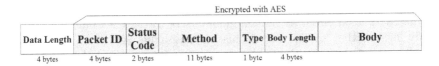

Fig. 1. LOCO packet structure

KakaoTalk uses a proprietary protocol over TCP/IP (called LOCO). Each packet is encrypted with AES [5] after a handshake between client and server (see Fig. 1). As for the encrypted traffic, we assume a computationally bounded adversary running in a polynomial time, and is not capable of breaking the encryption algorithm without knowing the key(s) used for packet encryption; this assumption is reasonable since breaking advanced encryption algorithms such as AES is computationally infeasible for the most powerful supercomputers.

Attacker's Goal. The attacker's goal is to infer a user's online activities on KakaoTalk by analyzing the network packets and communication patterns between the KakaoTalk messenger server and the KakaoTalk application running on the user's mobile device — users' private activities can be monitored. For example, a user's stalking behaviors (i.e., viewing other users' profiles) can be uncovered. The effectiveness of an inference attack is evaluated with the results of a multi-class classification for users' activities. In the next subsection, we present the target user activities on KokaoTalk in detail.

2.2   User Activities on KakaoTalk

KakaoTalk has many useful features. For example, a user sets his (or her) profile (and status message), views friends' profiles, and registers new friends based on either their KakaoTalk IDs or phone numbers [7,8]. Especially, the automatic friend registration feature can be misused for enumeration attacks [7,8].

Typical user activities on KakaoTalk are relevant to (1) communicating with others (including friends); (2) managing friends, and (3) customizing the user's application. In this paper, we are only interested in identifying some sensitive user activities in (1) and (2) categories because those activities have dominated in KakaoTalk users' actual behaviors, compared with (3). We briefly explain each user activity, respectively, that we looked at (see Table 1). The first four activities ("Receive a message", "Join a chat room", "Leave the chat room", and "Send a message") are in the category (1); and all the remaining activities are in the category (2).

Table 1. User activities on KakaoTalk that we considered in the inference attacks

Activity	Description
Join a chat room	Join a chat room from the list of chat rooms
Leave the chat room	Leave the chat room that you joined first
Receive a message	Receive a message such as text, photograph and emoticon from another user
Send a message	Send a message such as text, photograph and emoticon to others
Add a friend	Add a new user into the friend list
Hide a friend	Hide a specific friend from the friend list. After hiding the friend, the friend is not displayed in the friend list anymore
Block a user	Block a specific user. After blocking the user, the blocked user cannot send (and receive) messages to (from) the requesting user
Unblock a blocked user	Unblock a specific blocked user from the list of blocked users. After unblocking the user, the unblocked user can send (and receive) messages to (from) the requesting user
Re-add a blocked friend	Re-add a blocked friend into the friend list again. When a blocked friend is unblocked, this option is available
View a user's profile	View a specific user's profile (i.e., the user's status message and profile picture)
Synchronize friend list	Synchronize the friend list with the requesting user's contacts stored in the mobile device

3   Inference Attack Framework

In this section, we describe the proposed framework to infer users' activities on KakaoTalk with traffic analysis.

The proposed framework first filters out all the packets except the packets for the KakaoTalk application with several filtering rules in order to focus on inferring interesting activities on KakaoTalk (see Sect. 3.1). Next, given a sequence of packets, our problem can be reduced to a multiclass classification problem for identifying a KakaoTalk user' activity with the sequence of packets (see Sect. 3.2).

3.1   Traffic Filtering

Collecting Packets with IP Address. We found that the KakaoTalk servers have used four fixed IP addresses for the messaging service. Therefore, we can selectively capture only the desired packets for the KakaoTalk application with their IP addresses.

Filtering Out Unwanted Packets. As a next step, we carefully filtered out unnecessary packets such as acknowledgement and retransmitted packets; acknowledgement packets have a zero-length payload; and damaged packets (usually initiated by a time-out) are re-transmitted. We also need to particularly consider sending a large file (e.g., when a multimedia message is delivered); the large file must be broken up into several pieces since TCP protocol used on Ethernet limits the MSS (Maximum Segment Size) to 1460 bytes by default; however, even when more than one packet is generated per message, those packets are only relevant to a user's activity. Therefore, we regard a sequence of consecutive packets whose size is 1460 bytes as a single packet of 1460 bytes.

Separating Sequences of Packets. Since an adversary cannot exactly identify when a sequence of packets per user's activity on KakaoTalk is started, it is also challenging to determine a reasonable time threshold for separating packet sequences of different user activities. In general, if the arrival time of two subsequent packets is larger, the respective packets are considered as packets for different user activities. Therefore, separating sequences from the captured traffic is equivalent to setting cuts in the packet sequence and aggregating all packets which are within these borders to one sequence. According to the observation in the previous study [13], we selected a threshold of 4.43 s as the optimal parameter value for separating packet sequences of different user activities.

3.2 Classification of User Activities

For inferring user activities with packet sequences, we use a supervised learning method that requires a labeled training dataset; each sample of the dataset is labeled as a user activity.

Interestingly, whenever we repeatedly performed the same user activity on KakaoTalk, the generated packet sequences were not always identical. That is, a user activity can be mapped to several different packet sequences. To effectively manage such situations, we selected a Random Forest [2] classifier with a tree constructed by a hierarchical clustering method [6].

For efficient grouping of packet sequences generated by the KakaoTalk application, we opted for an agglomerative hierarchical clustering algorithm; similar sequences of packets are grouped together in the same cluster, while dissimilar sequences of packets are assigned to different clusters. Agglomerative hierarchical clustering provides a *nested sequence of clusters* with a single and all-inclusive cluster at the top and single-point clusters at the bottom, unlike partition-based clustering techniques such as k-means. This allows us to control the desired number of clusters based on cluster relationships to maximize the accuracy of the classification algorithm.

The key parameter in agglomerative hierarchical clustering algorithms is the clustering criterion function used to determine the pairs of clusters to be merged at each step. In most agglomerative algorithms, this is accomplished by selecting the most similar (or closest) pair of clusters. Many cluster selection schemes have been developed for computing the similarity between clusters. They mainly differ in how they update the similarity between existing and merged clusters. For example, the single linkage scheme [9] measures the distance of two clusters by computing the shortest distance between objects in the two clusters while the complete linkage clustering scheme uses the maximum distance between objects in the two clusters. In this paper, we used the average linkage scheme which is widely used in traffic analysis [3]. That is, the distance between two clusters A and B is given by

$$d(A, B) = \frac{1}{|A||B|} \sum_{a \in A} \sum_{b \in B} distance(a, b)$$

where A and B are clusters in a dataset.

In order to calculate the $distance(a, b)$ between two sequences of packets $a \in A$ and $b \in B$ for two clusters A and B, we used Dynamic Time Warping (DTW) [12] which is a well-known technique to measure the similarity between time series objects.

In order to speed up the classification process, the representative object of each cluster called *leader* is selected. Given a cluster A containing the sequences of packets $\{a_1, \cdots, a_n\}$, the leader is elected by selecting the sequence a_i that has minimum overall distance from the other objects of the cluster which is defined as:

$$leader(A) = \operatorname*{argmin}_{a_i \in A} \left(\sum_{a_j \in A} distance(a_i, a_j) \right)$$

After electing a leader for each cluster, we executed the Random Forest [2] algorithm with labeled leaders. For a given sequence s, we try to find the cluster C that minimizes the distance between s and the leader of the cluster $leader(C)$ and identify the user activity for s as the label of $leader(C)$.

4   Experiments

We present how the experiments were taken in Sect. 4.1 and evaluate the performance of our implementation in Sect. 4.2.

In order to analyze the network traffic for the KakaoTalk application running on an Android device, we used a PC (with running 64-bit Ubuntu) connected to the same network by configuring it as a NAT router and tried to capture all network traffic from the KakaoTalk application on the Android device by using the libpcap library (see Fig. 2). In our experiments, we used the KakaoTalk v4.8.4 running on the Android 4.1.2 version, and equipped with a non-congested 100 Mbit/s WiFi connection to a LAN that was connected to the Internet.

4.1   Dataset Collection

In June 2015, during the course of a day, we collected 1100 objects of packet sequences by repeatedly simulating 11 KakaoTalk activities (100 per activity) that we are interested in (see Table 1 in Sect. 2.2).

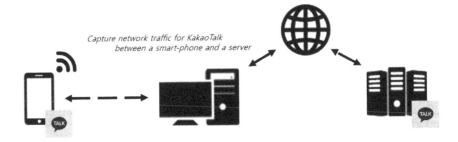

Fig. 2. Experimental environment

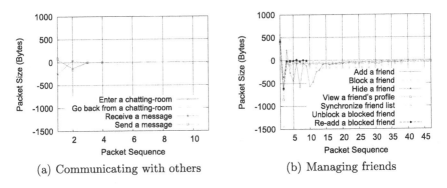

(a) Communicating with others   (b) Managing friends

Fig. 3. Packet sequence of behaviors

In the proposed framework, the simulated user activities were generated in a random manner to reduce the bias associated with specific data. For example, when we mimic *sending a message* to a friend, a friend is randomly selected and then a randomly generated (short) message is sent to the friend.

In most of user activities, we can see nearly unique patterns of packet sequences by analyzing the sizes of packets in sequence from the captured traffic dataset. Figure 3 demonstrates the average packet size of kth packets for each user activity. The results were presented by the two categories of "communicating with others" and "managing friends" (see Table 1 in Sect. 2.2). In those figures, the y-axis represents the packet size; positive values represent outgoing packets while negative values represent incoming packets.

Through the analysis of those patterns, we can find some interesting observations. For example, unlike the other user activities, a packet sequence for "Receive a message" has a negative integer at the first packet in the session (see Fig. 3(a)). In fact, it is obvious that this activity is triggered by an incoming packet. Also, we can see that the activities for "communicating with others" are completed within at most 12 packets; this short-term session behavior is totally different from some activities in the category of "managing friends", such as "View a user's profile" and "Synchronize friend list" which typically require more than 40 packet interactions on average (see Fig. 3(b)).

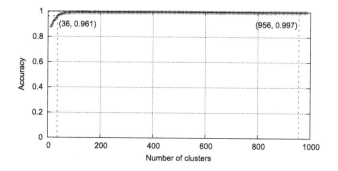

Fig. 4. Classification results with number of clusters

4.2 Classification Results

To evaluate the performance of the proposed classification method in Sect. 3, we use the *accuracy* measure that is the proportion of correctly classified activities. In general, the accuracy measure is acceptable if the test data is balanced.

For classification, we used a 10-fold cross-validation where the training samples are partitioned into 10 equal-sized blocks and each block in turn is then used as test data for the classifier generated from the remaining nine blocks. We analyzed the performance of the proposed classification method with varying the number of clusters from 11 to 990. This is because we consider the only 11 activities (see Sect. 2.2) and the 90 % of 1100 samples is 990. Figure 4 shows the accuracy of the proposed classification method with number of clusters.

As we can expect, the accuracy of the proposed classification method overall was improved as the number of clusters increased. We were finally capable of achieving an accuracy of 0.997 with 956 clusters. Using that multiclass classifier with 956 clusters, we analyzed the accuracy results of individual user activities. The results are presented in the confusion matrix (see Fig. 5; darker the color, higher the accuracy of the classification method for each activity). From looking at the confusion matrix, we can see that all user activities were very accurately identified even though some activities for "Hide a friend" were misclassified as "Receive a message". For more detailed analysis, in addition to the accuracy results, we analyzed the other classification measures (*precision, recall*, and *F-measure*). For each activity i, those measures are defined as:

- **Precision**: the proportion of activities classified as activity i that actually are i activities;
- **Recall**: the proportion of i activities that were accurately classified;
- **F-measure**: the harmonic mean of *Precision* and *Recall*; $(2*Precision*Recall) / (Precision+Recall)$.

The evaluation results are shown in Table 2. We can still see that all activities could be classified well even though we achieved a relatively low precision and F-measure for "Hide a friend".

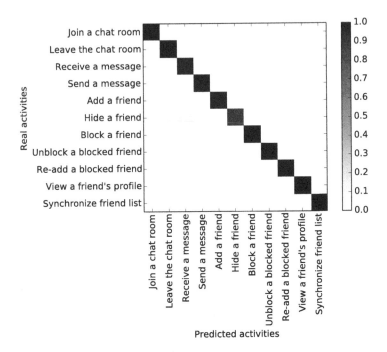

Fig. 5. Confusion matrix in 956 clusters

Table 2. Classification accuracy with 956 clusters

Behavior	Precision	Recall	F-measure	Accuracy
Join a chat room	1.000	1.000	1.000	1.000
Leave the chat room	0.990	0.952	0.971	0.995
Receive a message	0.960	0.923	0.941	0.989
Send a message	0.980	1.000	0.990	0.998
Add a friend	0.960	0.980	0.970	0.995
Hide a friend	**0.880**	0.931	**0.905**	0.984
Block a friend	0.990	1.000	0.995	0.999
Unblock a blocked friend	0.990	0.971	0.980	0.996
Re-add a blocked friend	0.990	1.000	0.995	0.999
View a friend's profile	1.000	1.000	1.000	1.000
Synchronize friend list	1.000	0.990	0.995	0.999

Although the multiclass classifier with 956 clusters produced the best classification results, it might be desirable to classify packet sequences with only a few clusters in terms of efficiency since the computation time of the classification increases (linearly) with the number of clusters used in the proposed method. Fortunately, we can see that an accuracy of 0.961 can still be achieved with a small number of clusters (e.g., 36 clusters), which is shown in Fig. 4.

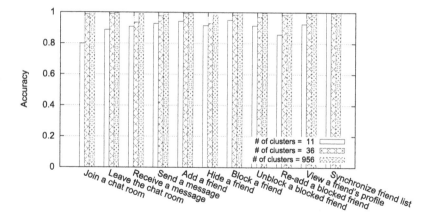

Fig. 6. Accuracy of the classification with 11, 36, and 956 clusters, respectively

To demonstrate the effects of the number of clusters for each activity, we analyzed the accuracy results with 11, 36, and 956 clusters, respectively. The results were shown in Fig. 6. With 11 clusters only, some activities such as "Join a chat room" and "Re-add a blocked friend" could be misclassified with a significant rate.

5   Countermeasures

The proposed framework can be used to infer user activities even with encrypted traffic. The key idea is to use an activity's network characteristics (e.g., number of packets, size of each packet, directions of packets in the network session) as its signature. With this idea, we proved that a popular instant messaging service named KakaoTalk could be vulnerable to our traffic analysis attacks.

In practice, however, preventing such traffic analysis is not an easy problem. Most conventional protocols have been carefully designed to minimize communication overhead by adjusting packet flows.

To mitigate such traffic analysis, the simplest defense solution is to use a proper padding scheme for fixed size packets. Also, dummy packets might be inserted so that packet sequences have nearly identical patterns. However, those solutions will inherently introduce additional communication overhead. Those techniques should be treated with caution: the communication cost they impose on a system is likely to be nontrivial, and they may indeed be unacceptable in competitive markets.

6   Limitation

The primary aim of this work was to demonstrate the feasibility of using network characteristics in a session for identifying user activities. However, some of the features (e.g., the time intervals between packets), which could significantly improve the accuracy, have not been considered in depth.

In evaluating the effectiveness of the proposed framework, we simulated user activities to collect labeled ground truth network traffic rather than using the actual users' packets. However, those stimulated user activities might significantly different from real users' activity patterns in several aspects. For example, when a large file is used for "Send a message", the number of packets and/or the size of each packet can be greatly increased. Also, we do not consider various message types such as text, emoticon, and image.

Finally, some activities might be more frequently appeared than the other activities in practice. In our experiments, however, we simply assumed that all user activities would be expected to occur equally. The performance of classification methods can typically be changed with a different distribution of samples.

7   Related Work

In conventional network environments, it has been already studied to identify online user activities. Zhang et al. [14] showed the risk of traffic analysis by identifying user applications with an accuracy of over 90 % if the eavesdropping lasts for 1 min.

Because of the increased use of smartphones, it is also challenging to perform traffic analysis with applications on smartphones. Lee et al. [11] studied the characteristic of smartphone traffic by particularly analyzing the proportion of smartphone traffic from the entire network traffic in a campus network. Their study analyzed the traffic proportion of most popular 50 smartphone applications and found that KakaoTalk was the third ranked in the experiment.

Stöber et al. [13] also proposed a traffic analysis technique to identify specific traffic for a smartphone application. In their work, they showed network traffic generated from the most popular applications (Facebook, WhatsApp, Skype, Dropbox, and others) can successfully be identified with a probability of 90 %. Conti et al. [3] developed a system to identify the specific actions that a user is doing on smartphone applications such as Gmail, Facebook and Twitter by using machine learning techniques. Similarly, Coulle et al. [4] focused on the traffic analysis of encrypted messages for instant messaging services such as WhatsApp, Viber, and Telegram to infer the message types and language used in chatting. Here, we extend their work by developing a framework to identify user activities on the KakaoTalk application in more detail.

8   Conclusion

In this paper, we proposed a framework to infer user activities in KakaoTalk by passively analyzing network traffic. From the experiment, we demonstrated that each activity generates a practically unique packet sequence and those packet sequences can be sufficiently used to infer user activities with 99.7 % accuracy by using a supervised machine learning technique.

In future, we plan to evaluate the effectiveness of the proposed technique on a larger scale so as to further extend this attack strategy.

Acknowledgments. This work was supported in part by the National Research Foundation of Korea (No. 2014R1A1A1003707), the ITRC (IITP-2015-H8501-15-1008, IITP-2015-R0992-15-1006), and the IITP (2014-044-072-003).

References

1. KakaoTalk: number of monthly active users 2013–2015 (2015). http://www.statista.com/statistics/278846/kakaotalk-monthly-active-users-mau/
2. Breiman, L.: Random forests. Mach. Learn. **45**(1), 5–32 (2001)
3. Conti, M., Mancini, L.V., Spolaor, R., Verde, N.V.: Can't you hear me knocking: Identification of user actions on Android apps via traffic analysis. In: Proceedings of the 5th ACM Conference on Data and Application Security and Privacy (2015)
4. Coull, S.E., Dyer, K.P.: Traffic analysis of encrypted messaging services: apple imessage and beyond. ACM SIGCOMM Comput. Commun. Rev. **44**(5), 5–11 (2014)
5. Daemen, J., Rijmen, V.: The Design of Rijndael: AES–The Advanced Encryption Standard. Springer, Heidelberg (2002)
6. Johnson, S.C.: Hierarchical clustering schemes. Psychometrika **32**(3), 241–254 (1967)
7. Kim, E., Park, K., Kim, H., Song, J.: I've got your number: Harvesting users' personal data via contacts sync for the kakaotalk messenger. In: Proceedings of the 15th International Workshop on Information Security Applications (2014)
8. Kim, E., Park, K., Kim, H., Song, J.: Design and analysis of enumeration attacks on finding friends with phone numbers: A case study with KakaoTalk. Comput. Secur. (in Press, 2015)
9. Lance, G.N., Williams, W.T.: A general theory of classificatory sorting strategies: 1. hierarchical systems. Comput. J. **9**(4), 373–380 (1967)
10. Landau, S.: Making sense from snowden: what's significant inthe NSA surveillance revelations. IEEE Secur. Priv. **11**(4), 54–63 (2013)
11. Lee, S.-W., Park, J.-S., Lee, H.-S., Kim, M.-S.: A study on smart-phone traffic analysis. In: Proceedings of the 13th Asia-Pacific Network Operations and Management Symposium (2011)
12. Müller, M.: Dynamic time warping. In: Information Retrieval for Musicand Motion, pp. 69–84 (2007)
13. Stöber, T., Frank, M., Schmitt, J., Martinovic, I.: Who do you sync you are?: smartphone fingerprinting via application behaviour. In: Proceedings of the 6th ACM Conference on Security and Privacy in Wireless and Mobile Networks (2013)
14. Zhang, F., He, W., Liu, X., Bridges, P.G.: Inferring users' online activities through traffic analysis. In: Proceedings of the 4th ACM Conference on Wireless Network Security (2011)

IoT Security

Challenges in Deploying CoAP Over DTLS in Resource Constrained Environments

Hyeokjin Kwon, Jiye Park, and Namhi Kang[(⊠)]

Digital Media Department, Duksung Women's University, Seoul, South Korea
{hyeok,jiyepark,kang}@duksung.ac.kr

Abstract. In the world of Internet of Things (IoT), huge number of resource constrained devices are directly accessible over the Internet. For allowing the constrained devices to exchange information, the IETF standard group has specified the CoAP which works on top of UDP/IP. Also, Datagram TLS (DTLS) binding is recommended to make the CoAP secure. When DTLS is enabled, a device can select one of three security modes that are PreSharedKey, RawPublicKey and Certificate mode. Especially, the RawPublicKey mode, which uses an asymmetric-key pair without a certificate, is mandatory to implement CoAP over DTLS. But there are several challenges in using the asymmetric-key based secure mode in resource constrained device. This paper compares the RawPublicKey mode and the PreSharedKey mode, which uses a symmetric-key, to discuss DTLS performance in resource constrained devices and networks. For the comparison, we implemented an experimental environment based on IEEE 802.15.4 wireless networks consisting of resource constrained devices in the Cooja Simulator and in the real test-bed as well. Then we analyze the comparison results with regard to code size, energy consumption and processing and receiving time.

Keywords: DTLS · Handshake · Energy consumption · Internet of things · Cooja simulator

1 Introduction

The Internet of Things (IoT) technology has been recently highlighted in the world. Each IoT object communicates with a human or an object by connecting to the Internet. The IoT provides context awareness services so the object should perform both functions of server or client depends on the service. Therefore, security threats in general server-client models and security technology should be considered in the IoT environment [1].

Today, various security technologies are being applied in a device which has enough computing resource. In particular, the asymmetric-key encryption algorithm is employed in TLS protocol which is widely used in web-based ecommerce, email and messenger [2]. The asymmetric-key encryption algorithm is known to be several hundred times slower than the symmetric-key encryption algorithm. It is not a problem to the device having adequate resource in existing Internet. However, three constraints should be overcome in order to apply security technologies in the IoT devices. First, the

© Springer International Publishing Switzerland 2016
H. Kim and D. Choi (Eds.): WISA 2015, LNCS 9503, pp. 269–280, 2016.
DOI: 10.1007/978-3-319-31875-2_22

IoT device has limited computing resources such as CPU, memory and battery. The IoT device is generally present as an embedded device so it has small size even if products containing the embedded devices such as vehicles or refrigerators are large. It means that CPU, memory or storage performance declines. The low performance of the device can be limitation for choosing security protocols. Second, the power supply is not guaranteed in many cases. Therefore, it depends on batteries and the operating time which can be accepted by users should be ensured. It means the energy consumption is a very important factor in the IoT security. Third, a security tends to be ignored by tradeoff between price and device performance. Despite the miniaturized device with the same size, the cost varies depending on the performance. The IoT device has the minimal performance due to the cost saving required for business operators who produce the products and the economic logics of consumers who want to buy less expensive products. It means that the security may be compromised. In this regards, the LWIG working group of IETF classified constrained devices with consideration of data size and code size as shown in Table 1 [3].

Table 1. Classes of constrained devices (Source: [3])

Name	Data size (e.g., RAM)	Code size (e.g., Flash)
Class 0 (C0)	≪ 10 KiB	≪ 100 KiB
Class 1 (C1)	∼ 10 KiB	∼ 100 KiB
Class 2 (C2)	∼ 50 KiB	∼ 250 KiB

Devices in Class 0 do not have enough resources to securely and directly connect to the Internet. It is completely constrained. Thus, the Class 0 devices need a help of infra-devices such as proxy or gateway. Class 1 still has some constraints to connect to the Internet using full protocol stacks such as HTTP, Transport Layer Security (TLS) and XML-based data representations. If it uses a Constrained Application Protocol (CoAP) over UDP protocol stack which is designed specifically for constrained nodes, Class 1 device can connect to the Internet without help of other devices. Devices belonging to Class 2 support most of protocols used in existing Internet. Nevertheless, it is recommended to use a lightweight protocol stack to reduce development costs and increase the interoperability [3].

CoAP is the application layer protocol for IoT device and it is standardized by the IETF [4]. CoAP is similar to HTTP, but it uses UDP instead of TCP with consideration for the transmission efficiency. In terms of the security, Datagram TLS (DTLS) which is a UDP based version of TLS is recommended as a de-facto standard security protocol for CoAP. It is similar to HTTP using TLS security protocol [5].

However, DTLS protocol is not designed for constrained environment unlike CoAP designed for constrained IoT environment. Furthermore, DTLS has lower performance than TLS in spite of using UDP. The reason is that the additional features are added in the DTLS to compensate the reliability not provided in the UDP unlike TLS dependent on the reliability provided by TCP. The DTLS protocol is classified into two separate phases [5] as follows. (1) A handshake phase that supports mutual authentication and key agreement. It creates security credentials (including symmetric keys). (2) Encrypted data transmission phase that sends authenticated and encrypted data using the security keys created in the handshake phase.

In the handshake phase, either symmetric-key or asymmetric-key based cipher suite can be used as an encryption key exchange algorithm. Depending on cipher suite selection, it causes a big difference in performance. If PSK based cipher suite is used, performance is excellent but there is limitation to set up a shared security key in advance. On the other hand, asymmetric-key based cipher suite can set up the security without setting the PSK system, but it has other burdens such as public key authentication and management. In addition, it has been well known that performance declines due to a high volume of calculation. There are not big performance differences which users feel when they use the TLS using asymmetric-key in personal computers and servers. However, general asymmetric-key algorithm is not easy to operate in constrained devices having $8 \sim 16$ MHz CPU. Nevertheless, four modes are defined for using DTLS security protocol to the CoAP. Especially, a RawPublicKey mode using asymmetric-key among four kinds of modes is designated as mandatory [4].

In this paper, we examine DTLS protocol performance issues that is recommended as a security protocol for IoT device by many international standard organizations such as IETF, oneM2M and OMA. In particular, we would like to discuss the specific issues for using DTLS in constrained environment, as follows.

- The code size which should be considered when the DTLS is implemented in devices with constrained resources.
- The energy consumption for using DTLS on constrained device.
- Data transmission efficiency in low power and lossy network (LLN).

This paper is organized as follows. In Sect. 2, we discuss standard trends recommended to use CoAP/DTLS and related works. In Sect. 3, we describe test environments for analysis. In Sect. 4, code size, energy consumption and data transmission rates are analyzed and discussed. Finally, we conclude with Sect. 5.

2   Preliminary

2.1   Standard Trends

Seven regional standard organizations such as TTA in Korea, TIA and ATIS in the US, ETSI in the Europe, CCSA in China, and TTC and ARIB of Japan have participated in OneM2M. It has defined common platform, Common Services Entities (CSE) and Application Entity (AE), for various IoT application services such as smart home, smart car and smart healthcare [6]. OneM2M considers TLS or DTLS for secure telecommunication between AE/CSE [7]. It has defined two cipher suites to be applied such as TLS_PSK_WITH_AES_128_CCM_8 and TLS_ECDHE_ ECDSA_-WITH_AES_128_CCM_8. Moreover, the technical plenaries of the oneM2M partnership project increases the compatibility of various protocols by providing the binding of various transmission technologies such as MQTT, CoAP, XMPP and HTPP as the telecommunication protocol [7].

Among protocols supporting CSE and binding in the OneM2M, MQTT provides the secure system using TLS while it has the TCP-based communication. However, as the UDP-based communication system is recently considered, the use of DTLS is naturally considered as a security protocol for MQTT protocol.

In addition, like IETF, DTLS is also considered as a de facto security protocol for CoAP. When the DTLS is used, four modes are proposed as follows [4]: NoSec, PreSharedKey, RawPublicKey, and Certificate modes. Among them, NoSec mode and RawPublicKey modes must be implemented [4]. NoSec mode does not provide encryption in the transport layer. PreSharedKey mode has a device with PSK and 1:1 node/key ratios are required. The pre shared key is used to examine whether it is the device of the group. In the RawPublicKey mode, it identifies the device by examining whether it is the appropriate device. In the Certificate mode, authentication and key exchange can be done through certificate based mechanism. However, under the IoT environment with constrained computing resources, the use of DTLS may cause various problems. Thus, it is required to analyze the performance upon the use of each cipher suite in the DTLS.

2.2   Related Works

Researches has been proposed for the analyzing and resolving the performance issues occurring when the DTLS is used in the constrained IoT environment. Existing researches compare time and memory size when the handshake is performed, and compares the amount of consumed power. Table 2 shows previous studies providing information about required memory, processing time and energy consumption for using DTLS.

Table 2. Related works

Papers	[8]	[9]	[10]	[11]	[12]	Proposal
Device	Opal sensor	TelosB	WisMote	WisMote, STGreenNet	WisMote	Z1, Sky
Security Mode	Certificate	Raw Public Key	Certificate	Raw Public Key	PSK	PSK & Raw Public Key
Library	OpenSSL, CyaSSL, tinyECC	tinyECC	TinyDTLS	tinyECC	Lithe	TinyDTLS
Code size	Tested	Not tested	Tested	Not tested	Tested	Tested
Processing Time	Tested	Not tested	Tested	Tested	Tested	Tested
Energy Consumption	Tested	Tested	Not tested	Tested	Tested	Tested

If the experiment has been carried out for each conditions, we marked 'test' in each row required memory, processing time and energy consumption in the Table 2.

While energy consumption is important factor in performance evaluation, there is no research accurately focusing on four modes proposed in [4] from the perspectives of energy consumption. In addition, because each study obtained the results by using different devices and different libraries, it is difficult to compare them.

3   Evaluation Environments

This chapter describes our evaluation environment used to analyze the code size, energy consumption in the DTLS handshake operations, and transmission efficiency in resource constrained networks. The DTLS handshake phase is made up of six sub-processes and each of the processes is called a flight as shown in Fig. 1. The handshake processing of DTLS is similar to those of TLS but the flight 2 and 3 have been added to the DTLS to prevent against denial of service attacks caused by UDP's characteristic. Like TLS, those indicated in a dotted line in the Flight 4 and 5 are used only when using the asymmetric-key based cipher suite, and it is ignored when using the symmetric-key based cipher suite.

In the experimental environment, we used TinyDTLS library which is known as the most lightweight DTLS implementation. We also used Contiki OS which is widely used as a lightweight operating system for IoT devices. Recent version of TinyDTLS (i.e. version 0.8.2) supports three main crypto primitives - AES as a symmetric-key and ECDHE, ECDSA as asymmetric-key based algorithms developed by C language.

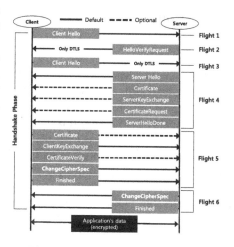

Fig. 1. DTLS handshake procedure

By using the primitives, current TinyDTLS supports only two cipher suites among them specified in DTLS standard [5]. Table 3 summarizes other components and tools used in our environment.

Note here that our evaluations are based on both simulation and real test-bed. We utilized Cooja Simulator contained in Contiki OS, especially for measurement of the energy consumption. In case of real test-bed network, IEEE 802.15.4 was used. The simulator provides the same virtual device as the specifications of the lightweight device that exists with IEEE 802.15.4 wireless environment.

Table 3. Experimental environment

Device	Zolteria Z1, Tmote Sky
Operating System	Contiki OS
Simulator	Cooja(for energy consumption)
Compiler	msp430-gcc
DTLS Standard	1.2 (RFC 6347 [5])
DTLS Library	TinyDTLS 0.8.2[a]
Ciphersuite	TLS_PSK_WITH_AES_128_CCM_8, TLS_ECDHE_ECDSA_WITH_AES_128_CCM_8
Wireless Access Network	802.15.4
Adaptation layer	6LowPAN (RFC 6282 [13])
IP Version	IPv6

[a]http://tinydtls.sourceforge.net/

4 Experiment Results and Analysis

4.1 Code Size

The code size of Contiki OS is about $36 \sim 44$KiB depending on whether provided features are activated, and method of optimizing the size of buffer and queue, etc. In this experiment, we analyzed the code size in applying DTLS into Zolteria Z1 device which is classified in Class 1. It is not possible to build a firmware with TinyDTLS in the configuration state that is basically provided in Contiki, because the firmware size exceeds the ROM size of the lightweight device. Therefore, we removed some unnecessary functions for our experiments to have sufficient memory space. In addition, we disabled TCP function and reduced some QUEUE size in 'contiki-conf.h' file. The firmware file in ELF format is made by using the msp430-gcc compiler. We obtained the firmware size to be uploaded to the ROM of device by utilizing the msp430-objcopy command to this firmware file.

Table 4 shows the firmware size for each cipher suite. The difference of code size between Client and Server is about 1 %. Also, using the asymmetric-key based cipher suite needs about 10 % higher memory size than when using the symmetric-key based cipher suite. If devices support both symmetric-key and asymmetric-key, it required ROM space of at least more than 77 KiB.

Table 4. TinyDTLS firmware size of Contiki OS (Unit: bytes)

Device Roles	PSK	ECC	PSK + ECC
Client	70,153	78,061	79,621
Server	69,119	77,143	78,885

Among the 13 lightweight devices provided in Cooja Simulator, devices which are actually available for simulation are five devices. Table 5 describes the five devices in detail. Devices that are capable of DTLS execution among them are three; Wismote,

Zolteria Z1, and Exp430F5438. Even though Tmote Sky is classified in Class 1 as same to Zolteria Z1, the performance is low as 2 times. It also cannot load even the code that only symmetric-key based cipher suite is applied due to small ROM size.

Table 5. Devices supported by Cooja Simulator

Mote	Flash	RAM	CPU	Class	TinyDTLS
MicaZ	128 KiB	4 Kib	7.37 MHz	C1	X
Exp430F5438	256 KiB	32 KiB	8 MHz	C2	O
Wismote	256 KiB	32 KiB	16 MHz	C2	O
Zolteria Z1	92 KiB	8 KiB	8 MHz	C1	O
Tmote Sky	48 KiB	10 KiB	3.9 MHz	C1	X

TinyDTLS is made up several modules such as algorithm, encryption, hash, session management, queue management in separate C files. Object files of each module generated from C files in the build process. By using the msp430-size command, we confirmed sizes of the section that are text, data, and bss. The source code name and size of the major modules that make up TinyDTLS are shown in Fig. 2.

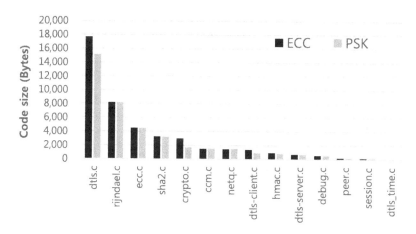

Fig. 2. The size of the major modules of TinyDTLS

The dtls.c is a core file in which DTLS protocol is implemented and it has the largest size. The rijndael.c, file includes symmetric-key algorithm and it has a size of two times larger than ecc.c file having asymmetric-key algorithm. Although computing amount is much more complex in ecc.c, the code size is even greater in rijndael.c due to Substitution-box(S-BOX) of fixed size that is used in rijndael.c.

Through this experiment, we confirmed that using TinyDTLS is impossible to be used in the Class 1 device without optimization as it is distributed condition. TinyDTLS currently supports only two cipher suites. However, according to The Internet Assigned Numbers Authority (IANA) that manages cipher suite conforming to the internet standard, currently more than about 300 cipher suites exist [14]. It means that if additional cipher suite is required for the mutual compatibility, the encryption-related algorithm codes must be added and it causes an increase of code sizes.

4.2 Energy Consumption

The energy consumption of DTLS in lightweight device is determined by key exchange algorithm of the handshake phase, data encryption algorithm, and network conditions. The energy consumption by the operations is always constant without great changes in repeated measurements after the hardware specifications and encryption algorithm are determined. However, in the wireless network, despite of same environment, the measurement results are much larger variation because of uncontrollable surrounding environmental factors. Therefore, this paper excluded the energy consumption by network device and considered only the energy consumption by the arithmetic operations of symmetric-key and asymmetric-key algorithms. In this experiment, we used Cooja Simulator and Zolteria Z1 device. To measure the energy consumption of DTLS in Contiki, we also used a built-in function, energest_type_time(). This function is known to have a 94 % accuracy as compared with hardware measuring instrument [15]. This function returns the CPU time from the time that the device is booted, until the time that the function itself is called. The CPU time is measured in clock ticks, which are a basic unit of time that the device actually used CPU. We could get the energy consumption to be used when the code is executed, when applying the obtained clock tick value to the energy consumption in the Datasheet provided by the device manufacturers.

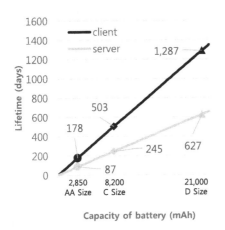
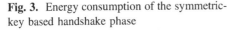

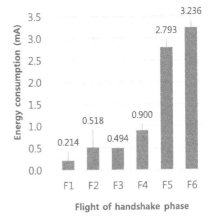

Fig. 3. Energy consumption of the symmetric-key based handshake phase

Fig. 4. Lifetime by battery sizes according to symmetric-key based hand-shaking

We analyzed the energy consumption when using the symmetric-key, and describe by comparing the energy consumption in asymmetric-key method. The Fig. 3 shows the amount of energy to be consumed in each flight of the handshake phase in milliamps, when using the symmetric-key algorithm.

The energy consumption's sum, 3.501 mA, in Flight 1, 3, 5 are the amount of energy that the client consumes in the handshake phase. Similarly, the sum of Flight 2, 4, 6, 4.654 mA, is the amount of energy that the server consumes. The time in the handshake phase took an average of 6.6 s. To get the energy consumption per second, we divide the energy consumption of the server and client by total elapsed handshake time. The Fig. 4 indicates lifetime depending on the types of battery sizes, when the server and client repeatedly execute DTLS sessions, based on the energy consumption measurements in Fig. 3.

TinyDTLS has a bug that the program stops as stack overflow occurs immediately after Flight 4 if using TLS_ECDHE_ECDSA_WITH_AES_128_CCM_8 cipher suite. Because of this problem, we could not obtain the energy consumption of the asymmetric-key in the lightweight devices belonging to Class $1 \sim 2$. TinyDTLS not only Contiki, but it also has a compatibility that can run on Linux. Therefore, in this paper, as an alternative, we estimated the energy consumption in lightweight devices by comparing each of CPU time between the symmetric-key and asymmetric-key algorithm, when running the same TinyDTLS in Linux environment. For the devices that are used in this asymmetric-key experiment, it used a Raspberry Pi with 700 MHz CPU, where Raspbian Linux is installed, and a general Personal Computer of 3.2 GHz CPU, where Ubuntu Linux is installed. The gcc was used for a compiler, the optimization option of compiler was applied in the same way as the options used in Contiki. Also, as same as energest_type_time() function in Contiki, it measured the amount of computation by using clock_gettime() function that returns CPU time that a process used.

Table 6 describes elapsed time and CPU time on average for the handshake phase when using the symmetric-key and asymmetric-key algorithm, in Raspberry Pi and Personal Computer respectively. In the case of elapsed time, it showed the increase rate of about 35 times in both Raspberry Pi and Personal Computer. However, they have each different rate in CPU time, while Raspberry Pi increased by about 343 times, Personal Computer increased by about 421 times. Because it is affected by optimization option of compiler that is dependent on CPU chipset. If not using the optimization option of compiler, both Raspberry Pi and Personal Computer, with 660 times, showed the same rate of CPU time increase rate.

When using the asymmetric-key algorithm in lightweight device by using the values in the Table 6, the expected values are as follows. First, if elapsed time for handshake is assumed to be increased by 35 times, the expected elapsed time is approximately 3 min

Table 6. The alternative results for the asymmetric-key based handshake

Experiment	Raspberry Pi		Personal Computer	
	PSK	ECC	PSK	ECC
Elapsed Time (seconds)	0.058	2.053	0.003	0.108
CPU Time (ticks)	5978	2,052,804	260	109,429

and 51 s. In the case of CPU time that is the biggest factor to determine the energy consumption, even if assuming the increase rate as 200 times in rough, unlike the symmetric-key that can be used for about 6 months in base of AA-size battery, the asymmetric-key is difficult to be used for more than one week.

4.3   Handshake Time

The data transmission performance in wireless environment is generally affected by the transmission delay and fragmentation. Especially, the more fragmentation increases the transmission-delay rate, and the more transmission quantity and multi-hop network environment increase the transmission-delay rate into NlogN. Similarly, if the DTLS handshake messages are fragmented, the data processing performance is exacerbated. When the asymmetric-key is used, as the parts indicated in solid lines in the Fig. 1 are processed, transmission data becomes larger.

In the Wireless Standards, IEEE 802.15.4, which has been developed as a personal network (low-power personal area networks), MTU is defined in 127 bytes for wireless performance efficiency. In other words, in larger frames than 127 bytes in the link layer, the fragmentation always occurs. In order not to have loss by fragmentation to be generated in the sub-layers, DTLS standards has been defined to support fragmentation directly in DTLS layer.

To confirm the effect that DTLS protocol receives from the 802.15.4 environment, we set up two separated 802.15.4 networks in the real test-bed as the following. First, two separated each LLN networks are connected to the Internet through a border-router

Table 7. Fragmentation occurred in each Flight

(a) asymmetric-key

No	Message Type	Size	Frag
1	ClientHello	97	O
2	HelloVerifyRequest	44	X
3	ClientHello	113	O
4	ServerHello	81	O
	Certificate	122	O
	ServerKeyExchange	170	O
	CertificateRequest	33	X
	ServerHelloDone	25	X
5	Certificate	122	O
	ClientKeyExchange	91	O
	CertificateVerify	99	O
	ChangeCipherSpec	14	X
	Finished	53	X
6	ChangeCipherSpec	14	X
	Finished	53	X

(b) symmetric-key

No	Message Type	Size	Frag
1	ClientHello	67	O
2	HelloVerifyRequest	44	X
3	ClientHello	83	O
	ServerHello	63	O
4	N/A		
	ServerHelloDone	25	X
5	N/A		
	ClientKeyExchange	42	X
	N/A		
	ChangeCipherSpec	14	X
	Finished	53	X
6	ChangeCipherSpec	14	X
	Finished	53	X

that acts as a gateway. TinyDTLS code has not been used for the efficiency of experiment, and we implement the fakeDTLS as a Contiki OS Server/Client program. The fakeDTLS mimics the transmission size of each Flight in TinyDTLS. By applying the fakeDTLS to Tmote Sky device, it made the server and client access to each other over the Internet. Also, by adding a device between the border-router and measuring device, we measured multi-hop based time. Each device was placed in an indoor laboratory corridor in the interval of 10 m.

Table 7 shows that compared the size and whether there is fragmentation to be sent by each Flight in the handshake phase. Through this, it can ascertain the effect that handshake transmission data size of DTLS receives from the 802.15.4 wireless environment. In the experimental environment of this paper, the fragmentation is occurred when the application data is exceeds 59 bytes. Unlike that three fragmentations occur out of 10 transmissions in the symmetric-key based handshake phase, eight fragmentations occur out of 15 transmissions in the asymmetric-key based handshake phase. This means that the probability of network delays is higher in the asymmetric-key based handshake phase.

The elapsed time for the handshake phase by each multi-hop when the fragmentation of Table 7 was applied, is shown in Fig. 5. The elapsed time is measured in fakeDTLS and does not include processing time. In the case of symmetric-key based handshake, the HOP4 time was increased by 9.05 s as compared with HOP 1. In contrast, the asymmetric-key based handshake time was increased by 22.76 s. This is because that the number of transmissions, amount of traffic, and fragmentation rate are all higher than those based on symmetric-key.

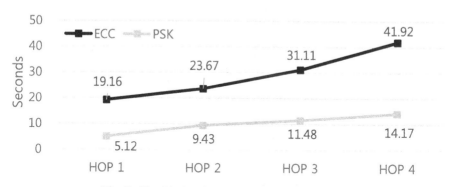

Fig. 5. Handshake Time required for each multi-hop

5   Conclusion

In this paper, we discussed DTLS performance issues in resource constrained environments. We compared the RawPublicKey mode and the PreSharedKey mode specified in CoAP/DTLS binding. We analyzed the comparison results with regard to code size, energy consumption and processing and receiving time. As a result, our analysis showed that devices classified in Class 1 (e.g. Zolteria Z1) can use the PreSharedKey mode. We also showed that the RawPublicKey mode cannot be well operated in

Class 1 and Class 2 devices although it is mandatory to implement CoAP over DTLS. As an alternative experiment, we could get the information about that usage of the RawPublicKey mode is difficult in resource constrained environments. We expect that our analysis results can be utilized for designing secure IoT environments.

Acknowledgement. This research was supported by the MSIP(Ministry of Science, ICT and Future Planning), Korea, under the ITRC(Information Technology Research Center) support program (IITP-2015-H8501-15-1008) supervised by the IITP(Institute for Information & communications Technology Promotion). Also, this research was supported by Basic Science Research Program through the National Research Foundation of Korea (NRF) funded by the Ministry of Education (no. 2014R1A1A2056961).

References

1. Heer, T., Garcia-Morchon, O., Hummen, R., Keoh, S.L., Kumar, S.S., Wehrle, K.: Security challenges in the IP-based internet of things. Wirel. Pers. Commun. **61**(3), 527–542 (2011)
2. Dierks, T., Rescorla, E.: The Transport Layer Security (TLS) Protocol Version 1.2. IETF. RFC 5246 (2008)
3. Bormann, C., Ersue, M., Keranen, A.: Terminology for Constrained-Node Networks. IETF. RFC 7228 (2014)
4. Shelby, Z., Hartke, K., Bormann, C.: The Constrained Application Protocol (CoAP). IETF. RFC 7252 (2014)
5. Rescorla, E., Modadugu, N.: Datagram Transport Layer Security Version 1.2. IETF. RFC 6347 (2012)
6. Swetina, J., Lu, G., Jacobs, P., Ennesser, F., Jaeseung, S.: Toward a standardized common m2 m service layer platform: Introduction to onem2 m. Wirel. Commun. IEEE **21**(3), 20–26 (2014)
7. oneM2M specifications. http://www.onem2m.org/technical/published-documents
8. Kothmayr, T., Schmitt, C., Hu, W., Brunig, M., Carle, G.: A DTLS based end-to-end security architecture for the Internet of Things with two-way authentication. In: IEEE 37th Conference Local Computer Networks Workshops, pp. 956–963 (2012)
9. Granjal, J., Monteiro, E., Silva, J.S.: A framework towards adaptable and delegated end-to-end transport-layer security for Internet-integrated Wireless Sensor Networks. In: 2nd Joint ERCIM eMobility and MobiSense Workshop, p. 34 (2013)
10. Hummen, R., Shafagh, H., Raza, S., Voig, T., Wehrle, K.: Delegation-based authentication and authorization for the IP-based internet of things. In: Sensing, Communication, and Networking, Eleventh Annual IEEE International Conference, pp. 284–292 (2014)
11. Vucinic, M., Tourancheau, B., Rousseau, F., Duda, A., Damon, L., Guizzetti, R.: OSCAR: Object security architecture for the Internet of Things. Ad Hoc Netw. **11**, 2724–2737 (2014)
12. Raza, S., Shafagh, H., Hewage, K., Hummen, R., Voigt, T.: Lithe: Lightweight secure CoAP for the internet of things. Sens. J. IEEE **13**(10), 3711–3720 (2013)
13. Hui, J., Thubert, P.: Compression Format for IPv6 Datagrams over IEEE 802.15.4-Based Networks. IETF. RFC 6282 (2011)
14. Transport Layer Security (TLS) Parameters. http://www.iana.org/assignments/tls-parameters/tls-parameters.xhtml
15. Dunkels, A., Eriksson, J., Finne, N., Tsiftes, N.: Powertrace: Network-level power profiling for low-powerwireless networks. SICS Technical Report T2011:05, ISSN 1100-3154 (2011)

A Study of OAuth 2.0 Risk Notification and Token Revocation from Resource Server

Jungsoo Park, Jinouk Kim, Minho Park, and Souhwan Jung[(✉)]

School of Electronic Engeneering, Soongsil University, Seoul, South Korea
{ddukki86,ouk92,mhp,souhwanj}@ssu.ac.kr

Abstract. OAuth was created to simplify authentication procedure. OAuth is a protocol that allows access to the user's assets in 3rd party web sites or applications without exposing the user's identity and credential. OAuth can be used to grant the access rights for the user without exposing the user's information to third parties. By utilizing the Token issued by the Authorization Server, client is able to gain access to the resources in the Resource Server. However, in current standards, the restrictions of token usage are not clearly defined. Although it specified Token expiration time, in reality, malicious client can reuse the Token to access Resource server. The existing Token Revocation operation has been carried out in a way that the client performs Revocation by requesting to the Authorization Server when special cases occur such as logout or identity change by resource owner. The revocation does not happen for the case that malicious code targets the Resource Server. This paper proposes a method for revoking the Token by requesting Revocation when the Resource Server performs abnormal behaviors by using Token.

1 Introduction

Diverse and professional services are being provided on the web site owing to the spread and universalization of the Internet. In many of these sites, the user has to be authenticated through the membership registration by entering their personal information. To solve these inconveniences, OAuth protocol that allows 3rd party services can access the user's protected data became to appear [1]. OAuth, as one of the standard techniques for authentication, provides a method capable of accessing a user's resource, in addition to the authentication linkage between the service providers and 3rd Party applications that provide the authentication-related system. As sites such as Google, Facebook, and Twitter provide OAuth protocol-based API, the cases that build Mash-Up Service by using their user resources are increasing [2]. Such OAuth Protocol, being supposed to work by using JWT (JSON Web Token), becomes to have a structure that transmits by entering a variety of information about Token in the Claim section of JWT, and authenticate by confirming these in the server. However, currently, the revocation determination of these Token is a method of operating between Client and Authorization Server when there are requests by Resource Owner, a method of terminating Token does not exist when the actual threats on the Resource Server

© Springer International Publishing Switzerland 2016
H. Kim and D. Choi (Eds.): WISA 2015, LNCS 9503, pp. 281–287, 2016.
DOI: 10.1007/978-3-319-31875-2_23

are detected. In this paper, prior to presenting a countermeasure for this problem, a short review of the OAuth 2.0 Protocol and operation procedure of Token revocation, will be given. A new Token Revocation operation procedure is proposed using the protocol when a threat at the Resource Server is detected. When receiving a threat notification from Resource Server, Resource Owner check the contents, determines whether to proceed Revocation of Token, and by stopping the token use at needs-base, it provides a more secure OAuth environment. This paper consists of as follows. In Sect. 2, it describes the OAuth 2.0 and operation procedure of existing Token Revocation. In Sect. 3, a threat problem was presented. In Sect. 4, the proposed protocol is presented. In Sect. 5, it describes the security aspects of this, and finally a conclusion is described in Sect. 6.

2   Introduction to OAuth 2.0

2.1   The OAuth 2.0 Authorization Framework

The OAuth is a protocol to provide access to the user's assets in 3rd party Web sites or applications without exposing the user's Identity and credential. For the method that sets the access rights for each user and does not expose the user information to a 3rd party, it has been revised up to OAuth 2.0 currently, with OAuth core 1.0 started on December 2007 [3]. OAuth 2.0 was standardized as RFC 6749 in order to overcome the limitations of OAuth 1.0a [4]. Existing OAuth 1.0a, not only complicate in the authentication and signature generation, but also supported in Web environment only, has difficulties in applying to various cases, and has a limit that large-scale service providers may have performance issues. In order to overcome this, OAuth 2.0, has simplified Token encryption method by using SSL channels, and it has been applied to diverse cases by authenticating the non browser's clients [5]. OAuth's basic operations are shown as in Fig. 1.

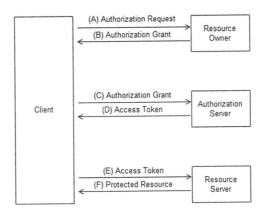

Fig. 1. OAuth 2.0 Flow

(A) The client requests authorization from the resource owner.
(B) The resource owner redirects the request to authorization server.
(C) The client requests authorization grant from the authorization server by presenting the client credentials.
(D) The authorization server validates the client credentials and the authorization grant, and if valid issues an access token.
(E) The client requests the protected resource from the resource server and authenticates by presenting the access token.
(F) The resource server validates the access token, and if valid, serves the request.

OAuth 2.0 provides four grant types [4] to be applied for different situations. Each of the grant methods is as follows. First, the authorization code method, as the most frequently used method, is used when long-term access is required, OAuth client must be a Web application server at that time, the responsibility for the API call is very important, and it is a method used when OAuth token should not be exposed to the Web browser that the user accesses. Second, the implicit method is used when the access to the data is required temporarily, which is used when the user logs in to API provider in a regular base, the reliability of Web browser is high, and there are less concerns that it is exposed to untrusted users or applications. However, since it can be exposed to risk during reissue, it does not issue the refresh token. In addition, if the authentication server expires the access token periodically, the applications must proceed the authentication flow again when the access is required. Third the resource owner password credential authentication method is used when the relationship between the resource owner and the client can be trusted, and usually is used in the official applications that API providers are distributed. Finally, the client credentials authentication method, a method that client owns the access rights on the resource, which is a method when there is no need for delegated access by the resource owner because it owns the data, or when delegating access to applications from the outside of OAuth flow is already permitted.

2.2   OAuth 2.0 Token Revocation

Token Revocation [RFC7009][6] describes the revocation for refresh and access tokens specified in the OAuth 2.0 core specification [RFC6749]. If a resource owner wants to revoke access given to a client in some cases: logout, identity change, or application uninstall, the client can request the token revocation to an authorization server. On receiving the request, the authorization server cleans up data associated with that token and the underlying authorization grant. Token Revocation operations are as follows in Fig. 2.

Fig. 2. Token revocation flow

3   Security Threat

Since OAuth gets a permission to access the resources of the resource owner by utilizing the token that client has got, many studies on malicious client have been performed. Malicious client can attack in various ways such as taking personal information of users by using phishing sites and giving an excessive load on the server by continually accessing the resources by using Token[7]. In particular, since OAuth protocol depends on Token, management of Token is important. OAuth security is based on the Token expiration time and revocation technique to protect against lost Token. The expire time for token is indicated within the area of JWT(JSON Web Token) [8] claim to prevent malignant client from reusing token continuously and to destroy the token that has remained exposed for a long time. Such expiry time is specified only as one-time or short time, which may be abused by client to launch attack. In addition, existing token revocation is activated at the request of resource owner through the revocation by client. However, there has been no way to cope with threats that may occur in resource server actually retaining important resources. In current systems, the only available method is to verify logs subsequently in relation to the attempts that resource server considers to be potential threats such as excessively many attempts to access server, unauthorized attempts to access resources, etc. That may be problematic as it is difficult to cope with potential threats immediately and allows the threats to be verified only after their occurrence. Therefore, in this paper, when the resource server senses a threat, it is able to immediately inform the risk to the user, and through this, it makes the user decide whether to use token or not.

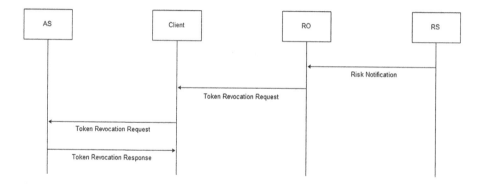

Fig. 3. Risk notification and revocation flow

4   Proposed Protocol

This paper supplements the Token Revocation with an additional revocation triggered by a resource server. We consider the case that a client accesses to resources legally with a malicious purpose, or tries to access unauthorized resources illegally. In most cases, a resource owner cannot know the clients behaviors after the access token is issued. Therefore, when the resource server detects abnormal behaviors of the client, it should send the risk notification including the risk type to the resource owner. According to the resource owners judgment, either the revocation process defined in OAuth token revocation flow may be followed or the risk notification may be discarded. If any abnormal behavior is detected in Resource Server (RS), RS sends Risk Notification to Resource Owner (RO), which enables RO to judge whether or not the issued access token should be revoked due to the reported behavior. Receiving Risk Notification, RO either may request the revocation of the access token to a client or may discard the Risk Notification. If the client receives the revocation request from RO, it revokes the access token in the way of OAuth token revocation flow. Figure 3 illustrates flow that is applicable to the case of doing Revocation. If it is determined for Revocation situation at RS, it will send a revocation request to AS through the client. AS is a form that performs the revocation operation after determining the situation. Each operation is supposed to operate by utilizing JWT, and the claim section of JWT is defined as following Table 1.

Figure 4 shows the flow corresponding to the case in which revocation is not activated. RS makes judgment on revocation situation and sends risk notification to RO. If RO decides not to revoke the access token, it sends Risk Notification Acknowledgement to RS in order to inform that the access token can be kept valid.

Table 1. Revocation JWT token claim

Token	Decide whenever when token revocation is performed
Token-risk-type	Type of risks in the server resource are specified and the content explanation are sent
Token-Issuer	Resource Server

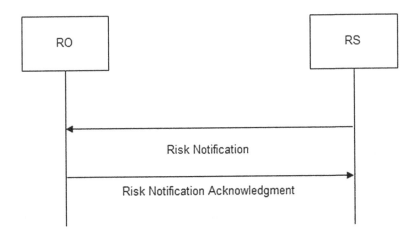

Fig. 4. Risk notification acknowledgment

5   Analysis of the Advantages Proposed Protocol

A client can access the privileged resources with the access token, which is the legal behavior. However, a malicious client might exploit the legal behavior to attack RS, e.g., a number of quarries to Database, or try to access unauthorized resources illegally. Although [RFC6819] mentioned about a malicious client, it does not consider these behaviors stated. Therefore, this proposed revocation can prevent those abnormal behaviors, and make up for this security vulnerability. It is noted that the main contribution of this paper is to provide a work-around for revocation issue, the detail of how to detect the malicious behaviours are not mentioned since this is the responsibility of the administrators of Resource Server.

6   Conclusion

Recently, OAuth protocol that allows third service to access protected data of the user has been actively used in having been applied on various websites such as Twitter, Google, etc. However, since Token Revocation in such OAuth protocol defines for problems that may occur between RO and the Client, such as logout, identity change, or application uninstall only, it has drawbacks that it is difficult to grasp the problems substantially occurring in RS. Also, various attacks of OAuth 2.0 protocol are defined in RFC6819 [9]. However, if RS notices the legal but malicious behaviors or the illegal behaviors other than those specified in Access Token, and alerts RO to such treats, the use of access token can be verified through the judgment of RO, and furthermore, potential threats from malicious clients can be prevented. Through the proposed protocol, since it allows not only immediate judgment on operations that occur from RS, but it also make judgment about the client's operations by giving a notification to RO, it can prevent so as not to reuse malicious Clients when RO tries to use clients later.

Acknowledgement. This research was supported by the MSIP(Ministry of Science, ICT and Future Planning), Korea, under the ITRC(Information Technology Research Center) support program (IITP-2015-H8501-15-1008) supervised by the IITP(Institute for Information & communications Technology Promotion).

This work was supported by the IT R&D program of ATC under the MOTIE/KEIT. [10045904, The development of Fundamental Technology for Security as a Service(SecaaS) Framework under cloud computing environment and the implementation of 1 Gbps mobile data loss prevention(DLP) service based on the SecaaS Framework.]

References

1. Pai, S., et al.: Formal verification of oauth 2.0 using alloy framework. In: International Conference on Communication Systems and Network Technologies (CSNT). IEEE (2011)
2. Yang, F., Manoharan, S.: A security analysis of the OAuth protocol. In: IEEE Pacific Rim Conference on Communications, Computers and Signal Processing (PACRIM). IEEE (2013)
3. Campbell, B., et al.: OAuth working group internet-draft intended status: standards track (2012)
4. Hardt, D.: The OAuth 2.0 authorization framework. RFC 6749, October 2012
5. Tassanaviboon, A., Gong, G.: Oauth and abe based authorization in semi-trusted cloud computing: aauth. In: Proceedings of the Second International Workshop on Data Intensive Computing in the Clouds. ACM (2011)
6. Lodderstedt, T., et al.: OAuth 2.0 token revocation. RFC 7009, August 2013
7. Sun, S.-T., Beznosov, K.: The devil is in the (implementation) details: an empirical analysis of oauth sso systems. In: Proceedings of the 2012 ACM Conference on Computer and Communications Security. ACM (2012)
8. Jones, M., et al.: JSON Web Token (JWT). RFCC 7519, May 2015
9. Lodderstedt, T., et al.: OAuth 2.0 threat model and security considerations. RFC 6819, January 2013

Cyber Security Considerations for Designing IoT-Based Control Systems

Kwangho Kim[✉]

National Security Research Institute, PO Box 1 Yuseong,
Daejeon 305-600, Korea
kkh57@nsr.re.kr

Abstract. It is critical to include cyber security measures at the designing stage of the real-life control systems in order to avail the application of the IoT-related devices, such as intelligent terminals or smart sensors, etc. to the system. This is due to the difference between the attributes of the IoT security measures and those of the Internet-related IT security. It requires a differentiated approach with new security concepts and operation methods. This paper outlines the security issues specific to of the hyper-connected society, where things are being applied to control systems, and suggest technical and organizational measures to be considered for designing of secure control system based on IoT.

Keywords: Hyper connectivity · Iot · SCADA · Key infrastructure

1 Introduction

In modern society, people communicate with objects free from time and space constraints. People enjoy faster access to broader information using technological innovations that allow access to things at any place. This phenomenon continues to evolve as new technologies such as cloud, big data, or IoT etc. are incorporated into the field. Hyper connectivity is increasingly being realized through the development of cutting-edge technologies and mobile interface, enabling connection from all around the world, including the outer space, ocean, or remote areas, beyond wired networks. Now the users have access to wider range of experiences and knowledge through the hyper connectivity, and can reproduce new cultures and things to enjoy through chatting, e-mail, Twitter, Facebook etc. Life has become richer as the imaginations from the past are being newly interpreted and reflected to it, moved to the cyberspace. The IoT started from this expansion of the hyper connectivity [1].

However, considering the adverse side-effects of IT, security considerations must be given to all aspects of the potential threats. Initially, when the Internet was designed and came into operation, the priority was devoted to the transmitting the information on the network in digital form, rather than in analogue form. The greatest concern for the founders of the Internet was to divide, transmit data in pieces through routing, and reassemble them at the end-terminals. Even after such technology became widespread, the focus of research has remained to increasing the speed of transmission for enabling audio, video and multimedia data transfer, rather than the cybersecurity issues. It was designed in economic perspective such as routing, speed or other efficiency, rather than

© Springer International Publishing Switzerland 2016
H. Kim and D. Choi (Eds.): WISA 2015, LNCS 9503, pp. 288–299, 2016.
DOI: 10.1007/978-3-319-31875-2_24

the security aspects. The initial security measures mostly depended on access control and encryption type rather than the cyber security against hacking and virus [2]. It was partially affected by the perception that it was possible to control access at the end of the terminal as they used to be UNIX series which some level of security was provided. However, as the number of users have increased, they have started being exposed to the cyber threats with the spread of personal computers with low-price operation systems such as Windows and LINUX (Fig. 1).

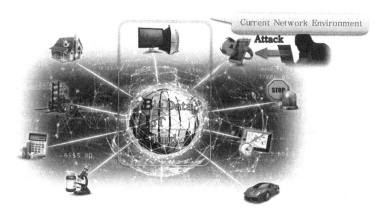

Fig. 1. Threats under IoT environment

A common misconception was that an impact of Internet incidents would be limited to the damage on the corporate images or the psychological impact to the society resulting from website modification or DDoS attacks. It was not considered as a direct threat to national security that could possibly cause casualties as well as economic crisis. As the era of IoT approaches, and humans being on the verge of creating an unprecedented attempt, connecting not only the things to the Internet, but also the control systems, the potential impacts of cyber threats could be catastrophic. Nonetheless, precise assessment of the threats and potential risks is insufficient, and the economic perspectives often impede the concerns on the overall impact on the society. Many people still assume that the impacts would be negligible, similarly to what has happened at the time of the Y2 K incident, or believe there exists a one-for-all solution to all the problems. However, when the IoT and the control system becomes connected, the risk of losing control of the system, as a result of intrusions by a large number of Trojan Horses, Time Bombs, or other malware could become real. People may become victims of mass surveillance or peeping through the IoT devices, and continuously be exposed to imminent risks [3].

A bigger problem is that, if the service errors or failures pertaining to the control system should occur, not only the control system itself but also other systems would be affected by them. In a hyper connected society, even if a system is constructed securely, it can still be damaged unintentionally by the linked systems or harm other systems, and it is more difficult to verify the attacker who caused the incident. It is more problematic that no absolute plans are in place to mitigate and cease the spread of damages in case of serious cyber attacks that may cause grave casualties. If the target is reached out to the control system closely related to our everyday life, including driverless cars, nuclear plants, railroads, water system, transportation, or airlines, the seriousness and the scale of the damages will proliferate correspondingly. Many analysts have warned these risks. For example, the HP had analyzed in its 2014 IoT Vulnerability Analysis Report, that 70 % of the currently-developed IoT devices have security vulnerabilities in themselves [4]. Another security expert insisted in March 2015 that he had succeeded in operating the engine of an airplane by hacking [5]. As it is expected that more than 50 billion things will be connected to the Internet and operated in year 2020, becoming the era of the IoT where all the things are connected, a failure to operate the future technologies in a secure way is likely to result in a dangerous situation, despite the convenience and efficiency they may provide to the human kind. There is a need to address the security problems in terms of the cyber security aspects when the IoT is applied to the control system, and to seek solutions for the analyzed problems.

2 Relevant Research (Problem Analysis)

Contrast to the past, where the use of the Internet was limited to computing devices such as PCs, tablets, and laptops etc., it is being applied to all things, including mobile devices and home appliances. In particular, smart sensors are starting to replace the sensors for industrial devices, equipped with functions to connect. Such smart sensors are linked to the information systems around us, and installed in various places. They are being increasingly installed in remote or restricted areas where people reside or access is complicated, controlled remotely and wirelessly, used in CCTV for monitoring facilities such as restaurants or kindergartens, and allows the operators or managers to access through the Internet anytime and anywhere. Smart home appliances such as TVs and refrigerators, as well as gas and boilers can already be controlled remotely, and in the nearest future, others like audios, vacuum cleaners, washing machines and rice cookers will also be able to be remote controlled, linked to smart sensors. Provided that the sensitive problems with regard to personal information are resolved, they will be used more widely around us, and subject to appropriate legal and policy measures, they will evolve further beyond merely starting or parking a vehicle to driving or calling traffic control centers in emergencies.

Furthermore, the technological advance will expand the functions of smart sensors from taking pictures or location detection, to the PLCs (Programmable Logic Controller) and the control devices of the physical devices such as turbine, gas valves, so that they can provide necessary service for effective management operation, rather than a simple control and manipulation. The problem is that the vulnerabilities that exist under such efficiency are likely to end up in exposure to serious threats from cyber attacks.

2.1   Legacy System

The past cyber incidents regarding the control system were mostly related to the disruption of the information systems related to the control or management systems, rather than the control system itself. The revelation of June 2010, that the serious malfunction in the Iranian nuclear power plant was indeed a cyber incident, occurred by a computer virus called Stuxnet, surfaced the issue of the control system security to the world (Fig. 2).

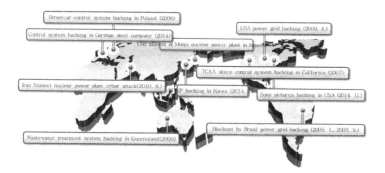

Fig. 2. Cyber incidents regarding control systems worldwide

So far, it has been hard to judge whether a failure on the control system was due to a simple crash as it was, or as a result of cyber attacks. Although the control system is usually automated, it is not designed to protect itself from cyber attacks, which would seem contrary to common perceptions. There has been hardly any systemized structure for investigation or analysis. As it is extremely burdensome to shut down for updating control systems and their physical components, the facilities are normally operated without any such reforms and depend on control systems with air-gapped networks. Therefore, it is not easy to reflect the growing security concerns and apply to the existing legacy systems, instead of replacing the whole system. The implementation of new security policies would be somewhat limited in these legacy systems, to introducing and improving smart terminals, while continuing to operate the facilities with an isolated network.

2.2   Interworking with Control System

Occurrence of new vulnerabilities is inevitable when IoT is applied to the control systems, as the structure of those in operation have not been designed with cybersecurity considerations. Internet-based technology for industrial purposes have been introduced in order to resolve the problem in the past. Many different approaches were taken to apply various solutions to the control systems, e.g. the industrial Ethernet, fieldbus, intelligence grid, or smart grid, etc. However, a switch-over of a system at the risk of the security has never been an easy choice. As a result, operation of an isolated network remained to be considered as the best available option as a security measure for control systems. But the newly-found vulnerabilities due to the technical advances caused other problems. Those vulnerabilities are mostly caused by the development and application of smart sensors and smart terminals, rather than the defects of the devices or the advanced technologies of the cyber attackers.

For instance, the intelligence sensor for measuring flood flow determines its location through GPS and transmits the information regarding its duty to the collecting terminals or Access Pointer near it. While such duty can be performed independently, as these sensors transmit information to the central server by communicating with surrounding devices, most of them may transmit false information or be exploited as an intrusion route.

2.3   Attribution of Responsibility

In case of a cyber-related incident, it should be clearly distinguished whether it is caused by the manufacturer or the user. In case of a traffic accident involving a driverless vehicle, it is hard to tell the cause of such incident: defects of the vehicle in the manufacturing or designing process, mistake or a negligence of the driver, or a problem of the road, which will hold the road managing organization accountable. An arrangement should be made for determining the responsibility of an incident. These procedural rules must contain information on by whom and how the investigation should be carried out. Resolution of such complex legal matters would be a precondition to the smooth dissemination of technologies.

The problem is that it is harder to establish a standard when the incident was caused by malicious cyber attacks by third parties. Where the court should act as the authority to confirm and label an incident as a cyber attack or a simple failure, it would often be frustrated by technical complexity, time-consuming investigations, and the difficulty of finding sufficient evidence. Moreover, if the acts were committed by terrorists or led by the government of an adversary, it is not easy to resolve the problems due to the lack of extraterritorial enforcement mechanisms.

Time-delays for more reliability of the security measures are also problematic for policy makers to prescribe the range of accountability for the manufacturers. For instance, more field tests are necessary to implement security measures for trains, cars, or other safety-related systems because of the potential collision between software due to the wrong information during the update process. On the contrary, ordinary PCs can be easily updated when a defect is discovered, and used by re-booting after removing the software with bugs or vulnerabilities. The manufacturer is not likely to be responsible for the incidents occurred by an unauthorized software hindering the operation of genuine software. Also it is practically impossible to expect that the manufacturer will perform security verification for the control programs on each and every product. This is in contrast with the PCs, as it is relatively easier to be verified because the operation systems are based on Windows and UNIX, and the same for mobile devices. However, it is nearly impossible to resolve all the issues related to smart sensors as there are too many vendors and manufacturers. Also, even if the safety of the "things" is achieved, problems still remain during the linkage procedure.

Because of the differences between the IoT products and the Internet products, the application of cyber security in the IoT environment requires much more sophisticated approach.

2.4   Sustainability (Self-awareness)

Assurance of proper functionality of the smart sensors is a key issue. Smart sensors are placed beyond visual monitoring devices, to a broader area such as flood control, water management in dams and reservoirs, traffic control, and observing polluting facilities. As the data from the devices becomes more critical and the location being widespread, it is necessary to guarantee that each of the sensors are operating properly. I would call this an element of sustainability, or self-awareness to put it another way, which would constitute the four security element in addition to the three traditional security factors of confidentiality, integrity, and availability (Fig. 3).

Fig. 3. The difference in security elements between the Internet and the IoT

Under extreme environments, the impact on the system is critical if the sensors don't function normally or provides false information. So the smart sensors are required to perform general self-diagnosis and transmit the result to the surrounding Access Pointer to report to the server. This process involves an encryption of the communication in order to safeguard the information and avoid cyber attacks from malicious hackers. While the technical method of communication remains the same, the difference is that the indication of authenticity of the information and the functionality of the device is added. It also needs to acknowledge the server that the communications with the surrounding access pointers are kept secure. Without such trust, security measures for transmission of the data *per se* acquired by the sensors may be insufficient and cause significant problems to the system when the smart sensors are abused.

2.5   Information Sharing and Standardization

Information sharing among industries and standardization is a precondition to linking the control system to IoT. Under current situation where copyright issues between vendors and companies are causing compatibility matters, it is not likely to be resolved easily. However, there is a common understanding that the cyber security problem in the IoT is not an option but an essential issue, and that the IoT market will not grow without resolving it. In the end, the only solution would be to share information and establish a unified standard. The necessary resources for establishing the security measures can be arranged only when such standards are in place.

Maintaining the operation of complex and insecure system continues to put risk also for the managing authorities. While in the past the operation of control systems have generally been conducted by a limited number of administrators with related information undisclosed, it is common nowadays that information on the sensors used in internal control systems, network, operating system, or identity of the operators are open public. With these information, a hacker can easily access the field network and paralyze the control system, despite the network is closed. For this reason, a unified response procedure regarding cyber threats must be prepared.

2.6 Emerging Threat Routes

Intrusions into local networks typically exploit the vulnerabilities of the connected terminals and the network, hidden inside and activated upon a specific event on the local network. They would cause shutting down of the system, intercepting and leaking data, or interrupting the operation of the local system. Therefore, it was assumed that the control system could be secured by separating from the network. The problem with the smart terminals used in the control systems is that they use regular commercial operating systems and are mass-produced, as well as being able to operate on a wireless basis. Moreover, the backdoors installed by the vendors in most of these products, originally designed for remote maintenance, is most likely to be abused as a security hole for cyber attacks. The next level of hacking will involve wider access points distributed across smart grids and at numerous levels.

3 Technical Measures

Based on the discussed problems, the response measures that are to be reflected to the design with regard to the IoT-applied control system are suggested as below.

3.1 Self-authentication of the Things

Adoption of self-authentication, where things themselves check whether they are functioning properly, is required when linking them to the system. This is a different concept from existing vaccine or anti-virus programs. For terminals such as PCs, the concept is to check the software on the system to detect worms or viruses, and to remove them in case of a contamination. On the contrary, when it comes to control systems, it is necessary that they assess their functionality by themselves. An analogy to explain the difference between the two could be going to a hospital to cure a specific symptom, and taking a general checkup to assess the whole body. In the same vein, things linked to a control system requires regular scans to detect whether their boot program or PLC information have been modified without being noticed by the system. In order to design an effective self-authenticating system, the following requirements must be met. First, the security must be confirmed by authorized power or regular checks. A process using hash function to self-test the security is used for this purpose. The system will read all the information regarding its execution files, produce a result value using a hash function, and confirm whether it matches the value stored on the server. Unfortunately, there is a constraint in using a public key protocol, as the processing speed would be severely affected by the limited space and processing capacity of the things when they communicate encrypted with the server. Indeed, a public key protocol is unnecessary. The things and the server would already be aware of the counterpart of the communications. As such, the server may store the key using a table method, while the things should store safely their own secret keys. This could be managed with installing a smart card or other chips to the thing. As every hash result value produced by self-assessment would normally be the same, a time stamp value will be inserted to the hash value. The server compares the result received from the terminal to the value of each device stored in itself, and when the values match, it allows the flow of information from the devices and maintain the interlinked status.

3.2   Password of the Things

A device cannot use passwords as humans do. Users, on the contrary, may change the password regularly to data values that other people cannot acquire. As "things" cannot create or change passwords on their own, IDs are randomly assigned using the name or location of the device, while extra methodology is required to create passwords. A simple way to do so is to set the initial value generated by random number sequence, and then to align by time synchronization between the passwords on the device and the server. Such method may, however, overload the server when it manages a large number of devices, as well as hindering access by the devices when time synchronization is unsuccessful. Where the devices are under a poor power condition, continuous synchronization may also affect the lifespan of them. Therefore, preference is given to sequential synchronization methods, where the password is changed at preset times.

3.3   Things and the Encryption of the Data Transmission/Reception

The data transmitted between the "things" and the server typically contain very simple and short messages, for example, quantity, speed, number of revolutions, or state of a motor, and are sent repeatedly and instantly. If excessive handshake protocols are used or the encryption is time-consuming, the system is likely to be overloaded. Thus, it is important to design the security measures at the level where the overhead and the impact on the speed is minimized.

As such, the size of the password for the sequential control signal within the control system must be determined first. General commercial block ciphers are inadequate for encrypting the control signals, as they consist of 64, 128, 256, or 512 bits. It would be desirable to set the size of the multiples in accordance with the length of control signals. It should also be sized to match the length of the control signals as available, in order to ensure the continuity of the control signal sequence. The intensity of the logic, e.g. the number of rounds of a block cipher, should be configured taking into account the maximum delay time for encryption when the control signal sequence is communicated between the server and the things.

3.4 Encryption Protocol

Pursuance of convenience and efficiency, often leading to focusing only on the inter-operability of the data is an extremely risky approach. Such an approach can expose other devices to cyber attacks through the smart sensors. When false information or process data is injected during sensitive sequential process of a control system, it may end up shutting down the whole system, not to mention a disruption.

The fact that the information is simple repetitive and that it occurs between a limited number of objects suggests a solution. As the scope of the targets are clear and limited, the bandwidth should be expanded to cover the overhead including the handshake protocols that occur during the use of encryption protocol. The sequence of control signals should be rearranged to prevent time over during the handshake.

3.5 Prohibition of the Remote Setting Modification

Control systems generally use data communication rather than packet communication, by direct connection between the terminal and the server. PLC is used for this process. As there is a possibility of malfunction if the PLC information is altered, the security configurations should be set to guarantee that the input execution information is managed safely and the integrity of the information. In addition, it is important that the information is not changed remotely. Where there is a need for a remote access, a method for changing the information through security protocols that are mutually applicable should be prepared, and executed with the log and change guidelines for the remote change.

3.6 Air Gap Linkage Analysis

It has been generally perceived safe if IoT and the control system are not physically linked. While such separation can provide security under the Internet environment, the same may not be true in IoT. The information coming through IoT may not be confirmed and feedback not be provided as well. It would result in an inefficiency for the operation of the control system in the real world. For instance, although an air traffic control system is obviously separated from the ticketing system which is operated on the Internet, a failure of the ticketing system for a day will paralyze the operation of the airport. Where the immigration control system relating to passport information is disrupted and cooperation with foreign customs agencies become impossible, it will also cause chaos in the airport.

Therefore, the monitoring system for figuring out the point of access to the control network by hackers and for chasing them should be applied as a complemented. Also, additional services which can buffer the physical separation, e.g. mirroring and back-up should be prepared and designed.

3.7 Risk Management Regarding the Control System

A risk management (risk analysis) must be performed in order to design the control system using IoT [6]. If the things were to transmit and receive information through the connection, it is important to identify the object. Generally, the control system exchanges information based on trust between the server and the sensor. In a typical method of the master–slave type, if the server is deceived by information spoofing between the terminals, the real control system can be overloaded due to the error.

Thus, the architecture of a system should be designed after assessing all potential risks in advance, deciding how the security between the devices, between things and the server, between servers will be transmitted, and whether a terminal-to-terminal security or an end-to-end security is better off. Also, depending on the characteristics of the things, the importance of the information is different. Information can be categorized into different levels, and it can be sensitive to the speed. So the security measures should reflect the different value levels of the information.

4 Organizational Measures

4.1 Domestic and Overseas Information Sharing Cooperation

When cyber attacks on a control system should occur, other control systems that use the similar IoT devices is likely to be exposed to the same cyber threats. A failure of a larger-scale control systems, not just one, will endanger the national security and the economy can be damaged seriously. Thus, a mutual information sharing system regarding control systems is necessary. An environment based on such system for the research and investigation of the cyber attacks should be established. Additionally, the vulnerabilities and the threats identified by epidemiological research should be eliminated, and the result should be shared with other control system operators.

The security of a control system cannot be achieved fully by a good security practices by a single individual or a group. In case of advanced cyber attacks, the blocking and the recovery should be performed simultaneously through information sharing and collective response. A single information system manager cannot become an expert to respond to all sorts of problems. Cooperation for information sharing and analysis, and joint response team of civil, governmental, and the military sector is required. Also, an international cooperation system should be maintained, and the preventive measures for heading off the cyber attacks of terrorists in advance should be prepared together. To do so, a domestic organization system where the civil sector, the government and the military can cooperate should be arranged, and regional and sectoral international consultative forum is desirable. An information-sharing system at 1.5 track process, including experts, would offer a better cooperation than depending on a government-level track 1 or a civil sector-oriented track 2.

4.2   Security Verification for Smart Terminals

A security verification system for smart terminals and sensors installed in the control systems must be developed. Smart terminals must be equipped with an ability to provide mutual trust, and be capable of protecting themselves, in addition to being able to communicate and deliver information. It should be guaranteed that there is no modification, insertion of illegal codes, or a possibility of backdoors to the smart sensors.

4.3   Research and Development

The security measures used in the Internet can also be used for the IoT-applied control systems, but to a limited extent. The reason is that the control system, from the operation system to the protocols, has unique attributes and fundamental difference in operating methods: that the network structure of the control system is operated in a grid type, rather than a web type. There are a number of difficulties to impose cyber security measures once the system is installed, as the operation system and protocols of a control system is sophisticated and designed sequentially.

Therefore, the security architecture should be designed tailored to a control system, and additional resources including bandwidth and memory should be reserved for the security measures when the control system is designed. The cyber security research and development should include, *inter alia*, lightweight encryption system and ultra-power encryption protocol, as well as near field wireless protocol security area.

4.4   Security Management of the Outsourcing and the Partner Companies

In a control system, the managing the security of partnering operators or contractors is a huge issue, as numerous entities are usually involved. In case of a large-scale project such as aircraft or nuclear plants, there are typically over 100 partner companies. In such projects, the security management on the parent company is usually well-designed and implemented. However, since those of relevant entities are relatively weaker, it is possible that the hackers can leak confidential business information, drawings and the program from them.

If the vulnerabilities of the smart terminals are exposed by the cyber attacks on these partner companies, many cyber attacks on the smart terminals can occur in various ways. Thus, there is a need for a stronger security management for the products developed and manufactured by the partners, and to ensure designs and data regarding critical products are not left unattended. In addition, a security manual should be prepared, and its implementation should be checked regularly and thoroughly.

5 Conclusion

Cyber attacks against control systems would be incomparable in size, method, and impacts to those under the Internet environment. In order to securely apply the IoT to control systems, the concept of cyber operation should be reflected from the beginning. Firewalls or intrusion detection systems in use would no longer protect systems from multi-directional cyber operations. Thus, a total system of monitoring, detecting, and responding operations and cooperative instruments to prevent proliferation of harms must be developed. It must also be noted that this goal cannot be reached by a single authority or a State, but only under the shared responsibility of all relevant actors and a coordinating authority.

Innovations IoT technologies will be continue to evolve in a fast pace. Unfortunately, the lack of adequate cyber security measures may delay the application of such technologies. Therefore, based on the precise forecasts on technology development, appropriate manpower recruitment and training plans should be prepared and implemented, as well as designing the cyber security structure. Failure to investment in cyber security itself can be a great threat in the future. The hyper connected society will continue to evolve and the control systems will be interlinked. Thus, it is a must, not an option, where the cyber security issues from being connected should be prevented, and the measures should be prepared in order to move forward to a safe future.

References

1. Atzori, L., Iera, A., Morabito, G.: The internet of things: A survey. Comput. Netw. **54**(15), 2787–2805 (2010)
2. Xu, T., Wendt, J.B., Potkonjak, M.: Security of IoT systems: Design challenges and opportunities. In: 2014 IEEE/ACM International Conference on Computer-Aided Design (ICCAD), 2–6 November 2014
3. Zhang, Y., Zou, W., Chen, X., Yang, C.: The security for power internet of things: Framework, policies, and countermeasures. In: 2014 International Conference on Cyber-Enabled Distributed Computing and Knowledge Discovery (CyberC), 13–15 October 2014
4. HP: Internet of Things Research Study. 2014 Report, July 29, 2014
5. United States District Court. Case 5:15-mj-00154-ATB Document 1, April, 15 2015
6. Kim, I.J., Chung, Y.-J., Lee, Y., Won, D.H.: A time-variant risk analysis and damage estimation for large-scale network systems. In: Gervasi, O., Gavrilova, M.L., Kumar, V., Laganá, A., Lee, H.P., Mun, Y., Taniar, D., Tan, C.J.K. (eds.) ICCSA 2005. LNCS, vol. 3481, pp. 92–101. Springer, Heidelberg (2005)

Frying PAN: Dissecting Customized Protocol for Personal Area Network

Kibum Choi[1], Yunmok Son[1], Jangjun Lee[2], Suryeon Kim[2],
and Yongdae Kim[1,2(✉)]

[1] School of Electrical and Engineering, KAIST, Daejeon, Republic of Korea
{kibumchoi,yunmok00,yongdaek}@kaist.ac.kr
[2] Graduate School of Information Security, KAIST, Daejeon, Republic of Korea
{baator.nine,c16192}@kaist.ac.kr

Abstract. A spoofing attack for a wireless communication system is the most common attack method for unauthorized access and control. IEEE 802.15.4 is a standard that defines only physical and medium access control layers for low rate, low power, and low cost wireless systems. This standard is widely used as lower layers for not only several wireless communication standards but also customized protocols by manufacturers. However, security has not been considered seriously in these customized protocols, due to other important features including efficiency and cost. In this paper, in order to empirically analyze the real world threat in these systems, we chose to study three IEEE 802.15.4 based wireless communication systems as targets. We manually analyzed the customized protocols above IEEE 802.15.4 if there exist vulnerabilities to be exploited. For all three systems, we discover significant vulnerabilities. We implemented a spoofing attack for two targets, and we successfully controlled the targets by our spoofing attack. For the last target, we chose not to run the experiment due to significant safety reasons.

Keywords: Security · Wireless spoofing attack · IEEE 802.15.4

1 Introduction

IEEE 802.15.4 is a standard that specifies the physical (PHY) and the medium access control (MAC) layer for Low-Rate Wireless Personal Area Networks (LR-WPAN) [1]. It operates on one of three frequency bands, 868–868.6 MHz, 902–928 MHz, or 2,400–2,483.5 MHz. IEEE 802.15.4 can provide up to 250 kbps at 10 m distance with low power and low cost. Due to the requirement of efficiency in power and cost, IEEE 802.15.4 is designed as a simple structure, and does not readily to support encryption or authentication.

Despite its absence of security features, IEEE 802.15.4 is still utilized in the field of Internet of Things (IoT) devices, such as wireless sensor networks, smart

This research was supported by Next-Generation Information Computing Development Program through the National Research Foundation of Korea (NRF) funded by the Ministry of Science, ICT & Future Planning (No. NRF-2014M3C4A7030648).

© Springer International Publishing Switzerland 2016
H. Kim and D. Choi (Eds.): WISA 2015, LNCS 9503, pp. 300–312, 2016.
DOI: 10.1007/978-3-319-31875-2_25

home network and industrial controlling systems, on the basis of its efficiency. Numerous wireless communication systems such as ZigBee, 6LoWPAN, WirelessHART, and MiWi have been built upon IEEE 802.15.4.

Notably, we found three critical applications that are using custom protocols upon IEEE 802.15.4. Our first target, Smart plug, is a smart power metering system. It can turn on and off a power supply, and collect the power usage information of users. The second target is a door lock system controlled by both its user and a manager. By the user's request or in an emergency situation, the manager can control the door lock system remotely using wireless communication. The last target is a Platform Screen Door (PSD) system that communicates with a control system using a wireless protocol in subway stations. Although, these systems are closely related to security and safety, they are implemented without any security concerns and only rely on their custom protocol.

In this work, we captured packets from three target systems using commercial RF transceivers. By analyzing these packets manually, it was possible to infer most fields of customized protocols, and we then implemented a spoofing attack to take control of them. We were able to successfully control the first and second targets, but we could not perform our an attack on the third, because of legal and safety issues. Note that all vulnerabilities are responsibly disclosed in advance.

To summarize, we made the following contributions.

– We derived general analysis methodology for customized protocols on top of IEEE 802.15.4, which is far different from that of TCP/IP packet analysis.
– We found nine security vulnerabilities from three real world targets using the proposed analysis methodology. Furthermore, we were able to exploit these vulnerabilities to spoof the protocol messages.
– We performed unauthorized control of critical applications which are linked directly with the citizen's safety.

The remainder of this paper is organized as follows. Section 2 describes related work on the attack of IEEE 802.15.4 networks. Section 3 provides background on IEEE 802.15.4 and tools for the spoofing attack we used. Sections 4 and 5 explain our analysis methodology and generalized vulnerabilities of customized protocols over IEEE 802.15.4. Section 6 presents a detailed analysis and attack against two target systems and the result of the attacks are presented in Sect. 7. Section 8 concludes the paper.

2   Related Work

Several works on attacking IEEE 802.15.4 based systems in both the PHY and MAC layers have been reported. While most PHY layer attacks are related to jamming that causes a denial of service for systems, our main concern is taking control or causing malfunctions against the target system by injecting well crafted packets. Spoofing attacks are usually related to upper layers rather than the PHY layer. Some papers related to security on the MAC layer of IEEE 802.15.4 systems have been published. Sastry et al. mentioned three problems that could reduce security in IEEE 802.15.4 specifications [2]. First, there is an initial vector (IV) management problem where the same key can be used in two different access control list (ACL) entries. The second problem is no support for group keying because each ACL entry can only be associated with one destination address. The third problem is that the standard supports an unauthenticated encryption mode that is vulnerable. Sokullu et al. suggested a Guaranteed Time Slots (GTS) attack in the IEEE 802.15.4 MAC layer [3]. GTS is a part of the superframe for collision-free transmission, and thus they are exclusively dedicated to a single device. An attacker can learn the GTS slot times from the beacon frame following a GTS request, and then she can cause interference or a collision when a legitimate node transmits a GTS data frame. A GTS attack is a denial of service against GTS requests. Jokar et al. presented Received Signal Strength (RSS) based spoofing detection and prevention techniques in static IEEE 802.15.4 networks [4,5].

Most related works are focused on the security of the IEEE 802.15.4 standard itself. In contrast to previous works, we point out that customized protocols on IEEE 802.15.4 are utilized for actual devices and they have security problems.

3 Background

In this section, we explain the basic information of the IEEE 802.15.4 architecture, data frame format, and platforms used for our spoofing attack.

IEEE 802.15.4 Architecture. The IEEE 802.15.4 architecture consists of only two layers, the PHY layer and the MAC layer. The PHY layer defines the physical specifications to transmit and receive radio frequency (RF) signals through a physical transmission medium. The MAC layer provides a reliable link between two nodes, and is responsible for encoding digital bits into packet frames to transmit, decoding them to receive frames, and controlling the access to data in a network. This architecture is utilized not only for the lower layer of several wireless communication standards but also for unknown customized protocols designed by device developers.

Data Frame Format. Figure 1 depicts a data frame format of the MAC layer. The MAC frame contains the MAC Header (MHR), MAC Service Data Unit (MSDU), and MAC Footer (MFR). The MHR has a Frame Control Field (FCF), data sequence number, and address information. MSDU is the actual data to transmit and MFR is Cyclic Redundancy Check (CRC) for error detection.

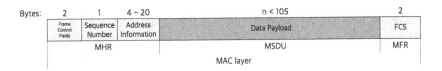

Fig. 1. IEEE 802.15.4 data frame format

In this work, the most important field is MSDU, because it carries a payload that is composed of the customized protocol data for the specific purpose or service of various manufacturers. Furthermore, FCF, the first two bytes in MHR, contains important information that is represented as a bit-map such as packet type, security enabled status, ACK request status, and addressing mode. If a security enabled field is '0', then data is not encrypted. This is the starting point of protocol reverse engineering.

Attack Platforms. We used two programmable RF transceiver devices to collect and inject IEEE 802.15.4 packets as attack platforms. The first is Universal Software Radio Peripheral (USRP) with "gr-ieee-802.15.4" GNU Radio module that fully supports the IEEE 802.15.4 standard. Another platform is KillerBee [6] which is a python based framework designed for the analysis of IEEE 802.15.4 and ZigBee protocol. By using these hardware and software platforms, we can obtain data frames of the MAC layer regardless of the PHY layer protocol. In addition, log files from these platforms are readable by Wireshark.

4   Methodology

Our analysis can be divided into three phases to make a spoofing attack possible for an IEEE 802.15.4 based customized protocol: collecting, grouping, and actual analysis. To understand the fields of a customized protocol as well as possible, it is necessary to control the variance of packets in known or predictable conditions in the first two phases. We strongly believe that this methodology with three phases can be considered as a generic approach for IEEE 802.15.4 based customized protocol reverse engineering.

4.1   Collecting Packets

The first step to take for a sniffing attack is to find a communication channel. By brute-forcing channels, we can find the active channel that the target system uses. The collecting phase is usually considered as a simple process, as it is supported in the hardware we use. However, the challenges in the next phases depend on this phase. There are variable factors or environments that feasibly affect the variance of the packet data such as function, date, timing, and place. Note that not all of these are necessary for building packets and all implementations are somewhat different.

Function is the most basic factor to distinguish command related fields, and date or time is related to the timestamp field. Sometimes it is necessary to capture packets within a limited time span to remove unnecessary packets that may not include critical information. Place is also an important factor, because the network topology can be one master to one client, one master to multiple client, or multiple masters to multiple clients. To control and identify the source and destination address fields among multiple communication pairs, the physical location should be addressed.

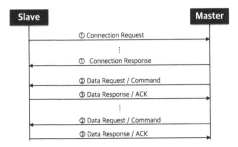

Fig. 2. IEEE 802.15.4 communication process in three steps

Both fixing and changing these factors may be necessary to identify the related fields in packets. Therefore, an attacker must control variable factors as much as possible.

4.2   Grouping Packets

The second phase is a grouping process for the collected packets. There are many types of packets in a common digital communication protocol such as request, response, command, acknowledgement, and so on. Because the formats of these various types usually have different fields, they make the protocol analysis more difficult. By classifying the collected packets according to the source or destination addresses, we can learn the information of request to response and command to acknowledgment relationships, which are shown in Fig. 2. The length of the packet can provide useful information, because the different fields lead to different packet lengths. For example, acknowledgement packets are usually very short for efficiency. It is also helpful to categorize the collected packets according to the factors mentioned in the previous phase.

4.3   Analysis Protocol

The last step is the actual analysis process of hex or ASCII valued byte data in the packets. In the case of customized protocols, most of this phase is conducted manually. The important elements in the sequence of grouped packets are the repeated data, periodic data, monotonically increasing or decreasing data, and other meaningful data. The repeated data can be related to the control features of the two previous phases including source or destination addresses, functional commands, and so on. Periodic data also can be interpreted to have various meanings by their timing characteristics such as the interval. Sequence number and timestamp of packets usually appear as monotonically increasing data, and they can be decoded according to their cycles. For example, the cycles of date or time data can be 12, 24, or 60 in decimal or hex, whereas that of sequence number can be a full byte size. In particular, repeated data in every packets without any change are important, because an attacker can use them as fixed values for a spoofing attack without detailed knowledge.

5   Vulnerabilities

During the protocol reverse engineering against three targets, we found several vulnerabilities in those customized protocols. We found features that in fact helped our protocol analysis. We listed these problems in Table 1.

Table 1. Vulnerabilities in custom protocols based on IEEE 802.15.4

Phase	Vulnerability	Smart plug	Door lock	PSD
Analysis	No encryption on payload	✓	✓	✓
	No packet fragmentation	✓	✓	✓
	Plaintext data (ASCII)	✓	✗	✓
	Repeated MAC layer data	✓	✓	✓
	Periodic increase (timestamp)	✗	✓	✓
	Sequential increase (seq num)	✓	✓	✓
Spoofing	Well-known CRC	✓	✓	✓
	Meaningless fixed field	△	✓	✓
	Poor authentication	✓	✗	△

5.1   Vulnerabilities in Analysis Phase

The most fundamental vulnerability in WPAN is the absence of encryption on the payload. This is the starting point of our protocol reverse engineering. When we analyzed the customized protocol, packet parsing was our basic approach. From an attacker's perspective, if packets are fragmented, then parsing is infeasible. If a packet shows plain text in ASCII, then we can easily infer the meaning of the packet or field. Even for packets that use non-ASCII range bytes, repeated byte fields were often detected. All three customized protocols use modified parts of the MAC address in their address fields, probably because using new address requires address to device binding. This would be an easy way to identify the source and destination field.

5.2   Vulnerabilities in Spoofing Phase

For a successful spoofing attack, normally we had to control two values, the sequence number and the CRC. The remaining fields were only copied from previous packets or could be hard-coded. If some fields use fixed bytes for every operation, then we do not have to guess the real meaning of fields. In addition, all three targets used well-known CRC methods. Moreover, some of them only check if the sequence number is larger than the current sequence number.

6 System Analysis

We now present our analysis following methodology consists of collecting packets, grouping packets, and protocol reverse engineering phases. This section contains three different customized systems based on IEEE 802.15.4.

6.1 Smart Plug Analysis

A. Smart Plug System Overview
Our first target is a wireless smart power metering system. This system consists of a Watt Checker Unit (WCU) and a Data Concentrate Unit (DCU). The WCU is set up between home appliances and a wall outlet, and it measures power usage data in real time and reports the data to the DCU. The DCU collects data from multiple WCU and displays the data. It can also remotely control each WCUs to turn it on or turn off.

B. Smart Plug System Analysis
Packet Capture. First, it was important to identify the communication channel to sniff packets. Because there are only 16 channels in the 2.4 GHz bands, we could easily brute force this. Initially, we found the source and destination address, packet length, and data type from the header fields of captured packets. Because the security option is disabled, we started reverse engineering.

On/Off Command. One on/off operation consists of three packets, the DCU on/off command request, response from WCU, and DCU ACK. After we found communication process, we sorted packets into two sets with address field and packet length. Figures 3 and 4 represent the arranged data from the two sets

0	1	2	3	4	5	6	7	8	9	10	11	12	13	14	15	16	17	18	19	20	21	22	23	
ID	CMD	sequence number				source address								destination address								PAN ID		ASCII representation
53	4F	32	31	31	34	17	04	00	00	00	55	43	44	64	0A	00	00	00	55	43	57	04	17	S02114.....UCDc.....UCW..
53	61	32	31	31	35	17	04	00	00	00	55	43	44	64	0A	00	00	00	55	43	57	04	17	Sa2115.....UCDc.....UCW..
53	46	32	31	31	36	17	04	00	00	00	55	43	44	64	0A	00	00	00	55	43	57	04	17	SF2116.....UCDc.....UCW..
53	61	32	31	31	37	17	04	00	00	00	55	43	44	64	0A	00	00	00	55	43	57	04	17	Sa2117.....UCDc.....UCW..

Fig. 3. Packet format of smart plug on/off command

0	1	2	3	4	5	6	7	8	9	10	11	12	13	14	15	16	17	18	19	20	21	22	
ID	CMD	sequence number				source address								destination address								stat	ASCII representation
57	73	32	30	39	32	63	0A	00	00	00	55	43	57	17	04	00	00	00	55	43	44	31	Ws2092c....UCW.....UCD1
57	73	32	30	39	33	63	0A	00	00	00	55	43	57	17	04	00	00	00	55	43	44	30	Ws2093c....UCW.....UCD0

Fig. 4. Packet format of smart plug on/off ACK

0	1	2	3	4	5	6	···	21	22	23	24	25	26	27	28	29	30	31	32	33	34	
ID	CMD	sequence number				address		Cumulative consumption				power consumption										ASCII representation
57	50	33	32	30	31	···		30	39	2E	34	30	30	30	30	30	2E	31	32	31		WP3201···09.400000.121
57	50	33	32	31	37	···		30	39	2E	38	30	30	30	30	30	2E	31	32	31		WP3217···09.800000.121
57	50	33	32	32	35	···		31	30	2E	34	30	30	30	30	30	2E	31	32	31		WP3325···10.400000.121

Fig. 5. Packet format of smart plug power consumption data

and protocol reversing results. After the sorting step, we had to cut packets into meaningful units. We used our analysis methodology in Sect. 4

We identified the address fields that are constantly repeated and have exactly the same values of source and destination address of header fields. Byte fields at positions 6–13 and 14–21 have exactly the same values of source and destination address, respectively.

Among the remaining bytes, bytes 1 and 5 are the only changing fields. In particular, byte 5 was changed from 0x30 ('0' in ASCII) to 0x39 ('9' in ASCII) circularly like a counter. After scanning numerous packets for long period, we found periodicity in 4 bytes from byte 2. From this, we determined that field to be the sequence number field with a decimal number.

The most important byte was byte 1 which prints 'O' and 'F'. Most of the fields used ASCII formats in the captured packets, and we could infer that 'O' and 'F' represent "ON" and "OFF". Likewise, 'a' may represents "answer" or "acknowledgment" (Fig. 5).

Sorted packets in the Fig. 4 are the WCU response for power control to the DCU. It has a similar format to that of the DCU. As a command in byte 1, the WCU uses 's', which may mean "success". The last byte in the WCU alternatively prints '0' and '1' in ASCII. This last byte likely means the power on/off status of the WCU. Another difference between the WCU and DCU formats is byte 0. The DCU uses 'S' and the WCU uses 'W' instead of 'S'. However, for a spoofing attack, fixed bytes were not our concern.

Power Monitoring Command. The DCU requests power consumption information to WCUs every minute. Like the power control operation, the power monitoring process is also divided into three steps. The DCU requests power consumption information, and then the WCU replies with power consumption information. Finally, the DCU sends an acknowledgment to the WCU. In this process, byte 1 changes as follows: 'P', 'P', and 'a'.

Power monitoring packets have almost an identical structure with the power control packet structure up to byte 21. The DCU only adds PAN ID at the end of the power request and ACK packets. The remaining bytes in the WCU have power consumption information. Two key features that we could understand the meaning of are the range of hexadecimal bytes and repeated bytes such as 0x30 ('0' in ASCII) and 0x2E ('.' in ASCII). From these, we determined that this field is using ASCII formats to represent cumulative power consumption and instant power consumption.

6.2   Door Lock Analysis

A. Door Lock System Overview

The second target is a wireless controlled digital door lock system. This system consists of a door lock, a transceiver and a central controller. When the central controller sends a door open signal to the transceiver, which is installed in each floor, the transceiver sends a wireless packet to a specific door lock.

B. Door Lock Protocol Analysis

Packet capture. In an apartment, the distance between a door to another door is close enough to receive packets in the same floor. After we found a channel, we could collect all packets between a transceiver and multiple door locks. However, since the door opening operation from the central controller is not a normal operation, we operated KillerBee until we collected enough packets.

0	1	2	3 4 5 6	7 8 9 10	11 12 13 14	15 16 17 18	19 20 21 22	23
ID	Seq	CMD	Lower 32bit of src MAC addr	Prefix (00:15:8d:00)	Lower 32bit of dst MAC addr	Prefix (00:15:8d:00)	Misc.	END

Fig. 6. Packet format of door lock open command

Door Status Monitoring Command. After gathering bunch of packets, we grouped packets according to packet length. We found six different length packets. We create a variety of situations to classify the different size of packets for further analysis. Majority of them are door status monitoring packets that consist of 2 phases. Firstly, request command packet of 47 byte length is transmitted from controller to door lock. Secondly, response command of 48 byte length is transmitted from door lock to controller. Packet of 47 bytes has a same feature with door open command which will be discussed right below. We disintegrated response packet of 48 bytes. Most of field was fixed making our work much easier. According to the change of command type between request and response the value of byte 0 repeats 0x02 and 0x05. Four bytes from byte 18 represent time field consisting of mm/dd/hh/mm meaningful as a status information. Each request and response command has a subsequent ACK packet of 5 byte length. ACK packet is simply configured with FCF, sequence number and CRC. The above procedure repeats every 5 min between controller and door locks.

Door Open Command. With repeated door open and close experiments, we could filter out status monitoring packets from the door lock to the central controller. In Fig. 6, we dissected the format of the door lock open command. From byte 3 to byte 18, we found that address fields consist of modified MAC layer addresses. The last byte is always fixed when packets have different lengths. We assumed that this field means the end of data. The remaining fields are variable fields. The value of byte 0 repeats 0x02 and 0x05 corresponding to request and response. Obviously, byte 1 is a sequence number. When the byte length is changed, byte 2 is changed. Therefore, it shows the type of packets or the kind of command code. Four bytes from byte 19 are important. In normal cases, it receives 0x02013B3B. When the door is opened with a signal sent from the central controller, then 0x02014848 is captured.

6.3   Platform Screen Door System Analysis

A. PSD System Overview
PSDs have been installed at subway platforms to separate the platform from the subway train for the safety of passengers and a pleasant air environment of subway stations. For citizen's safety, the PSD design must be secure. We found customized IEEE 802.15.4 based wireless communication in PSD installed in the subway station of the largest city of our country. The PSD system coincides with Fig. 2. The PSD controllers installed in a train and a station correspond to a master and slave, respectively. We found two subway lines use a customized protocol based on IEEE 802.15.4 and successfully reverse-engineered it.

B. PSD System Analysis
PSD Packet Capture. As a train approaches a platform, we try to detect an active channel by brute forcing. Fortunately, the train and the PSD exchange packets with a 20 ms interval for almost 2 to 3 s. Therefore, we scanned all 16 channels by changing the receiving channel for each 100 ms. Furthermore, the communication channel is fixed for the same line and for the same direction. We systematically collected packets against 20 subway stations and several trains to reverse the PSD protocol.

PSD System Protocol Reversing for Line X and Y. First, we analyzed captured packets from line X, due to the completeness of the captured packet sequences. (Line Y has an identical packet structure with line X). First, we verified the header of the MAC layer to obtain meta data. The value of FCF is 0x8841, which represents a disabled security option, no ACK, and a 16-bit source and destination address. We grouped PSD packets in three steps following Fig. 2.

① **Step 1 - Connection Request and Response.** Packets corresponding to step 1 from three different stations are depicted in Fig. 7. In the whole process, we found that a header field is 5 bytes.

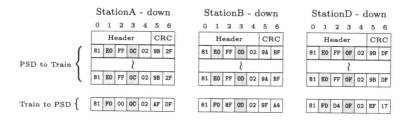

Fig. 7. PSD packet format - step 1

StationA - down

0	1	2	3	4	5	6	7	8	9	10	11	12	13	14
Header					Timestamp						Index		CRC	
81	E1	00	0C	02	14	05	18	22	54	44	2A	18	B9	A6
81	E1	00	0C	02	14	05	18	22	54	45	28	10	E8	C0
81	E1	00	0C	02	14	05	18	22	54	46	28	10	18	C0
81	E1	00	0C	02	14	05	18	22	54	47	28	10	49	00

StationB - down

0	1	2	3	4	5	6	7	8	9	10	11	12	13	14
Header					Timestamp						Index		CRC	
81	E1	8F	0D	02	14	05	18	23	07	35	2A	18	0D	2A
81	E1	8F	0D	02	14	05	18	23	07	36	2A	10	FC	EC
81	E1	8F	0D	02	14	05	18	23	07	37	2A	10	AD	2C
81	E1	8F	0D	02	14	05	18	23	07	38	28	10	9C	4F

Fig. 8. PSD packet format - step 2

Byte 1 represents the communication step. We could see the transition of byte 1 when the communication process changes. Byte 1 from PSD, 0xE0 in step 1 changed to 0xE1 in step 2 packets. Otherwise, byte 1 from the train changed from 0xF0 in step 1 to 0xF1 in step 3. Bytes 2 and 3 describe the lower 8 bits of the train MAC address and the station MAC address (each address is 16-bits), respectively. Thus, 0xFF in byte 2 indicates broadcasting address. We could also observe the increment in byte 3 when the train moved to the next station. Byte 4 is always 0x01 or 0x02. After numerous experiments in the same station, we found that byte 4 represents the direction of the train. Bytes 5 and 6 contained CRC-16, which is a well-known protocol.

② **Step 2 - Data Request of PSD.** In Fig. 8, the packet consists of a header, timestamp, and CRC. Byte 1 changed to 0xE1 from 0xE0 in step 1. We found the timestamp field was formed as yy/mm/dd/hh/mm/ss from the fact that the period is 60 in decimal. The index field changed following the status of the PSD. We assumed that field to be an index code for the purpose of PSD status monitoring.

StationA - Train1 - down

0	1	2	3	4	5	6	7	8	9	10
Header					Code					CRC
81	F1	00	11	02	11	20	40	82	67	F8
81	F1	00	11	02	11	20	42	82	66	98
81	F1	00	11	02	11	20	40	82	67	F8

StationA - Train2 - down

0	1	2	3	4	5	6	7	8	9	10
Header					Code					CRC
81	F1	00	11	02	13	20	40	82	66	40
81	F1	00	11	02	13	20	42	82	67	20
81	F1	00	11	02	13	20	40	82	66	40

StationA - Train3 - down

0	1	2	3	4	5	6	7	8	9	10
Header					Code					CRC
81	F1	00	11	02	15	20	40	82	14	0C
81	F1	00	11	02	15	20	42	82	15	6C
81	F1	00	11	02	15	20	40	82	14	0C

Fig. 9. PSD packet format - step 3

③ **Step 3 - Data Transmission of Train.** Figure 9 represents packets from train to the PSD. Byte 2 changed to 0xF1 from 0xF0. In the code field, bytes 6 and 8 are never changed. Although we could not find the meaning of the bytes, we can fill these fields with the same values for the spoofing attack. However, byte 5 increased by two as the next train entered the platform. Since the PSD closed when byte 7 changed to 0x42 from 0x40, we speculated that it was the practical PSD control code. This field is the only changing field of step 3. Thus, we believe byte 7 is a control message.

7   Attack Results

7.1   Spoofing Smart Plug

To implement a spoofer, we utilized the KillerBee framework. The only task that we need to perform is a simple payload forgery. We hard-coded constant fields such as addresses and inserted the command. We additionally attached sequence number and CRC code at last. We composed a malicious packet with the command we want and the suitable sequence number that is larger than the current sequence number. Using our spoofer, we could send a malicious packet and receive the corresponding ACK packet successfully. We also noticed that WCU only checks the addresses, sequence number, and CRC code. The sequence number only has to be larger than the previous sequence number. In this case, 0xFFFFFFFF is the best choice.

We implemented an attack against DCU to masquerade power usage information. This attack was a bit more challenging than the previous attack, because we needed to send the packet exactly on time when the DCU asked WCU. In addition, our spoofing packet should be sent faster than the legitimate packet with higher signal strength. Therefore, we sent five packets in 0.1 second immediately after the receiver sniffed the power consumption information request. Finally, we could inject the power consumption information to the DCU display.

7.2   Spoofing Door Lock

In the case of door lock, capturing a real command packet is the most difficult aspect. This is because the action followed after the "open" command itself is simple. We copied the door open packet from the central controller and only a brute-force one byte sequence number field. Brute-forcing a one byte field took less than one minute, and we opened the door lock with our spoofing packets. We collected packets during brute-forcing, and found interesting result. Sequence number of packet use the value increased by one greater than the previous packet in general. However, once packet having sequence number 00 was transmitted to central controller, the sequence number initialized and increased from the value 00. This means that we are able to open the door with just one packet having sequence number value 00. Moreover, with address modification, we successfully opened the other rooms as desired.

8   Conclusion

In this paper, we analyzed and implemented spoofing attacks against the real world applications using unknown customized protocols upon IEEE 802.15.4 stacks such as smart plug, door lock and PSD system. We collected the packets of the target devices wirelessly, and reverse-engineered most fields of unknown customized protocols to take control of the targets by spoofing.

The results of our reverse-engineering analysis are evaluated by successful spoofing attacks against real world systems. We were able to remotely turn on/off electric devices connected to Smart plug. Moreover, we could attack the target devices more ingeniously with power usage information modification by spoofing. Likewise, opening door lock is possible with simple brute-forcing in less than one minute. The custom protocol of a PSD system, the most critical application, was also successfully analyzed. We found enough information to implement a spoofing attack with two bytes brute-forcing. For public security and safety, we could not actually conduct a test against a PSD system. However, we believe that our spoofing attack would affect the PSD system and we specifically predict that closing the PSD system would be possible.

From the results of our analysis on IEEE 802.15.4 based customized protocols, we pointed out general security problems. Wireless communication over open standard protocols can be accessed by anyone. Therefore, it must be designed with elaborate security measures.

References

1. IEEE Standard for Local, metropolitan area networks - Part 15.4: Low-Rate Wireless Personal Area Networks (LR-WPANs) (2011)
2. Sastry, N., Wagner, D.: Security considerations for IEEE 802.15.4 networks. In: WiSe. IEEE (2004)
3. Sokullu, R., Dagdeviren, O., Korkmar, I.: On the IEEE 802.15. 4 MAC layer attacks: GTS attack. In: SENSORCOMM. ACM (2008)
4. Jokar, P., Arianpoo, N., Leung, V.C.: Spoofing detection in IEEE 802.15.4 networks based on received signal strength. Ad Hoc Netw. **11**(8), 2648–2660 (2013)
5. Jokar, P., Arianpoo, N., Leung, V.C.: Spoofing prevention using received signal strength for ZigBee-based home area networks. In: SmartGridComm. IEEE (2013)
6. KillerBee. https://code.google.com/p/killerbee/

Structured Design Approach for an Optimal Programmable Synchronous Security Processor

Mahmoud El-Hadidi[1], Hany El-Sayed[1]([⊠]), Heba Aslan[2],
and Karim Osama[1]

[1] Department of Electronics and Electrical Communication Engineering,
Cairo University, Giza, Egypt
hadidi@eun.eg, helsayed@ieee.org,
karim.central@gmail.com
[2] Electronic Research Institute, Cairo, Egypt
hebaaslan@yahoo.com

Abstract. A new security processor has been recently proposed which accepts the assembly code for arbitrary security algorithms, and executes it efficiently, thanks to its use of a data-flow architecture that distributes arithmetic and logical Function Units (FUs) over a number of Execution Regions (ERs). In this paper, a structured approach is presented to determine the optimal solution of the processor architecture in which one seeks the best combination of the number of ERs and the assignment of 27 FUs to these ERs. In order to cover the huge design space, a structured approach has been adopted which is based on the use of a powerful software simulator and the customization of the Genetic Algorithm NSGA-II for efficient optimization. Numerical results have been obtained and the optimal security processor architecture has been deduced by considering the AES Encryption algorithm as the reference assembly code.

Keywords: Structured design approach · Genetic algorithm NSGA-II · Data-Flow architecture · Synchronous security processor

1 Introduction

The ever-growing use of powerful applications over an ever-expanding global information network, has necessitated the deployment of effective security services such as confidentiality, integrity, authentication, access control, and non-repudiation [1]. Typically, these services are realized using sophisticated security algorithms such as AES, RSA, ECC, SHA3 and others. Contemporary processor families – whether based on CISC or RISC architectures – can be programmed to compute these algorithms [2–7]. Nonetheless, since these processors are not natively designed to efficiently perform arithmetic and logical operations encountered in security algorithms, researchers have looked for more effective implementation approaches. On one extreme, dedicated hardware designs have been developed for a specific security algorithm - such as AES [8, 9] - which offered optimized performance. However, these were not very attractive in view of the fact that typical security protocols – such as SSL

© Springer International Publishing Switzerland 2016
H. Kim and D. Choi (Eds.): WISA 2015, LNCS 9503, pp. 313–325, 2016.
DOI: 10.1007/978-3-319-31875-2_26

and IPSec [1] – can deploy one of several possible algorithms (e.g. 3DES or AES for Private Key Schemes, and RSA or ECC for Public Key schemes). The use of reconfigurable architectures (such as FPGA [10, 11], TTA [12], CGRA [13], and EGRA [14]) may relax this limitation. In this case, the same hardware can be re-utilized but it would necessitate making a new design (corresponding to a new hardware configuration) for each desired security algorithm.

A more effective approach is to use a programmable security processor, whose hardware is designed to run different security algorithms at wire-speed, but only one of these algorithms is executed depending on the program loaded into the processor. In [15], a 5-stage pipeline processor – called CryptoAeg – is proposed, which uses a basic ALU in the execution stage, along with one or more parallel dedicated special ALUs, as required by the security algorithms to be implemented. Such special units are determined by the designer based on analysis of the particular algorithm to be supported. In [16], a processor architecture – called sRISC – is deduced by analyzing the data flow of both SMS4 (the Chinese Encryption Standard for local wireless networks) and AES, then combining an ALU with 4 parallel lookup tables in the execution stage, and proposing a 16-bit instruction set that uses a number of predefined functions implemented by ALU. Distinct lookup-tables are dedicated for each of the two algorithms, which include 4 parallel lookup tables and an instruction lookup-table. The authors claim that their 3-stage pipeline architecture gives low code density, low hardware cost and low power consumption. In both designs, the security processor architecture depends on the specific security algorithms to be implemented, and attempts to optimize the hardware by benefiting from simplifications and enhancements associated with the specific underlying operations such as XOR and SHIFT. A different design methodology is proposed in [17], where a security processor architecture is built using a "Main Controller" (that manages all processor functions), an "Instruction Register" (that holds sets of instructions corresponding to 4 security algorithms, namely; DES, AES, RSA, and ECC), a number of "Computing Units" (corresponding to basic operations performed in security algorithm computations, such as ADD, XOR, SHIFT, …, etc.), a number of "Register Files" (that hold data to be processed, keys to be deployed, and values of S-Boxes), and a shared bus that interconnects all of the previous components. While this processor architecture is basically independent of the security algorithm to be deployed, and hence is scalable and flexible, it is not very efficient since it uses the Von Neuman design, in which instructions are fetched from registers and results are returned back to registers.

In the next section, we shall introduce the basic concepts of a new security processor that improves on the design of [17] above, and which has been previously published in [18]. In Sect. 3, we formulate the design of the new security processor as an optimization problem. Section 4, presents the formulas for calculating the objective functions of the optimization problem, while Sect. 5 briefly describes the software used for simulating the new processor to deduce information necessary for objective function calculations. Results of solving the design problem using the genetic algorithm (NSGA-II) are presented in Sect. 6. Final remarks and conclusions are summarized in Sect. 7.

2   A New Programmable Security Processor

A novel security processor has been proposed in [19], which suggested a new architecture for a programmable processor having the following features:

1. It consists of a collection of Function Units (FUs) that are selected based on arithmetic operations actually deployed in security algorithms.
2. It distributes these FUs in multiple "Execution Regions" (ERs) to allow parallel execution of arithmetic operations.
3. It applies data-flow concepts [20], whereby results of one FU are fed directly into other FUs, without having to be cashed in a centralized storage (which is the case for the classical Von Neumann architecture). This eliminates the unnecessary time delay and centralized resources that would be needed otherwise.
4. It reads an assembly code written using "standardized" instruction format, which can be used to encode any security algorithm. This assures the flexibility of the processor, and its ability to run arbitrary security algorithms.
5. It applies randomization logic to randomly alter the order of execution of instructions, as well as to randomly select between several candidate internal signals competing for the same FU. This provides increased protection against side channel attacks.
6. It allows different regions to run at different clocks, thereby encouraging the placement of FUs (having similar speeds) in the same region. This relieves fast FUs from the need to run at slower speeds - waiting for other slower FUs – leading to further improvement in the processor performance.

The architecture of the newly proposed security processor is depicted in Fig. 1. It is shown to consist of: ONE Instruction Region (IR), a number of Execution Regions (ERs), and ONE Global Interconnection Network (GIN). In order to support multiple-clock operation, special interfaces should be inserted at the boundaries between IR → ER, ER → GIN, and GIN → ER. Such design would correspond to a Globally Asynchronous-Locally Synchronous (GALS) processor. In the current paper, we direct our attention to the case where all regions run at the same clock, which corresponds to a multi-region synchronous processor.

A number of relevant observations are in order:

a. In the IR, instructions are fetched by the Instruction Fetcher from the Instruction Cache taking into consideration: # of ERs (hence allowing up to 4 new instructions in the case of 4 ERs); and the readiness of each ER to receive a new instruction (hence the use of an Instruction Arbiter to make a clock-by-clock check and decision).
b. In the ER, each incoming instruction is directed to the appropriate FU using an Instruction Switch (IS). Meanwhile, each FU has an area for receiving incoming operands and storing operands with the same tag in the same buffer (such area is called Matched Input Buffer, MIB). Moreover, a Local Interconnection Network (LIN) in each ER decides whether results from an FU are to be rerouted inside this ER, or else sent to another ER through GIN.

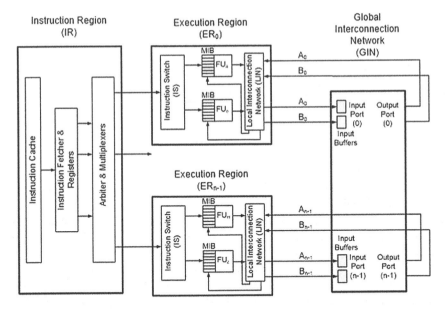

Fig. 1. Architecture of the newly proposed synchronous security processor [19]

c. In the GIN, incoming data is buffered at the input port before being forwarded to the appropriate ER via the appropriate output port.

3   The Synchronous Security Processor Optimization Problem

The design principles outlined in Sect. 2 do not give an answer to the following legitimate questions:

1. How many Execution Regions (ERs) should the security processor comprise in order to give an optimal performance? We shall use "n" to denote the number of ERs.
2. How to assign the various Function Units (FUs) among the ERs to get the optimal performance? We shall express the assignment of FUs to ERs as follows:

$$[\ FU_i(j), \text{ where } i \ = 1, 2, \ldots, 27, \ j\{1, 2, \ldots, n\} \ ]$$

and FU_i (j) designates the assignment of "FU_i" to region "j".(The set of FUs considered in the optimization problem are listed in Table 1 below.)

To answer the above questions, one should consider the following facts: The value of n determines the number of instructions fetched inside IR (and hence areas of Instruction Fetcher and Instruction Arbiter), the number of data and control buses

Table 1. Function Units (FUs) deployed in the synchronous security processor

FU₁	FU₂	FU₃	FU₄	FU₅	FU₆	FU₇	FU₈	FU₉
ADD	ADDMOD	AND	COMBINE 16	COMBINE 8	EXTRACT 16	EXTRACT 4	EXTRACT 8	GFMUL
FU₁₀	FU₁₁	FU₁₂	FU₁₃	FU₁₄	FU₁₅	FU₁₆	FU₁₇	FU₁₈
MUL	MULINV	MUX	NAND	OR	PUSHIMM	READREG	READSBOX	REPLICATE
FU₁₉	FU₂₀	FU₂₁	FU₂₂	FU₂₃	FU₂₄	FU₂₅	FU₂₆	FU₂₇
ROL	ROR	SHL	SHR	SUB	WRITEREG	WRITESBOX	XOR2	XOR3

between IR and ERs, and the number of ports and number of input buffers at GIN (and hence its area and power). On the other hand, the number of FUs inside an ER determines the number of ports of IS and the number of ports of LIN (and hence their area and power). Finally, the types of FUs inside an ER determines the corresponding region clock according to the slowest FU.

It follows that, for each value of n and for each assignment of FUs to ERs (corresponding to this n), one gets a corresponding: overall processor maximum clock and overall processor area. Moreover, for each security algorithm, there is an associated assembly code that invokes various FUs for certain time durations, in a certain sequence. In other words, the power (and energy) consumed, as well as the time delay for the algorithm execution are functions of the specific security algorithm under consideration, in addition to the dependency on the value of n and the assignment of FUs to ERs.

In view of the fact that the Advanced Encryption Standard (AES) is by far the most widely used algorithm for symmetric key encryption since its adoption in 2001 [21], it has been selected as the basis for the synchronous security processor optimization. More specifically, it is required to find:

$$n \text{ and } [FU_i(j), \text{ where } i = 1, 2, \ldots, 27, \ j \in \{1, 2, \ldots, n\}] \quad (1)$$

such that:

Processor Area is minimized
Processor Energy is minimized
Execution Delay is minimized
for the Advanced Encryption Standard (AES) in the encryption mode.

Equation (1) represents a multi-objective optimization problem which – in general – has no single unique solution. For such problems, there is a set of candidate solutions which form what is called a "Pareto Front" [22]. The evaluation of the objective functions for points in the huge combinatorial search space based on hardware implementations is a formidable and time consuming task. Therefore, we developed a software simulator that mimics the execution of instructions in the original data-flow processor, and used it to deduce energy and execution delay information. Moreover, the search inside the space of candidate points has to be carried out using an efficient optimization technique rather than by exhaustive search. The Non-dominated Sorting Genetic Algorithm Type 2 (NSGA-II) – which is a well-known evolutionary optimization algorithm [22] - has been adopted for that purpose.

Applying the above ideas, one can obtain the Pareto Front which still does not specify one single design as an answer. Therefore, we shall differentiate between the set of candidate solutions among the Pareto Front points based on the value of their metrics when executing AES Decryption, RC6 Encryption, RC6 Decryption, and SHA3 Hashing.

4 Objective Function Determination

The three metrics used as objective functions are determined – for each point in the search space – as follows:

$$\textbf{Total Area} = A_{IR}(n) + A_{GIN}(n) + \sum_{i=1}^{n} A_{IS}(f_i) + \sum_{i=1}^{n} A_{LIN}(f_i) + \sum_{j=1}^{f} A_{FU}(j) \qquad (2)$$

where n = number of ERs in the solution, f_i = number of FUs in region i. f = total number of FUs in processor (currently equal to 27), $A_{IR}(n)$ = area of IR as function of the number of regions in the design, $A_{GIN}(n)$ = area of GIN as function of the number of regions in the design, $A_{IS}(f_i)$ = area of IS in region i as function of the number of FUs inside this region, $A_{LIN}(f_i)$ = area of LIN in region i as function of the number of FUs inside this region, and $A_{FU}(j)$ = area of FU number j. The second metric is

$$\textbf{Total Energy} = \text{Total Power} \times D \qquad (3)$$

and

$$\text{Total Power} = P_{IR}(n) + P_{GIN}(n) + \sum_{i=1}^{n} P_{IS}(f_i) + \sum_{i=1}^{n} P_{LIN}(f_i) + \sum_{j=1}^{f} P_{FU}(j)$$

where P_{IR} = power consumed by IR, P_{GIN} = power consumed by GIN, $P_{IS}(f_i)$ = power consumed by IS in region i, as function of the number of FUs inside this region, $P_{LIN}(f_i)$ = power consumed by the LIN in region i, as function of the number of FUs inside this region, and $P_{FU}(j)$ = power consumed by FU number j.

The power consumed by each component can be obtained from the dynamic power and the static (idle) power consumed by the component, together with the busy and idle times for the component. Thus, any of the above power terms are obtained using the formula:

$$P = [(P_d * T_d) + (P_i * T_i)]]/D$$

where P_d = dynamic power of the component obtained from the power database, P_i = static power of the component obtained from the power database, T_d = busy time of the component, obtained from the simulator, T_i = idle time of the component, obtained from the simulator, and $D = T_d + T_i$ is the total delay between *Start* signal and *Done* signal.

As mentioned earlier, the usage times of each FU, as well as the usage time for IS, LIN, IR, and GIN depend on the specific assembly code used for the implementation of the particular security algorithm in use. Moreover, the only feasible way to determine such times is to actually execute the assembly code for the selected security algorithm and measure the associated times. This has been obtained from the Software Simulator for the Security Processor, which is described in Sect. 5. Finally, the third metric is

$$\textbf{Execution Delay} = D \tag{4}$$

where D is obtained from the Software Simulator according to formula:
# of IR Clocks to execute assembly code x Period of IR Clock

5 Software Simulator for Security Processor

The software simulator for the security processor was developed using C#, in order to meet the following requirements:

(a) GUI that allows user to specify # of ERs (n), specify the clock for each ER, assign each FU to any ER, specify size of MIB for each FU, and specify mode of operation for security processor (deterministic or random).
(b) Reading assembly code for the selected security algorithm
(c) Reading key and input message (plain or ciphered)
(d) Reading S-Box
(e) Executing assembly code and saving results in a .txt file
(f) Calculating simulation parameters, including execution delay and percentage utilization for IR, each FU, IS of each ER, LIN of each ER, and GIN.

In order to facilitate the integration of the software simulator for the security processor with NSGA-II optimization software, a special version of the code has been developed which accepts input files that specify assembly code for security algorithm, input message (plain or cipher), input key, and S-Box (if any), # of regions, assignment of FUs to regions, clock of each region, size of MIB, and mode of operation.

Upon the execution of the assembly code, the special version of the software simulator produces time delay and percentage utilization for various modules.

6 Optimal Design for the Synchronous Security Processor

The Assembly code for the AES Encryption security algorithm was selected as the basis for the optimization of the synchronous security processor architecture. For each configuration (i.e. selected point in the search space with corresponding # of regions "n", and assignment of FUs to these "n" regions), the software simulator is run and "Total Delay Time" is determined, as well as "Percentage Utilization" of components. The selected configuration also determines – in conjunction with the database for the areas of the various processor modules - the "Total Area" for such configuration. In addition, the selected configuration – in conjunction with the database for the powers of the various processor modules and by using the "Percentage Utilization" information – determines the "Total Energy". This process is repeated for all points in the search space corresponding to members of the population at the current generation of the evolutionary optimization algorithm NSGA-II. The following parameters have been chosen for deducing the optimal design of the synchronous security processor:

– Population = 100
– # of Generations = 200
– Initial Population = Chosen randomly in the search space.

Other assumptions invoked in the optimization are:

– All logical FUs (namely; AND, NAND, and OR) are placed in the same region.
– All memory-related FUs (namely; READREG, WRITREG, and READSBOX) are placed in the same region
– All versions of the COMBINE FU (namely; COMBINE8 and COMBINE16) are consolidated together
– All version of the EXTRACT FU (namely; EXTRACT4, EXTRACT8, and EXTRACT16) are consolidated together.

The above assumptions were inspired by hardware implementation considerations. Moreover, in order to have realistic database for area and power calculations, HDL codes for each of the FUs were synthesized using 130 nm technology.

As mentioned earlier, a special version of the simulator code was developed so that the modified NSGA-II code would call the software simulator for each point in the search space, use the outputs from the software simulator to compute the three objective functions of such point, then utilize these data to determine the best points for the current generation of the evolutionary algorithm. The results for the 200 generations were obtained, and Figs. 2 and 3 summarize the optimization results.

We observe the following:

– Initially (at Generation # 1), values for area, delay and energy were spread over wide ranges (6.7–8.0 mm^2 for area, 10.0–22.5 μs for delay, and 9.0–18.0 μJ for energy). As the optimization progressed (at Generation # 200), these ranges reduced to 6.7–7.3 mm^2 for area, 9.5–13.0 μs for delay, and 8.5–11.0 μJ for energy.
– Initially (at Generation # 1), members of the population had configurations that were spread over many regions (n = 3, 4, 5, 6, 7, 8, 9, 10). As the optimization progressed, the configurations clustered at four values of n: n = 4 (for minimum delay), n = 7 (for minimum area and minimum energy), and n = 5, and 6 (for points on the Pareto Front that are not at minimum area nor minimum delay nor minimum energy, but still they are not dominated by other points in the search space).

Note that each point in Fig. 3 gives the values of two objective functions for one solution on the obtained Pareto front. Solutions that appear to be dominated in these figures are in fact non-dominated if we consider the third objective function.

To reduce the set of candidate solutions for the optimal synchronous security processor, we proceeded as follows:

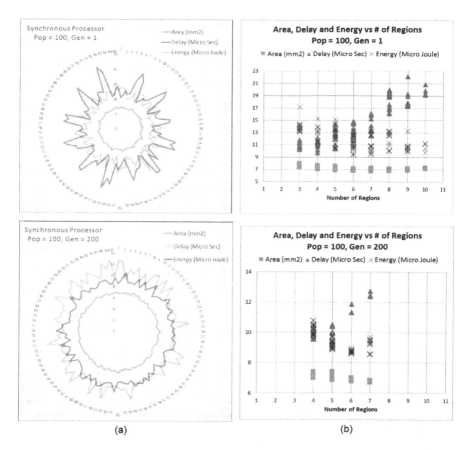

Fig. 2. Results of the synchronous security processor design optimization for initial generation and generation #200 of the NSGA-II algorithm: (a) Objective functions for each member of the 100 population, (b) Clustering of the 100 population based on # of regions "n".

1. Set of points with minimum area + set of points with minimum delay + set of points with minimum energy were identified.

2. Repeated members of the set were removed. This led to 6 distinct points in the search space (Candidate 1 to Candidate 6). As shown in Table 2, Candidates 1, 2 and 3 have minimum area, Candidates 4 and 5 have minimum delay, and Candidate 6 has minimum energy. These candidates have, respectively 7 regions, 4 regions, and 7 regions. The assignment of the FUs for each of these candidates are shown in Table 3.

3. To further differentiate between these 6 candidates, 4 other security algorithms have been implemented using these specific configurations (i.e. we have fixed the # of regions and FUs assignment to regions according to optimized AES Encryption algorithm). These algorithms are: AES Decryption, RC6 Encryption, RC6 Decryption, and SHA-3 Hashing. The resulting objective functions for each candidate and for the 4 additional security algorithms are shown to the right of Table 2. (Note that processor area is independent of the executed algorithm).

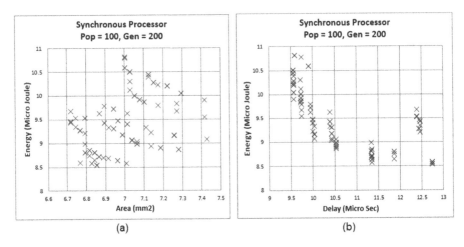

Fig. 3. Objective function values for generation #200 of the NSGA-II algorithm :(a) Distribution of energy as function of area (b) Distribution of energy as function of delay.

Table 2. Area, delay and energy values for the 6 candidate solutions.

Security Algorithm	AES Encryption			# of Regions		AES Decryption		RC6 Encryption		RC6 Decryption		SHA3 Hashing	
Objective Function	Area	Delay	Energy			Delay	Energy	Delay	Energy	Delay	Energy	Delay	Energy
	mm2	Micro Sec	Micro Joule			Micro Sec	Micro Joule	Micro Sec	Micro Joule	Micro Sec	Micro Joule	Micro Sec	Micro Joule
Candidate 1	6.7205	12.3890	9.6782	7	Min Area	14.742000	10.908170	8.073000	5.424328	8.749000	6.394790	41.379000	24.763410
Candidate 2	6.7205	12.4540	9.4673	7		14.729000	9.778723	8.515000	5.803341	9.347000	6.846887	40.859000	26.002300
Candidate 3	6.7205	12.4670	9.4339	7		14.729000	10.861750	8.541000	5.815966	9.542000	6.923053	40.859000	25.472960
Candidate 4	7.0297	9.5490	10.5034	4	Min Delay	11.853000	12.173380	5.427000	5.334890	5.841000	6.132699	38.889000	36.882750
Candidate 5	7.1265	9.5490	10.4476	4		11.853000	12.267640	5.247000	5.083223	5.670000	6.080751	38.259000	36.553450
Candidate 6	6.8533	12.7400	8.5430	7	Min Energy	16.081000	10.734830	8.229000	5.497724	8.333000	6.060592	54.821000	36.191670

Table 3. Assignment of FUs to various regions for the 6 candidate points in the search space.

	ADD	ADDMOD	AND	COMBINE 16	COMBINE8	EXTRACT 16	EXTRACT4	EXTRACT8	GFMUL	MUL	MULINV	MUX	NAND	OR	PUSHIMM	READREG	READSBOX	REPLICATE	ROL	ROR	SHL	SHR	SUB	WRITEREG	WRITESBOX	XOR2	XOR3
Candidate 1	3	4	4	0	0	6	6	6	3	0	0	4	4	5	5	2	1	1	2	5	6	5	1	3
Candidate 2	5	4	5	2	2	2	2	2	3	0	1	3	5	5	1	6	6	2	3	4	5	1	4	6	6	0	0
Candidate 3	3	5	3	0	0	2	2	2	6	4	4	0	3	3	4	5	5	2	0	6	2	3	6	5	5	1	1
Candidate 4	0	3	2	1	1	2	2	2	2	0	2	3	2	2	0	3	3	1	2	0	3	1	2	3	3	1	0
Candidate 5	0	3	2	1	1	2	2	2	2	0	2	3	2	2	0	3	3	1	0	0	2	2	2	3	3	1	0
Candidate 6	1	4	2	2	2	4	4	4	5	1	6	2	2	2	5	3	3	3	6	6	6	2	4	3	3	3	0

4. Inspection of the performance of the six candidates reveals that:

   – Candidates 1, 2 and 3 – while displaying minimum area for AES Encryption – behave differently in different algorithms. In particular, Candidate1 scores well in AES Encryption (Delay), RC6 Encryption (Delay and Energy), RC6 Decryption (Energy), and SHA-3 (Energy). Candidate 2 comes second by scoring well in AES Decryption (Delay and Energy), RC6 Decryption (Delay), and SHA-3 (Delay). Candidate 3 comes in third place by scoring well in AES Encryption (Energy), AES Decryption (Delay), and SHA-3 (Delay).
   – Candidates 4 and 5 exhibit lowest delays among all 6 Candidates for AES Encryption. However, it turns out that Candidate 5 outperforms Candidate 4 in RC6 Encryption (Delay and Energy), RC6 Decryption (Delay and Energy), and SHA-3 (Delay and Energy). Only for AES Encryption does Candidate 4 outperforms Candidate 5.
   – Candidate 6 exhibits lowest energy among all 6 Candidates for AES Encryption. This distinction in energy performance – compared to all other 5 candidates – continues to hold for AES Decryption and RC Decryption.

As expected in typical multi-objective optimization problems, no single solution would behave well for all performance measures. Nonetheless, we managed to narrow the alternatives to very few candidates by giving preference to the commonly used AES algorithm, and then differentiating among candidates having the same metric in AES Encryption, by comparing their performance when using other algorithms. Under the assumptions specified earlier, one concludes that for the synchronous security processor Candidate 1 (with 7 ERs) is to be used if area is of prime concern, Candidate 5 (with 4 ERs) is to be used to minimize delay, while Candidate 6 (with 5 ERs) is best for minimum energy.

7   Concluding Remarks

In this work, a systematic procedure has been developed to deduce the optimal architecture for a newly proposed programmable security processor, which is based on a data-flow architecture and exploits the parallelism resulting from the use of multiple execution regions (ERs) that host different function units (FUs). The processor design is formulated as a combinatorial grouping problem, and the genetic algorithm (NSGA-II) was used to efficiently search the design space. To facilitate the determination of the objective function at each candidate solution, a powerful simulator has been developed, and a comprehensive database for area, delay, and power was compiled based on ASIC 130 nm technology. The study showed that when all regions operate at the same clock (i.e. synchronous mode), the optimum processor would map 27 FUs into 4 ERs (for minimum delay), and it would map these FUs into 5 ERs (for minimum energy), while mapping these FUs into 7 ERs would give minimum area. As a follow-up to the current study, and realizing that the processor performance can benefit from the fact that some FUs may operate faster than others, thereby allowing some ERs to run at faster clocks, it would be interesting to investigate the optimal processor design when each region is allowed to run at the fastest clock it can support.

.

This corresponds to an asynchronous security processor, whose optimal design involves an additional dimension in the design space.

Acknowledgements. This work has been funded by the National Telecommunication Regulatory Authority (NTRA) of Egypt.

References

1. Stallings, W.: Cryptography and Network Security: Principles and Practice, 6th edn. Prentice-Hall, Boston (2013)
2. Keating, G.: Performance analysis of AES candidates on the 6805 CPU core. In: Proceedings of the Second AES Candidate Conference, Rome, Italy, pp. 109–114 (1999)
3. Woodbury, A.D., Bailey, D.V., Paar, C.: Elliptic curve cryptography on smart cards without coprocessors. In: Domingo-Ferrer, J., Chan, D., Watson, A. (eds.) Proceedings of the Fourth Working Conference on Smart Card Research and Advanced Applications, pp. 71–92. Springer, Heidelberg (2001)
4. Bertoni, G., Breveglieri, L., Fragneto, P., Macchetti, M., Marchesin, S.: Efficient software implementation of AES on 32-bit platforms. In: Kaliski Jr., Burton S., Koç, Çetin Kaya, Paar, Christof (eds.) CHES 2002. LNCS, vol. 2523. Springer, Heidelberg (2003)
5. Atasu, K., Breveglieri, L., Macchetti, M.: Efficient AES implementations for ARM based platforms. In: Proceedings of the 2004 ACM Symposium on Applied Computing, SAC 2004, Cyprus, pp. 841–845 (2004)
6. Tillich, S., Großschädl, J.: Instruction set extensions for efficient AES implementation on 32-bit processors. In: Goubin, L., Matsui, M. (eds.) CHES 2006. LNCS, vol. 4249, pp. 270–284. Springer, Heidelberg (2006)
7. Drutarovsky, M., Varchola, M.: Cryptographic system on a chip based on ACTEL ARM7 soft-core with embedded true random number generator. Design and Diagnostics of Electronic Circuits and Systems, 1–6 (2008)
8. Verbauwhede, I., Schaumont, P., Kuo, H.: Design and performance testing of a 2.29-GB/s rijndael processor. IEEE J. Solid-State Circ. **38**(3), 569–572 (2003)
9. Hämäläinen, P., Alho, T., Hännikäinen, M., Hämäläinen, T.D.: Design and implementation of low-area and low-power AES encryption hardware core. In: 9th EUROMICRO Conference on Digital System Design: Architectures, Methods and Tools, DSD 2006, pp. 577–583 (2006)
10. Elbirt, A.J., Yip, W., Chetwynd, B., Paar, C.: An FPGA implementation and performance evaluation of the AES block cipher candidate algorithm finalists. In: The Third Advance Encryption Standard (AES3) Candidate Conference, New York, USA, April 13–14, 2000
11. Purnaprajna, M., Puttmann, C., Porrmann, M.: Power aware reconfigurable multiprocessor for elliptic curve cryptography. In: Proceedings of the Conference on Design, Automation and Test in Europe (DATE 2008), pp. 1462–1467. Munich, Germany (2008)
12. Hamalainen, P., Heikkinen, J., Hannikainen, M., Hamalainen, T.D.: Design of transport triggered architecture processors for wireless encryption. In: Proceedings of the 8th Euromicro Conference on Digital System Design, Washington, DC, USA, pp. 144–152 (2005)
13. Mei, B., Lambrechts, A., Mignolet, J.-Y., Verkest, D., Lauwereins, R.: Architecture exploration for a reconfigurable architecture template. IEEE Des. Test Comput. **22**(2), 90–101 (2005)

14. Ansaloni, G., Bonzini, P., Pozzi, L.: EGRA: A coarse grained reconfigurable architectural template. IEEE Trans. VLSI **19**(6), 1062–1074 (2011)
15. Lu, R., Han, J., Zeng, X.: A low-cost cryptographic processor for security embedded system. In: Asia and South Pacific Design Automation Conference (ASPDAC), Seoul, South Korea, 21-24 January, pp. 113-114 (2008)
16. Han, L., Han, J., Zeng, X., Lu, R., Zhao, J.: A programmable security processor for cryptography algorithms. In: 9th International Conference on Solid-State and Integrated-Circuit Technology, ICSICT 2008, 20–23 October 2008, pp. 2144–2147 (2008)
17. Li, C., Jiang, Y., Su, D., Xu, Y., Luo, Z.: A new design of low cost security coprocessor for portable electronic devices. In: 2010 International Conference on Communications and Mobile Computing, (CMC), 12–14 April (2010)
18. Farouk, H., El-Hadidi, M.T., Abou El Farag, A.: GALS-based LPSP: Implementation of a novel architecture for low power high performance security processors. In: 25th IEEE International Parallel and Distributed Processing Symposium, Anchorage (USA), May 16–20 (2011)
19. Farouk, H.: Design and Implementation of a Novel Low-Power Security Processor, Ph. D. Thesis, submitted to Department of Electronics and Electrical Communication Engineering, Cairo University (2011)
20. Corporaal, H.: Design of transport triggered architectures. In: Proceedings of the Fourth Great Lakes Symposium on Design Automation of High Performance VLSI Systems. GLSV (1994)
21. Advanced Encryption Standard (AES), November 2001, Fed. Inf. Process. Standards Pub (2001)
22. Deb, K., Pratap, A., Agarwal, S., Meyarivan, T.: A fast and elitist multi-objective genetic algorithm: NSGA-II. IEEE Trans. Evol. Comput. **6**(2), 182–197 (2002)

On Zero Knowledge Argument with PQT Soundness

Guifang Huang[1,2(✉)] and Hongda Li[1,2]

[1] State Key Laboratory of Information Security,
Institute of Information Engineering, Chinese Academy of Sciences,
Beijing 100093, People's Republic of China
[2] Data Assurance and Communication Security Center,
Institute of Information Engineering, Chinese Academy of Sciences,
Beijing 100093, People's Republic of China
{huangguifang,lihongda}@iie.ac.cn

Abstract. Loosely speaking, an interactive argument is said to be *zero knowledge* if the view of every "efficient" verifier can be "efficiently" simulated. Recently, Pass relaxed the "efficient" adversaries and the simulator to be probabilistic quasi-polynomial time ($\mathcal{PQT}$)) machines and proposed such a relaxed zero knowledge argument with computational soundness. In this paper, we present a relaxed zero knowledge protocol which achieves $\mathcal{PQT}$ soundness, instead of computational soundness. Also, it can be regarded as a stand-alone version of PMV scheme, with the difference that it is 5-round while PMV scheme is 6-round in the stand-alone setting. In addition, the simulation way determines that it is secure against $\mathcal{PPT}$ resettable-soundness attackers.

Keywords: Zero knowledge · Σ-protocol · $\mathcal{PQT}$-soundness

1 Introduction

Zero knowledge (ZK) proof, brought out by Goldwasser, Micali and Rackoff [13], is a two-party protocol where prover convinces verifier the validity of a statement without revealing any *additional* knowledge. In the past three decades, ZK proof attracted much attention and many interesting results had been worked out. For example, it was shown that every language in $\mathcal{NP}$ has a ZK proof [14], which plays a fundamental role for applications of ZK proofs. Now, ZK proof has been an important tool in design of cryptographic protocols, and can be widely used in identification [9], multi-party secure computation [11,12], e-voting [7], etc.

Since its invention, the composition of ZK proofs has always been popular for many years. Resettable composition is such a case. In [3], Canetti et al. considered the security of ZK proof under resettable attacks and gave a resettable

---

Supported by NSFC under grant No. 61003276 and the Strategic Priority Program of Chinese Academy of Sciences (Grant No. XDA06010702).

H. Kim and D. Choi (Eds.): WISA 2015, LNCS 9503, pp. 326–335, 2016.
DOI: 10.1007/978-3-319-31875-2_27

ZK construction. Later, resettable soundness was defined and some resettable-soundness schemes were brought out [1,5,15]. It is believed that constructing efficient ZK protocols with resettable-soundness property would be very meaningful for applications of ZK proofs.

Originally, the definition of ZK is formalized in simulation paradigm. The intuition behind it is that what an *efficient* verifier V^* gets from the real interaction can be simulated by an *efficient* simulator S. As "efficient" adversaries are normally modeled as probabilistic polynomial time ($\mathcal{PPT}$) machines, in the classical definition of ZK, both the verifier and the simulator are $\mathcal{PPT}$ machines. Later, to overcome some limitations of ZK proof [2,16,17], Pass relaxed the definition by modeling the efficient verifier and simulator as probabilistic quasi-polynomial time ($\mathcal{PQT}$) machines [18].

The relaxed ZK property requires that the view of every malicious $\mathcal{PQT}$ verifier can be simulated by a $\mathcal{PQT}$ simulator. In [18], an efficient 4-round perfect relaxed ZK argument was presented (Pass scheme). It was computationally sound and secure under concurrent attacks. There the simulator performed its simulation in a straight-line way, by running an exhaustive search in $n^{poly(logn)}$ time to get a fake witness. However, the existence of such a simulator makes the $\mathcal{PQT}$ soundness property impossible. In [19], a relaxed concurrent zero knowledge argument was proposed (called PMV scheme). It has the soundness property w.r.t $\mathcal{PQT}$ adversarial prover. In order to guarantee the security in the concurrent setting [6], 3 slots are performed to provide enough chances for the simulator to rewind successfully. In the stand-alone setting, PMV scheme contains only 1 slot and is 6-round.

Our Results. In this paper, we aims at constructing a round-efficient relaxed ZK argument with $\mathcal{PQT}$ soundness in the stand-alone setting, instead of computational soundness in the concurrent setting. Our new scheme can be viewed as a stand-alone version of PMV scheme, with the higher round-efficiency. Specifically, the stand-alone version of PMV scheme is 6-round, while our new scheme is 5-round. In addition, the simulation way determines that our construction is also secure against $\mathcal{PPT}$ resettable-soundness attackers.

The new scheme is constructed in the FLS paradigm [8]. The intuition behind it is quite simple: At first, the verifier takes a Σ-protocol to proves that he knows the knowledge of a pre-image of v under g generated by himself or the message d committed in c by the prover. Then, the prover proves the knowledge of $x \in L$ or the pre-image of v. Such a construction is PQT sound and can be simulated by rewinding technique in expected polynomial time. However, the simulation way relying on rewinding techniques makes the scheme insecure against $\mathcal{PPT}$ resettable-soundness attacker. Then we modify it in the following way: instead of proving the knowledge of $x \in L$ or the pre-image of v, the prover proves that $x \in L$ or some part of pre-image of v is actually the image of q under one-way permutation f. On the whole, the simulator works in a combined way: Firstly, he extracts the pre-image of v by rewinding technique, then takes an exhaustive search to get q from some part of pre-image of v. At last, he proves his knowledge about (x, v, q) using the fake witness he obtained above.

It is organized as follows. In Sect. 2, some related notions and definitions are given. In Sect. 3 the 5-round relaxed zero knowledge argument is presented and the security proof is given in Sect. 4.

2   Preliminaries

If A is a probabilistic algorithm, then $y \leftarrow A(x_1, x_2, \ldots)$ denotes an experiment of choosing r randomly and y is the result of $A(x_1, x_2, \ldots; r)$. If S is a finite set, let $\alpha \leftarrow S$ be the process of choosing an element α uniformly from S. Let $s_1 \circ s_2$ denote the concatenation of s_1 and s_2.

A function $f(n)$ is called $\mathcal{C}$-negligible, if for every $T(n) \in \mathcal{C}$, there exists a positive integer N such that for all $n \geq N$, we have $f(n) \leq 1/T(n)$. Here $\mathcal{C}$ denotes some classes of functions.

In this paper, it is assumed that the reader is familiar with the notion of resettable-soundness [1].

Definition 1 *(one-way function secure against sub-exponential circuits [18]).* $f : \{0,1\}^\star \to \{0,1\}^\star$ *is called one-way function secure against 2^{n^k} adversary, if the following conditions hold:*

(1) $f(x)$ is computable in polynomial time.
(2) For any probabilistic algorithm B with running time 2^{n^k}, all sufficiently large n, every auxiliary input $z \in \{0,1\}^\star$, we have

$$Pr[B\left(f\left(U_n\right), z\right) \in f^{-1}\left(f(U_n)\right] < 2^{-n^k},$$

where U_n is a random variable uniformly distributed in $\{0,1\}^n$.

f is called one-way function secure against sub-exponential circuits iff there exists a constant k ($0 < k < 1$) such that f is secure against 2^{n^k} adversary.

2.1   Interactive Proof and Proof of Knowledge

Given a pair of interactive Turing machine P and V, we denote $< P(w), V(z) > (x)$ the random variable representing the view of V on auxiliary input z, when interacting with P on common input x and auxiliary input w.

Definition 2 *($T(\cdot)$-sound Interactive Argument [19]).* A pair of interactive machine (P, V) is called $T(\cdot)$-sound interactive argument for language L with relation R if V is a $\mathcal{PPT}$ machine and the following conditions hold:*

- *Completeness: For every $x \in L$ and $w \in R(x)$, $Pr[< P(w), V > (x) = 1] = 1$.*
- *Soundness: For $x \notin L$, and every $T(n)$-bounded machine B, $Pr[< B, V > (x) = 1] \leq \frac{1}{T(|x|)}$.*

(P, V) is a $\mathcal{C}$ sound interactive argument if for all $T(\cdot) \in \mathcal{C}$ it is $T(\cdot)$-sound.

Definition 3 *(Argument of knowledge w.r.t C). Let R be a binary relation, probabilistic polynomial time machine V is called knowledge verifier w.r.t C for language L with relation R, if the following conditions hold:*

(1) (non-triviality) There exists a machine P with running time $\overset{\bullet}{C}$, such that for every $(x, y) \in R$ all possible interactions of P with V on common input x and auxiliary input y are accepting.

(2) (knowledge soundness w.r.t C) There exists a probabilistic oracle machine K satisfying the following condition: For every P^* running in time $T(\cdot) \in C$ and every $x, y, r \in \{0, 1\}^*$, Let $p(x, y, r)$ be the probability that $P^*_{x,y,r}$ convinces V. If $p(x, y, r) > u(|x|)$ where $u(|x|)$ is a C-negligible function, then K outputs $s \in R(x)$ with probability at least $(1 - u(|x|))$ in $poly(T(n))$ time.

If V is a knowledge verifier w.r.t C for language L with relation R and P is a machine satisfying non-triviality condition, (P, V) is called an argument of knowledge w.r.t C for language L, and K is called knowledge extractor.

2.2   Zero Knowledge and Witness Indistinguishability

Definition 4 *(Strong $T(\cdot)$ Indistinguishability). Let X and Y be countable sets. Two ensembles $\{A_{x,y}\}_{x \in X, y \in Y}$ and $\{B_{x,y}\}_{x \in X, y \in Y}$ are said to be indistinguishable in time $T(\cdot)$ over $x \in X$, if for every probabilistic distinguisher D with running time $T(\cdot)$ in its first input, and every $x \in X, y \in Y$, it holds that*

$$|Pr[a \leftarrow A_{x,y} : D(x, y, a) = 1] - Pr[b \leftarrow B_{x,y} : D(x, y, b) = 1]| < \frac{1}{poly(T(|x|))}.$$

Two ensembles $\{A_{x,y}\}_{x \in X, y \in Y}$ and $\{B_{x,y}\}_{x \in X, y \in Y}$ are said to be strongly indistinguishable w.r.t C over $x \in X$ if they are strong $T(\cdot)$-indistinguishable for every function $T(\cdot) \in C$.

Strongly $T(n)$-simulatable argument is in fact zero knowledge in *on-line/off-line* model, where parties would be modeled as polynomial-time machines during on-line communication, while $T(n)$-time machines when off-line. For simplicity of expression, in this paper we call strongly $T(n)$-simulatable argument *zero knowledge* argument without distinguishing it from the classical definition of zero knowledge.

Definition 5 *(Zero Knowledge). A $T(n)$-sound interactive argument (P, V) for language $L \in NP$ with witness relation R is said to be strongly $T(n)$-simulatable, if for every $T(\cdot)$-time malicious verifier V^*, there exists a probabilistic machine S with running time $T(\cdot)$, such that for every $x \in L$, every $w \in R(x)$ and $z \in \{0, 1\}^*$, the following two ensembles are strongly $T(\cdot)$-indistinguishable*

(a) $\{< P(w), V(z) > (x)\}_{x \in L, w \in R(x), z \in \{0,1\}^*}$
(b) $\{S(x, z)\}_{x \in L, z \in \{0,1\}^*}$

If for every $T(\cdot) \in C$, (P, V) is strongly $T(n)$-simulatable with $T(n)$-soundness, then we call (P, V) is strongly C-simulatable argument with C-soundness.

Definition 6 (Witness Strong Indistinguishability w.r.t C ([10]). *Let (P, V) be an interactive proof system for language $L \in NP$ with witness relation R. We say that $< P, V >$ is witness strongly indistinguishable w.r.t C, if for every probabilistic machine $V^\star$ with running time $T(\cdot) \in C$, for every two sequences $\{w_x^1\}_{x \in L}$ and $\{w_x^2\}_{x \in L}$ such that $w_x^1, w_x^2 \in R(x)$, the ensembles $\{< P(w_x^1), V^\star(z) >\}_{x \in L, z \in \{0,1\}^*}$ and $\{< P(w_x^2), V^\star(z) >\}_{x \in L, z \in \{0,1\}^*}$ are strongly indistinguishable w.r.t C over $x \in L$.*

2.3 Other Primitives

We recall other primitives which will be used in our construction.

Commitment Scheme: A commitment scheme is a two-party interactive protocol consisting of two phases. In commitment phase, S commits to m and sends the commitment c to receiver R; In reveal phase, S reveals the value m along with the random coins used and R checks the validity of the de-commitment. The commitment scheme is required to satisfy the following properties:

(a) *Hiding*: Commitments to different values are computational indistinguishable; Furthermore, if commitments to different values are identically distributed, it is called perfect hiding property;

(b) *Binding*: Once having sent the commitment c to message m, except for negligible probability, any $\mathcal{PPT}$ S^* cannot reveal c as a different value $m' \neq m$. If for $m' \neq m$, the two sets $Com(m)$ and $Com(m')$ are disjoint, it is called perfect binding property, where $Com(m)$ and $Com(m')$ are sets of all possible commitments to m and m' respectively.

From [12], non-interactive commitment scheme with computational hiding property can be constructed from one-way permutation. If the one-way permutation is secure w.r.t $(\omega(\mathcal{PQT}))$, we can get a non-interactive commitment scheme with $\mathcal{PQT}$-hiding property. Also, a perfect hiding commitment can be constructed using claw-free permutation [12]. The scheme is computationally binding. In fact, if we require the claw-free permutation to be secure w.r.t $(\omega(\mathcal{PQT}))$, a 2-round perfect hiding commitment with $\mathcal{PQT}$-binding property is obtained.

Σ-Protocol ([4]): Σ-protocol for language $L \in \mathcal{NP}$ with relation R is a special witness indistinguishable proof (argument) of knowledge with the following conditions:

(a) (special soundness) For common input x, from any pair of accepting transcripts (a, e, z) and (a, e', z') where $e \neq e'$, one can efficiently compute w such that $(x, w) \in R$;

(b) (special honest-verifier computational zero knowledge) There exists a simulator M such that on input x and the challenge e, M can output a transcript which is computational indistinguishable from the real one.

From the zero knowledge protocol for Hamiltonian Cycle (HC) problem, we can get a Σ-protocol for every language in NP with $\frac{1}{n^{poly(\log n)}}$ knowledge error by independently parallel executing the HC protocol enough times.

(a) In HC protocol, if using a non-interactive $\mathcal{PQT}$-hiding commitment, we get a 3-round Σ-protocol with the witness strong indistinguishability w.r.t $\mathcal{PQT}$. Such a Σ-protocol is based on the existence of one-way permutation secure w.r.t $(\omega(\mathcal{PQT}))$.

(b) If the commitment scheme in HC protocol satisfies perfectly-hiding and $\mathcal{PQT}$-binding properties, the resulting Σ-protocol is a 4-round argument of knowledge w.r.t $\mathcal{PQT}$ with the special honest-verifier perfect zero knowledge property. Such a Σ-protocol is in turn based on the assumption of claw-free permutation secure against $(\omega(\mathcal{PQT}))$ adversary.

3   Zero Knowledge with $\mathcal{PQT}$ Soundness

In this section, we present the 5-round construction then give its proof security. The following tools will be used in the construction:

(1) Let $f : \{0,1\}^\star \to \{0,1\}^\star$ be a one-way permutation secure against 2^{n^k} adversary, where k is a constant $(0 < k < 1)$. Let g be a one-way function secure against $\omega(\mathcal{PQT})$.

(2) Suppose $Com(\cdot)$ be a $\mathcal{PQT}$-hiding commitment.

(3) The Languages are respectively defined as follows:
   a. $L_0 = \{(v,q) : \exists(s_1,s_2), s.t. v = g(s_1 \circ s_2) \wedge q = f^{-1}(s_2)\}$
   b. $L_1 = \{c : \exists r, d, s.t. c = Com(r,d)\} \vee \{v : \exists(s_1,s_2), s.t. v = g(s_1 \circ s_2)\}$
   c. $L_2 = L \vee L_0$

(4) Σ_1 and Σ_2 are two Σ-protocols to prove knowledge of L_1 and L_2 respectively. Here Σ_1 is witness strongly indistinguishable w.r.t $\mathcal{PQT}$ and Σ_2 is an argument of knowledge w.r.t $\mathcal{PQT}$ with the special honest-verifier perfect zero knowledge property.

Construction of Protocol Π:
Common Input: $x \in L$, where the length of x is n.
Auxiliary Input of Prover P: $y \in R(x)$.

(P1): P commits to a random string d and sends $c = Com(d)$ to V;

(V1): V randomly picks $s = s_1 \circ s_2 \in \{0,1\}^\star$ and computes $v = g(s)$. At the same time, he generates the first message a_1 of Σ_1 to prove that he knows the knowledge of $(c,v) \in L_1$. In addition, V generates the first message t of Σ_2. He sends (v, a_1, t) to prover.

(P2): P produces a random challenge e_1 to a_1 and a random string $q \in \{0,1\}^{(\log n)^m}$, where $m = 1 + \frac{1}{k}$. Also, he computes the second message a_2 of Σ_2 to prove $(x,v,q) \in L_2$. At last, he sends (e_1, a_2, q) to verifier;

(V2): V computes z_1 to answer challenge e_1 and produces a challenge e_2 to message a_2. At last, he sends (z_1, e_2) to P;

(P3): If (a_1, e_1, z_1) is an accepting conversation of statement $(c,v) \in L_1$, P produces z_2 and sends it to V; Otherwise, P aborts;

(V3): If (t, a_2, e_2, z_2) is an accepting conversation of statement $(x,v,q) \in L_2$, V outputs 1. Otherwise, he outputs 0.

4   Proof of Security

In this section, we give the proof of security of the above construction.

Lemma 1. *Protocol Π is an argument with $\mathcal{PQT}$-soundness property.*

Proof. Firstly, honest prover P cannot get any information about s from Σ_1. Therefore, if P succeeds in convincing V, what he proves is indeed $x \in L$. This implies the *correctness* of protocol Π.

Completeness of protocol Π comes from completeness of Σ_1 and $\Sigma 2$ for statement $(c, v) \in L_1$ and $(x, v, q) \in L_2$ respectively. For $x \in L$, P can use $y \in R(x)$ to prove $(x, v, q) \in L_3$ correctly.

Next we prove *the knowledge-soundness property* w.r.t $\mathcal{PQT}$. For any $\mathcal{PQT}$ machine $P^\star$ satisfying $p = Pr[< P^\star, V > (x) = 1] > \frac{1}{n^{poly(logn)}}$, by the knowledge soundness property of Σ_2, there exists a $\mathcal{PQT}$ oracle machine K which extracts a witness for statement $x \in L \vee (v, q) \in L_0$ with probability at least $1 - u(|x|)$, where $u(|x|)$ is a $n^{poly(logn)}$-negligible function. For the accepting transcript $(c, v, a_1, t, e_1, q, a_2, z_1, e_2, z_2)$ generated by $P^\star$ interacting with V, assume the probability that what K outputs is a witness of $(v, q) \in L_0$ is at least $\frac{1}{n^{poly(logn)}}$. Therefore there must be at least $\frac{1}{n^{poly(logn)}}$ fraction of (c, v) satisfying that K extracts the witnesses of $(v, q) \in L_0$ from the transcripts containing (c, v). For these (c, v), a malicious verifier $V^{\star\star}$ can be constructed to break the witness-indistinguishability of Σ_1 for $(c, v) \in L_1$.

Algorithm $V^{\star\star}$ works as follows: On input (c, v) and auxiliary input x, $V^{\star\star}$ interacts with the honest prover of Σ_1 externally for statement $(c, v \in L_1)$, and runs $P^\star$ and K internally for statement $x \in L \vee (v, q) \in L_0$.

(1) When receiving the message a_1, $V^{\star\star}$ forwards it to $P^\star$.
(2) $V^{\star\star}$ generates v, t in the same way as an honest verifier of protocol Π in step (P1) and forwards them to $P^\star$.
(3) Upon seeing (e_1, q, a_2) generated by $P^\star$, $V^{\star\star}$ sends e_1 to the honest prover of Σ_1.
(4) When receiving z_1 from outside, $V^{\star\star}$ forwards it to $P^\star$. At the same time, he generates a random challenge e_2 and sends to $P^\star$.
(5) Upon seeing z_2 from $P^\star$, he runs K to extract a witness w of $(x, v, q) \in L_2$. If w is a witness for $(v, q) \in L_0$, $V^{\star\star}$ outputs 1, otherwise outputs 0.

From above it can be seen that: when using a witness for $v = g(s)$ to interact with $V^{\star\star}$, the probability that $V^{\star\star}$ outputs 1 is at least $\frac{1}{n^{poly(logn)}}$. When using a witness for $c = Com(d)$ to interact with $V^{\star\star}$, the view of $V^{\star\star}$ is independent of witness of $(v, q) \in L_0$, in such case the probability that $V^{\star\star}$ outputs 1 is $n^{poly(logn)}$-negligible. Therefore, $V^{\star\star}$ can distinguish the witnesses for statement $(c, v) \in L_1$, which contradicts with witness indistinguishability of Σ_1. That is, except for $n^{poly(logn)}$-negligible probability, what K extracts from an accepting conversation is actually a witness for $x \in L$. □

Lemma 2. *In protocol Π, for every $\mathcal{PQT}$ machine V^*, there exists a $\mathcal{PQT}$ simulator S such that for every $x \in L$, $z \in \{0,1\}^*$ S can perfectly simulate the real interaction of $< P, V^*(z) > (x)$.*

Proof. For every $\mathcal{PQT}$ V^*, and every $x \in L$, simulator S works in the following way: S firstly commits to a random string and acts as an honest verifier of Σ_1 by asking a query e_1 to V^*. Upon getting an answer z_1 from V^*, if (a_1, e_1, z_1) is not accepting, S aborts. Otherwise, he rewinds V^* to get another accepting transcript (a_1, e_1', z_1') where $e_1 \neq e_1'$ and extracts the witness from (a_1, e_1, z_1) and (a_1, e_1', z_1'). From Lemma 3, we conclude that what S extracts is exactly the witness $s = s_1 \circ s_2$ for $(c, v) \in L_1$, where s_2 is of length $(logn)^m$. Then, S takes a brute-force search to get q' satisfying $s_2 = f(q')$. At last, S uses the fake witness s to the statement $(x, v, q') \in L_2$, which completes the simulation.

From the construction of S, we can see that its running time is $n^{poly(logn)}$. Because Σ_2 is witness independently w.r.t $n^{poly(logn)}$-adversaries, the simulated view $\{S(x,z)\}_{x \in L, z \in \{0,1\}^*}$ is identically distributed as the real interaction view $\{< P, V^*(z) > (x)\}_{x \in L, z \in \{0,1\}^*}$. $\qquad\square$

Lemma 3. *In protocol Π, for any $\mathcal{PQT}$ machine V^*, if he always convinces P the statement $(c, v) \in L_1$, then except for $n^{poly(logn)}$-negligible probability, what the extractor K_1 of Σ_1 extracts from V^* is actually a witness for $v = g(s)$.*

Proof. For a $\mathcal{PQT}$ machine V^* who convinces P the statement $(c, v) \in L_1$, let q be the probability that K_1 outputs a witness for $c = Com(d)$. Assume $q > \frac{1}{n^{poly(logn)}}$, we can construct a $\mathcal{PQT}$ algorithm B to break the hiding property of commitment scheme Com.

Algorithm B can be constructed as follows: On input c_b, r_0, r_1, where c_b is a commitment to r_0 or r_1 and b is hardwired in B, B runs the knowledge extractor K_1 of Σ_1 for statement $(c_b, v) \in L_1$. For simplicity, assume that K_1 can always succeed in extracting the witness for $(c, v) \in L_1$.

- When what K_1 outputs is a witness for $v = g(s)$, B outputs b' by flipping coins.
- When what K_1 outputs $m' = m_0$, B outputs $b' = 0$, otherwise outputs $b' = 1$.

From the construction of algorithm B, $Pr[b' = b : B(c_b, r_0, r_1) = b'] > \frac{1}{2} + \frac{q}{2} > \frac{1}{2} + \frac{1}{n^{poly(logn)}}$, which contradicts with the $\mathcal{PQT}$ hiding property of Com. Therefore, except for $n^{poly(logn)}$-negligible probability, what K_1 outputs is actually a witness for $v = g(s)$. $\qquad\square$

From above three lemmas, we can conclude that Π is a perfect $n^{poly(logn)}$-simulatable argument of knowledge w.r.t $\mathcal{PQT}$. Therefore, we have

Theorem 1. *Every language $L \in \mathcal{NP}$ has an efficient 5-round zero knowledge argument with $\mathcal{PQT}$ soundness.*

5   Conclusion

Strongly $n^{poly(logn)}$-simulatable argument is a relaxed zero knowledge argument and is very useful in constructing multi-party secure computation schemes and universal composable secure protocols. Under the assumption of the existence of claw-free permutation secure against $\omega(\mathcal{PQT})$, we present a 5-round relaxed zero knowledge argument with $\mathcal{PQT}$ soundness. In addition, the simulation way makes the scheme secure against $\mathcal{PPT}$ resettable-soundness attackers.

Acknowledgments. We thank anonymous referees for the helpful suggestions to improve this paper.

References

1. Barak, B., Goldreich, O., Goldwasser, S., Lindell, Y.: Resettably sound zero knowledge and its applications. In: Proceedings FOCS 2001, pp. 116–125 (2001)
2. Canetti, R., Kilian, J., Petrank, E., Rosen, A.: Black-box concurrent zero- knowledge requires (almost) logarithm many rounds. SIAM J. Comput. **32**(1), 1–47 (2002)
3. Canetti, R., Goldreich, O., Goldwasser, S., Micali, S.: Resettable zero knowledge. In: Proceedings STOC 2000, pp. 235–244 (2000)
4. Damgård, I.: On Sigma Protocols. http://www.daimi.au.dk/~ivan/CPT.html
5. Deng, Y., Goyal, V., Sahai, A.: Resolving the simultaneous resettability conjecture and a new non-black-box simulation strategy. In: Proceedings FOCS 2009, pp. 251–260 (2009)
6. Dwork, C., Naor, M., Sahai, A.: Concurrent zero-knowledge. In: Proceedins STOC 1998, pp. 409–418 (1998)
7. Fouard, L., Duclos, M., Lafourcade, P.: Survey on electronic voting schemes. http://www-verimag.imag.fr/~duclos/paper/e-vote.pdf
8. Feige, U., Lapidot, D., Shamir, A.: Multiple non-interactive zero knowledge proofs under general assumptions. SIAM J. Comput. **29**(1), 1–28 (1999)
9. Fiat, A., Shamir, A.: How to prove yourself: Practical solutions to identification and signature problems. In: Odlyzko, A.M. (ed.) CRYPTO 1986. LNCS, vol. 263, pp. 186–194. Springer, Heidelberg (1987)
10. Feige, U., Shamir, A.: Witness indinstinguishable and witness hiding protocols. In: Proceedins STOC 1990, pp. 416–426 (1990)
11. Secure Multi-Party Computation. http://www.wisdom.weizmann.ac.il
12. Goldreich, O.: Foundation of Cryptography-Basic Tools. Cambridge University Press, New York (2001)
13. Goldwasser, O., Micali, A., Rackoff, C.: The knowledge complexity of interactive proof system. SIAM J. Comput. **18**(1), 186–208 (1989)
14. Goldreich, O., Micali, S., Widerson, A.: Proofs that yields nothing but their validity or all languages in $\mathcal{NP}$ have zero knowledge proof systems. J. ACM **38**(3), 691–729 (1991)
15. Micali, S., Reyzin, L.: Soundness in the public-key model. In: Kilian, J. (ed.) CRYPTO 2001. LNCS, vol. 2139, pp. 542–565. springer, Heidelberg (2001)
16. Lindell, Y.: General composition and universal composability in secure multi- party computation. In: proceedins FOCS 2003, pp. 394–403 (2003)

17. Lindell, Y.: Lower bounds for concurrent self composition. In: Naor, M. (ed.) TCC 2004. LNCS, vol. 2951, pp. 203–222. Springer, Heidelberg (2004)
18. Pass, R.: Simulation in quasi-polynomial time, and its application to protocol composition. In: Biham, E. (ed.) Advances in Cryptology – EUROCRYPT 2003. LNCS, vol. 2656, pp. 160–176. Springer, Heidelberg (2003)
19. Pass, R., Venkitasubramaniam, M.: On constant-round concurrent zero-knowledge. In: Canetti, R. (ed.) TCC 2008. LNCS, vol. 4948, pp. 553–570. Springer, Heidelberg (2008)

Network Security

Performance Analysis of Multiple Classifier System in DoS Attack Detection

Bayu Adhi Tama and Kyung Hyune Rhee[✉]

Laboratory of Information Security and Internet Applications,
IT Convergence and Application Engineering,
Pukyong National University, Busan, South Korea
{bayuat,khrhee}@pknu.ac.kr
http://lisia21.net

Abstract. DoS attacks become a serious attack so as resource protection against this kind of attack is a compulsory task. The major challenge on designing detection scheme using machine learning technique is how to maximize detection rate with lower false alarm. In this paper, we employ and analyze the performance of multiple classifier system (MCS) to detect DoS attack. Several renowned base classifiers such as C4.5, SVM, and k-NN are combined using combination voting scheme and we compare the results with existing ensemble learning algorithms such as Bagging, Adaboost, and Rotation Forest. Based on the experiment using NSL-KDD dataset, MCS scheme has promising performance comparing to existing ensemble learner and single classifier.

Keywords: DoS attack detection · Multiple classifier systems · Accuracy

1 Introduction

The development of Internet technology posseses many advantages. However, it is like two sides of coin, huge risk of lossing or leaking data might also be faced by users. On one side internet brings opportunity for users to shift their business to online i.e. e-commerce, e-business, e-government, etc., on the contrary, lots of information are available to misbehave users. Fraudulent users might continuously perform various attacks so as systems unavailable to legitimate users. Such attacks are increasing rapidly nowadays and according to [1], Denial of Service (DoS) and Distributed Denial of Service (DDoS) attack have remarkably grown both in size and frequency.

DoS/DDoS attacks employed brute force attack techniques. It aims at exploiting computing resources vulnerability and earning dollars by sending too many requests so it will not be able for the victim systems to handle. This consequences profit loss, system performance decline, and services unavailability. Hence, because DoS/DDoS attacks are the most notable security threat, DoS/DDoS attack detection are essential component of computer network protection systems. Moreover, according to [2,3], DoS attack in present-day intelligent transportation systems

© Springer International Publishing Switzerland 2016
H. Kim and D. Choi (Eds.): WISA 2015, LNCS 9503, pp. 339–347, 2016.
DOI: 10.1007/978-3-319-31875-2_28

(ITS) technology such as vehicular ad-hoc network (VANET), has gained much attentions from the researchers since it can result severe danger both for driver and passengers.

Recently, detection approaches such as statistical, soft computing, knowledge-based, data mining, and machine learning methods have been proposed by community. Recent trends indicate that the soft computing approach has been frequently used for DoS/DDoS attack detection [4]. Some prior researches showed that no single classifier was optimal for all problems, so that in this paper we employ and thoroughly analyse the performance of multi classifier system (MCS) with respect to detect DoS attack. To improve high detection rate, single classifier such as Decision Tree (C4.5) [5], Support Vector Machine (SVM) [6], and k-Nearest Neighbors (k-NN) [7] are combined using different decision combination schemes such as majority voting and average of probability [8,9]. Selection criteria is based on the fact that these algorithms are the most influential data mining algorithms in the research community [10]. The performance of MCS classifier is compared with the ensemble learning algorithms such as Bagging [11], Adaboost [12], and Rotation Forest [13].

The objectives of this paper are as follows: firstly, to select the most relevant features for DoS attack using the combination of correlation-based feature selection (CFS) [14] and wrapper feature subset selection [15]; secondly, to introduce the fusion of well-known base classifiers in term of their performance on DoS attack detection, and thirdly, to analyze a suitable and applicable MCS scheme for classifying DoS attack.

The rest of the paper is organized as follows. Section 2 provides related work regarding ensemble methods in DoS/DDoS detection. Next, Sect. 3 briefly describes multiple classifiers system used in this study while Sect. 4 presents experimental design and attack detection framework. The result and analysis are given in Sect. 5 and finally, some concluding remarks is presented in Sect. 6.

2   Related Work

Soft computing methods such as neural network, fuzzy systems and genetic algorithm are heavily used in DoS/DDoS attack detection due to their abilities to perform classification accurately. However, a lack of interpretability of neural network and poor learning capability of fuzzy system are the major drawbacks of soft computing methods [16].

For instance, Toosi and Kahani [17] proposed neuro-fuzzy classifiers, making final decision of whether the network activity is normal or intrusive. Nevertheless, the experiments and evaluations of the proposed method were performed with obsolete KDD Cup 99 intrusion detection dataset [18] and relatively high false positive rate. Anomaly-based method using radial basis function (RBF) neural network was proposed by Karimazad and Farahi [19]. The method is applied to classify data to normal and anomaly categories. RBF neural network can be performed online with low false alarm rate.

Combining multi classifiers have been tremendously established to overcome the drawbacks of soft computing methods. The experiment conducted with public dataset using Resilient Back Propogation based (RPBoost) algorithm can achieve high detection rate (99.4 %) with lower false alarm rate and outperform the existing ensemble algorithms [20]. Ensemble of adaptive hybrid neuro-fuzzy systems called NFBoost algorithms was proposed by Kumar and Selvakumar [21]. The proposed method offers a lower detection accuracy compared to RPBoost, but achieves high detection accuracy when it was compared with different ensemble learning algorithms.

3   Multiple Classification Systems

In this section, MCS for solving classification problem is described. Section 3.1 provides a combination scheme in MCS, and Sect. 3.2 presents the base classifiers used in this study.

3.1   Combination Scheme

Strategies for combining classifiers can be defined as serial and parallel approach [22]. Serial (sequential) approach arranges classifiers sequentially and if the prior classifier does not meet sufficient confidence, it is fed to the next classifier. Parallel approach organizes classifiers in parallel. All classifiers are applied for the same input in parallel, and then the result from each classifier is then combined to yield the final output.

In classifier combination research, parallel approach has gained much attention. In the parallel approaches, a combination scheme is needed in order to incorporate the output of each classifiers. Various classifier combination schemes have been proposed such as majority voting [23], Weighted majority voting [24], Naive Bayes combiner [25], and Multinomial methods [26,27]. In this study, we focus on majority voting and average probability because these combination methods are straightforward but tremendously robust.

3.2   Base Classifiers

Base classifiers used in this study are C4.5 [5], SVM [6], and k-NN [7]. These base classifier were chosen due to their renowned performance. we will briefly discuss as follows.

- *Decision Tree (C4.5)*. The classifier generates decision tree using divide-and-conquer algorithm which consists of a number of internal nodes. These nodes correspond to attributes and leaf nodes. For attribute selection, either Gain ratio or Gini index (a measure based on information gain) are used for implementation. In this paper we use J48, the version of C4.5 algorithm which is implemented in java machine learning tool, Weka [28].
- *Support Vector Machine (SVM)*. The classifier is one of supervised learning algorithm which generates input-output mapping function (either classification or regression task) from a set of labeled dataset. According to Vapnik [29],

SVM uses a strategy to find the best separating hyperplane on the input vector space called structural minimization principle. To distinguish between two classes, the margin is defined by the hyperplane. The margin corresponds to the shortest distance between the closest data points to a point on the hyperplane. In this study, a library of SVM called LibSVM [30] is used because it has faster computation compared to SMO [31].

– k-NN. The classifier is also known as instant base learner or lazy learner. The example is assigned to the most common class among its k nearest neighbors using a distance function. The number k determines the number of classes. Therefore, if $k = 1$ then examples are assigned to one class. In this experiment, four different number of k are 1, 3, 5, and 7.

4   Experimental Design

4.1   Research Framework

In this section, we are going to describe the research design. Firstly, we introduce a general framework of DoS detection using various MCS schemes as depicted in Fig. 1. To achieve a higher accuracy and reduce a computational cost, a feature selection task using the combination of CFS and wrapper feature subset selection is applied. CFS and wrapper have been proven as the best among the feature subset selection methods. The best features then will be trained by MCS to generate classification model which can be further utilized to distinguish whether the traffic data is normal or DoS.

Specifying the aforementioned base classifiers, we consider the following approaches to implement different MCS schemes.

1. Six different base classifiers are arranged: C4.5, SVM, and k-NN with different values (1, 3, 5, and 7). It is denoted by MCS-6.

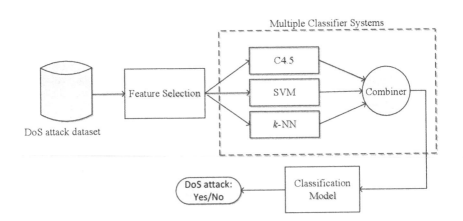

Fig. 1. Framework of DoS attack detection using MCS

2. Four MCS are denoted by MCSk-1, MCSk-3, MCSk-5, and MCSk-7 which are built by C4.5, SVM, and k-NN. Four values of k are specified (1, 3, 5, and 7).

The parameters for each base classifier are presented in Table 1. We considered the same parameters for base classifiers either as part of MCS or as an individual classifier.

Table 1. Parameter for base classifiers

C4.5	LibSVM	k-NN
confidence factor $c = 0.25$	cost $C = 1.0$	$k = 1, 3, 5, 7$
min. instances per leaf $i = 2$	tolerance $\epsilon = 0.001$	dist. function: Minkowski
pruning is performed	kernel type: radial basis function	no distance weighting
	type of SVM: $nu - SVC$	
	value of nu=0.5	

4.2 Dataset

DoS attack datasets, namely NSL-KDD [32] was employed in our study. The dataset was proposed in order to tackle the problem in respect to bias result of attack detection since many redundant records was contained in the dataset. It consists of selected records of KDD Cup 99 dataset [18]. The advantages of the dataset include no redundant records so as bias result can be avoided and records are selected inversely proportional to the percentage of records in KDD Cup 99 dataset. NSL-KDD possesses 41 attributes and one class label attribute. Five classes are normal and four types of attacks such as DoS, Probe, Remote to Local Attack (R2L), and User to Root Attack (U2R). In this study, we only considered 20 % (25192 instances) of dataset and extract only normal class and DoS class from the dataset. In the feature selection stage, the worth of attributes is evaluated using the combination of CFS and wrapper feature subset selection.

4.3 Evaluation Metrics

All MCS schemes will be evaluated using classification accuracy (CA) which is the percentage of correctly classified of samples for different number of attributes. Moreover, Recall, Precision, and F-measure for both positive and negative class are also considered. Recall refers to true positive rate (TPR) and false positive rate (FPR) for positive and negative class, respectively, whilst precision is also known as positive predictive value (PPV) and negative predictive value (NPV) for positve and negative class, respectively. F-measure denote the harmonic mean of precision and recall, is computed as,

$$F1 = 2 \cdot \frac{Precision \cdot Recall}{Precision + Recall}.$$

5   Result and Analysis

In this section, we presents the performance comparison between MCS and existing ensemble learning algorithms such as Bagging [11], Adaboost [12] and Rotation Forest [13], including the performance comparison between MCS and individual classifier. We considered C4.5 as base classifier when performing ensemble learning algorithms. Cross validation techniques with k=10 is used for model validation. All classifiers are implemented in open source data mining tool Weka [28] running on PC with processor Intel Core i5 3.5GHz, 16GB RAM, and Windows 7 operating system.

Based on the feature selection task using CFS and wrapper feature subset selection, 15 significant features out of 41 features have been successfully obtained. These features include service, flag, dst_bytes, wrong_fragment, hot, logged_in, num_compromised, num_root, num_file_creations, is_guest_login, count,

Table 2. Cross comparison of classifier's performance in %

Method	Accuracy	Positive class			Negative class		
		Precision	Recall	$F1$	Precision	Recall	$F1$
C4.5	99.17	99.1	99.4	99.2	99.3	98.9	99.1
SVM	97.14	97.2	97.5	97.3	97.1	96.7	96.9
1-NN	99.17	99.3	99.2	99.2	99.0	99.2	99.1
3-NN	99.01	99.1	99.1	99.1	98.9	98.9	98.9
5-NN	98.89	99.0	99.0	99.0	98.8	98.8	98.8
7-NN	98.73	98.8	98.8	98.8	98.6	98.6	98.6
Ensemble learners							
Bagging	99.18	99.1	99.4	99.2	99.3	98.9	99.1
AdaBoost	99.40	99.4	99.5	99.5	99.5	99.4	99.4
Rotation Forest	99.37	99.2	99.6	99.4	99.5	99.1	99.3
Majority voting							
MCS-6	99.41	99.1	99.3	99.2	99.2	98.9	99.1
MCSk-1	99.23	98.8	99.8	99.3	99.7	98.6	99.2
MCSk-3	99.21	98.8	99.7	99.3	99.7	98.6	99.2
MCSk-5	99.11	98.6	99.7	99.2	99.7	98.4	99.1
MCSk-7	98.95	98.4	99.7	99.0	99.6	98.1	98.9
Average probability							
MCS-6	99.45	99.4	99.5	99.3	99.5	99.0	99.2
MCSk-1	99.22	98.9	99.6	99.3	99.6	98.7	99.1
MCSk-3	99.21	98.8	99.7	99.3	99.7	98.6	99.2
MCSk-5	99.15	98.7	99.7	99.2	99.7	98.5	99.1
MCSk-7	98.95	98.4	99.7	99.0	99.6	98.1	98.9

same_srv _rate, dst_host_count, dst_host_srv_count, and dst_host_srv_diff_host_ rate. These 15 features then will be used for further classification analysis.

Table 2 summarizes the results of classification analysis experiment. It can be seen that different MCS schemes performed well in DoS detection. With respect to MCS scheme, the MCS-6 classifier with average probability voting scheme has higher accuracy rate compared to the MCS-6 with majority voting scheme. However, the MCS-6 either with majority or average probility voting scheme has significantly outperformed the current ensemble learners and single classifiers. In addition, as the number of k increases, the performance of MCS tends to decrease significantly regardless the voting scheme applied.

With respect to individual classifiers, we can see that C4.5 and 1-NN have better performance than others. Surprisingly, in many prior researches show that SVM is well-known robust algorithm and has good performance in a large number of real-word problems, but in our experiment result SVM perform worst than other individual classifiers. With reference to k-NN as single classifier, the results show that the higher the value of k, the lower the performance.

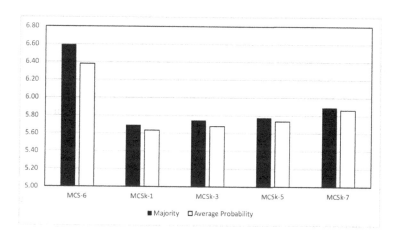

Fig. 2. Training time of each MCS voting scheme (minutes)

Besides the classification analysis, we also performed the training time of each MCS schemes for efficiency evaluation. Figure 2 shows training time comparison over NSL-KDD dataset between majority voting and average probalility scheme. Considering training time of MCS with majority voting, its training time in average is slightly longer than MCS with average probability scheme. However, in a real DoS attack detection, once model is built, it is not necessary to re-train. Therefore, the training time is still applicable and acceptable in real-life scenario.

From the experiment, it can be said that the proposed MCS with majority and average probability scheme are suitable for DoS attack detection. However, designing MCS for detecting DoS attack, similar to other applications, depends on the performance behavior of single classifiers. The performance of classifier depends on the characteristic of dataset used, in future work, we are going to compare and analyse several different public datasets and feature selection techniques.

6   Conclusion

In this paper, we analyze the performance of several MCS schemes in order to detect DoS attack by using the publicly available dataset, NSL-KDD. MCS was developed using well-known heterogenous machine learning algorithms such as C4.5, SVM, and k-NN. The performance of MCS have been compared with individual classifier. From the experiment result, it can be seen that combining MCS shows promising detection accuracy compared to exisiting ensemble learner and single classifier.

Acknowledgment. This work was supported by the National Research Foundation of Korea (NRF) grant funded by the Korea government (MSIP) No. NRF-2014R1A2A1A1 1052981.

References

1. Arbor Networks Worldwide infrastructure security report, April 2015. http://www.arbornetworks.com/images/documents/infographics/AttackTimeline_Final.pdf.
2. Aad, I., Hubaux, J.P., Knightly, E.W.: Impact of denial of service attacks on ad hoc networks. IEEE/ACM Trans. Netw. **16**(4), 791–802 (2008)
3. Samara, G., Al-Salihy, W.A., Sures, R.: Security analysis of vehicular ad hoc networks (vanet). In: 2010 Second International Conference on Network Applications Protocols and Services (NETAPPS), pp. 55–60. IEEE (2010)
4. Bhuyan, M.H., Kashyap, H.J., Bhattacharyya, D.K., Kalita, J.: Detecting distributed denial of service attacks: Methods, tools, and future directions. Comput. J. **57**, 537 (2013)
5. Quinlan, J.R.: C4.5: Programs for Machine Learning. Elsevier, Amsterdam (2014)
6. Cortes, C., Vapnik, V.: Support-vector networks. Mach. Learn. **20**(3), 273–297 (1995)
7. Aha, D.W., Kibler, D., Albert, M.K.: Instance-based learning algorithms. Mach. Learn. **6**(1), 37–66 (1991)
8. Kittler, J., Hatef, M., Duin, R.P., Matas, J.: On combining classifiers. IEEE Trans. Pattern Anal. Mach. Intell. **20**(3), 226–239 (1998)
9. Kuncheva, L.I.: Combining Pattern Classifiers: Methods and Algorithm. John Wiley & Sons, Chichester (2014)
10. Wu, X., Kumar, V., Quinlan, J.R., Ghosh, J., Yang, Q., Motoda, H., McLachlan, G.J., Ng, A., Liu, B., Philip, S.Y., et al.: Top 10 algorithms in data mining. Knowl. Inf. Syst. **14**(1), 1–37 (2008)
11. Breiman, L.: Bagging predictors. Mach. Learn. **24**(2), 123–140 (1996)
12. Freund, Y., Schapire, R.E.: A decision-theoretic generalization of on-line learning and an application to boosting. J. Comput. Syst. Sci. **55**(1), 119–139 (1997)

13. Rodriguez, J.J., Kuncheva, L.I., Alonso, C.J.: Rotation forest: A new classifier ensemble method. IEEE Trans. Pattern Anal. Mach. Intell. **28**(10), 1619–1630 (2006)
14. Hall, M.A.: Correlation-based feature selection for machine learning. Ph.D. thesis, The University of Waikato (1999)
15. Bermejo, P., Gámez, J.A., Puerta, J.M.: Speeding up incremental wrapper feature subset selection with naive bayes classifier. Knowl.-Based Syst. **55**, 140–147 (2014)
16. Aliev, R.A., Fazlollahi, B., Aliev, R.R.: Soft Computing and its Applications in Business and Economics, vol. 157. Springer Science & Business Media, Heidelberg (2004)
17. Toosi, A.N., Kahani, M.: A new approach to intrusion detection based on an evolutionary soft computing model using neuro-fuzzy classifiers. Comput. Commun. **30**(10), 2201–2212 (2007)
18. KDD cup 1999 data (1999). http://kdd.ics.uci.edu/databases/kddcup99/kddcup99.html
19. Karimazad, R., Faraahi, A.: An anomaly-based method for DDoS attacks detection using RBF neural networks. In: 2011 International Conference on Network and Electronics Engineering, IPCSIT, vol. 11 (2011)
20. Kumar, P.A.R., Selvakumar, S.: Distributed denial of service attack detection using an ensemble of neural classifier. Comput. Commun. **34**(11), 1328–1341 (2011)
21. Kumar, P.A.R., Selvakumar, S.: Detection of distributed denial of service attacks using an ensemble of adaptive and hybrid neuro-fuzzy systems. Comput. Commun. **36**(3), 303–319 (2013)
22. Ho, T.K., Hull, J.J., Srihari, S.N.: Decision combination in multiple classifier systems. IEEE Trans. Pattern Anal. Mach. Intell. **16**(1), 66–75 (1994)
23. Lachenbruch, P.A.: Multiple reading procedures: The performance of diagnostic tests. Stat. Med. **7**(5), 549–557 (1988)
24. Kim, H., Kim, H., Moon, H., Ahn, H.: A weight-adjusted voting algorithm for ensembles of classifiers. J. Korean Stat. Soc. **40**(4), 437–449 (2011)
25. Titterington, D., Murray, G., Murray, L., Spiegelhalter, D., Skene, A., Habbema, J., Gelpke, G.: Comparison of discrimination techniques applied to a complex data set of head injured patients. J. Roy. Stat. Soc.: Ser. A (Gen.) **144**, 145–175 (1981)
26. Raudys, Š.: Trainable fusion rules. I. large sample size case. Neural Netw. **19**(10), 1506–1516 (2006)
27. Raudys, Š.: Trainable fusion rules. II. small sample-size effects. Neural Netw. **19**(10), 1517–1527 (2006)
28. Hall, M., Frank, E., Holmes, G., Pfahringer, B., Reutemann, P., Witten, I.H.: The weka data mining software: An update. ACM SIGKDD Explor. Newslett. **11**(1), 10–18 (2009)
29. Vapnik, V.: The Nature of Statistical Learning Theory. Springer Science & Business Media, Heidelberg (2000)
30. Chang, C.C., Lin, C.J.: LIBSVM: A library for support vector machines. ACM Trans. Intell. Syst. Technol. (TIST) **2**(3), 27 (2011)
31. Keerthi, S.S., Shevade, S.K., Bhattacharyya, C., Murthy, K.R.K.: Improvements to Platt's SMO algorithm for SVM classifier design. Neural Comput. **13**(3), 637–649 (2001)
32. NSL-KDD dataset for network-based intrusion detection systems (2007). http://nsl.cs.unb.ca/KDD/NSLKDD.html

Changes of Cybersecurity Legal System in East Asia: Focusing on Comparison Between Korea and Japan

Kwangho Kim[1], Sangdon Park[1(✉)], and Jongin Lim[2]

[1] National Security Research Institute, Daejeon, Korea
{kkh57,sdpark}@nsr.re.kr
[2] Graduate School of Information Security, Korea University, Seoul, Korea
jilim@korea.ac.kr

Abstract. Efforts to improve cybersecurity legal system has been in progress in East Asian countries and there are some changes. In this paper, we compare 'National Anti-Cyberterrorism Act' of Korea with 'Basic Act on Cybersecurity' of Japan and examine the main features of them. Korea and Japan all intend to set each role to related entities and build up the foundation of cybersecurity through the law proposing the structure of implementation system for strong cybersecurity. In Japan, this law is applied actually but in Korea, that is currently pending at the National Assembly so we should wait for legislation of it additionally. In the future, we should improve the legal system of cybersecurity and make strong cybersecurity in Korea, and furthermore we should contribute to the development of cybersecurity in East Asia.

Keywords: Basic act on cybersecurity · National Anti-Cyberterrorism act · Korean cybersecurity law · Japanese cybersecurity law · Legal system for cybersecurity

1 Introduction

In East Asia, the Improvement of cybersecurity legal system is becoming an issue, and each country shows the movement for it concretely. In Korea, the legislative bills for for cybersecurity like National Anti-Cyberterrorism Act have been proposed to the National Assembly. However in Japan, Basic Act on Cybersecurity is enacted and enforced with lighting speed as a basic act for cybersecurity to strengthen cybersecurity.

In March, 2015, the Korean government announced to prompt the plan for strengthening cybersecurity readiness at the national level through press releases and requested to concentrate power to enact National Anti-Cyberterrorism Act. This shows that the Korean government thinks National Anti-Cyberterrorism Act as an institutional foundation to strengthen cybersecurity. So it is important to legislate National Anti-Cyberterrorism Act and as part of discussion for it, it is required to compare National Anti-Cyberterrorism Act with Basic Act on Cybersecurity in order to find the necessity of National Anti-Cyberterrorism Act and to lead the progressive direction. To understand the improvement of cybersecurity legal system of Korea and Japan and compare and analyze the improvement direction of it will

© Springer International Publishing Switzerland 2016
H. Kim and D. Choi (Eds.): WISA 2015, LNCS 9503, pp. 348–356, 2016.
DOI: 10.1007/978-3-319-31875-2_29

contribute to improve the legal system of cybersecurity in Korea and furthermore will contribute to lead the development of cybersecurity legal system in East Asia.

2   Efforts to Change Cybersecurity Legal System in Korea and Japan

2.1   Proposal of National Anti-cyberterrorism Act in Korea

For existing law for cybersecurity in Korea, its range of applicability and governance system for implementation are dispersed and also its completion of legal system is not enough. From various researches [1, 2], it has been suggested that cybersecurity legal system in Korea should be improved and its necessity has been already developed [3]. As a result, National Anti-Cyberterrorism Act was proposed at April, 2013 in the 19th National Assembly of Korea and is pending in the concerned committee now (as of August, 2015). National Anti-Cyberterrorism Act is composed of total 5 titles (General Provisions, National Anti-Cyberterrorism and Crisis Management Implementation System, Anti-Cyberterrorism and Crisis Management Activity, R&D and Support, Penal Regulations) of 26 articles with supplementary provisions of 2 articles.

2.2   Enactment of Basic Act on Cybersecurity in Japan

In Japan, the necessity for strong cybersecurity was raised by 2020 Tokyo Olympics [4]. As a result, Basic Act on Cybersecurity was submitted to the National Diet of Japan in June, 2014 and was promulgated and enforced by passing House of Representatives in November after passing the House of Councilors in October of the same year. Basic Act on Cybersecurity is composed of total 4 titles(General Provisions, Cybersecurity Strategy, Basic Policy, Cybersecurity Strategy Headquarters) of 35 articles with supplementary provisions of 4 articles.

After the passage of the Act, Japanese government takes various measures for cybersecurity. For example, the government designated 48 entities, including Nippon Telegram and Telephone Corp., operators of highways, parts of the Japan Railways group, NHK, the Bank of Japan and the Japanese Red Cross Society, as targets with which the government is seeking cooperation in coping with cyberattacks [5].

3   Analysis of Changes in Legal System by Comparing National Anti-cyberterrorism Act with Basic Act on Cybersecurity

3.1   Purpose of Law

The purpose of National Anti-Cyberterrorism Act of Korea and Basic Act on Cybersecurity of Japan is ultimately to contribute to the safety and interests of the nation and people through the policy for cybersecurity [6, 7].

3.2 Legal Interest

According to National Anti-Cyberterrorism Act, Cyber Safety indicates an activity including administrative, physical or technical measures and readiness implemented to protect information and communication facilities and information against cyberterror. Cyberterror means all offensive actions like intrusion, disruption, paralysis or destruction of information and communication facilities or theft, damaging or distorted transmission of information by electronic ways like hacking, computer virus, service interruption, and electromagnetic waves. That is, Cyber Safety can be defined to an activity including administrative, physical or technical measures and readiness implemented to protect information and communication facilities and information against all offensive actions like intrusion, disruption, paralysis or destruction of information and communication facilities or theft, damaging or distorted transmission of information by electronic ways like hacking, computer virus, service interruption, and electromagnetic waves [6].

And Basic Act on Cybersecurity suggests the definition of Cybersecurity as a similar term with Cyber Safety. Cybersecurity is defined to 'consideration, maintenance and management of needed measures to prevent the leakage, destruction or damaging of information reported or transmitted or received or transmitted by electronic way, magnetic way or other ways that human cannot recognize, or to manage safety control of that information, or to ensure safety and reliability of information systems or information and communication networks' [7].

In effect, information systems and information and communication networks calling for protection when defining Cyber Safety is in the same scope with information and communication facilities called as protection when defining cybersecurity. Additionally Information is designated for protection in common. Finally, it is ensured that the protection and benefit of law which National Anti-Cyberterrorism Act and Basic Act on Cybersecurity want to protect are the same.

3.3 Basic Concept of Cybersecurity and Basic Responsibility of Each Entity

National Anti-Cyberterrorism Act defines the organization which executes anti-cyberterrorism and crisis management to Anti-Cyberterrorism and Crisis Management Responsible Agency (hereafter, Responsible Agency) without defining the basic concept of cybersecurity and requires Responsible Agencies to take responsibility to keep the safety of concerned information and communication facilities and to consider needed actions [6].

However, Basic Act on Cybersecurity describes six basic concepts for cybersecurity as basic concept for implementation policy for cybersecurity. And this prescribes the responsibilities for cybersecurity which state, local public entity, critical infrastructure provider, cyber related provider, education research facility, and citizen should do respectively [7].

National Anti-Cyberterrorism Act and Basic Act on Cybersecurity all state the responsibility of each entity for cybersecurity. And especially Basic Act on Cybersecurity defines the responsibility of citizen.

3.4   Lead Organization of Cybersecurity Action

National Anti-Cyberterrorism Act defines to establish National Cyber Safety Strategy Council. National Cyber Safety Strategy Council deliberate policy establishment for anti-cyberterrorism and crisis management and role adjustment among organizations in order to direct cybersecurity policy. And this defines to establish National Cyber Security Center in order to support the operation of National Cyber Safety Strategy Council and perform practical roles in policy establishment [6].

And Basic Act on Cybersecurity defines to establish Cybersecurity Strategy Headquarters and carry out businesses for development of cybersecurity strategy plan and policy enforcement of national administrative agencies in order to direct cybersecurity policy. And this requires to legislate for existing National Information Security Center for practical business support of Cybersecurity Strategy Headquarters [7]. So the center is reorganized as National center of Incident readiness and Strategy for Cybersecurity.

Thus, National Anti-Cyberterrorism Act and Basic Act on Cybersecurity are similar in view of the fact that they have general policy organization and practical support organizations in cybersecurity organization system.

3.5   Policy Establishment and Implementation

In National Anti-Cyberterrorism Act, Korean government should establish National Anti-Cyberterrorism and Crisis Management Master Plan, and each central administrative agency should distribute the implementation plan of it to the concerned Responsible Agencies and then National Intelligence Service (NIS) should confirm the performance of plans and put together the results in order to report it to the National Assembly. And each Responsible Agency should consider anti-cyberterrorism measures. Meanwhile, Korean government should execute the exercise for anti-cyberterrorism and cyber crisis management with emergency preparatory exercise together [6].

In Basic Act on Cybersecurity, the Japanese government should consider the necessary measures like establishing the Cybersecurity Strategy through the Cabinet meeting, reporting the strategy to the National Diet, opening it to the public and securing budget for enforcement of the strategy. And the state should consider the needed policies to ensure cybersecurity of the central government, critical Infrastructure providers and local public entities. Commonly these include standards establishment, exercise and training and information sharing with especially used options for each entity. And the state should consider the policies to promote self-activities of private operators, education research institutes and individuals. Meanwhile, the government pushes ahead with the improvements for legislation, finance, tax system and the reorganization of administrative organization in order to enforce the policy for cybersecurity [7].

National Anti-Cyberterrorism Act and Basic Act on Cybersecurity all have something in common for the government to establish cybersecurity policy not only for the private sector but also the public sector including national agencies, and especially to establish the grand policy with the title of National Anti-Cyberterrorism and Crisis Management Master Plan and Cybersecurity Strategy all over the country. This can be analyzed to establish and enforce the systematic policy all over the country.

3.6   Cooperation and Support

National Anti-Cyberterrorism Act defines that the Korean government can make and operate a consultative group with the private sectors and set up and operate Private - Government-Military Joint Response Team in National Cyber Security Center. And the Act defines that the government can support the responsible agency and the related concerned central administrative agencies and NIS can request the support to the supporting agencies [6].

Basic Act on Cybersecurity defines that the state considers the needed policy to cooperate among various entities including the state, local public entities, critical infrastructure providers and cyber related providers connected. Also the Act defines that the organizations of public sector like concerned administrative agencies, local public entities and independent administrative institutions should cooperate with Cybersecurity Strategy Headquarters according to the request from the headquarters and the local public entities can request a cooperation to Cybersecurity Strategy Headquarters when it is permitted to be necessary to establish and enforce the policy for cybersecurity [7].

National Anti-Cyberterrorism Act and Basic Act on Cybersecurity all keep the supporting private-public cooperation and mutual support across related agencies in mind. However, These Acts have some difference. National Anti-Cyberterrorism Act focuses on the proposal of implementation system in the respect of specifying a specific type like a consultative group in private-government cooperation and Private-Government-Military Joint Response Team in connected activity all over the country, but Basic Act on Cybersecurity is flexible for definite implementation system of private-public cooperation and connected activity all over the country and it defines that Cybersecurity Strategy Headquarters is the center for various cooperation of support.

3.7   Monitoring and Information Sharing

National Anti-Cyberterrorism Act defines that the responsible agencies operate Security Monitoring and Control Center in order to detect cyberterror information and share it with related central administrative agency and NIS. And the Act defines to build up and operate Cyber Threat Information Integration and Sharing System [6].

Basic Act on Cybersecurity defines that the chiefs of related administrative agencies provides related data and information to Cybersecurity Strategy Headquarters and local public entities can request to provide them with the information to the Headquarters. And the Act defines that the state should consider the policies in order for monitoring of illegal activities for information systems of national administrative agencies and sharing Information [7].

National Anti-Cyberterrorism Act defines to establish the organization of Security Monitoring and Control Center and guarantee the implementation of security control responsibility, and defines a specific measure of Cyber Threat Information Integration and Sharing System for good information sharing. Basic Act on Cybersecurity has the same purpose with National Anti-Cyberterrorism Act but specific implementation of it follows the policy based on the law.

3.8   Incident Investigation

National Anti-Cyberterrorism Act defines that central administrative agencies can conduct the incident investigation for concerned agency damaged by cyberterror and NIS can conduct the investigation in a critical case [6].

Basic Act on Cybersecurity defines that Cybersecurity Strategy Headquarters evaluates the policies of a serious situation for cybersecurity occurred at national administrative agencies like investigating the cause [7].

National Anti-Cyberterrorism Act gives the autonomous right for incident investigation for concerned agencies to the central administrative agencies. Also Basic Act on Cybersecurity takes a similar stand. The activity of Cybersecurity Strategy Headquarters for a serious situation occurred at national administrative agencies is to evaluate the investigation not the investigation to find the cause directly, and this is possible in case that national administrative agencies investigate it.

3.9   Response to Critical Situation

National Anti-Cyberterrorism Act defines that NIS Director can issue the phased alert. Red level Alert is necessary to discuss with Chief Secretary in charge of Cybersecurity at Office of National Security and to report it to the National Assembly. And the Act defines to make and operate Cyber Crisis Task Force if an alert over Orange level is issued [6].

Basic Act on Cybersecurity defines that the state should consider the policiess to response to the situation affecting the national safety seriously and that the Japanese government should review the policies to strengthen the defensive ability in case of the emergency and the situation which may affect the people's living and economic activities seriously in a wide point of view [7].

National Anti-Cyberterrorism Act suggests specific ways of Alert and Task Force operation and defines concerned procedure. However, Basic Act on Cybersecurity suggests abstract ways of policy review and consideration and follows policy enforcement later on for its specific response and preparation.

3.10   Development of Economic, Technical and Social Foundation

National Anti-Cyberterrorism Act defines that the Korean government can push ahead with the policies for R&D, related industry promotion, manpower training and education promotion, and related institutes and specialized organizations can implement the work according to the field [6].

Basic Act on Cybersecurity defines that the Japanese government considers the policies necessary for industrial promotion and enhancement of national competitiveness R&D, securing of talent and public awareness [7].

National Anti-Cyberterrorism Act and Basic Act on Cybersecurity all specify to implement R&D, industrial development, manpower training and public awareness at the national level.

3.11 International Cooperation

National Anti-Cyberterrorism Act defines that the Korean government implements the work in order to increase the cooperation with international organizations and foreign countries and suggests the types of work to cooperation system construction, information exchange and joint response and cross outreach education [6].

Basic Act on Cybersecurity defines that the state implements the international cooperation and the policies in order to increase the understanding of foreign countries and suggests the fields requesting the international cooperation to international form establishment, trust building and information exchange, technical cooperation of developing country support and crime control [7].

National Anti-Cyberterrorism Act and Basic Act on Cybersecurity all specify the implementation of international cooperation. Basic Act on Cybersecurity specifies the support of developing countries and the establishment of international rule as matters of international cooperation, so it can be analyzed to participate in making international order positively and to get the initiative. But National Anti-Cyberterrorism Act focuses on the solution of current problems through increasing cooperation than making international order.

4 Implication by Analysis of Changes in Legislative System

4.1 Legislation of Control Tower-Centric Cooperation System

According to the result of comparison previously mentioned, Korea and Japan have organized general policy organization and practical Business organization and established the grand policy all over the country in order to strengthen cybersecurity. National Anti-Cyberterrorism Act designates those organizations under Director of NIS, the Intelligence Service, and Basic Act on Cybersecurity designates the Chief Cabinet Secretary to supervise all policies. These organizations make human resources from private, government and military participated and provides the condition which can act as control tower for policy and practical business including all private, government and military. Apart from the organization in charge of control tower and the implementation of specific works, the necessity itself of control tower is recognized commonly in Korea and Japan. And this control tower is requested to normal and emergency response all.

4.2 Extension of Concerned Entities by Generalization of Cybersecurity

The legal system in Korea and Japan reflects the consensus, that is, cyberspace is real space and cybersecurity is real security. That is, as the development of information and communication, cybersecurity reflects the situations that information and communication is generalized and cyberspace is just real space not virtual space isolated with the real world. So it is recognized that cybersecurity is not only a problem of the national agencies but also that of the privates. And the success and failure of cybersecurity depends on both of them. So the role of private sector is very important. For example, KEIDANREN, a comprehensive economic organization with a membership comprised of representative companies of Japan, suggested cybersecurity measures, including measures against important infrastructure and business community's efforts [8].

4.3 Promotion of Cooperation Among Entities for Cybersecurity Development

In Korea and Japan, setting up control tower and strengthening cybersecurity does not mean that only the control tower is in charge of all works. As previously explained, the effort to change legal system has been in progress to define the responsibilities of other entities related with cybersecurity together and increase mutual cooperation. This can be thought of mutual cooperation system construction, based on control tower. Japan realizes this change by Basic Act on Cybersecurity and Korea tries to enforce the change by legislation of National Anti-Cyberterrorism Act including it.

5   Conclusion

According to previous result of comparison, it is certain that Korea and Japan designates the role of each entities and develop the foundation of cybersecurity through the law suggesting the structure of implementation system to strengthen cybersecurity all. However there are some difference between Korea and Japan. It is noted that in Japan, the law is already in progress but in Korea, the law is pending in the National Assembly so it should be legislated additionally. So Korea should try to improve the legal system of cybersecurity.

Currently, cybersecurity is an important issue in the world. And cybersecurity is an important subject of nations. For Example, Minister for Foreign Affairs Fumio Kishida, Minister of Defense Gen Nakatani, Secretary of State John Kerry, and Secretary of Defense Ashton Carter said that a dynamic world requires a modern Alliance and called for continued progress in cooperation on cyberspace issues [9].

Therefore, the improvement of cybersecurity legal system becomes an important issue. Meaningful information is found much in order to improve the legal system of cybersecurity in Korea in the future by comparing National Anti-Cyberterrorism Act of Korea with Basic Act on Cybersecurity of Japan. If improving the legal system of Korean cybersecurity based on this, cybersecurity of Korea will be strengthen and furthermore this will contribute to the development of cybersecurity in East Asia.

References

1. Yook, S.-Y.: The necessity of enacting cyber security act. Public Law J. Vol. 11(2), Korea Comparative Public Law Association (2010)
2. A Study on Solutions for the Advancement of Security Legislation, Korea Communications Commission (2011)
3. Park, S.: A Contemporary Study on Comprehensive Cybersecurity Legislation: Focusing on the Legislative Trends in the United States, Legislation and Policy Studies, Vol. 6 No. 2, National Assembly Research Service, Republic of Korea (2014)
4. Japan holds first broad cybersecurity drill, frets over Olympics risks. Reuters (2014)
5. 48 infrastructure entities to get cybersecurity cooperation requests, The Japan Times (2015)

6. National Anti-Cyberterrorism Act of Korea
7. Basic Act on Cybersecurity of Japan
8. Proposals for Reinforcing Cybersecurity Measures, KEIDANREN (2015)
9. Nakatani, K., Carter, K.: Stronger Alliance for a Dynamic Security Environment: The New Guidelines for Japan-U.S. Defense Cooperation, Joint Statement of the Security Consultative Committee (2015)

Applying Recurrent Neural Network to Intrusion Detection with Hessian Free Optimization

Jihyun Kim and Howon Kim$^{(\boxtimes)}$

School of Computer Science and Engineering, Pusan National University,
San-30, Jangjeon-Dong, Geumjeong-Gu, Busan 609–735, Republic of Korea
{jihyunkim,howonkim}@pusan.ac.kr

Abstract. With developing a network communication technology, cyber attacks which threaten users safety are increasing. Consequently, many studies are being carried out to protect the user security. One of them is an intrusion detection system (IDS). In this paper, we apply recurrent neural network with hessian-free optimization which is one of the deep learning algorithm for intrusion detection. We use DARPA dataset in order to train and test the intrusion detection model. It was used for the 1999 KDD Cup contest dataset. It composed of 41 features and 22 different attacks. We chose salient features for training the model and analyzed a result of experiment with various metrics. We found that our result is superior to the existing studies through comparing the performance.

Keywords: Intrusion detection · Recurrent neural network · Hessian free optimization · Deep learning

1 Introduction

For many decades, information and communication technology (ICT) have been making great progress. With this development, ICT have been applied to human life. It makes peoples living more convenient and affluent. However, cyberattack by malicious people are increasing with high quality techniques [1]. These days, most of malicious people so-called hackers are attacking systems for pecuniary advantage. As a result, cybercrime has become an important social issue. The United States legislated the cybersecurity law in 2014. EU concluded a treaty of convention on cybercrime and emphasized the importance of cyber security.

This work was partly supported by Institute for Information & communications Technology Promotion (IITP) grant funded by the Korea government (MSIP) (No. 10043907, Development of high performance IoT device and Open Platform with Intelligent Software) and the MSIP (Ministry of Science, ICT and Future Planning), Korea, under the ITRC (Information Technology Research Center) support program (IITP-2015-H8501-15-1017) supervised by the IITP (Institute for Information & communications Technology Promotion).

© Springer International Publishing Switzerland 2016
H. Kim and D. Choi (Eds.): WISA 2015, LNCS 9503, pp. 357–369, 2016.
DOI: 10.1007/978-3-319-31875-2_30

Neighboring countries are also preparing an effective countermeasure of cyber-crime. Consequently, researches about an intrusion detection system (IDS) have been carried out actively. IDS is a malicious detection system through network traffic, system activity and policy violation monitoring [2]. Misuse detection and anomaly detection are usually used in IDS. Misuse detection construct a model about known attacks and detect an intrusion by using key stroke monitoring or state transition analysis [3]. Because this method detects the known attacks, it has a low false alarm. But it cannot detect unknown attacks. Anomaly detection constructs a normal system behavior model and detects an abnormal behavior by using threshold with statistical approach [4]. This method is able to detect unknown attacks. More precisely, it catches out of the normal behavior range. But it has a high false alarm due to modeling a simple pattern.

One alternative solution is using deep learning. Deep learning is an algorithm set based on neural network [5]. At first, it was introduced as a part of machine learning. However, the status of them are switched because remarkable accomplishments in image recognition and speech recognition field have been introduced [6,7]. Deep learning can model complex system behaviors due to training a high level data abstraction. Also, if we categorize the known attacks, the model could detect not only the attacks which are in the same category but also the unknown attacks which have a similar pattern. Recurrent neural network (RNN) is one of the deep learning algorithm and it is able to train the sequential data [8]. It unfolds a recurrent feed forward network and builds a deep neural network. However, if RNN has a long time step, errors could not be propagated to the end of the network while the model was in the training step. We call this vanishing gradient problem [9]. In order to overcome this problem, Martens et al. proposed hessian-free optimization [10]. This method used conjugate gradient for propagating the errors. As a result, we can use the longer time step than before.

In this paper, we do intrusion detection through applying hessian-free optimization to RNN. We use DARPA dataset which was used for 1999 KDD Cup contest as the training and test data [11]. We extract salient features toward 22 attacks in the dataset for training data. We measure a performance and verify the efficiency through comparing to the existing studies. The structure of this paper is the following manner. In Sect. 2, we introduce the studies about intrusion detection with machine learning. And we describe RNN and hessian-free optimization in Sect. 3. In Sect. 4, we explain the dataset. In Sect. 5, we show the result of experiment and make a conclusion in the last section.

2   Related Works

The conventional IDS using anomaly or misuse detection has an issue of unknown attack detection and low false alarm rate. To solve the problems, the researchers tried to apply machine learning to intrusion detection. DARPA dataset was opened to the public, lots of studies have carried on. A detailed description about DARPA dataset is in Sect. 4. Following studies are the research about IDS using DARPA dataset. Srinivas et al. combined artificial neural networks

(ANN) and support vector machines (SVM) for intrusion detection in 2003 [12]. They constructed IDS model using 3 types of ANN and 1 SVM with an ensemble approach. Because of using 4 algorithms, the IDS model has to be trained 4 times. It gives a prediction using the algorithm which has the least deviation. S.Chavan et al. used Fuzzy Inference System (FIS) with ANN for IDS in 2004 [13]. When FIS infers something, it depends on a priori knowledge. They adapted ANN because there is no proper way to convert a persons experience to knowledge. However, the performance was not so increased. Sandhya Peddabacchigari et al. merge Decision Tree (DT) and SVM for IDS in 2005 [14]. They applied specific rules to DT and generated some information about the data. After that, they detected the attacks by using SVM. The performance of hybrid DT-SVM was similar to SVMs. But the accuracy toward R2L (Remote Penetration) attack was higher when they use the ensemble approach with DT, SVM and hybrid DT-SVM. Pavel Kachurka et al. contructed IDS model by using recirculation neural network in 2011 [15]. They made 5 models for each attack including normal communication, and detected the attacks with threshold. The studies what we described above used machine learning approach but they made detection models for each attack. This method is inconvenient for IDS. And with increasing the category of attacks, the complexity of model is also increased. In this study, we are able to construct only one detection model for all attacks with deep learning approach.

3 Recurrent Neural Network with Hessian Free Optimization

RNN has an advantage in training the sequential data. However, the original RNN has a problem when it has a long step size. Hessian-free optimization was introduced as one potential solution. We explain the basic of RNN and explore the problem. Lastly, we describe how hessian-free optimization overcomes the problem.

3.1 Recurrent Neural Network

Feedforward neural network is the first artificial neural network [16]. It is composed of input layer, hidden layer, output layer and connections between layers so-called weight. When the form of feedforward network is a directed cycle, we call it is RNN. The basic key idea of RNN is unfolding a recurrent computation of cyclic feedforward network. Then RNN can be a deep neural network. It can learn patterns in sequences.

Figure 1 shows a basic concept of RNN and how to unfold the cyclic feedforward neural network. The original RNN is composed of input layer, hidden layer and output layer. Connections between units in each layer are weights. There are three kind of weights. A weight from input unit to hidden unit is input-to-hidden weight. The weight from hidden unit to output unit is hidden-to-output weight.

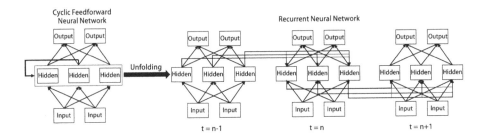

Fig. 1. Basic concept of RNN and unfolding

The weight from hidden unit to the next time step hidden unit is hidden-to-hidden weight. We can easily notice that hidden-to-hidden weight is computed recurrently. RNN updates the weights by training.

Table 1. Notations for RNN formulation

Notation	Description
x_t	Input vector (subscript t means a time sequence)
h_t	Hidden state
y_t	Output vector
$\overline{y_t}$	Predicted output vector by RNN
W_{xh}	Input-to-Hidden weight
W_{hh}	Hidden-to-Hidden weight
W_{hy}	Hidden-to-Output weight
b_h	Bias value of hidden state
b_y	Bias value of output vector
f	Hidden nonlinearity
g	Output nonlinearity

For more details, we define some notations. Table 1. shows the notations for RNN formulation. x_t is an input vector at time step t. y_t can be explained in the same manner. Training dataset can be defined as a list of $[x_t, y_t]$. RNN trains the training dataset and predicts $\overline{y_t}$. The forward propagation formulation is (3). f and g are nonlinearity function called an activation function in neural network. The activation functions usually used are sigmoid, hyperbolic tangent and rectifier linear unit (ReLU). Sigmoid and hyperbolic tangent are recommended for RNN.

$$h_t = f(W_{xh}x_t + W_{hh}h_{t-1} + b_h) \tag{1}$$
$$\overline{y_t} = g(W_{hy}h_t + b_y)$$

After forward propagation, the weights will be updated by using backpropagation through time (BPTT) [17]. However, the original RNN is hard to train. What makes it difficult is that the gradient is exploding or vanishing while doing BPTT. Bengio et al. addressed this problem [18]. Because we use nonlinearity function f and g, the forward propagation is nonlinear. Although the time step of RNN is long, this feature is able to prevent the exploding or vanishing activation values. However, backward propagation is linear. Therefore if the time step is long, the gradients would be exploded or vanished. For example, if the weights are big, the gradient would grow exponentially. On the contrary to this, if the weights are small, the gradient would become smaller exponentially. We call this exploding/vanishing problem of RNN.

3.2 Hessian Free Optimization

Because of exploding/vanishing problem of RNN, we need to find a way for training RNN. In gradient decent algorithm, it only use the first derivative of the error function. It cannot always be the best way to find a minimum error. Because sometimes it find a local minimum error depending on the hyper parameters. Therefore we have to consider the second derivatives of the error function for finding the minimum error. We usually use Newtons method [19]. Let the error function is $\mathbf{f} : \mathbb{R}^n \to R$. Then the update rule is as follows.

$$x_{t+1} = x_t - (f''(x))^{-1} f'(x) = x_t - (H(f)(x_t))^{-1} f'(x_t) \tag{2}$$

H is a hessian matrix which means the curvature matrix of f. And it also means the second derivatives of f. We can easily find a global minimum when we compute the inverse of hessian matrix. However H is a huge matrix. It is hard to compute the hessian matrix. To solve this problem, James Martens et al. proposed Hessian-free optimization in 2010 [20]. They used Conjugate Gradient (CG) method. CG method minimizes a quadratic function. Also, it can be applied to a non-quadratic function. By making a new direction is conjugate, the previous gradient was not affected. If a new direction is not conjugate, the gradients which are computed before are messed up. As a result, the error cannot be minimized.

4 Dataset

We use DARPA dataset which was used for 1999 KDD Cup contest as for training a model and verification [21,22]. The data was generated by the Defense Advanced Research Projects Agency and the Air Force Research Laboratory. There are training data for 7 weeks and test data for 2 weeks. The main purpose is to prove the high performance when RNN with hessian free optimization is applied to intrusion detection. Although the dataset is old, there are many studies with it due to the fact that it is the well-organized dataset for machine learning. It is good to compare the performance because all studies including ours experimented with the same dataset. Therefore we choose DARPA dataset as the training and test dataset.

4.1 Data Description

The data in DARPA dataset are tcp dump. Training data and test data are recorded for 5 million connections and 2 million connections. The dataset has 41 features. And 22 attacks are recorded in the dataset. Table 2. shows the features and their description and range except rate features such as *serror_rate* or *rerror_rate*. The descriptions of attacks in the dataset are given in Table 3. The attacks were categorized according to their feature. DoS means denial-of-service. Probe is a surveillance attack. U2R is an attack which tries to unauthorized access to superuser. R2L is an unauthorized remote access attack.

Table 2. The features of dataset

No	Feature	Description/Range
1	Duration	Connection time, [0-58329]
2	Protocol_type	Protocol types , [3 symbols]
3	Service	Network service, [70 symbols]
4	Flag	Error status of connection, [11 symbols]
5	Src_bytes	Source data size[0-1.3 billion]
6	Dst_bytes	Destination data size [0-1.3 billion]
7	Land	If connection with a same host or port, then 1, otherwise 0, [0,1]
8	Wrong_fragment	Wrong fragment number, [0-3]
9	Urgent	Urgent packet number, [0-14]
10	Hot	Hot indicator number, [0-101]
11	Num_failed_logins	Failed login number, [0-5]
12	Logged_in	1 means login successfully, otherwise 0, [0,1]
13	Num_compromized	Compromised conditions number, [0-9]
14	Root_shell	1 means root shell is obtained, otherwise 0, [0,1]
15	Su_attempted	1 means su root command is attempted, otherwise 0, [0,1]
16	Num_root	Root access number, [0-7468]
17	Num_file_creations	File creation number, [0-100]
18	Num_shells	Shell prompts number, [0-5]
19	Num_access_files	Access file operation number, [0-9]
20	Num_outbound_cmds	Outbound command in ftp session number
21	Is_host_login	1 means the host login, otherwise 0, [0,1]
22	Is_guest_login	1 means a guest login, otherwise 0, [0,1]
23	count	number of connections to the same host as the current connection in the past two seconds, [0-511]
24	srv_count	number of connections to the same service as the current connection in the past two seconds, [0-511]
25	serror_rate	SYN error connections percent (same host connection)
26	srv_serror_rate	SYN error connections percent (same service connection)

Table 2. (*Continued.*)

No	Feature	Description/Range
27	rerror_rate	REJ error connections percent (same host connection)
28	srv_rerror_rate	REJ error connections percent (same service connection)
29	same_srv_rate	Same service connections percent
30	diff_srv_rate	Different service connection percent
31	srv_diff_host_rate	Different host connection percent
32	dst_host_count	Same destination host connections number, [0-255]
33	dst_host_srv_count	Same destination host and service connections number, [0-255]
34	dst_host_same_srv_rate	Same destination host and service connections percent
35	dst_host_diff_srv_rate	Percent of different services on the current host
36	dst_host_same_src_port_rate	Current host having the same src port connections percent
37	dst_host_srv_diff_host_rate	Same service coming from different hosts connections percent
38	dst_host_serror_rate	Percent of connections to the current host that have an S0 error
39	dst_host_srv_serror_rate	Percent of connections to the current host and specified service that have an S0 error
40	dst_host_rerror_rate	Percent of connections to the current host that have an RST error
41	dst_host_srv_rerror_rate	Percent of connections to the current host and specified service that have an RST error

4.2 Feature Selection

For obtaining high accuracy, we have to reduce the features in Table 2. Some features are not associated with intrusion detection. These features lower the efficiency of IDS. Adetunmbi A. et al. analyzed DARPA dataset for selecting relevant features [23]. They removed redundant features by Rough set theory. And they selected relevance features for each attack through dependency ratio. We arranged the relevant features per category of the attacks in Table 4. The numbers in the column of relevant features are feature numbers in Table 2. In order to detect all categorized attacks using one detection model, we have to use all relevant features in Table 4. And we do not have to use 9 features (13,15,17,19,20,21,22,40, 41).

4.3 Preprocessing

If we want to use the features as an input vector of RNN, we should normalize them. The normalization range is from -1 to 1. There are 4 types feature in

Table 3. The attacks in the dataset

Category	Attacks	Description
DoS	land	Access the server with same IP address and Port number. And beat down the server
	neptune	A denial of service attack to TCP/IP vulnerable. Send only SYN packet to the victim then do not establish 3-hand shaking. Beat down the waiting queue
	pod	Ping Of Death (POD) is a kind of denial of service attack. Send a lot of ping (ICMP protocol) and beat down the server
	smurf	Attackers use ICMP echo request packets directed to IP broadcast addresses fromremote locations
	teardrop	The teardrop is a DoS attack that exploits a flaw in the implementation of older TCP/IP stacks
Probe	ipsweep	Send ping to certain group of network and waiting for response. Distinguish host is alive
	nmap	Network vulnerability scanning using nmap
	portsweep	Checking which port is open, or what kind of program is running on the system
	satan	Network vulnerability scanning using satan
U2R	buffer_overflow	Pour the data more than buffer size. And modify the data in buffer
	loadmodule	Load certain kernel driver module dynamically for acquiring root authority
	rootkit	The program that hide the backdoor
R2L	ftp_write	Overwrite or write another file to the ftp server in order to drive client to receive wrong file from the server
	guess_passwd	Guessing password by brute force or dictionary attack
	imap	Injecting imap protocol command to e-mail server for sending commands
	phf	Operating shell command by using phf cgi
	warezclient	Make users download the illegal warez software
	warezmaster	Exploits a system bug associated with a FTP server

the dataset. The first type is a symbolic feature such as protocol_type and service and flag. We convert these features to numerical value in the normalization range. The second type is a binary feature such as land, logged_in and root_shell. These feature values are already in range. Therefore we do not have to normalize them. The third type is a percentage feature. Like the second one, we do not mind it. The last feature is a numerical feature. We have to normalize all these feature values. We compute the center value (Table 5) for each feature from the feature

Table 4. Relevant features

Attack category	Relevant features
DoS	2,3,4,5,6,7,8,12,23,25,26,29,30,31,32,34,36,37, 38,39
Probe	5,27,28,36
U2R	3,5,6,14,16,18,23,24,36
R2L	1,3,4,5,6,9,10,11,14,23,24,26,39
Normal	3,6,12,23,25,26,29,30,33,34,35,36,37,38,39

Table 5. Center values

No	Feature	Center value
1	Duration	29164.5
5	Src_bytes	650000000
6	Dst_bytes	650000000
8	Wrong_fragment	1.5
9	Urgent	7
10	Hot	50.5
11	Num_failed_logins	2.5
16	Num_root	3734
18	Num_shells	2.5
23	count	255.5
24	srv_count	255.5
32	dst_host_count	127.5
33	dst_host_srv_count	127.5

value range in Table 2. Then we calculate a deviation. If we divide the deviation by the center value, the normalization value could be calculated.

5 Experiment

We take an experiment for measuring the performance of our model. We developed IDS by python using Theano [24]. Our experiment environment is as follows.

- CPU : intel i7
- GPU : NVIDIA GeForce GTX 970
- RAM : 8GB
- OS : Windows 7

5.1   Model Construction

As we explained in Sect. 4.2, we select 32 features as an input vector of the intrusion detection model. An output vector is composed of Dos, Probe, R2L, U2R and Normal. We use 'kddcup.data.txt' for constructing a training data and test data. The training data has 3100 samples and the test data has 400 samples. We applied softmax to the output of the model. So we made 5 classes from the output vector. We use hyperbolic tangent as an activation function. The number of hidden unit is 45 and a step size is 50. CG batch size is 1000.

5.2   Performance Metrics

We use accuracy, detection rate and false alarm rate as performance metrics of IDS by using a confusion matrix. The confusion matrix is composed of true positive (TP), true negative (TN), false positive (FP), and false negative (FN). Accuracy is a ratio of correct classification to the total test data. Detection rate is a ratio of the number of correct detection to the total number of attacks. False alarm rate is a ratio of the number of misclassification. All metrics are calculated using the following relation.

$$Accuracy = \frac{TP + TN}{TP + TN + FP + FN}$$
$$DetectionRate = \frac{TP}{TP + FN} \tag{3}$$
$$FalseAlarmRate = \frac{FP}{TN + FP}$$

5.3   Result

Table 6 is the confusion matrix of the experiment result. TP means when the attack is occurred the model predicts the correct answer. TN means when the connection is normal class the model predicts normal connection. FN means when the attack is occurred the model predicts normal connections. FP means when the attack is occurred the model predicts wrong attack. Figure 2 shows classification accuracies for each attack. The accuracies of DoS, U2R and Normal is outperform than other classes. There are small samples for Probe and R2L. We only trained 40 samples and 100 samples for R2L and Probe. If there

Table 6. Confusion Matrix of IDS model

	Positive (Predicted)	Negative (Predicted)
Positive (Actual Value)	289 (TP)	14 (FN)
Negative (Actual Value)	2 (FP)	95 (TN)

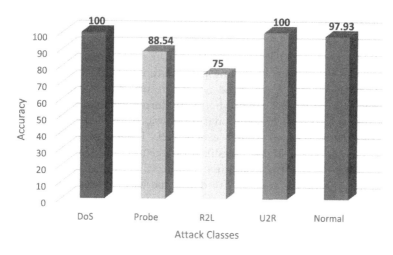

Fig. 2. Accuracy for each attack

Table 7. The performance comparison

Model	Detection rate	False alarm rate
KNN [25]	91	8
Fuzzy association rules [26]	91	3.34
Jordan ANN [27]	62.9	37.09
RNN [27]	73.1	26.85
Feed Forward Neural Network [28]	86.89	2.65
Generalized Regression Neural Network [28]	59.12	12.46
Probabilistic Neural Network [28]	78.95	3.34
Radial Basis Neural Network [28]	69.83	6.95
Our model	**95.37**	**2.1**

are plenty of samples, the accuracies would be higher. Table 7 shows the comparison of performance with other models. We can easily notice that our model is outperform than other model. The detection rate of our model is 95.37 % and false alarm rate is only 2.1 %.

6 Conclusion

In this paper, we applied RNN with Hessian-free optimization to IDS. Even though, we had a difficulty of finding proper step size, CG batch size and the number of hidden unit, it produced a good result. The result of experiment showed that our model has a quite better performance than other model. The detection rate was 95.37 % and false alarm rate was only 2.1 %. The classification accuracy of each attack was so high except R2L. If there are sufficient samples for R2L, we could get a higher classification accuracy. In this study, we could verify that using RNN with hessian-free optimization for intrusion detection is a quite good approach. We are going to detect modern attacks and malwares for further study.

References

1. US cybercrime : Rising risks, reduced readiness, white paper (2014)
2. Karen, S., Mell, P.: Guide to intrusion detection and prevention systems (idps). In: NIST special publication 800-94 (2007)
3. Kumar, S., Eugene, H., Spafford, A.: Pattern matching model for misuse intrusion detection. In: Proceedings of the 17th National Computer Security Conference (1994)
4. Mukherjee, B., Heberlein, L., Levitt, K.: Network intrusion detection. Netw. IEEE **8**(3), 2641 (1994)
5. Deng, L., Yu, D.: Deep learning: methods and applications. Found. Trends Signal Process. **7**(34), 197–387 (2014)
6. Krizhevsky, A., Sutskever, I., Hinton, G.E.: Imagenet classification with deep convolutional neural networks. In: Advances in Neural Information Processing Systems (2012)
7. Graves, A., Mohamed, A., Hinton, G.: Speech recognition with deep recurrent neural networks. In: 2013 IEEE International Conference on Acoustics, Speech and Signal Processing (ICASSP). IEEE (2013)
8. Funahashi, K., Nakamura, Y.: Approximation of dynamical systems by continuous time recurrent neural networks. Neural Netw. **6**(6), 801–806 (1993)
9. Hochreiter, S., et al.: Gradient flow in recurrent nets: the difficulty of learning long-term dependencies (2001)
10. Martens, J., Sutskever, I.: Learning recurrent neural networks with hessian-free optimization. In: Proceedings of the 28th International Conference on Machine Learning (ICML-11) (2011)
11. Thomas, C., Sharma, V., Balakrishnan, N.: Usefulness of DARPA dataset for intrusion detection system evaluation. In: SPIE Defense and Security Symposium. International Society for Optics and Photonics (2008)
12. Mukkamala, S., Sung, A.H., Abraham, A.: Intrusion detection using ensemble of soft computing paradigms. In: Abraham, A., Franke, K., Köppen, M. (eds.) Intelligent Systems Design and Applications. Advances in Intelligent and Soft Computing, vol. 23, pp. 239–248. Springer, Heidelberg (2003)
13. Chavan, S., et al.: Adaptive neuro-fuzzy intrusion detection systems. In: Proceedings of International Conference on Information Technology, Coding and Computing, ITCC 2004, vol. 1. IEEE (2004)

14. Peddabachigari, S., et al.: Modeling intrusion detection system using hybrid intelligent systems. J. Netw. Comput. Appl. **30**(1), 114–132 (2007)
15. Kachurka, P., Golovko, V.: Neural network approach to real-time network intrusion detection and recognition. In: 2011 IEEE 6th International Conference on Intelligent Data Acquisition and Advanced Computing Systems (IDAACS), vol. 1. IEEE (2011)
16. Hornik, K., Stinchcombe, M., White, H.: Multilayer feedforward networks are universal approximators. Neural Netw. **2**(5), 359–366 (1989)
17. Werbos, P.J.: Backpropagation through time: what it does and how to do it. Proc. IEEE **78**(10), 1550–1560 (1990)
18. Bengio, Y., Simard, P., Frasconi, P.: Learning long-term dependencies with gradient descent is difficult. IEEE Trans. Neural Netw. **5**(2), 157–166 (1994)
19. Battiti, R.: First-and second-order methods for learning: between steepest descent and Newton's method. Neural Comput. **4**(2), 141–166 (1992)
20. Martens, J.: Deep learning via Hessian-free optimization. In: Proceedings of the 27th International Conference on Machine Learning (ICML-10) (2010)
21. Lippmann, R., Haines, J., Fried, D., Korba, J., Das, K.: The 1999 darpa off-line intrusion detection evaluation. Comput. Netw. **34**(4), 579–595 (2000)
22. Lippmann, R., Fried, D., Graf, I., Haines, J., Kendall, K., McClung, D., Weber, D., Webster, S., Wyschogrod, D., Cunningham, R., et al.: Evaluating intrusion detection systems: The 1998 darpa off-line intrusion detection evaluation. In: Proceedings of DARPA Information Survivability Conference and Exposition, DISCEX 2000, vol. 2, p. 1226. IEEE (2000)
23. Olusola, A.A., Oladele, A.S., Abosede, D.O.: Analysis of KDD99 intrusion detection dataset for selection of relevance features. In: Proceedings of the World Congress on Engineering and Computer Science, vol. 1 (2010)
24. Bergstra, J., et al.: Theano : a CPU and GPU math expression compiler. In: Proceedings of the Python for Scientific Computing Conference (SciPy), vol. 4 (2010)
25. Han, S.-J., Cho, S.-B.: Detecting intrusion with rule-based integration of multiple models. Comput. Secur. **22**(7), 613–623 (2003)
26. Tajbakhsh, A., Rahmati, M., Mirzaei, A.: Intrusion detection using fuzzy association rules. Appl. Soft Comput. **9**(2), 462–469 (2009)
27. Beghdad, R.: Training all the KDD data set to classify and detect attacks. Neural Netw. World **17**(2), 81 (2007)
28. Devaraju, S., Ramakrishnan, S.: Performance comparison for intrusion detection system using neural network with KDD dataset. ICTACT J. Soft Comput. **4**, 743–752 (2014)

Application Security

Cost-Effective Modeling for Authentication and Its Application to Activity Tracker

Hiroya Susuki$^{(\boxtimes)}$ and Rie Shigetomi Yamaguchi

The University of Tokyo, 7-3-1 Hongo, Bunkyo-ku, Tokyo 113-8656, Japan
susuki.hiroya@sict.i.u-tokyo.ac.jp, yamaguchi.rie@i.u-tokyo.ac.jp,
http://www.sict.i.u-tokyo.ac.jp

Abstract. The growing popularity of multi-factor authentication, it makes the need for more cost-effective approach. The more authentication factors the system use, the higher cost for machine learning all of factors it require. We considered the behavioral authentication that is brought to attention as one of the authentication factors. The behavioral authentication works well with machine learning approaches. However, with machine learning, a model must be created, and the service provider must analyze each user individually; both adding to the cost. In this paper, we propose a cost-effective user modeling approach that uses a FuelBand to obtain activity information for behavioral authentication. This approach uses a clustering method that focuses on the characteristics of our behavioral authentication method. The performance of our system was compared to that of machine learning (70 users), and for no more than half the cost, the results had an accuracy of 89.28 %.

Keywords: User authentication · User behavior · Wearable device · Machine learning · Activity log

1 Introduction

Online services are increasing, and the use of mobile devices, such as smartphones and tablets, is spreading. In recent years, people have begun using these devices to access the Internet. In order to use online services, users have to complete an authentication process. When the information accessed by such services is sensitive, it is important that the user authentication process is both secure and easy to use. "Behavioral authentication" is one approach to this, such as implicit authentication [1]. This method classifies the unique patterns of each user's behavior, without requiring any additional actions by the users. Behavioral authentication is based on the unique behavioral tendencies that result from both the psychological and physiological differences between individuals [2,3]. Many types of behavioral authentication schemes have been proposed, such as gait recognition [4], location [5], usage characteristic of mobile devices [6], application-centric authentication [7] and risk-based authentication [8]. These schemes not only capture the features of a machine, such as its OS and browser,

© Springer International Publishing Switzerland 2016
H. Kim and D. Choi (Eds.): WISA 2015, LNCS 9503, pp. 373–385, 2016.
DOI: 10.1007/978-3-319-31875-2_31

but they can also obtain information collected by wearable devices. There are some authentication schemes that use the data obtained by wearable devices, in particular, data about the user's activities [9,10].

A problem with behavioral authentication is that the input data is ambiguous. The data from two samples for the same person will not be exactly the same, due to collecting data under imperfect conditions (e.g., sensor noise, changes in the physiology or behavior of the user, and the interaction of the user with the sensor) [11]. Instead of using rules or matching patterns, other proposed methods use machine learning for biometric authentication [12,13]. Machine learning is well suited for ambiguous input data, but it is difficult and expensive to create a model for each user.

In addition, the behavioral authentication is useful for one of the authentication factors for multi-factor authentication system because the factor is required to have diversity and be large in number. Also, service providers want to consider the security level of authentication systems depending on their services. In some practical cases, the cost is as important as security. However, the more factors the authentication system use, the higher cost for modeling all of factors it requires. The cost-effective model is important for reducing the required computing resources and time for modeling. For modeling the activity data of individual users, we propose a cost-effective scheme that is based on machine learning. When using machine learning to create a model, the data from each user must be analyzed individually. Our scheme is able to reduce the time required to create the models, because instead of creating models individually, it analyzes existing patterns to find an approximate match.

1.1   Related Work

Authentication methods based on machine learning have been proposed for biometric authentication such as fingerprint authentication [12], gait recognition [13], and keystroke authentication [14], and the primary motivation has been the security of authentication systems. However, machine learning is an expensive process, and is well known that there is a tradeoff between security and cost. For classifying multiple users, multiple binary classifiers, such as a one-against-one approach, and a one-against-the-rest (or one-against-all) approach, have been proposed [15–17]. In these methods, the number of classifiers is proportional to the number of users in the system, and so is not practical for use with a real-world large-scale authentication system.

There are two types of machine learning. One is supervised learning, which tries to make inferences based on the labeled training data, and the other is unsupervised learning, which tries to find hidden structure in unlabeled data. Supervised learning methods are used for authentication tasks, since there is a clear target to be classified [18]. The support vector machine (SVM) is a well-known supervised learning method that uses binary classification and has shown remarkable success in many applications [19]. Facial recognition is one area in which SVMs have been very successful [20–22]. When using an SVM, each item in a set of training data is marked as belonging to one of two classes (positive and negative examples).

The SVM then uses the training data to assign new examples into one of the two classes. Problems can occur when learning from imbalanced datasets, in which the positive data is heavily outnumbered by the negative data [23]. This also occurs in the field of user authentication, where positive examples are the data for the person who should be recognized, and negative examples are the data for everyone else; thus, the data will be unbalanced, with an excess number of negative examples. Previous studies have not considered the imbalanced dataset problem for authentication systems.

Fig. 1. The Nike+ FuelBand SE is a device meant to be worn on the wrist. The client application presents graphical output produced by the data from the FuelBand. Here we show an example of daily graphical output as it appears on an iPhone [26].

The number of SVM classifiers determines the learning cost. Authentication systems require multiclass classification for an ensemble of one-class classifiers, although some use ensemble methods [15,24,25]. However, the security of the existing methods is not comparable to that of current authentication systems.

Two issues that are important for the cost and performance of authentication systems are the number of classifiers and whether the dataset is imbalanced. We propose a user model that reduces the cost of machine learning by reducing the required computing resources and reducing the time required for learning.

1.2 Our Contribution

Our results show that it is possible to reduce the large learning cost in exchange for only a small loss of accuracy. The cost of machine learning depends on the number of classifiers. Our proposed model is based on the following three techniques: one-against-one approach with clustering using daily features, one-against-one approach with clustering using hourly features, one-against-the-rest approach. It is based on clustering and ensemble techniques for machine learning classification. We evaluated our proposed model by applying it to a system that uses a behavioral authentication method based on user activity data. We show that our proposed model could provide acceptable levels of both security

Table 1. Age and gender of participants

	20-	30-	40-	50-	60-	Total
Male	20	11	8	6	1	46
Female	10	7	5	1	1	24
Total	30	18	13	7	2	70

Table 2. Daily average Fuel

	20-	30-	40-	50-69	Average
Male	2287.6	2045.3	3182.6	2432.7	2407.3
Female	2208.4	1704.7	1691.5	2029.4	1938.9

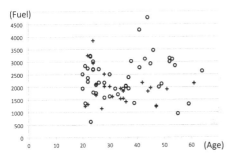

Fig. 2. Distribution of daily average Fuel by age and gender (male: circle sign; female: multiplication sign).

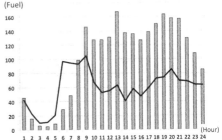

Fig. 3. Average Fuel per hour (average Fuel: bar graph; standard deviation: line graph).

and cost. As a result, we show our model can change that the balance of security and cost by selecting machine learning methods depending on the use case.

1.3 Authentication Model

Multi-factor authentication will spread more and more in this decade and beyond. The merit of multi-factor authentication is not only security but also flexibility. The flexibility of multi-factor authentication means that service providers determine the balance point of the selectability of security, usability and the cost by combination of authentication factors. The cost is one of the important things for multi-factor authentication. The more and more factors increase, the higher and higher the cost of machine learning will be. In the case of single-factor authentication, the accuracy is more important than the cost. On the other hand, there is necessarily no need for multi-factor authentication to have all of the factors are high accuracy. It needs secure authentication methods as a whole. Such multi-factor authentication systems, we can also consider not only security but also cost.

2 Data Collection and Baseline Authentication Method Using Activity Data

In this section, we discuss an activity data collection experiment and our proposed authentication method, which uses the collected data.

2.1   Activity Data Collection Using FuelBand

The data used in this paper was collected using a Nike+ FuelBand SE ("Fuel-Band") [27], a wearable device that contains triaxial accelerometers to monitor activity and is worn on the wrist (see Fig. 1). It measures human activity data at intervals of one minute, and it records the data in units of Fuel, a measure of the energy required to perform an activity. We obtained data from 70 volunteers (see Table 1). The experiment ran from Monday, May 26, 2014 to Sunday, July 6, 2014. The participants were asked to perform their normal daily activities, and they were told they could remove the FuelBand at any time, such as at bedtime.

Table 2 shows the average Fuel per day by age and gender. The overall average Fuel was 2246.7, and the standard deviation was 779.7. Figure 2 shows the relation between the daily average Fuel and participants by age and gender. There was no strong correlation between Fuel and age or gender of participants. Figure 3 shows hourly average Fuel of all participants.

2.2   Machine Learning Using Proposed Activity Features

For the learning, we used a SVM with a radial basis function (RBF) kernel and 10–fold cross validation. We used the SVM implementation for authentication systems, from the library LIBSVM [28]. The data sets of training examples and the test examples were obtained from the collected data. For the dataset, one entry consisted of one day, which was defined to be the period from 0:00 to 23:59. The FuelBand records data once per minute, so the number of data points in each entry was $60(minutes) \times 24(hours) = 1,440$.

For the baseline case, we used the one-against-one approach for multiclass classification. For this approach, since there were 70 participants and 69 classifiers for each participant, we need $(70 \times 69)/2 = 2,415$ classifiers. In this paper, we will define the accuracy of the system to be the average accuracy of all of the classifiers. The accuracy is the rate at which we correctly classify the data (positive data to the positive class and negative data to the negative class).

To compare the various learning approaches, we used the same data set for the learning in each approach. The learning data set had an accuracy of 93.98 % as a best case that is the baseline. Previous researches have not applied to FuelBand for behavioral authentication system without the study [10]. We used the baseline case as the highest accuracy and the highest cost case to evaluate the efficiency of our proposed method.

3   Machine Learning Using a User Model

In this section, we discuss our proposed machine learning approach that uses a user model for the authentication.

3.1 Multiclass Classification

If a multiclass classifier is used for user authentication, it is not necessary to use a multiple classifier for each user: a single classifier can be used for multiple user models. Thus, we performed a preliminary experiment to compare the performance of two machine learning methods when using multiclass (70-class) classification. Table 3 shows the results of multiclass classification using an ensemble machine learning method (Random Forest [29]) and SVM. Some implementations of SVM can use ensemble methods to preform multiclass classification [15]. In this preliminary experiment, we used two packages from R, which is a language and environment for statistical computing and graphics [30]; the packages were "randomForest" (a package for Random Forest), and "e1071" (a package for SVM). Compared to the accuracy of 93.98 % that has been shown for an ensemble of one-class (binary) classifiers, the results show that multiclass classification is not sufficiently accurate for user authentication.

Table 3. Comparison of the accuracy of multiclass classifications

	No. of classes	Accuracy
Multiclass SVM	70	32.41 %
Random Forest	70	37.14 %
Ensemble of One-Class SVM	-	93.98 %

Table 4. Comparison of the accuracy of the one-against-one and one-against-the-rest

	one-against-one	one-against-the-rest (random sampling)	difference between the two approaches
Accuracy	93.98%	81.59%	12.38%
Standard deviation	1.65%	5.86%	4.62%

3.2 Random Sampling

One-class SVM requires multiple classifiers, and the number depends on the number of users to be classified, since each person has their own unique model. If the number of classes to be classified is m, the one-against-one approach requires $m(m-1)/2$ classifiers, and the one-against-the-rest approach requires m classifiers. In the one-against-one approach, a set of training data consists of positive examples and negative examples, and each member of the set consists of the data for a single user. On the other hand, in the one-against-the-rest approach, a set of training data consists of positive examples that consist of the data from one user, and negative examples that consist of the data of all the other users. For comparison with the one-against-one approach, we evaluated the accuracy of classification when using the one-against-the-rest approach.

The one-against-the-rest approach must extract negative examples from the data of the nontargeted users, because of the problem of imbalanced datasets. To evaluate the performance of the one-against-the-rest approach, we obtained negative examples by random sampling. To compare the results with those of the one-against-one approach, we used the same data set, but in a random order (shuffled). We obtained the negative examples by random sampling from the shuffled data set. The results had an accuracy of 81.59 % (see Table 4). Compared with the one-against-one approach, the accuracy was reduced by 12.39 %.

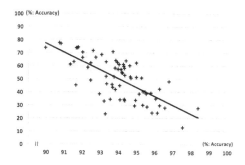

Fig. 4. Scatter plot of modified false acceptance rate; the line represents a linear approximation. Horizontal axis: accuracy (%) when using the third party data. Vertical axis: the regular accuracy (%) when using the data of the learned participants.

3.3 Evaluation of False Acceptance Rate

Unauthorized cases, such as login attempts by adversaries or by those who accidentally entered the wrong ID, should be denied, as such and we evaluated these cases. To evaluate the classification accuracy, we used the data that was not used for learning. The one-against-one approach to learning uses the data of two participants; one is considered to be a positive example, and the other, negative. In this experiment, the training data was that of a third participant. For example, we used the training data for participant ID:1 as positive examples and that of participant ID:2 as negative examples; the test data was that of participant ID:3. Generally, supervised learning methods should not use the data from a third party, because the learned classifiers lack information about it. However, it should be classified accurately if our proposed learning characteristics are effective for classifying each person.

Figure 4 shows that the modified false acceptance rate is strongly negatively correlated with the accuracy of the learned participants. As a result, although the average accuracy was 49.80 %, the best accuracy for any individual participant was 86.90 %. This is close to the result (93.98 %) obtained when using the data of learned participants as the test data. Therefore, even without using the data of participants as negative examples, our method can classify the unlearned negative data if the positive and negative examples are accurate. The results show that this method is effective for users who display characteristic behaviors.

3.4   Evaluation of the Clustering Approach

We evaluated the two proposed approaches to determine if there was a way to reduce the number of classifiers. When performing authentication using machine learning, it is problematic if the datasets are unbalanced. Both approaches cluster the data of users that have similar characteristic behaviors. This means that the approach can make a single user model that will work for multiple people. The clustered user is just a generalized user model. In the first approach, the task is to select the appropriate clustered user. As we can see from evaluating the modified false acceptance rate (FAR), this approach is not effective for users who have less accurate results. In the second approach, the model is extracted from all of the data of the clustered users. Below, we describe how to extract the negative examples from the users.

Selecting One User's Data from the Clustered Users. This approach is simple. The approach only selects one user from the clustered users. Only this selected user's behavior data affects the learning.

Extracting Data from All Clusters of Users. With this approach, the data from all clusters of users is allowed to affect the learning. A problem with this approach is that the information about individual users is mixed together.

In this section, we evaluate the second approach described above. There are two points of comparison. The first point is how the number of clusters compares to the number of users, and the second point is how the clusters are formed from multiple users. Below we list two types of clustering features that we used for this evaluation, and we propose their use for the authentication of behavior when using activity data collected by a FuelBand.

Daily Clustering Features. The features use daily statistics for the collected data (e.g., daily average Fuel, and the daily standard deviation).

Table 5. The number of clusters and the learning features used for clustering.

Number of clusters	Average number of members	Features used for clustering	
		daily features	hourly features
(baseline) 70	1.0	93.98%	
30	2.3	88.94%	89.28%
20	3.5	87.83%	88.44%
10	7.0	85.18%	86.93%

Hourly Clustering Features. The features use hourly statistics for the collected data (e.g., hourly average Fuel).

Table 5 shows the accuracy of each type of clustering. In this experiment, we used the "randomForest" package for clustering. This result is consistent with the assumption that the number of cluster members reduces the accuracy. When there were 30 clusters, our model achieved an accuracy of 89.28 %, and the cost was no more than half that of the baseline. The accuracy was only 4.7 % less than that of the baseline approach 93.98 %: reasonable for a cost-oriented system.

4   Discussions

In this section, we use activity data to evaluate our proposed user model.

4.1   Random Sampling

Figure 5 shows the relation between the simple baseline one-against-one approach and the one-against-the-rest approach; there is a positive correlation, as can be seen by the straight-line estimate. In this experiment, the one-against-the-rest approach used randomly sampled negative examples for learning. Therefore, it is assumed that its accuracy is less that of the baseline one-against-one approach. Classification of ID:23 was 96.42 % accurate with the one-against-the-rest approach, it was 98.38 % accurate with the one-against-one (baseline) approach. If the accuracy of the baseline one-against-one approach is high, then the accuracy of the one-against-the-rest approach will also be high, as is seen with ID:23. This shows the effectiveness of our method when the user is distinct.

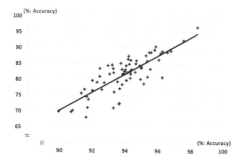

Fig. 5. Scatter plot of the classification accuracy per user of the one-against-one and one-against-the-rest (using random sampling) methods. The line is a linear approximation. Horizontal axis: the accuracy (%) of the one-against-one method. Vertical axis: the accuracy (%) of the one-against-the-rest method.

4.2   True Rejection Rate

Figure 6 shows the accuracy of the simple baseline one-against-one approach (bar graph) and the true rejection rate (TRR) (line graph) for each participant. As can be seen from the results, there are users with the low positive correlation and others with strong positive correlation. ID:53 has the highest classi-

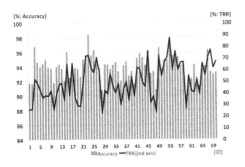

Table 6. Comparison of ID:23 and ID:53.

	ID: 23	ID: 53	All
Average TRR	72.23 %	86.90 %	49.80 %
Standard deviation	16.10 %	9.72 %	15.67 %
Average accuracy	98.14 %	96.67 %	93.89 %

Fig. 6. True Rejection Rate by ID. Horizontal axis: participant ID. Vertical axis: accuracy of the user ID.

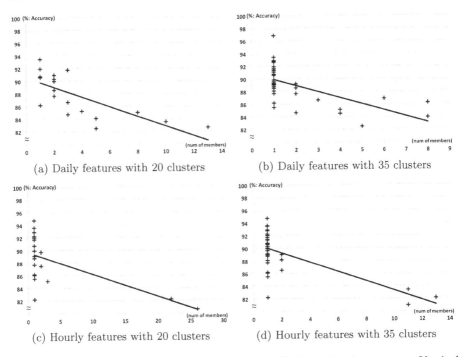

(a) Daily features with 20 clusters

(b) Daily features with 35 clusters

(c) Hourly features with 20 clusters

(d) Hourly features with 35 clusters

Fig. 7. Daily/Hourly features with 20/35 clusters. Horizontal axis: accuracy. Vertical axis: the number of members in a cluster.

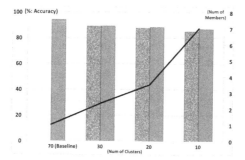

Fig. 8. The relation between the two clustering types (bar graph, reft stripe bar is daily, right bar is hourly) and the number of members per cluster (line graph, 2nd-axis).

fication accuracy, and it also has a high TRR with strong positive correlation (see Table 6). On the other hand, ID:23 has high accuracy but a slightly lower TRR. ID:23 has the highest accuracy. For ID:23, we can see a small variation in the accuracy, but a big variation in the TRR. Unlike ID:23, ID:53 shows a big variation in accuracy, but only a small variation in TRR. As described above, although there is a different trend for each user, the accuracy and TRR are generally positively correlated.

4.3 Clustering

As expected, the number of members in a cluster and the accuracy are negatively correlated. We proposed two clustering methods using data extraction: one uses daily features, and the other uses hourly features. The various combinations of the number of members in a cluster and the daily or hourly features are shown in Fig. 7. From these figures, it can be seen that the accuracy decreases as the number of cluster members increases. By balancing the number of cluster members, such as in Fig. 7(a), it is possible to reduce the loss in accuracy. Using the hourly features results in greater accuracy than using daily features (see Fig. 8). The result shows the authentication system can change the balance of security level and the cost by selecting the number of cluster members.

5   Conclusions

In this paper, we propose a cost-effective user model for a behavioral authentication system that obtains activity information from a wearable device (FuelBand). In accordance with the diversification of online services, service providers want to consider the security level of authentication systems depending on their services. The level should be able to change only security but also the cost of the system. We evaluated the relationship between accuracy and cost. The results showed that it is possible to reduce the learning cost in exchange for only a small loss of accuracy. Our model achieved an accuracy rate of 89.28 %, and did so at no more than half the cost. The accuracy rate was 4.7 % less than the accuracy rate of the baseline approach: reasonable for a cost-oriented system. By using our proposed model, administrators of authentication systems are able to select the machine learning cost that is suitable for their service.

Acknowledgments. We would like to thank Mitsubishi UFJ NICOS Co., Ltd. for a grant that made it possible to complete this work.

References

1. Jakobsson, M., Shi, E., Golle, P., Chow, R.: Implicit authentication for mobile devices. In: Proceedings of the 4th USENIX Conference on Hot Topics in Security, p. 9. USENIX Association (2009)
2. Zhang, F., Kondoro, A., Muftic, S.: Location-based authentication and authorization using smart phones. In: IEEE 11th International Conference on, Trust, Security and Privacy in Computing and Communications (TrustCom), pp. 1285–1292. IEEE (2012)
3. Bergadano, F., Gunetti, D., Picardi, C.: User authentication through keystroke dynamics. ACM Trans. Inf. Syst. Secur. (TISSEC) 5(4), 367–397 (2002)
4. Rong, L., Jianzhong, Z., Ming, L., Xiangfeng, H.: A wearable acceleration sensor system for gait recognition. In: 2nd IEEE Conference on Industrial Electronics and Applications, ICIEA 2007, pp. 2654–2659. IEEE (2007)
5. Hayashi, E., Das, S., Amini, S., Hong, J., Oakley, I.: Casa: context-aware scalable authentication. In: Proceedings of the Ninth Symposium on Usable Privacy and Security, p. 3. ACM (2013)
6. Shi, E., Niu, Y., Jakobsson, M., Chow, R.: Implicit authentication through learning user behavior. In: Burmester, M., Tsudik, G., Magliveras, S., Ilić, I. (eds.) ISC 2010. LNCS, vol. 6531, pp. 99–113. Springer, Heidelberg (2011)
7. Khan, H., Hengartner, U.: Towards application-centric implicit authentication on smartphones. In: Proceedings of the 15th Workshop on Mobile Computing Systems and Applications, p. 10. ACM (2014)
8. Last account activity. https://support.google.com/mail/answer/45938?hl=en Google. Accessed 10 March 2015
9. Riva, O., Qin, C., Strauss, K., Lymberopoulos, D.: Progressive authentication: deciding when to authenticate on mobile phones. In: USENIX Security Symposium, pp. 301–316 (2012)
10. Susuki, H., Yamaguchi, R.S.: Availability for user authentication by using user behavior of wearable devices (in japanese). In: The 32nd Symposium on Cryptography and Information Security (SCIS), p. 4C2-4 (2015)
11. Jain, A.K., Ross, A., Prabhakar, S.: An introduction to biometric recognition. IEEE Trans. Circ. Syst. Video Technol. 14(1), 4–20 (2004)
12. Jain, A.K., Prabhakar, S., Hong, L.: A multichannel approach to fingerprint classification. IEEE Trans. Pattern Anal. Mach. Intell. 21(4), 348–359 (1999)
13. Kale, A., Sundaresan, A., Rajagopalan, A.N., Cuntoor, N.P., Roy-Chowdhury, A.K., Kruger, V., Chellappa, R.: Identification of humans using gait. IEEE Trans. Image Process. 13(9), 1163–1173 (2004)
14. Monrose, F., Rubin, A.D.: Keystroke dynamics as a biometric for authentication. Future Gener. Comput. Syst. 16(4), 351–359 (2000)

15. Bottou, L., Cortes, C., Denker, J.S., Drucker, H., Guyon, I., Jackel, L.D., LeCun, Y., Muller, U.A., Sackinger, E., Simard, P., et al.: Comparison of classifier methods: a case study in handwritten digit recognition. In: International Conference on Pattern Recognition, p. 77. IEEE Computer Society Press (1994)

16. Weston, J., Watkins, C.: Multi-class support vector machines. Technical report, Citeseer (1998)

17. Hsu, C.-W., Lin, C.-J.: A comparison of methods for multiclass support vector machines. IEEE Trans. Neural Netw. **13**(2), 415–425 (2002)

18. Guo, G., Li, S.Z., Chan, K.L.: Face recognition by support vector machines. In: Proceedings. Fourth IEEE International Conference on Automatic Face and Gesture Recognition, pp. 196–201. IEEE (2000)

19. Vapnik, V.: The Nature of Statistical Learning Theory. Springer Science & Business Media, New York (2000)

20. Pusara, M., Brodley, C.E.: User re-authentication via mouse movements. In: Proceedings of the ACM Workshop on Visualization and Data Mining for Computer Security, pp. 1–8. ACM(2004)

21. Tefas, A., Kotropoulos, C., Pitas, I.: Using support vector machines to enhance the performance of elastic graph matching for frontal face authentication. IEEE Trans. Pattern Anal. Mach. Intell. **23**(7), 735–746 (2001)

22. Jonsson, K., Kittler, J., Li, Y.P., Matas, J.: Support vector machines for face authentication. Image Vis. Comput. **20**(5), 369–375 (2002)

23. Liu, Y., An, A., Huang, X.: Boosting prediction accuracy on imbalanced datasets with SVM ensembles. In: Ng, W.-K., Kitsuregawa, M., Li, J., Chang, K. (eds.) PAKDD 2006. LNCS (LNAI), vol. 3918, pp. 107–118. Springer, Heidelberg (2006)

24. Tian, M., Zhang, W., Liu, F.: On-line ensemble SVM for robust object tracking. In: Yagi, Y., Kang, S.B., Kweon, I.S., Zha, H. (eds.) ACCV 2007, Part I. LNCS, vol. 4843, pp. 355–364. Springer, Heidelberg (2007)

25. Yu, L., Yue, W., Wang, S., Lai, K.K.: Support vector machine based multiagent ensemble learning for credit risk evaluation. Expert Syst. Appl. **37**(2), 1351–1360 (2010)

26. Fuelband apps. https://itunes.apple.com/en/app/nike+-fuel/id493325070?mt=8. Accessed 30 June 2015

27. Fuelband. http://www.nike.com/us/en_us/c/nikeplus-fuel. Accessed 10 March 2015

28. Chang, C.-C., Lin, C.-J.: LIBSVM: A library for support vector machines. ACM Trans. Intell. Syst. Technol. **2**, 27: 1–27: 27 (2011). http://www.csie.ntu.edu.tw/~cjlin/libsvm

29. Breiman, L.: Random forests. Mach. Learn. **45**(1), 5–32 (2001)

30. R: The r project for statistical computing. http://www.r-project.org

Fully Batch Processing Enabled Memory Integrity Verification Algorithm Based on Merkle Tree

Se Hwan Kim[✉], Yonggon Kim, Ohmin Kwon, and Hyunsoo Yoon

School of Computing, Korea Advanced Institute of Science
and Technology (KAIST), Daejeon 305-701, Republic of Korea
{shkim,ygkim,omkwon,hyoon}@nslab.kaist.ac.kr

Abstract. Memory attacks have been increasing in number recently. Adversary can manipulate memory data or break system by doing active attacks. Especially, main memory is used as a target of attack, because main memory is more vulnerable than other components, such as CPU. To prevent adversary's active attack, memory integrity verification algorithm has been proposed. Protection of computer's memory integrity is important in situations where attacks on the computer systems are a threat. As technology has advanced, computer systems migrate from wire-based to wireless system. A lot of memory integrity verification algorithms are already developed, but these algorithms do not consider new wireless platform. Wireless platform is constrained by a lack of storage and power supply in comparison with wire-based system, therefore computational overhead and storage overhead must be considered when applying to algorithm, which is used in wireless system. In this study, integrity verification performance can be improved by doing batch-processing. Previous verification algorithms based on Merkle tree do not support fully batch processing verification. We propose fully batch processing enabled memory integrity verification algorithm based on Merkle tree. This algorithms can verify memory integrity in completely batches. For implement our algorithm, we use Incremental multiset hash function, and as a result, consume only 480-bit on-chip storage. Reducing consumption of on-chip storage leads to improving on the performance of computation. We implement our algorithm and previous memory integrity verification algorithms based on standard Merkle tree and lazy-processing Merkle tree in simulator to compare their performance. Our algorithm offers better system performance overall, especially when attack rarely occur.

Keywords: Memory integrity · Incremental multiset hash function · Temper-resistant · Merkle tree

1 Introduction

With the advancement of computer systems, the field of computer security has gained immense interest. Processors must ensure the correctness of computation under suspicious attack, not to mention fast computation. In other words, the importance of making secure processor is constantly increasing. The effort to take advantages by

© Springer International Publishing Switzerland 2016
H. Kim and D. Choi (Eds.): WISA 2015, LNCS 9503, pp. 386–398, 2016.
DOI: 10.1007/978-3-319-31875-2_32

attacking insecure processors has been prevalent since the past. Several conditions must be met in order to make secure processor. One of the conditions is secure input. Processor receives data from the memory and computes and processes the data. However, if the memory is vulnerable to the adversary so that the data is modifiable as the intention of the adversary, the processor no longer receives secure input. Thus, to make secure processor, the integrity of the data in the memory must be guaranteed. Recently, the advancement of computer systems must be based on the integrity of the memory.

In the past, the integrity of the data could be verified by the user in case of data modification due to the adversary because the computer managed few data. Currently, the number of data to manage has grown exponentially. Also, computers now computes data not related to the matching user due to grid computing technology [6]. Especially, unmanned system is fast girdling the world. Adversary can access machine easily, and modify machine's memory.

Figure 1 shows an example of memory integrity violation. In Fig. 1, 100 is right result, but by attacking block 'B', it has an effect entirely alien from the user intended. Because of these reasons, memory integrity verification is essential scheme for building secure processor, and it is still actively discussed and studied today. Merkle tree [9] is data structure which is used to verify data. It is often used to verify memory integrity [2]. A lot of memory integrity verification algorithms are already developed, but these algorithms do not consider new wireless platform. Wireless platform is constrained by a lack of storage and power supply in comparison with wire-based system, therefore computational overhead and storage overhead must be considered when applying to algorithm, which is used in wireless system. Because of new paradigm of technology, we need to revisit previous memory integrity verification algorithm.

Fig. 1. An example of integrity violation

Our key contributions can be summarized as follows:

- We implement fully batch verification enabled memory integrity verification algorithm. One by one verification is wasteful of scarce resources. While maintaining security, our scheme supports flexible setting of verification moment.
- Our scheme reduce computational overhead and On-chip storage overhead comparison with other schemes. Specifically, the proposed algorithm shows 9 % IPC improvement on average than the Lazy-processing technique, and 34 % IPC improvement on average than the standard algorithm. Moreover, our scheme use only 480-bit On-chip storage.

2 Preliminaries

2.1 Merkle Tree

Figure 2 is represents a basic structure of Merkle tree. Merkle tree is divided into three major parts, which are leaf node, internal node, and root node. First, Hash values of the data are immediately stored on leaf nodes to verify the data. Internal nodes are made through leaf nodes. The way of building internal nodes is summarized as follows. On the basis of binary Merkle tree, internal nodes are composed of their children nodes. To be more descriptive, after concatenating both children nodes, hash values of concatenating result are stored on internal node. By using hash functions, it can prevent growing the size of internal node. Root node can be made by repeating above process, and as a result, root node has an information of every data. Therefore, root node can be used as a means of verification by comparison. To do that, root node must be stored in On-chip and if it is clear that root node is secure, other nodes, which are internal nodes or leaf nodes, don't have to be stored in On-chip. Detail information of On-chip shows at 2.2.1.

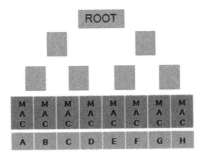

Fig. 2. The structure of Merkle tree

2.2 Incremental Multiset Hash Function

Incremental multiset hash function is the basis scheme of log hash [12], which is one of memory integrity verification algorithm. Incremental hash has some characteristic as follows. First, Let us assume that message X exists, and $H(X)$ is hash value of X. If modified message is $X' = X + m$, Incremental hash satisfy the condition, $H(X') = H(X) + H(m)$. That is, if we know $H(X)$, we don't have to know message value X for recalculating hash value of modified message X', and more easily update hash value. Incremental multiset hash function have multiset as input value, and has above characteristic. Multiset is analogous to a set, but multiset allows duplication of elements. In our study, we use $Mset - Add - Hash$, because it is simpler than other function, and suits our proposes.

2.3 Basic Assumptions of Memory Integrity Verification

The basic assumption for memory integrity verification is as follows. First, it is difficult for adversary to attack processor chip, that is, processor chip is secure, because processor chip is relatively inaccessible parts compared with others, and has complicated structure physically. Therefore, Adversary cannot attack parts in processor chip such as register and cache memory. This secure parts are called On-chip. Above this, other parts such as DRAM is unsecure and falsification can happen. This unsecure parts are called Off-chip. The best case for security is saving all data in On-chip, but On-chip is much more expensive than Off-chip. Therefore a minimum amount of data can load on the On-chip. For memory integrity verification using Merkle tree, small register in On-chip serves the role as secure place for saving root node.

2.4   Threat Model

Ways of adversary's attack can be largely categorized as passive and active. In case of passive attack, data modification does not happen, but adversary can access data and try to leak confidential information. On the other hand, adversary can do data modification by doing active attack. Depending on the situation, adversary can change existing data to certain value, which is what the adversary intended, and profiting from altered calculation result. Moreover, by using random value using modification, adversary can disable the entire system. As a result, an attack succeeds when system user cannot get desired result. Memory integrity verification algorithm aims at preventing from active attack. Figure 3 shows an example of active attacks. First is spoofing attack. Spoofing attack change from certain memory block to random value. Second is splicing attack. Splicing attack change from certain memory block to other memory block. Last is replay attack. Replay attack change from certain memory block's present value to previous value.

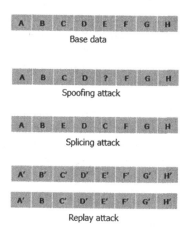

Fig. 3. An example of active attack

Memory modification attack can be divided into two, which are the attack through the Kernel and the physical attack. The attack through Kernel is the way of using the Kernel's access availability to the memory. Although Kernel's security has been improving, bugs still exist in the system. It is because the Kernel is too complicated to eliminate all the possibility of weakness. By using the fact, the adversary modifies the memory. Physical attack literally means the attack that modify data in the memory through the physical access. For example, modification can be occurred by analyzing traffics between CPU and main memories thorough external devices such as Bus analyzer. Since recently machines controlled automatically has increased and simultaneously been developed to mobile devices, the physical access to the target machine becomes easier. Therefore, the importance of the self-recognition of intrusion has risen. Suggesting algorithm that is able to verify those attacks is the purpose of this paper.

3 Related Works

3.1 Tree Based Algorithm

For verifying memory integrity, naïve method is using hash value of data to tag original data. In general, adversary cannot modify data easily, because these naïve approaches use keyed-hash, and it is difficult to get private key. However, these approaches have problems which cannot verify integrity of hash values. For example, Adversary can steal and save data and hash value of data, and at a particular point in time adversary change from present data to previous data adversary owned. Above attack is replay attack. Merkle tree using hash function is first introduced by Blum et al. to prevent attack [2] by using root node as a standard of comparison. Merkle tree is almost perfect from the aspect of security, but Merkle tree's computational performance is somewhat slow. The cause is seeking from leaf node to root node exactly. For improving computational performance, efficient memory integrity algorithm based on Merkle tree is developed by using characteristics of cache memory [7]. Also, Merkle tree has a problem about storage overhead, because of internal node. Rogers et al. propose Bonsai Merkle Tree(BMT) [11]. BMT is light-weight Merkle tree scheme by using 8bit counter instead of full data. In addition, many study about Merkle tree and memory integrity algorithm based on Merkle tree are ongoing, such as skewed Merkle tree [13].

Lazy-processing algorithm doesn't verify integrity immediately, but does it as a whole. Simply it waits and deals with process en bloc. This way of processing contributes to performance improvement, but has two problems as well. First problem is using On-chip storage. The more data system reads, the smaller available On-chip storage is. It incapacitates the On-chip storage such as cache memory. Also, before eviction occurs from cache to main memory, verification must be held. This breaks the integrity of verification.

3.2 Non-tree Based Algorithm

A new memory integrity verification algorithm which name is Log hashing (Lhash) was suggested by Suh et al. [12]. Giving solution for the problem risen from the integrity verification algorithm based on hash tree. Lhash is based on the Incremental multiset hash function suggested at Sect. 2.2. Two Incremental multiset hashes used in Lhash are ReadHash, and WriteHash. ReadHash is the value stored by recording loaded data from main memory to cache memory, and WriteHash is the value stored by recording evicted data from cache memory to main memory. It is called Log hash because it contains meaning of recording. Lhash ingenerates lower overhead in terms of time and space during the Run-time than the algorithm based on Merkle tree. On the other hand, it makes worse overhead during the initialization process than the Merkle tree based algorithm. Hence the assumption that the initialization process doesn't occur frequently is needed.

4 Proposed Scheme

4.1 Design Goal

Previous schemes do not support batch verification or support half-batch verification by using lazy-processing. Besides, incumbent half-batch verification systems by using lazy-processing consume too much on-chip storage. The above is one cause of performance degradation, because available on-chip storage decreases. Proposed scheme consider two aspects for improving performance. First is supporting fully batch verification. By doing fully batch verification, it can reduce the number of verification. Finally, costs of verification can be reduced. Second is reducing On-chip storage overhead. To doing batch verification, some data should be stored securely, that is algorithm variable. Naïve approach is using On-chip storage for saving these data, but this approach reduce available space of On-chip storage. Reduction of On-chip space be causative of slowing down computational performance. For example, cache memory is also On-chip storage, and reduction of On-chip space means reduction of cache memory space. Finally, reduction of cache memory space has a bad influence on computational performance. In our scheme, algorithm variable can be stored in Off-chip instead of On-chip, and at the same time our scheme keep this variable safe. Minimum data are stored in On-chip, it's size is about 480-bits. The purpose of saving this minimum data is verifying data stored in Off-chip.

4.2 Components

4.2.1 Variables

For implementing our algorithm, essential variables are tabulated as Table 1. *MAC_Table* is the space of saving necessary variable for our algorithm. This information should not be modified by adversary, so *MAC_Table* is stored in On-chip. *MAC_Table* consists of four sectors.

To supporting batch processing, the information of memory block which application read should be is logged. In previous scheme, this information is stored in On-chip. For expanding available space of On-chip storage, our scheme save this information in Off-chip. The problem of Off-chip storage is unsecure. To solve this problem, our algorithm calculates hash values of memory block which application read, and save hash values in *loaded_sector*. By using *loaded_sector*, we can check integrity of memory block which application read. *current_sector* is storage section of Merkle

Table 1. Components of proposed scheme

Name	Stored section
MAC_Table	On-chip
Internal node storage	Off-chip
Loaded_value	Off-chip
Evicted_value	Off-chip

Name
Loaded sector
Current sector
Updated sector
Deleted sector

tree's root node. Information of root node in current_sector can be comparison group further verification process. *updated_sector* is storage section about fetched memory block which application modify. If fetched memory block is modified by application, this modified data should be evicted and memory block should be updated. *deleted_sector* is storage section about the removing memory block. All sectors in *MAC_Table* consist of Incremental multiset hash value, therefore even if our algorithm calculate many times, the size of sectors does not change, Moreover, It is possible to update these sector freely by using Incremental multiset hash function.

Other components, which are original data and internal node of Merkle tree, are stored in Off-chip. *Loaded_value* is queue of saving data which application read for supporting batch verification. *Evicted_value* is also queue of saving evicted value.

4.2.2 Functions

Two functions are used in our scheme. First is HMAC(Hash Memory Authentication Code). Our paper address this function as $HMAC(x)$, which x is data. $HMAC(x)$ is exactly $HMAC(data_x|tag_x)$, which $tag_x = (address_x, counter_x)$. Second is Incremental multiset hash function. Our paper address this function as $H_K(x)$. Incremental multiset hash function is based on HMAC, and HMAC is keyed-hash function, therefore key is provided in every event.

4.3 Running Process

- Initiation

The coverage of verification is from the initiation, and it doesn't guarantee verification for the time before the initiation. Merkle tree is built for the whole memory blocks to be verified. Difference between the former Merkle tree and our scheme is the composition of the inner nodes. It has changed from the way using concatenation to incremental multiset hash function's addition to build internal nodes. Consequently, the root node contains information about all data blocks like Merkle tree's root. At the same time, it consists of addition of incremental multiset hash values of all data blocks.

```
Merkle-tree.Make(node)
{
    if node = leaf node then
        return data
    else if node = root then
        return H_K (Merkle-tree.Make(node.left
        + Merkle-tree.Make(node.right));
    else //not root but internal node
        Temp = H_K(Merkle_tree.Make(node.left)
        +Merkle-tree.Make(node.right))
        INS.Save(Temp);
        return Temp;
}
Root ← Merkle-tree.Make(node )
MAC-Table.Current_sector ← root
MAC-Table.Updated_sector ← root
```

- Data Fetching

  Data is fetched from main memory to cache memory. Incremental multiset hash value of fetched data is recorded in *Loadedvalue*.

  ```
  Fetch data X
  Loaded-value.Add(X, Address_X )
  MAC-Table.Loaded-sector ← H_K(Loaded-value)
  ```

- Modify Data in Cache

This process is modifying fetched data in cache memory by application. In our paper, it is assumed that system uses write-back cache. Modified value update at once, by saving these values in *evicted_value*.

```
Old-mac ← INS.get(address)
New-mac ← H_K(new-data)
Evicted-value.Add(new-data,address)
MAC-Table.Deleted-sector.Add(Old-mac)
MAC-Table.Updated-sector.Add(New-mac)
```

- Verification of Read Data

  Merkle tree is built on memory block. *Loaded_value*, and *Internal node storage*.

```
Check Loaded-value's integrity
Unclear-root ← Rebuild Merkle tree
CompareTo(Unclear-root,MAC-table.Current-sector)
if value is same then
     Integrity is guaranteed
else
     Integrity is not guaranteed
```

- Data Eviction

  In this process, temporarily stored eviction data in *Evicted_value* are evicted at once. *Evicted_value* should be verified because this value is Off-chip component.

```
Evict value in Evicted-value
Compute multiset hash value of
               Current + Evicted-value
CompareTo(result of above, MAC-Table.updated-sector)
if value is same then
     //Integrity is guaranteed
     MAC_Table.Current_sector ←
          MAC-Table.Updated-sector -
          MAC-Table.Deleted-sector
else
     //Integrity is not guaranteed
```

4.4 Security Analysis

This chapter will prove the security of our scheme against the memory modification attack mentioned in Sect. 2.4. Among the attacks, three attacks, Spoofing attack, Splicing attack, and Replay attack, were used. Merkle tree's configuration can verify hash values hierarchically. This makes it hard for adversary to intrude a system. Because adversary has to modify all ancestor nodes of a certain node to hide that modification was occurred. Besides, the highest node, root, is protected in the On-chip, so the modification becomes difficult.

- Security against Spoofing attack: Our scheme consist of MAC values based on hash function. Therefore MAC value changes when data is modified. That is why attacks get detected, and how the security is proved.
- Security against Splicing attack: When MAC values are calculated, the address of data is used as tag. It makes MAC value changed when the location of data is changed. That is why attacks get detected, and how the security is proved.

- Security against Replay attack: When MAC values are calculated, the time when data stored is used as tag. So, when time of data changes, MAC value differs. That is why attacks get detected, and how the security is proved.

5 Simulation

In this section, we conduct experiments on the proposed algorithm. To analyze the performance and the characteristics of the proposed integrity verification algorithm, we evaluate our algorithm compared with Standard Merkle tree and Lazy-Process Merkle tree. Furthermore, in contrast to the Merkle tree's composition of internal node using concatenation, we evaluate the efficiency of composition of internal node using incremental multiset hash. We measure the performance by comparing the number of comparisons between IPC and internal node when running a benchmark application.

5.1 Simulation Environment

We use MARSSx86 (Micro ARchitectural and System Simulator) [10] to compare the proposed system and the previous researches. MARSSx86 is a cycle-accurate simulator that implements a full-system and supports out-of-order execution. MARSSx86 can be divided into simulation framework and emulator framework. Simulation framework is a modified version of PTLSim [14] and the emulator framework is based on QEMU [1]. We choose MARSSx86 as the simulator for the convenience of applying the proposed algorithm as it is an open-source project, and the faster performance compared to other simulators. HMAC is based on SHA-1 [5] and requires 80-cycle latency. We refer to the results of [11] for 80-cycle latency. Table 2 shows specifications for real system and simulation system, which are used for evaluating the implementation and performance of the proposed algorithm. We use general desktop environment for evaluation and collect data using the stat file generated at the end of simulation in MARSSx86. To evaluate performance, we use SPEC2006 [8] binary file. We evaluate the performance in 5 benchmark binary files.

Table 2. Specifications for real system and simulator

Main machine configuration	
Processor	Intel® Core™ i3-3220 3.3 GHz
OS, Kernel	Ubuntu 13.04, Linux 3.13.0-46-generic
RAM	4 GB
Simulator configuration	
Processor	1 ooo(out-of-order) core, 3.3 GHz
L1 Cache	128 KB Inst/128 KB Data, 8-ways, 64B line
L2 Cache	2 MB, 8-ways, 64B line
Memory	4 GB, 165 cycles latency

5.2   Simulation Result

We choose IPC (Instructions Per Cycle) and the number of HMAC function called as performance measurements. We can evaluate general performance of the system using IPC. Also, we can evaluate the number of node updates and the number of node verifications using HMAC function as HMAC function is called when accessing internal node of the Merkle tree. We compare the number of verifications between batch verification algorithm and general verification algorithm. For our purpose, we end our simulation in 200 million instruction commits. Figure 4 is the evaluation result of normalized IPC when setting the performance of the algorithm without memory

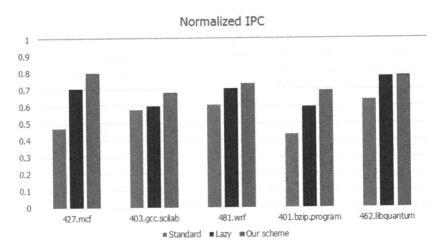

Fig. 4. Simulation result of normalized IPC

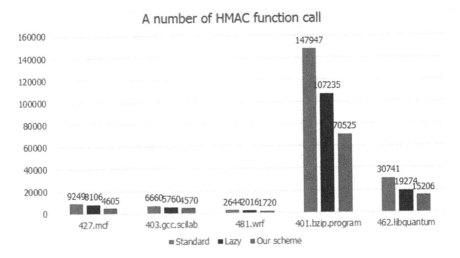

Fig. 5. The number of HMAC functions call

integrity verification technique as 1. Generally, algorithms that use batch verification, the proposed algorithm and the lazy-processing algorithm, show 9 % IPC improvement on average compared to the standard integrity verification algorithm, which does not use batch verification. Specifically, the proposed algorithm shows 9 % IPC improvement on average than the Lazy-processing technique, and 34 % IPC improvement on average than the standard algorithm.

Figure 5 shows the number of HMAC functions call. Algorithms implementing batch verification calls less number of HMAC functions. Specifically, the proposed algorithm calls HMAC functions 32 % less on average than the Lazy-processing technique, and 51 % less on average than the standard algorithm.

6   Conclusion

The existing integrity verification Algorithm based on Merkle tree verifies exterior falsification attacks and maintains the security by carrying out the integrity verification every time a system reads data blocks. However, fulfilling verification every time the data blocks are read leaded to the performance fall. To make up for this, Lazy-processing, which can verify better than the existing one, was introduced. But, to introduce the Lazy-processing technique on the existing algorithm, On-chip storage that is considered to be safe was needed. And as the amount of data to be read gets increasing, narrowed On-chip storage resulted in performance fall as well. Also, another problem was found from the existing algorithm that must be verified every time before data eviction occurs. To solve problems above and to attain the stability at the same time, On-chip stores only minimum hash value able to verify the storage's integrity, and the other is stored in Off-chip to minimize On-chip usage. To reduce calculation over heads during Merkle tree approach, we changed the inner configuration of Merkle tree from the concatenation to the addition of Incremental multiset hash function. As the result of the change, integrity verification become possible completely, so the unnecessary verification process was reduced. Moreover, instant verification was realized bringing usability of verification timing. The controllable verification timing makes it possible for users to find optimizing verification time. At the same time, we proved that our scheme outperform the algorithms which are Lazy-processing and the one which isn't supporting integrity verification.

Acknowledgements. This work was supported by the National Research Foundation of Korea Grant funded by the Korean Government (NRF-2014R1A2A2A01006957) and the Institute for Information & communication Technology Promotion (IITP) grant funded by the Korea government. (MSIP) (No. 10041244, SmartTV 2.0 Software Platform).

References

1. Bellard, F.: QEMU, a Fast and Portable Dynamic Translator. In: USENIX Annual Technical Conference, FREENIX Track, pp. 41–46 (2005)

2. Blum, M., Evans, W., Gemmell, P., Kannan, S., Naor, M.: Checking the cor-rectness of memories. In: Proceedings of the 32nd IEEE Symposium on Foundations of Computer Science 1991, pp. 90–99 (1991)

3. Clarke, D., Devadas, S., van Dijk, M., Gassend, B., Suh, G.: Incremental multiset hash functions and their application to memory integrity checking. In: Laih, C.-S. (ed.) ASIACRYPT 2003. LNCS, vol. 2894, pp. 188–207. Springer, Heidelberg (2003)

4. Clarke, D., Suh, G.E., Gassend, B., Sudan, A., Van Dijk, M., Devadas, S.: Towards constant bandwidth overhead integrity checking of untrusted data. In: IEEE Symposium on Security and Privacy, 2005, pp. 139–153 (2005)

5. Eastlake, D., Jones, P.: US secure hash algorithm 1 (SHA1) (2001). http://www.hjp.at/doc/rfc/rfc3174.html

6. Foster, I., Zhao, Y., Raicu, I., Lu, S.: Cloud computing and grid computing 360-degree compared. Grid Comput. Environ. Workshop **2008**, 1–10 (2008)

7. Gassend, B., Suh, G.E., Clarke, D., Van Dijk, M., Devadas, S.: Caches and hash trees for efficient memory integrity verification. High Perform. Comput. Archit. **2003**, 295–306 (2003)

8. Henning, J.L.: SPEC CPU2006 benchmark descriptions. ACM SIGARCH Comput. Architect. News **34**(4), 1–17 (2006)

9. Merkle, R.C.: Protocols for public key cryptosystems. IEEE Symp. Secur. Priv. **1980**, 122–123 (1980)

10. Patel, A., Afram, F., Ghose, K.: Marss-x86: A qemu-based micro-architectural and systems simulator for x86 multicore processors. In: 1st International Qemu Users' Forum, pp. 29–30 (2011)

11. Rogers, B., Chhabra, S., Prvulovic, M., Solihin, Y.: Using address independent seed encryption and bonsai merkle trees to make secure processors os and performance-friendly. In: Proceedings of the 40th Annual IEEE/ACM International Symposium on Microarchitecture 2007, pp. 183–196 (2007)

12. Suh, G.E., Clarke, D., Gassend, B., Dijk, M.V., Devadas, S.: Efficient memory integrity verification and encryption for secure processors. In: Proceedings of the 36th Annual IEEE/ACM International Symposium on Microarchitecture 2003, p. 339 (2003)

13. Szefer, J., Biedermann, S.: Towards fast hardware memory integrity checking with skewed Merkle trees. In: Proceedings of the Third Workshop on Hard-ware and Architectural Support for Security and Privacy 2014, p. 9 (2014)

14. Yourst, M.T.: PTLsim: A cycle accurate full system x86-64 microarchitec-tural simulator. In: IEEE International Symposium on Performance Analysis of Systems & Software, ISPASS 2007, pp. 23–34 (2007)

Automatic Security Classification with Lasso

Paal E. Engelstad[1,2]([✉]), Hugo Hammer[2], Kyrre Wahl Kongsgård[1],
Anis Yazidi[2], Nils Agne Nordbotten[1], and Aleksander Bai[2]

[1] Norwegian Defense Research Establishement (FFI), Kjeller, Norway
{paal.engelstad,kyrre-wahl.kongsgard,nils.nordbotten}@ffi.no
[2] Oslo and Akershus University College of Applied Sciences (HiOA), Oslo, Norway
{paal.engelstad,hugo.hammer,anis.yazidi,aleksander.bai}@hioa.no

Abstract. With an increasing amount of generated information, also
within security domains, there is a growing need for tools that can assist
with automatic security classification. The state-of-the art today is the
use of simple classification lists ("dirty word lists") for reactive content
checking. In the future, however, we expect there will be both proactive tools for security classification (assisting humans when creating the
information object) and reactive tools (i.e. double-checking the content
in a guard). This paper demonstrates the use of machine learning with
Lasso (Least Absolute Shrinkage and Selection Operator) [1,2] both to
two-class (binary) and multi-class security classification. We also explore
the ability of Lasso to create sparse solutions that are easy for humans
to analyze and interpret, in contrast to many other machine learning
techniques that do not possess an explanatory nature.

Keywords: Classification list · Machine learning · Feature selection ·
Multiclass · Guard · Multi-layer security · Cross-domain information
exchange

1 Introduction

Security classification is about classifying information objects, such as documents and text messages, into different groups, e.g. "Secret", "Confidential",
"Unclassified" etc. The concept is not only used by the military, government
agencies and international organizations, but also by private corporations, e.g.
see [3]. The classification indicates the sensitivity of the contents of different
information objects and mandates how the information object shall be treated
according to the governing security policy.

The content of an information object is typically classified by human inspection and assessment, and given a security label (e.g. "Public" vs "Confidential" or "Business Internal"). However, with an increasing amount of generated
information, there is a need for tools that can assist with automatic security
classification, which is the problem this paper addresses.

Organizations that implement security classifications might also use *guards*
to enforce information flow control according to the policy. The guard is typically

© Springer International Publishing Switzerland 2016
H. Kim and D. Choi (Eds.): WISA 2015, LNCS 9503, pp. 399–410, 2016.
DOI: 10.1007/978-3-319-31875-2_33

located on the border between two domains, e.g. a "high" domain and a "low" domain. It is responsible to protect the confidentiality of the "high" domain, by denying objects of a too high classification to leave the "high" domain and be released into the "low" domain.

There is a number of commercial guard solutions available, e.g., Lockheed Martin's Radiant Mercury (RM), BAE's DataSync Guard and Boeing's eXMeritus Hardware Wall, have been certified and officially approved for use by the Department of Defense (DoD) in the US [4]. In terms of content scanning, the guards typically support some type of basic "dirty word" checking, i.e. the classification lists in these guards are not very advanced. A review of such content scanning tools is undertaken in [5].

In the future, we expect there will be both proactive tools for security classification (assisting humans when creating the information object) and reactive tools (i.e. double-checking the content in the guard). However, the only tool that resembles automatic security classification today, is the content checking that takes place in the guard itself, which is based on "Dirty Word Lists".

However, in this paper we propose to use machine learning as a starting point instead of "Dirty-word lists". In doing so, we put focus on Lasso (Least Absolute Shrinkage and Selection Operator) [1,2], which has not been considered for this problem in previous work.

Lasso has a number of compelling features that are explored in this paper. For instance, it is easily expanded to multinomial regression.

However, perhaps the most attractive feature is the sparseness of the solution that Lasso provides, which makes it able to derive interpretable classifications lists as a outcome of the machine learning. A classification list, such as a "Dirty Word List", is with current state-of-the-art typically configured manually, because good human control with the list is critical. The disadvantage of manually constructed lists is that it is hard to construct lists with advanced functionality (e.g. introducing a weight factor to each word or an overall bias-term) which would force humans to take complex decisions (e.g. which values to assign). This paper demonstrates the use of machine learning to create more advanced classification lists automatically. A major obstacle for machine learning to be used is that they would create long lists that are difficult to inspect, analyze and control by humans. First, some of the most efficient machine learning techniques, such as Support Vector Machines (SVM), k-Nearest Neighbor (kNN) or Naïve Bayes (NB) [6] are hard to interpret by humans. SVM, for instance, is known to have notoriously poor interpretability, as noted by Kotsiantis [7].

The main contributions of this paper are as follows:

- Putting *Automatic Security Classification* as a topic on the research agenda. As pointed out in the next section, surprisingly little has been published on Automatic Security Classification.
- Constructing a well-described two-class benchmark experiment for a binary security classification problem, and exploring features of this experiment.
- Exploring the Lasso machine learner [1] as a method that has not yet been analyzed in literature for this problem.

- Exploring the multinomial regression of Lasso for situation with more than two security classes. This problem has not yet been analyzed in the literature.
- Taking false positives and negatives into account in the evaluation, which has not yet been done in the literature for this problem.
- Showing how machine learning in general, and Lasso in particular, can automatically create classification lists that are more advanced than the simple "dirty word lists" that are used today and that are still easy for humans to understand and assess.

2 Background

2.1 Introduction to Lasso

The main focus of the paper is exploring the use of Lasso as a novel approach to the automatic security classification problem. In terms of classification accuracy, we will compare Lasso with other state-of-the art machine learners, such as SVM.

For the sake of clarity, we should first briefly clarify how Lasso can be adopted for classification as it is mainly designed for solving regression problems. Lasso deals with feature selection by shrinkage methods which allow a variable to be partly included in the regression model.

We want to learn a text classifier, $y = f(x)$, from a set of n training examples $D = \{(x_1, y_1), ..., (x_i, y_i), ..., (x_n, y_n)\}$. For text categorization, x_{ij} represent an entry in the Document-Term Matrix (DTM). That is, each element in the vector $x_i = [x_{i1}, ..., x_{ij}, ..., x_{id}]^T$ contains the word frequency of term j in document i, and d is the total number of terms. Usually d is a huge number. The values $y_i \in \{-1, +1\}$ are class labels that indicate non-membership or membership to a class. The concept can easily be generalized to a multi-class problem. Due to space limitations, here we will focus on explaining how Lasso can be applied to solve a two-class/binary classification problem.

Logistic regression is a conditional probability model of the form:

$$p(y_i = +1|\beta, x_i) = \frac{1}{1 + exp(-\beta^T x_i))} \tag{1}$$

To estimate the unknown parameters in the Lasso model, we compute the following minimization

$$\widehat{\beta} = \arg\min_{\beta} \{-\sum_{i=1}^{n} \ln(1 + \exp(-\beta^T x_i)) + \lambda \sum_{j=1}^{d} |\beta_j|\} \tag{2}$$

where $\widehat{\beta}$ is the parameter estimates.

Lasso is a regularized regression method based on the L1-norm (second sum in Eq. 2). As we see, the expression consists of two sums. The first sum is for maximizing the likelihood estimation of the parameters $\beta_j, j = 1, 2, ..., d$ and the second sum is for controlling the sparsity of the solution. λ is a regularization parameter controlling the degree of sparsity.

2.2   Related Work on Automatic Security Classification

Little has been published on Automatic Security Classification, and all works we have seen make comments on the surprising lack of published data.

To the best of our knowledge, the only *published* work mentioning this issue dates to 2005. However, here Rhetorical Structure Theory is applied to the problem, which is not pertinent to the our work presented here [8]. In this paper, on the contrary, we employ a machine learning approach to the problem.

Other relevant available information - although not in the form of *published papers* - that we have found is a Master thesis from 2008 [9] and a (difficultly accessible) technical report [5] from 2010. The Master thesis did not make attempts to apply machine learning, but proposed an architecture for the problem. However, we use the technical report as a starting point for the work presented in this paper. The corpus used in this report was retrieved from the Digital National Security Archive - DNSA [10]. We will look closer at the corpus and their work in the following Sect. 2.3.

2.3   Experiments on Policy Documents from DNSA

The Digital National Security Archive (DNSA) contains the most comprehensive collection of historic and declassified US government documents available to the public [10]. These were chosen because they contain a mix of both classified and unclassified documents from three unrelated domains:

- AF, Afghanistan: The Making of U.S. Policy, 1973–1990
- CH, China and the United States: From Hostility to Engagement, 1960–1998
- PH, The Philippines: U.S. Policy during the Marcos Years, 1965–1986

The technical report from 2010 [5] used only 686 of the 5853 documents available DNSA documents within these three topics, but did not describe why so few documents were selected and what were the selection criteria. A number of other issues and parameters were also unclear from the report. We contacted the authors for further information, but due to the 5 years that have passed since the report was written, they informed us that most detail information about the experiment was now lost. Thus, a starting point of our introduction of automatic security classification into the public domain of published works was to re-conduct the experiments - however with less strict selection criteria - and thus with more documents in the corpus. Furthermore, we document in detail how the experiment is done. The experiment is presented in Sect. 3.1. Before we get to this, we will summarize the main pertinent information about their experiment as follows:

In the experiment of the technical report the "Unclassified" documents comprised one class, while all documents of higher classifications were aggregated into one class, thus reducing the security classification problem into one that only deals with two classes, i.e. into a *binary* classification problem. Being restricted to only the use of two different security classes is strictly limiting the applicability of the results presented in the report. To address this limitation, we will present a novel multi-class solution to the security classification problem later in this paper, in Sect. 4.

In these kinds of experiments, document texts are treated as bag of words, where punctuation marks, white spaces etc. are removed, and each document gives a term-vector with a dimensionality corresponding to the number of available words, and with each vector component providing the frequency of the word being used, i.e. it is typically a sparse vector. Vectors of all documents are comprising the Document-Term Matrix (DTM), where each row in the matrix is a word-frequency vector corresponding to one specific document.

In the technical report, three general classifiers, namely "k Nearest Neighbor" (kNN), "Naïve Bayes" (NB), and "Support Vector Machine" (SVM) [6] were applied for security classification and compared. They concluded that SVM performed best, with a best performance around 85 % classification accuracy. Other classifiers, such as Lasso, was not mentioned.

The report explored stemming of all the words in the DTM, i.e. every word in the documents are replaced with its word stem [5]. This means that sets of multiple columns in the DTM (corresponding to different word forms with the same stem) are aggregated into a single column corresponding the stem. This reduction of dimensionality of the DTM will increase calculation speed. In terms of classification accuracy, stemming might contribute positively by removing some words that introduce "noise", but might on the other hand also contribute negatively if the aggregation of words into the word stems leads to less precision in terms of conserving the exact meaning of each word form. The analysis in [5], however, concluded that word stemming does not influence classification accuracy considerably.

They also explored the use of "term frequency-inverse document frequency" (tfidt) [5] for term weighting (e.g. transforming the word frequencies metric in the original DTM into another metric), which is also a common technique in such experiments. Also on this point, they concluded that such term weighting does not affect the performance significantly.

3   Two-Class Benchmark Experiment

3.1   Experiment with Standard Machine Learners

The starting point of our analysis is to conduct a benchmark experiment. We base our experiment on the documents in the DNSA database from the same three topics as outlined in Sect. 2.3. Of the 5867 documents available within these three topics, we skip documents that are not very useful to the scenario we are targeting on to the analysis itself (Table 1).

For instance, 9 documents are removed since they are duplicates of other documents already in the set, while 620 documents are not useful for classification, since their classification is unknown (i.e. they are classified/marked as "UNKNOWN"). 1612 documents are removed because these documents are marked as "EXCISED" (i.e. the classified text sections are removed). The

Table 1. Documents used in the experiments

	Total docs	Dupl.	UN-KNOWN	EX-CISED	LIM.-OFF.	PUBL. USE	REST-RICT.	NON-CLASS.	UN-CLASS.	CONFI-DENT.	SEC-RET	TOP-SECR.
AF	2010	1	359	449	300	0	0	37	331	420	109	4
CH	1989		227	706	80	3	1	196	131	253	299	93
PH	1868	8	35	457	308	0	0	220	223	528	89	0
Sum	5867	9	621	1612	688	3	1	453	685	1201	497	97

"PUBLICUSE" documents could be considered as an unclassified class and the "RESTRICTED" document as classified, but since their sizes are so limited (3 docs and 1 doc, respectively), they are omitted. Furthermore, 688 documents are within the borderline classification "LIMITEDOFFICIAL", and therefore not considered. Thus we end up with 2933 documents in total, where 1138 documents (453 "NONCLASSIFIED" and 685 "UNCLASSIFIED") are aggregated to the "Unclassified" class of our analysis. The remaining 1795 documents (classified as either "CONFIDENTIAL", "SECRET" or "TOPSECRET") are aggregated into the other "Classified" class of the experiment. The number of documents per classes and per country (AF:Afghanistan, CH:China and PH:Philippines) is summarized in Table 1.

As part of our analysis algorithm, we also remove very short documents with only 30 word stems or less extracted. As a baseline, we remove 128 documents and end up with a corpus of 2805 documents constituting the 2805 rows of the DTM that is used for further analysis. As for the actual machine learning 70 % of the documents (i.e. 1964 documents) are used for the training set, while the remaining 30 % (i.e. 841 documents) constitute the test set. However, if we remove some additional keywords (as explained below in Sect. 3.2), a few more documents get to the limit of 30 word stems. Then we end up with 2793 documents (i.e. a DTM of 2793 rows), with 1955 documents in the training set, and 838 documents in the test set.

As DNSA contains pdf documents, we extracted the raw textual contents using the optical character recognition (OCR) service provided by Abbyy [11]. Since the scanned pdf documents are of poor quality, we used auto-correction to mend the many OCR errors occurring in the extracted text. The processed/auto-corrected text material is more concise, and less verbose than the raw text (i.e. mis-spelled words are merged into the same word for the analysis).

For all the experiments we used word stemming and resorted to the simple bag-of-words model [12], in which any word order was discarded, ending up with a corpus of 23477 word stems. Infrequent word stems, occurring less than 15 times in the entire corpus were also omitted to speed up calculations, by reducing the number of word stems (or columns in the DTM) from 23477 to 5840. Our analyses showed that this *term-frequency limitation* did not affect classification accuracy noticeably. Finally, each document (row in the DTM) was represented in the DTM merely by a vector of term frequency-inverse document frequency (tf-idf) weights [5].

Table 2. Classification performance for different machine learners.

Machine learner	Keywords ignored	Classification Accuracy	95 % conf.int.
SVM	No	0.84	(0.81, 0.87)
5 kNN	No	0.70	(0.66, 0.73)
Naive Bayes	No	0.65	(0.61, 0.69)
SVM	Yes	0.77	(0.74, 0.81)
5 kNN	Yes	0.66	(0.62, 0.69)
Naive Bayes	Yes	0.65	(0.61, 0.68)
Lasso	No	0.90	(0.88, 0.92)
Lasso	Yes	0.78	(0.75, 0.82)

Results are shown in Table 2. The upper pane of the table (i.e. upper three rows of results) confirms the conclusion in [5], i.e. that SVM displays an accuracy around 84 % (compared with around 85 % in [5]). Furthermore, our results confirm that SVM has better performance than k-Nearest Neighbor (kNN) and Naïve Bayes (NB), even though the performance difference is higher here than in [5]. Nevertheless, based on these results, SVM will be used as a benchmark machine learner throughout the rest of this paper, while we will focus less on kNN and NB in the following. (We also note that Lasso performs better than SVM, as discussed in more detail in Sect. 3.3 below).

3.2 Removing Favourable Keywords

In addition, we did analysis where we removed/ignored any keywords relating the classification labels/words ("SECRET", "UNCLASSIFIED" etc.) from all the textual contents prior to training the machine learning algorithm, i.e. we removed the word stems of such words.

The reason we did this is that we suspected that the policy documents might include words that describe explicitly if a topic is classified or secret, such as the label itself. If we were to leave these types of words in the text, it would potentially result in the classifiers yielding artificially good results, that effectively would only determine the security label based on absence or presence of such words.

The number of word stems is thus reduced from 23477 to 23473, and after applying the minimum term-frequency limitation from 5840 to 5836 word stems (cf. Sect. 3.1). Removing keywords also reduces the number of documents in the corpus from 2805 to 2793, as pointed out earlier in Sect. 3.1.

By removing these keywords, we think that our analysis results are more amenable to many other types of information objects where this is not the case. Not surprisingly, the classification performance is a little lower when reducing these keywords, as shown in the second pane of Table 2 (i.e. in rows 4–6), even though very few words are removed. Indeed, we observe that the classification accuracy of SVM drops from 84 % down to 77 %.

406   P.E. Engelstad et al.

Table 3. Confusion matrix of the two-class (binary) classification

| | | Predicted classes | | Row-sums |
		Classified	Unclassified	
Actual classes	Classified	460	59	519
	Unclassified	123	196	319
	Column sums	255	583	838

3.3 Experiment with Lasso

In addition to testing the standard machine learners explored in a previous technical report, we also explored the use of Lasso for the automatic security classification problem according to the model presented in Sect. 2.1.

The confusion matrix derived from the analysis is shown in Table 3, showing how the 838 test documents are classified ("Predicted class") compared to their actual classification ("Actual class"). Correct classification is along the diagonal, i.e. the *classification accuracy* is of $(460 + 196)/838 = 0.78$. Knowing the entire confusion matrix, other performance metrics can also be calculated, e.g. the *precision* is of $460/(460+123) = 0.79$, while the *recall* is of $460/(460+56) = 0.89$. We could go further into exploring ROC and AUC curves, but due to space limitations this is outside scope of this paper and left for future work. This paper focuses primarily on the classification accuracy.

For comparison with other methods, the Lasso results are summarized in bottom pane of Table 2. Here, we observe that Lasso has a classification accuracy of 90 %, and performs better compared to SVM at 84 %. However, in all analyses in the rest of the papers, the keywords related to the security classifications or security labels are ignored (cf. Sect. 3.2). Then, Lasso yields a classification performance of 78 %, compared to SVM at 77 %.

3.4 False Negatives

With a spam filter, which protects the confidentiality of a site from the outside world, one is often concerned with the problem of false positives. This is a legitimate message mistakenly marked as spam, which is critical if users miss critical information. A false negative, on the other hand, is usually not critical but mostly inconvenient, in terms of a spam message that reaches the inbox.

For guard, on the contrary, which protects against information leakage, false negatives must often be avoided at all costs. For instance, if a guard mistakenly releases a "Classified" document, due to the fact that it is mistakenly classified as "Unclassified", this false negative might have severe consequences for the organization. On the other hand, if the guard mistakenly blocks an "Unclassified" document from being released, this false positive is inconvenient - although probably not critical.

Analysis of false negatives of automatic security classification has not yet been tackled in previous work. From the confusion matrix, the false positives are given by the lower triangular part of the matrix, and is of $123/838 = 0.15$, while the false negatives are given by the upper triangular part of the matrix, and is of $59/838 = 0.07$. Thus, if we are only concerned with information leakage, and find a solution to tackle the inconvenience of false positives, the guard performs at 93 %.

4 Multi-Class Security Classification with Lasso

While previous work has only considered two classes, here we consider automatic security classification with multiple classes. Just as we used Lasso for the binomial logistic regression of the binary (two-class) classification problem above, we can easily use Lasso for multinomial logistic regression of the multi-class problem of automatic security classification. While we aggregated the classes "CONFIDENTIAL", "SECRET" and "TOPSECRET" into one common "Classified" class above, now we keep these as separate classes. Results of the Lasso multinomial regression are shown in Table 4.

Table 4. Confusion matrix of multi-class classification

		Predicted classes				Row-sums
		Top secret	Secret	Confidential	Unclassified	
Actual classes	Top Secret	14	13	4	3	34
	Secret	2	55	52	30	139
	Confidential	0	16	268	62	346
	Unclassified	0	14	71	234	319
	Column sums	16	98	395	329	838

Now the classification accuracy is of $(+14 + 55 + 268 + 234)/838 = 0.68$. The fact that it drops compared to the binomial analysis is not surprising, as we now have considerably fewer documents available of each class. However, if we are only concerned with information leakage, and find a solution to tackle the inconvenience of false positives, the guard performs at 80 %, derived from the classification accuracy on the diagonal (contributing 68 %) and the false positives in the lower triangular part of the matrix (contributing 12 %). Again, the confusion matrix allows us to calculate other metrics as well, but we leave an exploration of this to future work.

5 Lasso Feature Selection for Short Classification Lists

Lasso is a regularized regression method based on the L1-norm (second sum in Eq. 2 in Sect. 2.1.) L1 regularization is a compelling feature for creating

Table 5. The real classification list lengths generated by Lasso, when adjusting the λ parameter.

MinIndex	54	50	45	40	35	30	25	20	15	10	5
$log(\lambda)$	-4.60	-4.41	-4.18	-3.95	-3.72	-3.48	-3.25	-3.02	-2.79	-2.55	-2.32
ListLength	**479**	404	306	206	139	93	55	23	15	7	3
Class.Acc.	0.78	0.78	0.78	0.77	0.77	0.75	0.73	0.7	0.68	0.66	0.62
Low Conf.Int	0.75	0.75	0.75	0.74	0.74	0.71	0.69	0.67	0.65	0.63	0.59
High Conf.Int	0.81	0.81	0.81	0.80	0.8	0.77	0.76	0.73	0.72	0.69	0.66

brief classification lists, because it leads to sparse solutions where an additional automatic feature selection is performed within the Lasso learning algorithm. Lasso maximizes the likelihood, while constraining (i.e. penalizing) the sum of the absolute values (i.e. L1-norm) of the regression coefficients. Due to the L1-based regularization, we end up in a situation where some of the β_i-estimates becomes exactly zero and are removed from the solution. This leads to sparse solutions with many zero beta-values, effectively reducing the dimension of the solution.

Indeed, while other machine learners easily would create solutions with thousands of words corresponding to the thousands of columns in the DTM, the optimal solution of Lasso to our experiment is a list of only 479 words, or 479 non-zero β_i values. Table 5 shows that the optimal solution of 479 words

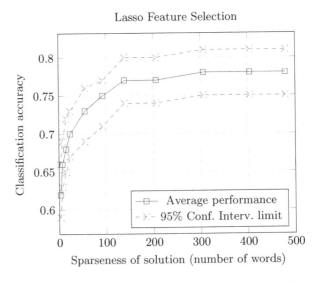

Fig. 1. The blue curve shows the classification accuracy (y-axis) as a function of number of words (with non-zero β-value) in the solution (x-axis)

correspond to a MinIndex of 54, where the MinIndex indicates the size of the λ parameter. (A value of 54 corresponds to $\lambda = 0.01005$, i.e. $log(\lambda) = -4.60$.)

The size of the penalty is controlled by the λ parameter; the larger the penalty applied (or the lower the MinIndex is in Table 5), the sparser is the solution. In Table 5, we explore doing feature selection in Lasso, by selecting a non-optimal λ parameter that increases the penalty, i.e. Lasso creates sparser solution at the expense of a reduced (non-opitmal) classification accuracy.

Table 5 shows that Lasso demonstrates good preservation of the classification accuracy when reducing dimensions by increasing the L1 norm penalty. As observed in the table, Lasso preserves its accuracy of around 75 % down to a classification list length of only 93 words, and the accuracy drops to only around 70 % with a list length of 23 words. The ability of Lasso of preserving classification accuracy even when going to quite sparse solutions is also illustrated in Fig. 1. In other words, Lasso is well adapted to creating advanced classification lists that are easily understood and inspected by humans, and the length of the classification list can be adjusted down at the expense of a moderately lower classification accuracy.

6   Conclusions and Future Work

This paper introduces Lasso into the solution space of automatic security classification. First, we observed an indication that Lasso might perform better than SVM and other commonly used machine learners in terms of classification accuracy (e.g. as shown in Table 2).

The paper confirms that with Lasso a classification accuracy around 80-90 % is realistic using machine learning for automatic security classification. However, we identified that some strict removal of some keywords (not identified in previous work) might make our analysis more amenable to other types of corpus. The requirement reduced classification accuracy to around 78 %, and we used this as a starting point for our general analysis.

In addition to the performance benefits of Lasso for this problem, Lasso is easy to extend to multi-class classification problems where more than two different security classes are present. This has not yet been studied in the literature, and the paper demonstrated that multi-class security classification is feasible with Lasso. We also shed light on the false negative problem of automatic security classification and guard functionality, which is opposite to the false positive problem that have been studied for spam filters. Both the topic of multi-class security classification and the false negative problem are issues for future work.

Due to the fact that Lasso tend to create sparse solution, we demonstrated that Lasso is able to automatically create advanced classification lists that might partly replace the simple "Dirty Word Lists" used in guards today. Creating short lists is an advantage since brief lists are easily to interpret by humans.

While other machine learners would easily create a classification list of thousands of words, Lasso automatically reduced the size to only 479 words (Table 5).

Furthermore, we showed that by adjusting the λ parameter of the L1 norm, we could create even considerably shorter lists with good preservation of the classification accuracy. Comparing this technique with other feature selection techniques is an issue for future work.

Acknowledgments. This work was partially funded by the University Graduate Center (UNIK).

References

1. Tibshirani, R.: Regression shrinkage and selection via the lasso. J. Royal. Statist. Soc B. **58**(1), 267–288 (1996)
2. Friedman, J., Hastie, T., Tibshirani, R.: Regularization paths for generalized linear models via coordinate descent. J. Stat. Softw. **33**(1), 1–22 (2010). http://www.jstatsoft.org/v33/i01/
3. Nicolls, W.: Implementing company classification policy with the S/MIME security label. RFC 3114, IETF, May 2002
4. UCDMO. Ucdmo cross domain baseline list. http://www.crossdomain.org (2011). Accessed 26 March 2015
5. Brown, J.D., Charlebois, D.: Security classification using automated learning (scale), DRDC Ottawa CR, Technical Report (2010)
6. Entezari-Maleki, C., Rezaei, A., Minaei-Bidgoli, B.: Comparison of classification methods based on the type of attributes and sample size. J. Convergence Inf. Technol. **4**(3), 94–102 (2009)
7. Kotsiantis, S.B.: Supervised machine learning: A review of classification techniques. Informatica **31**, 249–268 (2007)
8. Mathkour, H., Touir, A., Al-Sanie, W.: Automatic information classifier using rhetorical structure theory. In: Kłopotek, M.A., Wierzchoń, S.T., Trojanowski, K. (eds.) Intelligent Information Processing and Web Mining. Advances in Soft Computing, vol. 31, pp. 229–236. Springer, Heidelberg (2005)
9. Clark, K.: Automated security classification. Master's thesis, Vrije Universiteit (2008)
10. Digitial national security archive. http://nsarchive.chadwyck.com/home.do. Accessed 26 March 2015
11. Abbyy. http://www.abbyy.com/. Accessed 26 March 2015
12. Baeza-Yates, R., Ribeiro-Neto, B., et al.: Modern Information Retrieval, vol. 463. ACM Press, New York (1999)

Constructing Efficient PAKE Protocols from Identity-Based KEM/DEM

Kyu Young Choi[1], Jihoon Cho[1], Jung Yeon Hwang[2](✉), and Taekyoung Kwon[3]

[1] Network and Security Lab, Samsung SDS, Inc., Seoul, Korea
{ky12.choi,jihoon1.cho}@samsung.com
[2] Authentication Research Section, ETRI, Daejeon, Korea
videmot@etri.re.kr
[3] Graduate School of Information, Yonsei University, Seoul, Korea
taekyoung@yonsei.ac.kr

Abstract. In this paper, we propose an efficient identity-based password authenticated key exchange (IBPAKE) protocol using identity-based KEM/DEM. In IBPAKE, a client conducts authentication based on a human-memorable password and a server's identity. A distinctive feature of IBPAKE protocols, compared to the well-known EKE-like PAKE protocols, is that an adversary who even acquired a user's password cannot impersonate a server to further investigate user's sensitive information.

We first construct the new IBPAKE protocol using the Boneh-Franklin identity-based encryption (IBE) scheme, and then generalize the protocol by presenting a generic method to yield an efficient IBPAKE protocol from identity-based KEM/DEM. Our fine-grained approach has concrete advantages in terms of performance. First, unnecessary parameters can be removed easily. This allows a straightforward improvement on computational cost and communication bandwidth. Our protocol gives better performance, compared to previously known IBPAKE protocols.

1 Introduction

Backgrounds. A key exchange (KE) protocol is run by two parties who want to share a secret key over a public network. For security in KE, two basic security notions must be achieved: One is *key secrecy* and the other is *mutual authentication*, respectively, to resist passive and active adversaries that exist in the wild. The Diffie-Hellman (DH) KE protocol [16] is such a fundamental element that provides key secrecy even forward, but still needs to add authentication. Among various authentication factors, particularly when one party is a user in the client-server model, an ID/password pair is widely used for authentication because it can be memorized by user without any specific device. Consequently, a great

J.Y. Hwang—This work was supported by the ICT R and D program of MSIP/IITP [B1206-15-1007, Development of Universal Authentication Platform Technology with Context-Aware Multi-Factor Authentication and Digital Signature].

© Springer International Publishing Switzerland 2016
H. Kim and D. Choi (Eds.): WISA 2015, LNCS 9503, pp. 411–422, 2016.
DOI: 10.1007/978-3-319-31875-2_34

number of password-authenticated KE (PAKE) protocols have been proposed to extend the DH protocol in the password authentication paradigm. The well-known challenge in designing a PAKE protocol is to resist *dictionary attacks* due to the low entropy of a human-memorable password. An adversary can prepare a dictionary of password candidates and exhaustively try those words from the dictionary. On-line dictionary attacks can be deterred simply by counting the number of failed attempts up to the limit. However, off-line dictionary attacks are notoriously challenging to designing the PAKE protocols. The so-called 'Encrypted Key Exchange (EKE)' [5] is a typical example of PAKE that prevents off-line dictionary attacks effectively. The essential idea of EKE is to encrypt ephemeral DH keys by a password. Since ephemeral DH keys are generated from a random distribution, decryption by a guessed password does not reveal meaningful information about the original one.

Problems. Even in the case of using a secure PAKE protocol, there remain various kinds of threats that are possible to leak a password, for example, installing malware, hacking a system, shoulder-surfing a password entry, and investigating lost/stolen portable devices. When a password or its verifier is revealed, inevitably an adversary can impersonate either a client or a server. Although a client impersonation is unavoidable due to the intrinsic nature of password authentication, a server impersonation is quite different. If an adversary impersonates a server to the client who was stolen the password, saying that the adversary succeeds in running a secure PAKE protocol with the client, then she can further investigate the client through the useful services that may be allowed to gather sensitive information from the user, such as financial and healthcare services. In the previous EKE-like PAKE protocols, a client and a server authenticate each other by a shared password (or a password verifier). Therefore they are also vulnerable to server impersonation attacks when a password is revealed.

As an approach to resolve this problem, we can apply a hybrid method combining password authentication and asymmetric cryptographic schemes. For example, [18,20] use a public key encryption scheme in conjunction with password authentication. It uses a password for a client and a public key encryption scheme for a server. In a usual client-server model, a client is a human who can memorize a password and a server is a powerful machine which can store a high-entropy secret key. The hybrid structure fits for such *unbalanced computational* environments. A public key is set to be a random string for security. A client must check if the random public key is corresponding to a specific server by a certificate [21]. The maintenance of certificates entails additional computation and communication costs[1]. To simplify the certificate-based public key management, one can build an identity-based cryptosystem [4,25]. Here, a public key can be replaced with an arbitrary public string that a user chooses, such as an e-mail address or IP address.

Recently, an identity-based password authenticated key exchange (IBPAKE) protocol is introduced in a client-server model [28]. In the protocol, a server's

---

[1] For example, each client must verify a server's certificate (e.g., X.509 Certificates) via CRL (Certificate Revocation Lists) or OCSP (Online Certificate Status Protocol).

public identity is additionally used to encrypt a password. Since the server's public identity such as a company or brand name is typically well remembered, a client can perform a convenient authentication. However, the IBPAKE protocol of [28] is generically constructed from an identity-based encryption (IBE) scheme. Though it gives a conceptually simple design principle, efficiency is further studied.

Our Results. In this paper, we propose an efficient IBPAKE protocol using identity-based key encapsulation mechanism (KEM) and data encapsulation mechanism (DEM) [2]. Basically, identity-based KEM/DEM works in identity-based cryptosystem, that is, a public key is defined as an arbitrary string. Thus a client can do an easy authentication based on a human-memorable password and server's identity.

In contrast to the approach of [28], our approach has various advantages in terms of the performance. Intuitively, we can control a keying material from identity-based KEM/DEM more precisely and remove unnecessary parameters. This gives straightforward improvement on computational cost and communication bandwidth.

Our first IBPAKE protocol is constructed by using the well-known Boneh-Franklin IBE scheme [4]. Next, generalizing our first protocol, we present a generic method to yield an efficient IBPAKE protocol using identity-based KEM/ DEM. Our idea is to combine an identity-based KEM/DEM and a DH KE protocol. We formally prove its security. Using the generic method, we can flexibly and independently construct an IBPAKE protocol by combining any pair of identity-based KEM/DEM and KE protocols irrespective of their underlying structures or hardness assumptions. For example, an integer factorization-based identity-based KEM and a pairing-based KE can be combined together.

As shown in our performance analysis, our IBPAKE protocol gives better performance, compared to [28].

Organization. The remainder of this paper is organized as follows. In Sect. 2, we briefly review some preliminaries. In Sect. 3 we present an IBPAKE protocol over gap Diffie-Hellman groups and prove its security. In Sect. 4 we present a generalization of the IBPAKE protocol, i.e., a generic method to generate an IBPAKE protocol and its security. Finally we conclude in Sect. 5.

2   Preliminaries

In this section, we briefly review related work and some mathematical assumptions as preliminaries.

Related Work. Since Diffie-Hellman key agreement protocol [16], KE protocols have been proposed to achieve various authentication goals [6–8,22]. Authenticated KE protocols have been developed largely according to two authentication types, i.e., symmetric and asymmetric.

Symmetric authentication type assumes that participants have a same secret key in advance before running a KE protocol [6–8]. For example, we can consider

PAKE. Refer to [24] for a recent survey. Since the formal work of [6,11] for PAKE, lots of research has been conducted to provide useful features, e.g. resilience to server compromise [19], construction under standard assumption [23], and multi-party PAKE [1]. Recent research on PAKE protocols [9] focuses on meeting highly theoretical security requirement such as UC model [14] but the protocols are known to be relatively inefficient.

Asymmetric authentication type assumes that a participant has a secret key and its corresponding public key. The secret key is kept secret by the participant while the public key is set to be public and so anyone can access it. By construction, no information about the secret key should be extracted from the public key. For example, we can consider a standard public key based KE and identity-based KE [15].

Mathematical Assumptions. We review bilinear maps and some assumptions related to our protocol. Let $\mathbb{G}_1$ and $\mathbb{G}_2$ are two (multiplicative) cyclic group of prime order p. We assume that the discrete logarithm problems in both $\mathbb{G}_1$ and $\mathbb{G}_2$ are intractable.

Admissible Bilinear Map. We call $e : \mathbb{G}_1 \times \mathbb{G}_1 \to \mathbb{G}_2$ an *admissible (symmetric) bilinear* map if it satisfies the following properties:

- Bilinearity: $e(g^a, h^b) = e(g, h)^{ab}$ for all $g, h \in \mathbb{G}_1$ and $a, b \in \mathbb{Z}_p^*$.
- Non-degenerancy: There exists $g \in \mathbb{G}_1$ such that $e(g, g) \neq 1$.
- Computability: There exists an efficient algorithm to compute $e(g, h)$ for all $g, h \in \mathbb{G}_1$.

The modified Weil and Tate pairings in elliptic curve are examples of the admissible bilinear maps.

Computational Diffie-Hellman (CDH) Problem. A CDH problem is to compute g^{ab} when given g, g^a and g^b for some $a, b \in \mathbb{Z}_p^*$.

Bilinear Diffie-Hellman (BDH) Problem. A BDH problem in $[\mathbb{G}_1, \mathbb{G}_2, e]$ is to compute $e(g, g)^{abc}$ when given $g, g^a, g^b,$ and g^c for some $a, b, c \in \mathbb{Z}_p^*$.

We assume that the above CDH and BDH problems are intractable. That is, there is no probabilistic polynomial time (PPT) algorithm that solves the problems with non-negligible probability.

3   Proposed IBPAKE Protocol and Security Analysis

In this section, we propose an IBPAKE protocol, called iPAKE using the Boneh-Franklin IBE (BF-IBE) scheme [4]. The protocol makes an asymmetric key setting for a client and a server. That is, the server S has a long-term secret key to be used for BF-IBE scheme, while the client C has only a human-memorizable password without any secret key of high-entropy. In the following description, we denote by $x \xleftarrow{R} X$ the operation to pick an element x from set X uniformly at random.

3.1   Protocol Description

Our protocol, iPAKE consists of two phases, initialization and key establishment as follows.

Initialization Phase. A server, S obtains a secret key corresponding to its identity ID_S and a client, C with identity ID_C registers a password, i.e., a password verifier as its authentication key.

- Setup: To generate IBE system parameters, KGS chooses a random number $\kappa \in \mathbb{Z}_p^*$ and a random generator g of $\mathbb{G}_1$, and sets $g_{pub} = g^\kappa$. KGS also chooses four cryptographic hash functions $H_1 : \{0,1\}^* \rightarrow \mathbb{G}_1$, $H_2 : \mathbb{G}_2 \rightarrow \{0,1\}^t$, $H_3 : \{0,1\}^* \rightarrow \{0,1\}^t$, and $H_4 : \{0,1\}^* \rightarrow \{0,1\}^l$ where t is a security parameter and l is the bit length of a session key. The system parameters p and the master secret key msk are given by

$$\mathsf{msk} = \kappa, \qquad \mathsf{p} = (\lambda, p, e, \mathbb{G}_1, \mathbb{G}_2, g, g_{pub}, H_1, H_2, H_3, H_4).$$

- Extract: To generate a private key for ID_S, KGS computes $q_S = H_1(ID_S)$ and the private key $k_S = (q_S)^\kappa$ using msk$= \kappa$. KGS sends k_S to S over a secure channel.
- Registration: C chooses a password $pw_C \in$ Password and sends $H_3(pw_C)$ to S over a secure channel.

Key Establishment Phase. When C and S want to establish a session key, they execute the following protocol (See Fig. 1).

Client C		Server S
$[ID_C, pw_C]$		$[ID_S, k_S], [ID_C, H_3(pw_C)]$

$$x \xleftarrow{R} \mathbb{Z}_p$$
$$X = g^x,\ q_S = H_1(ID_S)$$
$$d_S = e(q_S, g_{pub}),\ \delta = (d_S)^x$$
$$W = H_2(\delta) \oplus H_3(pw_C) \qquad \xrightarrow{\ ID_C, W, X\ }$$

$$\delta' = e(X, k_S)$$
$$H_3(pw_C)' = W \oplus H_2(\delta')$$
$$H_3(pw_C)' \overset{?}{=} H_3(pw_C)$$
$$y \xleftarrow{R} \mathbb{Z}_p$$
$$\xleftarrow{\quad Y \quad} \qquad Y = g^y$$
$$Z = Y^x \qquad\qquad Z = X^y$$
$$\mathsf{sid}_C = W||X||Y \qquad \mathsf{sid}_S = W||X||Y$$
$$ssk = H_4(ID_C||ID_S||\mathsf{sid}_C||\delta||Z) \qquad ssk = H_4(ID_C||ID_S||\mathsf{sid}_S||\delta||Z)$$

Fig. 1. Our iPAKE protocol

1. C picks a random number $x \in \mathbb{Z}_p^*$, and computes $X = g^x$, $q_S = H_1(ID_S)$, $d_S = e(q_S, p_{pub})$, and $\delta = (d_S)^x$. Also, C computes $W = H_2(\delta) \oplus H_3(pw_C)$ by using his/her own password. C then sends $\langle ID_C, W, X \rangle$ to the server S.

2. When S receives $\langle ID_C, W, X \rangle$, S computes $\delta' = e(X, k_S)$ and $H_3(pw_C)' = W \oplus H_2(\delta')$ using its secret key k_S. S then checks if $H_3(pw_C)' = H_3(pw_C)$. If it is not true, S outputs FAIL and aborts. Otherwise, S picks a random number $y \in \mathbb{Z}_p^*$. S computes $(Y = g^y, Z = X^y)$, and sends Y to C. Finally, S computes the session secret key $ssk = H_4(ID_C || ID_S || \text{sid}_S || \delta || Z)$ with $\text{sid}_S = W || X || Y$.

3. C computes the session secret key $ssk = H_4(ID_C || ID_S || \text{sid}_C || \delta || Z)$ with $\text{sid}_C = W || X || Y$ and $Z = Y^x$.

In the above protocol, the transcript (W, X) is a ciphertext of BF-IBE scheme to encrypt the plaintext $H_3(pw_C)$, i.e., we have $(W, X) \leftarrow$ BF-IBE.Enc$(ID_S, H_3(pw_C))$ and $H_3(pw_C) \leftarrow$ BF-IBE.Dec$(k_S, (W, X))$.

The above IBPAKE protocol provides implicit authentication. A KE protocol is said to achieve *implicit key authentication* if a participant (a client or a server) is assured that no other entity except its partner can learn a session secret key. Note that implicit key authentication does not necessarily mean that partners have actually computed the key. For explicit key authentication, we can easily apply the known techniques to exchange authentication tags [22].

3.2 Security Analysis

We analyze our protocol based on the extended security model of a PAKE protocol by Bellare et al. [6], in order to treat an IBPAKE protocol. In the following security proof, we consider given identity attack[2] [10,12].

Theorem 1. *Let $\mathcal{A}$ be an adversary for given ID_C and ID_S attack to iPAKE in the random oracle model. Suppose $\mathcal{A}$ makes at most q_{H_4}, q_E, and q_S queries to H_4, Execute, and Sand oracles, respectively. Then, we have*

$$\mathsf{Adv}_{\mathcal{A},\text{iPAKE}}^{\text{IBPAKE}}(t) \leq q_E \mathsf{Adv}_{\mathcal{A},[\mathbb{G}_1,\mathbb{G}_2,e]}^{\text{BDH}}(t) + \frac{1}{2}q_{H_4}\mathsf{Adv}_{\mathcal{A},\mathbb{G}_1}^{\text{CDH}}(t) + q_S\mathsf{Adv}_{\mathcal{A},\text{BF-IBE}}(t) + \frac{q_S}{\mathcal{PW}}$$

where t is the adversary's running time and $\mathsf{Adv}_{\mathcal{A},\text{BF-IBE}}(t)$ is the maximum advantage of $\mathcal{A}$ against the BF-IBE scheme.

Proof. Let $\mathcal{A}$ be an active adversary that gets an advantage in attacking iPAKE. $\mathcal{A}$ can get the advantage (except negligible probability) by following cases:

– Case 1. Finding the password, namely impersonating the client.
– Case 2. Computing a server's secret value, namely impersonating the server.
– Case 3. Breaking the protocol without altering transcripts.

In Case 1, the adversary $\mathcal{A}$ can get information about a particular session key by finding the password pw_C. There are two ways $\mathcal{A}$ can get information about the password; either $\mathcal{A}$ executes on-line dictionary attacks using Send

---

[2] For the security of full adaptive identity attack, refer to the full version of this paper.

queries or $\mathcal{A}$ breaks a ciphertext (W, X) of the BF-IBE scheme. Let Succ_{pw} be the event that $\mathcal{A}$ succeeds in Case 1, and we assume that passwords are uniformly distributed. We then may obtain the probability of Succ_{pw} as follows:

$$\mathsf{Pr}_{\mathcal{A}}[\mathsf{Succ}_{pw}] \leq q_S \mathsf{Adv}_{\mathcal{A},\mathsf{BF\text{-}IBE}}(t) + \frac{q_S}{\mathcal{PW}}.$$

In Case 2, to impersonate the server or to get information about a session key, $\mathcal{A}$ may try to compute $\delta = e(q_S, g_{pub})^x$ from the transcript X and the public values (q_S, g_{pub}) of the protocol from Execute queries. It is the same as solving the BDH problem. Therefore, the upper bound about the advantage of $\mathcal{A}$ from Case 2 is $q_E \mathsf{Adv}_{\mathcal{A},[\mathbb{G}_1,\mathbb{G}_2,e]}^{\mathsf{BDH}}(t)$.

Next, we consider the advantage from Case 3. Note that, to get any information of a session secret key ssk in the random oracle model, $\mathcal{A}$ has to ask $\langle ID_C || ID_S || \mathsf{sid} || \delta || Z \rangle$ to the hash oracle H_4. We can construct $\mathcal{B}$ which succeeds in solving the CDH problem using $\mathcal{A}$ as a subroutine. $\mathcal{B}$ receives a CDH instance $(\mathbb{G}, N, g, U = g^u, V = g^v)$. $\mathcal{B}$ chooses two identities (ID_C, ID_S), a master secret key $\kappa \in \mathbb{Z}_p^*$, and a password $pw_C \in \mathsf{Password}$ of the client's identity ID_C. $\mathcal{B}$ sets $g_{pub} = g^\kappa$, and gives (ID_C, ID_S) and system parameters to $\mathcal{A}$. $\mathcal{B}$ then runs $\mathcal{A}$, answering its oracle queries as follows:

- For queries $H_1(ID_i)$ proceed as follows: if $[ID_i, q_i]$ exist in a list h_1-tuples, return q_i. Otherwise, return a random $q_i \in \mathbb{G}_1$ and store $[ID_i, q_i]$ in h_1-tuples. (If $ID_i = ID_S$, we denote $q_i = q_S$.)
- For queries $H_2(\delta_i)$ proceed as follows: if $[\delta_i, \alpha_i]$ exist in a list h_2-tuples, return α_i. Otherwise, return a random $\alpha_i \in \{0,1\}^t$ and store $[\delta_i, \alpha_i]$ in h_2-tuples.
- For queries $H_3(pw_i)$ proceed as follows: if $[pw_i, \beta_i]$ exist in a list h_3-tuples, return β_i. Otherwise, return a random $\beta_i \in \{0,1\}^t$ and store $[pw_i, \beta_i]$ in h_3-tuples.
- For queries $H_4(ID_C || ID_S || \mathsf{sid}_i || \delta_i || Z_i)$, return a random $\gamma_i \in \{0,1\}^l$. Store $[\mathsf{sid}_i, \gamma_i]$ in a list h_4-tuples.
- For queries $\mathsf{Extract}(ID_i)$ proceed as follows: find $[ID_i, q_i]$ in h_1-tuples and return $k_i = q_i^\kappa$. (We assume $\mathsf{Extract}$ queries are preceded by H_1 queries.)
- For queries $\mathsf{Execute}(ID_C, ID_S)$ proceed as follows: choose random $a, b \in \mathbb{Z}_p^*$ and $\alpha, \beta \in \{0,1\}^t$. Compute $X = Ug^a$, $\delta = e(X, k_S)$, $W = \alpha \oplus \beta$, and $Y = Vg^b$. Return $\langle ID_C, W, X, Y \rangle$ and store $[\delta, \alpha]$ and $[pw_C, \beta]$ in h_2-tuples and h_3-tuples, respectively. (We assume $\mathsf{Execute}$ queries are not preceded by H_2, H_3 queries.)
- Send, $\mathsf{Corrupt}$, Reveal, and Test queries are answered honestly.

The success probability of $\mathcal{B}$ depends on the event query that $\mathcal{A}$ issues H_4 oracle query on $ID_C || ID_S || \mathsf{sid} || \delta || Z$, where sid is a return value of $\mathsf{Execute}$ query and $Z = g^{(u+a)(v+b)}$. (Note that, $g^{uv} = Z/U^b V^a g^{ab}$.) If the advantage of $\mathcal{A}$ in Case 3 is ϵ, then $\mathcal{A}$ issues a query for $H_4(ID_C || ID_S || \mathsf{sid} || \delta || Z)$ with probability at least 2ϵ, i.e., $\mathsf{Pr}_{\mathcal{A}}[\mathsf{query}] \leq 2\epsilon$. (The details are in [4].) Thus, the provability that $\mathcal{B}$ outputs g^{uv} from the list h_4-tuples is at least $2\epsilon/q_{H_4}$. Therefore, the upper bound about the advantage of $\mathcal{A}$ from Case 3 is $\frac{1}{2}q_{H_4}\mathsf{Adv}_{\mathcal{A},[\mathbb{G}_1,\mathbb{G}_2,e]}^{\mathsf{BDH}}(t)$. Finally, we have

$$\mathsf{Adv}^{\mathrm{IBPAKE}}_{\mathcal{A},\mathrm{iPAKE}}(t) \le q_E \mathsf{Adv}^{\mathrm{BDH}}_{\mathcal{A},[\mathbb{G}_1,\mathbb{G}_2,e]}(t) + \frac{1}{2}q_{H_4}\mathsf{Adv}^{\mathrm{CDH}}_{\mathcal{A},\mathbb{G}_1}(t) + q_S \mathsf{Adv}_{\mathcal{A},\mathsf{BF\text{-}IBE}}(t) + \frac{q_S}{\mathcal{PW}}.$$

$\square$

4   Generic Construction

In this section, we present a generic method to construct an IBPAKE protocol from an identity-based KEM/DEM scheme. Before describing our construction in detail, we present an identity-based KEM/DEM scheme which extends the identity-based KEM scheme [2].

4.1   Identity-Based KEM/DEM Scheme

An identity-based KEM/DEM scheme is specified by six polynomial time algorithms, Setup, Extract, IBKEM.Enc, IBDEM.Enc, IBKEM.Dec, and IBDEM.Dec.

- Setup(λ). This algorithm takes a security parameter λ as input and returns a master secret key, msk and its corresponding public parameter, p.
- Extract(msk, p, ID). This algorithm takes the master secret key, msk, public parameter, p, and an identity, ID as input. It returns a secret key, sk_{ID}.
- IBKEM.Enc(p, ID). This algorithm takes p and an identity, ID as input. It returns a random *one-time* key, $k_p \in \mathcal{K}_P$ and its ciphertext, Δ_{KEM}, where $\mathcal{K}_P$ is a key space associated with p.
- IBDEM.Enc(k_p, p, m). This algorithm takes p, a key k_p, and a message, m as input. It returns a ciphertext Δ_{DEM} for m.
- IBKEM.Dec(sk_{ID}, p, Δ_{KEM}). This algorithm takes p, a private key sk_{ID}, and a ciphertext Δ_{KEM} as input. It returns a key, k_p.
- IBDEM.Dec(k_p, p, Δ_{DEM}). This algorithm takes p, a key k_p, and a ciphertext Δ_{DEM} as input. It returns a message m.

In the above identity-based KEM/DEM scheme, the full ciphertext for m is $(\Delta_{\mathsf{KEM}}, \Delta_{\mathsf{DEM}})$. IBE schemes [3,4,13,17,26,27] can be represented in the identity-based KEM/DEM framework [2].

4.2   Our Generic Construction for IBPAKE

The generic method to construct an IBPAKE protocol from an identity-based KEM/DEM scheme is described as follows:

1. C runs IBKEM.Enc(p, ID_S) to obtain a random one-time key k_p and its ciphertext Δ_{KEM}. C also runs IBDEM.Enc(k_p, p, $f(pw_C)$) to obtain a ciphertext Δ_{DEM} for a message $f(pw_C)$, where f is a one-way function. C then sends ID_C and $\Delta = (\Delta_{\mathsf{KEM}}, \Delta_{\mathsf{DEM}})$ to S.

$$
\begin{array}{ll}
\underline{\text{Client } C} & \underline{\text{Server } S} \\
[ID_C, pw_C] & [ID_S, sk_{ID_s}], [ID_C, f(pw_C)]
\end{array}
$$

$(k_p, \Delta_{\mathsf{KEM}}) \leftarrow \mathsf{IBKEM.Enc}(\mathsf{p}, ID_S)$
$\Delta_{\mathsf{DEM}} \leftarrow \mathsf{IBDEM.Enc}(k_p, \mathsf{p}, f(pw_C))$
$\Delta = (\Delta_{\mathsf{KEM}}, \Delta_{\mathsf{DEM}}) \quad \xrightarrow{ID_C, \Delta}$

$\qquad\qquad\qquad\qquad\qquad k_p \leftarrow \mathsf{IBKEM.Dec}(sk_{ID_s}, \mathsf{p}, \Delta_{\mathsf{KEM}})$
$\qquad\qquad\qquad\qquad\qquad f(pw_C)' \leftarrow \mathsf{IBDEM.Dec}(k_p, \mathsf{p}, \Delta_{\mathsf{DEM}})$
$\qquad\qquad\qquad\qquad\qquad \text{Check } f(pw_C)' \stackrel{?}{=} f(pw_C)$
$\qquad\qquad\qquad\quad \xleftarrow{r_S} \quad r_S \leftarrow \mathsf{RanGen}(\lambda)$
$ssk = H(ID_C\|ID_S\|\Delta\|r_S\|k_p) \qquad ssk = H(ID_C\|ID_S\|\Delta\|r_S\|k_p)$

Fig. 2. Generic construction for IBPAKE

2. S runs $\mathsf{IBKEM.Dec}(sk_{ID_s}, \mathsf{p}, \Delta_{\mathsf{KEM}})$ to obtain the one-time key k_p, where sk_{ID_s} is a server's secret key generated by $\mathsf{Extract}(\mathsf{msk}, \mathsf{p}, ID_S)$. S obtains $f(pw_C)'$ by running $\mathsf{IBDEM.Dec}(k_p, \mathsf{p}, \Delta_{\mathsf{DEM}})$ and then checks if $f(pw_C)' = f(pw_C)$. If it is not true, S outputs FAIL and aborts. Otherwise, S generates a random number r_S from a random number generator, and sends r_S to C. Finally, S computes a session secret key $ssk = H(ID_C\|ID_S\|\Delta\|r_S\|k_p)$.
3. C computes a session secret key, $ssk = H(ID_C\|ID_S\|\Delta\|r_S\|k_p)$.

The above generic protocol provides *half forward secrecy*. That is, if the secret key of the server is compromised, then all session keys are revealed using protocol transcripts. However, the exposure of client's password is not helpful to get the information about previous session keys. In practice, it is reasonable to assume that low-power devices held by clients are vulnerable to attacks, while a server is powerful and so more secure.

However, our generic construction can be modified to provide *forward secrecy* by using additional ephemeral DH KE. In fact, iPAKE can be viewed as a specific version of our generic protocol, in which BF-IBE is used as an identity-based KEM/DEM scheme. Note that BF-IBE can be represented as a identity-based KEM/DEM scheme as follows:

IBE-Enc
$$(k_p = e(q_S, g_{pub})^x, \Delta_{\mathsf{KEM}} = g^x) \leftarrow \mathsf{IBKEM.Enc}(\mathsf{p}, ID)$$
$$\Delta_{\mathsf{DEM}} = m \oplus H_2(k_p) \leftarrow \mathsf{IBDEM.Enc}(k_p, \mathsf{p}, m)$$
IBE-Dec
$$k_p = e(\Delta_{\mathsf{KEM}}, sk_{ID}) \leftarrow \mathsf{IBKEM.Dec}(sk_{ID}, \mathsf{p}, \Delta_{\mathsf{KEM}})$$
$$m = \Delta_{\mathsf{DEM}} \oplus H_2(k_p) \leftarrow \mathsf{IBDEM.Dec}(k_p, \mathsf{p}, \Delta_{\mathsf{DEM}})$$

The ciphertext element $X(= \Delta_{\mathsf{KEM}} = g^x)$ of BF-IBE is a public ephemeral DH value. Our iPAKE performs DH KE to compute g^{xy} by using g^y, instead of use of the random value r_S. It is known that the ephemeral key, g^{xy} is sufficient for perfect forward secrecy [22]. Similarly, by using such identity-based KEM/DEM schemes [3,13,17,26,27] that have public DH values in ciphertexts, we can also construct an IBPAKE protocol with perfect forward secrecy.

4.3 Comparison

We now compare performance between our IBPAKE protocol and the previous IBPAKE protocol [28][3]. To be fair, we assume that the IBPAKE protocols are constructed by using the BF-IBE [4] and Gentry IBE [17], respectively. The following table summarizes the results.

Table 1. Comparison of IBAKE protocols (e: pairing operation, Exp: modular exponentiation, Mul: modular multiplication, w.l.o.g, Exp and Mul contain the multiplication and the addition in a gap Diffie-Hellman group, respectively.)

Protocol		Client			Server		
		e	Exp	Mul	e	Exp	Mul
IBPAKE [28]	based on [4]	1	6	1	1	4	1
	based on [17]	2	8	3	1	5	3
Ours	based on [4](iPAKE)	1	3	0	1	2	0
	based on [17]	2	5	2	1	3	2

As shown in Table 1, although the IBPAKE protocol [28] can be constructed by using the IBE schemes [4,17], our protocols are more efficient.

5   Conclusion

We have proposed efficient IBPAKE protocols using identity-based KEM/DEM. A client can do an easy authentication based on only a human-memorable password and server's public identity. Our protocols give resistance to server impersonation attacks. That is, even if a password is revealed from a client, a server impersonation attack can be prevented effectively. The proposed protocols outperform the best-known IBPAKE protocol.

References

1. Abdalla, M., Pointcheval, D.: A scalable password-based group key exchange protocol in the standard model. In: Lai, X., Chen, K. (eds.) ASIACRYPT 2006. LNCS, vol. 4284, pp. 332–347. Springer, Heidelberg (2006)
2. Boyen, X.: A tapestry of identity-based encryption: practical frameworks compared. J. Appl. Crypt. 1(1), 3–21 (2008). Inderscience

---

[3] To the best of our knowledge, this is the only protocol with provable security.

3. Boneh, D., Boyen, X.: Efficient selective-ID secure identity-based encryption without random oracles. In: Cachin, C., Camenisch, J.L. (eds.) EUROCRYPT 2004. LNCS, vol. 3027, pp. 223–238. Springer, Heidelberg (2004)
4. Boneh, D., Franklin, M.: Identity-based encryption from the weil pairing. In: Kilian, J. (ed.) CRYPTO 2001. LNCS, vol. 2139, pp. 213–229. Springer, Heidelberg (2001)
5. Bellovin, S.M., Merritt, M.: Encrypted key exchange: Password-based protocol secure against dictionary attack. In: IEEE Symposium on Research in Security and Privacy, pp. 72–84 (1992)
6. Bellare, M., Pointcheval, D., Rogaway, P.: Authenticated key exchange secure against dictionary attacks. In: Preneel, B. (ed.) EUROCRYPT 2000. LNCS, vol. 1807, pp. 139–155. Springer, Heidelberg (2000)
7. Bellare, M., Rogaway, P.: Entity authentication and key distribution. In: Stinson, D.R. (ed.) CRYPTO 1993. LNCS, vol. 773, pp. 232–249. Springer, Heidelberg (1994)
8. Bellare, M., Rogaway, P.: Provably-secure session key distribution: the three party case. In: STOC 1995, pp. 57–66 (1995)
9. Benhamouda, F., Blazy, O., Chevalier, C., Pointcheval, D., Vergnaud, D.: New techniques for SPHFs and efficient one-round PAKE protocols. In: Canetti, R., Garay, J.A. (eds.) CRYPTO 2013, Part I. LNCS, vol. 8042, pp. 449–475. Springer, Heidelberg (2013)
10. Barreto, P.S.L.M., Libert, B., McCullagh, N., Quisquater, J.-J.: Efficient and provably-secure identity-based signatures and signcryption from bilinear maps. In: Roy, B. (ed.) ASIACRYPT 2005. LNCS, vol. 3788, pp. 515–532. Springer, Heidelberg (2005)
11. Boyko, V., MacKenzie, P.D., Patel, S.: Provably secure password-authenticated key exchange using diffie-hellman. In: Preneel, B. (ed.) EUROCRYPT 2000. LNCS, vol. 1807, p. 156. Springer, Heidelberg (2000)
12. Cha, J.C., Cheon, J.H.: An identity-based signature from gap diffie-hellman groups. In: Desmedt, Y.G. (ed.) PKC 2003. LNCS, vol. 2567, pp. 18–30. Springer, Heidelberg (2002)
13. Canetti, R., Halevi, S., Katz, J.: Chosen-ciphertext security from identity-based encryption. In: Cachin, C., Camenisch, J.L. (eds.) EUROCRYPT 2004. LNCS, vol. 3027, pp. 207–222. Springer, Heidelberg (2004)
14. Canetti, R., Halevi, S., Katz, J., Lindell, Y., MacKenzie, P.: Universally composable password-based key exchange. In: Cramer, R. (ed.) EUROCRYPT 2005. LNCS, vol. 3494, pp. 404–421. Springer, Heidelberg (2005)
15. Choi, K.Y., Hwang, J.Y., Lee, D.-H.: Efficient ID-based group key agreement with bilinear maps. In: Bao, F., Deng, R., Zhou, J. (eds.) PKC 2004. LNCS, vol. 2947, pp. 130–144. Springer, Heidelberg (2004)
16. Diffie, W., Hellman, M.: New directions in cryptography. IEEE Trans. Inf. Theor. **22**(6), 644–654 (1976)
17. Gentry, C.: Practical identity-based encryption without random oracles. In: Vaudenay, S. (ed.) EUROCRYPT 2006. LNCS, vol. 4004, pp. 445–464. Springer, Heidelberg (2006)
18. Gong, L.A., Lomas, T.M., Needham, R., Saltzwe, J.: Protecting poorly chosen secrets from guessing attacks. IEEE J. Sel. Areas Commun. **11**(5), 648–656 (1993)
19. Gentry, C., MacKenzie, P.D., Ramzan, Z.: A method for making password-based key exchange resilient to server compromise. In: Dwork, C. (ed.) CRYPTO 2006. LNCS, vol. 4117, pp. 142–159. Springer, Heidelberg (2006)
20. Halevi, S., Krawczyk, H.: Public-key cryptography and password protocols. ACM Trans. Inf. Syst. Secur. **2**(3), 230–268 (1999)

21. Housley, R., Polk, T.: Planning for PKI: Best Practices Guide for Deploying Public Key Infrastructure. John Wiley & Sons, Inc., New York (2001)

22. Katz, J., Yung, M.: Scalable protocols for authenticated group key exchange. In: Boneh, D. (ed.) CRYPTO 2003. LNCS, vol. 2729, pp. 110–125. Springer, Heidelberg (2003)

23. Katz, J., Ostrovsky, R., Yung, M.: Efficient password-authenticated key exchange using human-memorable passwords. In: Pfitzmann, B. (ed.) EUROCRYPT 2001. LNCS, vol. 2045, p. 475. Springer, Heidelberg (2001)

24. Pointcheval, D.: Password-based authenticated key exchange. In: Fischlin, M., Buchmann, J., Manulis, M. (eds.) PKC 2012. LNCS, vol. 7293, pp. 390–397. Springer, Heidelberg (2012)

25. Shamir, A.: Identity-based cryptosystems and signature schemes. In: Blakely, G.R., Chaum, D. (eds.) CRYPTO 1984. LNCS, vol. 196, pp. 47–53. Springer, Heidelberg (1985)

26. Sakai, R., Kasahara, M.: ID based cryptosystems with pairing over elliptic curve, Cryptology ePrint Archive, Report 2003/054. http://eprint.iacr.org/2003/054

27. Waters, B.: Efficient identity-based encryption without random oracles. In: Cramer, R. (ed.) EUROCRYPT 2005. LNCS, vol. 3494, pp. 114–127. Springer, Heidelberg (2005)

28. Yi, X., Tso, R., Okamoto, E.: Identity-based password-authenticated key exchange for client/server model. In: SECRYPT 2012, pp. 45–54 (2012)

How to Demonstrate Our Presence Without Disclosing Identity? Evidence from a Grouping-Proof Protocol

Yunhui Zhuang[1](✉), Gerhard P. Hancke[1], and Duncan S. Wong[2]

[1] Department of Computer Science, City University of Hong Kong,
Kowloon Tong, Hong Kong
yhzhuang2-c@my.cityu.edu.hk, gp.hancke@cityu.edu.hk
[2] Security and Data Sciences, ASTRI, Ma Liu Shui, Hong Kong
duncanwong@astri.org

Abstract. The recent hot debate on sharing economy has been an emergence in a dynamic ownership economy, which attracts lots of attentions in the news media. The concept and practice of resource sharing have been fast becoming a mainstream phenomenon across the world. People share assets to their friends via Internet or smartphones. Meanwhile, researchers are now beginning to weigh in with deeper analysis in terms of security and privacy, which turn out to be one critical area of argument when sharing the items with others. To securely track the location of an item is of high importance in many mobile applications, which rely heavily on the notion of device proximity. In addition to securely and precisely determining an item's location, it is also desirable to preserve the privacy and untraceability of the item. Grouping-proof protocols are often used to prove the presence of a group of Provers to the Verifier at the same time. In this paper, we propose a new grouping-proof protocol that is well deployed in proximity identification systems for sharing economy, where each Prover needs to demonstrate its presence to the Verifier without disclosing its real identity. Our protocol is mutually authenticated and secure against all known attacks in a grouping-proof setting. Furthermore, the protocol retains the untraceability of a tag through forward privacy and prevents de-synchronization attacks.

Keywords: Sharing economy · Wireless sensor networks · RFID · Grouping-proof · Forward privacy

1 Introduction

Mobile Technology + Sharing Economy + Security & Privacy

=

Future EconTech Boom

On May 31st, 2010, a San Francisco based startup launched its first ride sharing service via mobile app. As of the end of May, 2015, this service is available

© Springer International Publishing Switzerland 2016
H. Kim and D. Choi (Eds.): WISA 2015, LNCS 9503, pp. 423–435, 2016.
DOI: 10.1007/978-3-319-31875-2_35

through 300 cities in 58 countries worldwide. The startup has raised 2.8 billion US dollars in total funding at the beginning of 2015 and has a market capitalization of over 40 billion US dollars. The name of this startup is called "UBER". This success startup example not only shows the power of "sharing economy" as a fast-growing social medium, but also demonstrates that, the emerging mobile technology can beat even their mainstream competitors in terms of speed and flexibility, especially in securely and precisely tracking the location of people who are in need of the ride sharing service in real time. In addition to sharing the ride, the scope of what actually can be shared is continually widening, such as housing (e.g., Airbnb, 9Flats), rental sharing (e.g., Car2Go), or even durable goods (e.g., Ecomodo). According to Nielsen's report [14], more than 30,000 Internet survey respondents in 60 countries are willing to join and participate in the sharing economy; for any given category of goods (e.g., cars, bicycles, clothing, household items, etc.).

Thanks to rapid development of mobile technology, people enjoy these sharing services through mobile apps installed on their smartphones. How to ensure the security and protect personal privacy remain a big challenge. As the increasing demand of security and privacy of proximity identification system in wireless communication, Radio Frequency IDentification (RFID) technology has played an important role for automatic object identification with multiple applications related to secure localization.

A Prover's (e.g. an RFID tag) exact location relative to a Verifier (e.g. an RFID reader) is crucial to the secure and reliable operation of many Real-Time Location Systems (RTLSs). In an RFID environment, it can be cryptographically proved that a Prover is at the proximity of a Verifier, while in many RTLSs the verifier's ability to securely verify the physical distance of a Prover makes it critical in secure localization methods. During the last two decades, RTLSs have been actively used to track many high-value assets and play an important role in Wireless Sensor Networks (WSN). Most of the WSN applications require that the positions of a particular node is securely and precisely determined.

In the future, RFID technology will offer a huge potential for the development of sensor enabled tags in industry applications. It has a superior advantage over many other traditional technologies. For instance, temperature-enabled sensor tags provide a detailed temperature profile of the cold chain of perishable items; fragile items can be monitored during transportation to prevent breakage; an RFID reader uses a motion sensor detector to detect a pallet in a distribution warehouse. In addition, many mobile applications would benefit from the deployment of RFID technology through our daily life, such as building access control, home/hospital patient monitoring, building energy monitoring, library borrowing services, E-channel for immigration, and mobile payment, etc.

Our Contributions. In this paper, we propose a new grouping-proof protocol for proximity identification systems in sharing economy with the following properties:

1. Our protocol provides mutual authentication and forward privacy, which can be used to prove the presence of a group of tags at the same time and also protect their identity.
2. In particular, the protocol allows a reader to cryptographically generate a proof of presence of a group of tags simultaneously and protects a tag's privacy. It is secure against all known attacks in a grouping-proof setting. It also retains the untraceability of a tag through forward privacy and prevents de-synchronization attacks.
3. Section 2 revisits grouping-proof and forward privacy in proximity identification systems. Our protocol is described in Sect. 3, followed by a security and privacy analysis in Sect. 4, and a discussion on how it compares to other grouping-proof proposals in Sect. 5. Section 6 concludes the paper.

1.1 Brief Overview of an RFID System

In an RFID system, a reader identifies a set of RFID tags via the wireless channel and the identification is done automatically as long as the tag enters the legitimate area (e.g., communication range) of the RFID reader which is also called neighbor area. Each tag, consisting of a small chip and an antenna, is embedded in an object and contains some identifying information of its owner. Unlike barcodes, RFID tags do not need to be in sight of the reader, which makes easier, faster and more convenient the identification of objects.

The scope of RFID applications has been growing rapidly, but it may introduce various security and privacy concerns. The very basic security requirement for an RFID authentication protocol is to ensure data confidentiality, authentication and proof of proximity. Another important concern is the privacy of RFID tags: since RFID tags are usually attached to moving objects, it is desirable to keep them not only anonymous but also untraceable.

1.2 The RFID Grouping-Proof Protocol

A grouping-proof protocol is used to guarantee that two or more RFID tags are scanned simultaneously and thus are present at the same time. It is designed in such a way so that the reader would be able to create a proof of a group of tags being present at the same time. An adversary is not able to fake the presence of a tag (or more tags) and the generated proof can be verified at some later time. Nowadays, this technology has been widely used in various industry applications. For example, in Hong Kong's medical industry, local hospitals use RFID systems to track in-patients and medical equipments, and the routine delivery of drugs and specimens. These items should be proved along with their prescription or with their information leaflet. In the aviation industry, Hong Kong International Airport has adopted an RFID-enabled baggage handling system, which handles over 110,000 pieces of baggage every day from more than 60 airlines using RFID labels. Together with the boarding pass and a person's ID, the system can generate a proof to make sure each baggage is along with the presence of a person who is on board the aircraft. Otherwise, the baggage is removed from the aircraft for the sake of security.

There are different ways to name "grouping-proof", such as yoking-proof [10], grouping-proof [19], existence-proof [18], clumping-proof [16], and so on. In this paper, we define "yoking-proof" for only two tags to be proved in a system and "grouping-proof" when the protocol is designed for a set of tags (more than two tags) at the same time. One of the difficult parts in designing a secure grouping-proof protocol is to defend against various attack scenarios which can deteriorate the credibility of a proof when launching a successful attack. There are several essential criteria of security and privacy concerns in the design of a qualified grouping-proof protocol as analyzed in Sect. 4.1.

2   Related Work

This section serves as a brief revision of two prominent features in proximity identification systems. Section 2.1 presents a brief review of grouping-proof protocols. Next, Sect. 2.2 will revisit forward privacy.

2.1   Revisiting Grouping-Proof Protocol

In 2004, Juels [10] presented a new idea of generating an evidence that a pair of tags are being scanned simultaneously by the reader. Such evidence is called "Yoking-proof" with the meaning "to join together"; and is verifiable by a trusted third party in an offline setting, rather than requiring direct involvement. The paper proposed two protocols in terms of a tag's computation capabilities (e.g., tags with standard cryptographic primitives and basic EPC tags). Later in 2005 and 2006, Saito and Sakurai [19], and Bolotnyy and Robins [2] proved that [10]'s two protocols are not secure against replay attacks. In addition, Burmester et al. [3] showed that these two protocols may suffer from Denial-of-Service (DoS) and impersonation attacks.

Since "Yoking-proof" can only prove the presence of two tags at the same time, Saito and Sakurai [19] extended Juels's idea to "grouping-proof" so that the presence of a set of tags (more than two tags) can be proved simultaneously. However, their proposal was broken by Piramuthu [18] in the sense that it is vulnerable to replay attacks, since an adversary would be able to predict the used timestamps and therefore collect prior responses and combine them together to forge a partial proof of one particular tag. Therefore, Piramuthu suggested to use random values in the partial proof instead of timestamps. One year later, Peris-Lopez et al. [16] proved that [18] is vulnerable to multi-proof session replay attacks for improper use of random numbers. Accordingly, Peris-Lopez et al. [16] also proposed a new yoking-proof protocol to defeat these attacks. In 2007, Lin et al. [13] proposed two grouping-proof protocols for online and offline modes to avoid race conditions and showed how to determine whether tags are missing as they are supposed to be in a grouping-proof. Unfortunately, the protocol for offline mode is not secure to multiple impersonation attacks as proved in [17]. In 2008, Cho et al. [5] proposed a variant of [18] to make it secure against brute force attack. But it is still vulnerable to multi-proof session replay attacks.

The first anonymous grouping-proof protocol was introduced by Bolotnyy and Robins [2] in 2006. Two years later, Burmester *et al.* [3] stated that [2]'s proposal is not clear how the reader can identify a pair of tags from their pseudonyms and proposed a new protocol to fix this problem. In the same year, Burmester *et al.* [3] proposed three new grouping-proof protocols to guarantee the generation of real grouping-proof and preserve the anonymity for the proof and the tag. Later in 2011, Peris-Lopez *et al.* [17] showed that they are all vulnerable to multiple impersonation attacks. In 2009, Chien and Liu [4] proposed a tree-based anonymous yoking-proof protocol aiming to reduce a reader's computational cost of identifying a tag from $O(N)$ to $O(1)$. However, this protocol was also broken by Peris-Lopez *et al.* [17] for the traceability attacks. Since then a number of grouping-proof protocols have been proposed but none of them is formally cryptanalyzed yet.

2.2 Revisiting Forward Privacy for RFID Authentication Protocol

During the past decade, researchers have been putting many efforts on RFID privacy models and some of them have been formalized in the literature [7,8,11,21,22]. In 2005, Avoine [1] proposed a security notion for the privacy of RFID authentication protocols in terms of traceability. Later on, Juels and Weis [11] presented a even stronger privacy notion which is extended from [1]. Their model was based on the indistinguishability of two distinct tags, which means an adversary cannot distinguish between any two uncorrupted tags within its computational power. But Ha *et al.* [7] in 2008 pointed out that their model is vulnerable to location tracking in the sense that a tag's ID is sent through an insecure channel, and thus they proposed a new model based on the unpredictability of the outputs of a tag to fix this problem. The underlying idea is to see whether an adversary is able to distinguish the real transcripts generated between the reader and a challenge tag from the random ones. This model was further refined by many new privacy notions [8,12,23]. However, none of aforementioned proposals capture forward privacy.

Ohkubo *et al.* [15] proposed the first RFID forward private protocol (OSK protocol) in 2003. OSK takes advantage of a hash chain to update the secret key of a tag at each protocol execution. The number of times that a tag's secret key can be updated is limited by a threshold T. The authors also proposed a forward privacy model, under which the OSK protocol is proved to be forward private. However, the OSK protocol is vulnerable to a denial of service (DoS) attack, where an adversary can keep querying the tag for T+1 times until it stops refreshing its secret key such that the adversary could identify this tag. Two similar approaches were proposed by Le *et al.* [20] and D'Arco *et al.* [6], who introduced two lightweight RFID authentication protocols which are proven as forward private under their defined forward privacy models, respectively. However, both protocols restrict the number of times that the secret key of a tag can be updated.

3 Our Protocol

In this section, we introduce our proposed protocol, which includes the preliminaries in Sect. 3.1 and the protocol description in Sect. 3.2. Our protocol benefits
from the issues discussed in Sect. 2 as practical tips to preclude mistakes invoked
in previous proposals. Table 1 summarizes the notations used in the description.

Table 1. Notations

X_1 / X_j	:	tag's secret key, update after reader authentication is successful
X_{j1} / X_{j2}	:	tag's old and new keys stored in the reader
$F(\cdot)$ / $G(\cdot)$	:	pseudo-random function (PRF)
ID_1 / ID_j	:	tag's real identity
N_T	:	the counter initialized to zero
c	:	a random challenge message with length l generated by the reader
r_1 / r_2	:	a random number with length l generated by the reader/tag
$MAC(\cdot)$	:	a keyed message authentication code with tag's secret key X_1 or X_j
b_1 / b_{j-1} / b_j :		tag's partial proof
$P_{1,...,m}$	:	Grouping-proof for tag 1 to m

3.1 Preliminaries

System Description. The system consists of a reader associated with a back-
end server, and a set of tags Tag 1, Tag 2, $\cdots$, Tag j. Each Tag j stores a dynamic
secret key X_j, which is shared with the reader. If the grouping-proof is succeeded,
the secret key X_j is updated for each protocol execution. The reader stores each
tag's identity ID_j and two keys X_{j1}, X_{j2} in order to combat de-synchronization
attacks, where X_{j1} is the "old" key used in the last session and is initially set
equal to a random value in the Initialization Stage; X_{j2} is the current key which
is initially set to be equivalent to X_j. The speed of propagation is assumed to
be the speed of light.

Pseudo-Random Function (PRF). Our protocol uses a PRF as the underlying cryptographic primitive. A family of efficiently computable functions $f =
\{F_K : \mathcal{D} \to \mathcal{R} \mid K \in \mathcal{K} \}$ is called a pseudo-random function family, if for any
polynomial time algorithm $\mathcal{C}$,

$$\mathbf{Adv}_{f,\mathcal{C}}^{prf}(k) = \mathbf{Pr}[\mathcal{C}^{F_K(\cdot)}(1^k) = 1] - \mathbf{Pr}[\mathcal{C}^{\mathsf{RF}(\cdot)}(1^k) = 1].$$

is a negligible function of the security parameter k, where K is randomly selected
from the key space $\mathcal{K}$, F_K is an instance of function family f, and $\mathsf{RF} : \mathcal{D} \to \mathcal{R}$
is a truly random function.

Message Authentication Code (MAC). A MAC is an algorithm that is
applied to a message to prevent an adversary from modifying this message sent
by one party to another, in particular, no adversary can generate a valid MAC
tag on any message that was not sent by the legitimate communicating parties.
In addition, the encryption task is performed if two parties have some important

secret that the adversary should not find out. Let $MAC : \{0,1\}^m \times \{0,1\}^* \to \{0,1\}^m$ denote a standard keyed message authentication code. Let $MAC(x, m)$ denote the MAC computed by applying a secret key x to message m.

3.2   Protocol Description

The protocol is designed in such a way that it features mutual authentication and forward privacy, which is inspired by a provably secure construction for RFID forward privacy in [22]. Let F and G be two secure PRFs, and MAC as a message authentication code defined in Sect. 3.1. We separate Tag 1 and the other tags into two different figures. Figure 1 shows how the protocol runs for the first tag, and Fig. 2 shows how the protocol runs for the other tags.

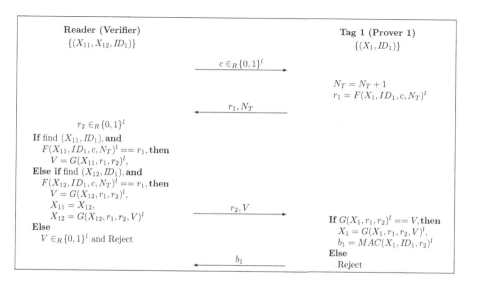

Fig. 1. The grouping-proof protocol (Tag 1)

The 1st Tag. Figure 1 describes the steps of generating a partial proof for the first tag. The protocol proceeds as follows:

1. The reader sends a random challenge message c with length l to the tag.
2. After receiving this challenge from the reader, the tag immediately updates its counter as $N_T = N_T + 1$, together with its identity ID_1, the challenge c from the reader, its current secret key X_1, as the input to compute an l bit "dynamic pseudonym" $r_1 = F(X_1, ID_1, c, N_T)^l$, which is then sent back to the reader with N_T.
3. Upon receiving $\{r_1, N_T\}$ from the tag, the reader picks another l-bit random challenge message r_2 and tries to search for the tag's identity.

4. The reader searches the database for the tuple (x_{11}, ID_1) such that $F(X_{11}, ID_1, c, N_T)^l == r_1$ holds. If such a tuple exists, it computes $V = G(X_{11}, r_1, r_2)^l$, then sends $\{r_2, V\}$ to the tag. If not, the reader searches for the tuple (x_{12}, ID_1) such that $F(X_{12}, ID_1, c, N_T)^l == r_1$ holds. If such a tuple exists, it computes $V = G(X_{12}, r_1, r_2)^l$. In the meantime, the reader updates two keys as follows: $X_{11} = X_{12}$, $X_{12} = G(X_{12}, r_1, r_2, V)^l$. After that the reader sends $\{r_2, V\}$ to the tag. Otherwise, the reader responds with $V \in_R \{0, 1\}^l$, r_2, rejects the tag, and terminates the proof session.

5. After receiving $\{r_2, V\}$, the tag computes the values of V and checks whether $G(X_1, r_1, r_2)^l == V$ holds. If yes, the tag updates its secret key $X_1 = G(X_1, r_1, r_2, V)^l$ and generates its partial proof by applying a MAC: $b_1 = MAC(X_1, ID_1, r_2)^l$, and sends b_1 to the reader. Otherwise, the tag rejects the reader and terminates the proof session.

6. The reader keeps $\{ID_1, b_1\}$ for the next protocol execution and the offline verification.

The Other Tags. Figure 2 shows the steps of generating partial proofs for the remaining tags (Tag 2, $\cdots$, Tag j).

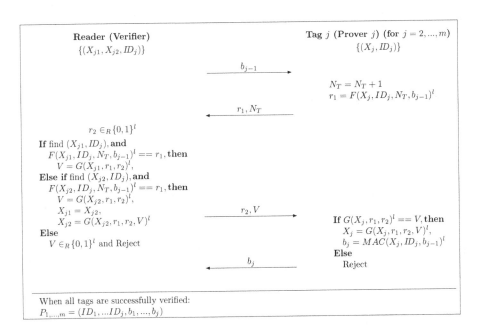

Fig. 2. The grouping-proof protocol (Tag 2, ..., m)

The main difference between the remaining tags and Tag 1 is that: instead of a random challenge message for Tag 1, the reader sends previous tag's partial proof b_{j-1} as "a challenge message" to Tag j, where $j = 2, ..., m$. This makes all the remaining tags' partial proof linked together in order to prevent different attack scenarios in a grouping-proof setting discussed in Sect. 4. After receiving b_{j-1}, Tag j will perform the same task as that of Tag 1. In the meantime, the reader is going to verify Tag j's identity the same way when verifying Tag 1 via several if-else decision makings. Finally, Tag j generates its partial proof by applying a MAC: $b_j = MAC(X_j, ID_j, b_{j-1})^l$, where one of the inputs is previous tag's partial proof b_{j-1}, and then sends b_j to the reader.

4 Security and Privacy Analysis

We start the security analysis by grouping-proof in Sect. 4.1, and then discuss how our protocol protects the tag's privacy in Sect. 4.2.

4.1 Grouping-Proof Security Analysis

Mutual Authentication. Many proposed grouping-proof protocols do not provide reader authentication. They focus on unilateral authentication where the tag tries to convince the reader of its identity and a genuine partial proof between them. The grouping-proof phase in our protocol provides reader authentication by introducing V. The presence of V let the legitimate tag be able to verify the reader's authenticity. This makes our protocol much more robust.

Resistance to Replay Attack. Our protocol for the 1st tag makes use of the reader's random challenge message c and tag's counter N_T. Even if a malicious tag deliberately chooses a counter that was used in a previous session, the reader's random challenge is always different during each grouping-proof session. In addition, the tag's dynamic secret key X_j is updated during each protocol execution when the authentication is successful, which means a repeated random challenge will yield a different r_2. For the remaining tags, the replay attack is also infeasible since each partial proof of previous tag is different.

Subset Replay Attack and Multiple Impersonation Attack. The partial proof for a tag is generated from a tag's "dynamic" secret key X_j, its identity ID_j, and the previous tag's partial proof b_{j-1}. Even if an adversary obtains b_{j-1}, she cannot compute a proof without knowing X_j and ID_j. In addition, the partial proof for current tag is depending on the previous tag's partial proof.

Denial-of-Service Attack. It is not straight-forward to protect against Denial-of-Service attack in grouping-proof protocols, but our protocol neutralizes the threats of Denial-of-Service attack in a simple manner. To be more specific, the dynamic secret key and mutual authentication prevent both parties from running any past runs or skip any runs. Moreover, the tag only updates its secret key if the reader authentication is successful. The grouping-proof phase in our protocol, in particular, involves a set of tags which may happen that some tags update their secret keys and some do not. Our protocol offers protection by having dynamic secrets for each tag, where both the old key X_{j1} and the new key X_{j2} are maintained in the reader side. An adversary won't be able to launch such attack to block either the reader or the tag form updating the secret key. This is due to the fact that the secret key X_j stored in the tag will always be equal to either X_{j1} or X_{j2} stored in the reader.

Race Conditions. Our protocol is resistant to the race conditions in the sense that each tag does not need to store V after the grouping-proof phase. Moreover, if the authentication during the grouping-proof phase fails, then no data will be stored on the tag either.

Denial of Proof (DoP). By putting n fake tags among legitimate tags, this attack cannot succeed since the reader cannot identify these fake tags' identities and thus the tag authentication will be failed. In addition, a passive adversary would not be able to simply draw a conclusion that the reader has rejected the tag in the sense that a pair of random message $\{r_2, V\}$ is still sent to the tag.

4.2 Privacy Analysis

Basic Privacy. First, we consider the basic privacy, where the adversary does not have the secret key of a tag T_j. We keep T_j's identifier ID_j secret and use it as an input to the PRF F and G. Given all the transaction messages, the adversary cannot determine whether this transaction coming from T_j under the assumption that F and G are secure PRF constructions. Hence our protocol supplies the property of untraceability for tags.

Forward Privacy. Forward privacy requires that even if the adversary can compromise a tag T_j's secret key, it cannot determine whether T_j's previous transactions belong to T_j. In our protocol, the tag will update its secret key after authenticating the reader. Suppose the adversary corrupts tag T_j at time t_j, obtaining T_j's secret key $X_{j_{t_j}}$ which is derived from the previous secret key by $X_{j_{t_j}} = G(X_{j_{t_{j-1}}}, r_1, r_2, V)$. The adversary cannot reveal the previous key $X_{j_{t_{j-1}}}$ at time t_{j-1} if G is a secure PRF construction. Without $X_{j_{t_{j-1}}}$, the adversary cannot tell whether a given transaction at time t_{j-1} belongs to the tag T_j or not, which means our protocol is forward secure.

De-Synchronization Attack. In addition, our protocol prevents the de-synchronization attack by using both the old key X_{j1} and the new key X_{j2} in the reader side. When launching a de-synchronization attack, the adversary either prevents the tag updating X_j, e.g., by modifying r_2, V sent from the reader to the tag, or prevents the reader updating X_{j1} and X_{j2}, e.g., by tampering the r_1 and N_T sent from the tag to the reader. It is obvious that even if the adversary somehow stops the tag or the reader from updating their data, the value of X_j stored in the tag will always be equal to either X_{j1} or X_{j2} stored in the reader. That is, the tag is always synchronized with the reader.

5   Comparison

It is difficult to compare our protocol with other grouping-proof protocols like-for-like and to take into account different operational or threat scenarios.

For example, one proposal's goal might be to minimise the communicated data, while another wishes to achieve an optimal security bound for only one or two attack scenarios. We therefore in this section provide a relative comparison in terms of grouping-proof scenarios. We highlight some of the positive features, and attempt to place it in context to related work.

Table 2. Comparison to selected grouping-proof protocols

Protocol	MA	Replay	Trace	Forward privacy	Forged proof	MI	m-DoP	DoS
1. Juels [10]	×	×	×	×	×	×	×	×
2. Saito and Sakurai [19]	×	×	√	×	×	×	×	×
3. Bolotnyy and Robins [2]	×	√	√	×	√	√	√	×
4. Peris-Lopez et al.[16]	×	√	√	×	√	√	×	×
5. Piramuthu [18]	×	√	×	×	√	√	×	×
6. Cho et al. [5]	×	√	×	×	√	√	×	×
7. Huang and Ku [9]	√	√	×	×	√	√	×	×
8. Chien and Liu [4]	×	√	×	×	√	√	×	√
9. Burmester et al. [3]	×	√	√	×	√	×	×	√
Our protocol	√	√	√	√	√	√	√	√

MA: Mutual Authentication MI: Multiple Impersonation Trace: Traceability attack m-DoP: Denial of Proof attack with m fake tags. DoS: Denial of Service attack

As shown in Table 2, our proposal outperforms others in terms of different attack scenarios, robust to all attacks in the context of a grouping-proof setting. Unfortunately, only Protocol 7 and ours provide mutual authentication, which is crucial to an RFID system as discussed in Sect. 4.1. Moreover, only our protocol features forward privacy and prevents the de-synchronization attack.

6   Conclusions and Future Work

In this paper, we propose a brand new grouping-proof protocol that features mutual authentication and forward privacy for social network users in mobile sharing economy, where each Prover needs to demonstrate its presence to the Verifier without disclosing its real identity. It is quite challenging nowadays since people care about protecting their identity more than ever. Many identity theft countermeasures have also been adopted. Our proposed protocol is secure against all known attacks in a grouping-proof setting. We provide a security analysis of our protocol considering the aforementioned attack scenarios.

Since the formal security analysis of grouping-proof protocols has lagged behind, we foresee that our protocol may be subject to new attacks in the future. Therefore, a unified framework that aims to improve analysis accuracy and better design of such protocols should be formalized. This includes a thorough terminology about different attacks, adversary's probabilities and strategies.

References

1. Avoine, G.: Adversarial model for radio frequency identification. Cryptology ePrint Archive, report 2005/049 (2005). http://eprint.iacr.org/
2. Bolotnyy, L., Robins, G.: Generalized "yoking-proofs" for a group of rfid tags. In: Third Annual International Conference on Mobile and Ubiquitous Systems: Networking Services, pp. 1–4, July 2006
3. Burmester, M., de Medeiros, B., Motta, R.: Provably secure grouping-proofs for RFID tags. In: Grimaud, G., Standaert, F.-X. (eds.) CARDIS 2008. LNCS, vol. 5189, pp. 176–190. Springer, Heidelberg (2008)
4. Chien, H.Y., Liu, S.B.: Tree-based RFID yoking proof. In: NSWCTC 2009. vol. 1, pp. 550–553 (2009)
5. Cho, J.S., Yeo, S.S., Hwang, S., Rhee, S.Y., Kim, S.K.: Enhanced yoking proof protocols for rfid tags and tag groups. In: Advanced Information Networking and Applications - Workshops, AINAW 2008, pp. 1591–1596, March 2008
6. D'Arco, P.: An almost-optimal forward-private RFID mutual authentication protocol with tag control. In: Ardagna, C.A., Zhou, J. (eds.) WISTP 2011. LNCS, vol. 6633, pp. 69–84. Springer, Heidelberg (2011)
7. Ha, J.H., Moon, S.-J., Zhou, J., Ha, J.C.: A new formal proof model for RFID location privacy. In: Jajodia, S., Lopez, J. (eds.) ESORICS 2008. LNCS, vol. 5283, pp. 267–281. Springer, Heidelberg (2008)
8. Hermans, J., Pashalidis, A., Vercauteren, F., Preneel, B.: A new RFID privacy model. In: Atluri, V., Diaz, C. (eds.) ESORICS 2011. LNCS, vol. 6879, pp. 568–587. Springer, Heidelberg (2011)
9. Huang, H.H., Ku, C.Y.: A RFID grouping proof protocol for medication safety of inpatient. J. Med. Syst. **33**(6), 467–474 (2009)
10. Juels, A.: "yoking-proofs" for RFID tags. In: International Workshop on Pervasive Computing and Communication Security - PerSec 2004, pp. 138–143. IEEE (2004)
11. Juels, A., Weis, S.A.: Defining strong privacy for RFID. ACM Trans. Inf. Syst. Secur. (TISSEC) **13**(1), 7:1–7:23 (2009)
12. Li, Y., Deng, R.H., Lai, J., Ma, C.: On two RFID privacy notions and their relations. ACM Trans. Inf. Syst. Secur. **14**(4), 30:1–30:23 (2008)
13. Lin, C.-C., Lai, Y.-C., Tygar, J.D., Yang, C.-K., Chiang, C.-L.: Coexistence proof using chain of timestamps for multiple RFID tags. In: Chang, K.C.-C., Wang, W., Chen, L., Ellis, C.A., Hsu, C.-H., Tsoi, A.C., Wang, H. (eds.) APWeb/WAIM 2007. LNCS, vol. 4537, pp. 634–643. Springer, Heidelberg (2007)
14. Nielsen: Global consumers embrace the share economy (2014). http://www.nielsen.com/lb/en/press-room/2014/global-consumers-embrace-the-share-economy.html
15. Ohkubo, M., Suzuki, K., Kinoshita, S.: Cryptographic approach to "privacy-friendly" tags. In: RFID Privacy Workshop. MIT, Massachusetts, USA (2003)
16. Peris-Lopez, P., Hernandez-Castro, J.C., Estevez-Tapiador, J.M., Ribagorda, A.: Solving the simultaneous scanning problem anonymously: Clumping proofs for RFID tags. In: 2007 Workshop on Security, Privacy and Trust in Pervasive and Ubiquitous Computing - SecPerU 2007, pp. 55–60. IEEE (2007)
17. Peris-Lopez, P., Orfila, A., Hernandez-Castro, J.C., van der Lubbe, J.C.A.: Flaws on RFID grouping-proofs. guidelines for future sound protocols. J. Netw. Comput. Appl. **34**(3), 833–845 (2011)
18. Piramuthu, S.: On existence proofs for multiple RFID tags. In: Workshop on Security, Privacy and Trust in Pervasive and Ubiquitous Computing - SecPerU 2006. IEEE, June 2006

19. Saito, J., Kouichi, S.: Grouping proof for RFID tags. In: Conference on Advanced Information Networking and Applications - AINA, vol. 2, pp. 621–624. IEEE, March 2005
20. Le, T., Burmester, M., Medeiros, B.: Universally composable and forward-secure RFID authentication and authenticated key exchange. In: ACM Symposium on Information. Computer and Communications Security - ASIACCS 2007, pp. 242–252. ACM, Singapore, March 2007
21. Vaudenay, S.: On privacy models for RFID. In: Kurosawa, K. (ed.) ASIACRYPT 2007. LNCS, vol. 4833, pp. 68–87. Springer, Heidelberg (2007)
22. Yang, A., Liang, K., Zhuang, Y., Wong, D.S., Jia, X.: A new unpredictability-based radio frequency identification forward privacy model and a provably secure construction. Secur. Commun. Netw. 8(16), 2836–2849 (2015)
23. Zhuang, Y., Yang, A., Wong, D.S., Yang, G., Xie, Q.: A highly efficient RFID distance bounding protocol without real-time PRF evaluation. In: Lopez, J., Huang, X., Sandhu, R. (eds.) NSS 2013. LNCS, vol. 7873, pp. 451–464. Springer, Heidelberg (2013)

Author Index

Printed in the United States
By Bookmasters